E L

EVERYMAN'S LIBRARY

EVERYMAN,
I WILL GO WITH THEE,
AND BE THY GUIDE,
IN THY MOST NEED
TO GO BY THY SIDE

MARK TWAIN

COLLECTED NONFICTION

VOLUME 2

SELECTIONS FROM THE MEMOIRS AND TRAVEL WRITINGS

WITH AN INTRODUCTION BY RICHARD RUSSO

EVERYMAN'S LIBRARY
Alfred A. Knopf New York London Toronto
376

THIS IS A BORZOI BOOK

PUBLISHED BY ALFRED A. KNOPF

First included in Everyman's Library, 2016

Typography by Peter B. Willberg

Illustrations courtesy of the Mark Twain Project, The Bancroft Library, University of California, Berkeley

The publishers are grateful to the Mark Twain Project for their assistance in the preparation of this two-volume Everyman edition of Mark Twain's collected nonfiction.

 Published in the United States by Alfred A. Knopf, a division of Penguin Random House LLC, New York, and in Canada by Penguin Random House Canada Ltd., Toronto. Distributed by Penguin Random House LLC, New York. Published in the United Kingdom by Everyman's Library, 50 Albemarle Street, London W1S 4DB and distributed by Penguin Random House UK, 20 Vauxhall Bridge Road, London SW1V 2SA.

www.randomhouse/everymans
www.everymanslibrary.co.uk

ISBN 978-1-101-90772-6 (US)
978-1-84159-376-0 (UK)

A CIP catalogue reference for this book is available from the British Library

Book design by Barbara de Wilde and Carol Devine Carson

Typeset in the UK by Input Data Services, 17 King Square, Bridgwater, Somerset TA6 3DJ
Printed and bound in Germany by GGP Media GmbH, Pössneck

MARK TWAIN

CONTENTS

INTRODUCTION

The novelist William Dean Howells once famously remarked that his friend Mark Twain was not a writer who performed so much as a performer who wrote. Perhaps surprisingly, this astute observation also holds true in Twain's nonfiction, a form that would seem to put less of a premium on both invention and performance. To read the passages from *The Innocents Abroad*, *Roughing It*, *A Tramp Abroad*, and *Life on the Mississippi* collected in this volume is to understand that Twain didn't lose much sleep over the idiosyncratic demands of fiction versus nonfiction. Both offered numerous and varied opportunities to an inspired, indeed unparalleled, bullshitter. To be sure, many of the set pieces that are included in the Everyman's Library volume of Twain's *Complete Short Stories* – "Buck Fanshaw's Funeral," "The Story of the Old Ram" – turn up in this volume as well. Classifying Twain's work into fiction or nonfiction is something we do for our own convenience; it was his own convenience to ignore ours.

So, are the events chronicled in *Roughing It* – which details Twain's journey by stagecoach to the Nevada territory, his stint there as a silver miner, and his apprenticeship to the newspaper trade – true? Once asked that same question about one of his own stories, David Sedaris replied, "They're true enough," and it's easy to imagine Twain saying the same thing about his youthful adventures in the American West. We know he traveled to Europe and the Holy Land as a correspondent, so it's not unreasonable to suppose that at least some of what he reports in *The Innocents Abroad* actually happened. I suspect, however, that the literally true parts are those he wasn't able to improve on through embellishment or outright invention. For Twain, "truth" was not just elastic but indeed designed to be stretched. He learned this lesson early on, writing for western newspapers. He explains the job to great comic effect in *Roughing It*, where, as a cub reporter, he wrote a story about a wagon full of immigrants attacked by Indians. At first, fearing that other reporters might recount the same story, he sticks pretty close to the facts, despite his conviction that the story could be improved upon by straying from them. Later, though, when he learns that the owner of the wagon meant to continue his journey the following morning (leaving no one to contradict Twain's account), all bets are off. His next draft describes an Indian fight that "to this day has no parallel in history." This is Twain we're talking about, so it's likely that he also exaggerated the extent of his exaggerations, but still. Buoyed by praise from the paper's editor, he expresses a willingness to murder every immigrant on the plains with his pen if "the interests of the paper demanded it." Thus the low bar of truth is established: *true enough*. For him. For his editor. For the paper's readership.

His approach to fiction was basically the same. At the beginning of the *Adventures of Huckleberry Finn*, Huck says that readers may have heard of him if they've read *The Adventures of Tom Sawyer*, which "was made by Mr. Mark Twain, and he told the truth, mainly. There were things which he stretched, but mainly he told the truth." That first assertion, it's worth remembering, was both the truth and a lie. The book was actually "made" by Samuel Clemens, and the parts Mr. Clemens "stretched" were the parts that needed stretching, beginning with his own identity as Mark Twain. Again, Twain is not so much a writer, at least the way the term is used today, as a storyteller whose primary duties are to the narrative and its audience. No story is likely to be instructive if it isn't entertaining, and the best way to gauge whether it's working or not is to watch it land with an actual audience, a lesson Twain learned long before he gave his first public lecture.

In *A Tramp Abroad* he recounts his first ride on a Mississippi steamboat as a ten-year-old boy. Falling asleep, he has a terrifying dream that the boat is ablaze, and he rushes into the ladies' salon, still under the nightmare's influence, screaming, "Fire!" The ladies there knew better, of course, and they advised him to return to his cabin and dress, lest he catch cold. It's a revealing memory. The humiliation of his story playing so badly, his audience rejecting both the tale and the teller, is still fresh in Twain's mind twenty-five years later as he's writing *Tramp*. Just as telling is the reason he recalls the episode in the first place. He's in Germany watching a production of *King Lear*, where the actor playing the title role "raged and wept and howled" about the stage. Twain admires the performance but feels sorry for the actor, who has to wait all the way to the end of the act for his applause.

Writers, by contrast, are used to silence. Their applause, if they're lucky enough to get any, comes long after their "performance" has concluded, in the form of reviews. True, authors who publish serially may to some degree interact with their audience. When readers loved Sam Weller in an early installment of *Pickwick Papers*, Dickens was happy to expand his role as the novel progressed, but that's hardly the same as telling the same stories on stage night after night, as Twain did on his speaking tours. Each audience provided him with valuable insight into what worked and why, allowing him to revise the material accordingly. His first public lecture triumph near the end of *Roughing It* is described almost completely in terms of the crowd's appreciation. The audience is with him from the start, he tells us, even the jokes he'd judged to be inferior, faring "royally." Near the end, though, the material grows more somber and serious, and Twain tells us that the "absorbed hush" that fell over the audience "gratified me more than any applause." Indeed, he's so pleased by the reaction that he can't help but smile, which the crowd took as a cue to laugh, thus ruining the moment.

Later in life, Twain's relationship with his audience would grow more complex. In *Life on the Mississippi*, he admits that being a river pilot was the best job he ever had, because the steamboat pilot has no master, whereas writers were "manacled servants of the public." That said, no writer ever courted his audience more assiduously nor drew more confidence and pleasure from public adulation (Twain courted honorary degrees, too, and shamelessly). Indeed one suspects that it was from his audience, as much as the work itself, that Twain derived his sense of accomplishment and well-being.

It's worth pointing out that the world has changed since Twain left it, and our attitudes towards "truth" and "fiction" have become more rigorous and stern. Mislabel your novel as a memoir (or allow your publisher to do so) and you'll likely find yourself in a world of hurt. Twain was no great fan of fraud and deception, but like Melville he understood that the world was steeped in both, and moreover he harbored more than a little admiration and affection for the world's charlatans. Reading *Huckleberry Finn* I often wonder if I judge the King and the Duke more harshly than their creator intended. At the very least Twain would've understood that people who get conned are often complicit in their own deception. Just as important, Twain would have recognized the paradox inherent in labeling some stories "made up" (fiction) and others "true" (nonfiction). Interestingly, audience often plays a role here, too. When you claim that a story is invented – especially one as elaborate as Twain's were – people will naturally suspect you of telling the truth (*Come on! You couldn't have made that up!*); conversely, when you claim to be telling the truth, those same folks shift gears and suspect you of lying (*Surely you embellished this?*). Storytelling thrives in this fundamental paradox and often resists attempts at clarification.

The world has changed in other ways, too, since Twain's departure. Seen in proper historical context, he appears in so many ways – in his embrace of technology, his use of the vernacular, his attitudes toward race, colonialism, and, later, the abomination of slavery – forward-thinking, a man ahead of his time. However, though it pains me to say it, there is, by contemporary standards, some pretty cringe-worthy stuff in these pages. In *The Innocents Abroad*, observing the two men in a Paris parade, Twain sees in Emperor Napoleon III "the representative of the highest modern civilization, progress, and refinement," whereas the Turkish sultan Abdul-Aziz, sized up from a distance as "stupid" and "unprepossessing," represents a people "filthy, brutish, ignorant, unprogressive, [and] superstitious." In Palestine, Twain's party comes upon a group of homeless, impoverished people by the side of the road. Among them are a mother and child; from afar, it looks like the child is wearing goggles, but up close they see that its eyes are infested with flies which the mother can't be bothered to shoo away. Twain notes how this "usual assemblage of squalid humanity ... sat in silence, and with tireless patience watched our every motion with that vile, uncomplaining impoliteness which is so truly Indian and which makes a white man so nervous and uncomfortable and savage that he wants to exterminate the whole tribe." Yikes.

Closer to home in *Roughing It*, he describes the western coyote as having a "blood kinship" with the American Indian, both of which will "eat anything they can bite." The Goshoot tribe of the Nevada territories are a "silent, sneaking, treacherous looking race ... always hungry, and yet never refusing anything that a hog would eat, though often eating what a hog would decline." From our privileged twenty-first-century vantage point, we can't help wishing our nineteenth-century literary hero would identify what he's witnessing as poverty and ignorance, not innate depravity. And female readers will surely note that women don't seem to register fully on Twain's consciousness and imagination. Nor do the poor and downtrodden always elicit the sympathy we might expect. Twain describes Parisian slum-dwellers as "savage-looking ruffians" who "take as much genuine pleasure in building a barricade as they do in cutting a throat or shoving a friend into the Seine." Nor, at times, is he above playing the least fortunate for laughs: "If you want dwarfs – I mean just a few dwarfs for a curiosity – go to Genoa. If you wish to buy them by the gross, for retail, go to Milan ... the crop [is] luxuriant."

But if Twain was a man of his time and not ours, it's also worth noting that his convictions evolved during his life. For instance, throughout *The Innocents Abroad*, he identifies himself as a Christian and as such compares himself and his fellow pilgrims favorably to non-Christians and pagans, who are typically depicted as superstitious, cruel, and violence-prone. But in *The Mysterious Stranger* fragments, which were among the last things he wrote, he has the angel Satan tell the story's protagonist that "two or three centuries from now it will be recognized that all the competent killers are Christians." And who is to blame? Why, the Christian God, "who could make good children as easily as bad, yet preferred to make bad ones."

More often, though, he is *our* Mark Twain, compassionate, broad-minded, and fatherly, more the man we've come to expect from reading *Huckleberry Finn* and *Pudd'nhead Wilson*, whose moral compass we can admire. In *Roughing It*, he recognizes as purest bigotry the shabby treatment of the Chinese, who were essential to both the building of the transcontinental railroad and the settlement of the West: "They are a harmless race when white men either let them alone or treat them no worse than dogs … A disorderly Chinaman is rare, and a lazy one does not exist." On their behalf he demands fairness, justice. "Any white man can swear a Chinaman's life away in the courts, but no Chinaman can testify against a white man." And once aroused, his sympathies are both righteous and fierce. "Only the scum of the population" abuse the Chinese, he asserts, they and "policemen and politicians … the dust-licking pimps and slaves of the scum." With very few exceptions he can be counted on to take the side of the oppressed over the oppressor. In *The Innocents Abroad*, the prisoner consigned for political reasons to the dungeons of the Doge's palace in Venice lives "without light, air, books; naked, unshaven, uncombed, covered with vermin; his useless tongue forgetting its office, with none to speak to." And his heart goes out to all abused animals, even to the notorious, much-maligned dogs of Constantinople: "I never saw such utterly wretched, starving, sad-visaged, broken-hearted looking curs in my life." "Do I contradict myself?" Walt Whitman asked in "Song of Myself," before immediately answering in the affirmative. If Twain embodies his own fair share of contradictions, we do well to remember that he too was "large" and "contained multitudes."

Of course the prevailing characteristic of Twain's storytelling is his witty, playful exuberance. He loves to tell us one thing while showing us another, ascribing, for instance, a laudable, benevolent motive to a human behavior when a baser one is actually on display. Again in Palestine, fearing an attack by Bedouins, he tells us, "My first impulse was to dash forward and destroy [them] … My second was to dash to the rear to see if there were any coming in that direction. I acted on the latter impulse. So did all the others. If any Bedouins had approached us, then, from that point on the compass, they would have paid dearly for their rashness." Taking painting lessons in *A Tramp Abroad*, he tells us, tongue firmly implanted in cheek, that he's been complimented by his teachers for having "a manner of my own ... that if I ever painted the commonest type of a dog, I should be sure to throw a something into the aspect of that dog which would keep him from being mistaken for the creation of any other artist," and after many months of arduous study, his German is described by one of his teachers as "very rare, possibly a 'unique.' " By the end of his life Twain would rail against the "damned human race," but in these pages we see a writer still buoyant and hopeful enough to regard human foolishness as grand entertainment, and far from considering himself exempt from folly, he's all too willing (as above) to make himself the butt of the joke. If others are fools and hypocrites, well, they have him (and, if we're honest, *us*) for company. In Gibraltar he buys a pair of kid gloves that are manifestly too small, tearing them to shreds as he tugs them on and off, all because the merchant keeps complimenting him on how perfect they look on him. Elsewhere he tells the story of a tiresome, grouchy fellow who keeps banging on about how perfectly wretched the coffee has been during their travels, offering as evidence the pale, transparent liquid he happens just then to be drinking. Taking a taste, his companion admits that as coffee it leaves a great deal to be desired, but that it's tolerably good *tea*. Only at the anecdote's conclusion does Twain identify the chastened fool as himself.

Such passages, together with unforgettable set pieces on shaving, dueling, profanity, singing gondoliers, Turkish baths, and the ridiculous German language, make apparent just how much *fun* Twain had writing. I mention this because not every writer does have fun, and not all that do are willing to admit it. For Twain, much of the sheer joy of storytelling is language itself. All good writers take pleasure in locating the precise right word for the occasion. Twain, who in a letter to William Dean Howells called a man "a quadrilateral, astronomical, incandescent son of a bitch," finds equal delight in locating the perfect *wrong* one. In order to tell the story of his grandfather's ram, it's necessary for the storyteller, Jim Blaine, to become "tranquilly, serenely, *symmetrically* drunk" [my emphasis], and in real life Twain takes particular delight in people like Mr. Ballou, also in *Roughing It*, who loves the *sound* of words, irrespective of their meaning and context. His ire up, he accuses a man named Ollendorf of being dumber than a "logarythm." That gentleman, deeply wounded, later admits he has no idea what the word means except that it's obviously "a thing considered disgraceful and unbecoming in America." When young Sam didn't learn the Mississippi River fast enough to suit his "gunpowdery" teacher and mentor, Mr. Bixby, Bixby "went off with a bang ... and then went on loading and firing until he was out of adjectives." Twain himself is never out of them. He describes a riverboat captain named Brown as a "middle-aged, long, slim, bony, smooth-shaven, horse-faced, ignorant, stingy, malicious, snarling, fault-hunting, mote-magnifying tyrant." *Who says, Show, don't tell*? In addition to words, Twain is deeply devoted to every sort of comic illogic and fallacy. "There is probably no pleasure equal to the pleasure of climbing a dangerous Alp; but it is a pleasure which is confined strictly to people who can find pleasure in it." His inability to *keep* promises, he explains (lest it be considered a character flaw) is the quite natural and understandable result of his too large and generous capacity to *make* them. "The surest way to stop writing about Rome," he informs us, as if we'll all have need of this advice one day, "is to stop."

Also on display throughout these pages is Twain the iconoclast, who has little use for received wisdom. Prone to invention and embellishment himself, he's naturally suspicious of the authority of others. Taking in the sights of Europe, he steadfastly refuses to allow professional guides (including, and especially, guidebooks) to trump the evidence of his own senses. Those who revere "the old masters" for their "sublimity," "feeling," and "richness of coloring," come under sharp, unrelenting attack. "I envy them their honest admiration, if it be honest – their delight, if they feel delight ... But at the same time the thought *will* intrude itself upon me, How can they see what is not visible? ... What would you think of a man who stared in ecstasy upon a desert of stumps and said: 'Oh ... what a noble forest is here!' " German opera? Twain finds it insufferable, though he has a theory as to its popularity across the Atlantic. Opera's ingenuity, he argues, is that "it deals so largely in pain that its scattered delights are prodigiously augmented by the contrasts . . . just as an honest man in politics shines more than he would elsewhere." He has little doubt that one day Americans will like opera, too: "One in fifty" already does, the other forty-nine attending "in order to learn to like it, and the rest in order to be able to talk knowingly about it." They hum along "so that their neighbors may perceive that they have been to operas before. The funerals of these do not occur often enough."

What's particularly thrilling to witness here is the emergence of Twain's voice, which he seems to have invented not just for himself but for the young nation he clearly feels at liberty to speak for. That voice, its distinctive attitude and posture, has become so much a part of us that it's hard to remember that there was ever a time when there was simply nothing like it. Its unexpected freshness, like the emergence, later, of jazz or rock and roll, was actually part of its message. In *The Innocents Abroad* and *A Tramp Abroad* he puts Europe and the rest of the world under the microscope, but the lens he peers through is strictly American, meaning that he has as much to say about us, the viewer, as the viewed. It's the American character – our energy, practicality, arrogance, competence, anti-intellectualism, and congenital optimism – that thus emerges. His use of arithmetic to suggest the fraudulence of European relics (added up, there are enough nails and slivers of the true cross to make dozens of them, and there appear to be at least two complete sets of the Apostle John's ashes) are hilarious enough in their own right, but they also make the case that America, a nation too young to have a past, really isn't missing much. At Heidelberg Castle he buys for a pittance a portrait of a duke and another of a princess so that he might start "a portrait gallery of my ancestors," remarking that "one can lay in ancestors at even cheaper rates than these." In Titian, Tintoretto, Raphael, Rubens and Veronese he sees men of "cringing spirit," toadies willing to genuflect before "such monsters as the French, Venetian, and Florentine Princes," something no American would do. Regarding the riches of the Vatican and "priest-ridden" Italy, he goes off (forgive me) like a Roman candle: "Raphael pictured such infernal villains as

Catherine and Marie de Medicis seated in heaven and conversing familiarly with the Virgin Mary and the angels." "Alas! those good old times are gone," he says elsewhere, "when a murderer could wipe the stain from his name ... by building an addition to a church."

When he's not busy mocking European snobbery and pretension he's having fun playing with the stereotype of the parochial, self-satisfied American abroad. Seeing Notre Dame Cathedral for the first time, he assures us, "We had heard of it before." Like Washington Irving before him, he often depicts his fellow pilgrims as slow-witted, a step behind (like Brom Bones), when in reality they're steps ahead. Throughout Europe they allow their guides – all of whom they call Ferguson, rather than learn to pronounce their names – to deliver long lectures about this or that Renaissance or medieval artist, only to inquire when Ferguson's voice finally falls, "Is he dead?"

And yet in the two books where America itself is put under the microscope – *Roughing It* and *Life on the Mississippi* – Twain displays both pride and profound misgivings about the American character that is surfacing. As in *Huckleberry Finn*, he recognizes violence as part of the nation's DNA. As a lover of tall tales, he immediately recognizes its inherent comic potential. On his first day in Carson City he witnesses a dispute between a man named Harris and another who had recently identified him as the robber of a stagecoach. The former "began to rebuke the stranger with a six-shooter, and the stranger began to explain with another." When both revolvers are empty Harris, full of "picturesque" bullet holes, rides on with a "polite nod." Twain's portrait of the fearsome outlaw Slade is similarly cartoonish. Real violence, which Twain equates with cruelty, is different, and he evinces little taste or stomach for either. He learns early that there's nothing romantic about death. Sneaking home late one night he discovers a corpse in his father's office: "A white human hand lay in the moonlight! Such an awful sinking at the heart – such a sudden gasp for breath! I felt – I can not tell *what* I felt." With cartoon violence, his instinct is to embellish; with real violence (in life or violence made real in fiction), he instead draws the curtain, as at the end of the Grangerford/Shepherdson feud in *Huckleberry Finn*, where Huck explains that he won't be telling us about all the things he witnessed because "it would make me sick again." In *Life on the Mississippi*, Twain is similarly reticent in describing the death of his brother Henry after a steamboat explosion. "On the evening of the sixth day his wandering mind busied itself with matters far away ... His hour had struck; we bore him to the death-room, poor boy." What's fascinating about his lengthy account of the explosion's aftermath is that most of Twain's attention is devoted not to his brother at all, but rather to the boat's chief mate, whose horrific injuries are described in harrowing detail. Three times the man is carried to the death-room, only to rally there and curse his attendant. Why focus on the mate instead of his own brother? Because the mate "lived to be mate of a steamboat again." Life trumps death – it's that simple.

Is such optimism a matter of youth? Faith? If the latter, faith in what? God? Perhaps, sometimes. In these early books, though he gleefully skewers conformist piety, Twain shows both respect and admiration for genuine faith, like that of the Dominican fathers who minister to the sick and dying during the plague. More often, though, his faith seems to reside in the seemingly incorruptible spirit and innocence of individuals like Tom and Huck, the unflagging devotion and love radiating from men like Jim. We sense that it's because of them he can believe in his fledgling nation, in the progress it represents. At the end of *Life on the Mississippi* he returns to Hannibal and locates the house he grew up in before he, like Huck, lit out for the territories. "The people who now occupy it are of no more value than I am; but in my time they would have been worth not less than five hundred dollars apiece. They are colored folk."

Should it trouble us that in the end Twain's optimism was unsustainable? Maybe. Should it surprise us? Probably not. If despair is not a potent source of comedy – and many argue that it is – it's all too often the fate of the comic artist. There comes a day when all that you've managed to keep at bay through humor just isn't funny anymore, which may be why comic geniuses often do their best work early. G. K. Chesterton preferred Dickens's first novel, *Pickwick Papers*, to all that followed. Not many would agree with that assessment, but there is much to be said for the novels that preceded *Bleak House*, their sheer delight in the world, their author's youthful chutzpah. The Mark Twain of these early- to mid-career books clearly felt equal to whatever task was put before him. Sure, even as a young man he was acquainted with loss and failure, but these had not yet begun to take their toll, which is another way of saying he'd not yet really begun to internalize them. That would come later.

Meanwhile, he was, like the nation he spoke for, confident, irreverent, exuberant, unapologetic, full of swagger, untroubled by self-doubt, and, perhaps most important, dead game. A force of nature. Something new in the world.

Richard Russo

RICHARD RUSSO is the author of eight novels, two collections of stories, and a memoir. In 2002 he received the Pulitzer Prize for *Empire Falls.*

SELECT BIBLIOGRAPHY

AUTOBIOGRAPHY

TWAIN, MARK, *Autobiography of Mark Twain*, Vols I–III, University of California Press, Berkeley, 2010, 2013, 2015.

BIOGRAPHY

BURNS, KEN; DUNCAN, DAYTON and WARD, GEOFFREY C., *Mark Twain: An Illustrated Biography*, Alfred A. Knopf, New York, 2001.

EMERSON, EVERETT, *Mark Twain: A Literary Life*, University of Pennsylvania Press, Philadelphia, 2000.

KAPLAN, FRED, *The Singular Mark Twain*, Doubleday, New York, 2003.

LOVING, JEROME, *Mark Twain: The Adventures of Samuel L. Clemens*, University of California Press, Berkeley, 2010.

KATZ, HARRY L. and The Library of Congress, *Mark Twain's America: A Celebration in Words and Images*, Little, Brown and Company, New York, 2014.

POWERS, RON, *Mark Twain, A Life*, Free Press, New York, 2005.

SHELDEN, MICHAEL, *Mark Twain: Man in White*, Random House, New York, 2010.

CRITICISM

BLOOM, HAROLD, ed., *Mark Twain*, Chelsea House Publishers, New York and Philadelphia, 1986.

BUDD, LOUIS J., *Mark Twain: The Contemporary Reviews*, Cambridge University Press, New York, 1999.

MESSENT, PETER, *The Short Works of Mark Twain: A Critical Study*, University of Pennsylvania Press, Philadelphia, 2001.

QUIRK, TOM, *Mark Twain: A Study of the Short Fiction*, Twayne Publishers, New York, 1997.

RAILTON, STEPHEN, *Mark Twain: A Short Introduction*, Blackwell Publishing, Oxford, UK, 2003.

ROBINSON, FORREST G., ed., *The Cambridge Companion to Mark Twain*, Cambridge University Press, New York, 1995.

SCHMITTER, DEAN MORGAN, ed., *Mark Twain: A Collection of Criticism*, McGraw-Hill Book Company, New York, 1974.

ANTHOLOGIES

BUDD, LOUIS J., ed., *Collected Tales, Sketches, Speeches, & Essays, 1852–1890*, The Library of America, New York, 1992; *Collected Tales, Sketches, Speeches, & Essays, 1891–1910*, The Library of America, New York, 1992.

DE VOTO, BERNARD, ed., *The Portable Mark Twain*, Viking, New York, 1946.

NEIDER, CHARLES, ed., *The Selected Letters of Mark Twain*, Cooper Square Press, New York, 1982.

TWAIN, MARK, *Autobiographical Writings*, Penguin Books, New York, 2012.

The Mark Twain Project, University of California Press, Berkeley.

CHRONOLOGY

DATE	AUTHOR'S LIFE	LITERARY CONTEXT
1803		Birth of Emerson.
1811		
1819		Birth of Whitman and Melville. Irving: *The Sketch Book* (to 1820). Scott: *Ivanhoe.*
1821		
1830		Birth of Emily Dickinson.
1832		F. Trollope: *Domestic Manners of the Americans.*
1833		
1834		
1835	Samuel Langhorne Clemens born in Florida, Missouri, sixth of seven children. His father is a country lawyer and merchant.	Tocqueville: *Democracy in America* (I). Browning: *Paracelsus.* Balzac: *Old Goriot.*
1837		Carlyle: *The French Revolution.*
1838		Dickens: *Oliver Twist.*
1839	Family moves to Hannibal, Missouri, a river town on the Mississippi. Death of his sister, Margaret (b. 1830).	Poe: *Tales of the Grotesque and Arabesque.* Stendhal: *The Charterhouse of Parma.* Darwin: *The Voyage of the "Beagle."*
1840		Cooper: *The Pathfinder.*
1841		Emerson: *Essays, First Series.* Thorpe: *The Big Bear of Arkansas.* Cooper: *The Deerslayer.* Dickens: *Barnaby Rudge.*

HISTORICAL EVENTS

Louisiana Purchase. Ohio becomes the 17th state to join the Union.
First Mississippi steamboat launched.
Florida Purchase. SS *Savannah* first steam-powered vessel to cross the Atlantic.

The State of Missouri admitted to the Union as the 24th state. Leads to the Missouri Compromise: slavery is accepted in the new state but prohibited in lands north of latitude 36°30' N.
President Andrew Jackson's Indian Removal Act to transfer all Indians to the west of the Mississippi. The Choctaw Nation is the first to be deported (1831–3).

Slavery abolished in the British Empire.
The Indian Territory (later to become Oklahoma) reserved by the Federal government.
Texan Revolution against Mexican rule (to 1836); a republic is declared.
Samuel Colt travels to England to patent his revolver.

Accession of Queen Victoria in Britain. Financial crisis in US (to 1843).
Seminole War in Florida. Osage War: Missouri militia forces out last remaining Osage Indians. Michigan becomes the 26th state.
The Underground Railway for runaway slaves set up in Ohio. Passage of the Personal Liberty Laws, impeding enforcement of the Federal Fugitive Slave Law of 1793. Deportation of Cherokee Nation from Georgia; some 4000 die on the "Trail of Tears" to the Indian Territory. Daguerre–Niepce method of photography first presented in Paris.
University of Missouri founded. Samuel Cunard wins contract to carry British Royal Mail to the USA and Canada.

John Tyler becomes US President.

DATE	AUTHOR'S LIFE	LITERARY CONTEXT
1842	Death of his brother, Benjamin (b. 1832).	Dickens tours the US. *American Notes.*
1843		Carlyle: *Past and Present.* Dickens: *Martin Chuzzlewitt* (to 1844). Ruskin: *Modern Painters* (I).
1845		
1846		Melville: *Typee.*
1847	Death of his father.	C. Brontë: *Jane Eyre.* E. Brontë: *Wuthering Heights.* Thackeray: *Vanity Fair* (to 1848).
1848	Sam goes to work as a printer's apprentice.	Lowell: *The Biglow Papers.* Marx and Engels: *The Communist Manifesto.*
1849		Death of Poe. Parkman: *The Oregon Trail.*
1850	His brother Orion, a printer, purchases the *Hannibal Western Union.*	Hawthorne: *The Scarlet Letter.* Dickens: *David Copperfield.*
1851	Working for Orion. Sam's first known published work, "A Gallant Fireman," appears in the paper.	Death of Cooper. Melville: *Moby-Dick.* Hawthorne: *The House of Seven Gables.*
1852		Stowe: *Uncle Tom's Cabin.* Turgenev: *A Sportsman's Notebook.*
1853	Travels to St. Louis, New York, Philadelphia and Washington, working as a jobbing printer (to 1856). Orion moves to Iowa, taking his mother and brother Henry with him.	Thackeray: *The English Humorists* (lectures given in England and the US 1852–3).
1854		Thoreau: *Walden.*
1855		Whitman: *Leaves of Grass.*

HISTORICAL EVENTS

Webster–Ashburton Treaty establishes the northeastern border of the US with British colonies in Canada; US promises co-operation in suppressing the slave trade.
The Oregon Trail – around 900 migrants travel more than 2000 miles from Missouri to settle in Oregon, with increasing numbers to follow during the 1840s.

Texas annexed by the US. James K. Polk becomes US President (to 1849).
White Star Line founded.
Mexican War (to 1848). Wilmot Proviso: unsuccessful attempt by northern abolitionists to ban slavery in any territory gained from Mexico. Treaty with Britain establishes 49th Parallel as boundary between Oregon and Canada.
Salt Lake City founded.

Treaty of Guadalupe Hidalgo: US makes huge territorial gains at the end of the war with Mexico, acquiring California, New Mexico and Arizona, and parts of Colarado, Nevada and Utah. Organization of the Free Soil Party. Gold first discovered in California. Year of Revolutions in Europe. Second Republic in France. Franz Josef becomes Austrian Emperor (to 1916).
Senator John C. Calhoun's Southern Address against Northern "acts of aggression and encroachment." California Gold Rush underway (to 1855); widespread violence against American Indian tribes leading to catastrophic decline in population.
Compromise of 1850: California admitted to the Union as a free state; Utah and New Mexico established as territories with the right to decide for themselves on the issue of slavery; a tighter Fugitive Slave Bill passed.
Louis Napoleon's *coup d'état* in France leads to re-establishment of Empire in 1852. Great Exhibition in London. Isaac Singer devises continuous stitch sewing machine. *New York Times* founded.

First world trade fair to be held in America opens in New York. Franklin Pierce becomes US President (to 1857). Gadsden Purchase.

Kansas–Nebraska Act effectively repeals the Missouri Compromise. Violent clashes over slavery in Kansas; Kansas–Missouri border troubles (to 1865).
Republican party founded.
Obed Hussey invents self-propelled steam engine for plowing.

DATE	AUTHOR'S LIFE	LITERARY CONTEXT
1855 *cont.*		Longfellow: *The Song of Hiawatha.* Spencer: *The Principles of Psychology.*
1856	Sam writing humorous articles for his brother's new paper, the *Keokuk Daily Post*, under the pseudonym Thomas Jefferson Snodgrass. Moves to Cincinnati in the fall.	Melville: *Piazza Tales.* Flaubert: *Madame Bovary.*
1857	Departs Cincinnati for New Orleans on the *Paul Jones*, piloted by Horace E. Bixby, whom he persuades to train him as a Mississippi River pilot.	Thackeray: *The Virginians* (to 1859). Trollope: *Barchester Towers.* *The Atlantic Monthly* founded.
1858	Younger brother Henry (working with him on the Mississippi as a junior clerk) killed in a steamboat explosion.	
1859	Becomes a licensed river pilot.	Death of Irving. Tennyson: *Idylls of the King.* Dickens: *A Tale of Two Cities.*
1860		Hawthorne: *The Marble Faun.* Emerson: *The Conduct of Life.* Eliot: *The Mill on the Floss.* Collins: *The Woman in White.*
1861	War halts river trade. Enlists briefly in the Confederate Militia. Accompanies Orion to Nevada, where Lincoln has appointed him Secretary. Prospects for gold and silver.	Wendell Holmes: *Elsie Venner.* Dostoevsky: *The House of the Dead.*
1862	Reporter on the *Territorial Enterprise*, Virginia City, Nevada.	Birth of Edith Wharton. Death of Thoreau. Hugo: *Les Misérables.*
1863	Adopts the *nom de plume* "Mark Twain" – the cry of a river boatman taking a sounding of two fathoms (twelve feet).	Longfellow: *Tales of a Wayside Inn.*
1864	Works as a journalist in San Francisco. Forms friendships with the writer Bret Harte, the professional lecturer Artemus Ward and raconteur Jim Gillis.	Death of Hawthorne. Tolstoy: *War and Peace* (to 1869). Verne: *Journey to the Centre of the Earth.*

CHRONOLOGY

HISTORICAL EVENTS

James Buchanan becomes US President (to 1861).

Beginning of the Raj: following the Indian Mutiny (1857) the British Crown takes control of India from the East India Company. First transatlantic cable laid.

Darwin publishes *On the Origin of Species*, propounding the theory of evolution. First commercial oil well in US, Titusville, Pennsylvania.

Abraham Lincoln elected US President. Pony Express founded.

Kansas admitted to the Union as a free state. Southern Congress at Montgomery, Alabama; Jefferson Davis elected President of the Confederate States of America. Missouri votes to stay in the Union but the population is divided over the issues. Outbreak of Civil War in US. Western Union completes first transcontinental telegraph line across North America. Apache Wars (to 1900). Italy united under Victor Emmanuel II. Tsar Alexander II emancipates the serfs in Russia.

Battle of Shiloh. Sioux uprising in Minnesota. Bismarck appointed Prime Minister of Prussia.

Lincoln issues Emancipation Proclamation (amendment to constitution passed 1865). Battle of Gettysburg.

US Civil War rages on. Lincoln re-elected President. Massacre of Cheyenne and Arapaho Indians at Sand Creek, Colorado. Karl Marx founds International Workingmen's Association in London. Louis Pasteur establishes connection between bacteria and disease.

DATE	AUTHOR'S LIFE	LITERARY CONTEXT
1865	His short story "Jim Smiley and His Jumping Frog" appears in the *New York Saturday Press* and elsewhere, to great popular acclaim.	Whitman: *Drum Taps.* Carroll: *Alice's Adventures in Wonderland.*
1866	Travels to Hawaii as correspondent of the *Alta California*. Takes up lecturing.	
1867	Becomes the paper's New York correspondent. Delivers first lecture in New York. Publishes his first book, *The Celebrated Jumping Frog of Calaveras County and Other Sketches.* Travels as correspondent to Europe and the Holy Land (June–Nov). Introduced to Olivia (Livy) Langdon in New York (Dec).	Marx: *Das Kapital* (I). Dickens's second American tour (to 1868).
1868	Livy and Twain hear Charles Dickens read. Twain lectures across the US.	Harte: "The Luck of Roaring Camp." Collins: *The Moonstone.*
1869	Publishes *The Innocents Abroad*, a collection of articles written during his recent voyage, which becomes a best-seller. Lecture tour of Midwest.	Harte: "The Outcasts of Poker Flat." Alcott: *Little Women.* Hugo: *L'Homme qui rit.*
1870	Marries Olivia Langdon in Elmira, New York. The couple settle briefly in Buffalo, New York. Writes an early version of *Tom Sawyer* entitled *A Boy's Manuscript.* Birth of son, Langdon.	Death of Dickens. Verne: *Twenty Thousand Leagues Under the Sea.*
1871	The family moves to Hartford, Connecticut, renting a house at Nook Farm. Summers in the 1870s and '80s are spent at Quarry Farm, Elmira, where Twain does much of his writing.	Darwin: *The Descent of Man.*
1872	Publishes *Roughing It.* Birth of daughter, Susy. Langdon contracts diphtheria and dies. First trip to England in the fall. Patents his self-pasting scrapbook, the only one of his inventions to make money.	Wendell Holmes: *The Autocrat at the Breakfast-Table.* Eliot: *Middlemarch.* Hardy: *Under the Greenwood Tree.* Butler: *Erewhon.*

HISTORICAL EVENTS

End of Civil War. Assassination of President Lincoln. Southern Democrat Andrew Johnson becomes President; favours a policy of Reconstruction lenient towards the South. Ku Klux Klan founded in Tennessee. Mississippi first Southern state to adopt a "Black Code" to re-establish white supremacy.
Civil Rights Bill passed by Congress in spite of presidential veto. Racial violence in Tennessee and New Orleans. Red Cloud's War in Wyoming (to 1868).
Increased Republican majority in Congress passes first Reconstruction Act (again in defiance of presidential veto), placing southern states under military rule and making readmittance to the Union dependant upon their acceptance of black suffrage. Building of the first elevated railroad (New York). Alaska purchased from Russia. British North American Act; self-governing dominion of Canada established. Dual monarchy of Austria-Hungary established.

14th Amendment ratified, defining US citizenship to include all those born or naturalized in the US. (Native Americans, however, were largely excluded.) Failed impeachment of President Johnson. Gladstone's first Liberal ministry in Britain (to 1874).
First Pacific Railroad completed, linking East and West coasts. Suez Canal opens. Ulysses S. Grant becomes US President (to 1877). Elizabeth Cady Stanton founds National Women's Suffrage Organization.

First African American admitted to Congress. Passage of the 15th Amendment: "no state shall deprive a citizen of the right to vote on grounds of race, color, or previous condition of servitude," a promised not fulfilled for another century. Franco-Prussian War (to 1871).

Fall of Paris; Napoleon III goes into exile; Third Republic in France. Paris Commune. Wilhelm I of Prussia proclaimed German Emperor. US and Britain sign Treaty of Washington, settling US–Canadian boundary and disputes dating from the Civil War. Meeting of Stanley and Livingstone in Ujiji.

Yellowstone National Park established. President signs amnesty bill for former Confederates. Grant is re-elected. "Cleveland Massacre" – Rockefeller's Standard Oil company buys out 22 of its 26 rivals in Cleveland, Ohio in a first move to achieve national, then multinational domination.

DATE	AUTHOR'S LIFE	LITERARY CONTEXT
1873	Publishes novel, *The Gilded Age*, written with Charles Dudley Warner. Travels with his family to England, Scotland and Ireland. Meets Trollope, Browning, and Spencer. (May–Nov). Returns alone to England for a lecture tour (to Jan 1874).	Tolstoy: *Anna Karenina* (to 1877). Trollope: *The Eustace Diamonds*. Verne: *Around the World in Eighty Days*.
1874	Birth of daughter, Clara. Moves into a mansion he has had built in Hartford, the family home until 1891.	Hugo: *Quatre-vingt-treize*.
1875	Writes *Old Times on the Mississippi* in seven installments for W. D. Havell's *Atlantic Monthly*.	
1876	Publishes *The Adventures of Tom Sawyer*.	Birth of Willa Cather. Henry James: *Roderick Hudson*.
1877	Makes ill-received speech at the 70th birthday dinner for John Greenleaf Whittier.	Turgenev: *Virgin Soil*.
1878	Takes his family to Europe (April). Twain and Joseph Twichell go on a "tramp abroad" through the Black Forest and Swiss Alps. Spends winter in Munich.	James: *Daisy Miller*.
1879	Visits Paris; meets Henry James, Whistler and Darwin. Returns to New York via England (August).	Stevenson: *Travels with a Donkey in the Cévennes*.
1880	Publishes *A Tramp Abroad*. Birth of daughter, Jean.	Maupassant: "Boule de Suif."
1881	*The Prince and the Pauper* (novel) published. Begins to invest in Paige typesetting machine.	James: *The Portrait of a Lady*; *Washington Square*.
1882	Visits the Mississippi with Horace Bixby.	Death of Emerson. Howells: *A Modern Instance*.
1883	Publishes an amended version of *Old Times* as *Life on the Mississippi*.	Riley: *The Old Swimmin'-Hole and 'Leven More Poems*. Stevenson: *Treasure Island*.
1884	*Adventures of Huckleberry Finn* published in London in December (and in the US two months later). Founds publishing company, Charles L. Webster & Co.	

HISTORICAL EVENTS

Colfax Massacre in Louisiana. Panic of 1873 – collapse of a Wall Street banking firm with interests in railroad investment has severe economic repercussions. Conviction of New York political racketeer "Boss" Tweed for corruption. Remington manufacture the first commercial typewriter. First cable car (San Francisco). G. A. Hansen discovers leprosy bacillus.

Disraeli British Prime Minister (to 1880). Impressionists' first exhibition in Paris.

A shortlived Civil Rights Act guarantees equal access, regardless of color, to public transport and recreation, and protects the right to serve on juries.

Great Sioux War (to 1877); US troops defeated at the Battle of Little Bighorn. Colorado becomes US state. Alexander Graham Bell patents the telephone.

Sioux lands officially annexed. Great Railroad Strike put down by militia and federal troops. Disraeli proclaims Queen Victoria Empress of India. Britain annexes the Transvaal. Thomas Edison invents phonograph. Republican Rutherford B. Hayes becomes President after a disputed election, having made a deal with his opponents to lift tough Reconstruction policies in the South. Southern states are free to introduce policies of segregation ("Jim Crow laws"); gradual disenfranchisement of blacks begins.

Zulu War (to 1880).

Gladstone again British Prime Minister (to 1885). First Boer War.

British troops defeated by Boers at Majuba Hill. Britain recognizes Boer Republic of Transvaal.

Chinese Exclusion Act suspends immigration of Chinese laborers.

Brooklyn Bridge opened. Southern Pacific and Northern Pacific transcontinental railroads completed. Supreme Court declares the 1875 Civil Rights Act unconstitutional.

Berlin Conference; the "Scamble for Africa" begins. Merganthaler invents the Linotype machine (first machine installed at the *New York Tribune* in 1886).

DATE	AUTHOR'S LIFE	LITERARY CONTEXT
1885	Webster & Co. publishes the memoirs of Ulysses S. Grant, a useful financial success. Twain pays the expenses of Walter McGuinn, first black student at Yale Law School. Susy begins to write a biography of her father.	Howell: *The Rise of Silas Lapham.* Riley: "Little Orphant Annie." Zola: *Germinal.*
1886	In pursuance of a long campaign to improve copyright protection for authors, appears before a congressional committee on copyright (and again in 1906).	James: *The Bostonians.* Jewett: *A White Heron.* Stevenson: *Dr. Jekyll and Mr. Hyde*; *Kidnapped.*
1887		
1888	Receives an honorary MA from Yale University.	Birth of O'Neill and T. S. Eliot. Kipling: *Plain Tales from the Hills.* Ward: *Robert Elsmere.*
1889	Publishes *A Connecticut Yankee in King Arthur's Court.* Meets Rudyard Kipling in Elmira.	Jerome: *Three Men in a Boat.* Stevenson: *The Master of Ballantrae.*
1890	Death of his mother.	Dickinson: *Poems* (to 1896).
1891	Financial difficulties drive the Clemens family to settle in Europe. They spend the winter of 1891–2 in Berlin.	Death of Melville. Conan Doyle: *The Adventures of Sherlock Holmes.*
1892	Twain dines with Kaiser Wilhelm II.	Death of Whitman and Tennyson. Kipling: *Barrack-Room Ballads.*
1893	Publishes *The $1,000,000 Bank-Note and Other New Stories.* Living in Italy but visiting the US on business.	Kipling: *Many Inventions.*
1894	Twain's publishing company and speculative enterprises, notably the Paige typesetting machine, are bankrupted by the crash of 1893. His health and that of his wife and daughters declines. Family moves to France. *The Tragedy of Pudd'nhead Wilson* published.	Chopin: *Bayou Folk.* Kipling: *The Jungle Book* (I).

CHRONOLOGY

HISTORICAL EVENTS

Leopold II of Belgium's personal rule in the Congo Free State (to 1908). Indian National Congress founded in Bombay. Pasteur successfully uses rabies vaccine to prevent humans developing the disease after a dog-bite. Gottlieb Daimler and Wilhelm Maybach patent high-speed internal combustion engine.

Geronimo signs peace treaty; end of last major Indian war.

Dawes Act enforces assimilation of American Indians by depriving them of their communal tribal lands in exchange for individual allotments. Dunlop patents pneumatic tyre.

Large central area of the Indian Territory opened for settlement; major land rush. Jane Addams and Ellen Gates Starr found Hull House in Chicago. Cecil Rhodes's British South African Company receives royal charter and a mandate to colonize further territories. First Kodak camera using roll film manufactured.

Massacre of Lakota Sioux at Wounded Knee. Fall of Bismarck. Monotype caster patented.

International Copyright Act.

Ellis Island opens as an immigration station.

Henry Ford and Karl Benz build their first cars. Serious economic depression in the US. British South African Company invades Matabeleland; First Matabele War (to 1894).

Dreyfus case begins in France.

DATE	AUTHOR'S LIFE	LITERARY CONTEXT
1895	Returns to the US in May. Embarks on worldwide lecture tour to restore finances (July). Livy and Clara accompany him. Visits Canada, Australia and New Zealand.	Crane: *The Red Badge of Courage.* Dunbar: *Majors and Minors.* Wells: *The Time Machine.* Wilde: *The Importance of Being Earnest.* Hardy: *Jude the Obscure.*
1896	Moves on to Ceylon, India and South Africa, arriving in England in July. Death of his daughter Susy at home in Hartford (August). Clemens family settle in England. Jean diagnosed with epilepsy. *Personal Recollections of Joan of Arc* serialized in *Harper's Magazine.*	Jewett: *The Country of the Pointed Firs.* Beerbohm: *The Works of Max Beerbohm.*
1897	Moves to Vienna where Clara pursues her musical studies and Twain enjoys being lionized. Publishes *How to Tell a Story and Other Essays* and *Following the Equator.* Death of his brother Orion.	Birth of Faulkner. Robinson: *Richard Cory.* Chopin: *A Night in Acadie.* Stoker: *Dracula.* Shaw: *The Devil's Disciple.*
1898	Discharges his debts. "Stirring Times in Austria" appears in *Harper's Magazine.* Working on *What is Man?* and *The Mysterious Stranger* (novel).	Birth of Hemingway. James: *The Turn of the Screw.* Wells: *The War of the Worlds.*
1899	Leaves Vienna (May); audience with Emperor Franz Josef I. Visits Sweden seeking treatment for Jean. "Concerning the Jews," an essay against anti-semitism, published in *Harper's.*	Chopin: *The Awakening.* Norris: *McTeague.* Chekhov: "The Lady with the Dog."
1900	Returns to the US to a national welcome. Lives in New York City. Publishes *The Man That Corrupted Hadleyburg and Other Stories and Essays* and *English As She Is Taught.*	Dreiser: *Sister Carrie.* Freud: *The Interpretation of Dreams.*

CHRONOLOGY

HISTORICAL EVENTS

Cuban War of Independence begins. In Britain, Conservative Lord Salisbury forms ministry in conjunction with the Liberal Unionists (to 1902). Jameson Raid on the Transvaal. "Rhodesia" founded. Freud's *Studies in Hysteria* inaugurates psychoanalysis. First public screening of a film by the Lumière brothers. Trial of Oscar Wilde.

Plessy v Ferguson: Supreme Court upholds conviction of Homer Plessy for contravening the Separate Cars Act in Louisiana, endorsing "separate but equal" policy. Utah becomes 45th state to join the Union. Second Matabele War (to 1897). Sudan War (to 1899). Anti-semitic Karl Lueger mayor of Vienna (to 1910). Marconi moves to England to conduct his experiments in wireless telegraphy.

Klondike gold rush (to 1899). Queen Victoria's Diamond Jubilee. Destruction of Benin City (West Africa) by the British. Aboriginal peoples in Australia confined to reserves, strictly controlled by government agencies or missionaries. Vienna Secession founded. Badeni language ordinances resisted by German nationalists, leading to riots throughout the Austrian Empire; Badeni is dismissed and the ordinances are repealed in 1899.

Brief Spanish–American War. By the Treaty of Paris, Spain renounces claim to Cuba and cedes Puerta Rico and Guam to the US; US purchases the Philippine Islands from Spain for $20 million. Curtis Act extends Dawes Act to the "Five Civilized Nations," hitherto exempt; tribal institutions dismantled. First German Navy Law; arms race with Britain begins. Britain and France clash in the Sudan (Fashoda incident). Britain granted 99-year lease on Hong Kong by Chinese government. Assassination of the Empress Elizabeth (Twain witnesses her funeral in Vienna). Emperor Franz Josef's Golden Jubilee. Pierre and Marie Curie discover radium. Machine for magnetic recording of sound patented by V. Poulsen.

Philippine–American War (to 1902). Second Boer War (to 1902). After a century of expansion the British Empire covers one fifth of the globe, and is home to one quarter of the world's population. Retrial of Dreyfus and national outcry in France at his conviction. Scott Joplin's "Maple Leaf Rag." Death of Johann Strauss II, "the waltz king," in Vienna.

US annexes Hawaii. Britain annexes Transvaal and Orange Free State. Boxer Rebellion in China. First "direct" election primary tried in Minneapolis. Texas hurricane kills 8000 – the worst natural disaster in US history.

DATE	AUTHOR'S LIFE	LITERARY CONTEXT
1901	Moves to Riverdale-on-the-Hudson. Publishes "To the Person Sitting in Darkness" and "To My Missionary Critics" in the *North American Review*. Becomes vice-president of the Anti-Imperialist League.	Washington: *Up From Slavery*. Conan Doyle: *The Hound of the Baskervilles*. Kipling: *Kim*.
1902	*A Double-Barrelled Detective Story*. Awarded an honorary degree by the University of Missouri. Travels to Hannibal, Missouri, for the last time. Livy seriously ill.	Conrad: *Heart of Darkness*; *Typhoon*.
1903	Moves with family to Florence for Livy's health. Harper and Brothers acquires exclusive rights to all of Twain's work. Hartford house sold.	London: *The Call of the Wild*. Dubois: *The Souls of Black Folk*. Butler: *The Way of All Flesh*.
1904	Publishes *Extracts from Adam's Diary*. Begins dictating autobiography. Death of his wife. Family returns to New York.	James: *The Golden Bowl*. O. Henry: *Cabbages and Kings*. London: *The Sea-Wolf*. Conrad: *Nostromo*. Saki: *Reginald*.
1905	*King Leopold's Soliloquy* published. Dines at the White House with President Roosevelt. Banquet at Delmonico's, New York, for his 70th birthday.	Wharton: *The House of Mirth*. Cather: *The Troll Garden*. Shaw: *Man and Superman*; *Major Barbara*.
1906	*Eve's Diary* published. Selected chapters from his autobiography appear in the *North American Review* (to 1907). Resumes dictations. Albert Bigelow Paine moves into Twain's home to begin work as his authorized biographer. *What is Man?* printed anonymously for private distribution.	O. Henry: *The Four Million*. Sinclair: *The Jungle*. London: *White Fang*.
1907	Trip to Bermuda with Joseph Twichell. Visits England to receive an honorary doctorate from Oxford University.	Adams: *The History of Henry Adams*. William James: *Pragmatism*. Conrad: *The Secret Agent*.
1908	Moves to "Stormfield," the house he had commissioned in Redding, Connecticut.	London: *The Iron Heel*. Forster: *A Room with a View*.

CHRONOLOGY

HISTORICAL EVENTS

Theodore Roosevelt becomes President after the assassination of William McKinley. First major oil discovery in Texas. Death of Queen Victoria and accession of Edward VII. First Nobel prizes awarded.

Roosevelt embarks on a conservation program to protect wildlife and public land. During his presidency (to 1909) 150 national forests, 51 federal bird reserves and 5 national parks are created. Treaty of Vereeniging ends Boer War. First celebration of Empire Day in Britain. Cuba gains formal independence from the US.

Wright brothers' first successful powered flight. Ford Motor Company set up. Marconi demonstrates wireless communication between Great Britain and the US when President Roosevelt sends a cable to King Edward VII.

Roosevelt wins landslide victory in general election. Panama Canal zone acquired by the US. Russo-Japanese War (to 1905). Congo Reform Association founded by Edmund Dene Morel and Roger Casement.

"Bloody Sunday" in St Petersburg; first Russian Revolution. Moroccan crisis.

Severe anti-Negro riots and martial law in Atlanta. Roosevelt awarded Nobel Peace Prize for negotiating end to the Russo-Japanese War. San Francisco earthquake.

Currency panic; run on banks; J. P. Morgan imports $100 million in gold from Europe to halt crisis. Lenin founds newspaper *The Proletarian* in Geneva. Oklahoma and the Indian Territory combine to become a state. Regular transatlantic radio telegraph service established.
Ford Model T marketed.

DATE	AUTHOR'S LIFE	LITERARY CONTEXT
1909	Holidays in Bermuda. Marriage of Clara. Death of Jean.	Wells: *Tono-Bungay.*
1910	Another trip to Bermuda. Dies at home on April 21. Birth of his only grandchild, Nina. William Dean Howells publishes *My Mark Twain.*	Forster: *Howards End.* Death of Tolstoy, William James and O. Henry.
1911		Wharton: *Ethan Frome.*
1912	Paine's biography published.	
1916	The unfinished *Mysterious Stranger* published, edited by Paine.	Joyce: *A Portrait of the Artist as a Young Man.*
1924	*Mark Twain's Autobiography* (ed. Paine) published.	

HISTORICAL EVENTS

Commercial manufacture of bakelite, the world's first synthetic plastic.
William Howard Taft becomes US President and instigates "Dollar Diplomacy" to extend US influence.
Culmination of the worst five years of mining disasters (2494 killed) in American history. Death of Edward VII.

W. C. Handy's revolutionary "Memphis Blues" published. RMS *Titanic* sinks.

Indian Citizenship Act grants citizenship to all Native Americans born in the US.

From

THE INNOCENTS ABROAD

1869

THE PILGRIM'S VISION.

PREFACE

THIS BOOK IS a record of a pleasure-trip. If it were a record of a solemn scientific expedition, it would have about it that gravity, that profundity, and that impressive incomprehensibility which are so proper to works of that kind, and withal so attractive. Yet notwithstanding it is only a record of a picnic, it has a purpose, which is, to suggest to the reader how *he* would be likely to see Europe and the East if he looked at them with his own eyes instead of the eyes of those who traveled in those countries before him. I make small pretence of showing any one how he *ought* to look at objects of interest beyond the sea – other books do that, and therefore, even if I were competent to do it, there is no need.

I offer no apologies for any departures from the usual style of travel-writing that may be charged against me – for I think I have seen with impartial eyes, and I am sure I have written at least honestly, whether wisely or not.

In this volume I have used portions of letters which I wrote for the *Daily Alta California*, of San Francisco, the proprietors of that journal having waived their rights and given me the necessary permission. I have also inserted portions of several letters written for the New York *Tribune* and the New York *Herald*.

THE AUTHOR
SAN FRANCISCO, 1869

CHAPTER I

FOR MONTHS THE great Pleasure Excursion to Europe and the Holy Land was chatted about in the newspapers every where in America, and discussed at countless firesides. It was a novelty in the way of Excursions – its like had not been thought of before, and it compelled that interest which attractive novelties always command. It was to be a picnic on a gigantic scale. The participants in it, instead of freighting an ungainly steam ferry-boat with youth and beauty and pies and doughnuts, and paddling up some obscure creek to disembark upon a grassy lawn and wear themselves out with a long summer day's laborious frolicking under the impression that it was fun, were to sail away in a great steamship with flags flying and cannon pealing, and take a royal holiday beyond the broad ocean, in many a strange clime and in many a land renowned in history! They were to sail for months over the breezy Atlantic and the sunny Mediterranean; they were to scamper about the decks by day, filling the ship with shouts and laughter – or read novels and poetry in the shade of the smoke-stacks, or watch for the jelly-fish and the nautilus, over the side, and the shark, the whale, and other strange monsters of the deep; and at night they were to dance in the open air, on the upper deck, in the midst of a ball-room that stretched from horizon to horizon, and was domed by the bending heavens and lighted by no meaner lamps than the stars and the magnificent moon – dance, and promenade, and smoke, and sing, and make love, and search the skies for constellations that never associate with the "Big Dipper" they were so tired of; and they were to see the ships of twenty navies – the customs and costumes of twenty curious peoples – the great cities of half a world – they were to hob-nob with nobility and hold friendly converse with kings and princes, Grand Moguls, and the anointed lords of mighty empires!

It was a brave conception; it was the offspring of a most ingenious brain. It was well advertised, but it hardly needed it: the bold originality, the extraordinary character, the seductive nature, and the vastness of the enterprise provoked comment every where and advertised it in every household in the land. Who could read the programme of the excursion without longing to make one of the party? I will insert it here. It is almost as good as a map. As a text for this book, nothing could be better:

EXCURSION TO THE HOLY LAND, EGYPT, THE CRIMEA, GREECE, AND INTERMEDIATE POINTS OF INTEREST

BROOKLYN, FEBRUARY 1*st*, 1867

The undersigned will make an excursion as above during the coming season, and begs to submit to you the following programme:

A first-class steamer, to be under his own command, and capable of accommodating at least one hundred and fifty cabin passengers, will be selected, in which will be taken a select company, numbering not more than three-fourths of the ship's capacity. There is good reason to believe that this company can be easily made up in this immediate vicinity, of mutual friends and acquaintances.

The steamer will be provided with every necessary comfort, including library and musical instruments.

An experienced physician will be on board.

Leaving New York about June 1st, a middle and pleasant route will be taken across the Atlantic, and passing through the group of Azores, St. Michael will be reached in about ten days. A day or two will be spent here, enjoying the fruit and wild scenery of these islands, and the voyage continued, and Gibraltar reached in three or four days.

A day or two will be spent here in looking over the wonderful subterraneous fortifications, permission to visit these galleries being readily obtained.

From Gibraltar, running along the coasts of Spain and France, Marseilles will be reached in three days. Here ample time will be given not only to look over the city, which was founded six hundred years before the Christian era, and its artificial port, the finest of the kind in the Mediterranean, but to visit Paris during the Great Exhibition; and the beautiful city of Lyons, lying intermediate, from the heights of which, on a clear day, Mont Blanc and the Alps can be distinctly seen. Passengers who may wish to extend the time at Paris can do so, and, passing down through Switzerland, rejoin the steamer at Genoa.

From Marseilles to Genoa is a run of one night. The excursionists will have an opportunity to look over this, the "magnificent city of palaces," and visit the birthplace of Columbus, twelve miles off, over a beautiful road built by Napoleon I. From this point, excursions may be made to Milan, Lakes Como and Maggiore, or to Milan, Verona, (famous for its extraordinary fortifications,) Padua, and Venice. Or, if passengers desire to visit Parma (famous for Correggio's frescoes,) and Bologna, they can by rail go on to Florence, and rejoin the steamer at Leghorn, thus spending about three weeks amid the cities most famous for art in Italy.

From Genoa the run to Leghorn will be made along the coast in one night, and time appropriated to this point in which to visit Florence, its palaces and galleries; Pisa, its Cathedral and "Leaning Tower," and Lucca and its baths, and Roman amphitheatre; Florence, the most remote, being distant by rail about sixty miles.

From Leghorn to Naples, (calling at Civita Vecchia to land any who may prefer to go to Rome from that point,) the distance will be made in about thirty-six hours; the route will lay along the coast of Italy, close by Caprera, Elba, and Corsica. Arrangements have been made to take on board at Leghorn a pilot for Caprera, and, if practicable, a call will be made there to visit the home of Garibaldi.

Rome, [by rail] Herculaneum, Pompeii, Vesuvius, Virgil's tomb, and possibly, the ruins of Pæstum, can be visited, as well as the beautiful surroundings of Naples and its charming bay.

The next point of interest will be Palermo, the most beautiful city of Sicily, which will be reached in one night from Naples. A day will be spent here, and leaving in the evening, the course will be taken towards Athens.

Skirting along the north coast of Sicily, passing through the group of Æolian Isles, in sight of Stromboli and Vulcania, both active volcanoes, through the Straits of Messina, with "Scylla" on the one hand and "Charybdis" on the other, along the east coast of Sicily, and in sight of Mount Ætna, along the south coast of Italy, the west and south coast of Greece, in sight of ancient Crete, up Athens Gulf, and into the Piræus, Athens will be reached in two and a half or three days. After tarrying here awhile, the Bay of Salamis will be crossed, and a day given to Corinth, whence the voyage will be continued to Constantinople, passing on the way through the Grecian Archipelago, the Dardanelles, the Sea of Marmora, and the mouth of the Golden Horn, and arriving in about forty-eight hours from Athens.

After leaving Constantinople, the way will be taken out through the beautiful Bosphorus, across the Black Sea to Sebastopol and Balaklava, a run of about twenty-four hours. Here it is proposed to remain two days, visiting the harbors, fortifications, and battle-fields of the Crimea; thence back through the Bosphorus, touching at Constantinople to take in any who may have preferred to remain there; down through the Sea of Marmora and the Dardanelles, along the coasts of ancient Troy and Lydia in Asia, to Smyrna, which will be reached in two or two and a half days from Constantinople. A sufficient stay will be made here to give opportunity of visiting Ephesus, fifty miles distant by rail.

From Smyrna towards the Holy Land the course will lay through the Grecian Archipelago, close by the Isle of Patmos, along the coast of Asia, ancient Pamphylia, and the Isle of Cyprus. Beirout will be reached in three days. At Beirout time will be given to visit Damascus; after which the steamer will proceed to Joppa.

From Joppa, Jerusalem, the River Jordan, the Sea of Tiberias, Nazareth, Bethany, Bethlehem, and other points of interest in the Holy Land can be visited, and here those who may have preferred to make the journey from Beirout *through* the country, passing through Damascus, Galilee, Capernaum, Samaria, and by the River Jordan and Sea of Tiberias, can rejoin the steamer.

Leaving Joppa, the next point of interest to visit will be Alexandria, which will be reached in twenty-four hours. The ruins of Cæsar's Palace, Pompey's Pillar, Cleopatra's Needle, the Catacombs, and ruins of ancient Alexandria, will be found worth the visit. The journey to Cairo, one hundred and thirty miles by rail, can be made in a few hours, and from which can be visited the site of ancient Memphis, Joseph's Granaries, and the Pyramids.

From Alexandria the route will be taken homeward, calling at Malta, Cagliari (in Sardinia,) and Parma (in Majorca,) all magnificent harbors, with charming scenery, and abounding in fruits.

A day or two will be spent at each place, and leaving Parma in the evening, Valencia in Spain will be reached the next morning. A few days will be spent in this, the finest city of Spain.

From Valencia, the homeward course will be continued, skirting along the coast of Spain. Alicant, Carthagena, Palos, and Malaga, will be passed but a mile or two distant, and Gibraltar reached in about twenty-four hours.

A stay of one day will be made here, and the voyage continued to Madeira, which will be reached in about three days. Captain Marryatt writes: "I do not know a spot on the globe which so much astonishes and delights upon first arrival as Madeira." A stay of one or two days will be made here, which, if time permits, may be extended, and passing on through the islands, and probably in sight of the Peak of Teneriffe, a southern track will be taken, and the Atlantic crossed within the latitudes of the Northeast trade winds, where mild and pleasant weather, and a smooth sea, can always be expected.

A call will be made at Bermuda, which lies directly in this route homeward, and will be reached in about ten days from Madeira, and after spending a short time with our friends the Bermudians, the final departure will be made for home, which will be reached in about three days.

Already, applications have been received from parties in Europe wishing to join the Excursion there.

The ship will at all times be a home, where the excursionists, if sick, will be surrounded by kind friends, and have all possible comfort and sympathy.

Should contagious sickness exist in any of the ports named in the programme, such ports will be passed, and others of interest substituted.

The price of passage is fixed at $1,250, currency, for each adult passenger. Choice of rooms and of seats at the tables apportioned in the order in which passages are engaged, and no passage considered engaged until ten per cent. of the passage money is deposited with the treasurer.

Passengers can remain on board of the steamer, at all ports, if they desire, without additional expense, and all boating at the expense of the ship.

All passages must be paid for when taken, in order that the most perfect arrangements be made for starting at the appointed time.

Applications for passage must be approved by the committee before tickets are issued, and can be made to the undersigned.

Articles of interest or curiosity, procured by the passengers during the voyage, may be brought home in the steamer free of charge.

Five dollars per day, in gold, it is believed, will be a fair calculation to make for *all* traveling expenses on shore, and at the various points where passengers may wish to leave the steamer for days at a time.

The trip can be extended, and the route changed, by *unanimous* vote of the passengers.

CHAS. C. DUNCAN,
117 Wall Street, New York

R. R. G******, Treasurer.

COMMITTEE ON APPLICATIONS

J. T. H*****, Esq., R. R. G*****, Esq., C. C. Duncan.

COMMITTEE ON SELECTING STEAMER

CAPT. W. W. S****, *Surveyor for Board of Underwriters.*
C. W. C*******, *Consulting Engineer for U. S. and Canada.*
J. T. H*****, ESQ.
C. C. Duncan.

P.S. – The very beautiful and substantial side wheel steamship *"Quaker City"* has been chartered for the occasion, and will leave New York, June 8th. Letters have been issued by the government commending the party to courtesies abroad.

What was there lacking about that programme, to make it perfectly irresistible? Nothing, that any finite mind could discover. Paris, England, Scotland, Switzerland, Italy – Garibaldi! The Grecian archipelago! Vesuvius! Constantinople! Smyrna! The Holy Land! Egypt and "our friends the Bermudians!" People in Europe desiring to join the Excursion – contagious sickness to be avoided – boating at the expense of the ship – physician on board – the circuit of the globe to be made if the passengers unanimously desired it – the company to be rigidly selected by a pitiless "Committee on Applications" – the vessel to be as rigidly selected by as pitiless a "Committee on Selecting Steamer." Human nature could not withstand these bewildering temptations. I hurried to the Treasurer's office and deposited my ten per cent. I rejoiced to know that a few vacant state-rooms were still left. I *did* avoid a critical personal examination into my character, by that bowelless committee, but I referred to all the people of high standing I could think of in the community who would be least likely to know any thing about me.

Shortly a supplementary programme was issued which set forth that the Plymouth Collection of Hymns would be used on board the ship. I then paid the balance of my passage money.

I was provided with a receipt, and duly and officially accepted as an excursionist. There was happiness in that, but it was tame compared to the novelty of being "select."

This supplementary programme also instructed the excursionists to provide themselves with light musical instruments for amusement in the ship; with saddles for Syrian travel; green spectacles and umbrellas; veils for Egypt; and substantial clothing to use in rough pilgrimizing in the Holy Land. Furthermore, it was suggested that although the ship's library would afford a fair amount of reading matter, it would still be well if each passenger would provide himself with a few guide-books, a Bible and some standard works of travel. A list was appended, which consisted chiefly of books relating to the Holy Land, since the Holy Land was part of the excursion and seemed to be its main feature.

Rev. Henry Ward Beecher was to have accompanied the expedition, but urgent duties obliged him to give up the idea. There were other passengers who could have been spared better, and would have been spared more willingly. Lieut. Gen. Sherman was to have been of the party, also, but the Indian war compelled his presence on the plains. A popular actress had entered her name on the ship's books, but something interfered, and *she* couldn't go. The "Drummer Boy of the Potomac" deserted, and lo, we had never a celebrity left!

However, we were to have a "battery of guns" from the Navy Department, (as per advertisement,) to be used in answering royal salutes; and the document furnished by the Secretary of the Navy, which was to make "Gen. Sherman and party" welcome guests in the courts and camps of the old world, was still left to us, though both document and battery, I think, were shorn of somewhat of their original august proportions. However, had not we the seductive programme, still, with its Paris, its Constantinople, Smyrna, Jerusalem, Jericho, and "our friends the Bermudians?" What did we care?

CHAPTER II

OCCASIONALLY, DURING THE following month, I dropped in at 117 Wall-street to inquire how the repairing and refurnishing of the vessel was coming on; how additions to the passenger list were averaging; how many people the committee were decreeing not "select," every day, and banishing in sorrow and tribulation. I was glad to know that we were to have a little printing-press on board and issue a daily newspaper of our own. I was glad to learn that our piano, our parlor organ and our melodeon were to be the best instruments of the kind that could be had in the market. I was proud to observe that among our excursionists were three ministers of the gospel, eight doctors, sixteen or eighteen ladies, several military and naval chieftains with sounding titles, an ample crop of "Professors" of various kinds, and a gentleman who had "COMMISSIONER OF THE UNITED STATES OF

AMERICA TO EUROPE, ASIA, AND AFRICA" thundering after his name in one awful blast! I had carefully prepared myself to take rather a back seat in that ship, because of the uncommonly select material that would alone be permitted to pass through the camel's eye of that committee on credentials; I had schooled myself to expect an imposing array of military and naval heroes, and to have to set that back seat still further back in consequence of it, may be; but I state frankly that I was all unprepared for *this* crusher.

I fell under that titular avalanche a torn and blighted thing. I said that if that potentate *must* go over in our ship, why, I supposed he must – but that to my thinking, when the United States considered it necessary to send a dignitary of that tonnage across the ocean, it would be in better taste, and safer, to take him apart and cart him over in sections, in several ships.

Ah, if I had only known, then, that he was only a common mortal, and that his mission had nothing more overpowering about it than the collecting of seeds, and uncommon yams and extraordinary cabbages and peculiar bullfrogs for that poor, useless, innocent, mildewed old fossil, the Smithsonian Institute, I would have felt *so* much relieved.

During that memorable month I basked in the happiness of being for once in my life drifting with the tide of a great popular movement. Every body was going to Europe – I, too, was going to Europe. Every body was going to the famous Paris Exposition – I, too, was going to the Paris Exposition. The steamship lines were carrying Americans out of the various ports of the country at the rate of four or five thousand a week, in the aggregate. If I met a dozen individuals, during that month, who were not going to Europe shortly, I have no distinct remembrance of it now. I walked about the city a good deal with a young Mr. Blucher, who was booked for the excursion. He was confiding, good-natured, unsophisticated, companionable; but he was not a man to set the river on fire. He had the most extraordinary notions about this European exodus, and came at last to consider the whole nation as packing up for emigration to France. We stepped into a store in Broadway, one day, where he bought a handkerchief, and when the man could not make change, Mr. B. said:

"Never mind, I'll hand it to you in Paris."

"But I am not going to Paris."

"How is – what did I understand you to say?"

"I said I am not going to Paris."

"Not going to *Paris*! Not g—well then, where in the nation *are* you going to?"

"Nowhere at all."

"Not any where whatsoever? – not any place on earth but this?"

"Not any place at all but just this – stay here all summer."

My comrade took his purchase and walked out of the store without a word – walked out with an injured look upon his countenance. Up the street apiece he broke silence and said impressively: "It was a lie – that is my opinion of it!"

In the fullness of time the ship was ready to receive her passengers. I was introduced to the young gentleman who was to be my room mate, and found him to be intelligent, cheerful of spirit, unselfish, full of generous impulses, patient, considerate, and wonderfully good-natured. Not any passenger that sailed in the *Quaker City* will withhold his indorsement of what I have just said. We selected a state-room forward of the wheel, on the starboard side, "below decks." It had two berths in it, a dismal dead-light, a sink with a wash-bowl in it, and a long, sumptuously cushioned locker, which was to do service as a sofa – partly, and partly as a hiding-place for our things. Notwithstanding all this furniture, there was still room to turn around in, but not to swing a cat in, at least with entire security to the cat. However, the room was large, for a ship's state-room, and was in every way satisfactory.

The vessel was appointed to sail on a certain Saturday early in June.

A little after noon, on that distinguished Saturday, I reached the ship and went on board. All was bustle and confusion. [I have seen that remark before, somewhere.] The pier was crowded with carriages and men; passengers were arriving and hurrying on board; the vessel's decks were encumbered with trunks and valises; groups of excursionists, arrayed in unattractive traveling costumes, were moping about in a drizzling rain and looking as droopy and woe-begone as so many molting chickens. The gallant flag was up, but it was under the spell, too, and hung limp and disheartened by the mast. Altogether, it was the bluest, bluest spectacle! It was a pleasure excursion – there was no gainsaying that, because the programme said so – it was so nominated in the bond – but it surely hadn't the general aspect of one.

Finally, above the banging, and rumbling, and shouting and hissing of steam, rang the order to "cast off!" – a sudden rush to the gangways – a scampering ashore of visitors – a revolution of the wheels, and we were off – the picnic was begun! Two very mild cheers went up from the dripping crowd on the pier; we answered them gently from the slippery decks; the flag made an effort to wave, and failed; the "battery of guns" spake not – the ammunition was out.

We steamed down to the foot of the harbor and came to anchor. It was still raining. And not only raining, but storming. "Outside" we could see, ourselves, that there was a tremendous sea on. We must lie still, in the calm harbor, till the storm should abate. Our passengers hailed from fifteen States; only a few of them had ever been to sea before; manifestly it would not do to pit them against a full-blown tempest until they had got their sea-legs on. Toward evening the two steam-tugs that had accompanied us with a rollicking champagne-party of young New Yorkers on board who wished to bid farewell to one of our number in due and ancient form, departed, and we were alone on the deep. On deep five fathoms, and anchored fast to the bottom. And out in the solemn rain, at that. This was pleasuring with a vengeance.

It was an appropriate relief when the gong sounded for prayer-meeting. The first Saturday night of any other pleasure excursion might have been devoted to whist and dancing; but I submit it to the unprejudiced mind if it would have been in good taste for *us* to engage in such frivolities, considering what we had gone through and the frame of mind we were in. We would have shone at a wake, but not at any thing more festive.

However, there is always a cheering influence about the sea; and in my berth, that night, rocked by the measured swell of the waves, and lulled by the murmur of the distant surf, I soon passed tranquilly out of all consciousness of the dreary experiences of the day and damaging premonitions of the future.

CHAPTER III

ALL DAY SUNDAY at anchor. The storm had gone down a great deal, but the sea had not. It was still piling its frothy hills high in air "outside," as we could plainly see with the glasses. We could not properly begin a pleasure excursion on Sunday; we could not offer untried stomachs to so pitiless a sea as that. We must lie still till Monday. And we did. But we had repetitions of church and prayer-meetings; and so, of course, we were just as eligibly situated as we could have been any where.

I was up early that Sabbath morning, and was early to breakfast. I felt a perfectly natural desire to have a good, long, unprejudiced look at the passengers, at a time when they should be free from self-consciousness – which is at breakfast, when such a moment occurs in the lives of human beings at all.

I was greatly surprised to see so many elderly people – I might almost say, so many venerable people. A glance at the long lines of heads was apt to make one think it was *all* gray. But it was not. There was a tolerably fair sprinkling of young folks, and another fair sprinkling of gentlemen and ladies who were non-committal as to age, being neither actually old or absolutely young.

The next morning, we weighed anchor and went to sea. It was a great happiness to get away, after this dragging, dispiriting delay. I thought there never was such gladness in the air before, such brightness in the sun, such beauty in the sea. I was satisfied with the picnic, then, and with all its belongings. All my malicious instincts were dead within me; and as America faded out of sight, I think a spirit of charity rose up in their place that was as boundless, for the time being, as the broad ocean that was heaving its billows about us. I wished to express my feelings – I wished to lift up my voice and sing; but I did not know any thing to sing, and so I was obliged to give up the idea. It was no loss to the ship though, perhaps.

It was breezy and pleasant, but the sea was still very rough. One could not promenade without risking his neck; at one moment the bowsprit was taking a deadly aim at the sun in mid-heaven, and at the next it was trying to harpoon a shark in the bottom of the ocean. What a weird sensation it is to feel the stern of a ship sinking swiftly from under you and see the bow climbing high away among the clouds! One's safest course, that day, was to clasp a railing and hang on; walking was too precarious a pastime.

By some happy fortune I was not seasick. – That was a thing to be proud of. I had not always escaped before. If there is one thing in the world that will make a man peculiarly and insufferably self-conceited, it is to have his stomach behave itself, the first day at sea, when nearly all his comrades are seasick. Soon, a venerable fossil, shawled to the chin and bandaged like a mummy, appeared at the door of the after deck-house, and the next lurch of the ship shot him into my arms. I said:

"Good-morning, Sir. It is a fine day."

He put his hand on his stomach and said, "*Oh*, my!" and then staggered away and fell over the coop of a skylight.

Presently another old gentleman was projected from the same door, with great violence. I said:

"Calm yourself, Sir – There is no hurry. It is a fine day, Sir."

He, also, put his hand on his stomach and said "*Oh*, my!" and reeled away.

In a little while another veteran was discharged abruptly from the same door, clawing at the air for a saving support. I said:

"Good-morning, Sir. It is a fine day for pleasuring. You were about to say—"

"*Oh*, my!"

I thought so. I anticipated *him*, any how. I staid there and was bombarded with old gentlemen for an hour perhaps; and all I got out of any of them was "*Oh*, my!"

I went away, then, in a thoughtful mood. I said, this is a good pleasure excursion. I like it. The passengers are not garrulous, but still they are sociable. I like those old people, but somehow they all seem to have the "Oh, my" rather bad.

I knew what was the matter with them. They were seasick. And I was glad of it. We all like to see people seasick when we are not, ourselves. Playing whist by the cabin lamps when it is storming outside, is pleasant; walking the quarter-deck in the moonlight, is pleasant; smoking in the breezy foretop is pleasant, when one is not afraid to go up there; but these are all feeble and commonplace compared with the joy of seeing people suffering the miseries of seasickness.

I picked up a good deal of information during the afternoon. At one time I was climbing up the quarter-deck when the vessel's stern was in the sky; I was smoking a cigar and feeling passably comfortable. Somebody ejaculated:

"Come, now, *that* won't answer. Read the sign up there – NO SMOKING ABAFT THE WHEEL!"

It was Capt. Duncan, chief of the expedition. I went forward, of course. I saw a long spy-glass lying on a desk in one of the upper-deck state-rooms back of the pilot-house, and reached after it – there was a ship in the distance:

"Ah, ah – hands off! Come out of that!"

I came out of that. I said to a deck-sweep – but in a low voice:

"Who is that overgrown pirate with the whiskers and the discordant voice?"

"It's Capt. Bursley – executive officer – sailing-master."

I loitered about awhile, and then, for want of something better to do, fell to carving a railing with my knife. Somebody said, in an insinuating, admonitory voice:

"Now *say* – my friend – don't you know any better than to be whittling the ship all to pieces that way? *You* ought to know better than that."

I went back and found the deck-sweep:

"Who is that smooth-faced animated outrage yonder in the fine clothes?"

"That's Capt. L****, the owner of the ship – he's one of the main bosses."

In the course of time I brought up on the starboard side of the pilot-house, and found a sextant lying on a bench. Now, I said, they "take the sun" through this thing; I should think I might see that vessel through it. I had hardly got it to my eye when some one touched me on the shoulder and said, deprecatingly:

"I'll have to get you to give that to me, Sir. If there's any thing you'd like to know about taking the sun, I'd as soon tell you as not – but I don't like to trust any body with that instrument. If you want any figuring done – Aye-aye, Sir!"

He was gone, to answer a call from the other side. I sought the deck-sweep:

"Who is that spider-legged gorilla yonder with the sanctimonious countenance?"

"It's Capt. Jones, Sir – the chief mate."

"Well. This goes clear away ahead of any thing I ever heard of before. Do you – now I ask you as a man and a brother – *do* you think I could venture to throw a rock here in any given direction without hitting a captain of this ship?"

"Well, Sir, I don't know – I think likely you'd fetch the captain of the watch, may be, because he's a-standing right yonder in the way."

I went below – meditating, and a little down-hearted. I thought, if five cooks can spoil a broth, what may not five captains do with a pleasure excursion.

CHAPTER VII

A WEEK OF buffeting a tempestuous and relentless sea; a week of seasickness and deserted cabins; of lonely quarter-decks drenched with spray – spray so ambitious that it even coated the smoke-stacks thick with a white crust of salt to their very tops; a week of shivering in the shelter of the life-boats and deck-houses by day, and blowing suffocating "clouds" and boisterously performing at dominoes in the smoking room at night.

And the last night of the seven was the stormiest of all. There was no thunder, no noise but the pounding bows of the ship, the keen whistling of the gale through the cordage, and the rush of the seething waters. But the vessel climbed aloft as if she would climb to heaven – then paused an instant that seemed a century, and plunged headlong down again, as from a precipice. The sheeted sprays drenched the decks like rain. The blackness of darkness was every where. At long intervals a flash of lightning clove it with a quivering line of fire, that revealed a heaving world of water where was nothing before, kindled the dusky cordage to glittering silver, and lit up the faces of the men with a ghastly lustre!

Fear drove many on deck that were used to avoiding the night-winds and the spray. Some thought the vessel could not live through the night, and it seemed less dreadful to stand out in the midst of the wild tempest and *see* the peril that threatened than to be shut up in the sepulchral cabins, under the dim lamps and imagine the horrors that were abroad on the ocean. And once out – once where they could see the ship struggling in the strong grasp of the storm – once where they could hear the shriek of the winds, and face the driving spray and look out upon the majestic picture the lightnings disclosed, they were prisoners to a fierce fascination they could not resist, and so remained. It was a wild night – and a very, very long one.

Every body was sent scampering to the deck at seven o'clock this lovely morning of the 30th of June with the glad news that land was in sight! It was a rare thing and a joyful, to see *all* the ship's family abroad once more, albeit the happiness that sat upon every countenance could only partly conceal the ravages which that long siege of storms had wrought there. But dull eyes soon sparkled with pleasure, pallid cheeks flushed again, and frames weakened by sickness gathered new life from the quickening influences of the bright, fresh morning. Yea, and from a still more potent influence: the worn castaways were to see the blessed land again! – and to see it was to bring back that mother-land that was in all their thoughts.

Within the hour we were fairly within the Straits of Gibraltar, the tall yellow-splotched hills of Africa on our right, with their bases veiled in a blue haze and their summits swathed in clouds – the same being according to Scripture, which says that "clouds and darkness are over the land." The words were spoken of this particular portion of Africa, I believe. On our left were the granite-ribbed domes of old Spain. The Strait is only thirteen miles wide in its narrowest part.

At short intervals, along the Spanish shore, were quaint-looking old stone towers – Moorish, we thought – but learned better afterwards. In former times the Morocco rascals used to coast along the Spanish Main in their boats till a safe opportunity seemed to present itself, and then dart in and capture a Spanish village, and carry off all the pretty women they could find. It was a pleasant business, and was very popular. The Spaniards built these watchtowers on the hills to enable them to keep a sharper lookout on the Moroccan speculators.

The picture on the other hand was very beautiful to eyes weary of the changeless sea, and bye and bye the ship's company grew wonderfully cheerful. But while we stood admiring the cloud-capped peaks and the lowlands robed in misty gloom, a finer picture burst upon us and chained every eye like a magnet – a stately ship, with canvas piled on canvas till she was one towering mass of bellying sail! She came speeding over the sea like a great bird. Africa and Spain were forgotten. All homage was for the beautiful stranger. While every body gazed, she swept superbly by and flung the Stars and Stripes to the breeze! Quicker than thought, hats and handkerchiefs flashed in the air, and a cheer went up! She was beautiful before – she was radiant now. Many a one on our decks knew then for the first time how tame a sight his country's flag is at home compared to what it is in a foreign land. To see it is to see a vision of home itself and all its idols, and feel a thrill that would stir a very river of sluggish blood!

We were approaching the famed Pillars of Hercules, and already the African one, "Ape's Hill," a grand old mountain with summit streaked with granite ledges, was in sight. The other, the great Rock of Gibraltar, was yet to come. The ancients considered the Pillars of Hercules the head of navigation and the end of the world. The information the ancients didn't have was very voluminous. Even the prophets wrote book after book and epistle after epistle, yet never once hinted at the existence of a great continent on our side of the water; yet they must have known it was there, I should think.

In a few moments a lonely and enormous mass of rock, standing seemingly in the centre of the wide strait and apparently washed on all sides by the sea, swung magnificently into view, and we needed no tedious traveled parrot to tell us it was Gibraltar. There could not be two rocks like that in one kingdom.

The Rock of Gibraltar is about a mile and a half long, I should say, by 1,400 to 1,500 feet high, and a quarter of a mile wide at its base. One side and one end of it come about as straight up out of the sea as the side of a house, the other end is irregular and the other side is a steep slant which an army would find very difficult to climb. At the foot of this slant is the walled town of Gibraltar – or rather the town occupies part of the slant. Every where – on hillside, in the precipice, by the sea, on the heights, – every where you choose to look, Gibraltar is clad with masonry and bristling with guns. It makes a striking and lively picture, from whatsoever point you contemplate it. It is pushed out into the sea on the end of a flat, narrow strip of land, and is suggestive of a "gob" of mud on the end of a shingle. A few hundred yards of this flat ground at its base belongs to the English, and then, extending across the strip from the Atlantic to the Mediterranean, a distance of a quarter of a mile, comes the "Neutral Ground," a space two or three hundred yards wide, which is free to both parties.

"Are you going through Spain to Paris?" That question was bandied about the ship day and night from Fayal to Gibraltar, and I thought I never could get so tired of hearing any one combination of words again, or more tired of answering, "I don't know." At the last moment six or seven had sufficient decision of character to make up their minds to go, and did go, and I felt a sense of relief at once – it was forever too late, now, and I could make up my mind at my leisure, not to go. I must have a prodigious quantity of mind; it takes me as much as a week, sometimes, to make it up.

But behold how annoyances repeat themselves. We had no sooner gotten rid of the Spain distress than the Gibraltar guides started another – a tiresome repetition of a legend that had nothing very astonishing about it, even in the first place: "That high hill yonder is called the Queen's Chair; it is because one of the Queens of Spain placed her chair there when the French and Spanish troops were besieging Gibraltar, and said she would never move from the spot till the English flag was lowered from the fortresses. If the English hadn't been gallant enough to lower the flag for a few hours one day, she'd have had to break her oath or die up there."

We rode on asses and mules up the steep, narrow streets and entered the subterranean galleries the English have blasted out in the rock. These galleries are like spacious railway tunnels, and at short intervals in them great guns frown out upon sea and town through port-holes five or six hundred feet above the ocean. There is a mile or so of this subterranean work, and it must have cost a vast deal of money and labor. The gallery guns command the peninsula and the harbors of both oceans, but they might as well not be there, I should think, for an army could hardly climb the perpendicular wall of the rock any how. Those lofty port-holes afford superb views of the sea, though. At one place, where a jutting crag was hollowed out into a great chamber whose furniture was huge cannon and whose windows were port-holes, a glimpse was caught of a hill not far away, and a soldier said:

"That high hill yonder is called the Queen's Chair; it is because a Queen of Spain placed her chair there, once, when the French and Spanish troops were besieging Gibraltar, and said she would never move from the spot till the English flag was lowered from the fortresses. If the English hadn't been gallant enough to lower the flag for a few hours, one day, she'd have had to break her oath or die up there."

On the topmost pinnacle of Gibraltar we halted a good while, and no doubt the mules were tired. They had a right to be. The military road was good, but rather steep, and there was a good deal of it. The view from the narrow ledge was magnificent; from it vessels seeming like the tiniest little toy-boats, were turned into noble ships by the telescopes; and other vessels that were fifty miles away, and even sixty, they said, and invisible to the naked eye, could be clearly distinguished through those same telescopes. Below, on one side, we looked down upon an endless mass of batteries, and on the other straight down to the sea.

While I was resting ever so comfortably on a rampart, and cooling my baking head in the delicious breeze, an officious guide belonging to another party came up and said:

"Senor, that high hill yonder is called the Queen's Chair"—

"Sir, I am a helpless orphan in a foreign land. Have pity on me. Don't – now *don't* inflict that most in-FERNAL old legend on me any more to-day!"

There – I had used strong language, after promising I would never do so again; but the provocation was more than human nature could bear. If you had been bored so, when you had the noble panorama of Spain and Africa and the blue Mediterranean, spread abroad at your feet, and wanted to gaze, and enjoy, and surfeit yourself with its beauty in silence, you might have even burst into stronger language than I did.

Gibraltar has stood several protracted sieges, one of them of nearly four years duration (it failed,) and the English only captured it by stratagem. The wonder is that any body should ever dream of trying so impossible a project as the taking it by assault – and yet it has been tried more than once.

The Moors held the place twelve hundred years ago, and a stanch old castle of theirs of that date still frowns from the middle of the town, with moss-grown battlements and sides well scarred by shots fired in battles and sieges that are forgotten now. A secret chamber, in the rock behind it, was discovered some time ago, which contained a sword of exquisite workmanship, and some quaint old armor of a fashion that antiquaries are not acquainted with, though it is supposed to be Roman. Roman armor and Roman relics, of various kinds, have been found in a cave in the sea extremity of Gibraltar; history says Rome held this part of the country about the Christian era, and these things seem to confirm the statement.

In that cave, also, are found human bones, crusted with a very thick, stony coating, and wise men have ventured to say that those men not only lived before the flood, but as much as ten thousand years before it. It may be true – it looks reasonable enough – but as long as those parties can't vote any more, the matter can be of no great public interest. In this cave, likewise, are found skeletons and fossils of animals that exist in every part of Africa, yet within memory and tradition have never existed in any portion of Spain save this lone peak of Gibraltar! So the theory is that the channel between Gibraltar and Africa was once dry land, and that the low, neutral neck between Gibraltar and the Spanish hills behind it was once ocean, and of course that these African animals, being over at Gibraltar (after rock, perhaps – there is plenty there,) got closed out when the great change occurred. The hills in Africa, across the channel, are full of apes, and there are now, and always have been, apes on the rock of Gibraltar – but not elsewhere in Spain! The subject is an interesting one.

There is an English garrison at Gibraltar of 6,000 or 7,000 men, and so uniforms of flaming red are plenty; and red and blue, and undress costumes of snowy white, and also the queer uniform of the bare-kneed Highlander; and one sees soft-eyed Spanish girls from San Roque, and veiled Moorish beauties (I suppose they are beauties) from Tarifa, and turbaned, sashed and trowsered Moorish merchants from Fez, and long-robed, bare-legged, ragged Mohammedan vagabonds from Tetouan and Tangier, some brown, some yellow and some as black as virgin ink – and Jews from all around, in gaberdine, skull-cap and slippers, just as they are in pictures and theatres, and just as they were three thousand years ago, no doubt. You can easily understand that a tribe (somehow our pilgrims suggest that expression, because they march in a straggling procession through these foreign places with such an Indian-like air of complacency and independence about them,) like ours, made up from fifteen or sixteen States of the Union, found enough to stare at in this shifting panorama of fashion to-day.

Speaking of our pilgrims reminds me that we have one or two people among us who are sometimes an annoyance. However, I do not count the Oracle in that list. I will explain that the Oracle is an innocent old ass who eats for four and looks wiser than the whole Academy of France would have any right to look, and never uses a one-syllable word when he can think of a longer one, and never by any possible chance knows the meaning of any long word he uses, or ever gets it in the right place: yet he will serenely venture an opinion on the most abstruse subject, and back it up complacently with quotations from authors who never existed, and finally when cornered will slide to the other side of the question, say he has been there all the time, and come back at you with your own spoken arguments, only with the big words all tangled, and play them in your very teeth as original with himself. He reads a chapter in the guide-books, mixes the facts all up, with his bad memory, and then goes off to inflict the whole mess on somebody as wisdom which has been festering in his brain for years, and which he gathered in college from erudite authors who are dead, now, and out of print. This morning at breakfast he pointed out of the window, and said:

"Do you see that there hill out there on that African coast? – It's one of them Pillows of Herkewls, I should say – and there's the ultimate one alongside of it."

"The ultimate one – that is a good word – but the Pillars are not both on the same side of the strait." (I saw he had been deceived by a carelessly written sentence in the Guide Book.)

"Well, it ain't for you to say, nor for me. Some authors states it that way, and some states it different. Old Gibbons don't say nothing about it, – just shirks it complete – Gibbons always done that when he got stuck – but there is Rolampton, what does *he* say? Why, he says that they was both on the same side, and Trinculian, and Sobaster, and Syraccus, and Langomarganbl—"

"Oh, that will do – that's enough. If you have got your hand in for inventing authors and testimony, I have nothing more to say – let them *be* on the same side."

We don't mind the Oracle. We rather like him. We can tolerate the Oracle very easily; but we have a poet and a good-natured enterprising idiot on board, and they *do* distress the company. The one gives copies of his verses to Consuls, commanders, hotel keepers, Arabs, Dutch, – to any body, in fact, who will submit to a grievous infliction most kindly meant. His poetry is all very well on shipboard, notwithstanding when he wrote an "Ode to the Ocean in a Storm" in one half-hour, and an "Apostrophe to the Rooster in the Waist of the Ship" in the next, the transition was considered to be rather abrupt; but when he sends an invoice of rhymes to the Governor of Fayal and another to the commander-in-chief and other dignitaries in Gibraltar, with the compliments of the Laureate of the Ship, it is not popular with the passengers.

The other personage I have mentioned is young and green, and not bright, not learned and not wise. He will be, though, some day, if he recollects the answers to all his questions. He is known about the ship as the "Interrogation Point," and this by constant use has become shortened to "Interrogation." He has distinguished himself twice already. In Fayal they pointed out a hill and told him it was eight hundred feet high and eleven hundred feet long. And they told him there was a tunnel two thousand feet long and one thousand feet high running through the hill, from end to end. He believed it. He repeated it to every body, discussed it, and read it from his notes. Finally, he took a useful hint from this remark which a thoughtful old pilgrim made:

"Well, yes, it *is* a little remarkable – singular tunnel altogether – stands up out of the top of the hill about two hundred feet, and one end of it sticks out of the hill about nine hundred!"

Here in Gibraltar he corners these educated British officers and badgers them with braggadocio about America and the wonders she can perform. He told one of them a couple of our gunboats could come here and knock Gibraltar into the Mediterranean Sea!

At this present moment, half a dozen of us are taking a private pleasure excursion of our own devising. We form rather more than half the list of white passengers on board a small steamer bound for the venerable Moorish town of Tangier, Africa. Nothing could be more absolutely certain than that we are enjoying ourselves. One can not do otherwise who speeds over these sparkling waters, and breathes the soft atmosphere of this sunny land. Care can not assail us here. We are out of its jurisdiction.

We even steamed recklessly by the frowning fortress of Malabat, (a stronghold of the Emperor of Morocco,) without a twinge of fear. The whole garrison turned out under arms, and assumed a threatening attitude – yet still we did not fear. The entire garrison marched and counter-marched, within the rampart, in full view – yet notwithstanding even this, we never flinched.

I suppose we really do not know what fear is. I inquired the name of the garrison of the fortress of Malabat, and they said it was

Mehemet Ali Ben Sancom. I said it would be a good idea to get some more garrisons to help him; but they said no; he had nothing to do but hold the place, and he was competent to do that; had done it two years already. That was evidence which one could not well refute. There is nothing like reputation.

Every now and then, my glove purchase in Gibraltar last night intrudes itself upon me. Dan and the ship's surgeon and I had been up to the great square, listening to the music of the fine military bands, and contemplating English and Spanish female loveliness and fashion, and, at 9 o'clock, were on our way to the theatre, when we met the General, the Judge, the Commodore, the Colonel, and the Commissioner of the United States of America to Europe, Asia, and Africa, who had been to the Club House, to register their several titles and impoverish the bill of fare; and they told us to go over to the little variety store, near the Hall of Justice, and buy some kid gloves. They said they were elegant, and very moderate in price. It seemed a stylish thing to go to the theatre in kid gloves, and we acted upon the hint. A very handsome young lady in the store offered me a pair of blue gloves. I did not want blue, but she said they would look very pretty on a hand like mine. The remark touched me tenderly. I glanced furtively at my hand, and somehow it did seem rather a comely member. I tried a glove on my left, and blushed a little. Manifestly the size was too small for me. But I felt gratified when she said:

"Oh, it is just right!" – yet I knew it was no such thing.

I tugged at it diligently, but it was discouraging work. She said:

"Ah! I see *you* are accustomed to wearing kid gloves – but some gentlemen are *so* awkward about putting them on."

It was the last compliment I had expected. I only understand putting on the buckskin article perfectly. I made another effort, and tore the glove from the base of the thumb into the palm of the hand – and tried to hide the rest. She kept up her compliments, and I kept up my determination to deserve them or die:

"Ah, you have had experience!" [A rip down the back of the hand.] "They are just right for you – your hand is very small – if they tear you need not pay for them." [A rent across the middle.] "I can always tell when a gentleman understands putting on kid gloves. There is a grace about it that only comes with long practice. [The whole after-guard of the glove "fetched away," as the sailors say, the fabric parted across the knuckles, and nothing was left but a melancholy ruin.]

I was too much flattered to make an exposure, and throw the merchandise on the angel's hands. I was hot, vexed, confused, but still happy; but I hated the other boys for taking such an absorbing interest in the proceedings. I wished they were in Jericho. I felt exquisitely mean when I said cheerfully, –

"This one does very well; it fits elegantly. I like a glove that fits. No, never mind, ma'am, never mind; I'll put the other on in the street. It is warm here."

It *was* warm. It was the warmest place I ever was in. I paid the bill, and as I passed out with a fascinating bow, I thought I detected a light in the woman's eye that was gently ironical; and when I looked back from the street, and she was laughing all to herself about something or other, I said to myself, with withering sarcasm, "Oh, certainly; *you* know how to put on kid gloves, don't you? – a self-complacent ass, ready to be flattered out of your senses by every petticoat that chooses to take the trouble to do it!"

The silence of the boys annoyed me. Finally, Dan said, musingly:

"Some gentlemen don't know how to put on kid gloves at all; but some do."

And the doctor said (to the moon, I thought,)

"But it is always easy to tell when a gentleman is used to putting on kid gloves."

Dan soliloquized, after a pause:

"Ah, yes; there is a grace about it that only comes with long, very long practice."

"Yes, indeed, I've noticed that when a man hauls on a kid glove like he was dragging a cat out of an ash-hole by the tail, *he* understands putting on kid gloves; *he's* had ex—"

"Boys, enough of a thing's enough! You think you are very smart, I suppose, but I don't. And if you go and tell any of those old gossips in the ship about this thing, I'll never forgive you for it; that's all."

They let me alone then, for the time being. We always let each other alone in time to prevent ill feeling from spoiling a joke. But they had bought gloves, too, as I did. We threw all the purchases away together this morning. They were coarse, unsubstantial, freckled all over with broad yellow splotches, and could neither stand wear nor public exhibition. We had entertained an angel unawares, but we did not take her in. She did that for us.

Tangier! A tribe of stalwart Moors are wading into the sea to carry us ashore on their backs from the small boats.

CHAPTER VIII

THIS IS ROYAL! Let those who went up through Spain make the best of it – these dominions of the Emperor of Morocco suit our little party well enough. We have had enough of Spain at Gibraltar for the present. Tangier is the spot we have been longing for all the time. Elsewhere we have found foreign-looking things and foreign-looking people, but always with things and people intermixed that we were familiar with before, and so the novelty of the situation lost a deal of its force. We wanted something thoroughly and uncompromisingly foreign – foreign from top to bottom – foreign from centre to circumference – foreign inside and outside and all around – nothing any where about it to dilute its foreignness – nothing to remind us of any other people or any other land under the sun. And lo! in Tangier we have found it. Here is not the slightest thing that ever we have seen save in pictures – and we always mistrusted the pictures before. We can not any more. The pictures used to seem exaggerations – they seemed too weird and fanciful for reality. But behold, they were not wild enough – they were not fanciful enough – they have not told half the story. Tangier is a foreign land if ever there was one; and the true spirit of it can never be found in any book save the Arabian Nights. Here are no white men visible, yet swarms of humanity are all about us. Here is a packed and jammed city inclosed in a massive stone wall which is more than a thousand years old. All the houses nearly are one and two-story; made of thick walls of stone; plastered outside; square as a dry-goods box; flat as a floor on top; no cornices; whitewashed all over – a crowded city of snowy tombs! And the doors are arched with the peculiar arch we see in Moorish pictures; the floors are laid in varicolored diamond-flags; in tesselated many-colored porcelain squares wrought in the furnaces of Fez; in red tiles and broad bricks that time can not wear; there is no furniture in the rooms (of Jewish dwellings) save divans – what there is in Moorish ones no man may know; within their sacred walls no Christian dog can enter. And the streets are oriental – some of them three feet wide, some six, but only two that are over a dozen; a man can blockade the most of them by extending his body across them. Isn't it an oriental picture?

There are stalwart Bedouins of the desert here, and stately Moors, proud of a history that goes back to the night of time; and

Jews, whose fathers fled hither centuries upon centuries ago; and swarthy Riffians from the mountains – born cutthroats – and original, genuine negroes, as black as Moses; and howling dervishes, and a hundred breeds of Arabs – all sorts and descriptions of people that are foreign and curious to look upon.

And their dresses are strange beyond all description. Here is a bronzed Moor in a prodigious white turban, curiously embroidered jacket, gold and crimson sash, of many folds, wrapped round and round his waist, trowsers that only come a little below his knee, and yet have twenty yards of stuff in them, ornamented scimetar, bare shins, stockingless feet, yellow slippers, and gun of preposterous length – a mere soldier! – I thought he was the Emperor at least. And here are aged Moors with flowing white beards, and long white robes with vast cowls; and Bedouins with long, cowled, striped cloaks, and negroes and Riffians with heads clean-shaven, except a kinky scalp-lock back of the ear, or rather up on the after corner of the skull, and all sorts of barbarians in all sorts of weird costumes, and all more or less ragged. And here are Moorish women who are enveloped from head to foot in coarse white robes and whose sex can only be determined by the fact that they only leave one eye visible, and never look at men of their own race, or are looked at by them in public. Here are five thousand Jews in blue gaberdines, sashes about their waists, slippers upon their feet, little skull-caps upon the backs of their heads, hair combed down on the forehead, and cut straight across the middle of it from side to side – the self-same fashion their Tangier ancestors have worn for I don't know how many bewildering centuries. Their feet and ankles are bare. Their noses are all hooked, and hooked alike. They all resemble each other so much that one could almost believe they were of one family. Their women are plump and pretty, and do smile upon a Christian in a way which is in the last degree comforting.

What a funny old town it is! It seems like profanation to laugh, and jest, and bandy the frivolous chat of our day amid its hoary relics. Only the stately phraseology and the measured speech of the sons of the Prophet are suited to a venerable antiquity like this. Here is a crumbling wall that was old when Columbus discovered America; was old when Peter the Hermit roused the knightly men of the Middle Ages to arm for the first Crusade; was old when Charlemagne and his paladins beleaguered enchanted castles and battled with giants and genii in the fabled days of the olden time; was old when Christ and his disciples walked the earth; stood where it stands to-day when the lips of Memnon were vocal, and men bought and sold in the streets of ancient Thebes!

The Phœnicians, the Carthagenians, the English, Moors, Romans, all have battled for Tangier – all have won it and lost it. Here is a ragged, oriental-looking negro from some desert place in interior Africa, filling his goat-skin with water from a stained and battered fountain built by the Romans twelve hundred years ago. Yonder is a ruined arch of a bridge built by Julius Cæsar nineteen hundred years ago. Men who had seen the infant Saviour in the Virgin's arms, have stood upon it, may be.

Near it are the ruins of a dock-yard where Cæsar repaired his ships and loaded them with grain when he invaded Britain, fifty years before the Christian era.

Here, under the quiet stars, these old streets seem thronged with the phantoms of forgotten ages. My eyes are resting upon a spot where stood a monument which was seen and described by Roman historians less than two thousand years ago, whereon was inscribed:

> "WE ARE THE CANAANITES. WE ARE THEY THAT HAVE BEEN DRIVEN OUT OF THE LAND OF CANAAN BY THE JEWISH ROBBER, JOSHUA."

Joshua drove them out, and they came here. Not many leagues from here is a tribe of Jews whose ancestors fled thither after an unsuccessful revolt against King David, and these their descendants are still under a ban and keep to themselves.

Tangier has been mentioned in history for three thousand years. And it was a town, though a queer one, when Hercules, clad in his lion-skin, landed here, four thousand years ago. In these streets he met Anitus, the king of the country, and brained him with his club, which was the fashion among gentlemen in those days. The people of Tangier (called Tingis, then,) lived in the rudest possible huts, and dressed in skins and carried clubs, and were as savage as the wild beasts they were constantly obliged to war with. But they were a gentlemanly race, and did no work. They lived on the natural products of the land. Their king's country residence was at the famous Garden of Hesperides, seventy miles down the coast from here. The garden, with its golden apples, (oranges,) is gone now – no vestige of it remains. Antiquarians concede that such a personage as Hercules did exist in ancient times, and agree that he was an enterprising and energetic man, but decline to believe him a good, bona fide god, because that would be unconstitutional.

Down here at Cape Spartel is the celebrated cave of Hercules, where that hero took refuge when he was vanquished and driven out of the Tangier country. It is full of inscriptions in the dead languages, which fact makes me think Hercules could not have traveled much, else he would not have kept a journal.

Five days' journey from here – say two hundred miles – are the ruins of an ancient city, of whose history there is neither record nor tradition. And yet its arches, its columns, and its statues, proclaim it to have been built by an enlightened race.

The general size of a store in Tangier is about that of an ordinary shower-bath in a civilized land. The Mohammedan merchant, tinman, shoemaker, or vendor of trifles, sits cross-legged on the floor, and reaches after any article you may want to buy. You can rent a whole block of these pigeon-holes for fifty dollars a month. The market people crowd the marketplace with their baskets of figs, dates, melons, apricots, etc., and among them file trains of laden asses, not much larger, if any, than a Newfoundland dog. The scene is lively, is picturesque, and smells like a police court. The Jewish money-changers have their dens close at hand; and all day long are counting bronze coins and transferring them from one bushel basket to another. They don't coin much money now-a-days, I think. I saw none but what was dated four or five hundred years back, and was badly worn and battered. These coins are not very valuable. Jack went out to get a Napoleon changed, so as to have money suited to the general cheapness of things, and came back and said he had "swamped the bank; had bought eleven quarts of coin, and the head of the firm had gone on the street to negotiate for the balance of the change." I bought nearly half a pint of their money for a shilling myself. I am not proud on account of having so much money, though. I care nothing for wealth.

The Moors have some small silver coins, and also some silver slugs worth a dollar each. The latter are exceedingly scarce – so much so that when poor ragged Arabs see one they beg to be allowed to kiss it.

They have also a small gold coin worth two dollars. And that reminds me of something. When Morocco is in a state of war, Arab couriers carry letters through the country, and charge a liberal postage. Every now and then they fall into the hands of marauding bands and get robbed. Therefore, warned by experience, as soon as they have collected two dollars' worth of money they exchange it for one of those little gold pieces, and when robbers come upon them, swallow it. The stratagem was good while it was unsuspected, but after that the marauders simply gave the sagacious United States mail an emetic and sat down to wait.

The Emperor of Morocco is a soulless despot, and the great officers under him are despots on a smaller scale. There is no regular system of taxation, but when the Emperor or the Bashaw want money, they levy on some rich man, and he has to furnish the cash or go to prison. Therefore, few men in Morocco dare to be rich. It is too dangerous a luxury. Vanity occasionally leads a man to display wealth, but sooner or later the Emperor trumps up a charge against him – any sort of one will do – and confiscates his property. Of course, there are many rich men in the empire, but their money is buried, and they dress in rags and counterfeit poverty. Every now and then the Emperor imprisons a man who is suspected of the crime of being rich, and makes things so uncomfortable for him that he is forced to discover where he has hidden his money.

Moors and Jews sometimes place themselves under the protection of the foreign consuls, and then they can flout their riches in the Emperor's face with impunity.

CHAPTER XII

WE HAVE COME five hundred miles by rail through the heart of France. What a bewitching land it is! – What a garden! Surely the leagues of bright green lawns are swept and brushed and watered every day and their grasses trimmed by the barber. Surely the hedges are shaped and measured and their symmetry preserved by the most architectural of gardeners. Surely the long straight rows of stately poplars that divide the beautiful landscape like the squares of a checker-board are set with line and plummet, and their uniform height determined with a spirit level. Surely the straight, smooth, pure white turnpikes are jack-planed and sandpapered every day. How else are these marvels of symmetry, cleanliness and order attained? It is wonderful. There are no unsightly stone walls, and never a fence of any kind. There is no dirt, no decay, no rubbish any where – nothing that even hints at untidiness – nothing that ever suggests neglect. All is orderly and beautiful – every thing is charming to the eye.

We had such glimpses of the Rhone gliding along between its grassy banks; of cosy cottages buried in flowers and shrubbery; of quaint old red-tiled villages with mossy mediæval cathedrals looming out of their midst; of wooded hills with ivy-grown towers and turrets of feudal castles projecting above the foliage; such glimpses of Paradise, it seemed to us, such visions of fabled fairy-land!

We knew, then, what the poet meant, when he sang of –

> " – thy cornfields green, and sunny vines,
> O pleasant land of France!"

And it *is* a pleasant land. No word describes it so felicitously as that one. They say there is no word for "home" in the French language. Well, considering that they have the article itself in such an attractive aspect, they ought to manage to get along without the word. Let us not waste too much pity on "homeless" France. I have observed that Frenchmen abroad seldom wholly give up the idea of going back to France some time or other. I am not surprised at it now.

We are not infatuated with these French railway cars, though. We took first-class passage, not because we wished to attract attention by doing a thing which is uncommon in Europe, but because we could make our journey quicker by so doing. It is hard to make railroading pleasant, in any country. It is too tedious. Stage-coaching is infinitely more delightful. Once I crossed the plains and deserts and mountains of the West, in a stage-coach, from the Missouri line to California, and since then all my pleasure trips must be measured to that rare holiday frolic. Two thousand miles of ceaseless rush and rattle and clatter, by night and by day, and never a weary moment, never a lapse of interest! The first seven hundred miles a level continent, its grassy carpet greener and softer and smoother than any sea, and figured with designs fitted to its magnitude – the shadows of the clouds. Here were no scenes but summer scenes, and no disposition inspired by them but to lie at full length on the mail sacks, in the grateful breeze, and dreamily smoke the pipe of peace – what other, where all was repose and contentment? In cool mornings, before the sun was fairly up, it was worth a lifetime of city toiling and moiling, to perch in the foretop with the driver and see the six mustangs scamper under the sharp snapping of a whip that never touched them; to scan the blue distances of a world that knew no lords but us; to cleave the wind with uncovered head and feel the sluggish pulses rousing to the spirit of a speed that pretended to the resistless rush of a typhoon! Then thirteen hundred miles of desert solitudes; of limitless panoramas of bewildering perspective; of mimic cities, of pinnacled cathedrals, of massive fortresses, counterfeited in the eternal rocks and splendid with the crimson and gold of the setting sun; of dizzy altitudes among fog-wreathed peaks and never-melting snows, where thunders and lightnings and tempests warred magnificently at our feet and the storm-clouds above swung their shredded banners in our very faces!

But I forgot. I am in elegant France, now, and not skurrying through the great South Pass and the Wind River Mountains, among antelopes and buffaloes, and painted Indians on the war path. It is not meet that I should make too disparaging comparisons between hum-drum travel on a railway and that royal summer flight across a continent in a stage-coach. I meant in the beginning, to say that railway journeying is tedious and tiresome, and so it is – though at the time, I was thinking particularly of a dismal fifty-hour pilgrimage between New York and St. Louis. Of course our trip through France was not really tedious, because all its scenes and experiences were new and strange; but as Dan says, it had its "discrepancies."

The cars are built in compartments that hold eight persons each. Each compartment is partially subdivided, and so there are two tolerably distinct parties of four in it. Four face the other four. The seats and backs are thickly padded and cushioned and are very comfortable; you can smoke, if you wish; there are no bothersome peddlers; you are saved the infliction of a multitude of disagreeable fellow-passengers. So far, so well. But then the conductor locks you in when the train starts; there is no water to drink, in the car; there is no heating apparatus for night travel; if a drunken rowdy should get in, you could not remove a matter of twenty seats from him, or enter another car; but above all, if you are worn out and must sleep, you must sit up and do it in naps, with cramped legs and in a torturing misery that leaves you withered and lifeless the next day – for behold they have not that culmination of all charity and human kindness, a sleeping car, in all France. I prefer the American system. It has not so many grievous "discrepancies."

In France, all is clockwork, all is order. They make no mistakes. Every third man wears a uniform, and whether he be a Marshal of the Empire or a brakeman, he is ready and perfectly willing to answer all your questions with tireless politeness, ready to tell you which car to take, yea, and ready to go and put you into it to make sure that you shall not go astray. You can not pass into the waiting-room of the depot till you have secured your ticket, and you can not pass from its only exit till the train is at its threshold to receive you. Once on board, the train will not start till your ticket has been examined – till every passenger's ticket has been inspected. This is chiefly for your own good. If by any possibility you have managed to take the wrong train, you will be handed over to a polite official who will take you whither you belong, and bestow you with many an affable bow. Your ticket will be inspected every now and then along the route, and when it is time to change cars you will know it. You are in the hands of officials who zealously study your welfare and your interest, instead of turning their talents to the invention of new methods of discommoding and snubbing you, as is very often the main employment of that exceedingly self-satisfied monarch, the railroad conductor of America.

But the happiest regulation in French railway government, is – thirty minutes to dinner! No five-minute boltings of flabby rolls, muddy coffee, questionable eggs, gutta-percha beef, and pies whose conception and execution are a dark and bloody mystery to all save the cook that created them! No; we sat calmly down – it was in old Dijon, which is so easy to spell and so impossible to pronounce, except when you civilize it and call it Demijohn – and poured out rich Burgundian wines and munched calmly through a long table d'hote bill of fare, snail-patties, delicious fruits and all, then paid the trifle it cost and stepped happily aboard the train again, without once cursing the railroad company. A rare experience, and one to be treasured forever.

They say they do not have accidents on these French roads, and I think it must be true. If I remember rightly, we passed high above wagon roads, or through tunnels under them, but never crossed them on their own level. About every quarter of a mile, it seemed to me, a man came out and held up a club till the train went by, to signify that every thing was safe ahead. Switches were changed a mile in advance, by pulling a wire rope that passed along the ground by the rail, from station to station. Signals for the day and signals for the night gave constant and timely notice of the position of switches.

No, they have no railroad accidents to speak of in France. But why? Because when one occurs, *somebody* has to hang for it!* Not

*They go on the principle that it is better that one innocent man should suffer than five hundred.

hang, may be, but be punished at least with such vigor of emphasis as to make negligence a thing to be shuddered at by railroad officials for many a day thereafter. "No blame attached to the officers" – that lying and disaster-breeding verdict so common to our soft-hearted juries, is seldom rendered in France. If the trouble occurred in the conductor's department, that officer must suffer if his subordinate can not be proven guilty; if in the engineer's department, and the case be similar, the engineer must answer.

The Old Travelers – those delightful parrots who have "been here before," and know more about the country than Louis Napoleon knows now or ever will know, – tell us these things, and we believe them because they are pleasant things to believe, and because they are plausible and savor of the rigid subjection to law and order which we behold about us every where.

But we love the Old Travelers. We love to hear them prate, and drivel and lie. We can tell them the moment we see them. They always throw out a few feelers; they never cast themselves adrift till they have sounded every individual and know that he has not traveled. Then they open their throttle-valves, and how they do brag, and sneer, and swell, and soar, and blaspheme the sacred name of Truth! Their central idea, their grand aim, is to subjugate you, keep you down, make you feel insignificant and humble in the blaze of their cosmopolitan glory! They will not let you know any thing. They sneer at your most inoffensive suggestions; they laugh unfeelingly at your treasured dreams of foreign lands; they brand the statements of your traveled aunts and uncles as the stupidest absurdities; they deride your most trusted authors and demolish the fair images they have set up for your willing worship with the pitiless ferocity of the fanatic iconoclast! But still I love the Old Travelers. I love them for their witless platitudes; for their supernatural ability to bore; for their delightful asinine vanity; for their luxuriant fertility of imagination; for their startling, their brilliant, their overwhelming mendacity!

By Lyons and the Saone (where we saw the lady of Lyons and thought little of her comeliness;) by Villa Franca, Tonnere, venerable Sens, Melun, Fontainebleau, and scores of other beautiful cities, we swept, always noting the absence of hog-wallows, broken fences, cowlots, unpainted houses and mud, and always noting, as well, the presence of cleanliness, grace, taste in adorning and beautifying, even to the disposition of a tree or the turning of a hedge, the marvel of roads in perfect repair, void of ruts and guiltless of even an inequality of surface – we bowled along, hour after hour, that brilliant summer day, and as night-fall approached we entered a wilderness of odorous flowers and shrubbery, sped through it, and then, excited, delighted, and half persuaded that we were only the sport of a beautiful dream, lo, we stood in magnificent Paris!

What excellent order they kept about that vast depot! There was no frantic crowding and jostling, no shouting and swearing, and no swaggering intrusion of services by rowdy hackmen. These latter gentry stood outside – stood quietly by their long line of vehicles and said never a word. A kind of hackman-general seemed to have the whole matter of transportation in his hands. He politely received the passengers and ushered them to the kind of conveyance they wanted, and told the driver where to deliver them. There was no "talking back," no dissatisfaction about overcharging, no grumbling about any thing. In a little while we were speeding through the streets of Paris, and delightfully recognizing certain names and places with which books had long ago made us familiar. It was like meeting an old friend when we read *"Rue de Rivoli"* on the street corner; we knew the genuine vast palace of the Louvre as well as we knew its picture; when we passed by the Column of July we needed no one to tell us what it was, or to remind us that on its site once stood the grim Bastile, that grave of human hopes and happiness, that dismal prison-house within whose dungeons so many young faces put on the wrinkles of age, so many proud spirits grew humble, so many brave hearts broke.

We secured rooms at the hotel, or rather, we had three beds put into one room, so that we might be together, and then we went out to a restaurant, just after lamp-lighting, and ate a comfortable, satisfactory, lingering dinner. It was a pleasure to eat where every thing was so tidy, the food so well cooked, the waiters so polite, and the coming and departing company so moustached, so frisky, so affable, so fearfully and wonderfully Frenchy! All the surroundings were gay and enlivening. Two hundred people sat at little tables on the sidewalk, sipping wine and coffee; the streets were thronged with light vehicles and with joyous pleasure seekers; there was music in the air, life and action all about us, and a conflagration of gaslight every where!

After dinner we felt like seeing such Parisian specialties as we might see without distressing exertion, and so we sauntered through the brilliant streets and looked at the dainty trifles in variety stores and jewelry shops. Occasionally, merely for the pleasure of being cruel, we put unoffending Frenchmen on the rack with questions framed in the incomprehensible jargon of their native language, and while they writhed, we impaled them, we peppered them, we scarified them, with their own vile verbs and participles.

We noticed that in the jewelry stores they had some of the articles marked "gold," and some labeled "imitation." We wondered at this extravagance of honesty, and inquired into the matter. We were informed that inasmuch as most people are not able to tell false gold from the genuine article, the government compels jewelers to have their gold work assayed and stamped officially according to its fineness, and their imitation work duly labeled with the sign of its falsity. They told us the jewelers would not dare to violate this law, and that whatever a stranger bought in one of their stores might be depended upon as being strictly what it was represented to be. – Verily, a wonderful land is France!

Then we hunted for a barber-shop. From earliest infancy it had been a cherished ambition of mine to be shaved some day in a palatial barber-shop of Paris. I wished to recline at full length in a cushioned invalid chair, with pictures about me, and sumptuous furniture; with frescoed walls and gilded arches above me, and vistas of Corinthian columns stretching far before me; with perfumes of Araby to intoxicate my senses, and the slumbrous drone of distant noises to soothe me to sleep. At the end of an hour I would wake up regretfully and find my face as smooth and as soft as an infant's. Departing, I would lift my hands above that barber's head and say, "Heaven bless you, my son!"

So we searched high and low, for a matter of two hours, but never a barber-shop could we see. We saw only wig-making establishments, with shocks of dead and repulsive hair bound upon the heads of painted waxen brigands who stared out from glass boxes upon the passer-by, with their stony eyes, and scared him with the ghostly white of their countenances. We shunned these signs for a time, but finally we concluded that the wig-makers must of necessity be the barbers as well, since we could find no single legitimate representative of the fraternity. We entered and asked, and found that it was even so.

I said I wanted to be shaved. The barber inquired where my room was. I said, never mind where my room was, I wanted to be shaved – there, on the spot. The doctor said he would be shaved also. Then there was an excitement among those two barbers! There was a wild consultation, and afterwards a hurrying to and fro and a feverish gathering up of razors from obscure places and a ransacking for soap. Next they took us into a little mean, shabby back room; they got two ordinary sitting-room chairs and placed us in them, with our coats on. My old, old dream of bliss vanished into thin air!

I sat bolt upright, silent, sad, and solemn. One of the wig-making villains lathered my face for ten terrible minutes and finished by plastering a mass of suds into my mouth. I expelled the nasty stuff with a strong English expletive and said, "Foreigner, beware!" Then this outlaw stropped his razor on his boot, hovered over me ominously for six fearful seconds, and then swooped down upon me like the genius of destruction. The first rake of his razor loosened the very hide from my face and lifted me out of the chair. I stormed and raved, and the other boys enjoyed it. Their beards are not strong and thick. Let us draw the curtain over this harrowing scene. Suffice it that I submitted, and went through with the cruel infliction of a shave by a French barber; tears of exquisite agony coursed down my cheeks, now and then, but I survived. Then the incipient assassin held a basin of water under my chin and slopped its contents over my face, and into my bosom, and down the back of my neck, with a mean pretense of washing away the soap and blood. He dried my features with a towel, and was going to comb my hair; but I asked to be excused. I said, with withering irony, that it was sufficient to be skinned – I declined to be scalped.

I went away from there with my handkerchief about my face, and never, never, never desired to dream of palatial Parisian barber-shops any more. The truth is, as I believe I have since found out, that they have no barber-shops worthy of the name, in Paris – and no barbers, either, for that matter. The impostor who does duty as a barber, brings his pans and napkins and implements of torture to your residence and deliberately skins you in your private apartments. Ah, I have suffered, suffered, suffered, here in Paris, but never mind – the time is coming when I shall have a dark and bloody revenge. Some day a Parisian barber will come to my room to skin me, and from that day forth, that barber will never be heard of more.

At eleven o'clock we alighted upon a sign which manifestly referred to billiards. Joy! We had played billiards in the Azores with balls that were not round, and on an ancient table that was very little smoother than a brick pavement – one of those wretched old things with dead cushions, and with patches in the faded cloth and invisible obstructions that made the balls describe the most astonishing and unsuspected angles and perform feats in the way of unlooked-for and almost impossible "scratches," that were perfectly bewildering. We had played at Gibraltar with balls the size of a walnut, on a table like a public square – and in both instances we achieved far more aggravation than amusement. We expected to fare better here, but we were mistaken. The cushions were a good deal higher than the balls, and as the balls had a fashion of always stopping under the cushions, we accomplished very little in the way of caroms. The cushions were hard and unelastic, and the cues were so crooked that in making a shot you had to allow for the curve or you would infallibly put the "English" on the wrong side of the ball. Dan was to mark while the doctor and I played. At the end of an hour neither of us had made a count, and so Dan was tired of keeping tally with nothing to tally, and we were heated and angry and disgusted. We paid the heavy bill – about six cents – and said we would call around some time when we had a week to spend, and finish the game.

We adjourned to one of those pretty cafés and took supper and tested the wines of the country, as we had been instructed to do, and found them harmless and unexciting. They might have been exciting, however, if we had chosen to drink a sufficiency of them.

To close our first day in Paris cheerfully and pleasantly, we now sought our grand room in the Grand Hotel du Louvre and climbed into our sumptuous bed, to read and smoke – but alas!

It was pitiful,
In a whole city-full,
Gas we had none.

No gas to read by – nothing but dismal candles. It was a shame. We tried to map out excursions for the morrow; we puzzled over French "Guides to Paris;" we talked disjointedly, in a vain endeavor to make head or tail of the wild chaos of the day's sights and experiences; we subsided to indolent smoking; we gaped and yawned, and stretched – then feebly wondered if we were really and truly in renowned Paris and drifted drowsily away into that vast mysterious void which we call sleep.

CHAPTER XIII

THE NEXT MORNING we were up and dressed at ten o'clock. We went to the *commissionaire* of the hotel – I don't know what a *commissionaire* is, but that is the man we went to – and told him we wanted a guide. He said the great International Exposition had drawn such multitudes of Englishmen and Americans to Paris that it would be next to impossible to find a good guide unemployed. He said he usually kept a dozen or two on hand, but he only had three now. He called them. One looked so like a very pirate that we let him go at once. The next one spoke with a simpering precision of pronunciation that was irritating, and said:

"If ze zhentlemans will to me make ze grande honneur to me rattain in hees serveece, I shall show to him every sing zat is magnifique to look upon in ze beautiful Parree. I speaky ze Angleesh pairfaitemaw."

He would have done well to have stopped there, because he had that much by heart and said it right off without making a mistake. But his self-complacency seduced him into attempting a flight into regions of unexplored English, and the reckless experiment was his ruin. Within ten seconds he was so tangled up in a maze of mutilated verbs and torn and bleeding forms of speech that no human ingenuity could ever have gotten him out of it with credit. It was plain enough that he could not "speaky" the English quite as "pairfaitemaw" as he had pretended he could.

The third man captured us. He was plainly dressed, but he had a noticeable air of neatness about him. He wore a high silk hat which was a little old, but had been carefully brushed. He wore second-hand kid gloves, in good repair, and carried a small rattan cane with a curved handle – a female leg, of ivory. He stepped as gently and as daintily as a cat crossing a muddy street; and oh, he was urbanity; he was quiet, unobtrusive self-possession; he was deference itself! He spoke softly and guardedly; and when he was about to make a statement on his sole responsibility, or offer a suggestion, he weighed it by drachms and scruples first, with the crook of his little stick placed meditatively to his teeth. His opening speech was perfect. It was perfect in construction, in phraseology, in grammar, in emphasis, in pronunciation – every thing. He spoke little and guardedly, after that. We were charmed. We were more than charmed – we were overjoyed. We hired him at once. We never even asked him his price. This man – our lackey, our servant, our unquestioning slave though he was, was still a gentleman – we could see that – while of the other two one was coarse and awkward, and the other was a born pirate. We asked our man Friday's name. He drew from his pocket-book a snowy little card, and passed it to us with a profound bow:

A. Billfinger,
Guide to Paris, France, Germany,
Spain, &c., &c.,
Grande Hotel du Louvre

"Billfinger! Oh, carry me home to die!"

That was an "aside" from Dan. The atrocious name grated harshly on my ear, too. The most of us can learn to forgive, and even to like, a countenance that strikes us unpleasantly at first, but few of us, I fancy, become reconciled to a jarring name so easily. I was almost sorry we had hired this man, his name was so unbearable. However, no matter. We were impatient to start. Billfinger stepped to the door to call a carriage, and then the doctor said:

"Well, the guide goes with the barber-shop, with the billiard-table, with the gasless room, and may be with many another pretty romance of Paris. I expected to have a guide named Henri de Montmorency, or Armand de la Chartreuse, or something that would sound grand in letters to the villagers at home; but to think of a Frenchman by the name of Billfinger! Oh! this is absurd, you know. This will never do. We can't say Billfinger; it is nauseating. Name him over again: what had we better call him? Alexis du Caulaincourt?"

"Alphonse Henri Gustave de Hauteville," I suggested.

"Call him Ferguson," said Dan.

That was practical, unromantic good sense. Without debate, we expunged Billfinger *as* Billfinger, and called him Ferguson.

The carriage – an open barouche – was ready. Ferguson mounted beside the driver, and we whirled away to breakfast. As was proper, Mr. Ferguson stood by to transmit our orders and answer questions. Bye and bye, he mentioned casually – the artful adventurer – that he would go and get his breakfast as soon as we had finished ours. He knew we could not get along without him, and that we would not want to loiter about and wait for him. We asked him to sit down and eat with us. He begged, with many a bow, to be excused. It was not proper, he said; he would sit at another table. We ordered him peremptorily to sit down with us.

Here endeth the first lesson. It was a mistake.

As long as we had that fellow after that, he was always hungry; he was always thirsty. He came early; he stayed late; he could not pass a restaurant; he looked with a lecherous eye upon every wine shop. Suggestions to stop, excuses to eat and to drink were forever on his lips. We tried all we could to fill him so full that he would have no room to spare for a fortnight; but it was a failure. He did not hold enough to smother the cravings of his superhuman appetite.

He had another "discrepancy" about him. He was always wanting us to buy things. On the shallowest pretenses, he would inveigle us into shirt stores, boot stores, tailor shops, glove shops – any where under the broad sweep of the heavens that there seemed a chance of our buying any thing. Any one could have guessed that the shopkeepers paid him a per centage on the sales; but in our blessed innocence we didn't, until this feature of his conduct grew unbearably prominent. One day, Dan happened to mention that he thought of buying three or four silk dress patterns for presents. Ferguson's hungry eye was upon him in an instant. In the course of twenty minutes, the carriage stopped.

"What's this?"

"Zis is ze finest silk magazin in Paris – ze most celebrate."

"What did you come here for? We told you to take us to the palace of the Louvre."

"I suppose ze gentleman say he wish to buy some silk."

"You are not required to 'suppose' things for the party, Ferguson. We do not wish to tax your energies too much. We will bear some of the burden and heat of the day ourselves. We will endeavor to do such 'supposing' as is really necessary to be done. Drive on." So spake the doctor.

Within fifteen minutes the carriage halted again, and before another silk store. The doctor said:

"Ah, the palace of the Louvre: beautiful, beautiful edifice! Does the Emperor Napoleon live here now, Ferguson?"

"Ah, doctor! you do jest; zis is not ze palace; we come there directly. But since we pass right by zis store, where is such beautiful silk—"

"Ah! I see, I see. I meant to have told you that we did not wish to purchase any silks to-day; but in my absentmindedness I forgot it. I also meant to tell you we wished to go directly to the Louvre; but I forgot that also. However, we will go there now. Pardon my seeming carelessness, Ferguson. Drive on."

Within the half-hour, we stopped again – in front of another silk store. We were angry; but the doctor was always serene, always smooth-voiced. He said:

"At last! How imposing the Louvre is, and yet how small! how exquisitely fashioned! how charmingly situated! – Venerable, venerable pile—"

"Pairdon, doctor, zis is not ze Louvre – it is—"

"*What* is it?"

"I have ze idea – it come to me in a moment – zat ze silk in zis magazin—"

"Ferguson, how heedless I am. I fully intended to tell you that we did not wish to buy any silks to-day, and I also intended to tell you that we yearned to go immediately to the palace of the Louvre, but enjoying the happiness of seeing you devour four breakfasts this morning has so filled me with pleasurable emotions that I neglect the commonest interests of the time. However, we will proceed now to the Louvre, Ferguson."

"But doctor," (excitedly,) "it will take not a minute – not but one small minute! Ze gentleman need not to buy if he not wish to – but only *look* at ze silk – *look* at ze beautiful fabric," [Then pleadingly.] "*Sair* – just only one *leetle* moment!"

Dan said, "Confound the idiot! I don't want to see any silks to-day, and I *won't* look at them. Drive on."

And the doctor: "We need no silks now, Ferguson. Our hearts yearn for the Louvre. Let us journey on – let us journey on."

"But *doctor*! it is only one moment – one leetle moment. And ze time will be save – entirely save! Because zere is nothing to see, now – it is too late. It want ten minute to four and ze Louvre close at four – *only* one leetle moment, doctor!"

The treacherous miscreant! After four breakfasts and a gallon of champagne, to serve us such a scurvy trick. We got no sight of the countless treasures of art in the Louvre galleries that day, and our only poor little satisfaction was in the reflection that Ferguson sold not a solitary silk dress pattern.

I am writing this chapter partly for the satisfaction of abusing that accomplished knave, Billfinger, and partly to show whosoever shall read this how Americans fare at the hands of the Paris guides, and what sort of people Paris guides are. It need not be supposed that we were a stupider or an easier prey than our countrymen generally are, for we were not. The guides deceive and defraud every American who goes to Paris for the first time and sees its sights alone or in company with others as little experienced as himself. I shall visit Paris again some day, and then let the guides beware! I shall go in my war-paint – I shall carry my tomahawk along.

I think we have lost but little time in Paris. We have gone to bed every night tired out. Of course we visited the renowned International Exposition. All the world did that. We went there on our third day in Paris – and we stayed there *nearly two hours*. That was our first and last visit. To tell the truth, we saw at a glance that one would have to spend weeks – yea, even months – in that monstrous establishment, to get an intelligible idea of it. It was a wonderful show, but the moving masses of people of all nations we saw there were a still more wonderful show. I discovered that if I were to stay there a month, I should still find myself looking at the people instead of the inanimate objects on exhibition. I got a little interested in some curious old tapestries of the thirteenth century, but a party of Arabs came by, and their dusky faces and quaint costumes called my attention away at once. I watched a silver swan, which had a living grace about his movements, and a living intelligence in his eyes – watched him swimming about as comfortably and as unconcernedly as if he had been born in a morass instead of a jeweller's shop – watched him seize a silver fish from under the water and hold up his head and go through all the customary and elaborate motions of swallowing it – but the moment it disappeared down his throat some tattooed South Sea Islander approached and I yielded to their attractions. Presently I found a revolving pistol several hundred years old which looked strangely like a modern Colt, but just then I heard that the Empress of the French was in another part of the building, and hastened away to see what she might look like. We heard martial music – we saw an unusual number of soldiers walking hurriedly about – there was a general movement among the people. We inquired what it was all about, and learned that the Emperor of the French and the Sultan of Turkey were about to review twenty-five thousand troops at the *Arc de l'Etoile*. We immediately departed. I had a greater anxiety to see these men than I could have had to see twenty Expositions.

We drove away and took up a position in an open space opposite the American Minister's house. A speculator bridged a couple of barrels with a board and we hired standing-places on it. Presently there was a sound of distant music; in another minute a pillar of dust came moving slowly toward us; a moment more, and then, with colors flying and a grand crash of military music, a gallant array of cavalrymen emerged from the dust and came down the street on a gentle trot. After them came a long line of artillery; then more cavalry, in splendid uniforms; and then their Imperial Majesties

Napoleon III. and Abdul-Aziz. The vast concourse of people swung their hats and shouted – the windows and house-tops in the wide vicinity burst into a snow-storm of waving handkerchiefs, and the wavers of the same mingled their cheers with those of the masses below. It was a stirring spectacle.

But the two central figures claimed all my attention. Was ever such a contrast set up before a multitude till then? Napoleon, in military uniform – a long-bodied, short-legged man, fiercely moustached, old, wrinkled, with eyes half closed, and *such* a deep, crafty, scheming expression about them! – Napoleon, bowing ever so gently to the loud plaudits, and watching every thing and every body with his cat-eyes from under his depressed hat-brim, as if to discover any sign that those cheers were not heartfelt and cordial.

Abdul-Aziz, absolute lord of the Ottoman Empire, – clad in dark green European clothes, almost without ornament or insignia of rank; a red Turkish fez on his head – a short, stout, dark man, black-bearded, black-eyed, stupid, unprepossessing – a man whose whole appearance somehow suggested that if he only had a cleaver in his hand and a white apron on, one would not be at all surprised to hear him say: "A mutton-roast to-day, or will you have a nice porter-house steak?"

Napoleon III., the representative of the highest modern civilization, progress, and refinement; Abdul-Aziz, the representative of a people by nature and training filthy, brutish, ignorant, unprogressive, superstitious – and a government whose Three Graces are Tyranny, Rapacity, Blood. Here in brilliant Paris, under this majestic Arch of Triumph, the First Century greets the Nineteenth!

NAPOLEON III., Emperor of France! Surrounded by shouting thousands, by military pomp, by the splendors of his capital city, and companioned by kings and princes – this is the man who was sneered at, and reviled, and called Bastard – yet who was dreaming of a crown and an Empire all the while; who was driven into exile – but carried his dreams with him; who associated with the common herd in America, and ran foot-races for a wager – but still sat upon a throne, in fancy; who braved every danger to go to his dying mother – and grieved that she could not be spared to see him cast aside his plebeian vestments for the purple of royalty; who kept his faithful watch and walked his weary beat a common policeman of London – but dreamed the while of a coming night when he should tread the long-drawn corridors of the Tuileries; who made the miserable *fiasco* of Strasbourg; saw his poor, shabby eagle, forgetful of its lesson, refuse to perch upon his shoulder; delivered his carefully-prepared, sententious burst of eloquence, unto unsympathetic ears; found himself a prisoner, the butt of small wits, a mark for the pitiless ridicule of all the world – yet went on dreaming of coronations and splendid pageants, as before; who lay a forgotten captive in the dungeons of Ham – and still schemed and planned and pondered over future glory and future power; President of France at last! a *coup d'état*, and surrounded by applauding armies, welcomed by the thunders of cannon, he mounts a throne and waves before an astounded world the sceptre of a mighty Empire! Who talks of the marvels of fiction? Who speaks of the wonders of romance? Who prates of the tame achievements of Aladdin and the Magii of Arabia?

ABDUL-AZIZ, Sultan of Turkey, Lord of the Ottoman Empire! Born to a throne; weak, stupid, ignorant, almost, as his meanest slave; chief of a vast royalty, yet the puppet of his Premier and the obedient child of a tyrannical mother; a man who sits upon a throne – the beck of whose finger moves navies and armies – who holds in his hands the power of life and death over millions – yet who sleeps, sleeps, eats, eats, idles with his eight hundred concubines, and when he is surfeited with eating and sleeping and idling, and would rouse up and take the reins of government and threatens to *be* a Sultan, is charmed from his purpose by wary Fuad Pacha with a pretty plan for a new palace or a new ship – charmed away with a new toy, like any other restless child; a man who sees his people robbed and oppressed by soulless tax-gatherers, but speaks no word to save them; who believes in gnomes, and genii and the wild fables of the Arabian Nights, but has small regard for the mighty magicians of to-day, and is nervous in the presence of their mysterious railroads and steamboats and telegraphs; who would see undone in Egypt all that great Mehemet Ali achieved, and would prefer rather to forget than emulate him; a man who found his great Empire a blot upon the earth – a degraded, poverty-stricken, miserable, infamous agglomeration of ignorance, crime, and brutality, and will idle away the allotted days of his trivial life, and then pass to the dust and the worms and leave it so!

Napoleon has augmented the commercial prosperity of France, in ten years, to such a degree that figures can hardly compute it. He has rebuilt Paris, and has partly rebuilt every city in the State. He condemns a whole street at a time, assesses the damages, pays them and rebuilds superbly. Then speculators buy up the ground and sell, but the original owner is given the first choice by the government at a stated price before the speculator is permitted to purchase. But above all things, he has taken the sole control of the Empire of France into his hands, and made it a tolerably free land – for people who will not attempt to go too far in meddling with government affairs. No country offers greater security to life and property than France, and one has all the freedom he wants, but no license – no license to interfere with any body, or make any one uncomfortable.

As for the Sultan, one could set a trap any where and catch a dozen abler men in a night.

The bands struck up, and the brilliant adventurer, Napoleon III., the genius of Energy, Persistence, Enterprise; and the feeble Abdul-Aziz, the genius of Ignorance, Bigotry and Indolence, prepared for the Forward – March!

We saw the splendid review, we saw the white-moustached old Crimean soldier, Canrobert, Marshal of France, we saw – well, we saw every thing, and then we went home satisfied.

CHAPTER XIV

WE WENT TO see the Cathedral of Notre Dame. – We had heard of it before. It surprises me, sometimes, to think how much we *do* know, and how intelligent we are. We recognized the brown old Gothic pile in a moment; it was like the pictures. We stood at a little distance and changed from one point of observation to another, and gazed long at its lofty square towers and its rich front, clustered thick with stony, mutilated saints who had been looking calmly down from their perches for ages. The Patriarch of Jerusalem stood under them in the old days of chivalry and romance, and preached the third Crusade, more than six hundred years ago; and since that day they have stood there and looked quietly down upon the most thrilling scenes, the grandest pageants, the most extraordinary spectacles that have grieved or delighted Paris. These battered and broken-nosed old fellows saw many and many a cavalcade of mail-clad knights come marching home from Holy Land; they heard the bells above them toll the signal for the St. Bartholomew's Massacre, and they saw the slaughter that followed; later, they saw the Reign of Terror, the carnage of the Revolution, the overthrow of a king, the coronation of two Napoleons, the christening of the young prince that lords it over a regiment of servants in the Tuileries to-day – and they may possibly continue to stand there until they see the Napoleon dynasty swept away and the banners of a great Republic floating above its ruins. I wish these old parties could speak. They could tell a tale worth the listening to.

They say that a pagan temple stood where Notre Dame now stands, in the old Roman days, eighteen or twenty centuries ago – remains of it are still preserved in Paris; and that a Christian church took its place about A. D. 300; another took the place of that in A. D. 500; and that the foundations of the present Cathedral were laid about A. D. 1100. The ground ought to be measurably sacred by this time, one would think. One portion of this noble old edifice is suggestive of the quaint fashions of ancient times. It was built by Jean Sans-Peur, Duke of Burgundy, to set his conscience at rest – he had assassinated the Duke of Orleans. Alas! those good old times are gone, when a murderer could wipe the stain from his name and soothe his troubles to sleep simply by getting out his bricks and mortar and building an addition to a church.

The portals of the great western front are bisected by square pillars. They took the central one away, in 1852, on the occasion of thanksgivings for the reinstitution of the Presidential power – but precious soon they had occasion to reconsider that motion and put it back again! And they did.

We loitered through the grand aisles for an hour or two, staring up at the rich stained glass windows embellished with blue and yellow and crimson saints and martyrs, and trying to admire the numberless great pictures in the chapels, and then we were admitted to the sacristy and shown the magnificent robes which the Pope wore when he crowned Napoleon I.; a wagon-load of solid gold and silver utensils used in the great public processions and ceremonies of the church; some nails of the true cross, a fragment of the cross itself, a part of the crown of thorns. We had already seen a large piece of the true cross in a church in the Azores, but no nails. They showed us likewise the bloody robe which that Archbishop of Paris wore who exposed his sacred person and braved the wrath of the insurgents of 1848, to mount the barricades and hold aloft the olive branch of peace in the hope of stopping the slaughter. His noble effort cost him his life. He was shot dead. They showed us a cast of his face, taken after death, the bullet that killed him, and the two vertebræ in which it lodged. These people have a somewhat singular taste in the matter of relics. Ferguson told us that the silver cross which the good Archbishop wore at his girdle was seized and thrown into the Seine, where it lay embedded in the mud for fifteen years, and then an angel appeared to a priest and told him where to dive for it; he *did* dive for it and got it, and now it is there on exhibition at Notre Dame, to be inspected by any body who feels an interest in inanimate objects of miraculous intervention.

Next we went to visit the Morgue, that horrible receptacle for the dead who die mysteriously and leave the manner of their taking off a dismal secret. We stood before a grating and looked through into a room which was hung all about with the clothing of dead men; coarse blouses, water-soaked; the delicate garments of women and children; patrician vestments, hacked and stabbed and stained with red; a hat that was crushed and bloody. On a slanting stone lay a drowned man, naked, swollen, purple; clasping the fragment of a broken bush with a grip which death had so petrified that human strength could not unloose it – mute witness of the last despairing effort to save the life that was doomed beyond all help. A stream of water trickled ceaselessly over the hideous face. We knew that the body and the clothing were there for identification by friends, but still we wondered if any body could love that repulsive object or grieve for its loss. We grew meditative and wondered if, some forty years ago, when the mother of that ghastly thing was dandling it upon her knee, and kissing it and petting it and displaying it with satisfied pride to the passers-by, a prophetic vision of this dread ending ever flitted through her brain. I half feared that the mother, or the wife or a brother of the dead man might come while we stood there, but nothing of the kind occurred. Men and women came, and some looked eagerly in, and pressed their faces against the bars; others glanced carelessly at the body, and turned away with a disappointed look – people, I thought, who live upon strong excitements, and who attend the exhibitions of the Morgue regularly, just as other people go to see theatrical spectacles every night. When one of these looked in and passed on, I could not help thinking –

"Now this don't afford you any satisfaction – a party with his head shot off is what *you* need."

One night we went to the celebrated *Jardin Mabille*, but only staid a little while. We wanted to see some of this kind of Paris life, however, and therefore, the next night we went to a similar place of entertainment in a great garden in the suburb of Asnières. We went to the railroad depot, toward evening, and Ferguson got tickets for a second-class carriage. Such a perfect jam of people I have not often seen – but there was no noise, no disorder, no rowdyism. Some of the women and young girls that entered the train we knew to be of the *demi-monde*, but others we were not at all sure about.

The girls and women in our carriage behaved themselves modestly and becomingly, all the way out, except that they smoked. When we arrived at the garden in Asnières, we paid a franc or two admission, and entered a place which had flower-beds in it, and grass plats, and long, curving rows of ornamental shrubbery, with here and there a secluded bower convenient for eating ice-cream in. We moved along the sinuous gravel walks, with the great concourse of girls and young men, and suddenly a domed and filagreed white temple, starred over and over and over again with brilliant gas-jets, burst upon us like a fallen sun. Near by was a large, handsome house with its ample front illuminated in the same way, and above its roof floated the Star Spangled Banner of America.

"Well!" I said. "How is this?" It nearly took my breath away.

Ferguson said an American – a New Yorker – kept the place, and was carrying on quite a stirring opposition to the *Jardin Mabille*.

Crowds, composed of both sexes and nearly all ages, were frisking about the garden or sitting in the open air in front of the flag-staff and the temple, drinking wine and coffee, or smoking. The dancing had not begun, yet. Ferguson said there was to be an exhibition. The famous Blondin was going to perform on a tight-rope in another part of the garden. We went thither. Here the light was dim, and the masses of people were pretty closely packed together. And now I made a mistake which any donkey might make, but a sensible man never. I committed an error which I find myself repeating every day of my life. – Standing right before a young lady, I said –

"Dan, just look at this girl, how beautiful she is!"

"I thank you more for the evident sincerity of the compliment, sir, than for the extraordinary publicity you have given to it!" This in good, pure English.

We took a walk, but my spirits were very, very sadly dampened. I did not feel right comfortable for some time afterward. Why *will* people be so stupid as to suppose themselves the only foreigners among a crowd of ten thousand persons?

But Blondin came out shortly. He appeared on a stretched cable, far away above the sea of tossing hats and handkerchiefs, and in the glare of the hundreds of rockets that whizzed heavenward by him he looked like a wee insect. He balanced his pole and walked the length of his rope – two or three hundred feet; he came back and got a man and carried him across; he returned to the centre and danced a jig; next he performed some gymnastic and balancing feats too perilous to afford a pleasant spectacle; and he finished by fastening to his person a thousand Roman candles, Catherine wheels, serpents and rockets of all manner of brilliant colors, setting them on fire all at once and walking and waltzing across his rope again in a blinding blaze of glory that lit up the garden and the people's faces like a great conflagration at midnight.

The dance had begun, and we adjourned to the temple. Within it was a drinking saloon; and all around it was a broad circular platform for the dancers. I backed up against the wall of the temple, and waited. Twenty sets formed, the music struck up, and then – I placed my hands before my face for very shame. But I looked through my fingers. They were dancing the renowned *"Can-can."* A handsome girl in the set before me tripped forward lightly to meet the opposite gentleman – tripped back again, grasped her dresses vigorously on both sides with her hands, raised them pretty high, danced an extraordinary jig that had more activity and exposure about it than any jig I ever saw before, and then, drawing her clothes still higher, she advanced gaily to the centre and launched a vicious kick full at her *vis-a-vis* that must infallibly have removed his nose if he had been seven feet high. It was a mercy he was only six.

That is the *can-can.* The idea of it is to dance as wildly, as noisily, as furiously as you can; expose yourself as much as possible if you are a woman; and kick as high as you can, no matter which sex you belong to. There is no word of exaggeration in this. Any of the staid, respectable, aged people who were there that night can testify to the truth of that statement. There were a good many such people present. I suppose French morality is not of that strait-laced description which is shocked at trifles.

I moved aside and took a general view of the *can-can.* Shouts, laughter, furious music, a bewildering chaos of darting and intermingling forms, stormy jerking and snatching of gay dresses, bobbing heads, flying arms, lightning-flashes of white-stockinged calves and dainty slippers in the air, and then a grand final rush, riot, a terrific hubbub and a wild stampede! Heavens! Nothing like it has been seen on earth since trembling Tam O'Shanter saw the devil and the witches at their orgies that stormy night in "Alloway's auld haunted kirk."

We visited the Louvre, at a time when we had no silk purchases in view, and looked at its miles of paintings by the old masters.

Some of them were beautiful, but at the same time they carried such evidences about them of the cringing spirit of those great men that we found small pleasure in examining them. Their nauseous adulation of princely patrons was more prominent to me and chained my attention more surely than the charms of color and expression which are claimed to be in the pictures. Gratitude for kindnesses is well, but it seems to me that some of those artists carried it so far that it ceased to be gratitude, and became worship. If there is a plausible excuse for the worship of men, then by all means let us forgive Rubens and his brethren.

But I will drop the subject, lest I say something about the old masters that might as well be left unsaid.

Of course we drove in the *Bois de Boulogne*, that limitless park, with its forests, its lakes, its cascades, and its broad avenues. There were thousands upon thousands of vehicles abroad, and the scene was full of life and gayety. There were very common hacks, with father and mother and all the children in them; conspicuous little open carriages with celebrated ladies of questionable reputation in them; there were Dukes and Duchesses abroad, with gorgeous footmen perched behind, and equally gorgeous outriders perched on each of the six horses; there were blue and silver, and green and gold, and pink and black, and all sorts and descriptions of stunning and startling liveries out, and I almost yearned to be a flunkey myself, for the sake of the fine clothes.

But presently the Emperor came along and he out-shone them all. He was preceded by a body-guard of gentlemen on horseback in showy uniforms, his carriage-horses (there appeared to be somewhere in the remote neighborhood of a thousand of them,) were bestridden by gallant-looking fellows, also in stylish uniforms, and after the carriage followed another detachment of body-guards. Every body got out of the way; every body bowed to the Emperor and his friend the Sultan, and they went by on a swinging trot and disappeared.

I will not describe the *Bois de Boulogne*. I can not do it. It is simply a beautiful, cultivated, endless, wonderful wilderness. It is an enchanting place. It is in Paris, now, one may say, but a crumbling old cross in one portion of it reminds one that it was not always so. The cross marks the spot where a celebrated troubadour was waylaid and murdered in the fourteenth century. It was in this park that that fellow with an unpronounceable name made the attempt upon the Russian Czar's life last spring with a pistol. The bullet struck a tree. Ferguson showed us the place. Now in America that interesting tree would be chopped down or forgotten within the next five years, but it will be treasured here. The guides will point it out to visitors for the next eight hundred years, and when it decays and falls down they will put up another there and go on with the same old story just the same.

CHAPTER XVI

VERSAILLES! IT IS wonderfully beautiful! You gaze, and stare, and try to understand that it is real, that it is on the earth, that it is not the Garden of Eden – but your brain grows giddy, stupefied by the world of beauty around you, and you half believe you are the dupe of an exquisite dream. The scene thrills one like military music! A noble palace, stretching its ornamented front block upon block away, till it seemed that it would never end; a grand promenade before it, whereon the armies of an empire might parade; all about it rainbows of flowers, and colossal statues that were almost numberless, and yet seemed only scattered over the ample space; broad flights of stone steps leading down from the promenade to lower grounds of the park – stairways that whole regiments might stand to arms upon and have room to spare; vast fountains whose great bronze effigies discharged rivers of sparkling water into the air and mingled a hundred curving jets together in forms of matchless beauty; wide grass-carpeted avenues that branched hither and thither in every direction and wandered to seemingly interminable distances, walled all the way on either side with compact ranks of leafy trees whose branches met above and formed arches as faultless and as symmetrical as ever were carved in stone; and here and there were glimpses of sylvan lakes with miniature ships glassed in their surfaces. And every where – on the palace steps, and the great promenade, around the fountains, among the trees, and far under the arches of the endless avenues, hundreds and hundreds of people in gay costumes walked or ran or danced, and gave to the fairy picture the life and animation which was all of perfection it could have lacked.

It was worth a pilgrimage to see. Every thing is on so gigantic a scale. Nothing is small – nothing is cheap. The statues are all large; the palace is grand; the park covers a fair-sized county; the avenues are interminable. All the distances and all the dimensions about Versailles are vast. I used to think the pictures exaggerated these distances and these dimensions beyond all reason, and that they made Versailles more beautiful than it was possible for any place in the world to be. I know now that the pictures never came up to the subject in any respect, and that no painter could represent Versailles on canvas as beautiful as it is in reality. I used to abuse Louis XIV. for spending two hundred millions of dollars in creating this marvelous park, when bread was so scarce with some of his subjects; but I have forgiven him now. He took a tract of land sixty miles in circumference and set to work to make this park and build this palace and a road to it from Paris. He kept 36,000 men employed daily on it, and the labor was so unhealthy that they used to die and be hauled off by cart-loads every night. The wife of a nobleman of the time speaks of this as an "*inconvenience*," but naively remarks that "it does not seem worthy of attention in the happy state of tranquillity we now enjoy."

I always thought ill of people at home, who trimmed their shrubbery into pyramids, and squares, and spires, and all manner of unnatural shapes, and when I saw the same thing being practiced in this great park I began to feel dissatisfied. But I soon saw the idea of the thing and the wisdom of it. They seek the *general* effect. We distort a dozen sickly trees into unaccustomed shapes in a little yard no bigger than a dining-room, and then surely they look absurd enough. But here they take two hundred thousand tall forest trees and set them in a double row; allow no sign of leaf or branch to grow on the trunk lower down than six feet above the ground; from that point the boughs begin to project, and very gradually they extend outward further and further till they meet overhead, and a faultless tunnel of foliage is formed. The arch is mathematically precise. The effect is then very fine. They make trees take fifty different shapes, and so these quaint effects are infinitely varied and picturesque. The trees in no two avenues are shaped alike, and consequently the eye is not fatigued with any thing in the nature of monotonous uniformity. I will drop this subject now, leaving it to others to determine how these people manage to make endless ranks of lofty forest trees grow to just a certain thickness of trunk (say a foot and two-thirds;) how they make them spring to precisely the same height for miles; how they make them grow so close together; how they compel one huge limb to spring from the same identical spot on each tree and form the main sweep of the arch; and how all these things are kept exactly in the same condition, and in the same exquisite shapeliness and symmetry month after month and year after year – for I have tried to reason out the problem, and have failed.

We walked through the great hall of sculpture and the one hundred and fifty galleries of paintings in the palace of Versailles, and felt that to be in such a place was useless unless one had a whole year at his disposal. These pictures are all battle-scenes, and only one solitary little canvas among them all treats of anything but great French victories. We wandered, also, through the Grand Trianon and the Petit Trianon, those monuments of royal prodigality, and with histories so mournful – filled, as it is, with souvenirs of Napoleon the First, and three dead Kings and as many Queens. In one sumptuous bed they had all slept in succession, but no one occupies it now. In a large dining-room stood the table at which Louis XIV. and his mistress, Madame Maintenon, and after them Louis XV., and Pompadour, had sat at their meals naked and unattended – for the table stood upon a trap-door, which descended with it to regions below when it was necessary to replenish its dishes. In a room of the Petit Trianon stood the furniture, just as poor Marie Antoinette left it when the mob came and dragged her and the King to Paris, never to return. Near at hand, in the stables, were prodigious carriages that showed no color but gold – carriages used by former Kings of France on state occasions, and never used now save when a kingly head is to be crowned, or an imperial infant christened. And with them were some curious sleighs, whose bodies were shaped like lions, swans, tigers, etc. – vehicles that had once been handsome with pictured designs and fine workmanship, but were dusty and decaying now. They had their history. When Louis XIV. had finished the Grand Trianon, he told Maintenon he had created a Paradise for her, and asked if she could think of any thing now to wish for. He said he wished the Trianon to be perfection – nothing less. She said she could think of but one thing – it was summer, and it was balmy France – yet she would like well to sleigh-ride in the leafy avenues of Versailles! The next morning found miles and miles of grassy avenues spread thick with snowy salt and sugar, and a procession of those quaint sleighs waiting to receive the chief concubine of the gayest and most unprincipled court that France has ever seen!

From sumptuous Versailles, with its palaces, its statues, its gardens and its fountains, we journeyed back to Paris and sought its antipodes – the Faubourg St. Antoine. Little, narrow streets; dirty children blockading them; greasy, slovenly women capturing and spanking them; filthy dens on first floors, with rag stores in them (the heaviest business in the Faubourg is the chiffonier's;) other filthy dens where whole suits of second-1 and third-hand clothing are sold at prices that would ruin any proprietor who did not steal his stock; still other filthy dens where they sold groceries – sold them by the half-pennyworth – five dollars would buy the man out, good-will and all. Up these little crooked streets they will murder a man for seven dollars and dump the body in the Seine. And up some other of these streets – most of them, I should say – live lorettes.

All through this Faubourg St. Antoine, misery, poverty, vice and crime go hand in hand, and the evidences of it stare one in the face from every side. Here the people live who begin the revolutions. Whenever there is any thing of that kind to be done, they are always ready. They take as much genuine pleasure in building a barricade as they do in cutting a throat or shoving a friend into the Seine. It is these savage-looking ruffians who storm the splendid halls of the Tuileries, occasionally, and swarm into Versailles when a King is to be called to account.

But they will build no more barricades, they will break no more soldiers' heads with paving-stones. Louis Napoleon has taken care of all that. He is annihilating the crooked streets, and building in their stead noble boulevards as straight as an arrow – avenues which a cannon ball could traverse from end to end without meeting an obstruction more irresistible than the flesh and bones of men – boulevards whose stately edifices will never afford refuges and plotting-places for starving, discontented revolution-breeders. Five of these great thoroughfares radiate from one ample centre – a centre which is exceedingly well adapted to the accommodation of heavy artillery. The mobs used to riot there, but they must seek another rallying-place in future. And this ingenious Napoleon paves the streets of his great cities with a smooth, compact composition of asphaltum and sand. No more barricades of flag-stones – no more assaulting his Majesty's troops with cobbles. I can not feel friendly toward my quondam fellow-American, Napoleon III., especially at this time,* when in fancy I see his credulous victim, Maximilian, lying stark and stiff in Mexico, and his maniac widow watching eagerly from her French asylum for the form that will never come – but I do admire his nerve, his calm self-reliance, his shrewd good sense.

*July, 1867.

CHAPTER XVII

WE HAD A pleasant journey of it seaward again. We found that for the three past nights our ship had been in a state of war. The first night the sailors of a British ship, being happy with grog, came down on the pier and challenged our sailors to a free fight. They accepted with alacrity, repaired to the pier and gained – their share of a drawn battle. Several bruised and bloody members of both parties were carried off by the police, and imprisoned until the following morning. The next night the British boys came again to renew the fight, but our men had had strict orders to remain on board and out of sight. They did so, and the besieging party grew noisy, and more and more abusive as the fact became apparent (to them,) that our men were afraid to come out. They went away, finally, with a closing burst of ridicule and offensive epithets. The third night they came again, and were more obstreperous than ever. They swaggered up and down the almost deserted pier, and hurled curses, obscenity and stinging sarcasms at our crew. It was more than human nature could bear. The executive officer ordered our men ashore – with instructions not to fight. They charged the British and gained a brilliant victory. I probably would not have mentioned this war had it ended differently. But I travel to learn, and I still remember that they picture no French defeats in the battle-galleries of Versailles.

It was like home to us to step on board the comfortable ship again, and smoke and lounge about her breezy decks. And yet it was not altogether like home, either, because so many members of the family were away. We missed some pleasant faces which we would rather have found at dinner, and at night there were gaps in the euchre-parties which could not be satisfactorily filled. "Moult." was in England, Jack in Switzerland, Charley in Spain. Blucher was gone, none could tell where. But we were at sea again, and we had the stars and the ocean to look at, and plenty of room to meditate in.

In due time the shores of Italy were sighted, and as we stood gazing from the decks early in the bright summer morning, the stately city of Genoa rose up out of the sea and flung back the sunlight from her hundred palaces.

Here we rest, for the present – or rather, here we have been trying to rest, for some little time, but we run about too much to accomplish a great deal in that line.

I would like to remain here. I had rather not go any further. There may be prettier women in Europe, but I doubt it. The population of Genoa is 120,000; two-thirds of these are women, I think, and at least two-thirds of the women are beautiful. They are as dressy, and as tasteful and as graceful as they could possibly be without being angels. However, angels are not very dressy, I believe. At least the angels in pictures are not – they wear nothing but wings. But these Genoese women do look so charming. Most of the young demoiselles are robed in a cloud of white from head to foot, though many trick themselves out more elaborately. Nine-tenths of them wear nothing on their heads but a filmy sort of veil, which falls down their backs like a white mist. They are very fair, and many of them have blue eyes, but black and dreamy dark brown ones are met with oftenest.

The ladies and gentlemen of Genoa have a pleasant fashion of promenading in a large park on the top of a hill in the centre of the city, from six till nine in the evening, and then eating ices in a neighboring garden an hour or two longer. We went to the park on Sunday evening. Two thousand persons were present, chiefly young ladies and gentlemen. The gentlemen were dressed in the very latest Paris fashions, and the robes of the ladies glinted among the trees like so many snowflakes. The multitude moved round and round the park in a great procession. The bands played, and so did the fountains; the moon and the gas lamps lit up the scene, and altogether it was a brilliant and an animated picture. I scanned every female face that passed, and it seemed to me that all were handsome. I never saw such a freshet of loveliness before. I do not see how a man of only ordinary decision of character could marry here, because, before he could get his mind made up he would fall in love with somebody else.

Never smoke any Italian tobacco. Never do it on any account. It makes me shudder to think what it must be made of. You can not throw an old cigar "stub" down any where, but some vagabond will pounce upon it on the instant. I like to smoke a good deal, but it wounds my sensibilities to see one of these stub-hunters watching me out of the corners of his hungry eyes and calculating how long my cigar will be likely to last. It reminded me too painfully of that San Francisco undertaker who used to go to sick-beds with his watch in his hand and time the corpse. One of these stub-hunters followed us all over the park last night, and we never had a smoke that was worth any thing. We were always moved to appease him with the stub before the cigar was half gone, because he looked so viciously anxious. He regarded us as his own legitimate prey, by right of discovery, I think, because he drove off several other professionals who wanted to take stock in us.

Now, they surely must chew up those old stubs, and dry and sell them for smoking-tobacco. Therefore, give your custom to other than Italian brands of the article.

"The Superb" and the "City of Palaces" are names which Genoa has held for centuries. She is full of palaces, certainly, and the palaces are sumptuous inside, but they are very rusty without, and make no pretensions to architectural magnificence. "Genoa, the Superb," would be a felicitous title if it referred to the women.

We have visited several of the palaces – immense thick-walled piles, with great stone staircases, tesselated marble pavements on the floors, (sometimes they make a mosaic work, of intricate designs, wrought in pebbles, or little fragments of marble laid in cement,) and grand *salons* hung with pictures by Rubens, Guido, Titian, Paul Veronese, and so on, and portraits of heads of the family, in plumed helmets and gallant coats of mail, and patrician ladies, in stunning costumes of centuries ago. But, of course, the folks were all out in the country for the summer, and might not have known enough to ask us to dinner if they had been at home, and so all the grand empty *salons*, with their resounding pavements, their grim pictures of dead ancestors, and tattered banners with the dust of bygone centuries upon them, seemed to brood solemnly of death and the grave, and our spirits ebbed away, and our cheerfulness passed from us. We never went up to the eleventh story. We always began to suspect ghosts. There was always an undertaker-looking servant along, too, who handed us a programme, pointed to the picture that began the list of the *salon* he was in, and then stood stiff and stark and unsmiling in his petrified livery till we were ready to move on to the next chamber, whereupon he marched sadly ahead and took up another malignantly respectful position as before. I wasted so much time praying that the roof would fall in on these dispiriting flunkeys that I had but little left to bestow upon palace and pictures.

And besides, as in Paris, we had a guide. Perdition catch all the guides. This one said he was the most gifted linguist in Genoa, as far as English was concerned, and that only two persons in the city beside himself could talk the language at all. He showed us the birthplace of Christopher Columbus, and after we had reflected in silent awe before it for fifteen minutes, he said it was not the birthplace of Columbus, but of Columbus's grandmother! When we demanded an explanation of his conduct he only shrugged his shoulders and answered in barbarous Italian. I shall speak further of this guide in a future chapter. All the information we got out of him we shall be able to carry along with us, I think.

I have not been to church so often in a long time as I have in the last few weeks. The people in these old lands seem to make churches their specialty. Especially does this seem to be the case with the citizens of Genoa. I think there is a church every three or four hundred yards all over town. The streets are sprinkled from end to end with shovel-hatted, long-robed, well-fed priests, and the church bells by dozens are pealing all the day long, nearly. Every now and then one comes across a friar of orders gray, with shaven head, long, coarse robe, rope girdle and beads, and with feet cased in sandals or entirely bare. These worthies suffer in the flesh, and do penance all their lives, I suppose, but they look like consummate famine-breeders. They are all fat and serene.

The old Cathedral of San Lorenzo is about as notable a building as we have found in Genoa. It is vast, and has colonnades of noble pillars, and a great organ, and the customary pomp of gilded moldings, pictures, frescoed ceilings, and so forth. I can not describe it, of course – it would require a good many pages to do that. But it is a curious place. They said that half of it – from the front door half way down to the altar – was a Jewish Synagogue before the Saviour was born, and that no alteration had been made in it since that time. We doubted the statement, but did it reluctantly. We would much rather have believed it. The place looked in too perfect repair to be so ancient.

The main point of interest about the Cathedral is the little Chapel of St. John the Baptist. They only allow women to enter it on one day in the year, on account of the animosity they still cherish against the sex because of the murder of the Saint to gratify a caprice of Herodias. In this Chapel is a marble chest, in which, they told us, were the ashes of St. John; and around it was wound a chain, which, they said, had confined him when he was in prison. We did not desire to disbelieve these statements, and yet we could not feel certain that they were correct – partly because we could have broken that chain, and so could St. John, and partly because we had seen St. John's ashes before, in another church. We could not bring ourselves to think St. John had two sets of ashes.

They also showed us a portrait of the Madonna which was painted by St. Luke, and it did not look half as old and smoky as some of the pictures by Rubens. We could not help admiring the Apostle's modesty in never once mentioning in his writings that he could paint.

But isn't this relic matter a little overdone? We find a piece of the true cross in every old church we go into, and some of the nails that held it together. I would not like to be positive, but I think we have seen as much as a keg of these nails. Then there is the crown of thorns; they have part of one in Sainte Chapelle, in Paris, and part of one, also, in Notre Dame. And as for bones of St. Denis, I feel certain we have seen enough of them to duplicate him, if necessary.

I only meant to write about the churches, but I keep wandering from the subject. I could say that the Church of the Annunciation is a wilderness of beautiful columns, of statues, gilded moldings, and pictures almost countless, but that would give no one an entirely perfect idea of the thing, and so where is the use? One family built the whole edifice, and have got money left. There is where the mystery lies. We had an idea at first that only a mint could have survived the expense.

These people here live in the heaviest, highest, broadest, darkest, solidest houses one can imagine. Each one might "laugh a siege to scorn." A hundred feet front and a hundred high is about the style, and you go up three flights of stairs before you begin to come upon signs of occupancy. Every thing is stone, and stone of the heaviest – floors, stairways, mantels, benches – every thing. The walls are four to five feet thick. The streets generally are four or five to eight feet wide and as crooked as a corkscrew. You go along one of these gloomy cracks, and look up and behold the sky like a mere ribbon of light, far above your head, where the tops of the tall houses on either side of the street bend almost together. You feel as if you were at the bottom of some tremendous abyss, with all the world far above you. You wind in and out and here and there, in the most mysterious way, and have no more idea of the points of the compass than if you were a blind man. You can never persuade yourself that these are actually streets, and the frowning, dingy, monstrous houses dwellings, till you see one of these beautiful, prettily dressed women emerge from them – see her emerge from a dark, dreary-looking den that looks dungeon all over, from the ground away half way up to heaven. And then you wonder that such a charming moth could come from such a forbidding shell as that. The streets are wisely made narrow and the houses heavy and thick and stony, in order that the people may be cool in this roasting climate. And they are cool, and stay so. And while I think of it – the men wear hats and have very dark complexions, but the women wear no head-gear but a flimsy veil like a gossamer's web, and yet are exceedingly fair as a general thing. Singular, isn't it?

The huge palaces of Genoa are each supposed to be occupied by one family, but they could accommodate a hundred, I should think. They are relics of the grandeur of Genoa's palmy days – the days when she was a great commercial and maritime power several centuries ago. These houses, solid marble palaces though they be, are in many cases of a dull pinkish color, outside, and from pavement to eaves are pictured with Genoese battle-scenes, with monstrous Jupiters and Cupids and with familiar illustrations from Grecian mythology. Where the paint has yielded to age and exposure and is peeling off in flakes and patches, the effect is not happy. A noseless Cupid, or a Jupiter with an eye out, or a Venus with a fly-blister on her breast, are not attractive features in a picture. Some of these painted walls reminded me somewhat of the tall van, plastered with fanciful bills and posters, that follows the bandwagon of a circus about a country village. I have not read or heard that the outsides of the houses of any other European city are frescoed in this way.

I can not conceive of such a thing as Genoa in ruins. Such massive arches, such ponderous substructions as support these towering broad-winged edifices, we have seldom seen before; and surely the great blocks of stone of which these edifices are built can never decay; walls that are as thick as an ordinary American doorway is high, can not crumble.

The Republics of Genoa and Pisa were very powerful in the middle ages. Their ships filled the Mediterranean, and they carried on an extensive commerce with Constantinople and Syria. Their warehouses were the great distributing depots from whence the costly merchandise of the East was sent abroad over Europe. They were warlike little nations, and defied, in those days, governments that overshadow them now as mountains overshadow molehills. The Saracens captured and pillaged Genoa nine hundred years ago, but during the following century Genoa and Pisa entered into an offensive and defensive alliance and besieged the Saracen colonies in Sardinia and the Balearic Isles with an obstinacy that maintained its pristine vigor and held to its purpose for forty long years. They were victorious at last, and divided their conquests equably among their great patrician families. Descendants of some of those proud families still inhabit the palaces of Genoa, and trace in their own features a resemblance to the grim knights whose portraits hang in their stately halls, and to pictured beauties with pouting lips and merry eyes whose originals have been dust and ashes for many a dead and forgotten century.

The hotel we live in belonged to one of those great orders of knights of the Cross in the times of the Crusades, and its mailed sentinels once kept watch and ward in its massive turrets and woke the echoes of these halls and corridors with their iron heels.

But Genoa's greatness has degenerated into an unostentatious commerce in velvets and silver filigree work. They say that each European town has its specialty. These filigree things are Genoa's specialty. Her smiths take silver ingots and work them up into all manner of graceful and beautiful forms. They make bunches of flowers, from flakes and wires of silver, that counterfeit the delicate creations the frost weaves upon a window pane; and we were shown a miniature silver temple whose fluted columns, whose Corinthian capitals and rich entablatures, whose spire, statues, bells, and ornate lavishness of sculpture were wrought in polished silver, and with such matchless art that every detail was a fascinating study, and the finished edifice a wonder of beauty.

We are ready to move again, though we are not really tired, yet, of the narrow passages of this old marble cave. Cave is a good word – when speaking of Genoa under the stars. When we have been prowling at midnight through the gloomy crevices they call streets, where no foot falls but ours were echoing, where only ourselves were abroad, and lights appeared only at long intervals and at a distance, and mysteriously disappeared again, and the houses at our elbows seemed to stretch upward farther than ever toward the heavens, the memory of a cave I used to know at home was always in my mind, with its lofty passages, its silence and solitude, its shrouding gloom, its sepulchral echoes, its flitting lights, and more than all, its sudden revelations of branching crevices and corridors where we least expected them.

We are not tired of the endless processions of cheerful, chattering gossipers that throng these courts and streets all day long, either; nor of the coarse-robed monks; nor of the "Asti" wines, which that old doctor (whom we call the Oracle,) with customary felicity in the matter of getting every thing wrong, misterms "nasty." But we must go, nevertheless.

Our last sight was the cemetery, (a burial-place intended to accommodate 60,000 bodies,) and we shall continue to remember it after we shall have forgotten the palaces. It is a vast marble colonnaded corridor extending around a great unoccupied square of ground; its broad floor is marble, and on every slab is an inscription – for every slab covers a corpse. On either side, as one walks down the middle of the passage, are monuments, tombs, and sculptured figures that are exquisitely wrought and are full of grace and beauty. They are new, and snowy; every outline is perfect, every feature guiltless of mutilation, flaw or blemish; and therefore, to us these far-reaching ranks of bewitching forms are a hundred fold more lovely than the damaged and dingy statuary they have saved from the wreck of ancient art and set up in the galleries of Paris for the worship of the world.

Well provided with cigars and other necessaries of life, we are now ready to take the cars for Milan.

CHAPTER XVIII

ALL DAY LONG we sped through a mountainous country whose peaks were bright with sunshine, whose hillsides were dotted with pretty villas sitting in the midst of gardens and shrubbery, and whose deep ravines were cool and shady, and looked ever so inviting from where we and the birds were winging our flight through the sultry upper air.

We had plenty of chilly tunnels wherein to check our perspiration, though. We timed one of them. We were twenty minutes passing through it, going at the rate of thirty to thirty-five miles an hour.

Beyond Alessandria we passed the battle-field of Marengo.

Toward dusk we drew near Milan, and caught glimpses of the city and the blue mountain peaks beyond. But we were not caring for these things – they did not interest us in the least. We were in a fever of impatience; we were dying to see the renowned Cathedral! We watched – in this direction and that – all around – every where. We needed no one to point it out – we did not wish any one to point it out – we would recognize it, even in the desert of the great Sahara.

At last, a forest of graceful needles, shimmering in the amber sunlight, rose slowly above the pigmy house-tops, as one sometimes sees, in the far horizon, a gilded and pinnacled mass of cloud lift itself above the waste of waves, at sea, – the Cathedral! We knew it in a moment.

Half of that night, and all of the next day, this architectural autocrat was our sole object of interest.

What a wonder it is! So grand, so solemn, so vast! And yet so delicate, so airy, so graceful! A very world of solid weight, and yet it seems in the soft moonlight only a fairy delusion of frost-work that might vanish with a breath! How sharply its pinnacled angles and its wilderness of spires were cut against the sky, and how richly their shadows fell upon its snowy roof! It was a vision! – a miracle! – an anthem sung in stone, a poem wrought in marble!

Howsoever you look at the great Cathedral, it is noble, it is beautiful! Wherever you stand in Milan, or within seven miles of Milan, it is visible – and when it is visible, no other object can chain your whole attention. Leave your eyes unfettered by your will but a single instant and they will surely turn to seek it. It is the first thing you look for when you rise in the morning, and the last your lingering gaze rests upon at night. Surely, it must be the princeliest creation that ever brain of man conceived.

At nine o'clock in the morning we went and stood before this marble colossus. The central one of its five great doors is bordered with a bas-relief of birds and fruits and beasts and insects, which have been so ingeniously carved out of the marble that they seem like living creatures – and the figures are so numerous and the design so complex, that one might study it a week without exhausting its interest. On the great steeple – surmounting the myriad of spires – inside of the spires – over the doors, the windows – in nooks and corners – every where that a niche or a perch can be found about the enormous building, from summit to base, there is a marble statue, and every statue is a study in itself! Raphael, Angelo, Canova – giants like these gave birth to the designs, and their own pupils carved them. Every face is eloquent with expression, and every attitude is full of grace. Away above, on the lofty roof, rank on rank of carved and fretted spires spring high in the air, and through their rich tracery one sees the sky beyond. In their midst the central steeple towers proudly up like the mainmast of some great Indiaman among a fleet of coasters.

We wished to go aloft. The sacristan showed us a marble stairway (of course it was marble, and of the purest and whitest – there is no other stone, no brick, no wood, among its building materials,) and told us to go up one hundred and eighty-two steps and stop till he came. It was not necessary to say stop – we should have done that any how. We were tired by the time we got there. This was the roof.

Here, springing from its broad marble flag-stones, were the long files of spires, looking very tall close at hand, but diminishing in the distance like the pipes of an organ. We could see, now, that the statue on the top of each was the size of a large man, though they all looked like dolls from the street. We could see, also, that from the inside of each and every one of these hollow spires, from sixteen to thirty-one beautiful marble statues looked out upon the world below.

From the eaves to the comb of the roof stretched in endless succession great curved marble beams, like the fore-and-aft braces of a steamboat, and along each beam from end to end stood up a row of richly carved flowers and fruits – each separate and distinct in kind, and over 15,000 species represented. At a little distance these rows seem to close together like the ties of a railroad track, and then the mingling together of the buds and blossoms of this marble garden forms a picture that is very charming to the eye.

We descended and entered. Within the church, long rows of fluted columns, like huge monuments, divided the building into broad aisles, and on the figured pavement fell many a soft blush from the painted windows above. I knew the church was very large, but I could not fully appreciate its great size until I noticed that the men standing far down by the altar looked like boys, and seemed to glide, rather than walk. We loitered about gazing aloft at the monster windows all aglow with brilliantly colored scenes in the lives of the Saviour and his followers. Some of these pictures are mosaics, and so artistically are their thousand particles of tinted glass or stone put together that the work has all the smoothness and finish of a painting. We counted sixty panes of glass in one window, and each pane was adorned with one of these master achievements of genius and patience.

The guide showed us a coffee-colored piece of sculpture which he said was considered to have come from the hand of Phidias, since it was not possible that any other artist, of any epoch, could have copied nature with such faultless accuracy. The figure was that of a man without a skin; with every vein, artery, muscle, every fibre and tendon and tissue of the human frame, represented in minute detail. It looked natural, because somehow it looked as if it were in pain. A skinned man would be likely to look that way, unless his attention were occupied with some other matter. It was a hideous thing, and yet there was a fascination about it some where. I am very sorry I saw it, because I shall always see it, now. I shall dream of it, sometimes. I shall dream that it is resting its corded arms on the bed's head and looking down on me with its dead eyes; I shall dream that it is stretched between the sheets with me and touching me with its exposed muscles and its stringy cold legs.

It is hard to forget repulsive things. I remember yet how I ran off from school once, when I was a boy, and then, pretty late at night, concluded to climb into the window of my father's office and sleep on a lounge, because I had a delicacy about going home and getting thrashed. As I lay on the lounge and my eyes grew accustomed to the darkness, I fancied I could see a long, dusky, shapeless thing stretched upon the floor. A cold shiver went through me. I turned my face to the wall. That did not answer. I was afraid that that thing would creep over and seize me in the dark. I turned back and stared at it for minutes and minutes – they seemed hours. It appeared to me that the lagging moonlight never, never would get to it. I turned to the wall and counted twenty, to pass the feverish time away. I looked – the pale square was nearer. I turned again and counted fifty – it was almost touching it. With desperate will I turned again and counted one hundred, and faced about, all in a tremble. A white human hand lay in the moonlight! Such an awful sinking at the heart – such a sudden gasp for breath! I felt – I can not tell *what* I felt. When I recovered strength enough, I faced the wall again. But no boy could have remained so, with that mysterious hand behind him. I counted again, and looked – the most of a naked arm was exposed. I put my hands over my eyes and counted till I could stand it no longer, and then – the pallid face of a man was there, with the corners of the mouth drawn down, and the eyes fixed and glassy in death! I raised to a sitting posture and glowered on that corpse till the light crept down the bare breast, – line by line – inch by inch – past the nipple, – and then it disclosed a ghastly stab!

I went away from there. I do not say that I went away in any sort of a hurry, but I simply went – that is sufficient. I went out at the window, and I carried the sash along with me. I did not need the sash, but it was handier to take it than it was to leave it, and so I took it. – I was not scared, but I was considerably agitated.

When I reached home, they whipped me, but I enjoyed it. It seemed perfectly delightful. That man had been stabbed near the office that afternoon, and they carried him in there to doctor him, but he only lived an hour. I have slept in the same room with him often, since then – in my dreams.

Now we will descend into the crypt, under the grand altar of Milan Cathedral, and receive an impressive sermon from lips that have been silent and hands that have been gestureless for three hundred years.

The priest stopped in a small dungeon and held up his candle. This was the last resting-place of a good man, a warm-hearted, unselfish man; a man whose whole life was given to succoring the poor, encouraging the faint-hearted, visiting the sick; in relieving distress, whenever and wherever he found it. His heart, his hand and his purse were always open. With his story in one's mind he can almost see his benignant countenance moving calmly among the haggard faces of Milan in the days when the plague swept the city, brave where all others were cowards, full of compassion where pity had been crushed out of all other breasts by the instinct of self-preservation gone mad with terror, cheering all, praying with all, helping all, with hand and brain and purse, at a time when parents forsook their children, the friend deserted the friend, and the brother turned away from the sister while her pleadings were still wailing in his ears.

This was good St. Charles Borroméo, Bishop of Milan. The people idolized him; princes lavished uncounted treasures upon him. We stood in his tomb. Near by was the sarcophagus, lighted by the dripping candles. The walls were faced with bas-reliefs representing scenes in his life done in massive silver. The priest put on a short white lace garment over his black robe, crossed himself, bowed reverently, and began to turn a windlass slowly. The sarcophagus separated in two parts, length-wise, and the lower part sank down and disclosed a coffin of rock crystal as clear as the atmosphere. Within lay the body, robed in costly habiliments covered with gold embroidery and starred with scintillating gems. The decaying head was black with age, the dry skin was drawn tight to the bones, the eyes were gone, there was a hole in the temple and another in the cheek, and the skinny lips were parted as in a ghastly smile! Over this dreadful face, its dust and decay, and its mocking grin, hung a crown sown thick with flashing brilliants; and upon the breast lay crosses and croziers of solid gold that were splendid with emeralds and diamonds.

How poor, and cheap, and trivial these gew-gaws seemed in presence of the solemnity, the grandeur, the awful majesty of Death! Think of Milton, Shakespeare, Washington, standing before a reverent world tricked out in the glass beads, the brass ear-rings and tin trumpery of the savages of the plains!

Dead Bartoloméo preached his pregnant sermon, and its burden was: You that worship the vanities of earth – you that long for worldly honor, worldly wealth, worldly fame – behold their worth!

To us it seemed that so good a man, so kind a heart, so simple a nature, deserved rest and peace in a grave sacred from the intrusion of prying eyes, and believed that he himself would have preferred to have it so, but peradventure our wisdom was at fault in this regard.

As we came out upon the floor of the church again, another priest volunteered to show us the treasures of the church. What, more? The furniture of the narrow chamber of death we had just visited, weighed six millions of francs in ounces and carats alone, without a penny thrown into the account for the costly workmanship bestowed upon them! But we followed into a large room filled with tall wooden presses like wardrobes. He threw them open, and behold, the cargoes of "crude bullion" of the assay offices of Nevada faded out of my memory. There were Virgins and bishops there, above their natural size, made of solid silver, each worth, by weight, from eight hundred thousand to two millions of francs, and bearing gemmed books in their hands worth eighty thousand; there were bas-reliefs that weighed six hundred pounds, carved in solid silver; croziers and crosses, and candlesticks six and eight feet high, all of virgin gold, and brilliant with precious stones; and beside these were all manner of cups and vases, and such things, rich in proportion. It was an Aladdin's palace. The treasures here, by simple weight, without counting workmanship, were valued at fifty millions of francs! If I could get the custody of them for a while, I fear me the market price of silver bishops would advance shortly, on account of their exceeding scarcity in the Cathedral of Milan.

The priests showed us two of St. Paul's fingers, and one of St. Peter's; a bone of Judas Iscariot, (it was black,) and also bones of all the other disciples; a handkerchief in which the Saviour had left the impression of his face. Among the most precious of the relics were a stone from the Holy Sepulchre, part of the crown of thorns, (they have a whole one at Notre Dame,) a fragment of the purple robe worn by the Saviour, a nail from the Cross, and a picture of the Virgin and Child painted by the veritable hand of St. Luke. This is the second of St. Luke's Virgins we have seen. Once a year all these holy relics are carried in procession through the streets of Milan.

I like to revel in the dryest details of the great cathedral. The building is five hundred feet long by one hundred and eighty wide, and the principal steeple is in the neighborhood of four hundred feet high. It has 7,148 marble statues, and will have upwards of three thousand more when it is finished. In addition, it has one thousand five hundred bas-reliefs. It has one hundred and thirty-six spires – twenty-one more are to be added. Each spire is surmounted by a statue six and a half feet high. Every thing about the church is marble, and all from the same quarry; it was bequeathed to the Archbishopric for this purpose centuries ago. So nothing but the mere workmanship costs; still that is expensive – the bill foots up six hundred and eighty-four millions of francs, thus far (considerably over a hundred millions of dollars,) and it is estimated that it will take a hundred and twenty years yet to finish the cathedral. It looks complete, but is far from being so. We saw a new statue put in its niche yesterday, alongside of one which had been standing these four hundred years, they said. There are four staircases leading up to the main steeple, each of which cost a hundred thousand dollars, with the four hundred and eight statues which adorn them. Marco Compioni was the architect who designed the wonderful structure more than five hundred years ago, and it took him forty-six years to work out the plan and get it ready to hand over to the builders. He is dead now. The building was begun a little less than five hundred years ago, and the third generation hence will not see it completed.

The building looks best by moonlight, because the older portions of it being stained with age, contrast unpleasantly with the newer and whiter portions. It seems somewhat too broad for its height, but may be familiarity with it might dissipate this impression.

They say that the Cathedral of Milan is second only to St. Peter's at Rome. I can not understand how it can be second to any thing made by human hands.

We bid it good-bye, now – possibly for all time. How surely, in some future day, when the memory of it shall have lost its vividness, shall we half believe we have seen it in a wonderful dream, but never with waking eyes!

CHAPTER XIX

"DO YOU WIS zo haut can be?"

That was what the guide asked, when we were looking up at the bronze horses on the Arch of Peace. It meant, do you wish to go up there? I give it as a specimen of guide-English. These are the people that make life a burthen to the tourist. Their tongues are never still. They talk forever and forever, and that is the kind of billingsgate they use. Inspiration itself could hardly comprehend them. If they would only show you a masterpiece of art, or a venerable tomb, or a prison-house, or a battle-field, hallowed by touching memories or historical reminiscences, or grand traditions, and then step aside and hold still for ten minutes and let you think, it would not be so bad. But they interrupt every dream, every pleasant train of thought, with their tiresome cackling. Sometimes when I have been standing before some cherished old idol of mine that I remembered years and years ago in pictures in the geography at school, I have thought I would give a whole world if the human parrot at my side would suddenly perish where he stood and leave me to gaze, and ponder, and worship.

No, we did not "wis zo haut can be." We wished to go to La Scala, the largest theatre in the world, I think they call it. We did so. It was a large place. Seven separate and distinct masses of humanity – six great circles and a monster parquette.

We wished to go to the Ambrosian Library, and we did that also. We saw a manuscript of Virgil, with annotations in the handwriting of Petrarch, the gentleman who loved another man's Laura, and lavished upon her all through life a love which was a clear waste of the raw material. It was sound sentiment, but bad judgment. It brought both parties fame, and created a fountain of commiseration for them in sentimental breasts that is running yet. But who says a word in behalf of poor Mr. Laura? (I do not know his other name.) Who glorifies him? Who bedews him with tears? Who writes poetry about him? Nobody. How do you suppose *he* liked the state of things that has given the world so much pleasure? How did he enjoy having another man following his wife every where and making her name a familiar word in every garlic-exterminating mouth in Italy with his sonnets to her pre-empted eyebrows? *They* got fame and sympathy – he got neither. This is a peculiarly felicitous instance of what is called poetical justice. It is all very fine; but it does not chime with my notions of right. It is too one-sided – too ungenerous. Let the world go on fretting about Laura and Petrarch if it will; but as for me, my tears and my lamentations shall be lavished upon the unsung defendant.

We saw also an autograph letter of Lucrezia Borgia, a lady for whom I have always entertained the highest respect, on account of her rare histrionic capabilities, her opulence in solid gold goblets made of gilded wood, her high distinction as an operatic screamer, and the facility with which she could order a sextuple funeral and get the corpses ready for it. We saw one single coarse yellow hair from Lucrezia's head, likewise. It awoke emotions, but we still live. In this same library we saw some drawings by Michael Angelo (these Italians call him Mickel Angelo,) and Leonardo da Vinci. (They spell it Vinci and pronounce it Vinchy; foreigners always spell better than they pronounce.) We reserve our opinion of these sketches.

In another building they showed us a fresco representing some lions and other beasts drawing chariots; and they seemed to project so far from the wall that we took them to be sculptures. The artist had shrewdly heightened the delusion by painting dust on the creatures' backs, as if it had fallen there naturally and properly. Smart fellow – if it be smart to deceive strangers.

Elsewhere we saw a huge Roman amphitheatre, with its stone seats still in good preservation. Modernized, it is now the scene of more peaceful recreations than the exhibition of a party of wild beasts with Christians for dinner. Part of the time, the Milanese use it for a race track, and at other seasons they flood it with water and have spirited yachting regattas there. The guide told us these things, and he would hardly try so hazardous an experiment as the telling of a falsehood, when it is all he can do to speak the truth in English without getting the lock-jaw.

In another place we were shown a sort of summer arbor, with a fence before it. We said that was nothing. We looked again, and saw, through the arbor, an endless stretch of garden, and shrubbery, and grassy lawn. We were perfectly willing to go in there and rest, but it could not be done. It was only another delusion – a painting by some ingenious artist with little charity in his heart for tired folk. The deception was perfect. No one could have imagined the park was not real. We even thought we smelled the flowers at first.

We got a carriage at twilight and drove in the shaded avenues with the other nobility, and after dinner we took wine and ices in a fine garden with the great public. The music was excellent, the flowers and shrubbery were pleasant to the eye, the scene was vivacious, every body was genteel and well-behaved, and the ladies were slightly moustached, and handsomely dressed, but very homely.

We adjourned to a café and played billiards an hour, and I made six or seven points by the doctor pocketing his ball, and he made as many by my pocketing my ball. We came near making a carom sometimes, but not the one we were trying to make. The table was of the usual European style – cushions dead and twice as high as the balls; the cues in bad repair. The natives play only a sort of pool on them. We have never seen any body playing the French three-ball game yet, and I doubt if there is any such game known in France, or that there lives any man mad enough to try to play it on one of these European tables. We had to stop playing, finally, because Dan got to sleeping fifteen minutes between the counts and paying no attention to his marking.

Afterward we walked up and down one of the most popular streets for some time, enjoying other people's comfort and wishing we could export some of it to our restless, driving, vitality-consuming marts at home. Just in this one matter lies the main charm of life in Europe – comfort. In America, we hurry – which is well; but when the day's work is done, we go on thinking of losses and gains, we plan for the morrow, we even carry our business cares to bed with us, and toss and worry over them when we ought to be restoring our racked bodies and brains with sleep. We burn up our energies with these excitements, and either die early or drop into a lean and mean old age at a time of life which they call a man's prime in Europe. When an acre of ground has produced long and well, we let it lie fallow and rest for a season; we take no man clear across the continent in the same coach he started in – the coach is stabled somewhere on the plains and its heated machinery allowed to cool for a few days; when a razor has seen long service and refuses to hold an edge, the barber lays it away for a few weeks, and the edge comes back of its own accord. We bestow thoughtful care upon inanimate objects, but none upon ourselves. What a robust people, what a nation of thinkers we might be, if we would only lay ourselves on the shelf occasionally and renew our edges!

I do envy these Europeans the comfort they take. When the work of the day is done, they forget it. Some of them go, with wife and children, to a beer hall, and sit quietly and genteelly drinking a mug or two of ale and listening to music; others walk the streets, others drive in the avenues; others assemble in the great ornamental squares in the early evening to enjoy the sight and the fragrance of flowers and to hear the military bands play – no European city being without its fine military music at eventide; and yet others of the populace sit in the open air in front of the refreshment houses and eat ices and drink mild beverages that could not harm a child. They go to bed moderately early, and sleep well. They are always quiet, always orderly, always cheerful, comfortable, and appreciative of life and its manifold blessings. One never sees a drunken man among them. The change that has come over our little party is surprising. Day by day we lose some of our restlessness and absorb some of the spirit of quietude and ease that is in the tranquil atmosphere about us and in the demeanor of the people. We grow wise apace. We begin to comprehend what life is for.

We have had a bath in Milan, in a public bath-house. They were going to put all three of us in one bath-tub, but we objected. Each of us had an Italian farm on his back. We could have felt affluent if we had been officially surveyed and fenced in. We chose to have three bath-tubs, and large ones – tubs suited to the dignity of aristocrats who had real estate, and brought it with them. After we were stripped and had taken the first chilly dash, we discovered that haunting atrocity that has embittered our lives in so many cities and villages of Italy and France – there was no soap. I called. A woman answered, and I barely had time to throw myself against the door – she would have been in, in another second. I said:

"Beware, woman! Go away from here – go away, now, or it will be the worse for you. I am an unprotected male, but I will preserve my honor at the peril of my life!"

These words must have frightened her, for she skurried away very fast.

Dan's voice rose on the air:

"Oh, bring some soap, why don't you!"

The reply was Italian. Dan resumed:

"Soap, you know – soap. That is what I want – soap. S-o-a-p, soap; s-o-p-e, soap; s-o-u-p, soap. Hurry up! I don't know how you Irish spell it, but I want it. Spell it to suit yourself, but fetch it. I'm freezing."

I heard the doctor say, impressively:

"Dan, how often have we told you that these foreigners can not understand English? Why will you not depend upon us? Why will you not tell *us* what you want, and let us ask for it in the language of the country? It would save us a great deal of the humiliation your reprehensible ignorance causes us. I will address this person in his mother tongue: 'Here, cospetto! corpo di Bacco! Sacramento!

Solferino! – Soap, you son of a gun!' Dan, if you would let *us* talk for you, you would never expose your ignorant vulgarity."

Even this fluent discharge of Italian did not bring the soap at once, but there was a good reason for it. There was not such an article about the establishment. It is my belief that there never had been. They had to send far up town, and to several different places before they finally got it, so they said. We had to wait twenty or thirty minutes. The same thing had occurred the evening before, at the hotel. I think I have divined the reason for this state of things at last. The English know how to travel comfortably, and they carry soap with them; other foreigners do not use the article.

At every hotel we stop at we always have to send out for soap, at the last moment, when we are grooming ourselves for dinner, and they put it in the bill along with the candles and other nonsense. In Marseilles they make half the fancy toilet soap we consume in America, but the Marseillaise only have a vague theoretical idea of its use, which they have obtained from books of travel, just as they have acquired an uncertain notion of clean shirts, and the peculiarities of the gorilla, and other curious matters. This reminds me of poor Blucher's note to the landlord in Paris:

"PARIS, *le 7 Juillet.*

"*Monsieur le Landlord* – Sir: *Pourquoi* don't you *mettez* some *savon* in your bedchambers? *Est-ce que vous pensez* I will steal it? *La nuit passée* you charged me *pour deux chandelles* when I only had one; *hier vous avez* charged me *avec glace* when I had none at all; *tout les jours* you are coming some fresh game or other on me, *mais vous ne pouvez pas* play this *savon* dodge on me twice. *Savon* is a necessary *de la vie* to any body but a Frenchman, *et je l'aurai hors de cet hôtel* or make trouble. You hear *me. Allons.*

BLUCHER."

I remonstrated against the sending of this note, because it was so mixed up that the landlord would never be able to make head or tail of it; but Blucher said he guessed the old man could read the French of it and average the rest.

Blucher's French is bad enough, but it is not much worse than the English one finds in advertisements all over Italy every day. For instance, observe the printed card of the hotel we shall probably stop at on the shores of Lake Como:

"NOTISH."

"This hotel which the best it is in Italy and most superb, is handsome locate on the best situation of the lake, with the most splendid view near the Villas Melzy, to the King of Belgian, and Serbelloni. This hotel have recently enlarge, do offer all commodities on moderate price, at the strangers gentlemen who whish spend the seasons on the Lake Come."

How is that, for a specimen? In the hotel is a handsome little chapel where an English clergyman is employed to preach to such of the guests of the house as hail from England and America, and this fact is also set forth in barbarous English in the same advertisement. Wouldn't you have supposed that the adventurous linguist who framed the card would have known enough to submit it to that clergyman before he sent it to the printer?

Here, in Milan, in an ancient tumble-down ruin of a church, is the mournful wreck of the most celebrated painting in the world – "The Last Supper," by Leonardo da Vinci. We are not infallible judges of pictures, but of course we went there to see this wonderful painting, once so beautiful, always so worshipped by masters in art, and forever to be famous in song and story. And the first thing that occurred was the infliction on us of a placard fairly reeking with wretched English. Take a morsel of it:

> "Bartholomew (that is the first figure on the left hand side at the spectator,) uncertain and doubtful about what he thinks to have heard, and upon which he wants to be assured by himself at Christ and by no others."

Good, isn't it? And then Peter is described as "argumenting in a threatening and angrily condition at Judas Iscariot."

This paragraph recalls the picture. "The Last Supper" is painted on the dilapidated wall of what was a little chapel attached to the main church in ancient times, I suppose. It is battered and scarred in every direction, and stained and discolored by time, and Napoleon's horses kicked the legs off most the disciples when they (the horses, not the disciples,) were stabled there more than half a century ago.

I recognized the old picture in a moment – the Saviour with bowed head seated at the centre of a long, rough table with scattering fruits and dishes upon it, and six disciples on either side in their long robes, talking to each other – the picture from which all engravings and all copies have been made for three centuries. Perhaps no living man has ever known an attempt to paint the Lord's Supper differently. The world seems to have become settled in the belief, long ago, that it is not possible for human genius to outdo this creation of Da Vinci's. I suppose painters will go on copying it as long as any of the original is left visible to the eye. There were a dozen easels in the room, and as many artists transferring the great picture to their canvases. Fifty proofs of steel engravings and lithographs were scattered around, too. And as usual, I could not help noticing how superior the copies were to the original, that is, to my inexperienced eye. Wherever you find a Raphael, a Rubens, a Michael Angelo, a Caracci, or a Da Vinci (and we see them every day,) you find artists copying them, and the copies are always the handsomest. May be the originals were handsome when they were new, but they are not now.

This picture is about thirty feet long, and ten or twelve high, I should think, and the figures are at least life size. It is one of the largest paintings in Europe.

The colors are dimmed with age; the countenances are scaled and marred, and nearly all expression is gone from them; the hair is a dead blur upon the wall, and there is no life in the eyes. Only the attitudes are certain.

People come here from all parts of the world, and glorify this masterpiece. They stand entranced before it with bated breath and parted lips, and when they speak, it is only in the catchy ejaculations of rapture:

"O, wonderful!"

"Such expression!"

"Such grace of attitude!"

"Such dignity!"

"Such faultless drawing!"

"Such matchless coloring!"

"Such feeling!"

"What delicacy of touch!"

"What sublimity of conception!"

"A vision! a vision!"

I only envy these people; I envy them their honest admiration, if it be honest – their delight, if they feel delight. I harbor no animosity toward any of them. But at the same time the thought *will* intrude itself upon me, How can they see what is not visible? What would you think of a man who looked at some decayed, blind, toothless, pock-marked Cleopatra, and said: "What matchless beauty! What soul! What expression!" What would you think of a man who gazed upon a dingy, foggy sunset, and said: "What sublimity! what feeling! what richness of coloring!" What would you think of a man who stared in ecstasy upon a desert of stumps and said: "Oh, my soul, my beating heart, what a noble forest is here!"

You would think that those men had an astonishing talent for seeing things that had already passed away. It was what I thought when I stood before the Last Supper and heard men apostrophizing wonders, and beauties and perfections which had faded out of the picture and gone, a hundred years before they were born. We can imagine the beauty that was once in an aged face; we can imagine the forest if we see the stumps; but we can not absolutely *see* these things when they are not there. I am willing to believe that the eye of the practiced artist can rest upon the Last Supper and renew a lustre where only a hint of it is left, supply a tint that has faded away, restore an expression that is gone; patch, and color, and add, to the dull canvas until at last its figures shall stand before him aglow with the life, the feeling, the freshness, yea, with all the noble beauty that was theirs when first they came from the hand of the master. But *I* can not work this miracle. Can those other uninspired visitors do it, or do they only happily imagine they do?

After reading so much about it, I am satisfied that the Last Supper was a very miracle of art once. But it was three hundred years ago.

It vexes me to hear people talk so glibly of "feeling," "expression," "tone," and those other easily acquired and inexpensive technicalities of art that make such a fine show in conversations concerning pictures. There is not one man in seventy-five hundred that can tell *what* a pictured face is intended to express. There is not one man in five hundred that can go into a court-room and be sure that he will not mistake some harmless innocent of a juryman for the black-hearted assassin on trial. Yet such people talk of "character" and presume to interpret "expression" in pictures. There is an old story that Matthews, the actor, was once lauding the ability of the human face to express the passions and emotions hidden in the breast. He said the countenance could disclose what was passing in the heart plainer than the tongue could.

"Now," he said, "observe my face – what does it express?"

"Despair!"

"Bah, it expresses peaceful resignation! What does *this* express?"

"Rage!"

"Stuff! it means terror! *This!*"

"Imbecility!"

"Fool! It is smothered ferocity! Now *this!*"

"Joy!"

"Oh, perdition! *Any* ass can see it means insanity!"

Expression! People coolly pretend to read it who would think themselves presumptuous if they pretended to interpret the hieroglyphics on the obelisks of Luxor – yet they are fully as competent to do the one thing as the other. I have heard two very intelligent critics speak of Murillo's Immaculate Conception (now in the museum at Seville,) within the past few days. One said:

"Oh, the Virgin's face is full of the ecstasy of a joy that is complete – that leaves nothing more to be desired on earth!"

The other said:

"Ah, that wonderful face is so humble, so pleading – it says as plainly as words could say it: 'I fear; I tremble; I am unworthy. But Thy will be done; sustain Thou Thy servant!' "

The reader can see the picture in any drawing-room; it can be easily recognized: the Virgin (the only young and really beautiful Virgin that was ever painted by one of the old masters, some of us think,) stands in the crescent of the new moon, with a multitude of cherubs hovering about her, and more coming; her hands are crossed upon her breast, and upon her uplifted countenance falls a glory out of the heavens. The reader may amuse himself, if he chooses, in trying to determine which of these gentlemen read the Virgin's "expression" aright, or if either of them did it.

Any one who is acquainted with the old masters will comprehend how much the Last Supper is damaged when I say that the spectator can not really tell, now, whether the disciples are Hebrews or Italians. These ancient painters never succeeded in denationalizing themselves. The Italian artists painted Italian Virgins, the Dutch painted Dutch Virgins, the Virgins of the French painters were French women – none of them ever put into the face of the Madonna that indescribable something which proclaims the Jewess, whether you find her in New York, in Constantinople, in Paris, Jerusalem, or in the Empire of Morocco. I saw in the Sandwich Islands, once, a picture, copied by a talented German artist from an engraving in one of the American illustrated papers. It was an allegory, representing Mr. Davis in the act of signing a secession act or some such document. Over him hovered the ghost of Washington in warning attitude, and in the background a troop of shadowy soldiers in Continental uniform were limping with shoeless, bandaged feet through a driving snow-storm. Valley Forge was suggested, of course. The copy seemed accurate, and yet there was a discrepancy somewhere. After a long examination I discovered what it was – the shadowy soldiers were all Germans! Jeff Davis was a German! even the hovering ghost was a German ghost! The artist had unconsciously worked his nationality into the picture. To tell the truth, I am getting a little perplexed about John the Baptist and his portraits. In France I finally grew reconciled to him as a Frenchman; here he is unquestionably an Italian. What next? Can it be possible that the painters make John the Baptist a Spaniard in Madrid and an Irishman in Dublin?

We took an open barouche and drove two miles out of Milan to "see ze echo," as the guide expressed it. The road was smooth, it was bordered by trees, fields, and grassy meadows, and the soft air was filled with the odor of flowers. Troops of picturesque peasant girls, coming from work, hooted at us, shouted at us, made all manner of game of us, and entirely delighted me. My long-cherished judgment was confirmed. I always did think those frowsy, romantic, unwashed peasant girls I had read so much about in poetry were a glaring fraud.

We enjoyed our jaunt. It was an exhilarating relief from tiresome sight-seeing.

We distressed ourselves very little about the astonishing echo the guide talked so much about. We were growing accustomed to encomiums on wonders that too often proved no wonders at all. And so we were most happily disappointed to find in the sequel that the guide had even failed to rise to the magnitude of his subject.

We arrived at a tumble-down old rookery called the Palazzo Simonetti – a massive hewn-stone affair occupied by a family of ragged Italians. A good-looking young girl conducted us to a window on the second floor which looked out on a court walled on three sides by tall buildings. She put her head out at the window and shouted. The echo answered more times than we could count. She took a speaking trumpet and through it she shouted, sharp and quick, a single

"Ha!" The echo answered:

"Ha!———ha!——ha!——ha!–ha!-ha! ha! h-a-a-a-a-a!" and finally went off into a rollicking convulsion of the jolliest laughter that could be imagined. It was so joyful – so long continued – so perfectly cordial and hearty, that every body was forced to join in. There was no resisting it.

Then the girl took a gun and fired it. We stood ready to count the astonishing clatter of reverberations. We could not say one, two, three, fast enough, but we could dot our notebooks with our pencil points almost rapidly enough to take down a sort of short-hand report of the result. My page revealed the following account. I could not keep up, but I did as well as I could:

I set down fifty-two distinct repetitions, and then the echo got the advantage of me. The doctor set down sixty-four, and thenceforth the echo moved too fast for him, also. After the separate concussions could no longer be noted, the reverberations dwindled to a wild, long-sustained clatter of sounds such as a watchman's rattle produces. It is likely that this is the most remarkable echo in the world.

The doctor, in jest, offered to kiss the young girl, and was taken a little aback when she said he might for a franc! The commonest gallantry compelled him to stand by his offer, and so he paid the franc and took the kiss. She was a philosopher. She said a franc was a good thing to have, and she did not care any thing for one paltry kiss, because she had a million left. Then our comrade, always a shrewd business man, offered to take the whole cargo at thirty days, but that little financial scheme was a failure.

CHAPTER XXII

THIS VENICE, WHICH was a haughty, invincible, magnificent Republic for nearly fourteen hundred years; whose armies compelled the world's applause whenever and wherever they battled; whose navies well nigh held dominion of the seas, and whose merchant fleets whitened the remotest oceans with their sails and loaded these piers with the products of every clime, is fallen a prey to poverty, neglect and melancholy decay. Six hundred years ago, Venice was the Autocrat of Commerce; her mart was the great commercial centre, the distributing-house from whence the enormous trade of the Orient was spread abroad over the Western world. To-day her piers are deserted, her warehouses are empty, her merchant fleets are vanished, her armies and her navies are but memories. Her glory is departed, and with her crumbling grandeur of wharves and palaces about her she sits among her stagnant lagoons, forlorn and beggared, forgotten of the world. She that in her palmy days commanded the commerce of a hemisphere and made the weal or woe of nations with a beck of her puissant finger, is become the humblest among the peoples of the earth, – a peddler of glass beads for women, and trifling toys and trinkets for school-girls and children.

The venerable Mother of the Republics is scarce a fit subject for flippant speech or the idle gossiping of tourists. It seems a sort of sacrilege to disturb the glamour of old romance that pictures her to us softly from afar off as through a tinted mist, and curtains her ruin and her desolation from our view. One ought, indeed, to turn away from her rags, her poverty and her humiliation, and think of her only as she was when she sunk the fleets of Charlemagne; when she humbled Frederick Barbarossa or waved her victorious banners above the battlements of Constantinople.

We reached Venice at eight in the evening, and entered a hearse belonging to the Grand Hotel d'Europe. At any rate, it was more like a hearse than any thing else, though to speak by the card, it was a gondola. And this was the storied gondola of Venice! – the fairy boat in which the princely cavaliers of the olden time were wont to cleave the waters of the moonlit canals and look the eloquence of love into the soft eyes of patrician beauties, while the gay gondolier in silken doublet touched his guitar and sang as only gondoliers can sing! This the famed gondola and this the gorgeous gondolier! – the one an inky, rusty old canoe with a sable hearse-body clapped on to the middle of it, and the other a mangy, barefooted guttersnipe with a portion of his raiment on exhibition which should have been sacred from public scrutiny. Presently, as he turned a corner and shot his hearse into a dismal ditch between two long rows of towering, untenanted buildings, the gay gondolier began to sing, true to the traditions of his race. I stood it a little while. Then I said:

"Now, here, Roderigo Gonzales Michael Angelo, I'm a pilgrim, and I'm a stranger, but I am not going to have my feelings lacerated by any such caterwauling as that. If that goes on, one of us has got to take water. It is enough that my cherished dreams of Venice have been blighted forever as to the romantic gondola and the gorgeous gondolier; this system of destruction shall go no farther; I will accept the hearse, under protest, and you may fly your flag of truce in peace, but here I register a dark and bloody oath that you shan't sing. Another yelp, and overboard you go."

I began to feel that the old Venice of song and story had departed forever. But I was too hasty. In a few minutes we swept gracefully out into the Grand Canal, and under the mellow moonlight the Venice of poetry and romance stood revealed. Right from the water's edge rose long lines of stately palaces of marble; gondolas were gliding swiftly hither and thither and disappearing suddenly through unsuspected gates and alleys; ponderous stone bridges threw their shadows athwart the glittering waves. There was life and motion everywhere, and yet everywhere there was a hush, a stealthy sort of stillness, that was suggestive of secret enterprises of bravoes and of lovers; and clad half in moonbeams and half in mysterious shadows, the grim old mansions of the Republic seemed to have an expression about them of having an eye out for just such enterprises as these at that same moment. Music came floating over the waters – Venice was complete.

It was a beautiful picture – very soft and dreamy and beautiful. But what was this Venice to compare with the Venice of midnight? Nothing. There was a fête – a grand fête in honor of some saint who had been instrumental in checking the cholera three hundred years ago, and all Venice was abroad on the water. It was no common affair, for the Venetians did not know how soon they might need the saint's services again, now that the cholera was spreading every where. So in one vast space – say a third of a mile wide and two miles long – were collected two thousand gondolas, and every one of them had from two to ten, twenty and even thirty colored lanterns suspended about it, and from four to a dozen occupants. Just as far as the eye could reach, these painted lights were massed together – like a vast garden of many-colored flowers, except that these blossoms were never still; they were ceaselessly gliding in and out, and mingling together, and seducing you into bewildering attempts to follow their mazy evolutions. Here and there a strong red, green, or blue glare from a rocket that was struggling to get away, splendidly illuminated all the boats around it. Every gondola that swam by us, with its crescents and pyramids and circles of colored lamps hung aloft, and lighting up the faces of the young and the sweet-scented and lovely below, was a picture; and the reflections of those lights, so long, so slender, so numberless, so many-colored and so distorted and wrinkled by the waves, was a picture likewise, and one that was enchantingly beautiful. Many and many a party of young ladies and gentlemen had their state gondolas handsomely decorated, and ate supper on board, bringing their swallow-tailed, white-cravatted varlets to wait upon them, and having their tables tricked out as if for a bridal supper. They had brought along the costly globe lamps from their drawing-rooms, and the lace and silken curtains from the same places, I suppose. And they had also brought pianos and guitars, and they played and sang operas, while the plebeian paper-lanterned gondolas from the suburbs and the back alleys crowded around to stare and listen.

There was music every where – choruses, string bands, brass bands, flutes, every thing. I was so surrounded, walled in, with music, magnificence and loveliness, that I became inspired with the spirit of the scene, and sang one tune myself. However, when I observed that the other gondolas had sailed away, and my gondolier was preparing to go overboard, I stopped.

The fête was magnificent. They kept it up the whole night long, and I never enjoyed myself better than I did while it lasted.

What a funny old city this Queen of the Adriatic is! Narrow streets, vast, gloomy marble palaces, black with the corroding damps of centuries, and all partly submerged; no dry land visible any where, and no sidewalks worth mentioning; if you want to go to church, to the theatre, or to the restaurant, you must call a gondola. It must be a paradise for cripples, for verily a man has no use for legs here.

For a day or two the place looked so like an overflowed Arkansas town, because of its currentless waters laving the very doorsteps of all the houses, and the cluster of boats made fast under the windows, or skimming in and out of the alleys and by-ways, that I could not get rid of the impression that there was nothing the matter here but a spring freshet, and that the river would fall in a few weeks and leave a dirty high-water mark on the houses, and the streets full of mud and rubbish.

In the glare of day, there is little poetry about Venice, but under the charitable moon her stained palaces are white again, their battered sculptures are hidden in shadows, and the old city seems crowned once more with the grandeur that was hers five hundred years ago. It is easy, then, in fancy, to people these silent canals with plumed gallants and fair ladies – with Shylocks in gaberdine and sandals, venturing loans upon the rich argosies of Venetian commerce – with Othellos and Desdemonas, with Iagos and Roderigos – with noble fleets and victorious legions returning from the wars. In the treacherous sunlight we see Venice decayed, forlorn, poverty-stricken, and commerceless – forgotten and utterly insignificant. But in the moonlight, her fourteen centuries of greatness fling their glories about her, and once more is she the princeliest among the nations of the earth.

> "There is a glorious city in the sea;
> The sea is in the broad, the narrow streets,
> Ebbing and flowing; and the salt-sea weed
> Clings to the marble of her palaces.
> No track of men, no footsteps to and fro,
> Lead to her gates! The path lies o'er the sea,
> Invisible: and from the land we went,
> As to a floating city – steering in,
> And gliding up her streets, as in a dream,
> So smoothly, silently – by many a dome,
> Mosque-like, and many a stately portico,
> The statues ranged along an azure sky;
> By many a pile, in more than Eastern pride,
> Of old the residence of merchant kings;
> The fronts of some, tho' time had shatter'd them,
> Still glowing with the richest hues of art,
> As tho' the wealth within them had run o'er."

What would one naturally wish to see first in Venice? The Bridge of Sighs, of course – and next the Church and the Great Square of St. Mark, the Bronze Horses, and the famous Lion of St. Mark.

We intended to go to the Bridge of Sighs, but happened into the Ducal Palace first – a building which necessarily figures largely in Venetian poetry and tradition. In the Senate Chamber of the ancient Republic we wearied our eyes with staring at acres of historical paintings by Tintoretto and Paul Veronese, but nothing struck us forcibly except the one thing that strikes *all* strangers forcibly – a black square in the midst of a gallery of portraits. In one long row, around the great hall, were painted the portraits of the Doges of Venice (venerable fellows, with flowing white beards, for of the three hundred Senators eligible to the office, the oldest was usually chosen Doge,) and each had its complimentary inscription attached – till you came to the place that should have had Marino Faliero's picture in it, and that was blank and black – blank, except that it bore a terse inscription, saying that the conspirator had died for his crime. It seemed cruel to keep that pitiless inscription still staring from the walls after the unhappy wretch had been in his grave five hundred years.

At the head of the Giant's Staircase, where Marino Faliero was beheaded, and where the Doges were crowned in ancient times, two small slits in the stone wall were pointed out – two harmless, insignificant orifices that would never attract a stranger's attention – yet these were the terrible Lions' Mouths! The heads were gone (knocked off by the French during their occupation of Venice,) but these were the throats, down which went the anonymous accusation, thrust in secretly at dead of night by an enemy, that doomed many an innocent man to walk the Bridge of Sighs and descend into the dungeon which none entered and hoped to see the sun again. This was in the old days when the Patricians alone governed Venice – the common herd had no vote and no voice. There were one thousand five hundred Patricians; from these, three hundred Senators were chosen; from the Senators a Doge and a Council of Ten were selected, and by secret ballot the Ten chose from their own number a Council of Three. All these were Government spies, then, and every spy was under surveillance himself – men spoke in whispers in Venice, and no man trusted his neighbor – not always his own brother. No man knew who the Council of Three were – not even the Senate, not even the Doge; the members of that dread tribunal met at night in a chamber to themselves, masked, and robed from head to foot in scarlet cloaks, and did not even know each other, unless by voice. It was their duty to judge heinous political crimes, and from their sentence there was no appeal. A nod to the executioner was sufficient. The doomed man was marched down a hall and out at a door-way into the covered Bridge of Sighs, through it and into the dungeon and unto his death. At no time in his transit was he visible to any save his conductor. If a man had an enemy in those old days, the cleverest thing he could do was to slip a note for the Council of Three into the Lion's mouth, saying "This man is plotting against the Government." If the awful Three found no proof, ten to one they would drown him anyhow, because he was a deep rascal, since his plots were unsolvable. Masked judges and masked executioners, with unlimited power, and no appeal from their judgments, in that hard, cruel age, were not likely to be lenient with men they suspected yet could not convict.

We walked through the hall of the Council of Ten, and presently entered the infernal den of the Council of Three.

The table around which they had sat was there still, and likewise the stations where the masked inquisitors and executioners formerly stood, frozen, upright and silent, till they received a bloody order, and then, without a word, moved off, like the inexorable machines they were, to carry it out. The frescoes on the walls were startlingly suited to the place. In all the other saloons, the halls, the great state chambers of the palace, the walls and ceilings were bright with gilding, rich with elaborate carving, and resplendent with gallant pictures of Venetian victories in war, and Venetian display in foreign courts, and hallowed with portraits of the Virgin, the Saviour of men, and the holy saints that preached the Gospel of Peace upon earth – but here, in dismal contrast, were none but pictures of death and dreadful suffering! – not a living figure but was writhing in torture, not a dead one but was smeared with blood, gashed with wounds, and distorted with the agonies that had taken away its life!

From the palace to the gloomy prison is but a step – one might almost jump across the narrow canal that intervenes. The ponderous stone Bridge of Sighs crosses it at the second story – a bridge that is a covered tunnel – you can not be seen when you walk in it. It is partitioned length-wise, and through one compartment walked such as bore light sentences in ancient times, and through the other marched sadly the wretches whom the Three had doomed to lingering misery and utter oblivion in the dungeons, or to sudden and mysterious death. Down below the level of the water, by the light of smoking torches, we were shown the damp, thick-walled cells where many a proud patrician's life was eaten away by the long-drawn miseries of solitary imprisonment – without light, air, books; naked, unshaven, uncombed, covered with vermin; his useless tongue forgetting its office, with none to speak to; the days and nights of his life no longer marked, but merged into one eternal eventless night; far away from all cheerful sounds, buried in the silence of a tomb; forgotten by his helpless friends, and his fate a dark mystery to them forever; losing his own memory at last, and knowing no more who he was or how he came there; devouring the loaf of bread and drinking the water that were thrust into the cell by unseen hands, and troubling his worn spirit no more with hopes and fears and doubts and longings to be free; ceasing to scratch vain prayers and complainings on walls where none, not even himself, could see them, and resigning himself to hopeless apathy, driveling childishness, lunacy! Many and many a sorrowful story like this these stony walls could tell if they could but speak.

In a little narrow corridor, near by, they showed us where many a prisoner, after lying in the dungeons until he was forgotten by all save his persecutors, was brought by masked executioners and garroted, or sewed up in a sack, passed through a little window to a boat, at dead of night, and taken to some remote spot and drowned.

They used to show to visitors the implements of torture wherewith the Three were wont to worm secrets out of the accused – villainous machines for crushing thumbs; the stocks where a prisoner sat immovable while water fell drop by drop upon his head till the torture was more than humanity could bear; and a devilish contrivance of steel, which inclosed a prisoner's head like a shell, and crushed it slowly by means of a screw. It bore the stains of blood that had trickled through its joints long ago, and on one side it had a projection whereon the torturer rested his elbow comfortably and bent down his ear to catch the moanings of the sufferer perishing within.

Of course we went to see the venerable relic of the ancient glory of Venice, with its pavements worn and broken by the passing feet of a thousand years of plebeians and patricians – The Cathedral of St. Mark. It is built entirely of precious marbles, brought from the Orient – nothing in its composition is domestic. Its hoary traditions make it an object of absorbing interest to even the most careless stranger, and thus far it had interest for me; but no further. I could not go into ecstasies over its coarse mosaics, its unlovely Byzantine architecture, or its five hundred curious interior columns from as many distant quarries. Every thing was worn out – every block of stone was smooth and almost shapeless with the polishing hands and shoulders of loungers who devoutly idled here in by-gone centuries and have died and gone to the dev—no, simply died, I mean.

Under the altar repose the ashes of St. Mark – and Matthew, Luke and John, too, for all I know. Venice reveres those relics above all things earthly. For fourteen hundred years St. Mark has been her patron saint. Every thing about the city seems to be named after him or so named as to refer to him in some way – so named, or some purchase rigged in some way to scrape a sort of hurrahing acquaintance with him. That seems to be the idea. To be on good terms with St. Mark, seems to be the very summit of Venetian ambition. They say St. Mark had a tame lion, and used to travel with him – and every where that St. Mark went, the lion was sure to go. It was his protector, his friend, his librarian. And so the Winged Lion of St. Mark, with the open Bible under his paw, is a favorite emblem in the grand old city. It casts its shadow from the most ancient pillar in Venice, in the Grand Square of St. Mark, upon the throngs of free citizens below, and has so done for many a long century. The winged lion is found every where – and doubtless here, where the winged lion is, no harm can come.

St. Mark died at Alexandria, in Egypt. He was martyred, I think. However, that has nothing to do with my legend. About the founding of the city of Venice – say four hundred and fifty years after Christ – (for Venice is much younger than any other Italian city,) a priest dreamed that an angel told him that until the remains of St. Mark were brought to Venice, the city could never rise to high distinction among the nations; that the body must be captured, brought to the city, and a magnificent church built over it; and that if ever the Venetians allowed the Saint to be removed from his new resting-place, in that day Venice would perish from off the face of the earth. The priest proclaimed his dream, and forthwith Venice set about procuring the corpse of St. Mark. One expedition after another tried and failed, but the project was never abandoned during four hundred years. At last it was secured by stratagem, in the year eight hundred and something. The commander of a Venetian expedition disguised himself, stole the bones, separated them, and packed them in vessels filled with lard. The religion of Mahomet causes its devotees to abhor anything that is in the nature of pork, and so when the Christian was stopped by the officers at the gates of the city, they only glanced once into his precious baskets, then turned up their noses at the unholy lard, and let him go. The bones were buried in the vaults of the grand cathedral, which had been waiting long years to receive them, and thus the safety and the greatness of Venice were secured. And to this day there be those in Venice who believe that if those holy ashes were stolen away, the ancient city would vanish like a dream, and its foundations be buried forever in the unremembering sea.

CHAPTER XXIII

THE VENETIAN GONDOLA is as free and graceful, in its gliding movement, as a serpent. It is twenty or thirty feet long, and is narrow and deep, like a canoe; its sharp bow and stern sweep upward from the water like the horns of a crescent with the abruptness of the curve slightly modified.

The bow is ornamented with a steel comb with a battle-ax attachment which threatens to cut passing boats in two occasionally, but never does. The gondola is painted black because in the zenith of Venetian magnificence the gondolas became too gorgeous altogether, and the Senate decreed that all such display must cease, and a solemn, unembellished black be substituted. If the truth were known, it would doubtless appear that rich plebeians grew too prominent in their affectation of patrician show on the Grand Canal, and required a wholesome snubbing. Reverence for the hallowed Past and its traditions keeps the dismal fashion in force now that the compulsion exists no longer. So let it remain. It is the color of mourning. Venice mourns. The stern of the boat is decked over and the gondolier stands there. He uses a single oar – a long blade, of course, for he stands nearly erect. A wooden peg, a foot and a half high, with two slight crooks or curves in one side of it and one in the other, projects above the starboard gunwale. Against that peg the gondolier takes a purchase with his oar, changing it at intervals to the other side of the peg or dropping it into another of the crooks, as the steering of the craft may demand – and how in the world he can back and fill, shoot straight ahead, or flirt suddenly around a corner, and make the oar stay in those insignificant notches, is a problem to me and a never diminishing matter of interest. I am afraid I study the gondolier's marvelous skill more than I do the sculptured palaces we glide among. He cuts a corner so closely, now and then, or misses another gondola by such an imperceptible hair-breadth that I feel myself "scrooching," as the children say, just as one does when a buggy wheel grazes his elbow. But he makes all his calculations with the nicest precision, and goes darting in and out among a Broadway confusion of busy craft with the easy confidence of the educated hackman. He never makes a mistake.

Sometimes we go flying down the great canals at such a gait that we can get only the merest glimpses into front doors, and again, in obscure alleys in the suburbs, we put on a solemnity suited to the silence, the mildew, the stagnant waters, the clinging weeds, the deserted houses and the general lifelessness of the place, and move to the spirit of grave meditation.

The gondolier *is* a picturesque rascal for all he wears no satin harness, no plumed bonnet, no silken tights. His attitude is stately; he is lithe and supple; all his movements are full of grace. When his long canoe, and his fine figure, towering from its high perch on the stern, are cut against the evening sky, they make a picture that is very novel and striking to a foreign eye.

We sit in the cushioned carriage-body of a cabin, with the curtains drawn, and smoke, or read, or look out upon the passing boats, the houses, the bridges, the people, and enjoy ourselves much more than we could in a buggy jolting over our cobble-stone pavements at home. This is the gentlest, pleasantest locomotion we have ever known.

But it seems queer – ever so queer – to see a boat doing duty as a private carriage. We see business men come to the front door, step into a gondola, instead of a street car, and go off down town to the counting-room.

We see visiting young ladies stand on the stoop, and laugh, and kiss good-bye, and flirt their fans and say "Come soon – now *do* – you've been just as mean as ever you can be – mother's dying to see you – and we've moved into the new house, O such a love of a place! – so convenient to the post-office and the church, and the Young Men's Christian Association; and we do have such fishing, and such carrying on, and *such* swimming-matches in the back yard – Oh, you *must* come – no distance at all, and if you go down through by St. Mark's and the Bridge of Sighs, and cut through the alley and come up by the church of Santa Maria dei Frari, and into the Grand Canal, there isn't a *bit* of current – now *do* come, Sally Maria – by-bye!" and then the little humbug trips down the steps, jumps into the gondola, says, under her breath, "Disagreeable old thing, I hope she *won't*!" goes skimming away, round the corner; and the other girl slams the street door and says, "Well, *that* infliction's over, any way, – but I suppose I've got to go and see her – tiresome stuck-up thing!" Human nature appears to be just the same, all over the world. We see the diffident young man, mild of moustache, affluent of hair, indigent of brain, elegant of costume, drive up to *her* father's mansion, tell his hackman to bail out and wait, start fearfully up the steps and meet "the old gentleman" right on the threshold! – hear him ask what street the new British Bank is in – as if *that* were what he came for – and then bounce into his boat and skurry away with his coward heart in his boots! – see him come sneaking around the corner again, directly, with a crack of the curtain open toward the old gentleman's disappearing gondola, and out scampers his Susan with a flock of little Italian endearments fluttering from her lips, and goes to drive with him in the watery avenues down toward the Rialto.

We see the ladies go out shopping, in the most natural way, and flit from street to street and from store to store, just in the good old fashion, except that they leave the gondola, instead of a private carriage, waiting at the curbstone a couple of hours for them, – waiting while they make the nice young clerks pull down tons and tons of silks and velvets and moire antiques and those things; and then they buy a paper of pins and go paddling away to confer the rest of their disastrous patronage on some other firm. And they always have their purchases sent home just in the good old way. Human nature is *very* much the same all over the world; and it is *so* like my dear native home to see a Venetian lady go into a store and buy ten cents' worth of blue ribbon and have it sent home in a scow. Ah, it is these little touches of nature that move one to tears in these far-off foreign lands.

We see little girls and boys go out in gondolas with their nurses, for an airing. We see staid families, with prayer-book and beads, enter the gondola dressed in their Sunday best, and float away to church. And at midnight we see the theatre break up and discharge its swarm of hilarious youth and beauty; we hear the cries of the hackman-gondoliers, and behold the struggling crowd jump aboard, and the black multitude of boats go skimming down the moonlit avenues; we see them separate here and there, and disappear up divergent streets; we hear the faint sounds of laughter and of shouted farewells floating up out of the distance; and then, the strange pageant being gone, we have lonely stretches of glittering water – of stately buildings – of blotting shadows – of weird stone faces creeping into the moonlight – of deserted bridges – of motionless boats at anchor. And over all broods that mysterious stillness, that stealthy quiet, that befits so well this old dreaming Venice.

We have been pretty much every where in our gondola. We have bought beads and photographs in the stores, and wax matches in the Great Square of St. Mark. The last remark suggests a digression. Every body goes to this vast square in the evening. The military bands play in the centre of it and countless couples of ladies and gentlemen promenade up and down on either side, and platoons of them are constantly drifting away toward the old Cathedral, and by the venerable column with the Winged Lion of St. Mark on its top, and out to where the boats lie moored; and other platoons are as constantly arriving from the gondolas and joining the great throng. Between the promenaders and the sidewalks are seated hundreds and hundreds of people at small tables, smoking and taking *granita*, (a first cousin to ice-cream;) on the sidewalks are more employing themselves in the same way. The shops in the first floor of the tall rows of buildings that wall in three sides of the square are brilliantly lighted, the air is filled with music and merry voices, and altogether the scene is as bright and spirited and full of cheerfulness as any man could desire. We enjoy it thoroughly. Very many of the young women are exceedingly pretty and dress with rare good taste. We are gradually and laboriously learning the ill-manners of staring them unflinchingly in the face – not because such conduct is agreeable to us, but because it is the custom of the country and they say the girls like it. We wish to learn all the curious, outlandish ways of all the different countries, so that we can "show off" and astonish people when we get home. We wish to excite the envy of our untraveled friends with our strange foreign fashions which we can't shake off. All our passengers are paying strict attention to this thing, with the end in view which I have mentioned. The gentle reader will never, never know what a consummate ass he can become, until he goes abroad. I speak now, of course, in the supposition that the gentle reader has not been abroad, and therefore is not already a consummate ass. If the case be otherwise, I beg his pardon and extend to him the cordial hand of fellowship and call him brother. I shall always delight to meet an ass after my own heart when I shall have finished my travels.

On this subject let me remark that there are Americans abroad in Italy who have actually forgotten their mother tongue in three months – forgot it in France. They can not even write their address in English in a hotel register. I append these evidences, which I copied *verbatim* from the register of a hotel in a certain Italian city:

"John P. Whitcomb, *Etats Unis*.
"Wm. L. Ainsworth, *travailleur* (he meant traveler, I suppose,) *Etats Unis*.
"George P. Morton *et fils, d'Amerique*.
"Lloyd B. Williams, *et trois amis, ville de* Boston, *Amerique*.
"J. Ellsworth Baker, *tout de suite de France, place de naissance Amerique, destination la Grand Bretagne*."

I love this sort of people. A lady passenger of ours tells of a fellow-citizen of hers who spent eight weeks in Paris and then returned home and addressed his dearest old bosom friend Herbert as Mr. "Er-bare!" He apologized, though, and said, "'Pon my soul it is aggravating, but I cahn't help it – I have got so used to speaking nothing but French, my dear Erbare – damme there it goes again! – got so used to French pronunciation that I cahn't get rid of it – it is positively annoying, I assure you." This entertaining idiot, whose name was Gordon, allowed himself to be hailed three times in the street before he paid any attention, and then begged a thousand pardons and said he had grown so accustomed to hearing himself addressed as "M'sieu Gor-r-*dong*," with a roll to the r, that he had forgotten the legitimate sound of his name! He wore a rose in his button-hole; he gave the French salutation – two flips of the hand in front of the face; he called Paris *Pairree* in ordinary English conversation; he carried envelopes bearing foreign postmarks protruding from his breast pocket; he cultivated a moustache and imperial, and did what else he could to suggest to the beholder his pet fancy that he resembled Louis Napoleon – and in a spirit of thankfulness which is entirely unaccountable, considering the slim foundation there was for it, he praised his Maker that he was *as* he was, and went on enjoying his little life just the same as if he really *had* been deliberately designed and erected by the great Architect of the Universe.

Think of our Whitcombs, and our Ainsworths and our Williamses writing themselves down in dilapidated French in foreign hotel registers! We laugh at Englishmen, when we are at home, for sticking so sturdily to their national ways and customs, but we look back upon it from abroad very forgivingly. It is not pleasant to see an American thrusting his nationality forward *obtrusively* in a foreign land, but Oh, it is pitiable to see him making of himself a thing that is neither male nor female, neither fish, flesh, nor fowl – a poor, miserable, hermaphrodite Frenchman!

Among a long list of churches, art galleries, and such things, visited by us in Venice, I shall mention only one – the church of Santa Maria dei Frari. It is about five hundred years old, I believe, and stands on twelve hundred thousand piles. In it lie the body of Canova and the heart of Titian, under magnificent monuments. Titian died at the age of almost one hundred years. A plague which swept away fifty thousand lives was raging at the time, and there is notable evidence of the reverence in which the great painter was held, in the fact that to him alone the state permitted a public funeral in all that season of terror and death.

In this church, also, is a monument to the doge Foscari, whose name a once resident of Venice, Lord Byron, has made permanently famous.

The monument to the doge Giovanni Pesaro, in this church, is a curiosity in the way of mortuary adornment. It is eighty feet high and is fronted like some fantastic pagan temple. Against it stand four colossal Nubians, as black as night, dressed in white marble garments. The black legs are bare, and through rents in sleeves and breeches, the skin, of shiny black marble, shows. The artist was as ingenious as his funeral designs were absurd. There are two bronze skeletons bearing scrolls, and two great dragons uphold the sarcophagus. On high, amid all this grotesqueness, sits the departed doge.

In the conventual buildings attached to this church are the state archives of Venice. We did not see them, but they are said to number millions of documents. "They are the records of centuries of the most watchful, observant and suspicious government that ever existed – in which every thing was written down and nothing spoken out." They fill nearly three hundred rooms. Among them are manuscripts from the archives of nearly two thousand families, monasteries and convents. The secret history of Venice for a thousand years is here – its plots, its hidden trials, its assassinations, its commissions of hireling spies and masked bravoes – food, ready to hand, for a world of dark and mysterious romances.

Yes, I think we have seen all of Venice. We have seen, in these old churches, a profusion of costly and elaborate sepulchre ornamentation such as we never dreamed of before. We have stood in the dim religious light of these hoary sanctuaries, in the midst of long ranks of dusty monuments and effigies of the great dead of Venice, until we seemed drifting back, back, back, into the solemn past, and looking upon the scenes and mingling with the peoples of a remote antiquity. We have been in a half-waking sort of dream all the time. I do not know how else to describe the feeling. A part of our being has remained still in the nineteenth century, while another part of it has seemed in some unaccountable way walking among the phantoms of the tenth.

We have seen famous pictures until our eyes are weary with looking at them and refuse to find interest in them any longer. And what wonder, when there are twelve hundred pictures by Palma the Younger in Venice and fifteen hundred by Tintoretto? And behold there are Titians and the works of other artists in proportion. We have seen Titian's celebrated Cain and Abel, his David and Goliath, his Abraham's Sacrifice. We have seen Tintoretto's monster picture, which is seventy-four feet long and I do not know how many feet high, and thought it a very commodious picture. We have seen pictures of martyrs enough, and saints enough, to regenerate the world. I ought not to confess it, but still, since one has no opportunity in America to acquire a critical judgment in art, and since I could not hope to become educated in it in Europe in a few short weeks, I may therefore as well acknowledge with such apologies as may be due, that to me it seemed that when I had seen one of these martyrs I had seen them all. They all have a marked family resemblance to each other, they dress alike, in coarse monkish robes and sandals, they are all bald headed, they all stand in about the same attitude, and without exception they are gazing heavenward with countenances which the Ainsworths, the Mortons and the Williamses, *et fils*, inform me are full of "expression." To me there is nothing tangible about these imaginary portraits, nothing that I can grasp and take a living interest in. If great Titian had only been gifted with prophecy, and had skipped a martyr, and gone over to England and painted a portrait of Shakespeare, even as a youth, which we could all have confidence in now, the world down to the latest generations would have forgiven him the lost martyr in the rescued seer. I think posterity could have spared one more martyr for the sake of a great historical picture of Titian's time and painted by his brush – such as Columbus returning in chains from the discovery of a world, for instance. The old masters did paint some Venetian historical pictures, and these we did not tire of looking at, notwithstanding representations of the formal introduction of defunct doges to the Virgin Mary in regions beyond the clouds clashed rather harshly with the proprieties, it seemed to us.

But humble as we are, and unpretending, in the matter of art, our researches among the painted monks and martyrs have not been wholly in vain. We have striven hard to learn. We have had some success. We have mastered some things, possibly of trifling import in the eyes of the learned, but to us they give pleasure, and we take as much pride in our little acquirements as do others who have learned far more, and we love to display them full as well. When we see a monk going about with a lion and looking tranquilly up to heaven, we know that that is St. Mark. When we see a monk with a book and a pen, looking tranquilly up to heaven, trying to think of a word, we know that that is St. Matthew. When we see a monk sitting on a rock, looking tranquilly up to heaven, with a human skull beside him, and without other baggage, we know that that is St. Jerome. Because we know that he always went flying light in the matter of baggage. When we see a party looking tranquilly up to heaven, unconscious that his body is shot through and through with arrows, we know that that is St. Sebastian. When we see other monks looking tranquilly up to heaven, but having no trademark, we always ask who those parties are. We do this because we humbly wish to learn. We have seen thirteen thousand St. Jeromes, and twenty-two thousand St. Marks, and sixteen thousand St. Matthews, and sixty thousand St. Sebastians, and four millions of assorted monks, undesignated, and we feel encouraged to believe that when we have seen some more of these various pictures, and had a larger experience, we shall begin to take an absorbing interest in them like our cultivated countrymen from *Amerique*.

Now it does give me real pain to speak in this almost unappreciative way of the old masters and their martyrs, because good friends of mine in the ship – friends who do thoroughly and conscientiously appreciate them and are in every way competent to discriminate between good pictures and inferior ones – have urged me for my own sake not to make public the fact that I lack this appreciation and this critical discrimination myself. I believe that what I have written and may still write about pictures will give them pain, and I am honestly sorry for it. I even promised that I would hide my uncouth sentiments in my own breast. But alas! I never could keep a promise. I do not blame myself for this weakness, because the fault must lie in my physical organization. It is likely that such a very liberal amount of space was given to the organ which enables me to *make* promises, that the organ which should enable me to keep them was crowded out. But I grieve not. I like no half-way things. I had rather have one faculty nobly developed than two faculties of mere ordinary capacity. I certainly meant to keep that promise, but I find I can not do it. It is impossible to travel through Italy without speaking of pictures, and can I see them through others' eyes?

If I did not so delight in the grand pictures that are spread before me every day of my life by that monarch of all the old masters, Nature, I should come to believe, sometimes, that I had in me no appreciation of the beautiful, whatsoever.

It seems to me that whenever I glory to think that for once I have discovered an ancient painting that is beautiful and worthy of all praise, the pleasure it gives me is an infallible proof that it is *not* a beautiful picture and not in any wise worthy of commendation. This very thing has occurred more times than I can mention, in Venice. In every single instance the guide has crushed out my swelling enthusiasm with the remark:

"It is nothing – it is of the *Renaissance*."

I did not know what in the mischief the Renaissance was, and so always I had to simply say,

"Ah! so it is – I had not observed it before."

I could not bear to be ignorant before a cultivated negro, the offspring of a South Carolina slave. But it occurred too often for even my self-complacency, did that exasperating "It is nothing – it is of the *Renaissance*." I said at last:

"*Who* is this Renaissance? Where did he come from? Who gave him permission to cram the Republic with his execrable daubs?"

We learned, then, that Renaissance was not a man; that *renaissance* was a term used to signify what was at best but an imperfect rejuvenation of art. The guide said that after Titian's time and the time of the other great names we had grown so familiar with, high art declined; then it partially rose again – an inferior sort of painters sprang up, and these shabby pictures were the work of their hands. Then I said, in my heat, that I "wished to goodness high art had declined five hundred years sooner." The Renaissance pictures suit me very well, though sooth to say its school were too much given to painting real men and did not indulge enough in martyrs.

The guide I have spoken of is the only one we have had yet who knew any thing. He was born in South Carolina, of slave parents. They came to Venice while he was an infant. He has grown up here. He is well educated. He reads, writes, and speaks English, Italian, Spanish, and French, with perfect facility; is a worshipper of art and thoroughly conversant with it; knows the history of Venice by heart and never tires of talking of her illustrious career. He dresses better than any of us, I think, and is daintily polite. Negroes are deemed as good as white people, in Venice, and so this man feels no desire to go back to his native land. His judgment is correct.

I have had another shave. I was writing in our front room this afternoon and trying hard to keep my attention on my work and refrain from looking out upon the canal. I was resisting the soft influences of the climate as well as I could, and endeavoring to overcome the desire to be indolent and happy. The boys sent for a barber. They asked me if I would be shaved. I reminded them of my tortures in Genoa, Milan, Como; of my declaration that I would suffer no more on Italian soil. I said "Not any for me, if you please."

I wrote on. The barber began on the doctor. I heard him say:

"Dan, this is the easiest shave I have had since we left the ship."

He said again, presently:

"Why Dan, a man could go to sleep with this man shaving him."

Dan took the chair. Then he said:

"Why this is Titian. This is one of the old masters."

I wrote on. Directly Dan said:

"Doctor, it is perfect luxury. The ship's barber isn't any thing to him."

My rough beard was distressing me beyond measure. The barber was rolling up his apparatus. The temptation was too strong. I said:

"Hold on, please. Shave me also."

I sat down in the chair and closed my eyes. The barber soaped my face, and then took his razor and gave me a rake that well nigh threw me into convulsions. I jumped out of the chair: Dan and the doctor were both wiping blood off their faces and laughing.

I said it was a mean, disgraceful fraud.

They said that the misery of this shave had gone so far beyond any thing they had ever experienced before, that they could not bear the idea of losing such a chance of hearing a cordial opinion from me on the subject.

It was shameful. But there was no help for it. The skinning was begun and had to be finished. The tears flowed with every rake, and so did the fervent execrations. The barber grew confused, and brought blood every time. I think the boys enjoyed it better than any thing they have seen or heard since they left home.

We have seen the Campanile, and Byron's house and Balbi's the geographer, and the palaces of all the ancient dukes and doges of Venice, and we have seen their effeminate descendants airing their nobility in fashionable French attire in the Grand Square of St. Mark, and eating ices and drinking cheap wines, instead of wearing gallant coats of mail and destroying fleets and armies as their great ancestors did in the days of Venetian glory. We have seen no bravoes with poisoned stilettos, no masks, no wild carnival; but we have seen the ancient pride of Venice, the grim Bronze Horses that figure in a thousand legends. Venice may well cherish them, for they are the only horses she ever had. It is said there are hundreds of people in this curious city who never have seen a living horse in their lives. It is entirely true, no doubt.

And so, having satisfied ourselves, we depart to-morrow, and leave the venerable Queen of the Republics to summon her vanished ships, and marshal her shadowy armies, and know again in dreams the pride of her old renown.

CHAPTER XXV

THERE ARE A good many things about this Italy which I do not understand – and more especially I can not understand how a bankrupt Government can have such palatial railroad depots and such marvels of turnpikes. Why, these latter are as hard as adamant, as straight as a line, as smooth as a floor, and as white as snow. When it is too dark to see any other object, one can still see the white turnpikes of France and Italy; and they are clean enough to eat from, without a table-cloth. And yet no tolls are charged.

As for the railways – we have none like them. The cars slide as smoothly along as if they were on runners. The depots are vast palaces of cut marble, with stately colonnades of the same royal stone traversing them from end to end, and with ample walls and ceilings richly decorated with frescoes. The lofty gateways are graced with statues, and the broad floors are all laid in polished flags of marble.

These things win me more than Italy's hundred galleries of priceless art treasures, because I can understand the one and am not competent to appreciate the other. In the turnpikes, the railways, the depots, and the new boulevards of uniform houses in Florence and other cities here, I see the genius of Louis Napoleon, or rather, I see the works of that statesman imitated. But Louis has taken care that in France there shall be a foundation for these improvements – money. He has always the wherewithal to back up his projects; they strengthen France and never weaken her. Her material prosperity is genuine. But here the case is different. This country is bankrupt. There is no real foundation for these great works. The prosperity they would seem to indicate is a pretence. There is no money in the treasury, and so they enfeeble her instead of strengthening. Italy has achieved the dearest wish of her heart and become an independent State – and in so doing she has drawn an elephant in the political lottery. She has nothing to feed it on. Inexperienced in government, she plunged into all manner of useless expenditure, and swamped her treasury almost in a day. She squandered millions of francs on a navy which she did not need, and the first time she took her new toy into action she got it knocked higher than Gilderoy's kite – to use the language of the Pilgrims.

But it is an ill-wind that blows nobody good. A year ago, when Italy saw utter ruin staring her in the face and her greenbacks hardly worth the paper they were printed on, her Parliament ventured upon a *coup de main* that would have appalled the stoutest of her statesmen under less desperate circumstances. They, in a manner, confiscated the domains of the Church! This in priest-ridden Italy! This in a land which has groped in the midnight of priestly superstition for sixteen hundred years! It was a rare good fortune for Italy, the stress of weather that drove her to break from this prison-house.

They do not call it *confiscating* the Church property. That would sound too harshly yet. But it amounts to that. There are thousands of churches in Italy, each with untold millions of treasures stored away in its closets, and each with its battalion of priests to be supported. And then there are the estates of the Church – league on league of the richest lands and the noblest forests in all Italy – all yielding immense revenues to the Church, and none paying a cent in taxes to the State. In some great districts the Church owns *all* the property – lands, watercourses, woods, mills and factories. They buy, they sell, they manufacture, and since they pay no taxes, who can hope to compete with them?

Well, the Government has seized all this in effect, and will yet seize it in rigid and unpoetical reality, no doubt. Something must be done to feed a starving treasury, and there is no other resource in all Italy – none but the riches of the Church. So the Government intends to take to itself a great portion of the revenues arising from priestly farms, factories, etc., and also intends to take possession of the churches and carry them on, after its own fashion and upon its own responsibility. In a few instances it will leave the establishments of great pet churches undisturbed, but in all others only a handful of priests will be retained to preach and pray, a few will be pensioned, and the balance turned adrift.

Pray glance at some of these churches and their embellishments, and see whether the Government is doing a righteous thing or not. In Venice, to-day, a city of a hundred thousand inhabitants, there are twelve hundred priests. Heaven only knows how many there were before the Parliament reduced their numbers. There was the great Jesuit Church. Under the old regime it required sixty priests to engineer it – the Government does it with five, now, and the others are discharged from service. All about that church wretchedness and poverty abound. At its door a dozen hats and bonnets were doffed to us, as many heads were humbly bowed, and as many hands extended, appealing for pennies – appealing with foreign words we could not understand, but appealing mutely, with sad eyes, and sunken cheeks, and ragged raiment, that no words were needed to translate. Then we passed within the great doors, and it seemed that the riches of the world were before us! Huge columns carved out of single masses of marble, and inlaid from top to bottom with a hundred intricate figures wrought in costly verde antique; pulpits of the same rich materials, whose draperies hung down in many a pictured fold, the stony fabric counterfeiting the delicate work of the loom; the grand altar brilliant with polished facings and balustrades of oriental agate, jasper, verde antique, and other precious stones, whose names, even, we seldom hear – and slabs of priceless lapis lazuli lavished every where as recklessly as if the church had owned a quarry of it. In the midst of all this magnificence, the solid gold and silver furniture of the altar seemed cheap and trivial. Even the floors and ceilings cost a princely fortune.

Now, where is the use of allowing all those riches to lie idle, while half of that community hardly know, from day to day, how they are going to keep body and soul together? And, where is the wisdom in permitting hundreds upon hundreds of millions of francs to be locked up in the useless trumpery of churches all over Italy, and the people ground to death with taxation to uphold a perishing Government?

As far as I can see, Italy, for fifteen hundred years, has turned all her energies, all her finances, and all her industry to the building up of a vast array of wonderful church edifices, and starving half her citizens to accomplish it. She is to-day one vast museum of magnificence and misery. All the churches in an ordinary American city put together could hardly buy the jeweled frippery in one of her hundred cathedrals. And for every beggar in America, Italy can show a hundred – and rags and vermin to match. It is the wretchedest, princeliest land on earth.

Look at the grand Duomo of Florence – a vast pile that has been sapping the purses of her citizens for five hundred years, and is not nearly finished yet. Like all other men, I fell down and worshipped it, but when the filthy beggars swarmed around me the contrast was too striking, too suggestive, and I said, "O, sons of classic Italy, *is* the spirit of enterprise, of self-reliance, of noble endeavor, utterly dead within ye? Curse your indolent worthlessness, why don't you rob your church?"

Three hundred happy, comfortable priests are employed in that Cathedral.

And now that my temper is up, I may as well go on and abuse every body I can think of. They have a grand mausoleum in Florence, which they built to bury our Lord and Saviour and the Medici family in. It sounds blasphemous, but it is true, and here they *act* blasphemy. The dead and damned Medicis who cruelly tyrannized over Florence and were her curse for over two hundred years, are salted away in a circle of costly vaults, and in their midst the Holy Sepulchre was to have been set up. The expedition sent to Jerusalem to seize it got into trouble and could not accomplish the burglary, and so the centre of the mausoleum is vacant now. They say the entire mausoleum was intended for the Holy Sepulchre, and was only turned into a family burying place after the Jerusalem expedition failed – but you will excuse me. Some of those Medicis would have smuggled themselves in sure. – What *they* had not the effrontery to do, was not worth doing. Why, they had their trivial, forgotten exploits on land and sea pictured out in grand frescoes (as did also the ancient Doges of Venice) with the Saviour and the Virgin throwing bouquets to them out of the clouds, and the Deity himself applauding from his throne in Heaven! And who painted these things? Why, Titian, Tintoretto, Paul Veronese, Raphael – none other than the world's idols, the "old masters."

Andrea del Sarto glorified his princes in pictures that must save them for ever from the oblivion they merited, and they let him starve. Served him right. Raphael pictured such infernal villains as Catherine and Marie de Medicis seated in heaven and conversing familiarly with the Virgin Mary and the angels, (to say nothing of higher personages,) and yet my friends abuse me because I am a little prejudiced against the old masters – because I fail sometimes to see the beauty that is in their productions. I can not help but see it, now and then, but I keep on protesting against the groveling spirit that could persuade those masters to prostitute their noble talents to the adulation of such monsters as the French, Venetian and Florentine Princes of two and three hundred years ago, all the same.

I am told that the old masters had to do these shameful things for bread, the princes and potentates being the only patrons of art. If a grandly gifted man may drag his pride and his manhood in the dirt for bread rather than starve with the nobility that is in him untainted, the excuse is a valid one. It would excuse theft in Washingtons and Wellingtons, and unchastity in women as well.

But somehow, I can not keep that Medici mausoleum out of my memory. It is as large as a church; its pavement is rich enough for the pavement of a King's palace; its great dome is gorgeous with frescoes; its walls are made of – what? Marble? – plaster? – wood? – paper? No. Red porphyry – verde antique – jasper – oriental agate – alabaster – mother-of-pearl – chalcedony – red coral – lapis lazuli! All the vast walls are made wholly of these precious stones, worked in, and in and in together in elaborate patterns and figures, and polished till they glow like great mirrors with the pictured splendors reflected from the dome overhead. And before a statue of one of those dead Medicis reposes a crown that blazes with diamonds and emeralds enough to buy a ship-of-the-line, almost. These are the things the Government has its evil eye upon, and a happy thing it will be for Italy when they melt away in the public treasury.

And now—. However, another beggar approaches. I will go out and destroy him, and then come back and write another chapter of vituperation.

Having eaten the friendless orphan – having driven away his comrades – having grown calm and reflective at length – I now feel in a kindlier mood. I feel that after talking so freely about the priests and the churches, justice demands that if I know any thing good about either I ought to say it. I *have* heard of many things that redound to the credit of the priesthood, but the most notable matter that occurs to me now is the devotion one of the mendicant orders showed during the prevalence of the cholera last year. I speak of the Dominican friars – men who wear a coarse, heavy brown robe and a cowl, in this hot climate, and go barefoot. They live on alms altogether, I believe. They must unquestionably love their religion, to suffer so much for it. When the cholera was raging in Naples; when the people were dying by hundreds and hundreds every day; when every concern for the public welfare was swallowed up in selfish private interest, and every citizen made the taking care of himself his sole object, these men banded themselves together and went about nursing the sick and burying the dead. Their noble efforts cost many of them their lives. They laid them down cheerfully, and well they might. Creeds mathematically precise, and hair-splitting niceties of doctrine, are absolutely necessary for the salvation of some kinds of souls, but surely the charity, the purity, the unselfishness that are in the hearts of men like these would save their souls though they were bankrupt in the true religion – which is ours.

One of these fat barefooted rascals came here to Civita Vecchia with us in the little French steamer. There were only half a dozen of us in the cabin. He belonged in the steerage. He was the life of the ship, the bloody-minded son of the Inquisition! He and the leader of the marine band of a French man-of-war played on the piano and sang opera turn about; they sang duets together; they rigged impromptu theatrical costumes and gave us extravagant farces and pantomimes. We got along first-rate with the friar, and were excessively conversational, albeit he could not understand what we said, and certainly he never uttered a word that we could guess the meaning of.

This Civita Vecchia is the finest nest of dirt, vermin and ignorance we have found yet, except that African perdition they call Tangier, which is just like it. The people here live in alleys two yards wide, which have a smell about them which is peculiar but not entertaining. It is well the alleys are not wider, because they hold as much smell now as a person can stand, and of course, if they were wider they would hold more, and then the people would die. These alleys are paved with stone, and carpeted with deceased cats, and decayed rags, and decomposed vegetable-tops, and remnants of old boots, all soaked with dish-water, and the people sit around on stools and enjoy it. They are indolent, as a general thing, and yet have few pastimes. They work two or three hours at a time, but not hard, and then they knock off and catch flies. This does not require any talent, because they only have to grab – if they do not get the one they are after, they get another. It is all the same to them. They have no partialities. Whichever one they get is the one they want.

They have other kinds of insects, but it does not make them arrogant. They are very quiet, unpretending people. They have more of these kind of things than other communities, but they do not boast.

They are very uncleanly – these people – in face, in person and dress. When they see any body with a clean shirt on, it arouses their scorn. The women wash clothes, half the day, at the public tanks in the streets, but they are probably somebody else's. Or may be they keep one set to wear and another to wash; because they never put on any that have ever been washed. When they get done washing, they sit in the alleys and nurse their cubs. They nurse one ash-cat at a time, and the others scratch their backs against the door-post and are happy.

All this country belongs to the Papal States. They do not appear to have any schools here, and only one billiard-table. Their education is at a very low stage. One portion of the men go into the military, another into the priesthood, and the rest into the shoe-making business.

They keep up the passport system here, but so they do in Turkey. This shows that the Papal States are as far advanced as Turkey. This fact will be alone sufficient to silence the tongues of malignant calumniators. I had to get my passport *vised* for Rome in Florence, and then they would not let me come ashore here until a policeman had examined it on the wharf and sent me a permit. They did not even dare to let me take my passport in my hands for twelve hours, I looked so formidable. They judged it best to let me cool down. They thought I wanted to take the town, likely. Little did they know me. I wouldn't have it. They examined my baggage at the depot. They took one of my ablest jokes and read it over carefully twice and then read it backwards. But it was too deep for them. They passed it around, and every body speculated on it awhile, but it mastered them all.

It was no common joke. At length a veteran officer spelled it over deliberately and shook his head three or four times and said that in his opinion it was seditious. That was the first time I felt alarmed. I immediately said I would explain the document, and they crowded around. And so I explained and explained and explained, and they took notes of all I said, but the more I explained the more they could not understand it, and when they desisted at last, I could not even understand it myself. They said they believed it was an incendiary document, leveled at the government. I declared solemnly that it was not, but they only shook their heads and would not be satisfied. Then they consulted a good while; and finally they confiscated it. I was very sorry for this, because I had worked a long time on that joke, and took a good deal of pride in it, and now I suppose I shall never see it any more. I suppose it will be sent up and filed away among the criminal archives of Rome, and will always be regarded as a mysterious infernal machine which would have blown up like a mine and scattered the good Pope all around, but for a miraculous providential interference. And I suppose that all the time I am in Rome the police will dog me about from place to place because they think I am a dangerous character.

It is fearfully hot in Civita Vecchia. The streets are made very narrow and the houses built very solid and heavy and high, as a protection against the heat. This is the first Italian town I have seen which does not appear to have a patron saint. I suppose no saint but the one that went up in the chariot of fire could stand the climate.

There is nothing here to see. They have not even a cathedral, with eleven tons of solid silver archbishops in the back room; and they do not show you any moldy buildings that are seven thousand years old; nor any smoke-dried old fire-screens which are *chef d'œuvres* of Reubens or Simpson, or Titian or Ferguson, or any of those parties; and they haven't any bottled fragments of saints, and not even a nail from the true cross. We are going to Rome. There is nothing to see here.

CHAPTER XXVII

SO FAR, GOOD. If any man has a right to feel proud of himself, and satisfied, surely it is I. For I have written about the Coliseum, and the gladiators, the martyrs, and the lions, and yet have never once used the phrase "butchered to make a Roman holyday." I am the only free white man of mature age who has accomplished this since Byron originated the expression.

Butchered to make a Roman holyday sounds well for the first seventeen or eighteen hundred thousand times one sees it in print, but after that it begins to grow tiresome. I find it in all the books concerning Rome – and here latterly it reminds me of Judge Oliver. Oliver was a young lawyer, fresh from the schools, who had gone out to the deserts of Nevada to begin life. He found that country, and our ways of life, there, in those early days, different from life in New England or Paris. But he put on a woollen shirt and strapped a navy revolver to his person, took to the bacon and beans of the country, and determined to do in Nevada as Nevada did. Oliver accepted the situation so completely that although he must have sorrowed over many of his trials, he never complained – that is, he never complained but once. He, two others, and myself, started to the new silver mines in the Humboldt mountains – he to be Probate Judge of Humboldt county, and we to mine. The distance was two hundred miles. It was dead of winter. We bought a two-horse wagon and put eighteen hundred pounds of bacon, flour, beans, blasting-powder, picks and shovels in it; we bought two sorry-looking Mexican "plugs," with the hair turned the wrong way and more corners on their bodies than there are on the mosque of Omar; we hitched up and started. It was a dreadful trip. But Oliver did not complain. The horses dragged the wagon two miles from town and then gave out. Then we three pushed the wagon seven miles, and Oliver moved ahead and pulled the horses after him by the bits. We complained, but Oliver did not. The ground was frozen, and it froze our backs while we slept; the wind swept across our faces and froze our noses.

Oliver did not complain. Five days of pushing the wagon by day and freezing by night brought us to the bad part of the journey – the Forty Mile Desert, or the Great American Desert, if you please. Still, this mildest-mannered man that ever was, had not complained. We started across at eight in the morning, pushing through sand that had no bottom; toiling all day long by the wrecks of a thousand wagons, the skeletons of ten thousand oxen; by wagon-tires enough to hoop the Washington Monument to the top, and ox-chains enough to girdle Long Island; by human graves; with our throats parched always, with thirst; lips bleeding from the alkali dust; hungry, perspiring, and very, very weary – so weary that when we dropped in the sand every fifty yards to rest the horses, we could hardly keep from going to sleep – no complaints from Oliver: none the next morning at three o'clock, when we got across, tired to death. Awakened two or three nights afterward at midnight, in a narrow canon, by the snow falling on our faces, and appalled at the imminent danger of being "snowed in," we harnessed up and pushed on till eight in the morning, passed the "Divide" and knew we were saved. No complaints. Fifteen days of hardship and fatigue brought us to the end of the two hundred miles, and the Judge had not complained. We wondered if any thing *could* exasperate him. We built a Humboldt house. It is done in this way. You dig a square in the steep base of the mountain, and set up two uprights and top them with two joists. Then you stretch a great sheet of "cotton domestic" from the point where the joists join the hill-side down over the hoists to the ground; this makes the roof and the front of the mansion; the sides and back are the dirt walls your digging has left. A chimney is easily made by turning up one corner of the roof. Oliver was sitting alone in this dismal den, one night, by a sage-brush fire, writing poetry; he was very fond of digging poetry out of himself – or blasting it out when it came hard. He heard an animal's footsteps close to the roof; a stone or two and some dirt came through and fell by him. He grew uneasy and said "Hi! – clear out from there, can't you!" – from time to time. But by and by he fell asleep where he sat, and pretty soon a mule fell down the chimney! The fire flew in every direction, and Oliver went over backwards. About ten nights after that, he recovered confidence enough to go to writing poetry again. Again he dozed off to sleep, and again a mule fell down the chimney. This time, about half of that side of the house came in with the mule. Struggling to get up, the mule kicked the candle out and smashed most of the kitchen furniture, and raised considerable dust. These violent awakenings must have been annoying to Oliver, but he never complained. He moved to a mansion on the opposite side of the canon, because he had noticed the mules did not go there. One night about eight o'clock he was endeavoring to finish his poem, when a stone rolled in – then a hoof appeared below the canvas – then part of a cow – the after part. He leaned back in dread, and shouted "Hooy! hooy! get out of this!" and the cow struggled manfully – lost ground steadily – dirt and dust streamed down, and before Oliver could get well away, the entire cow crashed through on to the table and made a shapeless wreck of every thing!

Then, for the first time in his life, I think, Oliver complained. He said,

"This thing is growing monotonous!"

Then he resigned his judgeship and left Humboldt county. "Butchered to make a Roman holyday" has grown monotonous to me.

In this connection I wish to say one word about Michael Angelo Buonarotti. I used to worship the mighty genius of Michael Angelo – that man who was great in poetry, painting, sculpture, architecture – great in every thing he undertook. But I do not want Michael Angelo for breakfast – for luncheon – for dinner – for tea – for supper – for between meals. I like a change, occasionally. In Genoa, he designed every thing; in Milan he or his pupils designed every thing; he designed the Lake of Como; in Padua, Verona, Venice, Bologna, who did we ever hear of, from guides, but Michael Angelo? In Florence, he painted every thing, designed every thing, nearly, and what he did not design he used to sit on a favorite stone and look at, and they showed us the stone. In Pisa he designed every thing but the old shot-tower, and they would have attributed that to him if it had not been so awfully out of the perpendicular. He designed the piers of Leghorn and the custom house regulations of Civita Vecchia. But, here – here it is frightful. He designed St. Peter's; he designed the Pope; he designed the Pantheon, the uniform of the Pope's soldiers, the Tiber, the Vatican, the Coliseum, the Capitol, the Tarpeian Rock, the Barberini Palace, St. John Lateran, the Campagna, the Appian Way, the Seven Hills, the Baths of Caracalla, the Claudian Aqueduct, the Cloaca Maxima – the eternal bore designed the Eternal City, and unless all men and books do lie, he painted every thing in it! Dan said the other day to the guide, "Enough, enough, enough! Say no more! Lump the whole thing! say that the Creator made Italy from designs by Michael Angelo!"

I never felt so fervently thankful, so soothed, so tranquil, so filled with a blessed peace, as I did yesterday when I learned that Michael Angelo was dead.

But we have taken it out of this guide. He has marched us through miles of pictures and sculpture in the vast corridors of the Vatican; and through miles of pictures and sculpture in twenty other palaces; he has shown us the great picture in the Sistine Chapel, and frescoes enough to frescoe the heavens – pretty much all done by Michael Angelo. So with him we have played that game which has vanquished so many guides for us – imbecility and idiotic questions. These creatures never suspect – they have no idea of a sarcasm.

He shows us a figure and says: "Statoo brunzo." (Bronze statue.)

We look at it indifferently and the doctor asks: "By Michael Angelo?"

"No – not know who."

Then he shows us the ancient Roman Forum. The doctor asks: "Michael Angelo?"

A stare from the guide. "No – thousan' year before he is born."

Then an Egyptian obelisk. Again: "Michael Angelo?"

"Oh, *mon dieu*, genteelmen! Zis is *two* thousan' year before he is born!"

He grows so tired of that unceasing question sometimes, that he dreads to show us any thing at all. The wretch has tried all the ways he can think of to make us comprehend that Michael Angelo is only responsible for the creation of a *part* of the world, but somehow he has not succeeded yet. Relief for overtasked eyes and brain from study and sight-seeing is necessary, or we shall become idiotic sure enough. Therefore this guide must continue to suffer. If he does not enjoy it, so much the worse for him. We do.

In this place I may as well jot down a chapter concerning those necessary nuisances, European guides. Many a man has wished in his heart he could do without his guide; but knowing he could not, has wished he could get some amusement out of him as a remuneration for the affliction of his society. We accomplished this latter matter, and if our experience can be made useful to others they are welcome to it.

Guides know about enough English to tangle every thing up so that a man can make neither head or tail of it. They know their story by heart – the history of every statue, painting, cathedral or other wonder they show you. They know it and tell it as a parrot would – and if you interrupt, and throw them off the track, they have to go back and begin over again. All their lives long, they are employed in showing strange things to foreigners and listening to their bursts of admiration. It is human nature to take delight in exciting admiration. It is what prompts children to say "smart" things, and do absurd ones, and in other ways "show off" when company is present. It is what makes gossips turn out in rain and storm to go and be the first to tell a startling bit of news. Think, then, what a passion it becomes with a guide, whose privilege it is, every day, to show to strangers wonders that throw them into perfect ecstasies of admiration! He gets so that he could not by any possibility live in a soberer atmosphere. After we discovered this, we *never* went into ecstasies any more – we never admired any thing – we never showed any but impassible faces and stupid indifference in the presence of the sublimest wonders a guide had to display. We had found their weak point. We have made good use of it ever since. We have made some of those people savage, at times, but we have never lost our own serenity.

The doctor asks the questions, generally, because he can keep his countenance, and look more like an inspired idiot, and throw more imbecility into the tone of his voice than any man that lives. It comes natural to him.

The guides in Genoa are delighted to secure an American party, because Americans so much wonder, and deal so much in sentiment and emotion before any relic of Columbus. Our guide there fidgeted about as if he had swallowed a spring mattress. He was full of animation – full of impatience. He said:

"Come wis me, genteelmen! – come! I show you ze letter writing by Christopher Colombo! – write it himself! – write it wis his own hand! – come!"

He took us to the municipal palace. After much impressive fumbling of keys and opening of locks, the stained and aged document was spread before us. The guide's eyes sparkled. He danced about us and tapped the parchment with his finger:

"What I tell you, genteelmen! Is it not so? See! handwriting Christopher Colombo! – write it himself!"

We looked indifferent – unconcerned. The doctor examined the document very deliberately, during a painful pause. – Then he said, without any show of interest:

"Ah – Ferguson – what – what did you say was the name of the party who wrote this?"

"Christopher Colombo! ze great Christopher Colombo!"

Another deliberate examination.

"Ah – did he write it himself, or – or how?"

"He write it himself! – Christopher Colombo! he's own handwriting, write by himself!"

Then the doctor laid the document down and said:

"Why, I have seen boys in America only fourteen years old that could write better than that."

"But zis is ze great Christo—"

"I don't care who it is! It's the worst writing I ever saw. Now you mustn't think you can impose on us because we are strangers. We are not fools, by a good deal. If you have got any specimens of penmanship of real merit, trot them out! – and if you haven't, drive on!"

We drove on. The guide was considerably shaken up, but he made one more venture. He had something which he thought would overcome us. He said:

"Ah, genteelmen, you come wis me! I show you beautiful, O, magnificent bust Christopher Colombo! – splendid, grand, magnificent!"

He brought us before the beautiful bust – for it *was* beautiful – and sprang back and struck an attitude:

"Ah, look, genteelmen! – beautiful, grand, – bust Christopher Colombo! – beautiful bust, beautiful pedestal!"

The doctor put up his eye-glass – procured for such occasions:

"Ah – what did you say this gentleman's name was?"

"Christopher Colombo! – ze great Christopher Colombo!"

"Christopher Colombo – the great Christopher Colombo. Well, what did *he* do?"

"Discover America! – discover America, Oh, ze devil!"

"Discover America. No – that statement will hardly wash. We are just from America ourselves. We heard nothing about it. Christopher Colombo – pleasant name – is – is he dead?"

"Oh, corpo di Baccho! – three hundred year!"

"What did he die of?"

"I do not know! – I can not tell."

"Small-pox, think?"

"I do not know, genteelmen! – I do not know *what* he die of!"

"Measles, likely?"

"May be – may be – I do *not* know – I think he die of somethings."

"Parents living?"

"Im-posseeble!"

"Ah – which is the bust and which is the pedestal?"

"Santa Maria! – *zis* ze bust! – *zis* ze pedestal!"

"Ah, I see, I see – happy combination – very happy combination, indeed. Is – is this the first time this gentleman was ever on a bust?"

That joke was lost on the foreigner – guides can not master the subtleties of the American joke.

We have made it interesting for this Roman guide. Yesterday we spent three or four hours in the Vatican, again, that wonderful world of curiosities. We came very near expressing interest, sometimes – even admiration – it was very hard to keep from it. We succeeded though. Nobody else ever did, in the Vatican museums. The guide was bewildered – non-plussed. He walked his legs off, nearly, hunting up extraordinary things, and exhausted all his ingenuity on us, but it was a failure; we never showed any interest in any thing. He had reserved what he considered to be his greatest wonder till the last – a royal Egyptian mummy, the best preserved in the world, perhaps. He took us there. He felt so sure, this time, that some of his old enthusiasm came back to him:

"See, genteelmen! – Mummy! Mummy!"

The eye-glass came up as calmly, as deliberately as ever.

"Ah, – Ferguson – what did I understand you to say the gentleman's name was?"

"Name? – he got no name! – Mummy! – 'Gyptian mummy!"

"Yes, yes. Born here?"

"No! *'Gyptian* mummy!"

"Ah, just so. Frenchman, I presume?"

"No! – *not* Frenchman, not Roman! – born in Egypta!"

"Born in Egypta. Never heard of Egypta before. Foreign locality, likely. Mummy – mummy. How calm he is – how self-possessed. Is, ah – is he dead?"

"Oh, *sacre bleu,* been dead three thousan' year!"

The doctor turned on him savagely:

"Here, now, what do you mean by such conduct as this! Playing us for Chinamen because we are strangers and trying to learn! Trying to impose your vile second-hand carcasses on *us!* – thunder and lightning, I've a notion to – to – if you've got a nice *fresh* corpse, fetch him out! – or by George we'll brain you!"

We make it exceedingly interesting for this Frenchman. However, he has paid us back, partly, without knowing it. He came to the hotel this morning to ask if we were up, and he endeavored as well as he could to describe us, so that the landlord would know which persons he meant. He finished with the casual remark that we were lunatics. The observation was so innocent and so honest that it amounted to a very good thing for a guide to say.

There is one remark (already mentioned,) which never yet has failed to disgust these guides. We use it always, when we can think of nothing else to say. After they have exhausted their enthusiasm pointing out to us and praising the beauties of some ancient bronze image or broken-legged statue, we look at it stupidly and in silence for five, ten, fifteen minutes – as long as we can hold out, in fact – and then ask:

"Is – is he dead?"

That conquers the serenest of them. It is not what they are looking for – especially a new guide. Our Roman Ferguson is the most patient, unsuspecting, long-suffering subject we have had yet. We shall be sorry to part with him. We have enjoyed his society very much. We trust he has enjoyed ours, but we are harassed with doubts.

We have been in the catacombs. It was like going down into a very deep cellar, only it was a cellar which had no end to it. The narrow passages are roughly hewn in the rock, and on each hand as you pass along, the hollowed shelves are carved out, from three to fourteen deep; each held a corpse once. There are names, and Christian symbols, and prayers, or sentences expressive of Christian hopes, carved upon nearly every sarcophagus. The dates belong away back in the dawn of the Christian era, of course. Here, in these holes in the ground, the first Christians sometimes burrowed to escape persecution. They crawled out at night to get food, but remained under cover in the day time. The priest told us that St. Sebastian lived under ground for some time while he was being hunted; he went out one day, and the soldiery discovered and shot him to death with arrows. Five or six of the early Popes – those who reigned about sixteen hundred years ago – held their papal courts and advised with their clergy in the bowels of the earth. During seventeen years – from A. D. 235 to A. D. 252 – the Popes did not appear above ground. Four were raised to the great office during that period. Four years apiece, or thereabouts. It is very suggestive of the unhealthiness of underground graveyards as places of residence. One Pope afterward spent his entire pontificate in the catacombs – eight years. Another was discovered in them and murdered in the episcopal chair. There was no satisfaction in being a Pope in those days. There were too many annoyances. There are one hundred and sixty catacombs under Rome, each with its maze of narrow passages crossing and recrossing each other and each passage walled to the top with scooped graves its entire length. A careful estimate makes the length of the passages of all the catacombs combined foot up nine hundred miles, and their graves number seven millions. We did not go through all the passages of all the catacombs. We were very anxious to do it, and made the necessary arrangements, but our too limited time obliged us to give up the idea. So we only groped through the dismal labyrinth of St. Callixtus, under the Church of St. Sebastian. In the various catacombs are small chapels rudely hewn in the stones, and here the early Christians often held their religious services by dim, ghostly lights. Think of mass and a sermon away down in those tangled caverns under ground!

In the catacombs were buried St. Cecilia, St. Agnes, and several other of the most celebrated of the saints. In the catacomb of St. Callixtus, St. Bridget used to remain long hours in holy contemplation, and St. Charles Borroméo was wont to spend whole nights in prayer there. It was also the scene of a very marvelous thing.

> "Here the heart of St. Philip Neri was so inflamed with divine love as to burst his ribs."

I find that grave statement in a book published in New York in 1858, and written by "Rev. William H. Neligan, LL.D., M. A., Trinity College, Dublin; Member of the Archæological Society of Great Britain." Therefore, I believe it. Otherwise, I could not. Under other circumstances I should have felt a curiosity to know what Philip had for dinner.

This author puts my credulity on its mettle every now and then. He tells of one St. Joseph Calasanctius whose house in Rome he visited; he visited only the house – the priest has been dead two hundred years. He says the Virgin Mary appeared to this saint. Then he continues:

> "His tongue and his heart, which were found after nearly a century to be whole, when the body was disinterred before his canonization, are still preserved in a glass case, and after two centuries the heart is still whole. When the French troops came to Rome, and when Pius VII. was carried away prisoner, blood dropped from it."

To read that in a book written by a monk far back in the Middle Ages, would surprise no one; it would sound natural and proper;

but when it is seriously stated in the middle of the nineteenth century, by a man of finished education, an LL.D., M. A., and an Archæological magnate, it sounds strangely enough. Still, I would gladly change my unbelief for Neligan's faith, and let him make the conditions as hard as he pleased.

The old gentleman's undoubting, unquestioning simplicity has a rare freshness about it in these matter-of-fact railroading and telegraphing days. Hear him, concerning the church of Ara Cœli:

> "In the roof of the church, directly above the high altar, is engraved, *'Regina Cœli laetare Alleluia.'* In the sixth century Rome was visited by a fearful pestilence. Gregory the Great urged the people to do penance, and a general procession was formed. It was to proceed from Ara Cœli to St. Peter's. As it passed before the mole of Adrian, now the Castle of St. Angelo, the sound of heavenly voices was heard singing (it was Easter morn.) *'Regina Cœli, laetare! alleluia! quia quem meruisti portare, alleluia! Resurrexit sicut dixit; alleluia!'* The Pontiff, carrying in his hands the portrait of the Virgin, (which is over the high altar and is said to have been painted by St. Luke,) answered, with the astonished people, *'Ora pro nobis Deum, alleluia!'* At the same time an angel was seen to put up a sword in a scabbard, and the pestilence ceased on the same day. There are four circumstances which *confirm** this miracle: the annual procession which takes place in the western church on the feast of St. Mark; the statue of St. Michael, placed on the mole of Adrian, which has since that time been called the Castle of St. Angelo; the antiphon Regina Cœli, which the Catholic church sings during paschal time; and the inscription in the church."

CHAPTER XXVIII

FROM THE SANGUINARY sports of the Holy Inquisition; the slaughter of the Coliseum; and the dismal tombs of the Catacombs, I naturally pass to the picturesque horrors of the Capuchin Convent. We stopped a moment in a small chapel in the church to admire a

*The italics are mine. – M. T.

picture of St. Michael vanquishing Satan – a picture which is so beautiful that I can not but think it belongs to the reviled *"Renaissance,"* notwithstanding I believe they told us one of the ancient old masters painted it – and then we descended into the vast vault underneath.

Here was a spectacle for sensitive nerves! Evidently the old masters had been at work in this place. There were six divisions in the apartment, and each division was ornamented with a style of decoration peculiar to itself – and these decorations were in every instance formed of human bones! There were shapely arches, built wholly of thigh bones; there were startling pyramids, built wholly of grinning skulls; there were quaint architectural structures of various kinds, built of shin bones and the bones of the arm; on the wall were elaborate frescoes, whose curving vines were made of knotted human vertebræ; whose delicate tendrils were made of sinews and tendons; whose flowers were formed of knee-caps and toenails. Every lasting portion of the human frame was represented in these intricate designs (they were by Michael Angelo, I think,) and there was a careful finish about the work, and an attention to details that betrayed the artist's love of his labors as well as his schooled ability. I asked the good-natured monk who accompanied us, who did this? And he said, "*We* did it" – meaning himself and his brethren up stairs. I could see that the old friar took a high pride in his curious show. We made him talkative by exhibiting an interest we never betrayed to guides.

"Who were these people?"

"We – up stairs – Monks of the Capuchin order – my brethren."

"How many departed monks were required to upholster these six parlors?"

"These are the bones of four thousand."

"It took a long time to get enough?"

"Many, many centuries."

"Their different parts are well separated – skulls in one room, legs in another, ribs in another – there would be stirring times here for a while if the last trump should blow. Some of the brethren might get hold of the wrong leg, in the confusion, and the wrong skull, and find themselves limping, and looking through eyes that were wider apart or closer together than they were used to. You can not tell any of these parties apart, I suppose?"

"Oh, yes, I know many of them."

He put his finger on a skull. "This was Brother Anselmo – dead three hundred years – a good man."

He touched another. "This was Brother Alexander – dead two hundred and eighty years. This was Brother Carlo – dead about as long."

Then he took a skull and held it in his hand, and looked reflectively upon it, after the manner of the grave-digger when he discourses of Yorick.

"This," he said, "was Brother Thomas. He was a young prince, the scion of a proud house that traced its lineage back to the grand old days of Rome well nigh two thousand years ago. He loved beneath his estate. His family persecuted him; persecuted the girl, as well. They drove her from Rome; he followed; he sought her far and wide; he found no trace of her. He came back and offered his broken heart at our altar and his weary life to the service of God. But look you. Shortly his father died, and likewise his mother. The girl returned, rejoicing. She sought every where for him whose eyes had used to look tenderly into hers out of this poor skull, but she could not find him. At last, in this coarse garb we wear, she recognized him in the street. He knew her. It was too late. He fell where he stood. They took him up and brought him here. He never spoke afterward. Within the week he died. You can see the color of his hair – faded, somewhat – by this thin shred that clings still to the temple. This," [taking up a thigh bone,] "was his. The veins of this leaf in the decorations over your head, were his finger-joints, a hundred and fifty years ago."

This business-like way of illustrating a touching story of the heart by laying the several fragments of the lover before us and naming them, was as grotesque a performance, and as ghastly, as any I ever witnessed. I hardly knew whether to smile or shudder. There are nerves and muscles in our frames whose functions and whose methods of working it seems a sort of sacrilege to describe by cold physiological names and surgical technicalities, and the monk's talk suggested to me something of this kind. Fancy a surgeon, with his nippers lifting tendons, muscles and such things into view, out of the complex machinery of a corpse, and observing, "Now this little nerve quivers – the vibration is imparted to this muscle – from here it is passed to this fibrous substance; here its ingredients are separated by the chemical action of the blood – one part goes to the heart and thrills it with what is popularly termed emotion, another part follows this nerve to the brain and communicates intelligence of a startling character – the third part glides along this passage and touches the spring connected with the fluid receptacles that lie in the rear of the eye. Thus, by this simple and beautiful process, the party is informed that his mother is dead, and he weeps." Horrible!

I asked the monk if all the brethren up stairs expected to be put in this place when they died. He answered quietly:

"We must all lie here at last."

See what one can accustom himself to. – The reflection that he must some day be taken apart like an engine or a clock, or like a house whose owner is gone, and worked up into arches and pyramids and hideous frescoes, did not distress this monk in the least. I thought he even looked as if he were thinking, with complacent vanity, that his own skull would look well on top of the heap and his own ribs add a charm to the frescoes which possibly they lacked at present.

Here and there, in ornamental alcoves, stretched upon beds of bones, lay dead and dried-up monks, with lank frames dressed in the black robes one sees ordinarily upon priests. We examined one closely. The skinny hands were clasped upon the breast; two lustreless tufts of hair stuck to the skull; the skin was brown and sunken; it stretched tightly over the cheek bones and made them stand out sharply; the crisp dead eyes were deep in the sockets; the nostrils were painfully prominent, the end of the nose being gone; the lips had shriveled away from the yellow teeth: and brought down for us through the circling years, and petrified there, was a weird laugh a full century old!

It was the jolliest laugh, but yet the most dreadful, that one can imagine. Surely, I thought, it must have been a most extraordinary joke this veteran produced with his latest breath, that he has not got done laughing at it yet. At this moment I saw that the old instinct was strong upon the boys, and I said we had better hurry to St. Peter's. They were trying to keep from asking, "Is – is he dead?"

It makes me dizzy, to think of the Vatican – of its wilderness of statues, paintings, and curiosities of every description and every age. The "old masters" (especially in sculpture,) fairly swarm, there. I can not write about the Vatican. I think I shall never remember any thing I saw there distinctly but the mummies, and the Transfiguration, by Raphael, and some other things it is not necessary to mention now. I shall remember the Transfiguration partly because it was placed in a room almost by itself; partly because it is acknowledged by all to be the first oil painting in the world; and partly because it was wonderfully beautiful. The colors are fresh and rich, the "expression," I am told, is fine, the "feeling" is lively, the "tone" is good, the "depth" is profound, and the width is about four and a half feet, I should judge. It is a picture that really holds one's attention; its beauty is fascinating. It is fine enough to be a *Renaissance*. A remark I made a while ago suggests a thought – and a hope. Is it not possible that the reason I find such charms in this picture is because it is out of the crazy chaos of the galleries? If some of the others were set apart, might not they be beautiful? If this were set in the midst of the tempest of pictures one finds in the vast galleries of the Roman palaces, would I think it so handsome? If, up to this time, I had seen only one "old master" in each palace, instead of acres and acres of walls and ceilings fairly papered with them, might I not have a more civilized opinion of the old masters than I have now? I think so. When I was a school-boy and was to have a new knife, I could not make up my mind as to which was the prettiest in the show-case, and I did not think any of them were particularly pretty; and so I chose with a heavy heart. But when I looked at my purchase, at home, where no glittering blades came into competition with it, I was astonished to see how handsome it was. To this day my new hats look better out of the shop than they did in it with other new hats. It begins to dawn upon me, now, that possibly, what I have been taking for uniform ugliness in the galleries may be uniform beauty after all. I honestly hope it is, to others, but certainly it is not to me. Perhaps the reason I used to enjoy going to the Academy of Fine Arts in New York was because there were but a few hundred paintings in it, and it did not surfeit me to go through the list. I suppose the Academy was bacon and beans in the Forty-Mile Desert, and a European gallery is a state dinner of thirteen courses. One leaves no sign after him of the one dish, but the thirteen frighten away his appetite and give him no satisfaction.

There is one thing I am certain of, though. With all the Michael Angelos, the Raphaels, the Guidos and the other old masters, the sublime history of Rome remains unpainted! They painted Virgins enough, and popes enough and saintly scarecrows enough, to people Paradise, almost, and these things are all they did paint. "Nero fiddling o'er burning Rome," the assassination of Cæsar, the stirring spectacle of a hundred thousand people bending forward with rapt interest, in the Coliseum, to see two skillful gladiators hacking away each other's lives, a tiger springing upon a kneeling martyr – these and a thousand other matters which we read of with a living interest, must be sought for only in books – not among the rubbish left by the old masters – who are no more, I have the satisfaction of informing the public.

They did paint, and they did carve in marble, one historical scene, and one only, (of any great historical consequence.) And what was it and why did they choose it, particularly? It was the Rape of the Sabines, and they chose it for the legs and busts.

I like to look at statues, however, and I like to look at pictures, also – even of monks looking up in sacred ecstasy, and monks looking down in meditation, and monks skirmishing for something to eat – and therefore I drop ill nature to thank the papal government for so jealously guarding and so industriously gathering up these things; and for permitting me, a stranger and not an entirely friendly one, to roam at will and unmolested among them, charging me nothing, and only requiring that I shall behave myself simply as well as I ought to behave in any other man's house. I thank the Holy Father right heartily, and I wish him long life and plenty of happiness.

The Popes have long been the patrons and preservers of art, just as our new, practical Republic is the encourager and upholder of mechanics. In their Vatican is stored up all that is curious and beautiful in art; in our Patent Office is hoarded all that is curious or useful in mechanics. When a man invents a new style of horse-collar or discovers a new and superior method of telegraphing, our government issues a patent to him that is worth a fortune; when a man digs up an ancient statue in the Campagna, the Pope gives him a fortune in gold coin. We can make something of a guess at a man's character by the style of nose he carries on his face. The Vatican and the Patent Office are governmental noses, and they bear a deal of character about them.

The guide showed us a colossal statue of Jupiter, in the Vatican, which he said looked so damaged and rusty – so like the God of the Vagabonds – because it had but recently been dug up in the Campagna. He asked how much we supposed this Jupiter was worth? I replied, with intelligent promptness, that he was probably worth about four dollars – may be four and a half. "A hundred thousand dollars!" Ferguson said. Ferguson said, further, that the Pope permits no ancient work of this kind to leave his dominions. He appoints a commission to examine discoveries like this and report upon the value; then the Pope pays the discoverer one-half of that assessed value and takes the statue. He said this Jupiter was dug from a field which had just been bought for thirty-six thousand dollars, so the first crop was a good one for the new farmer. I do not know whether Ferguson always tells the truth or not, but I suppose he does. I know that an exorbitant export duty is exacted upon all pictures painted by the old masters, in order to discourage the sale of those in the private collections. I am satisfied, also, that genuine old masters hardly exist at all, in America, because the cheapest and most insignificant of them are valued at the price of a fine farm. I proposed to buy a small trifle of a Raphael, myself, but the price of it was eighty thousand dollars, the export duty would have made it considerably over a hundred, and so I studied on it awhile and concluded not to take it.

I wish here to mention an inscription I have seen, before I forget it:

"Glory to God in the highest, peace on earth TO MEN OF GOOD WILL!" It is not good scripture, but it is sound Catholic and human nature.

This is in letters of gold around the apsis of a mosaic group at the side of the *scala santa*, church of St. John Lateran, the Mother and Mistress of all the Catholic churches of the world. The group represents the Saviour, St. Peter, Pope Leo, St. Silvester, Constantine and Charlemagne. Peter is giving the *pallium* to the Pope, and a standard to Charlemagne. The Saviour is giving the keys to St. Silvester, and a standard to Constantine. No prayer is offered to the Saviour, who seems to be of little importance any where in Rome; but an inscription below says, *"Blessed Peter, give life to Pope Leo and victory to King Charles."* It does not say, "*Intercede for us*, through the Saviour, with the Father, for this boon," but "Blessed Peter, *give it* us."

In all seriousness – without meaning to be frivolous – without meaning to be irreverent, and more than all, without meaning to be blasphemous, – I state as my simple deduction from the things I have seen and the things I have heard, that the Holy Personages rank thus in Rome:

First – "The Mother of God" – otherwise the Virgin Mary.

Second – The Deity.

Third – Peter.

Fourth – Some twelve or fifteen canonized Popes and martyrs.

Fifth – Jesus Christ the Saviour – (but always as an infant in arms.)

I may be wrong in this – my judgment errs often, just as is the case with other men's – but it *is* my judgment, be it good or bad.

Just here I will mention something that seems curious to me. There are no "Christ's Churches" in Rome, and no "Churches of the Holy Ghost," that I can discover. There are some four hundred churches, but about a fourth of them seem to be named for the Madonna and St. Peter. There are so many named for Mary that they have to be distinguished by all sorts of affixes, if I understand the matter rightly. Then we have churches of St. Louis; St. Augustine; St. Agnes; St. Calixtus; St. Lorenzo in Lucina; St. Lorenzo in Damaso; St. Cecilia; St. Athanasius; St. Philip Neri; St. Catherine, St. Dominico, and a multitude of lesser saints whose names are not familiar in the world – and away down, clear out of the list of the churches, comes a couple of hospitals: one of them is named for the Saviour and the other for the Holy Ghost!

Day after day and night after night we have wandered among the crumbling wonders of Rome; day after day and night after night we have fed upon the dust and decay of five-and-twenty centuries – have brooded over them by day and dreamed of them by night till sometimes we seemed moldering away ourselves, and growing defaced and cornerless, and liable at any moment to fall a prey to some antiquary and be patched in the legs, and "restored" with an unseemly nose, and labeled wrong and dated wrong, and set up in the Vatican for poets to drivel about and vandals to scribble their names on forever and forevermore.

But the surest way to stop writing about Rome is to stop. I wished to write a real "guide-book" chapter on this fascinating city, but I could not do it, because I have felt all the time like a boy in a candy-shop – there was every thing to choose from, and yet no choice. I have drifted along hopelessly for a hundred pages of manuscript without knowing where to commence. I will not commence at all. Our passports have been examined. We will go to Naples.

CHAPTER XXXII

HOME, AGAIN! FOR the first time, in many weeks, the ship's entire family met and shook hands on the quarter-deck. They had gathered from many points of the compass and from many lands, but not one was missing; there was no tale of sickness or death among the flock to dampen the pleasure of the reunion. Once more there was a full audience on deck to listen to the sailors' chorus as they got the anchor up, and to wave an adieu to the land as we sped away from Naples. The seats were full at dinner again, the domino parties were complete, and the life and bustle on the upper deck in the fine moonlight at night was like old times – old times that had been gone weeks only, but yet they were weeks so crowded with incident, adventure and excitement, that they seemed almost like years. There was no lack of cheerfulness on board the *Quaker City*. For once, her title was a misnomer.

At seven in the evening, with the western horizon all golden from the sunken sun, and specked with distant ships, the full moon sailing high over head, the dark blue of the sea under foot, and a strange sort of twilight affected by all these different lights and colors around us and about us, we sighted superb Stromboli. With what majesty the monarch held his lonely state above the level sea! Distance clothed him in a purple gloom, and added a veil of shimmering mist that so softened his rugged features that we seemed to see him through a web of silver gauze. His torch was out; his fires were smoldering; a tall column of smoke that rose up and lost itself in the growing moonlight was all the sign he gave that he was a living Autocrat of the Sea and not the spectre of a dead one.

At two in the morning we swept through the Straits of Messina, and so bright was the moonlight that Italy on the one hand and Sicily on the other seemed almost as distinctly visible as though we looked at them from the middle of a street we were traversing. The city of Messina, milk-white, and starred and spangled all over with gaslights, was a fairy spectacle. A great party of us were on deck smoking and making a noise, and waiting to see famous Scylla and Charybdis. And presently the Oracle stepped out with his eternal spy-glass and squared himself on the deck like another Colossus of Rhodes. It was a surprise to see him abroad at such an hour. Nobody supposed he cared any thing about an old fable like that of Scylla and Charybdis. One of the boys said:

"Hello, doctor, what are you doing up here at this time of night? – What do you want to see this place for?"

"What do *I* want to see this place for? Young man, little do you know me, or you wouldn't ask such a question. I wish to see *all* the places that's mentioned in the Bible."

"Stuff – this place isn't mentioned in the Bible."

"It ain't mentioned in the Bible! – *this* place ain't – well now, what place *is* this, since you know so much about it?"

"Why it's Scylla and Charybdis."

"Scylla and Cha—confound it, I thought it was Sodom and Gomorrah!"

And he closed up his glass and went below. The above is the ship story. Its plausibility is marred a little by the fact that the Oracle was not a biblical student, and did not spend much of his time instructing himself about Scriptural localities. – They say the Oracle complains, in this hot weather, lately, that the only beverage in the ship that is passable, is the butter. He did not mean butter, of course, but inasmuch as that article remains in a melted state now since we are out of ice, it is fair to give him the credit of getting one long word in the right place, anyhow, for once in his life. He said, in Rome, that the Pope was a noble-looking old man, but he never *did* think much of his Iliad.

We spent one pleasant day skirting along the Isles of Greece. They are very mountainous. Their prevailing tints are gray and brown, approaching to red. Little white villages surrounded by trees, nestle in the valleys or roost upon the lofty perpendicular sea-walls.

We had one fine sunset – a rich carmine flush that suffused the western sky and cast a ruddy glow far over the sea. – Fine sunsets seem to be rare in this part of the world – or at least, striking ones. They are soft, sensuous, lovely – they are exquisite, refined, effeminate, but we have seen no sunsets here yet like the gorgeous conflagrations that flame in the track of the sinking sun in our high northern latitudes.

But what were sunsets to us, with the wild excitement upon us of approaching the most renowned of cities! What cared we for outward visions, when Agamemnon, Achilles, and a thousand other heroes of the great Past were marching in ghostly procession through our fancies? What were sunsets to us, who were about to live and breathe and walk in actual Athens; yea, and go far down into the dead centuries and bid in person for the slaves, Diogenes and Plato, in the public marketplace, or gossip with the neighbors about the siege of Troy or the splendid deeds of Marathon? We scorned to consider sunsets.

We arrived, and entered the ancient harbor of the Piræus at last. We dropped anchor within half a mile of the village. Away off, across the undulating Plain of Attica, could be seen a little square-topped hill with a something on it, which our glasses soon discovered to be the ruined edifices of the citadel of the Athenians, and most prominent among them loomed the venerable Parthenon.

So exquisitely clear and pure is this wonderful atmosphere that every column of the noble structure was discernible through the telescope, and even the smaller ruins about it assumed some semblance of shape. This at a distance of five or six miles. In the valley, near the Acropolis, (the square-topped hill before spoken of), Athens itself could be vaguely made out with an ordinary lorgnette. Every body was anxious to get ashore and visit these classic localities as quickly as possible. No land we had yet seen had aroused such universal interest among the passengers.

But bad news came. The commandant of the Piræus came in his boat, and said we must either depart or else get outside the harbor and remain imprisoned in our ship, under rigid quarantine, for eleven days! So we took up the anchor and moved outside, to lie a dozen hours or so, taking in supplies, and then sail for Constantinople. It was the bitterest disappointment we had yet experienced. To lie a whole day in sight of the Acropolis, and yet be obliged to go away without visiting Athens! Disappointment was hardly a strong enough word to describe the circumstances.

All hands were on deck, all the afternoon, with books and maps and glasses, trying to determine which "narrow rocky ridge" was the Areopagus, which sloping hill the Pnyx, which elevation the Museum Hill, and so on. And we got things confused. Discussion became heated, and party spirit ran high. Church members were gazing with emotion upon a hill which they said was the one St. Paul preached from, and another faction claimed that that hill was Hymettus, and another that it was Pentelicon! After all the trouble, we could be certain of only one thing – the square-topped hill was the Acropolis, and the grand ruin that crowned it was the Parthenon, whose picture we knew in infancy in the school books.

We inquired of every body who came near the ship, whether there were guards in the Piræus, whether they were strict, what the chances were of capture should any of us slip ashore, and in case any of us made the venture and were caught, what would be probably done to us? The answers were discouraging: There was a strong guard or police force; the Piræus was a small town, and any stranger seen in it would surely attract attention – capture would be certain. The commandant said the punishment would be "heavy;" when asked "how heavy?" he said it would be "very severe" – that was all we could get out of him.

At eleven o'clock at night, when most of the ship's company were abed, four of us stole softly ashore in a small boat, a clouded moon favoring the enterprise, and started two and two, and far apart, over a low hill, intending to go clear around the Piræus, out of the range of its police. Picking our way so stealthily over that rocky, nettle-grown eminence, made me feel a good deal as if I were on my way somewhere to steal something. My immediate comrade and I talked in an undertone about quarantine laws and their penalties, but we found nothing cheering in the subject. I was posted. Only a few days before, I was talking with our captain, and he mentioned the case of a man who swam ashore from a quarantined ship somewhere, and got imprisoned six months for it; and when he was in Genoa a few years ago, a captain of a quarantined ship went in his boat to a departing ship, which was already outside of the harbor, and put a letter on board to be taken to his family, and the authorities imprisoned him three months for it, and then conducted him and his ship fairly to sea, and warned him never to show himself in that port again while he lived. This kind of conversation did no good, further than to give a sort of dismal interest to our quarantine-breaking expedition, and so we dropped it. We made the entire circuit of the town without seeing any body but one man, who stared at us curiously, but said nothing, and a dozen persons asleep on the ground before their doors, whom we walked among and never woke – but we woke up dogs enough, in all conscience – we always had one or two barking at our heels, and several times we had as many as ten and twelve at once. They made such a preposterous din that persons aboard our ship said they could tell how we were progressing for a long time, and where we were, by the barking of the dogs. The clouded moon still favored us. When we had made the whole circuit, and were passing among the houses on the further side of the town, the moon came out splendidly, but we no longer feared the light. As we approached a well, near a house, to get a drink, the owner merely glanced at us and went within. He left the quiet, slumbering town at our mercy. I record it here proudly, that we didn't do any thing to it.

Seeing no road, we took a tall hill to the left of the distant Acropolis for a mark, and steered straight for it over all obstructions, and over a little rougher piece of country than exists any where else outside of the State of Nevada, perhaps. Part of the way it was covered with small, loose stones – we trod on six at a time, and they all rolled. Another part of it was dry, loose, newly-ploughed ground. Still another part of it was a long stretch of low grape-vines, which were tangle-some and troublesome, and which we took to be brambles. The Attic Plain, barring the grape-vines, was a barren, desolate, unpoetical waste – I wonder what it was in Greece's Age of Glory, five hundred years before Christ?

In the neighborhood of one o'clock in the morning, when we were heated with fast walking and parched with thirst, Denny exclaimed, "Why, these weeds are grape-vines!" and in five minutes we had a score of bunches of large, white, delicious grapes, and were reaching down for more when a dark shape rose mysteriously up out of the shadows beside us and said "Ho!" And so we left.

In ten minutes more we struck into a beautiful road, and unlike some others we had stumbled upon at intervals, it led in the right direction. We followed it. It was broad, and smooth, and white – handsome and in perfect repair, and shaded on both sides for a mile or so with single ranks of trees, and also with luxuriant vineyards. Twice we entered and stole grapes, and the second time somebody shouted at us from some invisible place. Whereupon we left again. We speculated in grapes no more on that side of Athens.

Shortly we came upon an ancient stone aqueduct, built upon arches, and from that time forth we had ruins all about us – we were approaching our journey's end. We could not see the Acropolis now or the high hill, either, and I wanted to follow the road till we were abreast of them, but the others overruled me, and we toiled laboriously up the stony hill immediately in our front – and from its summit saw another – climbed it and saw another! It was an hour of exhausting work. Soon we came upon a row of open graves, cut in the solid rock – (for a while one of them served Socrates for a prison) – we passed around the shoulder of the hill, and the citadel, in all its ruined magnificence, burst upon us! We hurried across the ravine and up a winding road, and stood on the old Acropolis, with the prodigious walls of the citadel towering above our heads. We did not stop to inspect their massive blocks of marble, or measure their height, or guess at their extraordinary thickness, but passed at once through a great arched passage like a railway tunnel, and went straight to the gate that leads to the ancient temples. It was locked! So, after all, it seemed that we were not to see the great Parthenon face to face. We sat down and held a council of war. Result: the gate was only a flimsy structure of wood – we would break it down. It seemed like desecration, but then we had traveled far, and our necessities were urgent. We could not hunt up guides and keepers – we must be on the ship before daylight. So we argued. This was all very fine, but when we came to break the gate, we could not do it. We moved around an angle of the wall and found a low bastion – eight feet high without – ten or twelve within. Denny prepared to scale it, and we got ready to follow. By dint of hard scrambling he finally straddled the top, but some loose stones crumbled away and fell with a crash into the court within. There was instantly a banging of doors and a shout. Denny dropped from the wall in a twinkling, and we retreated in disorder to the gate. Xerxes took that mighty citadel four hundred and eighty years before Christ, when his five millions of soldiers and camp-followers followed him to Greece, and if we four Americans could have remained unmolested five minutes longer, we would have taken it too.

The garrison had turned out – four Greeks. We clamored at the gate, and they admitted us. [Bribery and corruption.]

We crossed a large court, entered a great door, and stood upon a pavement of purest white marble, deeply worn by footprints. Before us, in the flooding moonlight, rose the noblest ruins we had ever looked upon – the Propylæ; a small Temple of Minerva; the Temple of Hercules, and the grand Parthenon. [We got these names from the Greek guide, who didn't seem to know more than seven men ought to know.] These edifices were all built of the whitest Pentelic marble, but have a pinkish stain upon them now. Where any part is broken, however, the fracture looks like fine loaf sugar. Six caryatides, or marble women, clad in flowing robes, support the portico of the Temple of Hercules, but the porticos and colonnades of the other structures are formed of massive Doric and Ionic pillars, whose flutings and capitals are still measurably perfect, notwithstanding the centuries that have gone over them and the sieges they have suffered. The Parthenon, originally, was two hundred and twenty-six feet long, one hundred wide, and seventy high, and had two rows of great columns, eight in each, at either end, and single rows of seventeen each down the sides, and was one of the most graceful and beautiful edifices ever erected.

Most of the Parthenon's imposing columns are still standing, but the roof is gone. It was a perfect building two hundred and fifty years ago, when a shell dropped into the Venetian magazine stored here, and the explosion which followed wrecked and unroofed it. I remember but little about the Parthenon, and I have put in one or two facts and figures for the use of other people with short memories. Got them from the guide-book.

As we wandered thoughtfully down the marble-paved length of this stately temple, the scene about us was strangely impressive. Here and there, in lavish profusion, were gleaming white statues of men and women, propped against blocks of marble, some of them armless, some without legs, others headless – but all looking mournful in the moonlight, and startlingly human! They rose up and confronted the mid-night intruder on every side – they stared at him with stony eyes from unlooked-for nooks and recesses; they peered at him over fragmentary heaps far down the desolate corridors; they barred his way in the midst of the broad forum, and solemnly pointed with handless arms the way from the sacred fane; and through the roofless temple the moon looked down, and banded the floor and darkened the scattered fragments and broken statues with the slanting shadows of the columns.

What a world of ruined sculpture was about us! Set up in rows – stacked up in piles – scattered broadcast over the wide area of the Acropolis – were hundreds of crippled statues of all sizes and of the most exquisite workmanship; and vast fragments of marble that once belonged to the entablatures, covered with bas-reliefs representing battles and sieges, ships of war with three and four tiers of oars, pageants and processions – every thing one could think of. History says that the temples of the Acropolis were filled with the noblest works of Praxiteles and Phidias, and of many a great master in sculpture besides – and surely these elegant fragments attest it.

We walked out into the grass-grown, fragment-strewn court beyond the Parthenon. It startled us, every now and then, to see a stony white face stare suddenly up at us out of the grass with its dead eyes. The place seemed alive with ghosts. I half expected to see the Athenian heroes of twenty centuries ago glide out of the shadows and steal into the old temple they knew so well and regarded with such boundless pride.

The full moon was riding high in the cloudless heavens, now. We sauntered carelessly and unthinkingly to the edge of the lofty battlements of the citadel, and looked down – a vision! And such a vision! Athens by moonlight! The prophet that thought the splendors of the New Jerusalem were revealed to him, surely saw this instead! It lay in the level plain right under our feet – all spread abroad like a picture – and we looked down upon it as we might have looked from a balloon. We saw no semblance of a street, but every house, every window, every clinging vine, every projection, was as distinct and sharply marked as if the time were noonday; and yet there was no glare, no glitter, nothing harsh or repulsive – the noiseless city was flooded with the mellowest light that ever streamed from the moon, and seemed like some living creature wrapped in peaceful slumber. On its further side was a little temple, whose delicate pillars and ornate front glowed with a rich lustre that chained the eye like a spell; and nearer by, the palace of the king reared its creamy walls out of the midst of a great garden of shrubbery that was flecked all over with a random shower of amber lights – a spray of golden sparks that lost their brightness in the glory of the moon, and glinted softly upon the sea of dark foliage like the pallid stars of the milky-way. Overhead the stately columns, majestic still in their ruin – under foot the dreaming city – in the distance the silver sea – not on the broad earth is there another picture half so beautiful!

As we turned and moved again through the temple, I wished that the illustrious men who had sat in it in the remote ages could visit it again and reveal themselves to our curious eyes – Plato, Aristotle, Demosthenes, Socrates, Phocion, Pythagoras, Euclid, Pindar, Xenophon, Herodotus, Praxiteles and Phidias, Zeuxis the painter. What a constellation of celebrated names! But more than all, I wished that old Diogenes, groping so patiently with his lantern, searching so zealously for one solitary honest man in all the world, might meander along and stumble on our party. I ought not to say it, may be, but still I suppose he would have put out his light.

We left the Parthenon to keep its watch over old Athens, as it had kept it for twenty-three hundred years, and went and stood outside the walls of the citadel. In the distance was the ancient, but still almost perfect Temple of Theseus, and close by, looking to the west, was the Bema, from whence Demosthenes thundered his philippics and fired the wavering patriotism of his countrymen. To the right was Mars Hill, where the Areopagus sat in ancient times, and where St. Paul defined his position, and below was the marketplace where he "disputed daily" with the gossip-loving Athenians. We climbed the stone steps St. Paul ascended, and stood in the square-cut place he stood in, and tried to recollect the Bible account of the matter – but for certain reasons, I could not recall the words. I have found them since:

> "Now while Paul waited for them at Athens, his spirit was stirred in him, when he saw the city wholly given up to idolatry.
>
> "Therefore disputed he in the synagogue with the Jews, and with the devout persons, and in the market daily with them that meet with him.

* * *

"And they took him and brought him unto Areopagus, saying, May we know what this new doctrine whereof thou speakest is?

* * *

"Then Paul stood in the midst of Mars hill, and said, Ye men of Athens, I perceive that in all things ye are too superstitious;

"For as I passed by and beheld your devotions, I found an altar with this inscription: TO THE UNKNOWN GOD. Whom, therefore, ye ignorantly worship, him declare I unto you." – *Acts*, ch. xvii."

It occurred to us, after a while, that if we wanted to get home before daylight betrayed us, we had better be moving. So we hurried away. When far on our road, we had a parting view of the Parthenon, with the moonlight streaming through its open colonnades and touching its capitals with silver. As it looked then, solemn, grand, and beautiful it will always remain in our memories.

As we marched along, we began to get over our fears, and ceased to care much about quarantine scouts or any body else. We grew bold and reckless; and once, in a sudden burst of courage, I even threw a stone at a dog. It was a pleasant reflection, though, that I did not hit him, because his master might just possibly have been a policeman. Inspired by this happy failure, my valor became utterly uncontrollable, and at intervals I absolutely whistled, though on a moderate key. But boldness breeds boldness, and shortly I plunged into a vineyard, in the full light of the moon, and captured a gallon of superb grapes, not even minding the presence of a peasant who rode by on a mule. Denny and Birch followed my example. Now I had grapes enough for a dozen, but then Jackson was all swollen up with courage, too, and he was obliged to enter a vineyard presently. The first bunch he seized brought trouble. A frowsy, bearded brigand sprang into the road with a shout, and flourished a musket in the light of the moon! We sidled toward the Piræus – not running, you understand, but only advancing with celerity. The brigand shouted again, but still we advanced. It was getting late, and we had no time to fool away on every ass that wanted to drivel Greek platitudes to us. We would just as soon have talked with him as not if we had not been in a hurry. Presently Denny said, "Those fellows are following us!"

We turned, and, sure enough, there they were – three fantastic pirates armed with guns. We slackened our pace to let them come up, and in the meantime I got out my cargo of grapes and dropped them firmly but reluctantly into the shadows by the wayside. But I was not afraid. I only felt that it was not right to steal grapes. And all the more so when the owner was around – and not only around, but with his friends around also. The villains came up and searched a bundle Dr. Birch had in his hand, and scowled upon him when they found it had nothing in it but some holy rocks from Mars Hill, and these were not contraband. They evidently suspected him of playing some wretched fraud upon them, and seemed half inclined to scalp the party. But finally they dismissed us with a warning, couched in excellent Greek, I suppose, and dropped tranquilly in our wake. When they had gone three hundred yards they stopped, and we went on rejoiced. But behold, another armed rascal came out of the shadows and took their place, and followed us two hundred yards. Then he delivered us over to another miscreant, who emerged from some mysterious place, and he in turn to another! For a mile and a half our rear was guarded all the while by armed men. I never traveled in so much state before in all my life.

It was a good while after that before we ventured to steal any more grapes, and when we did we stirred up another troublesome brigand, and then we ceased all further speculation in that line. I suppose that fellow that rode by on the mule posted all the sentinels, from Athens to the Piræus, about us.

Every field on that long route was watched by an armed sentinel, some of whom had fallen asleep, no doubt, but were on hand, nevertheless. This shows what sort of a country modern Attica is – a community of questionable characters. These men were not there to guard their possessions against strangers, but against each other; for strangers seldom visit Athens and the Piræus, and when they do, they go in daylight, and can buy all the grapes they want for a trifle. The modern inhabitants are confiscators and falsifiers of high repute, if gossip speaks truly concerning them, and I freely believe it does.

Just as the earliest tinges of the dawn flushed the eastern sky and turned the pillared Parthenon to a broken harp hung in the pearly horizon, we closed our thirteenth mile of weary, round-about marching, and emerged upon the sea-shore abreast the ships, with our usual escort of fifteen hundred Piræan dogs howling at our heels. We hailed a boat that was two or three hundred yards from shore, and discovered in a moment that it was a police-boat on the lookout for any quarantine-breakers that might chance to be abroad. So we dodged – we were used to that by this time – and when the scouts reached the spot we had so lately occupied, we were absent. They cruised along the shore, but in the wrong direction, and shortly our own boat issued from the gloom and took us aboard. They had heard our signal on the ship. We rowed noiselessly away, and before the police-boat came in sight again, we were safe at home once more.

Four more of our passengers were anxious to visit Athens, and started half an hour after we returned; but they had not been ashore five minutes till the police discovered and chased them so hotly that they barely escaped to their boat again, and that was all. They pursued the enterprise no further.

We set sail for Constantinople to-day, but some of us little care for that. We have seen all there was to see in the old city that had its birth sixteen hundred years before Christ was born, and was an old town before the foundations of Troy were laid – and saw it in its most attractive aspect. Wherefore, why should *we* worry?

Two other passengers ran the blockade successfully last night. So we learned this morning. They slipped away so quietly that they were not missed from the ship for several hours. They had the hardihood to march into the Piræus in the early dusk and hire a carriage. They ran some danger of adding two or three months' imprisonment to the other novelties of their Holy Land Pleasure Excursion. I admire "cheek."* But they went and came safely, and never walked a step.

CHAPTER XXXIII

FROM ATHENS ALL through the islands of the Grecian Archipelago, we saw little but forbidding sea-walls and barren hills, sometimes surmounted by three or four graceful columns of some ancient temple, lonely and deserted – a fitting symbol of the desolation that has come upon all Greece in these latter ages. We saw no ploughed fields, very few villages, no trees or grass or vegetation of any kind, scarcely, and hardly ever an isolated house. Greece is a bleak, unsmiling desert, without agriculture, manufactures or commerce,

*Quotation from the Pilgrims.

apparently. What supports its poverty-stricken people or its Government, is a mystery.

I suppose that ancient Greece and modern Greece compared, furnish the most extravagant contrast to be found in history. George I., an infant of eighteen, and a scraggy nest of foreign office holders, sit in the places of Themistocles, Pericles, and the illustrious scholars and generals of the Golden Age of Greece. The fleets that were the wonder of the world when the Parthenon was new, are a beggarly handful of fishing-smacks now, and the manly people that performed such miracles of valor at Marathon are only a tribe of unconsidered slaves to-day. The classic Illyssus has gone dry, and so have all the sources of Grecian wealth and greatness. The nation numbers only eight hundred thousand souls, and there is poverty and misery and mendacity enough among them to furnish forty millions and be liberal about it. Under King Otho the revenues of the State were five millions of dollars – raised from a tax of *one-tenth* of all the agricultural products of the land (which tenth the farmer had to bring to the royal granaries on pack-mules any distance not exceeding six leagues) and from extravagant taxes on trade and commerce. Out of that five millions the small tyrant tried to keep an army of ten thousand men, pay all the hundreds of useless Grand Equerries in Waiting, First Grooms of the Bedchamber, Lord High Chancellors of the Exploded Exchequer, and all the other absurdities which these puppy-kingdoms indulge in, in imitation of the great monarchies; and in addition he set about building a white marble palace to cost about five millions itself. The result was, simply: ten into five goes no times and none over. All these things could not be done with five millions, and Otho fell into trouble.

The Greek throne, with its unpromising adjuncts of a ragged population of ingenious rascals who were out of employment eight months in the year because there was little for them to borrow and less to confiscate, and a waste of barren hills and weed-grown deserts, went begging for a good while. It was offered to one of Victoria's sons, and afterwards to various other younger sons of royalty who had no thrones and were out of business, but they all had the charity to decline the dreary honor, and veneration enough for Greece's ancient greatness to refuse to mock her sorrowful rags and dirt with a tinsel throne in this day of her humiliation – till they came to this young Danish George, and he took it. He has finished the splendid palace I saw in the radiant moonlight the other night, and is doing many other things for the salvation of Greece, they say.

We sailed through the barren Archipelago, and into the narrow channel they sometimes call the Dardanelles and sometimes the Hellespont. This part of the country is rich in historic reminiscences, and poor as Sahara in every thing else. For instance, as we approached the Dardanelles, we coasted along the Plains of Troy and past the mouth of the Scamander; we saw where Troy had stood (in the distance,) and where it does not stand now – a city that perished when the world was young. The poor Trojans are all dead, now. They were born too late to see Noah's ark, and died too soon to see our menagerie. We saw where Agamemnon's fleets rendezvoused, and away inland a mountain which the map said was Mount Ida. Within the Hellespont we saw where the original first shoddy contract mentioned in history was carried out, and the "parties of the second part" gently rebuked by Xerxes. I speak of the famous bridge of boats which Xerxes ordered to be built over the narrowest part of the Hellespont (where it is only two or three miles wide.) A moderate gale destroyed the flimsy structure, and the King, thinking that to publicly rebuke the contractors might have a good effect on the next set, called them out before the army and had them beheaded. In the next ten minutes he let a new contract for the bridge. It has been observed by ancient writers that the second bridge was a very good bridge. Xerxes crossed his host of five millions of men on it, and if it had not been purposely destroyed, it would probably have been there yet. If our Government would rebuke some of our shoddy contractors occasionally, it might work much good. In the Hellespont we saw where Leander and Lord Byron swam across, the one to see her upon whom his soul's affections were fixed with a devotion that only death could impair, and the other merely for a flyer, as Jack says. We had two noted tombs near us, too. On one shore slept Ajax, and on the other Hecuba.

We had water batteries and forts on both sides of the Hellespont, flying the crimson flag of Turkey, with its white crescent, and occasionally a village, and sometimes a train of camels; we had all these to look at till we entered the broad sea of Marmora, and then the land soon fading from view, we resumed euchre and whist once more.

We dropped anchor in the mouth of the Golden Horn at daylight in the morning. Only three or four of us were up to see the great Ottoman capital. The passengers do not turn out at unseasonable hours, as they used to, to get the earliest possible glimpse of strange foreign cities. They are well over that. If we were lying in sight of the Pyramids of Egypt, they would not come on deck until after breakfast, now-a-days.

The Golden Horn is a narrow arm of the sea, which branches from the Bosphorus (a sort of broad river which connects the Marmora and Black Seas,) and, curving around, divides the city in the middle. Galata and Pera are on one side of the Bosphorus, and the Golden Horn; Stamboul (ancient Byzantium) is upon the other. On the other bank of the Bosphorus is Scutari and other suburbs of Constantinople. This great city contains a million inhabitants, but so narrow are its streets, and so crowded together are its houses, that it does not cover much more than half as much ground as New York City. Seen from the anchorage or from a mile or so up the Bosphorus, it is by far the handsomest city we have seen. Its dense array of houses swells upward from the water's edge, and spreads over the domes of many hills; and the gardens that peep out here and there, the great globes of the mosques, and the countless minarets that meet the eye every where, invest the metropolis with the quaint Oriental aspect one dreams of when he reads books of eastern travel. Constantinople makes a noble picture.

But its attractiveness begins and ends with its picturesqueness. From the time one starts ashore till he gets back again, he execrates it. The boat he goes in is admirably miscalculated for the service it is built for. It is handsomely and neatly fitted up, but no man could handle it well in the turbulent currents that sweep down the Bosphorus from the Black Sea, and few men could row it satisfactorily even in still water. It is a long, light canoe (caique,) large at one end and tapering to a knife blade at the other. They make that long sharp end the bow, and you can imagine how these boiling currents spin it about. It has two oars, and sometimes four, and no rudder. You start to go to a given point and you run in fifty different directions before you get there. First one oar is backing water, and then the other; it is seldom that both are going ahead at once. This kind of boating is calculated to drive an impatient man mad in a week. The boatmen are the awkwardest, the stupidest, and the most unscientific on earth, without question.

Ashore, it was – well, it was an eternal circus. People were thicker than bees, in those narrow streets, and the men were dressed in all the outrageous, outlandish, idolatrous, extravagant, thunder-and-lightning costumes that ever a tailor with the delirium tremens and seven devils could conceive of. There was no freak in dress too crazy to be indulged in; no absurdity too absurd to be tolerated; no frenzy in ragged diabolism too fantastic to be attempted. No two men were dressed alike. It was a wild masquerade of all imaginable costumes – every struggling throng in every street was a dissolving view of stunning contrasts. Some patriarchs wore awful turbans, but the grand mass of the infidel horde wore the fiery red skull-cap they call a fez. All the remainder of the raiment they indulged in was utterly indescribable.

The shops here are mere coops, mere boxes, bath-rooms, closets – any thing you please to call them – on the first floor. The Turks sit cross-legged in them, and work and trade and smoke long pipes, and smell like – like Turks. That covers the ground. Crowding the narrow streets in front of them are beggars, who beg forever, yet never collect any thing; and wonderful cripples, distorted out of all semblance of humanity, almost; vagabonds driving laden asses; porters carrying dry-goods boxes as large as cottages on their backs; peddlers of grapes, hot corn, pumpkin seeds, and a hundred other things, yelling like fiends; and sleeping happily, comfortably, serenely, among the hurrying feet, are the famed dogs of Constantinople; drifting noiselessly about are squads of Turkish women, draped from chin to feet in flowing robes, and with snowy veils bound about their heads, that disclose only the eyes and a vague, shadowy notion of their features. Seen moving about, far away in the dim, arched aisles of the Great Bazaar, they look as the shrouded dead must have looked when they walked forth from their graves amid the storms and thunders and earthquakes that burst upon Calvary that awful night of the Crucifixion. A street in Constantinople is a picture which one ought to see once – not oftener.

And then there was the goose-rancher – a fellow who drove a hundred geese before him about the city, and tried to sell them. He had a pole ten feet long, with a crook in the end of it, and occasionally a goose would branch out from the flock and make a lively break around the corner, with wings half lifted and neck stretched to its utmost. Did the goose-merchant get excited? No. He took his pole and reached after that goose with unspeakable *sang froid* – took a hitch round his neck, and "yanked" him back to his place in the flock without an effort. He steered his geese with that stick as easily as another man would steer a yawl. A few hours afterward we saw him sitting on a stone at a corner, in the midst of the turmoil, sound asleep in the sun, with his geese squatting around him, or dodging out of the way of asses and men. We came by again, within the hour, and he was taking account of stock, to see whether any of his flock had strayed or been stolen. The way he did it was unique. He put the end of his stick within six or eight inches of a stone wall, and made the geese march in single file between it and the wall. He counted them as they went by. There was no dodging that arrangement.

If you want dwarfs – I mean just a few dwarfs for a curiosity – go to Genoa. If you wish to buy them by the gross, for retail, go to Milan. There are plenty of dwarfs all over Italy, but it did seem to me that in Milan the crop was luxuriant. If you would see a fair average style of assorted cripples, go to Naples, or travel through the Roman States. But if you would see the very heart and home of cripples and human monsters, both, go straight to Constantinople. A beggar in Naples who can show a foot which has all run into one horrible toe, with one shapeless nail on it, has a fortune – but such an exhibition as that would not provoke any notice in Constantinople. The man would starve. Who would pay any attention to attractions like his among the rare monsters that throng the bridges of the Golden Horn and display their deformities in the gutters of Stamboul? O, wretched impostor! How could he stand against the three-legged woman, and the man with his eye in his cheek? How would he blush in presence of the man with fingers on his elbow? Where would he hide himself when the dwarf with seven fingers on each hand, no upper lip, and his under-jaw gone, came down in his majesty? Bismillah! The cripples of Europe are a delusion and a fraud. The truly gifted flourish only in the by-ways of Pera and Stamboul.

That three-legged woman lay on the bridge, with her stock in trade so disposed as to command the most striking effect – one natural leg, and two long, slender, twisted ones with feet on them like somebody else's fore-arm. Then there was a man further along who had no eyes, and whose face was the color of a fly-blown beefsteak, and wrinkled and twisted like a lava-flow – and verily so tumbled and distorted were his features that no man could tell the wart that served him for a nose from his cheek bones. In Stamboul was a man with a prodigious head, an uncommonly long body, legs eight inches long and feet like snow-shoes. He traveled on those feet and his hands, and was as sway-backed as if the Colossus of Rhodes had been riding him. Ah, a beggar has to have exceedingly good points to make a living in Constantinople. A blue-faced man, who had nothing to offer except that he had been blown up in a mine, would be regarded as a rank impostor, and a mere damaged soldier on crutches would never make a cent. It would pay him to get a piece of his head taken off, and cultivate a wen like a carpet sack.

The Mosque of St. Sophia is the chief lion of Constantinople. You must get a firman and hurry there the first thing. We did that. We did not get a firman, but we took along four or five francs apiece, which is much the same thing.

I do not think much of the Mosque of St. Sophia. I suppose I lack appreciation. We will let it go at that. It is the rustiest old barn in heathendom. I believe all the interest that attaches to it comes from the fact that it was built for a Christian church and then turned into a mosque, without much alteration, by the Mohammedan conquerors of the land. They made me take off my boots and walk into the place in my stocking-feet. I caught cold, and got myself so stuck up with a complication of gums, slime and general corruption, that I wore out more than two thousand pair of boot-jacks getting my boots off that night, and even then some Christian hide peeled off with them. I abate not a single boot-jack.

St. Sophia is a colossal church, thirteen or fourteen hundred years old, and unsightly enough to be very, very much older. Its immense dome is said to be more wonderful than St. Peter's, but its dirt is much more wonderful than its dome, though they never mention it. The church has a hundred and seventy pillars in it, each a single piece, and all of costly marbles of various kinds, but they came from ancient temples at Baalbec, Heliopolis, Athens and Ephesus, and are battered, ugly and repulsive. They were a thousand years old when this church was new, and then the contrast must have been ghastly – if Justinian's architects did not trim them any. The inside of the dome is figured all over with a monstrous inscription in Turkish characters, wrought in gold mosaic, that looks as glaring as a circus bill; the pavements and the marble balustrades are all battered and dirty; the perspective is marred every where by a web of ropes that depend from the dizzy height of the dome, and suspend countless dingy, coarse oil lamps, and ostrich-eggs, six or seven feet above the floor. Squatting and sitting in groups, here and there and far and near, were ragged Turks reading books, hearing sermons, or receiving lessons like children, and in fifty places were more of the same sort bowing and straightening up, bowing again and getting down to kiss the earth, muttering prayers the while, and keeping up their gymnastics till they ought to have been tired, if they were not.

Every where was dirt, and dust, and dinginess, and gloom; every where were signs of a hoary antiquity, but with nothing touching or beautiful about it; every where were those groups of fantastic pagans; overhead the gaudy mosaics and the web of lamp-ropes – nowhere was there any thing to win one's love or challenge his admiration.

The people who go into ecstasies over St. Sophia must surely get them out of the guide-book (where every church is spoken of as being "considered by good judges to be the most marvelous structure, in many respects, that the world has ever seen.") Or else they are those old connoisseurs from the wilds of New Jersey who laboriously learn the difference between a fresco and a fire-plug and from that day forward feel privileged to void their critical bathos on painting, sculpture and architecture forever more.

We visited the Dancing Dervishes. There were twenty-one of them. They wore a long, light-colored loose robe that hung to their heels. Each in his turn went up to the priest (they were all within a large circular railing) and bowed profoundly and then went spinning away deliriously and took his appointed place in the circle, and continued to spin. When all had spun themselves to their places, they were about five or six feet apart – and so situated, the entire circle of spinning pagans spun itself three separate times around the room. It took twenty-five minutes to do it. They spun on the left foot, and kept themselves going by passing the right rapidly before it and digging it against the waxed floor. Some of them made incredible "time." Most of them spun around forty times in a minute, and one artist averaged about sixty-one times a minute, and kept it up during the whole twenty-five. His robe filled with air and stood out all around him like a balloon.

They made no noise of any kind, and most of them tilted their heads back and closed their eyes, entranced with a sort of devotional ecstasy. There was a rude kind of music, part of the time, but the musicians were not visible. None but spinners were allowed within the circle. A man had to either spin or stay outside. It was about as barbarous an exhibition as we have witnessed yet. Then sick persons came and lay down, and beside them women laid their sick children (one a babe at the breast,) and the patriarch of the Dervishes walked upon their bodies. He was supposed to cure their diseases by trampling upon their breasts or backs or standing on the back of their necks. This is well enough for a people who think all their affairs are made or marred by viewless spirits of the air – by giants, gnomes, and genii – and who still believe, to this day, all the wild tales in the Arabian Nights. Even so an intelligent missionary tells me.

We visited the Thousand and One Columns. I do not know what it was originally intended for, but they said it was built for a reservoir. It is situated in the centre of Constantinople. You go down a flight of stone steps in the middle of a barren place, and there you are. You are forty feet under ground, and in the midst of a perfect wilderness of tall, slender, granite columns, of Byzantine architecture. Stand where you would, or change your position as often as you pleased, you were always a centre from which radiated a dozen long archways and colonnades that lost themselves in distance and the sombre twilight of the place. This old dried-up reservoir is occupied by a few ghostly silk-spinners now, and one of them showed me a cross cut high up in one of the pillars. I suppose he meant me to understand that the institution was there before the Turkish occupation, and I thought he made a remark to that effect; but he must have had an impediment in his speech, for I did not understand him.

We took off our shoes and went into the marble mausoleum of the Sultan Mahmoud, the neatest piece of architecture, inside, that I have seen lately. Mahmoud's tomb was covered with a black velvet pall, which was elaborately embroidered with silver; it stood within a fancy silver railing; at the sides and corners were silver candlesticks that would weigh more than a hundred pounds, and they supported candles as large as a man's leg; on the top of the sarcophagus was a fez, with a handsome diamond ornament upon it, which an attendant said cost a hundred thousand pounds, and lied like a Turk when he said it. Mahmoud's whole family were comfortably planted around him.

We went to the great Bazaar in Stamboul, of course, and I shall not describe it further than to say it is a monstrous hive of little shops – thousands, I should say – all under one roof, and cut up into innumerable little blocks by narrow streets which are arched overhead. One street is devoted to a particular kind of merchandise, another to another, and so on. When you wish to buy a pair of shoes you have the swing of the whole street – you do not have to walk yourself down hunting stores in different localities. It is the same with silks, antiquities, shawls, etc. The place is crowded with people all the time, and as the gay-colored Eastern fabrics are lavishly displayed before every shop, the great Bazaar of Stamboul is one of the sights that are worth seeing. It is full of life, and stir, and business, dirt, beggars, asses, yelling peddlers, porters, dervishes, high-born Turkish female shoppers, Greeks, and weird-looking and weirdly dressed Mohammedans from the mountains and the far provinces–and the only solitary thing one does not smell when he is in the Great Bazaar, is something which smells good.

CHAPTER XXXIV

MOSQUES ARE PLENTY, churches are plenty, graveyards are plenty, but morals and whiskey are scarce. The Koran does not permit Mohammedans to drink. Their natural instincts do not permit them to be moral. They say the Sultan has eight hundred wives. This almost amounts to bigamy. It makes our cheeks burn with shame to see such a thing permitted here in Turkey. We do not mind it so much in Salt Lake, however.

Circassian and Georgian girls are still sold in Constantinople by their parents, but not publicly. The great slave marts we have all read so much about – where tender young girls were stripped for inspection, and criticized and discussed just as if they were horses at an agricultural fair – no longer exist. The exhibition and the sales are private now. Stocks are up, just at present, partly because of a brisk demand created by the recent return of the Sultan's suite from the courts of Europe; partly on account of an unusual abundance of breadstuffs, which leaves holders untortured by hunger and enables them to hold back for high prices; and partly because buyers are too weak to bear the market, while sellers are amply prepared to bull it. Under these circumstances, if the American metropolitan newspapers were published here in Constantinople, their next commercial report would read about as follows, I suppose:

SLAVE GIRL MARKET REPORT

"Best brands Circassians, crop of 1850, £200; 1852, £250; 1854, £300. Best brands Georgian, none in market; second quality, 1851, £180. Nineteen fair to middling Wallachian girls offered at £130 @ 150, but no takers; sixteen prime A 1 sold in small lots to close out – terms private.

"Sales of one lot Circassians, prime to good, 1852 to 1854, at £240 @ 242½, buyer 30; one forty-niner – damaged – at £23, seller ten, no deposit. Several Georgians, fancy brands, 1852, changed hands to fill orders. The Georgians now on hand are mostly last year's crop, which was unusually poor. The new crop is a little backward, but will be coming in shortly. As regards its quantity and quality, the accounts are most encouraging. In this connection we can safely say, also, that the new crop of Circassians is looking extremely well. His Majesty the Sultan has already sent in large orders for his new harem, which will be finished within a fortnight, and this has naturally strengthened the market and given Circassian stock a strong upward tendency. Taking advantage of the inflated market, many of our shrewdest operators are selling short. There are hints of a 'corner' on Wallachians.

"There is nothing new in Nubians. Slow sale.

"Eunuchs – None offering; however, large cargoes are expected from Egypt today."

I think the above would be about the style of the commercial report. Prices are pretty high now, and holders firm; but, two or three years ago, parents in a starving condition brought their young daughters down here and sold them for even twenty and thirty dollars, when they could do no better, simply to save themselves and the girls from dying of want. It is sad to think of so distressing a thing as this, and I for one am sincerely glad the prices are up again.

Commercial morals, especially, are bad. There is no gainsaying that. Greek, Turkish and Armenian morals consist only in attending church regularly on the appointed Sabbaths, and in breaking the ten commandments all the balance of the week. It comes natural to them to lie and cheat in the first place, and then they go on and improve on nature until they arrive at perfection. In recommending his son to a merchant as a valuable salesman, a father does not say he is a nice, moral, upright boy, and goes to Sunday School and is honest, but he says, "This boy is worth his weight in broad pieces of a hundred – for behold, he will cheat whomsoever hath dealings with him, and from the Euxine to the waters of Marmora there abideth not so gifted a liar!" How is that for a recommendation? The Missionaries tell me that they hear encomiums like that passed upon people every day. They say of a person they admire, "Ah, he is a charming swindler, and a most exquisite liar!"

Every body lies and cheats – every body who is in business, at any rate. Even foreigners soon have to come down to the custom of the country, and they do not buy and sell long in Constantinople till they lie and cheat like a Greek. I say like a Greek, because the Greeks are called the worst transgressors in this line. Several Americans long resident in Constantinople contend that most Turks are pretty trustworthy, but few claim that the Greeks have any virtues that a man can discover – at least without a fire assay.

I am half willing to believe that the celebrated dogs of Constantinople have been misrepresented – slandered. I have always been led to suppose that they were so thick in the streets that they blocked the way; that they moved about in organized companies, platoons and regiments, and took what they wanted by determined and ferocious assault; and that at night they drowned all other sounds with their terrible howlings. The dogs I see here can not be those I have read of.

I find them every where, but not in strong force. The most I have found together has been about ten or twenty. And night or day a fair proportion of them were sound asleep. Those that were not asleep always looked as if they wanted to be. I never saw such utterly wretched, starving, sad-visaged, broken-hearted looking curs in my life. It seemed a grim satire to accuse such brutes as these of taking things by force of arms. They hardly seemed to have strength enough or ambition enough to walk across the street – I do not know that I have seen one walk that far yet. They are mangy and bruised and mutilated, and often you see one with the hair singed off him in such wide and well defined tracts that he looks like a map of the new Territories. They are the sorriest beasts that breathe – the most abject – the most pitiful. In their faces is a settled expression of melancholy, an air of hopeless despondency. The hairless patches on a scalded dog are preferred by the fleas of Constantinople to a wider range on a healthier dog; and the exposed places suit the fleas exactly. I saw a dog of this kind start to nibble at a flea – a fly attracted his attention, and he made a snatch at him; the flea called for him once more, and that forever unsettled him; he looked sadly at his flea-pasture, then sadly looked at his bald spot. Then he heaved a sigh and dropped his head resignedly upon his paws. He was not equal to the situation.

The dogs sleep in the streets, all over the city. From one end of the street to the other, I suppose they will average about eight or ten to a block. Sometimes, of course, there are fifteen or twenty to a block. They do not belong to any body, and they seem to have no close personal friendships among each other. But they district the city themselves, and the dogs of each district, whether it be half a block in extent, or ten blocks, have to remain within its bounds. Woe to a dog if he crosses the line! His neighbors would snatch the balance of his hair off in a second. So it is said. But they don't look it.

They sleep in the streets these days. They are my compass – my guide. When I see the dogs sleep placidly on, while men, sheep, geese, and all moving things turn out and go around them, I know I am not in the great street where the hotel is, and must go further. In the Grand Rue the dogs have a sort of air of being on the look-out – an air born of being obliged to get out of the way of many carriages every day – and that expression one recognizes in a moment. It does not exist upon the face of any dog without the confines of that street. All others sleep placidly and keep no watch. They would not move, though the Sultan himself passed by.

In one narrow street (but none of them are wide) I saw three dogs lying coiled up, about a foot or two apart. End to end they lay, and so they just bridged the street neatly, from gutter to gutter. A drove of a hundred sheep came along. They stepped right over the dogs, the rear crowding the front, impatient to get on. The dogs looked lazily up, flinched a little when the impatient feet of the sheep touched their raw backs – sighed, and lay peacefully down again. No talk could be plainer than that. So some of the sheep jumped over them and others scrambled between, occasionally chipping a leg with their sharp hoofs, and when the whole flock had made the trip, the dogs sneezed a little, in the cloud of dust, but never budged their bodies an inch. I thought I was lazy, but I am a steam-engine compared to a Constantinople dog. But was not that a singular scene for a city of a million inhabitants?

These dogs are the scavengers of the city. That is their official position, and a hard one it is. However, it is their protection. But for their usefulness in partially cleansing these terrible streets, they would not be tolerated long. They eat any thing and every thing that comes in their way, from melon rinds and spoiled grapes up through all the grades and species of dirt and refuse to their own dead friends and relatives – and yet they are always lean, always hungry, always despondent. The people are loath to kill them – do not kill them, in fact. The Turks have an innate antipathy to taking the life of any dumb animal, it is said. But they do worse. They hang and kick and stone and scald these wretched creatures to the very verge of death, and then leave them to live and suffer.

Once a Sultan proposed to kill off all the dogs here, and did begin the work – but the populace raised such a howl of horror about it that the massacre was stayed. After a while, he proposed to remove them all to an island in the Sea of Marmora. No objection was offered, and a ship-load or so was taken away. But when it came to be known that somehow or other the dogs never got to the island, but always fell overboard in the night and perished, another howl was raised and the transportation scheme was dropped.

So the dogs remain in peaceable possession of the streets. I do not say that they do not howl at night, nor that they do not attack people who have not a red fez on their heads. I only say that it would be mean for *me* to accuse them of these unseemly things who have not seen them do them with my own eyes or heard them with my own ears.

I was a little surprised to see Turks and Greeks playing newsboy right here in the mysterious land where the giants and genii of the Arabian Nights once dwelt – where winged horses and hydra-headed dragons guarded enchanted castles – where Princes and Princesses flew through the air on carpets that obeyed a mystic talisman – where cities whose houses were made of precious stones sprang up in a night under the hand of the magician, and where busy marts were suddenly stricken with a spell and each citizen lay or sat, or stood with weapon raised or foot advanced, just as he was, speechless and motionless, till time had told a hundred years!

It was curious to see newsboys selling papers in so dreamy a land as that. And, to say truly, it is comparatively a new thing here. The selling of newspapers had its birth in Constantinople about a year ago, and was a child of the Prussian and Austrian war.

There is one paper published here in the English language – *The Levant Herald* – and there are generally a number of Greek and a few French papers rising and falling, struggling up and falling again. Newspapers are not popular with the Sultan's Government. They do not understand journalism. The proverb says, "The unknown is always great." To the court, the newspaper is a mysterious and rascally institution. They know what a pestilence is, because they have one occasionally that thins the people out at the rate of two thousand a day, and they regard a newspaper as a mild form of pestilence. When it goes astray, they suppress it – pounce upon it without warning, and throttle it. When it don't go astray for a long time, they get suspicious and throttle it anyhow, because they think it is hatching deviltry. Imagine the Grand Vizier in solemn council with the magnates of the realm, spelling his way through the hated newspaper, and finally delivering his profound decision: "This thing means mischief – it is too darkly, too suspiciously inoffensive – suppress it! Warn the publisher that we can not have this sort of thing: put the editor in prison!"

The newspaper business has its inconveniences in Constantinople. Two Greek papers and one French one were suppressed here within a few days of each other. No victories of the Cretans are allowed to be printed. From time to time the Grand Vizier sends a notice to the various editors that the Cretan insurrection is entirely suppressed, and although that editor knows better, he still has to print the notice. The *Levant Herald* is too fond of speaking praisefully of Americans to be popular with the Sultan, who does not relish our sympathy with the Cretans, and therefore that paper has to be particularly circumspect in order to keep out of trouble. Once the editor, forgetting the official notice in his paper that the Cretans were crushed out, printed a letter of a very different tenor, from the American Consul in Crete, and was fined two hundred and fifty dollars for it. Shortly he printed another from the same source and was imprisoned three months for his pains. I think I could get the assistant editorship of the *Levant Herald*, but I am going to try to worry along without it.

To suppress a paper here involves the ruin of the publisher, almost. But in Naples I think they speculate on misfortunes of that kind. Papers are suppressed there every day, and spring up the next day under a new name. During the ten days or a fortnight we staid there one paper was murdered and resurrected twice. The newsboys are smart there, just as they are elsewhere. They take advantage of popular weaknesses. When they find they are not likely to sell out, they approach a citizen mysteriously, and say in a low voice – "Last copy, sir: double price; paper just been suppressed!" The man buys it, of course, and finds nothing in it. They do say – I do not vouch for it – but they do say that men sometimes print a vast edition of a paper, with a ferociously seditious article in it, distribute it quickly among the newsboys, and clear out till the Government's indignation cools. It pays well. Confiscation don't amount to any thing. The type and presses are not worth taking care of.

There is only one English newspaper in Naples. It has seventy subscribers. The publisher is getting rich very deliberately – very deliberately indeed.

I never shall want another Turkish lunch. The cooking apparatus was in the little lunch room, near the bazaar, and it was all open to the street. The cook was slovenly, and so was the table, and it had no cloth on it. The fellow took a mass of sausage-meat and coated it round a wire and laid it on a charcoal fire to cook. When it was done, he laid it aside and a dog walked sadly in and nipped it. He smelt it first, and probably recognized the remains of a friend. The cook took it away from him and laid it before us. Jack said, "I pass" – he plays euchre sometimes – and we all passed in turn. Then the cook baked a broad, flat, wheaten cake, greased it well with the sausage, and started towards us with it. It dropped in the dirt, and he picked it up and polished it on his breeches, and laid it before us. Jack said, "I pass." We all passed. He put some eggs in a frying pan, and stood pensively prying slabs of meat from between his teeth with a fork. Then he used the fork to turn the eggs with – and brought them along. Jack said "Pass again." All followed suit. We did not know what to do, and so we ordered a new ration of sausage. The cook got out his wire, apportioned a proper amount of sausage-meat, spat it on his hands and fell to work! This time, with one accord, we all passed out. We paid and left. That is all I learned about Turkish lunches. A Turkish lunch is good, no doubt, but it has its little drawbacks.

When I think how I have been swindled by books of Oriental travel, I want a tourist for breakfast. For years and years I have dreamed of the wonders of the Turkish bath; for years and years I have promised myself that I would yet enjoy one. Many and many a time, in fancy, I have lain in the marble bath, and breathed the slumbrous fragrance of Eastern spices that filled the air; then passed through a weird and complicated system of pulling and hauling, and drenching and scrubbing, by a gang of naked savages who loomed vast and vaguely through the steaming mists, like demons; then rested for a while on a divan fit for a king; then passed through another complex ordeal, and one more fearful than the first; and, finally, swathed in soft fabrics, been conveyed to a princely saloon and laid on a bed of eider down, where eunuchs, gorgeous of costume, fanned me while I drowsed and dreamed, or contentedly gazed at the rich hangings of the apartment, the soft carpets, the sumptuous furniture, the pictures, and drank delicious coffee, smoked the soothing narghili, and dropped, at the last, into tranquil repose, lulled by sensuous odors from unseen censers, by the gentle influence of the narghili's Persian tobacco, and by the music of fountains that counterfeited the pattering of summer rain.

That was the picture, just as I got it from incendiary books of travel. It was a poor, miserable imposture. The reality is no more like it than the Five Points are like the Garden of Eden. They received me in a great court, paved with marble slabs; around it were broad galleries, one above another, carpeted with seedy matting, railed with unpainted balustrades, and furnished with huge rickety chairs, cushioned with rusty old mattresses, indented with impressions left by the forms of nine successive generations of men who had reposed upon them. The place was vast, naked, dreary; its court a barn, its galleries stalls for human horses. The cadaverous, half-nude varlets that served in the establishment had nothing of poetry in their appearance, nothing of romance, nothing of Oriental splendor. They shed no entrancing odors – just the contrary. Their hungry eyes and their land forms continually suggested one glaring, unsentimental fact – they wanted what they term in California "a square meal."

I went into one of the racks and undressed. An unclean starveling wrapped a gaudy table-cloth about his loins, and hung a white rag over my shoulders. If I had had a tub then, it would have come natural to me to take in washing. I was then conducted down stairs into the wet, slippery court, and the first things that attracted my attention were my heels. My fall excited no comment. They expected it, no doubt. It belonged in the list of softening, sensuous influences peculiar to this home of Eastern luxury. It was softening enough, certainly, but its application was not happy. They now gave me a pair of wooden clogs – benches in miniature, with leather straps over them to confine my feet (which they would have done, only I do not wear No. 13s.) These things dangled uncomfortably by the straps when I lifted up my feet, and came down in awkward and unexpected places when I put them on the floor again, and sometimes turned sideways and wrenched my ankles out of joint. However, it was all Oriental luxury, and I did what I could to enjoy it.

They put me in another part of the barn and laid me on a stuffy sort of pallet, which was not made of cloth of gold, or Persian shawls, but was merely the unpretending sort of thing I have seen in the negro quarters of Arkansas. There was nothing whatever in this dim marble prison but five more of these biers. It was a very solemn place. I expected that the spiced odors of Araby were going to steal over my senses now, but they did not. A copper-colored skeleton, with a rag around him, brought me a glass decanter of water, with a lighted tobacco pipe in the top of it, and a pliant stem a yard long, with a brass mouth-piece to it.

It was the famous "narghili" of the East – the thing the Grand Turk smokes in the pictures. This began to look like luxury. I took one blast at it, and it was sufficient; the smoke went in a great volume down into my stomach, my lungs, even into the uttermost parts of my frame. I exploded one mighty cough, and it was as if Vesuvius had let go. For the next five minutes I smoked at every pore, like a frame house that is on fire on the inside. Not any more narghili for me. The smoke had a vile taste, and the taste of a thousand infidel tongues that remained on that brass mouthpiece was viler still. I was getting discouraged. Whenever, hereafter, I see the cross-legged Grand Turk smoking his narghili, in pretended bliss, on the outside of a paper of Connecticut tobacco, I shall know him for the shameless humbug he is.

This prison was filled with hot air. When I had got warmed up sufficiently to prepare me for a still warmer temperature, they took me where it was – into a marble room, wet, slippery and steamy, and laid me out on a raised platform in the centre. It was very warm. Presently my man sat me down by a tank of hot water, drenched me well, gloved his hand with a coarse mitten, and began to polish me all over with it. I began to smell disgreeably. The more he polished the worse I smelt. It was alarming. I said to him:

"I perceive that I am pretty far gone. It is plain that I ought to be buried without any unnecessary delay. Perhaps you had better go after my friends at once, because the weather is warm, and I can not 'keep' long."

He went on scrubbing and paid no attention. I soon saw that he was reducing my size. He bore hard on his mitten, and from under it rolled little cylinders, like maccaroni. It could not be dirt, for it was too white. He pared me down in this way for a long time. Finally I said:

"It is a tedious process. It will take hours to trim me to the size you want me; I will wait; go and borrow a jack-plane."

He paid no attention at all.

After a while he brought a basin, some soap, and something that seemed to be the tail of a horse. He made up a prodigious quantity of soap-suds, deluged me with them from head to foot, without warning me to shut my eyes, and then swabbed me viciously with the horse-tail. Then he left me there, a snowy statue of lather, and went away. When I got tired of waiting I went and hunted him up. He was propped against the wall, in another room, asleep. I woke him. He was not disconcerted. He took me back and flooded me with hot water, then turbaned my head, swathed me with dry table-cloths, and conducted me to a latticed chicken-coop in one of the galleries, and pointed to one of those Arkansas beds. I mounted it, and vaguely expected the odors of Araby again. They did not come.

The blank, unornamented coop had nothing about it of that oriental voluptuousness one reads of so much. It was more suggestive of the county hospital than any thing else. The skinny servitor brought a narghili, and I got him to take it out again without wasting any time about it. Then he brought the world-renowned Turkish coffee that poets have sung so rapturously for many generations, and I seized upon it as the last hope that was left of my old dreams of Eastern luxury. It was another fraud. Of all the unchristian beverages that ever passed my lips, Turkish coffee is the worst. The cup is small, it is smeared with grounds; the coffee is black, thick, unsavory of smell, and execrable in taste. The bottom of the cup has a muddy sediment in it half an inch deep. This goes down your throat, and portions of it lodge by the way, and produce a tickling aggravation that keeps you barking and coughing for an hour.

Here endeth my experience of the celebrated Turkish bath, and here also endeth my dream of the bliss the mortal revels in who passes through it. It is a malignant swindle. The man who enjoys it is qualified to enjoy any thing that is repulsive to sight or sense, and he that can invest it with a charm of poetry is able to do the same with any thing else in the world that is tedious, and wretched, and dismal, and nasty.

CHAPTER XXXV

WE LEFT A dozen passengers in Constantinople, and sailed through the beautiful Bosphorus and far up into the Black Sea. We left them in the clutches of the celebrated Turkish guide, "FAR-AWAY MOSES," who will seduce them into buying a ship-load of ottar of roses, splendid Turkish vestments, and all manner of curious things they can never have any use for. Murray's invaluable guide-books have mentioned Far-away Moses' name, and he is a made man. He rejoices daily in the fact that he is a recognized celebrity. However, we can not alter our established customs to please the whims of guides; we can not show partialities this late in the day. Therefore, ignoring this fellow's brilliant fame, and ignoring the fanciful name he takes such pride in, we called him Ferguson, just as we had done with all other guides. It has kept him in a state of smothered exasperation all the time. Yet we meant him no harm. After he has gotten himself up regardless of expense, in showy, baggy trowsers, yellow, pointed slippers, fiery fez, silken jacket of blue, voluminous waist-sash of fancy Persian stuff filled with a battery of silver-mounted horse-pistols, and has strapped on his terrible scimetar, he considers it an unspeakable humiliation to be called Ferguson. It can not be helped. All guides are Fergusons to us. We can not master their dreadful foreign names.

Sebastopol is probably the worst battered town in Russia or any where else. But we ought to be pleased with it, nevertheless, for we have been in no country yet where we have been so kindly received, and where we felt that to be Americans was a sufficient *visé* for our passports. The moment the anchor was down, the Governor of the town immediately dispatched an officer on board to inquire if he could be of any assistance to us, and to invite us to make ourselves at home in Sebastopol! If you know Russia, you know that this was a wild stretch of hospitality. They are usually so suspicious of strangers that they worry them excessively with the delays and aggravations incident to a complicated passport system. Had we come from any other country we could not have had permission to enter Sebastopol and leave again under three days – but as it was, we were at liberty to go and come when and where we pleased. Every body in Constantinople warned us to be very careful about our passports, see that they were strictly *en regle*, and never to mislay them for a moment: and they told us of numerous instances of Englishmen and others who were delayed days, weeks, and even months, in Sebastopol, on account of trifling informalities in their passports, and for which they were not to blame. I had lost my passport, and was traveling under my room mate's, who stayed behind in Constantinople to await our return. To read the description of him in that passport and then look at me, any man could see that I was no more like him than I am like Hercules. So I went into the harbor of Sebastopol with fear and trembling – full of a vague, horrible apprehension that I was going to be found out and hanged. But all that time my true passport had been floating gallantly overhead – and behold it was only our flag. They never asked us for any other.

We have had a great many Russian and English gentlemen and ladies on board to-day, and the time has passed cheerfully away. They were all happy-spirited people, and I never heard our mother tongue sound so pleasantly as it did when it fell from those English lips in this far-off land. I talked to the Russians a good deal, just to be friendly, and they talked to me from the same motive; I am sure that both enjoyed the conversation, but never a word of it either of us understood. I did most of my talking to those English people though, and I am sorry we can not carry some of them along with us.

We have gone whithersoever we chose, to-day, and have met with nothing but the kindest attentions. Nobody inquired whether we had any passports or not.

Several of the officers of the Government have suggested that we take the ship to a little watering-place thirty miles from here, and pay the Emperor of Russia a visit. He is rusticating there. These officers said they would take it upon themselves to insure us a cordial reception. They said if we would go, they would not only telegraph the Emperor, but send a special courier overland to announce our coming. Our time is so short, though, and more especially our coal is so nearly out, that we judged it best to forgo the rare pleasure of holding social intercourse with an Emperor.

Ruined Pompeii is in good condition compared to Sebastopol. Here, you may look in whatsoever direction you please, and your eye encounters scarcely any thing but ruin, ruin, ruin! – fragments of houses, crumbled walls, torn and ragged hills, devastation every where! It is as if a mighty earthquake had spent all its terrible forces upon this one little spot. For eighteen long months the storms of war beat upon the helpless town, and left it at last the saddest wreck that ever the sun has looked upon. Not one solitary house escaped unscathed – not one remained habitable, even. Such utter and complete ruin one could hardly conceive of. The houses had all been solid, dressed stone structures; most of them were ploughed through and through by cannon balls – unroofed and sliced down from eaves to foundation – and now a row of them, half a mile long, looks merely like an endless procession of battered chimneys. No semblance of a house remains in such as these. Some of the larger buildings had corners knocked off; pillars cut in two; cornices smashed; holes driven straight through the walls. Many of these holes are as round and as cleanly cut as if they had been made with an auger. Others are half pierced through, and the clean impression is there in the rock, as smooth and as shapely as if it were done in putty. Here and there a ball still sticks in a wall, and from it iron tears trickle down and discolor the stone.

The battle-fields were pretty close together. The Malakoff tower is on a hill which is right in the edge of the town. The Redan was within rifle-shot of the Malakoff; Inkerman was a mile away; and Balaklava removed but an hour's ride. The French trenches, by which they approached and invested the Malakoff were carried so close under its sloping sides that one might have stood by the Russian guns and tossed a stone into them. Repeatedly, during three terrible days, they swarmed up the little Malakoff hill, and were beaten back with terrible slaughter. Finally, they captured the place, and drove the Russians out, who then tried to retreat into the town, but the English had taken the Redan, and shut them off with a wall of flame; there was nothing for them to do but go back and retake the Malakoff or die under its guns. They did go back; they took the Malakoff and retook it two or three times, but their desperate valor could not avail, and they had to give up at last.

These fearful fields, where such tempests of death used to rage, are peaceful enough now; no sound is heard, hardly a living thing moves about them, they are lonely and silent – their desolation is complete.

There was nothing else to do, and so every body went to hunting relics. They have stocked the ship with them. They brought them from the Malakoff, from the Redan, Inkerman, Balaklava – every where. They have brought cannon balls, broken ramrods, fragments of shell – iron enough to freight a sloop. Some have even brought bones – brought them laboriously from great distances, and were grieved to hear the surgeon pronounce them only bones of mules and oxen. I knew Blucher would not lose an opportunity like this. He brought a sack full on board and was going for another. I prevailed upon him not to go. He has already turned his stateroom into a museum of worthless trumpery, which he has gathered up in his travels. He is labeling his trophies, now. I picked up one a while ago, and found it marked "Fragment of a Russian General." I carried it out to get a better light upon it – it was nothing but a couple of teeth and part of the jaw-bone of a horse. I said with some asperity:

"Fragment of a Russian General! This is absurd. Are you never going to learn any sense?"

He only said: "Go slow – the old woman won't know any different." [His aunt.]

This person gathers mementoes with a perfect recklessness, now-a-days; mixes them all up together, and then serenely labels them without any regard to truth, propriety, or even plausibility. I have found him breaking a stone in two, and labeling half of it "Chunk busted from the pulpit of Demosthenes," and the other half "Darnick from the Tomb of Abelard and Heloise." I have known him to gather up a handful of pebbles by the roadside, and bring them on board ship and label them as coming from twenty celebrated localities five hundred miles apart. I remonstrate against these outrages upon reason and truth, of course, but it does no good. I get the same tranquil, unanswerable reply every time:

"It don't signify – the old woman won't know any different."

Ever since we three or four fortunate ones made the midnight trip to Athens, it has afforded him genuine satisfaction to give every body in the ship a pebble from the Mars-hill where St. Paul preached. He got all those pebbles on the sea-shore, abreast the ship, but professes to have gathered them from one of our party. However, it is not of any use for me to expose the deception – it affords him pleasure, and does no harm to any body. He says he never expects to run out of mementoes of St. Paul as long as he is in reach of a sandbank. Well, he is no worse than others. I notice that all travelers supply deficiencies in their collections in the same way. I shall never have any confidence in such things again while I live.

CHAPTER XXXVI

WE HAVE GOT so far east, now – a hundred and fifty-five degrees of longitude from San Francisco – that my watch can not "keep the hang" of the time any more. It has grown discouraged, and stopped. I think it did a wise thing. The difference in time between Sebastopol and the Pacific coast is enormous. When it is six o'clock in the morning here, it is somewhere about week before last in California. We are excusable for getting a little tangled as to time. These distractions and distresses about the time have worried me so much that I was afraid my mind was so much affected that I never would have any appreciation of time again; but when I noticed how handy I was yet about comprehending when it was dinner-time, a blessed tranquillity settled down upon me, and I am tortured with doubts and fears no more.

Odessa is about twenty hours' run from Sebastopol, and is the most northerly port in the Black Sea. We came here to get coal, principally. The city has a population of one hundred and thirty-three thousand, and is growing faster than any other small city out of America. It is a free port, and is the great grain mart of this particular part of the world. Its roadstead is full of ships. Engineers are at work, now, turning the open roadstead into a spacious artificial harbor. It is to be almost inclosed by massive stone piers, one of which will extend into the sea over three thousand feet in a straight line.

I have not felt so much at home for a long time as I did when I "raised the hill" and stood in Odessa for the first time. It looked just like an American city; fine, broad streets, and straight as well; low houses (two or three stories,) wide, neat, and free from any quaintness of architectural ornamentation; locust trees bordering the sidewalks (they call them acacias;) a stirring, business-look about the streets and the stores; fast walkers; a familiar *new* look about the houses and every thing; yea, and a driving and smothering cloud of dust that was so like a message from our own dear native land that we could hardly refrain from shedding a few grateful tears and execrations in the old time-honored American way. Look up the street or down the street, this way or that way, we saw only America! There was not one thing to remind us that we were in Russia. We walked for some little distance, reveling in this home vision, and then we came upon a church and a hack-driver, and presto! the illusion vanished! The church had a slender-spired dome that rounded inward at its base, and looked like a turnip turned upside down, and the hackman seemed to be dressed in a long petticoat without any hoops. These things were essentially foreign, and so were the carriages – but every body knows about these things, and there is no occasion for my describing them.

We were only to stay here a day and a night and take in coal; we consulted the guide-books and were rejoiced to know that there were no sights in Odessa to see; and so we had one good, untrammeled holy-day on our hands, with nothing to do but idle about the city and enjoy ourselves. We sauntered through the markets and criticized the fearful and wonderful costumes from the back country; examined the populace as far as eyes could do it; and closed the entertainment with an ice-cream debauch. We do not get ice-cream every where, and so, when we do, we are apt to dissipate to excess. We never cared any thing about ice-cream at home, but we look upon it with a sort of idolatry now that it is so scarce in these red-hot climates of the East.

We only found two pieces of statuary, and this was another blessing. One was a bronze image of the Duc de Richelieu, grand-nephew of the splendid Cardinal. It stood in a spacious, handsome promenade, overlooking the sea, and from its base a vast flight of stone steps led down to the harbor – two hundred of them, fifty feet long, and a wide landing at the bottom of every twenty. It is a noble staircase, and from a distance the people toiling up it looked like insects. I mention this statue and this stairway because they have their story. Richelieu founded Odessa – watched over it with paternal care – labored with a fertile brain and a wise understanding for its best interests – spent his fortune freely to the same end – endowed it with a sound prosperity, and one which will yet make it one of the great cities of the Old World – built this noble stairway with money from his own private purse – and——. Well, the people for whom he had done so much, let him walk down these same steps, one day, unattended, old, poor, without a second coat to his back; and when, years afterwards, he died in Sebastopol in poverty and neglect, they called a meeting, subscribed liberally, and immediately erected this tasteful monument to his memory, and named a great street after him. It reminds me of what Robert Burns' mother said when they erected a stately monument to his memory: "Ah, Robbie, ye asked them for bread and they hae gi'en ye a stane."

The people of Odessa have warmly recommended us to go and call on the Emperor, as did the Sebastopolians. They have telegraphed his Majesty, and he has signified his willingness to grant us an audience. So we are getting up the anchors and preparing to sail to his watering-place. What a scratching around there will be, now! what a holding of important meetings and appointing of solemn committees! – and what a furbishing up of claw-hammer coats and white silk neck-ties! As this fearful ordeal we are about to pass through pictures itself to my fancy in all its dread sublimity, I begin to feel my fierce desire to converse with a genuine Emperor cooling down and passing away. What am I to do with my hands? What am I to do with my feet? What in the world am I to do with myself?

CHAPTER XL

THIS HAS BEEN a stirring day. The Superintendent of the railway put a train at our disposal, and did us the further kindness of accompanying us to Ephesus and giving to us his watchful care. We brought sixty scarcely perceptible donkeys in the freight cars, for we had much ground to go over. We have seen some of the most grotesque costumes, along the line of the railroad, that can be imagined. I am glad that no possible combination of words could describe them, for I might then be foolish enough to attempt it.

At ancient Ayassalook, in the midst of a forbidding desert, we came upon long lines of ruined aqueducts, and other remnants of architectural grandeur, that told us plainly enough we were nearing what had been a metropolis, once. We left the train and mounted the donkeys, along with our invited guests – pleasant young gentlemen from the officers' list of an American man-of-war.

The little donkeys had saddles upon them which were made very high in order that the rider's feet might not drag the ground. The preventative did not work well in the cases of our tallest pilgrims, however. There were no bridles – nothing but a single rope, tied to the bit. It was purely ornamental, for the donkey cared nothing for it. If he were drifting to starboard, you might put your helm down hard the other way, if it were any satisfaction to you to do it, but he would continue to drift to starboard all the same. There was only one process which could be depended on, and that was to get down and lift his rear around until his head pointed in the right direction, or take him under your arm and carry him to a part of the road which he could not get out of without climbing. The sun flamed down as hot as a furnace, and neck-scarfs, veils and umbrellas seemed hardly any protection; they served only to make the long procession look more than ever fantastic – for be it known the ladies were all riding astride because they could not stay on the shapeless saddles sidewise, the men were perspiring and out of temper, their feet were banging against the rocks, the donkeys were capering in every direction but the right one and being belabored with clubs for it, and every now and then a broad umbrella would suddenly go down out of the cavalcade, announcing to all that one more pilgrim had bitten the dust. It was a wilder picture than those solitudes had seen for many a day. No donkeys ever existed that were as hard to navigate as these, I think, or that had so many vile, exasperating instincts. Occasionally we grew so tired and breathless with fighting them that we had to desist, – and immediately the donkey would come down to a deliberate walk. This, with the fatigue, and the sun, would put a man asleep; and as soon as the man was asleep, the donkey would lie down. My donkey shall never see his boyhood's home again. He has lain down once too often. He must die.

We all stood in the vast theatre of ancient Ephesus, – the stone-benched amphitheatre I mean – and had our picture taken. We looked as proper there as we would look any where, I suppose. We do not embellish the general desolation of a desert much. We add what dignity we can to a stately ruin with our green umbrellas and jackasses, but it is little. However, we mean well.

I wish to say a brief word of the aspect of Ephesus.

On a high, steep hill, toward the sea, is a gray ruin of ponderous blocks of marble, wherein, tradition says, St. Paul was imprisoned eighteen centuries ago. From these old walls you have the finest view of the desolate scene where once stood Ephesus, the proudest city of ancient times, and whose Temple of Diana was so noble in design, and so exquisite of workmanship, that it ranked high in the list of the Seven Wonders of the World.

Behind you is the sea; in front is a level green valley, (a marsh, in fact,) extending far away among the mountains; to the right of the front view is the old citadel of Ayassalook, on a high hill; the ruined Mosque of the Sultan Selim stands near it in the plain, (this is built over the grave of St. John, and was formerly a Christian Church;) further toward you is the hill of Pion, around whose front is clustered all that remains of the ruins of Ephesus that still stand; divided from it by a narrow valley is the long, rocky, rugged mountain of Coressus. The scene is a pretty one, and yet desolate – for in that wide plain no man can live, and in it is no human habitation. But for the crumbling arches and monstrous piers and broken walls that rise from the foot of the hill of Pion, one could not believe that in this place once stood a city whose renown is older than tradition itself. It is incredible to reflect that things as familiar all over the world to-day as household words, belong in the history and in the shadowy legends of this silent, mournful solitude. We speak of Apollo and of Diana – they were born here; of the metamorphosis of Syrinx into a reed – it was done here; of the great god Pan – he dwelt in the caves of this hill of Coressus; of the Amazons – this was their best prized home; of Bacchus and Hercules – both fought the warlike women here; of the Cyclops – they laid the ponderous marble blocks of some of the ruins yonder; of Homer – this was one of his many birthplaces; of Cimon of Athens; of Alcibiades, Lysander, Agesilaus – they visited here; so did Alexander the Great; so did Hannibal and Antiochus, Scipio, Lucullus and Sylla; Brutus, Cassius, Pompey, Cicero, and Augustus; Antony was a judge in this place, and left his seat in the open court, while the advocates were speaking, to run after Cleopatra, who passed the door; from this city these two sailed on pleasure excursions, in galleys with silver oars and perfumed sails, and with companies of beautiful girls to serve them, and actors and musicians to amuse them; in days that seem almost modern, so remote are they from the early history of this city, Paul the Apostle preached the new religion here, and so did John, and here it is supposed the former was pitted against wild beasts, for in 1 Corinthians, xv. 32 he says:

> "If after the manner of men I have fought with beasts at Ephesus," &c.,

when many men still lived who had seen the Christ; here Mary Magdalen died, and here the Virgin Mary ended her days with John, albeit Rome has since judged it best to locate her grave elsewhere; six or seven hundred years ago – almost yesterday, as it were – troops of mail-clad Crusaders thronged the streets; and to come down to trifles, we speak of meandering streams, and find a new interest in a common word when we discover that the crooked river Meander, in yonder valley, gave it to our dictionary. It makes me feel as old as these dreary hills to look down upon these moss-hung ruins, this historic desolation. One may read the Scriptures and believe, but he can not go and stand yonder in the ruined theatre and in imagination people it again with the vanished multitudes who mobbed Paul's comrades there and shouted, with one voice, "Great is Diana of the Ephesians!" The idea of a shout in such a solitude as this almost makes one shudder.

It was a wonderful city, this Ephesus. Go where you will about these broad plains, you find the most exquisitely sculptured marble fragments scattered thick among the dust and weeds; and protruding from the ground, or lying prone upon it, are beautiful fluted columns of porphyry and all precious marbles; and at every step you find elegantly carved capitals and massive bases, and polished tablets engraved with Greek inscriptions. It is a world of precious relics, a wilderness of marred and mutilated gems. And yet what are these things to the wonders that lie buried here under the ground? At Constantinople, at Pisa, in the cities of Spain, are great mosques and cathedrals, whose grandest columns came from the temples and palaces of Ephesus, and yet one has only to scratch the ground here to match them. We shall never know what magnificence is, until this imperial city is laid bare to the sun.

The finest piece of sculpture we have yet seen and the one that impressed us most, (for we do not know much about art and can not easily work up ourselves into ecstasies over it,) is one that lies in this old theatre of Ephesus which St. Paul's riot has made so celebrated. It is only the headless body of a man, clad in a coat of mail, with a Medusa head upon the breast-plate, but we feel persuaded that such dignity and such majesty were never thrown into a form of stone before.

What builders they were, these men of antiquity! The massive arches of some of these ruins rest upon piers that are fifteen feet square and built entirely of solid blocks of marble, some of which are as large as a Saratoga trunk, and some the size of a boarding-house sofa. They are not shells or shafts of stone filled inside with rubbish, but the whole pier is a mass of solid masonry. Vast arches, that may have been the gates of the city, are built in the same way. They have braved the storms and sieges of three thousand years, and have been shaken by many an earthquake, but still they stand. When they dig alongside of them, they find ranges of ponderous masonry that are as perfect in every detail as they were the day those old Cyclopian giants finished them. An English Company is going to excavate Ephesus – and then!

And now am I reminded of –

THE LEGEND OF THE SEVEN SLEEPERS

In the Mount of Pion, yonder, is the Cave of the Seven Sleepers. Once upon a time, about fifteen hundred years ago, seven young men lived near each other in Ephesus, who belonged to the despised sect of the Christians. It came to pass that the good King Maximilianus, (I am telling this story for nice little boys and girls,) it came to pass, I say, that the good King Maximilianus fell to persecuting the Christians, and as time rolled on he made it very warm for them. So the seven young men said one to the other, let us get up and travel. And they got up and traveled. They tarried not to bid their fathers and mothers good-bye, or any friend they knew. They only took certain moneys which their parents had, and garments that belonged unto their friends, whereby they might remember them when far away; and they took also the dog Ketmehr, which was the property of their neighbor Malchus, because the beast did run his head into a noose which one of the young men was carrying carelessly, and they had not time to release him; and they took also certain chickens that seemed lonely in the neighboring coops, and likewise some bottles of curious liquors that stood near the grocer's window; and then they departed from the city. By-and-by they came to a marvelous cave in the Hill of Pion and entered into it and feasted, and presently they hurried on again. But they forgot the bottles of curious liquors, and left them behind. They traveled in many lands, and had many strange adventures. They were virtuous young men, and lost no opportunity that fell in their way to make their livelihood. Their motto was in these words, namely, "Procrastination is the thief of time." And so, whenever they did come upon a man who was alone, they said, Behold, this person hath the wherewithal – let us go through him. And they went through him. At the end of five years they had waxed tired of travel and adventure, and longed to revisit their old home again and hear the voices and see the faces that were dear unto their youth. Therefore they went through such parties as fell in their way where they sojourned at that time, and journeyed back toward Ephesus again. For the good King Maximilianus was become converted unto the new faith, and the Christians rejoiced because they were no longer persecuted. One day as the sun went down, they came to the cave in the Mount of Pion, and they said, each to his fellow, Let us sleep here, and go and feast and make merry with our friends when the morning cometh. And each of the seven lifted up his voice and said, It is a whiz. So they went in, and lo, where they had put them, there lay the bottles of strange liquors, and they judged that age had not impaired their excellence. Wherein the wanderers were right, and the heads of the same were level. So each of the young men drank six bottles, and behold they felt very tired, then, and lay down and slept soundly.

When they awoke, one of them, Johannes – surnamed Smithianus – said, We are naked. And it was so. Their raiment was all gone, and the money which they had gotten from a stranger whom they had proceeded through as they approached the city, was lying upon the ground, corroded and rusted and defaced. Likewise the dog Ketmehr was gone, and nothing save the brass that was upon his collar remained. They wondered much at these things. But they took the money, and they wrapped about their bodies some leaves, and came up to the top of the hill. Then were they perplexed. The wonderful temple of Diana was gone; many grand edifices they had never seen before stood in the city; men in strange garbs moved about the streets, and every thing was changed.

Johannes said, It hardly seems like Ephesus. Yet here is the great gymnasium; here is the mighty theatre, wherein I have seen seventy thousand men assembled; here is the Agora; there is the font where the sainted John the Baptist immersed the converts; yonder is the prison of the good St. Paul, where we all did use to go to touch the ancient chains that bound him and be cured of our distempers; I see the tomb of the disciple Luke, and afar off is the church wherein repose the ashes of the holy John, where the Christians of Ephesus go twice a year to gather the dust from the tomb, which is able to make bodies whole again that are corrupted by disease, and cleanse the soul from sin; but see how the wharves encroach upon the sea, and what multitudes of ships are anchored in the bay; see, also, how the city hath stretched abroad, far over the valley behind Pion, and even unto the walls of Ayassalook; and lo, all the hills are white with palaces and ribbed with colonnades of marble. How mighty is Ephesus become!

And wondering at what their eyes had seen, they went down into the city and purchased garments and clothed themselves. And when they would have passed on, the merchant bit the coins which they had given him, with his teeth, and turned them about and looked curiously upon them, and cast them upon his counter, and listened if they rang; and then he said, These be bogus. And they said, Depart thou to Hades, and went their way. When they were come to their houses, they recognized them, albeit they seemed old and mean; and they rejoiced, and were glad. They ran to the doors, and knocked, and strangers opened, and looked inquiringly upon them. And they said, with great excitement, while their hearts beat high, and the color in their faces came and went, Where is my father? Where is my mother? Where are Dionysius and Serapion, and Pericles, and Decius? And the strangers that opened said, We know not these. The Seven said, How, you know them not? How long have ye dwelt here, and whither are they gone that dwelt here before ye? And the strangers said, Ye play upon us with a jest, young men; we and our fathers have sojourned under these roofs these six generations; the names ye utter rot upon the tombs, and they that bore them have run their brief race, have laughed and sung, have borne the sorrows and the weariness that were allotted them, and are at rest; for nine-score years the summers have come and gone, and the autumn leaves have fallen, since the roses faded out of their cheeks and they laid them to sleep with the dead.

Then the seven young men turned them away from their homes, and the strangers shut the doors upon them. The wanderers marveled greatly, and looked into the faces of all they met, as hoping to find one that they knew; but all were strange, and passed them by and spake no friendly word. They were sore distressed and sad. Presently they spake unto a citizen and said, Who is King in Ephesus? And the citizen answered and said, Whence come ye that ye know not that great Laertius reigns in Ephesus? They looked one at the other, greatly perplexed, and presently asked again, Where, then, is the good King Maximilianus? The citizen moved him apart, as one who is afraid, and said, Verily these men be mad, and dream dreams, else would they know that the King whereof they speak is dead above two hundred years agone.

Then the scales fell from the eyes of the Seven, and one said, Alas, that we drank of the curious liquors. They have made us weary, and in dreamless sleep these two long centuries have we lain. Our homes are desolate, our friends are dead. Behold, the jig is up – let us die. And that same day went they forth and laid them down and died. And in that self-same day, likewise, the Seven-up did cease in Ephesus, for that the Seven that were up were down again, and departed and dead withal. And the names that be upon their tombs, even unto this time, are Johannes Smithianus, Trumps, Gift, High, and Low, Jack, and The Game. And with the sleepers lie also the bottles wherein were once the curious liquors; and upon them is writ, in ancient letters, such words as these – names of heathen gods of olden time, perchance: Rumpunch, Jinsling, Egnog.

Such is the story of the Seven Sleepers, (with slight variations,) and I know it is true, because I have seen the cave myself.

Really, so firm a faith had the ancients in this legend, that as late as eight or nine hundred years ago, learned travelers held it in superstitious fear. Two of them record that they ventured into it, but ran quickly out again, not daring to tarry lest they should fall asleep and outlive their great grand-children a century or so. Even at this day the ignorant denizens of the neighboring country prefer not to sleep in it.

CHAPTER XLIV

THE NEXT DAY was an outrage upon men and horses both. It was another thirteen-hour stretch (including an hour's "nooning.") It was over the barrenest chalk-hills and through the baldest canons that even Syria can show. The heat quivered in the air every where. In the canons we almost smothered in the baking atmosphere. On high ground, the reflection from the chalk-hills was blinding. It was cruel to urge the crippled horses, but it had to be done in order to make Damascus Saturday night. We saw ancient tombs and temples of fanciful architecture carved out of the solid rock high up in the face of precipices above our heads, but we had neither time nor strength to climb up there and examine them. The terse language of my notebook will answer for the rest of this day's experiences:

> "Broke camp at 7 A.M., and made a ghastly trip through the Zeb Dana valley and the rough mountains – horses limping and that Arab screech-owl that does most of the singing and carries the water-skins, always a thousand miles ahead, of course, and no water to drink – will he *never* die? Beautiful stream in a chasm, lined thick with pomegranate, fig, olive and quince orchards, and nooned an hour at the celebrated Baalam's Ass Fountain of Figia, second in size in Syria, and the coldest water out of Siberia – guide-books do not say Baalam's ass ever drank there – somebody been imposing on the pilgrims, may be. Bathed in it – Jack and I. Only a second – ice-water. It is the principal source of the Abana river – only one-half mile down to where it joins. Beautiful place – giant trees all around – *so* shady and cool, if one could keep awake – vast stream gushes straight out from under the mountain in a torrent. Over it is a very ancient ruin, with no known history – supposed to have been for the worship of the deity of the fountain or Baalam's ass or somebody. Wretched nest of human vermin about the fountain – rags, dirt, sunken cheeks, pallor of sickness, sores, projecting bones, dull, aching misery in their eyes and ravenous hunger speaking from every eloquent fibre and muscle from head to foot. How they sprang upon a bone, how they crunched the bread we gave them! Such as these to swarm about one and watch every bite he takes, with greedy looks, and swallow unconsciously every time he swallows, as if they half fancied the precious morsel went down their own throats – hurry up the caravan! – I never shall enjoy a meal in this distressful country. To think of eating three times every day under *such* circumstances for three weeks yet – it is worse punishment than riding all day in the sun. There are sixteen starving babies from one to six years old in the party, and their legs are no larger than broom handles. Left the fountain at 1 P.M. (the

fountain took us at least two hours out of our way,) and reached Mahomet's lookout perch, over Damascus, in time to get a good long look before it was necessary to move on. Tired? Ask of the winds that far away with fragments strewed the sea."

As the glare of day mellowed into twilight, we looked down upon a picture which is celebrated all over the world. I think I have read about four hundred times that when Mahomet was a simple camel-driver he reached this point and looked down upon Damascus for the first time, and then made a certain renowned remark. He said man could enter only one paradise; he preferred to go to the one above. So he sat down there and feasted his eyes upon the earthly paradise of Damascus, and then went away without entering its gates. They have erected a tower on the hill to mark the spot where he stood.

Damascus *is* beautiful from the mountain. It is beautiful even to foreigners accustomed to luxuriant vegetation, and I can easily understand how unspeakably beautiful it must be to eyes that are only used to the God-forsaken barrenness and desolation of Syria. I should think a Syrian would go wild with ecstasy when such a picture bursts upon him for the first time.

From his high perch, one sees before him and below him, a wall of dreary mountains, shorn of vegetation, glaring fiercely in the sun; it fences in a level desert of yellow sand, smooth as velvet and threaded far away with fine lines that stand for roads, and dotted with creeping mites we know are camel-trains and journeying men; right in the midst of the desert is spread a billowy expanse of green foliage; and nestling in its heart sits the great white city, like an island of pearls and opals gleaming out of a sea of emeralds. This is the picture you see spread far below you, with distance to soften it, the sun to glorify it, strong contrasts to heighten the effects, and over it and about it a drowsing air of repose to spiritualize it and make it seem rather a beautiful estray from the mysterious worlds we visit in dreams than a substantial tenant of our coarse, dull globe. And when you think of the leagues of blighted, blasted, sandy, rocky, sun-burnt, ugly, dreary, infamous country you have ridden over to get here, you think it is the most beautiful, beautiful picture that ever human eyes rested upon in all the broad universe! If I were to go to Damascus again, I would camp on Mahomet's hill about a week, and then go away. There is no need to go inside the walls. The Prophet was wise without knowing it when he decided not to go down into the paradise of Damascus.

There is an honored old tradition that the immense garden which Damascus stands in was the Garden of Eden, and modern writers have gathered up many chapters of evidence tending to show that it really was the Garden of Eden, and that the rivers Pharpar and Abana are the "two rivers" that watered Adam's Paradise. It may be so, but it is not paradise now, and one would be as happy outside of it as he would be likely to be within. It is so crooked and cramped and dirty that one can not realize that he is in the splendid city he saw from the hill-top. The gardens are hidden by high mud-walls, and the paradise is become a very sink of pollution and uncomeliness. Damascus has plenty of clear, pure water in it, though, and this is enough, of itself, to make an Arab think it beautiful and blessed. Water is scarce in blistered Syria. We run railways by our large cities in America; in Syria they curve the roads so as to make them run by the meagre little puddles they call "fountains," and which are not found oftener on a journey than every four hours. But the "rivers" of Pharpar and Abana of Scripture (mere creeks,) run through Damascus, and so every house and every garden have their sparkling fountains and rivulets of water. With her forest of foliage and her abundance of water, Damascus must be a wonder of wonders to the Bedouin from the deserts. Damascus is simply an oasis – that is what it is. For four thousand years its waters have not gone dry or its fertility failed. Now we can understand why the city has existed so long. It could not die. So long as its waters remain to it away out there in the midst of that howling desert, so long will Damascus live to bless the sight of the tired and thirsty wayfarer.

> "Though old as history itself, thou art fresh as the breath of spring, blooming as thine own rose-bud, and fragrant as thine own orange flower, O Damascus, pearl of the East!"

Damascus dates back anterior to the days of Abraham, and is the oldest city in the world. It was founded by Uz, the grandson of Noah. "The early history of Damascus is shrouded in the mists of a hoary antiquity." Leave the matters written of in the first eleven chapters of the Old Testament out, and no recorded event has occurred in the world but Damascus was in existence to receive the news of it. Go back as far as you will into the vague past, there was always a Damascus. In the writings of every century for more than four thousand years, its name has been mentioned and its praises sung. To Damascus, years are only moments, decades are only flitting trifles of time. She measures time, not by days and months and years, but by the empires she has seen rise, and prosper and crumble to ruin. She is a type of immortality. She saw the foundations of Baalbec, and Thebes, and Ephesus laid; she saw these villages grow into mighty cities, and amaze the world with their grandeur – and she has lived to see them desolate, deserted, and given over to the owls and the bats. She saw the Israelitish empire exalted, and she saw it annihilated. She saw Greece rise, and flourish two thousand years, and die. In her old age she saw Rome built; she saw it overshadow the world with its power; she saw it perish. The few hundreds of years of Genoese and Venetian might and splendor were, to grave old Damascus, only a trifling scintillation hardly worth remembering. Damascus has seen all that has ever occurred on earth, and still she lives. She has looked upon the dry bones of a thousand empires, and will see the tombs of a thousand more before she dies. Though another claims the name, old Damascus is by right the Eternal City.

We reached the city gates just at sundown. They do say that one can get into any walled city of Syria, after night, for bucksheesh, except Damascus. But Damascus, with its four thousand years of respectability in the world, has many old fogy notions. There are no street lamps there, and the law compels all who go abroad at night to carry lanterns, just as was the case in old days, when heroes and heroines of the Arabian Nights walked the streets of Damascus, or flew away toward Bagdad on enchanted carpets.

It was fairly dark a few minutes after we got within the wall, and we rode long distances through wonderfully crooked streets, eight to ten feet wide, and shut in on either side by the high mud-walls of the gardens. At last we got to where lanterns could be seen flitting about here and there, and knew we were in the midst of the curious old city. In a little narrow street, crowded with our pack-mules and with a swarm of uncouth Arabs, we alighted, and through a kind of a hole in the wall entered the hotel. We stood in a great flagged court, with flowers and citron trees about us, and a huge tank in the centre that was receiving the waters of many pipes. We crossed the court and entered the rooms prepared to receive four of us. In a large marble-paved recess between the two rooms was a tank of clear, cool water, which was kept running over all the time by the streams that were pouring into it from half a dozen pipes. Nothing, in this scorching, desolate land could look so refreshing as this pure water flashing in the lamp-light; nothing could look so beautiful, nothing could sound so delicious as this mimic rain to ears long unaccustomed to sounds of such a nature. Our rooms were large, comfortably furnished, and even had their floors clothed with soft, cheerful-tinted carpets. It was a pleasant thing to see a carpet again, for if there is any thing drearier than the tomb-like, stone-paved parlors and bed-rooms of Europe and Asia, I do not know what it is. They make one think of the grave all the time. A very broad, gaily caparisoned divan, some twelve or fourteen feet long, extended across one side of each room, and opposite were single beds with spring mattresses. There were great looking-glasses and marble-top tables. All this luxury was as grateful to systems and senses worn out with an exhausting day's travel, as it was unexpected – for one can not tell what to expect in a Turkish city of even a quarter of a million inhabitants.

I do not know, but I think they used that tank between the rooms to draw drinking water from; that did not occur to me, however, until I had dipped my baking head far down into its cool depths. I thought of it then, and superb as the bath was, I was sorry I had taken it, and was about to go and explain to the landlord. But a finely curled and scented poodle dog frisked up and nipped the calf of my leg just then, and before I had time to think, I had soused him to the bottom of the tank, and when I saw a servant coming with a pitcher I went off and left the pup trying to climb out and not succeeding very well. Satisfied revenge was all I needed to make me perfectly happy, and when I walked in to supper that first night in Damascus I was in that condition. We lay on those divans a long time, after supper, smoking narghilies and long-stemmed chibouks, and talking about the dreadful ride of the day, and I knew then what I had sometimes known before – that it is worth while to get tired out, because one so enjoys resting afterward.

In the morning we sent for donkeys. It is worthy of note that we had to *send* for these things. I said Damascus was an old fossil, and she is. Any where else we would have been assailed by a clamorous army of donkey-drivers, guides, peddlers and beggars – but in Damascus they so hate the very sight of a foreign Christian that they want no intercourse whatever with him; only a year or two ago, his person was not always safe in Damascus streets. It is the most fanatical Mohammedan purgatory out of Arabia. Where you see one green turban of a Hadji elsewhere (the honored sign that my lord has made the pilgrimage to Mecca,) I think you will see a dozen in Damascus. The Damascenes are the ugliest, wickedest-looking villains we have seen. All the veiled women we had seen yet, nearly, left their eyes exposed, but numbers of these in Damascus completely hid the face under a close-drawn black veil that made the woman look like a mummy. If ever we caught an eye exposed it was quickly hidden from our contaminating Christian vision; the beggars actually passed us by without demanding bucksheesh; the merchants in the bazaars did not hold up their goods and cry out eagerly, "Hey, John!" or "Look this, Howajji!" On the contrary, they only scowled at us and said never a word.

The narrow streets swarmed like a hive with men and women in strange Oriental costumes, and our small donkeys knocked them right and left as we plowed through them, urged on by the merciless donkey-boys. These persecutors run after the animals, shouting and goading them for hours together; they keep the donkey in a gallop always, yet never get tired themselves or fall behind. The donkeys fell down and spilt us over their heads occasionally, but there was nothing for it but to mount and hurry on again. We were banged against sharp corners, loaded porters, camels, and citizens generally; and we were so taken up with looking out for collisions and casualties that we had no chance to look about us at all. We rode half through the city and through the famous "street which is called Straight" without seeing any thing, hardly. Our bones were nearly knocked out of joint, we were wild with excitement, and our sides ached with the jolting we had suffered. I do not like riding in the Damascus street cars.

We were on our way to the reputed house of Judas and Ananias. About eighteen or nineteen hundred years ago, Saul, a native of Tarsus, was particularly bitter against the new sect called Christians, and he left Jerusalem and started across the country on a furious crusade against them. He went forth "breathing threatenings and slaughter against the disciples of the Lord."

> "And as he journeyed, he came near Damascus, and suddenly there shined round about him a light from heaven:
>
> "And he fell to the earth and heard a voice saying unto him, 'Saul, Saul, why persecutest thou me?'

"And when he knew that it was Jesus that spoke to him he trembled, and was astonished, and said, 'Lord, what wilt thou have me do?'"

He was told to arise and go into the ancient city and one would tell him what to do. In the meantime his soldiers stood speechless and awe-stricken, for they heard the mysterious voice but saw no man. Saul rose up and found that that fierce supernatural light had destroyed his sight, and he was blind, so "they led him by the hand and brought him to Damascus." He was converted.

Paul lay three days, blind, in the house of Judas, and during that time he neither ate nor drank.

There came a voice to a citizen of Damascus, named Ananias, saying, "Arise, and go into the street which is called Straight, and inquire at the house of Judas, for one called Saul, of Tarsus; for behold, he prayeth."

Ananias did not wish to go at first, for he had heard of Saul before, and he had his doubts about that style of a "chosen vessel" to preach the gospel of peace. However, in obedience to orders, he went into the "street called Straight" (how he ever found his way into it, and after he did, how he ever found his way out of it again, are mysteries only to be accounted for by the fact that he was acting under Divine inspiration.) He found Paul and restored him, and ordained him a preacher; and from this old house we had hunted up in the street which is miscalled Straight, he had started out on that bold missionary career which he prosecuted till his death. It was not the house of the disciple who sold the Master for thirty pieces of silver. I make this explanation in justice to Judas, who was a far different sort of man from the person just referred to. A very different style of man, and lived in a very good house. It is a pity we do not know more about him.

I have given, in the above paragraphs, some more information for people who will not read Bible history until they are defrauded into it by some such method as this. I hope that no friend of progress and education will obstruct or interfere with my peculiar mission.

The street called Straight is straighter than a corkscrew, but not as straight as a rainbow. St. Luke is careful not to commit himself; he does not say it is the street which *is* straight, but the "street which is *called* Straight." It is a fine piece of irony; it is the only facetious remark in the Bible, I believe. We traversed the street called Straight a good way, and then turned off and called at the reputed house of Ananias. There is small question that a part of the original house is there still; it is an old room twelve or fifteen feet under ground, and its masonry is evidently ancient. If Ananias did not live there in St. Paul's time, somebody else did, which is just as well. I took a drink out of Ananias' well, and singularly enough, the water was just as fresh as if the well had been dug yesterday.

We went out toward the north end of the city to see the place where the disciples let Paul down over the Damascus wall at dead of night – for he preached Christ so fearlessly in Damascus that the people sought to kill him, just as they would to-day for the same offense, and he had to escape and flee to Jerusalem.

Then we called at the tomb of Mahomet's children and at a tomb which purported to be that of St. George who killed the dragon, and so on out to the hollow place under a rock where Paul hid during his flight till his pursuers gave him up; and to the mausoleum of the five thousand Christians who were massacred in Damascus in 1861 by the Turks. They say those narrow streets ran blood for several days, and that men, women and children were butchered indiscriminately and left to rot by hundreds all through the Christian quarter; they say, further, that the stench was dreadful. All the Christians who could get away fled from the city, and the Mohammedans would not defile their hands by burying the "infidel dogs." The thirst for blood extended to the high lands of Hermon and Anti-Lebanon, and in a short time twenty-five thousand more Christians were massacred and their possessions laid waste. How they hate a Christian in Damascus! – and pretty much all over Turkeydom as well. And how they will pay for it when Russia turns her guns upon them again!

It is soothing to the heart to abuse England and France for interposing to save the Ottoman Empire from the destruction it has so richly deserved for a thousand years. It hurts my vanity to see these pagans refuse to eat of food that has been cooked for us; or to eat from a dish we have eaten from; or to drink from a goat-skin which we have polluted with our Christian lips, except by filtering the water through a rag which they put over the mouth of it or through a sponge! I never disliked a Chinaman as I do these degraded Turks and Arabs, and when Russia is ready to war with them again, I hope England and France will not find it good breeding or good judgment to interfere.

In Damascus they think there are no such rivers in all the world as their little Abana and Pharpar. The Damascenes have always thought that way. In 2 Kings, chapter v., Naaman boasts extravagantly about them. That was three thousand years ago. He says: "Are not Abana and Pharpar, rivers of Damascus, better than all the waters of Israel? May I not wash in them and be clean?" But some of my readers have forgotten who Naaman was, long ago. Naaman was the commander of the Syrian armies. He was the favorite of the king and lived in great state. "He was a mighty man of valor, but he was a leper." Strangely enough, the house they point out to you now as his, has been turned into a leper hospital, and the inmates expose their horrid deformities and hold up their hands and beg for buck-sheesh when a stranger enters.

One can not appreciate the horror of this disease until he looks upon it in all its ghastliness, in Naaman's ancient dwelling in Damascus. Bones all twisted out of shape, great knots protruding from face and body, joints decaying and dropping away – horrible!

CHAPTER XLV

THE LAST TWENTY-FOUR hours we staid in Damascus I lay prostrate with a violent attack of cholera, or cholera morbus, and therefore had a good chance and a good excuse to lie there on that wide divan and take an honest rest. I had nothing to do but listen to the pattering of the fountains and take medicine and throw it up again. It was dangerous recreation, but it was pleasanter than traveling in Syria. I had plenty of snow from Mount Hermon, and as it would not stay on my stomach, there was nothing to interfere with my eating it – there was always room for more. I enjoyed myself very well. Syrian travel has its interesting features, like travel in any other part of the world, and yet to break your leg or have the cholera adds a welcome variety to it.

We left Damascus at noon and rode across the plain a couple of hours, and then the party stopped a while in the shade of some fig trees to give me a chance to rest. It was the hottest day we had seen yet – the sun-flames shot down like the shafts of fire that stream out before a blow-pipe; the rays seemed to fall in a steady deluge on the head and pass downward like rain from a roof. I imagined I could distinguish between the floods of rays – I thought I could tell when each flood struck my head, when it reached my shoulders, and when the next one came. It was terrible. All the desert glared so fiercely that my eyes were swimming in tears all the time. The boys had white umbrellas heavily lined with dark green. They were a priceless blessing. I thanked fortune that I had one, too, notwithstanding it was packed up with the baggage and was ten miles ahead. It is madness to travel in Syria without an umbrella. They told me in Beirout (these people who always gorge you with advice) that it was madness to travel in Syria without an umbrella. It was on this account that I got one.

But, honestly, I think an umbrella is a nuisance any where when its business is to keep the sun off. No Arab wears a brim to his fez, or uses an umbrella, or any thing to shade his eyes or his face, and he always looks comfortable and proper in the sun. But of all the ridiculous sights I ever have seen, our party of eight is the most so – they do cut such an outlandish figure. They travel single file; they all wear the endless white rag of Constantinople wrapped round and round their hats and dangling down their backs; they all wear thick green spectacles, with side-glasses to them; they all hold white umbrellas, lined with green, over their heads; without exception their stirrups are too short – they are the very worst gang of horsemen on earth; their animals to a horse trot fearfully hard – and when they get strung out one after the other; glaring straight ahead and breathless; bouncing high and out of turn, all along the line; knees well up and stiff, elbows flapping like a rooster's that is going to crow, and the long file of umbrellas popping convulsively up and down – when one sees this outrageous picture exposed to the light of day, he is amazed that the gods don't get out their thunderbolts and destroy them off the face of the earth! I do – I wonder at it. I wouldn't let any such caravan go through a country of mine.

And when the sun drops below the horizon and the boys close their umbrellas and put them under their arms, it is only a variation of the picture, not a modification of its absurdity.

But may be you can not see the wild extravagance of my panorama. You could if you were here. Here, you feel all the time just as if you were living about the year 1200 before Christ – or back to the patriarchs – or forward to the New Era. The scenery of the Bible is about you – the customs of the patriarchs are around you – the same people, in the same flowing robes, and in sandals, cross your path – the same long trains of stately camels go and come – the same impressive religious solemnity and silence rest upon the desert and the mountains that were upon them in the remote ages of antiquity, and behold, intruding upon a scene like this, comes this fantastic mob of green-spectacled Yanks, with their flapping elbows and bobbing umbrellas! It is Daniel in the lion's den with a green cotton umbrella under his arm, all over again.

My umbrella is with the baggage, and so are my green spectacles – and there they shall stay. I will not use them. I will show some respect for the eternal fitness of things. It will be bad enough to get sun-struck, without looking ridiculous into the bargain. If I fall, let me fall bearing about me the semblance of a Christian, at least.

Three or four hours out from Damascus we passed the spot where Saul was so abruptly converted, and from this place we looked back over the scorching desert, and had our last glimpse of beautiful Damascus, decked in its robes of shining green. After night-fall we reached our tents, just outside of the nasty Arab village of Jonesborough. Of course the real name of the place is El something or other, but the boys still refuse to recognize the Arab names or try to pronounce them. When I say that that village is of the usual style, I mean to insinuate that all Syrian villages within fifty miles of Damascus are alike – so much alike that it would require more than human intelligence to tell wherein one differed from another. A Syrian village is a hive of huts one story high (the height of a man,) and as square as a dry-goods box; it is mud-plastered all over, flat roof and all, and generally white-washed after a fashion. The same roof often extends over half the town, covering many of the *streets*, which are generally about a yard wide. When you ride through one of these villages at noonday, you first meet a melancholy dog, that looks up at you and silently begs that you won't run over him, but he does not offer to get out of the way; next you meet a young boy without any clothes on, and he holds out his hand and says "Bucksheesh!" – he don't really expect a cent, but then he learned to say that before he learned to say mother, and now he can not break himself of it; next you meet a woman with a black veil drawn closely over her face, and her bust exposed; finally, you come to several sore-eyed children and children in all stages of mutilation and decay; and sitting humbly in the dust, and all fringed with filthy rags, is a poor devil whose arms and legs are gnarled and twisted like grape-vines. These are all the people you are likely to see. The balance of the population are asleep within doors, or abroad tending goats in the plains and on the hill-sides. The village is built on some consumptive little watercourse, and about it is a little fresh-looking vegetation. Beyond this charmed circle, for miles on every side, stretches a weary desert of sand and gravel, which produces a gray bunchy shrub like sage-brush. A Syrian village is the sorriest sight in the world, and its surroundings are eminently in keeping with it.

I would not have gone into this dissertation upon Syrian villages but for the fact that Nimrod, the Mighty Hunter of Scriptural notoriety, is buried in Jonesborough, and I wished the public to know about how he is located. Like Homer, he is said to be buried in many other places, but this is the only true and genuine place his ashes inhabit.

When the original tribes were dispersed, more than four thousand years ago, Nimrod and a large party traveled three or four hundred miles, and settled where the great city of Babylon afterwards stood. Nimrod built that city. He also began to build the famous Tower of Babel, but circumstances over which he had no control put it out of his power to finish it. He ran it up eight stories high, however, and two of them still stand, at this day – a colossal mass of brickwork, rent down the centre by earthquakes, and seared and vitrified by the lightnings of an angry God. But the vast ruin will still stand for ages, to shame the puny labors of these modern generations of men. Its huge compartments are tenanted by owls and lions, and old Nimrod lies neglected in this wretched village, far from the scene of his grand enterprise.

We left Jonesborough very early in the morning, and rode forever and forever and forever, it seemed to me, over parched deserts and rocky hills, hungry, and with no water to drink. We had drained the goat-skins dry in a little while. At noon we halted before the wretched Arab town of El Yuba Dam, perched on the side of a mountain, but the dragoman said if we applied there for water we would be attacked by the whole tribe, for they did not love Christians. We had to journey on. Two hours later we reached the foot of a tall isolated mountain, which is crowned by the crumbling castle of Banias, the stateliest ruin of that kind on earth, no doubt. It is a thousand feet long and two hundred wide, all of the most symmetrical, and at the same time the most ponderous masonry. The massive towers and bastions are more than thirty feet high, and have been sixty. From the mountain's peak its broken turrets rise above the groves of ancient oaks and olives, and look wonderfully picturesque. It is of such high antiquity that no man knows who built it or when it was built. It is utterly inaccessible, except in one place, where a bridle-path winds upward among the solid rocks to the old portcullis. The horses' hoofs have bored holes in these rocks to the depth of six inches during the hundreds and hundreds of years that the castle was garrisoned. We wandered for three hours among the chambers and crypts and dungeons of the fortress, and trod where the mailed heels of many a knightly Crusader had rang, and where Phenician heroes had walked ages before them.

We wondered how such a solid mass of masonry could be affected even by an earthquake, and could not understand what agency had made Banias a ruin; but we found the destroyer, after a while, and then our wonder was increased tenfold. Seeds had fallen in crevices in the vast walls; the seeds had sprouted; the tender, insignificant sprouts had hardened; they grew larger and larger, and by a steady, imperceptible pressure forced the great stones apart, and now are bringing sure destruction upon a giant work that has even mocked the earthquakes to scorn! Gnarled and twisted trees spring from the old walls every where, and beautify and overshadow the gray battlements with a wild luxuriance of foliage.

From these old towers we looked down upon a broad, far-reaching green plain, glittering with the pools and rivulets which are the sources of the sacred river Jordan. It was a grateful vision, after so much desert.

And as the evening drew near, we clambered down the mountain, through groves of the Biblical oaks of Bashan, (for we were just stepping over the border and entering the long-sought Holy Land,) and at its extreme foot, toward the wide valley, we entered this little execrable village of Banias and camped in a great grove of olive trees near a torrent of sparkling water whose banks are arrayed in fig trees, pomegranates and oleanders in full leaf. Barring the proximity of the village, it is a sort of paradise.

The very first thing one feels like doing when he gets into camp, all burning up and dusty, is to hunt up a bath. We followed the stream up to where it gushes out of the mountain side, three hundred yards from the tents, and took a bath that was so icy that if I did not know this was the main source of the sacred river, I would expect harm to come of it. It was bathing at noonday in the chilly source of the Abana, "River of Damascus," that gave me the cholera, so Dr. B. said. However, it generally does give me the cholera to take a bath.

The incorrigible pilgrims have come in with their pockets full of specimens broken from the ruins. I wish this vandalism could be stopped. They broke off fragments from Noah's tomb; from the exquisite sculptures of the temples of Baalbec; from the houses of

Judas and Ananias, in Damascus; from the tomb of Nimrod the Mighty Hunter in Jonesborough; from the worn Greek and Roman inscriptions set in the hoary walls of the Castle of Banias; and now they have been hacking and chipping these old arches here that Jesus looked upon in the flesh. Heaven protect the Sepulchre when this tribe invades Jerusalem!

The ruins here are not very interesting. There are the massive walls of a great square building that was once the citadel; there are many ponderous old arches that are so smothered with debris that they barely project above the ground; there are heavy-walled sewers through which the crystal brook of which Jordan is born still runs; in the hillside are the substructions of a costly marble temple that Herod the Great built here – patches of its handsome mosaic floors still remain; there is a quaint old stone bridge that was here before Herod's time, may be; scattered every where, in the paths and in the woods, are Corinthian capitals, broken porphyry pillars, and little fragments of sculpture; and up yonder in the precipice where the fountain gushes out, are well-worn Greek inscriptions over niches in the rock where in ancient times the Greeks, and after them the Romans, worshipped the sylvan god Pan. But trees and bushes grow above many of these ruins now; the miserable huts of a little crew of filthy Arabs are perched upon the broken masonry of antiquity, the whole place has a sleepy, stupid, rural look about it, and one can hardly bring himself to believe that a busy, substantially built city once existed here, even two thousand years ago. The place was nevertheless the scene of an event whose effects have added page after page and volume after volume to the world's history. For in this place Christ stood when he said to Peter:

> "Thou art Peter; and upon this rock will I build my church, and the gates of hell shall not prevail against it. And I will give unto thee the keys of the Kingdom of Heaven; and whatsoever thou shalt bind on earth shall be bound in heaven, and whatsoever thou shalt loose on earth shall be loosed in heaven."

On those little sentences have been built up the mighty edifice of the Church of Rome; in them lie the authority for the imperial power of the Popes over temporal affairs, and their godlike power to curse a soul or wash it white from sin. To sustain the position of "the only true Church," which Rome claims was thus conferred upon her, she has fought and labored and struggled for many a century, and will continue to keep herself busy in the same work to the end of time. The memorable words I have quoted give to this ruined city about all the interest it possesses to people of the present day.

It seems curious enough to us to be standing on ground that was once actually pressed by the feet of the Saviour. The situation is suggestive of a reality and a tangibility that seem at variance with the vagueness and mystery and ghostliness that one naturally attaches to the character of a god. I can not comprehend yet that I am sitting where a god has stood, and looking upon the brook and the mountains which that god looked upon, and am surrounded by dusky men and women whose ancestors saw him, and even talked with him, face to face, and carelessly, just as they would have done with any other stranger. I can not comprehend this; the gods of my understanding have been always hidden in clouds and very far away.

This morning, during breakfast, the usual assemblage of squalid humanity sat patiently without the charmed circle of the camp and waited for such crumbs as pity might bestow upon their misery. There were old and young, brown-skinned and yellow. Some of the men were tall and stalwart, (for one hardly sees any where such splendid-looking men as here in the East,) but all the women and children looked worn and sad, and distressed with hunger. They reminded me much of Indians, did these people. They had but little clothing, but such as they had was fanciful in character and fantastic in its arrangement. Any little absurd gew-gaw or gimcrack they had they disposed in such a way as to make it attract attention most readily. They sat in silence, and with tireless patience watched our every motion with that vile, uncomplaining impoliteness which is so truly Indian, and which makes a white man so nervous and uncomfortable and savage that he wants to exterminate the whole tribe.

These people about us had other peculiarities, which I have noticed in the noble red man, too: they were infested with vermin, and the dirt had caked on them till it amounted to bark.

The little children were in a pitiable condition – they all had sore eyes, and were otherwise afflicted in various ways. They say that hardly a native child in all the East is free from sore eyes, and that thousands of them go blind of one eye or both every year. I think this must be so, for I see plenty of blind people every day, and I do not remember seeing any children that hadn't sore eyes. And, would you suppose that an American mother could sit for an hour, with her child in her arms, and let a hundred flies roost upon its eyes all that time undisturbed? I see that every day. It makes my flesh creep.

Yesterday we met a woman riding on a little jackass, and she had a little child in her arms; honestly, I thought the child had goggles on as we approached, and I wondered how its mother could afford so much style. But when we drew near, we saw that the goggles were nothing but a camp meeting of flies assembled around each of the child's eyes, and at the same time there was a detachment prospecting its nose. The flies were happy, the child was contented, and so the mother did not interfere.

As soon as the tribe found out that we had a doctor in our party, they began to flock in from all quarters. Dr. B., in the charity of his nature, had taken a child from a woman who sat near by, and put some sort of a wash upon its diseased eyes. That woman went off and started the whole nation, and it was a sight to see them swarm! The lame, the halt, the blind, the leprous – all the distempers that are bred of indolence, dirt, and iniquity – were represented in the Congress in ten minutes, and still they came! Every woman that had a sick baby brought it along, and every woman that hadn't, borrowed one. What reverent and what worshipping looks they bent upon that dread, mysterious power, the Doctor! They watched him take his phials out; they watched him measure the particles of white powder; they watched him add drops of one precious liquid, and drops of another; they lost not the slightest movement; their eyes were riveted upon him with a fascination that nothing could distract. I believe they thought he was gifted like a god. When each individual got his portion of medicine, his eyes were radiant with joy – notwithstanding by nature they are a thankless and impassive race – and upon his face was written the unquestioning faith that nothing on earth could prevent the patient from getting well now.

Christ knew how to preach to these simple, superstitious, disease-tortured creatures: He healed the sick. They flocked to our poor human doctor this morning when the fame of what he had done to the sick child went abroad in the land, and they worshipped him with their eyes while they did not know as yet whether there was virtue in his simples or not. The ancestors of these – people precisely like them in color, dress, manners, customs, simplicity – flocked in vast multitudes after Christ, and when they saw Him make the afflicted whole with a word, it is no wonder they worshipped Him. No wonder His deeds were the talk of the nation. No wonder the multitude that followed Him was so great that at one time – thirty miles from here – they had to let a sick man down through the roof because no approach could be made to the door; no wonder his audiences were so great at Galilee that He had to preach from a ship removed a little distance from the shore; no wonder that even in the desert places about Bethsaida, five thousand invaded His solitude, and He had to feed them by a miracle or else see them suffer for their confiding faith and devotion; no wonder when there was a great commotion in a city in those days, one neighbor explained it to another in words to this effect: "They say that Jesus of Nazareth is come!"

Well, as I was saying, the doctor distributed medicine as long as he had any to distribute, and his reputation is mighty in Galilee this day. Among his patients was the child of the Sheik's daughter – for even this poor, ragged handful of sores and sin has its royal Sheik – a poor old mummy that looked as if he would be more at home in a poor-house than in the Chief Magistracy of this tribe of hopeless, shirtless savages. The princess – I mean the Sheik's daughter – was only thirteen or fourteen years old, and had a very sweet face and a pretty one. She was the only Syrian female we have seen yet who was not so sinfully ugly that she couldn't smile after ten o'clock Saturday night without breaking the Sabbath. Her child was a hard specimen, though – there wasn't enough of it to make a pie, and the poor little thing looked so pleadingly up at all who came near it (as if it had an idea that now was its chance or never,) that we were filled with compassion which was genuine and not put on.

But this last new horse I have got is trying to break his neck over the tent-ropes, and I shall have to go out and anchor him. Jericho and I have parted company. The new horse is not much to boast of, I think. One of his hind legs bends the wrong way, and the other one is as straight and stiff as a tent-pole. Most of his teeth are gone, and he is as blind as a bat. His nose has been broken at some time or other, and is arched like a culvert now. His under lip hangs down like a camel's, and his ears are chopped off close to his head. I had some trouble at first to find a name for him, but I finally concluded to call him Baalbec, because he is such a magnificent ruin. I can not keep from talking about my horses, because I have a very long and tedious journey before me, and they naturally occupy my thoughts about as much as matters of apparently much greater importance.

We satisfied our pilgrims by making those hard rides from Baalbec to Damascus, but Dan's horse and Jack's were so crippled we had to leave them behind and get fresh animals for them. The dragoman says Jack's horse died. I swapped horses with Mohammed, the kingly-looking Egyptian who is our Ferguson's lieutenant. By Ferguson I mean our dragoman Abraham, of course. I did not take this horse on account of his personal appearance, but because I have not seen his back. I do not wish to see it. I have seen the backs of all the other horses, and found most of them covered with dreadful saddle-boils which I know have not been washed or doctored for years. The idea of riding all day long over such ghastly inquisitions of torture is sickening. My horse must be like the others, but I have at least the consolation of not knowing it to be so.

I hope that in future I may be spared any more sentimental praises of the Arab's idolatry of his horse. In boyhood I longed to be an Arab of the desert and have a beautiful mare, and call her Selim or Benjamin or Mohammed, and feed her with my own hands, and let her come into the tent, and teach her to caress me and look fondly upon me with her great tender eyes; and I wished that a stranger might come at such a time and offer me a hundred thousand dollars for her, so that I could do like the other Arabs – hesitate, yearn for the money, but overcome by my love for my mare, at last say, "Part with thee, my beautiful one! Never with my life! Away, tempter, I scorn thy gold!" and then bound into the saddle and speed over the desert like the wind!

But I recall those aspirations. If these Arabs be like the other Arabs, their love for their beautiful mares is a fraud. These of my acquaintance have no love for their horses, no sentiment of pity for them, and no knowledge of how to treat them or care for them. The Syrian saddle-blanket is a quilted mattress two or three inches thick. It is never removed from the horse, day or night. It gets full of dirt and hair, and becomes soaked with sweat. It is bound to breed sores. These pirates never think of washing a horse's back. They do not shelter the horses in the tents, either; they must stay out and take the weather as it comes. Look at poor cropped and dilapidated "Baalbec," and weep for the sentiment that has been wasted upon the Selims of romance!

CHAPTER LII

THE NARROW CANON in which Nablous, or Shechem, is situated, is under high cultivation, and the soil is exceedingly black and fertile. It is well watered, and its affluent vegetation gains effect by contrast with the barren hills that tower on either side. One of these hills is the ancient Mount of Blessings and the other the Mount of Curses; and wise men who seek for fulfillments of prophecy think they find here a wonder of this kind – to wit, that the Mount of Blessings is strangely fertile and its mate as strangely unproductive. We could not see that there was really much difference between them in this respect, however.

Shechem is distinguished as one of the residences of the patriarch Jacob, and as the seat of those tribes that cut themselves loose from their brethren of Israel and propagated doctrines not in conformity with those of the original Jewish creed. For thousands of years this clan have dwelt in Shechem under strict *tabu*, and having little commerce or fellowship with their fellow-men of any religion or nationality. For generations they have not numbered more than one or two hundred, but they still adhere to their ancient faith and maintain their ancient rites and ceremonies. Talk of family and old descent! Princes and nobles pride themselves upon lineages they can trace back some hundreds of years. What is this trifle to this handful of old first families of Shechem, who can name their fathers straight back without a flaw for thousands – straight back to a period so remote that men reared in a country where the days of two hundred years ago are called "ancient" times grow dazed and bewildered when they try to comprehend it! Here is respectability for you – here is "family" – here is high descent worth talking about. This sad, proud remnant of a once mighty community still hold themselves aloof from all the world; they still live as their fathers lived, labor as their fathers labored, think as they did, feel as they did, worship in the same place, in sight of the same landmarks, and in the same quaint, patriarchal way their ancestors did more than thirty centuries ago. I found myself gazing at any straggling scion of this strange race with a riveted fascination, just as one would stare at a living mastodon, or a megatherium that had moved in the gray dawn of creation and seen the wonders of that mysterious world that was before the flood.

Carefully preserved among the sacred archives of this curious community is a MSS. copy of the ancient Jewish law, which is said to be the oldest document on earth. It is written on vellum, and is some four or five thousand years old. Nothing but bucksheesh can purchase a sight. Its fame is somewhat dimmed in these latter days, because of the doubts so many authors of Palestine travels have felt themselves privileged to cast upon it. Speaking of this MSS. reminds me that I procured from the high-priest of this ancient Samaritan community, at great expense, a secret document of still higher antiquity and far more extraordinary interest, which I propose to publish as soon as I have finished translating it.

Joshua gave his dying injunction to the children of Israel at Shechem, and buried a valuable treasure secretly under an oak tree there about the same time. The superstitious Samaritans have always been afraid to hunt for it. They believe it is guarded by fierce spirits invisible to men.

About a mile and a half from Shechem we halted at the base of Mount Ebal, before a little square area, inclosed by a high stone wall, neatly white-washed. Across one end of this inclosure is a tomb built after the manner of the Moslems. It is the tomb of Joseph. No truth is better authenticated than this.

When Joseph was dying he prophesied that exodus of the Israelites from Egypt which occurred four hundred years afterwards. At the same time he exacted of his people an oath that when they journeyed to the land of Canaan, they would bear his bones with them and bury them in the ancient inheritance of his fathers. The oath was kept.

> "And the bones of Joseph, which the children of Israel brought up out of Egypt, buried they in Shechem, in a parcel of ground which Jacob bought of the sons of Hamor the father of Shechem, for a hundred pieces of silver."

Few tombs on earth command the veneration of so many races and men of divers creeds as this of Joseph. "Samaritan and Jew, Moslem and Christian alike, revere it, and honor it with their visits. The tomb of Joseph, the dutiful son, the affectionate, forgiving brother, the virtuous man, the wise Prince and ruler. Egypt felt his influence – the world knows his history."

In this same "parcel of ground" which Jacob bought of the sons of Hamor for a hundred pieces of silver, is Jacob's celebrated well. It is cut in the solid rock, and is nine feet square and ninety feet deep. The name of this unpretending hole in the ground, which one might pass by and take no notice of, is as familiar as household words to even the children and the peasants of many a far-off country. It is more famous than the Parthenon; it is older than the Pyramids.

It was by this well that Jesus sat and talked with a woman of that strange, antiquated Samaritan community I have been speaking of, and told her of the mysterious water of life. As descendants of old English nobles still cherish in the traditions of their houses how that this king or that king tarried a day with some favored ancestor three hundred years ago, no doubt the descendants of the woman of Samaria, living there in Shechem, still refer with pardonable vanity to this conversation of their ancestor, held some little time gone by, with the Messiah of the Christians. It is not likely that they under-value a distinction such as this. Samaritan nature is human nature, and human nature remembers contact with the illustrious, always.

For an offense done to the family honor, the sons of Jacob exterminated all Shechem once.

We left Jacob's Well and traveled till eight in the evening, but rather slowly, for we had been in the saddle nineteen hours, and the horses were cruelly tired. We got so far ahead of the tents that we had to camp in an Arab village, and sleep on the ground. We could have slept in the largest of the houses; but there were some little drawbacks: it was populous with vermin, it had a dirt floor, it was in no respect cleanly, and there was a family of goats in the only bed-room, and two donkeys in the parlor. Outside there were no inconveniences, except that the dusky, ragged, earnest-eyed villagers of both sexes and all ages grouped themselves on their haunches all around us, and discussed us and criticized us with noisy tongues till midnight. We did not mind the noise, being tired, but, doubtless, the reader is aware that it is almost an impossible thing to go to sleep when you know that people are looking at you. We went to bed at ten, and got up again at two and started once more. Thus are people persecuted by dragomen, whose sole ambition in life is to get ahead of each other.

About daylight we passed Shiloh, where the Ark of the Covenant rested three hundred years, and at whose gates good old Eli fell down and "brake his neck" when the messenger, riding hard from the battle, told him of the defeat of his people, the death of his sons, and, more than all, the capture of Israel's pride, her hope, her refuge, the ancient Ark her forefathers brought with them out of Egypt. It is little wonder that under circumstances like these he fell down and brake his neck. But Shiloh had no charms for us. We were so cold that there was no comfort but in motion, and so drowsy we could hardly sit upon the horses.

After a while we came to a shapeless mass of ruins, which still bears the name of Beth-el. It was here that Jacob lay down and had that superb vision of angels flitting up and down a ladder that reached from the clouds to earth, and caught glimpses of their blessed home through the open gates of Heaven.

The pilgrims took what was left of the hallowed ruin, and we pressed on toward the goal of our crusade, renowned Jerusalem.

The further we went the hotter the sun got, and the more rocky and bare, repulsive and dreary the landscape became. There could not have been more fragments of stone strewn broadcast over this part of the world, if every ten square feet of the land had been occupied by a separate and distinct stonecutter's establishment for an age. There was hardly a tree or a shrub any where. Even the olive and the cactus, those fast friends of a worthless soil, had almost deserted the country. No landscape exists that is more tiresome to the eye than that which bounds the approaches to Jerusalem. The only difference between the roads and the surrounding country, perhaps, is that there are rather more rocks in the roads than in the surrounding country.

We passed Ramah, and Beroth, and on the right saw the tomb of the prophet Samuel, perched high upon a commanding eminence. Still no Jerusalem came in sight. We hurried on impatiently. We halted a moment at the ancient Fountain of Beira, but its stones, worn deeply by the chins of thirsty animals that are dead and gone centuries ago, had no interest for us – we longed to see Jerusalem. We spurred up hill after hill, and usually began to stretch our necks minutes before we got to the top – but disappointment always followed: – more stupid hills beyond – more unsightly landscape – no Holy City.

At last, away in the middle of the day, ancient bits of wall and crumbling arches began to line the way – we toiled up one more hill, and every pilgrim and every sinner swung his hat on high! Jerusalem!

Perched on its eternal hills, white and domed and solid, massed together and hooped with high gray walls, the venerable city gleamed in the sun. So small! Why, it was no larger than an American village of four thousand inhabitants, and no larger than an ordinary Syrian city of thirty thousand. Jerusalem numbers only fourteen thousand people.

We dismounted and looked, without speaking a dozen sentences, across the wide intervening valley for an hour or more; and noted those prominent features of the city that pictures make familiar to all men from their school days till their death. We could recognize the Tower of Hippicus, the Mosque of Omar, the Damascus Gate, the Mount of Olives, the Valley of Jehoshaphat, the Tower of David, and the Garden of Gethsemane – and dating from these landmarks could tell very nearly the localities of many others we were not able to distinguish.

I record it here as a notable but not discreditable fact that not even our pilgrims wept. I think there was no individual in the party whose brain was not teeming with thoughts and images and memories invoked by the grand history of the venerable city that lay before us, but still among them all was no "voice of them that wept."

There was no call for tears. Tears would have been out of place. The thoughts Jerusalem suggests are full of poetry, sublimity, and more than all, dignity. Such thoughts do not find their appropriate expression in the emotions of the nursery.

Just after noon we entered these narrow, crooked streets, by the ancient and the famed Damascus Gate, and now for several hours I have been trying to comprehend that I am actually in the illustrious old city where Solomon dwelt, where Abraham held converse with the Deity, and where walls still stand that witnessed the spectacle of the Crucifixion.

CHAPTER LV

WE CAST UP the account. It footed up pretty fairly. There was nothing more at Jerusalem to be seen, except the traditional houses of Dives and Lazarus of the parable, the Tombs of the Kings, and those of the Judges; the spot where they stoned one of the disciples to death, and beheaded another; the room and the table made celebrated by the Last Supper; the fig tree that Jesus withered; a number of historical places about Gethsemane and the Mount of Olives, and fifteen or twenty others in different portions of the city itself.

We were approaching the end. Human nature asserted itself, now. Overwork and consequent exhaustion began to have their natural effect. They began to master the energies and dull the ardor of the party. Perfectly secure now, against failing to accomplish any detail of the pilgrimage, they felt like drawing in advance upon the holy-day soon to be placed to their credit. They grew a little lazy. They were late to breakfast and sat long at dinner. Thirty or forty pilgrims had arrived from the ship, by the short routes, and much swapping of gossip had to be indulged in. And in hot afternoons, they showed a strong disposition to lie on the cool divans in the hotel and smoke and talk about pleasant experiences of a month or so gone by – for even thus early do episodes of travel which were sometimes annoying, sometimes exasperating and full as often of no consequence at all when they transpired, begin to rise above the dead level of monotonous reminiscences and become shapely landmarks in one's memory. The fog-whistle, smothered among a million of trifling sounds, is not noticed a block away, in the city, but the sailor hears it far at sea, whither none of those thousands of trifling sounds can reach. When one is in Rome, all the domes are alike; but when he has gone away twelve miles, the city fades utterly from sight and leaves St. Peter's swelling above the level plain like an anchored balloon. When one is traveling in Europe, the daily incidents seem all alike; but when he has placed them all two months and two thousand miles behind him, those that were worthy of being remembered are prominent, and those that were really insignificant have vanished. This disposition to smoke, and idle and talk, was not well. It was plain that it must not be allowed to gain ground. A diversion must be tried, or demoralization would ensue. The Jordan, Jericho and the Dead Sea were suggested. The remainder of Jerusalem must be left unvisited, for a little while. The journey was approved at once. New life stirred in every pulse. In the saddle – abroad on the plains – sleeping in beds bounded only by the horizon: fancy was at work with these things in a moment. – It was painful to note how readily these town-bred men had taken to the free life of the camp and the desert. The nomadic instinct is a human instinct; it was born with Adam and transmitted through the patriarchs, and after thirty centuries of steady effort, civilization has not educated it entirely out of us yet. It has a charm which, once tasted, a man will yearn to taste again. The nomadic instinct can not be educated out of an Indian at all.

The Jordan journey being approved, our dragoman was notified.

At nine in the morning the caravan was before the hotel door and we were at breakfast. There was a commotion about the place. Rumors of war and bloodshed were flying every where. The lawless Bedouins in the Valley of the Jordan and the deserts down by the Dead Sea were up in arms, and were going to destroy all comers. They had had a battle with a troop of Turkish cavalry and defeated them; several men killed. They had shut up the inhabitants of a village and a Turkish garrison in an old fort near Jericho, and were besieging them. They had marched upon a camp of our excursionists by the Jordan, and the pilgrims only saved their lives by stealing away and flying to Jerusalem under whip and spur in the darkness of the night. Another of our parties had been fired on from an ambush and then attacked in the open day. Shots were fired on both sides. Fortunately there was no bloodshed. We spoke with the very pilgrim who had fired one of the shots, and learned from his own lips how, in this imminent deadly peril, only the cool courage of the pilgrims, their strength of numbers and imposing display of war material, had saved them from utter destruction. It was reported that the Consul had requested that no more of our pilgrims should go to the Jordan while this state of things lasted; and further, that he was unwilling that any more should go, at least without an unusually strong military guard. Here was trouble. But with the horses at the door and every body aware of what they were there for, what would *you* have done? Acknowledged that you were afraid, and backed shamefully out? Hardly. It would not be human nature, where there were so many women. You would have done as we did: said you were not afraid of a million Bedouins – and made your will and proposed quietly to yourself to take up an unostentatious position in the rear of the procession.

I think we must all have determined upon the same line of tactics, for it did seem as if we never would get to Jericho. I had a notoriously slow horse, but somehow I could not keep him in the rear, to save my neck. He was forever turning up in the lead. In such cases I trembled a little, and got down to fix my saddle. But it was not of any use. The others all got down to fix their saddles, too. I never saw such a time with saddles. It was the first time any of them had got out of order in three weeks, and now they had all broken down at once. I tried walking, for exercise – I had not had enough in Jerusalem searching for holy places. But it was a failure. The whole mob were suffering for exercise, and it was not fifteen minutes till they were all on foot and I had the lead again. It was very discouraging.

This was all after we got beyond Bethany. We stopped at the village of Bethany, an hour out from Jerusalem. They showed us the tomb of Lazarus. I had rather live in it than in any house in the town. And they showed us also a large "Fountain of Lazarus," and in the centre of the village the ancient dwelling of Lazarus. Lazarus appears to have been a man of property. The legends of the Sunday Schools do him great injustice; they give one the impression that he was poor. It is because they get him confused with that Lazarus who had no merit but his virtue, and virtue never has been as respectable as money. The house of Lazarus is a three-story edifice, of stone masonry, but the accumulated rubbish of ages has buried all of it but the upper story. We took candles and descended to the dismal cell-like chambers where Jesus sat at meat with Martha and Mary, and conversed with them about their brother. We could not but look upon these old dingy apartments with a more than common interest.

We had had a glimpse, from a mountain top, of the Dead Sea, lying like a blue shield in the plain of the Jordan, and now we were marching down a close, flaming, rugged, desolate defile, where no living creature could enjoy life, except, perhaps, a salamander. It was such a dreary, repulsive, horrible solitude! It was the "wilderness" where John preached, with camel's hair about his loins – raiment enough – but he never could have got his locusts and wild honey here. We were moping along down through this dreadful place, every man in the rear. Our guards – two gorgeous young Arab sheiks, with cargoes of swords, guns, pistols and daggers on board – were loafing ahead.

"Bedouins!"

Every man shrunk up and disappeared in his clothes like a mud-turtle. My first impulse was to dash forward and destroy the Bedouins. My second was to dash to the rear to see if there were any coming in that direction. I acted on the latter impulse. So did all the others. If any Bedouins had approached us, then, from that point of the compass, they would have paid dearly for their rashness. We all remarked that, afterwards. There would have been scenes of riot and bloodshed there that no pen could describe. I know that, because each man told what he would have done, individually; and such a medley of strange and unheard-of inventions of cruelty you could not conceive of. One man said he had calmly made up his mind to perish where he stood, if need be, but never yield an inch; he was going to wait, with deadly patience, till he could count the stripes upon the first Bedouin's jacket, and then count them and let him have it. Another was going to sit still till the first lance reached within an inch of his breast, and then dodge it and seize it. I forbear to tell what he was going to do to that Bedouin that owned it. It makes my blood run cold to think of it. Another was going to scalp such Bedouins as fell to his share, and take his bald-headed sons of the desert home with him alive for trophies. But the wild-eyed pilgrim rhapsodist was silent. His orbs gleamed with a deadly light, but his lips moved not. Anxiety grew, and he was questioned. If he had got a Bedouin, what would he have done with him – shot him?

He smiled a smile of grim contempt and shook his head. Would he have stabbed him? Another shake. Would he have quartered him – flayed him? More shakes. Oh! horror, what *would* he have done?

"Eat him!"

Such was the awful sentence that thundered from his lips. What was grammar to a desperado like that? I was glad in my heart that I had been spared these scenes of malignant carnage. No Bedouins attacked our terrible rear. And none attacked the front. The new-comers were only a reinforcement of cadaverous Arabs, in shirts and bare legs, sent far ahead of us to brandish rusty guns, and shout and brag, and carry on like lunatics, and thus scare away all bands of marauding Bedouins that might lurk about our path. What a shame it is that armed white Christians must travel under guard of vermin like this as a protection against the prowling vagabonds of the desert – those sanguinary outlaws who are always going to do something desperate, but never do it. I may as well mention here that on our whole trip we saw no Bedouins, and had no more use for an Arab guard than we could have had for patent leather boots and white kid gloves. The Bedouins that attacked the other parties of pilgrims so fiercely were provided for the occasion by the Arab guards of those parties, and shipped from Jerusalem for temporary service as Bedouins. They met together in full view of the pilgrims, after the battle, and took lunch, divided the bucksheesh extorted in the season of danger, and then accompanied the cavalcade home to the city! The nuisance of an Arab guard is one which is created by the Sheiks and the Bedouins together, for mutual profit, it is said, and no doubt there is a good deal of truth in it.

We visited the fountain the prophet Elisha sweetened (it is sweet yet;) where he remained some time and was fed by the ravens.

Ancient Jericho is not very picturesque as a ruin. When Joshua marched around it seven times, some three thousand years ago, and blew it down with his trumpet, he did the work so well and so completely that he hardly left enough of the city to cast a shadow. The curse pronounced against the rebuilding of it, has never been removed. One King, holding the curse in light estimation, made the attempt, but was stricken sorely for his presumption. Its site will always remain unoccupied; and yet it is one of the very best locations for a town we have seen in all Palestine.

At two in the morning they routed us out of bed – another piece of unwarranted cruelty – another stupid effort of our dragoman to get ahead of a rival. It was not two hours to the Jordan. However, we were dressed and under way before any one thought of looking to see what time it was, and so we drowsed on through the chill night air and dreamed of camp fires, warm beds, and other comfortable things.

There was no conversation. People do not talk when they are cold, and wretched, and sleepy. We nodded in the saddle, at times, and woke up with a start to find that the procession had disappeared in the gloom. Then there was energy and attention to business until its dusky outlines came in sight again. Occasionally the order was passed in a low voice down the line: "Close up – close up! Bedouins lurk here, every where!" What an exquisite shudder it sent shivering along one's spine!

We reached the famous river before four o'clock, and the night was so black that we could have ridden into it without seeing it. Some of us were in an unhappy frame of mind. We waited and waited for daylight, but it did not come. Finally we went away in the dark and slept an hour on the ground, in the bushes, and caught cold. It was a costly nap, on that account, but otherwise it was a paying investment because it brought unconsciousness of the dreary minutes and put us in a somewhat fitter mood for a first glimpse of the sacred river.

With the first suspicion of dawn, every pilgrim took off his clothes and waded into the dark torrent, singing:

"On Jordan's stormy banks I stand,
And cast a wistful eye
To Canaan's fair and happy land,
Where my possessions lie."

But they did not sing long. The water was so fearfully cold that they were obliged to stop singing and scamper out again. Then they stood on the bank shivering, and so chagrined and so grieved, that they merited honest compassion. Because another dream, another cherished hope, had failed. They had promised themselves all along that they would cross the Jordan where the Israelites crossed it when they entered Canaan from their long pilgrimage in the desert. They would cross where the twelve stones were placed in memory of that great event. While they did it they would picture to themselves that vast army of pilgrims marching through the cloven waters, bearing the hallowed ark of the covenant and shouting hosannahs, and singing songs of thanksgiving and praise. Each had promised himself that he would be the first to cross. They were at the goal of their hopes at last, but the current was too swift, the water was too cold!

It was then that Jack did them a service. With that engaging recklessness of consequences which is natural to youth, and so proper and so seemly, as well, he went and led the way across the Jordan, and all was happiness again. Every individual waded over, then, and stood upon the further bank. The water was not quite breast deep, any where. If it had been more, we could hardly have accomplished the feat, for the strong current would have swept us down the stream, and we would have been exhausted and drowned before reaching a place where we could make a landing. The main object compassed, the drooping, miserable party sat down to wait for the sun again, for all wanted to see the water as well as feel it. But it was too cold a pastime. Some cans were filled from the holy river, some canes cut from its banks, and then we mounted and rode reluctantly away to keep from freezing to death. So we saw the Jordan very dimly. The thickets of bushes that bordered its banks threw their shadows across its shallow, turbulent waters ("stormy," the hymn makes them, which is rather a complimentary stretch of fancy,) and we could not judge of the width of the stream by the eye. We knew by our wading experience, however, that many streets in America are double as wide as the Jordan.

Daylight came, soon after we got under way, and in the course of an hour or two we reached the Dead Sea. Nothing grows in the flat, burning desert around it but weeds and the Dead Sea apple the poets say is beautiful to the eye, but crumbles to ashes and dust when you break it. Such as we found were not handsome, but they were bitter to the taste. They yielded no dust. It was because they were not ripe, perhaps.

The desert and the barren hills gleam painfully in the sun, around the Dead Sea, and there is no pleasant thing or living creature upon it or about its borders to cheer the eye. It is a scorching, arid, repulsive solitude. A silence broods over the scene that is depressing to the spirits. It makes one think of funerals and death.

The Dead Sea is small. Its waters are very clear, and it has a pebbly bottom and is shallow for some distance out from the shores. It yields quantities of asphaltum; fragments of it lie all about its banks; this stuff gives the place something of an unpleasant smell.

All our reading had taught us to expect that the first plunge into the Dead Sea would be attended with distressing results – our bodies would feel as if they were suddenly pierced by millions of red-hot needles; the dreadful smarting would continue for hours; we might even look to be blistered from head to foot, and suffer miserably for many days. We were disappointed. Our eight sprang in at the same time that another party of pilgrims did, and nobody screamed once. None of them ever did complain of any thing more than a slight pricking sensation in places where their skin was abraded, and then only for a short time. My face smarted for a couple of hours, but it was partly because I got it badly sun-burned while I was bathing, and staid in so long that it became plastered over with salt.

No, the water did not blister us; it did not cover us with a slimy ooze and confer upon us an atrocious fragrance; it was not very slimy; and I could not discover that we smelt really any worse than we have always smelt since we have been in Palestine. It was only a different kind of smell, but not conspicuous on that account, because we have a great deal of variety in that respect. We didn't smell, there on the Jordan, the same as we do in Jerusalem; and we don't smell in Jerusalem just as we did in Nazareth, or Tiberias, or Cesarea Philippi, or any of those other ruinous ancient towns in Galilee. No, we change all the time, and generally for the worse. We do our own washing.

It was a funny bath. We could not sink. One could stretch himself at full length on his back, with his arms on his breast, and all of his body above a line drawn from the corner of his jaw past the middle of his side, the middle of his leg and through his ankle bone, would remain out of water. He could lift his head clear out, if he chose. No position can be retained long; you lose your balance and whirl over, first on your back and then on your face, and so on. You can lie comfortably, on your back, with your head out, and your legs out from your knees down, by steadying yourself with your hands. You can sit, with your knees drawn up to your chin and your arms clasped around them, but you are bound to turn over presently, because you are top-heavy in that position. You can stand up straight in water that is over your head, and from the middle of your breast upward you will not be wet. But you can not remain so. The water will soon float your feet to the surface. You can not swim on your back and make any progress of any consequence, because your feet stick away above the surface, and there is nothing to propel yourself with but your heels. If you swim on your face, you kick up the water like a stern-wheel boat. You make no headway. A horse is so top-heavy that he can neither swim nor stand up in the Dead Sea. He turns over on his side at once. Some of us bathed for more than an hour, and then came out coated with salt till we shone like icicles. We scrubbed it off with a coarse towel and rode off with a splendid brand-new smell, though it was one which was not any more disagreeable than those we have been for several weeks enjoying. It was the variegated villainy and novelty of it that charmed us. Salt crystals glitter in the sun about the shores of the lake. In places they coat the ground like a brilliant crust of ice.

When I was a boy I somehow got the impression that the river Jordan was four thousand miles long and thirty-five miles wide. It is only ninety miles long, and so crooked that a man does not know which side of it he is on half the time. In going ninety miles it does not get over more than fifty miles of ground. It is not any wider than Broadway in New York. There is the Sea of Galilee and this Dead Sea – neither of them twenty miles long or thirteen wide. And yet when I was in Sunday School I thought they were sixty thousand miles in diameter.

Travel and experience mar the grandest pictures and rob us of the most cherished traditions of our boyhood. Well, let them go. I have already seen the Empire of King Solomon diminish to the size of the State of Pennsylvania; I suppose I can bear the reduction of the seas and the river.

We looked every where, as we passed along, but never saw grain or crystal of Lot's wife. It was a great disappointment. For many and many a year we had known her sad story, and taken that interest in her which misfortune always inspires. But she was gone. Her picturesque form no longer looms above the desert of the Dead Sea to remind the tourist of the doom that fell upon the lost cities.

I can not describe the hideous afternoon's ride from the Dead Sea to Mars Saba. It oppresses me yet, to think of it. The sun so pelted us that the tears ran down our cheeks once or twice. The ghastly, treeless, grassless, breathless canons smothered us as if we had been in an oven. The sun had positive *weight* to it, I think. Not a man could sit erect under it. All drooped low in the saddles. John preached in this "Wilderness!" It must have been exhausting work. What a very heaven the massy towers and ramparts of vast Mars Saba looked to us when we caught a first glimpse of them!

We staid at this great convent all night, guests of the hospitable priests. Mars Saba, perched upon a crag, a human nest stuck high up against a perpendicular mountain wall, is a world of grand masonry that rises, terrace upon terrace away above your head, like the terraced and retreating colonnades one sees in fanciful pictures of Belshazzar's Feast and the palaces of the ancient Pharaohs. No other human dwelling is near. It was founded many ages ago by a holy recluse who lived at first in a cave in the rock – a cave which is inclosed in the convent walls, now, and was reverently shown to us by the priests. This recluse, by his rigorous torturing of his flesh, his diet of bread and water, his utter withdrawal from all society and from the vanities of the world, and his constant prayer and saintly contemplation of a skull, inspired an emulation that brought about him many disciples. The precipice on the opposite side of the canon is well perforated with the small holes they dug in the rock to live in. The present occupants of Mars Saba, about seventy in number, are all hermits. They wear a coarse robe, an ugly, brimless stove-pipe of a hat, and go without shoes. They eat nothing whatever but bread and salt; they drink nothing but water. As long as they live they can never go outside the walls, or look upon a woman – for no woman is permitted to enter Mars Saba, upon any pretext whatsoever.

Some of those men have been shut up there for thirty years. In all that dreary time they have not heard the laughter of a child or the blessed voice of a woman; they have seen no human tears, no human smiles; they have known no human joys, no wholesome human sorrows. In their hearts are no memories of the past, in their brains no dreams of the future. All that is lovable, beautiful, worthy, they have put far away from them; against all things that are pleasant to look upon, and all sounds that are music to the ear, they have barred their massive doors and reared their relentless walls of stone forever. They have banished the tender grace of life and left only the sapped and skinny mockery. Their lips are lips that never kiss and never sing; their hearts are hearts that never hate and never love; their breasts are breasts that never swell with the sentiment, "I have a country and a flag." They are dead men who walk.

I set down these first thoughts because they are natural – not because they are just or because it is right to set them down. It is easy for book-makers to say "I thought so and so as I looked upon such and such a scene" – when the truth is, they thought all those fine things afterwards. One's first thought is not likely to be strictly accurate, yet it is no crime to think it and none to write it down, subject to modification by later experience. These hermits *are* dead men, in several respects, but not in all; and it is not proper, that, thinking ill of them at first, I should go on doing so, or, speaking ill of them I should reiterate the words and stick to them. No, they treated us too kindly for that. There is something human about them somewhere. They knew we were foreigners and Protestants, and not likely to feel admiration or much friendliness toward them. But their large charity was above considering such things. They simply saw in us men who were hungry, and thirsty, and tired, and that was sufficient. They opened their doors and gave us welcome. They asked no questions, and they made no self-righteous display of their hospitality. They fished for no compliments. They moved quietly about, setting the table for us, making the beds, and bringing water to wash in, and paid no heed when we said it was wrong for them to do that when we had men whose business it was to perform such offices. We fared most comfortably, and sat late at dinner. We walked all over the building with the hermits afterward, and then sat on the lofty battlements and smoked while we enjoyed the cool air, the wild scenery and the sunset. One or two chose cosy bed-rooms to sleep in, but the nomadic instinct prompted the rest to sleep on the broad divan that extended around the great hall, because it seemed like sleeping out of doors, and so was more cheery and inviting. It was a royal rest we had.

When we got up to breakfast in the morning, we were new men. For all this hospitality no strict charge was made. We could give something if we chose; we need give nothing, if we were poor or if we were stingy. The pauper and the miser are as free as any in the Catholic Convents of Palestine. I have been educated to enmity toward every thing that is Catholic, and sometimes, in consequence of this, I find it much easier to discover Catholic faults than Catholic merits. But there is one thing I feel no disposition to overlook, and no disposition to forget: and that is, the honest gratitude I and all pilgrims owe, to the Convent Fathers in Palestine. Their doors are always open, and there is always a welcome for any worthy man who comes, whether he comes in rags or clad in purple. The Catholic Convents are a priceless blessing to the poor. A pilgrim without money, whether he be a Protestant or a Catholic, can travel the length and breadth of Palestine, and in the midst of her desert wastes find wholesome food and a clean bed every night, in these buildings. Pilgrims in better circumstances are often stricken down by the sun and the fevers of the country, and then their saving refuge is the Convent. Without these hospitable retreats, travel in Palestine would be a pleasure which none but the strongest men could dare to undertake. Our party, pilgrims and all, will always be ready and always willing, to touch glasses and drink health, prosperity and long life to the Convent Fathers of Palestine.

So, rested and refreshed, we fell into line and filed away over the barren mountains of Judea, and along rocky ridges and through sterile gorges, where eternal silence and solitude reigned. Even the scattering groups of armed shepherds we met the afternoon before, tending their flocks of long-haired goats, were wanting here. We saw but two living creatures. They were gazelles, of "soft-eyed" notoriety. They looked like very young kids, but they annihilated distance like an express train. I have not seen animals that moved faster, unless I might say it of the antelopes of our own great plains.

At nine or ten in the morning we reached the Plain of the Shepherds, and stood in a walled garden of olives where the shepherds were watching their flocks by night, eighteen centuries ago, when the multitude of angels brought them the tidings that the Saviour was born. A quarter of a mile away was Bethlehem of Judea, and the pilgrims took some of the stone wall and hurried on.

The Plain of the Shepherds is a desert, paved with loose stones, void of vegetation, glaring in the fierce sun. Only the music of the angels it knew once could charm its shrubs and flowers to life again and restore its vanished beauty. No less potent enchantment could avail to work this miracle.

In the huge Church of the Nativity, in Bethlehem, built fifteen hundred years ago by the inveterate St. Helena, they took us below ground, and into a grotto cut in the living rock. This was the "manger" where Christ was born. A silver star set in the floor bears a Latin inscription to that effect. It is polished with the kisses of many generations of worshipping pilgrims. The grotto was tricked out in the usual tasteless style observable in all the holy places of Palestine. As in the Church of the Holy Sepulchre, envy and uncharitableness were apparent here. The priests and the members of the Greek and Latin Churches can not come by the same corridor to kneel in the sacred birthplace of the Redeemer, but are compelled to approach and retire by different avenues, lest they quarrel and fight on this holiest ground on earth.

I have no "meditations," suggested by this spot where the very first "Merry Christmas!" was uttered in all the world, and from whence the friend of my childhood, Santa Claus, departed on his first journey, to gladden and continue to gladden roaring firesides on wintry mornings in many a distant land forever and forever. I touch, with reverent finger, the actual spot where the infant Jesus lay, but I think – nothing.

You *can not* think in this place any more than you can in any other in Palestine that would be likely to inspire reflection. Beggars, cripples and monks compass you about, and make you think only of buck-sheesh when you would rather think of something more in keeping with the character of the spot.

I was glad to get away, and glad when we had walked through the grottoes where Eusebius wrote, and Jerome fasted, and Joseph prepared for the flight into Egypt, and the dozen other distinguished grottoes, and knew we were done. The Church of the Nativity is almost as well packed with exceeding holy places as the Church of the Holy Sepulchre itself. They even have in it a grotto wherein twenty thousand children were slaughtered by Herod when he was seeking the life of the infant Saviour.

We went to the Milk Grotto, of course – a cavern where Mary hid herself for a while before the flight into Egypt. Its walls were black before she entered, but in suckling the Child, a drop of her milk fell upon the floor and instantly changed the darkness of the walls to its own snowy hue. We took many little fragments of stone from here, because it is well known in all the East that a barren woman hath need only to touch her lips to one of these and her failing will depart from her. We took many specimens, to the end that we might confer happiness upon certain households that we wot of.

We got away from Bethlehem and its troops of beggars and relic-peddlers in the afternoon, and after spending some little time at Rachel's tomb, hurried to Jerusalem as fast as possible. I never was *so* glad to get home again before. I never have enjoyed rest as I have enjoyed it during these last few hours. The journey to the Dead Sea, the Jordan and Bethlehem was short, but it was an exhausting one. Such roasting heat, such oppressive solitude, and such dismal desolation can not surely exist elsewhere on earth. And *such* fatigue!

The commonest sagacity warns me that I ought to tell the customary pleasant lie, and say I tore myself reluctantly away from every noted place in Palestine. Every body tells that, but with as little ostentation as I may, I doubt the word of every he who tells it. I could take a dreadful oath that I have never heard any one of our forty pilgrims say any thing of the sort, and they are as worthy and as sincerely devout as any that come here. They will say it when they get home, fast enough, but why should they not? They do not wish to array themselves against all the Lamartines and Grimeses in the world. It does not stand to reason that men are reluctant to leave places where the very life is almost badgered out of them by importunate swarms of beggars and peddlers who hang in strings to one's sleeves and coat-tails and shriek and shout in his ears and horrify his vision with the ghastly sores and malformations they exhibit. One is *glad* to get away. I have heard shameless people say they were glad to get away from Ladies' Festivals where they were importuned to buy by bevies of lovely young ladies. Transform those houris into dusky hags and ragged savages, and replace their rounded forms with shrunken and knotted distortions, their soft hands with scarred and hideous deformities, and the persuasive music of their voices with the discordant din of a hated language, and *then* see how much lingering reluctance to leave could be mustered. No, it is the neat thing to say you were reluctant, and then append the profound thoughts that "struggled for utterance," in your brain; but it is the true thing to say you were not reluctant, and found it impossible to think at all – though in good sooth it is not respectable to say it, and not poetical, either.

We do not think, in the holy places; we think in bed, afterwards, when the glare, and the noise, and the confusion are gone, and in fancy we revisit alone, the solemn monuments of the past, and summon the phantom pageants of an age that has passed away.

CHAPTER LX

TEN OR ELEVEN o'clock found us coming down to breakfast one morning in Cadiz. They told us the ship had been lying at anchor in the harbor two or three hours. It was time for us to bestir ourselves. The ship could wait only a little while because of the quarantine. We were soon on board, and within the hour the white city and the pleasant shores of Spain sank down behind the waves and passed out of sight. We had seen no land fade from view so regretfully.

It had long ago been decided in a noisy public meeting in the main cabin that we could not go to Lisbon, because we must surely be quarantined there. We did every thing by mass-meeting, in the good old national way, from swapping off one empire for another on the programme of the voyage down to complaining of the cookery and the scarcity of napkins. I am reminded, now, of one of these complaints of the cookery made by a passenger. The coffee had been steadily growing more and more execrable for the space of three weeks, till at last it had ceased to be coffee altogether and had assumed the nature of mere discolored water – so this person said. He said it was so weak that it was transparent an inch in depth around the edge of the cup. As he approached the table one morning he saw the transparent edge – by means of his extraordinary vision – long before he got to his seat. He went back and complained in a high-handed way to Capt. Duncan. He said the coffee was disgraceful. The Captain showed his. It seemed tolerably good. The incipient mutineer was more outraged than ever, then, at what he denounced as the partiality shown the captain's table over the other tables in the ship. He flourished back and got his cup and set it down triumphantly, and said:

"Just try that mixture once, Captain Duncan."

He smelt it – tasted it – smiled benignantly – then said:

"It *is* inferior – for *coffee* – but it is pretty fair *tea.*"

The humbled mutineer smelt it, tasted it, and returned to his seat. He had made an egregious ass of himself before the whole ship. He did it no more. After that he took things as they came. That was me.

The old-fashioned ship-life had returned, now that we were no longer in sight of land. For days and days it continued just the same, one day being exactly like another, and, to me, every one of them pleasant. At last we anchored in the open roadstead of Funchal, in the beautiful islands we call the Madeiras.

The mountains looked surpassingly lovely, clad as they were in living green; ribbed with lava ridges; flecked with white cottages; riven by deep chasms purple with shade; the great slopes dashed with sunshine and mottled with shadows flung from the drifting squadrons of the sky, and the superb picture fitly crowned by towering peaks whose fronts were swept by the trailing fringes of the clouds.

But we could not land. We staid all day and looked, we abused the man who invented quarantine, we held half a dozen mass-meetings and crammed them full of interrupted speeches, motions that fell still-born, amendments that came to nought and resolutions that died from sheer exhaustion in trying to get before the house. At night we set sail.

We averaged four mass-meetings a week for the voyage – we seemed always in labor in this way, and yet so often fallaciously that whenever at long intervals we were safely delivered of a resolution, it was cause for public rejoicing, and we hoisted the flag and fired a salute.

Days passed – and nights; and then the beautiful Bermudas rose out of the sea, we entered the tortuous channel, steamed hither and thither among the bright summer islands, and rested at last under the flag of England and were welcome. We were not a nightmare here, where were civilization and intelligence in place of Spanish and Italian superstition, dirt and dread of cholera. A few days among the breezy groves, the flower gardens, the coral caves, and the lovely vistas of blue water that went curving in and out, disappearing and anon again appearing through jungle walls of brilliant foliage, restored the energies dulled by long drowsing on the ocean, and fitted us for our final cruise – our little run of a thousand miles to New York – America – HOME.

We bade good-bye to "our friends the Bermudians," as our programme hath it – the majority of those we were most intimate with were negroes – and courted the great deep again. I said the majority. We knew more negroes than white people, because we had a deal of washing to be done, but we made some most excellent friends among the whites, whom it will be a pleasant duty to hold long in grateful remembrance.

We sailed, and from that hour all idling ceased. Such another system of overhauling, general littering of cabins and packing of trunks we had not seen since we let go the anchor in the harbor of Beirout. Every body was busy. Lists of all purchases had to be made out, and values attached, to facilitate matters at the custom-house. Purchases bought by bulk in partnership had to be equitably divided, outstanding debts canceled, accounts compared, and trunks, boxes and packages labeled. All day long the bustle and confusion continued.

And now came our first accident. A passenger was running through a gangway, between decks, one stormy night, when he caught his foot in the iron staple of a door that had been heedlessly left off a hatchway, and the bones of his leg broke at the ankle. It was our first serious misfortune. We had traveled much more than twenty thousand miles, by land and sea, in many trying climates, without a single hurt, without a serious case of sickness and without a death among five and sixty passengers. Our good fortune had been wonderful. A sailor had jumped overboard at Constantinople one night, and was seen no more, but it was suspected that his object was to desert, and there was a slim chance, at least, that he reached the shore. But the passenger list was complete. There was no name missing from the register.

At last, one pleasant morning, we steamed up the harbor of New York, all on deck, all dressed in Christian garb – by special order, for there was a latent disposition in some quarters to come out as Turks – and amid a waving of handkerchiefs from welcoming friends, the glad pilgrims noted the shiver of the decks that told that ship and pier had joined hands again and the long, strange cruise was over. Amen.

CHAPTER LXI

IN THIS PLACE I will print an article which I wrote for the New York *Herald* the night we arrived. I do it partly because my contract with my publishers makes it compulsory; partly because it is a proper, tolerably accurate, and exhaustive summing up of the cruise of the ship and the performances of the pilgrims in foreign lands; and partly because some of the passengers have abused me for writing it, and I wish the public to see how thankless a task it is to put one's self to trouble to glorify unappreciative people. I was charged with "rushing into print" with these compliments. I did not rush. I had written news letters to the *Herald* sometimes, but yet when I visited the office that day I did not say any thing about writing a valedictory. I did go to the *Tribune* office to see if such an article was wanted, because I belonged on the regular staff of that paper and it was simply a duty to do it. The managing editor was absent, and so I thought no more about it. At night when the *Herald*'s request came for an article, I did not "rush." In fact, I demurred for a while, because I did not feel like writing compliments then, and therefore was afraid to speak of the cruise lest I might be betrayed into using other than complimentary language. However, I reflected that it would be a just and righteous thing to go down and write a kind word for the Hadjis – Hadjis are people who have made the pilgrimage – because parties not interested could not do it so feelingly as I, a fellow-Hadji, and so I penned the valedictory. I have read it, and read it again; and if there is a sentence in it that is not fulsomely complimentary to captain, ship and passengers, *I* can not find it. If it is not a chapter that any company might be proud to have a body write about them, my judgment is fit for nothing. With these remarks I confidently submit it to the unprejudiced judgment of the reader:

RETURN OF THE HOLY LAND EXCURSIONISTS – THE STORY OF THE CRUISE

TO THE EDITOR OF THE HERALD:

The steamer Quaker City has accomplished at last her extraordinary voyage and returned to her old pier at the foot of Wall street. The expedition was a success in some respects, in some it was not. Originally it was advertised as a "pleasure excursion."

Well, perhaps, it was a pleasure excursion, but certainly it did not look like one; certainly it did not act like one. Any body's and every body's notion of a pleasure excursion is that the parties to it will of a necessity be young and giddy and somewhat boisterous. They will dance a good deal, sing a good deal, make love, but sermonize very little. Any body's and every body's notion of a well conducted funeral is that there must be a hearse and a corpse, and chief mourners and mourners by courtesy, many old people, much solemnity, no levity, and a prayer and a sermon withal. Three-fourths of the Quaker City's passengers were between forty and seventy years of age! There was a picnic crowd for you! It may be supposed that the other fourth was composed of young girls. But it was not. It was chiefly composed of rusty old bachelors and a child of six years. Let us average the ages of the Quaker City's pilgrims and set the figure down as fifty years. Is any man insane enough to imagine that this picnic of patriarchs sang, made love, danced, laughed, told anecdotes, dealt in ungodly levity? In my experience they sinned little in these matters. No doubt it was presumed here at home that these frolicsome veterans laughed and sang and romped all day, and day after day, and kept up a noisy excitement from one end of the ship to the other; and that they played blind-man's buff or danced quadrilles and waltzes on moonlight evenings on the quarter-deck; and that at odd moments of unoccupied time they jotted a laconic item or two in the journals they opened on such an elaborate plan when they left home, and then skurried off to their whist and euchre labors under the cabin lamps. If these things were presumed, the presumption was at fault. The venerable excursionists were not gay and frisky. They played no blind-man's buff; they dealt not in whist; they shirked not the irksome journal, for alas! most of them were even writing books. They never romped, they talked but little, they never sang, save in the nightly prayer-meeting. The pleasure ship was a synagogue, and the pleasure-trip was a funeral excursion without a corpse. (There is nothing exhilarating about a funeral excursion without a corpse.) A free, hearty laugh was a sound that was not heard oftener than once in seven days about those decks or in those cabins, and when it was heard it met with precious little sympathy. The excursionists danced, on three separate evenings, long, long ago, (it seems an age,) quadrilles, of a single set, made up of three ladies and five gentlemen, (the latter with handkerchiefs around their arms to signify their sex,) who timed their feet to the solemn wheezing of a melodeon; but even this melancholy orgie was voted to be sinful, and dancing was discontinued.

The pilgrims played dominoes when too much Josephus or Robinson's Holy Land Researches, or book-writing, made recreation necessary – for dominoes is about as mild and sinless a game as any in the world, perhaps, excepting always the ineffably insipid diversion they call croquet, which is a game where you don't pocket any balls and don't carom on any thing of any consequence, and when you are done nobody has to pay, and there are no refreshments to saw off, and, consequently, there isn't any satisfaction whatever about it – they played dominoes till they were rested, and then they blackguarded each other privately till prayer-time. When they were not seasick they were uncommonly prompt when the dinner-gong sounded. Such was our daily life on board the ship – solemnity, decorum, dinner, dominoes, devotions, slander. It was not lively enough for a pleasure-trip; but if we had only had a corpse it would have made a noble funeral excursion. It is all over now; but when I look back, the idea of these venerable fossils skipping forth on a six months' picnic, seems exquisitely refreshing. The advertised title of the expedition – "The Grand Holy Land Pleasure Excursion" – was a misnomer. "The Grand Holy Land Funeral Procession" would have been better – much better.

Wherever we went, in Europe, Asia, or Africa, we made a sensation, and, I suppose I may add, created a famine. None of us had ever been any where before; we all hailed from the interior; travel was a wild novelty to us, and we conducted ourselves in accordance with the natural instincts that were in us, and trammeled ourselves with no ceremonies, no conventionalities. We always took care to make it understood that we were Americans – Americans! When we found that a good many foreigners had hardly ever heard of America, and that a good many more knew it only as a barbarous province away off somewhere, that had lately been at war with somebody, we pitied the ignorance of the Old World, but abated no jot of our importance. Many and many a simple community in the Eastern hemisphere will remember for years the incursion of the strange horde in the year of our Lord 1867, that called themselves Americans, and seemed to imagine in some unaccountable way that they had a right to be proud of it. We generally created a famine, partly because the coffee on the Quaker City was unendurable, and sometimes the more substantial fare was not strictly first-class; and partly because one naturally tires of sitting long at the same board and eating from the same dishes.

The people of those foreign countries are very, very ignorant. They looked curiously at the costumes we had brought from the wilds of America. They observed that we talked loudly at table sometimes. They noticed that we looked out for expenses, and got what we conveniently could out of a franc, and wondered where in the mischief we came from. In Paris they just simply opened their eyes and stared when we spoke to them in French! We never did succeed in making those idiots understand their own language. One of our passengers said to a shopkeeper, in reference to a proposed return to buy a pair of gloves, "*Allong restay trankeel – may be ve coom Moonday;*" and would you believe it, that shopkeeper, a born Frenchman, had to ask what it was that had been said. Sometimes it seems to me, somehow, that there must be a difference between Parisian French and Quaker City French.

The people stared at us every where, and we stared at them. We generally made them feel rather small, too, before we got done with them, because we bore down on them with America's greatness until we crushed them. And yet we took kindly to the manners and customs, and especially to the fashions of the various people we visited. When we left the Azores, we wore awful capotes and used fine tooth combs – successfully. When we came back from Tangier, in Africa, we were topped with fezzes of the bloodiest hue, hung with tassels like an Indian's scalp-lock. In France and Spain we attracted some attention in these costumes. In Italy they naturally took us for distempered Garibaldians, and set a gunboat to look for any thing significant in our changes of uniform. We made Rome howl. We could have made any place howl when we had all our clothes on. We got no fresh raiment in Greece – they had but little there of any kind. But at Constantinople, how we turned out! Turbans, scimetars, fezzes, horse-pistols, tunics, sashes, baggy trowsers, yellow slippers – Oh, we were gorgeous! The illustrious dogs of Constantinople barked their under-jaws off, and even then failed to do us justice. They are all dead by this time. They could not go through such a run of business as we gave them and survive.

And then we went to see the Emperor of Russia. We just called on him as comfortably as if we had known him a century or so, and when we had finished our visit we variegated ourselves with selections from Russian costumes and sailed away again more picturesque than ever. In Smyrna we picked up camel's hair shawls and other dressy things from Persia; but in Palestine – ah, in Palestine – our splendid career ended. They didn't wear any clothes there to speak of. We were satisfied, and stopped. We made no experiments. We did not try their costume. But we astonished the natives of that country. We astonished them with such eccentricities of dress as we could muster. We prowled through the Holy Land, from Cesarea Philippi to Jerusalem and the Dead Sea, a weird procession of pilgrims, gotten up regardless of expense, solemn, gorgeous, green-spectacled, drowsing under blue umbrellas, and astride of a sorrier lot of horses, camels and asses than those that came out of Noah's ark, after eleven months of seasickness and short rations. If ever those children of Israel in Palestine forget when Gideon's Band went through there from America, they ought to be cursed once more and finished. It was the rarest spectacle that ever astounded mortal eyes, perhaps.

Well, we were at home in Palestine. It was easy to see that that was the grand feature of the expedition. We had cared nothing much about Europe. We galloped through the Louvre, the Pitti, the Ufizzi, the Vatican – all the galleries – and through the pictured and frescoed churches of Venice, Naples, and the cathedrals of Spain; some of us said that certain of the great works of the old masters were glorious creations of genius, (we found it out in the guide-book, though we got hold of the wrong picture sometimes,) and the others said they were disgraceful old daubs. We examined modern and ancient statuary with a critical eye in Florence, Rome, or any where we found it, and praised it if we saw fit, and if we didn't we said we preferred the wooden Indians in front of the cigar stores of America. But the Holy Land brought out all our enthusiasm. We fell into raptures by the barren shores of Galilee; we pondered at Tabor and at Nazareth; we exploded into poetry over the questionable loveliness of Esdraelon; we meditated at Jezreel and Samaria over the missionary zeal of Jehu; we rioted – fairly rioted among the holy places of Jerusalem; we bathed in Jordan and the Dead Sea, reckless whether our accident-insurance policies were extra-hazardous or not, and brought away so many jugs of precious water from both places that all the country from Jericho to the mountains of Moab will suffer from drouth this year, I think. Yet, the pilgrimage part of the excursion was its pet feature – there is no question about that. After dismal, smileless Palestine, beautiful Egypt had few charms for us. We merely glanced at it and were ready for home.

They wouldn't let us land at Malta – quarantine; they would not let us land in Sardinia; nor at Algiers, Africa; nor at Malaga, Spain, nor Cadiz, nor at the Madeira islands. So we got offended at all foreigners and turned our backs upon them and came home. I suppose we only stopped at the Bermudas because they were in the programme. We did not care any thing about any place at all. We wanted to go home. Homesickness was abroad in the ship – it was epidemic. If the authorities of New York had known how badly we had it, they would have quarantined us here.

The grand pilgrimage is over. Good-bye to it, and a pleasant memory to it, I am able to say in all kindness. I bear no malice, no ill-will toward any individual that was connected with it, either as passenger or officer. Things I did not like at all yesterday I like very well to-day, now that I am at home, and always hereafter I shall be able to poke fun at the whole gang if the spirit so moves me to do, without ever saying a malicious word. The expedition accomplished all that its programme promised that it should accomplish, and we ought all to be satisfied with the management of the matter, certainly. Bye-bye!

MARK TWAIN

I call that complimentary. It *is* complimentary; and yet I never have received a word of thanks for it from the Hadjis; on the contrary I speak nothing but the serious truth when I say that many of them even took exceptions to the article. In endeavoring to please them I slaved over that sketch for two hours, and had my labor for my pains. I never will do a generous deed again.

CONCLUSION

NEARLY ONE YEAR has flown since this notable pilgrimage was ended; and as I sit here at home in San Francisco thinking, I am moved to confess that day by day the mass of my memories of the excursion have grown more and more pleasant as the disagreeable incidents of travel which encumbered them flitted one by one out of my mind – and now, if the *Quaker City* were weighing her anchor to sail away on the very same cruise again, nothing could gratify me more than to be a passenger. With the same captain and even the same pilgrims, the same sinners. I was on excellent terms with eight or nine of the excursionists (they are my staunch friends yet,) and was even on speaking terms with the rest of the sixty-five. I have been at sea quite enough to know that that was a very good average. Because a long sea-voyage not only brings out all the mean traits one has, and exaggerates them, but raises up others which he never suspected he possessed, and even creates new ones. A twelve months' voyage at sea would make of an ordinary man a very miracle of meanness. On the other hand, if a man has good qualities, the spirit seldom moves him to exhibit them on shipboard, at least with any sort of emphasis. Now I am satisfied that our pilgrims are pleasant old people on shore; I am also satisfied that at sea on a second voyage they would be pleasanter, somewhat, than they were on our grand excursion, and so I say without hesitation that I would be glad enough to sail with them again. I could at least enjoy life with my handful of old friends. They could enjoy life with *their* cliques as well – passengers invariably divide up into cliques, on *all* ships.

And I will say, here, that I would rather travel with an excursion party of Methuselahs than have to be changing ships and comrades constantly, as people do who travel in the ordinary way. Those latter are always grieving over some *other* ship they have known and lost, and over *other* comrades whom diverging routes have separated from them. They learn to love a ship just in time to change it for another, and they become attached to a pleasant traveling companion only to lose him. They have that most dismal experience of being in a strange vessel, among strange people who care nothing about them, and of undergoing the customary bullying by strange officers and the insolence of strange servants, repeated over and over again within the compass of every month. They have also that other misery of packing and unpacking trunks – of running the distressing gauntlet of custom-houses – of the anxieties attendant upon getting a mass of baggage from point to point on land in safety. I had rather sail with a whole brigade of patriarchs than suffer so. We never packed our trunks but twice – when we sailed from New York, and when we returned to it. Whenever we made a land journey, we estimated how many days we should be gone and what amount of clothing we should need, figured it down to a mathematical nicety, packed a valise or two accordingly, and left the trunks on board. We chose our comrades from among our old, tried friends, and started. We were never dependent upon strangers for companionship. We often had occasion to pity Americans whom we found traveling drearily among strangers with no friends to exchange pains and pleasures with. Whenever we were coming back from a land journey, our eyes sought one thing in the distance first – the ship – and when we saw it riding at anchor with the flag apeak, we felt as a returning wanderer feels when he sees his home. When we stepped on board, our cares vanished, our troubles were at an end – for the ship was home to us. We always had the same familiar old stateroom to go to, and feel safe and at peace and comfortable again.

I have no fault to find with the manner in which our excursion was conducted. Its programme was faithfully carried out – a thing which surprised me, for great enterprises usually promise vastly more than they perform. It would be well if such an excursion could be gotten up every year and the system regularly inaugurated. Travel is fatal to prejudice, bigotry and narrow-mindedness, and many of our people need it sorely on these accounts. Broad, wholesome, charitable views of men and things can not be acquired by vegetating in one little corner of the earth all one's lifetime.

The Excursion is ended, and has passed to its place among the things that were. But its varied scenes and its manifold incidents will linger pleasantly in our memories for many a year to come. Always on the wing, as we were, and merely pausing a moment to catch fitful glimpses of the wonders of half a world, we could not hope to receive or retain vivid impressions of all it was our fortune to see. Yet our holy-day flight has not been in vain – for above the confusion of vague recollections, certain of its best prized pictures lift themselves and will still continue perfect in tint and outline after their surroundings shall have faded away.

We shall remember something of pleasant France; and something also of Paris, though it flashed upon us a splendid meteor, and was gone again, we hardly knew how or where. We shall remember, always, how we saw majestic Gibraltar glorified with the rich coloring of a Spanish sunset and swimming in a sea of rainbows. In fancy we shall see Milan again, and her stately Cathedral with its marble wilderness of graceful spires. And Padua – Verona – Como, jeweled with stars; and patrician Venice, afloat on her stagnant flood – silent, desolate, haughty – scornful of her humbled state – wrapping herself in memories of her lost fleets, of battle and triumph, and all the pageantry of a glory that is departed.

We can not forget Florence – Naples – nor the foretaste of heaven that is in the delicious atmosphere of Greece – and surely not Athens and the broken temples of the Acropolis. Surely not venerable Rome – nor the green plain that compasses her round about, contrasting its brightness with her gray decay – nor the ruined arches that stand apart in the plain and clothe their looped and windowed raggedness with vines. We shall remember St. Peter's: not as one sees it when he walks the streets of Rome and fancies all her domes are just alike, but as he sees it leagues away, when every meaner edifice has faded out of sight and that one dome looms superbly up in the flush of sunset, full of dignity and grace, strongly outlined as a mountain.

We shall remember Constantinople and the Bosphorus – the colossal magnificence of Baalbec – the Pyramids of Egypt – the prodigious form, the benignant countenance of the Sphynx – Oriental Smyrna – sacred Jerusalem – Damascus, the "Pearl of the East," the pride of Syria, the fabled Garden of Eden, the home of princes and genii of the Arabian Nights, the oldest metropolis on earth, the one city in all the world that has kept its name and held its place and looked serenely on while the Kingdoms and Empires of four thousand years have risen to life, enjoyed their little season of pride and pomp, and then vanished and been forgotten!

From

ROUGHING IT

1872

THE MINER'S DREAM.

PREFATORY

THIS BOOK IS merely a personal narrative and not a pretentious history or a philosophical dissertation. It is a record of several years of variegated vagabondizing, and its object is rather to help the resting reader wile away an idle hour than afflict him with metaphysics, or goad him with science. Still, there is information in the volume; information concerning an interesting episode in the history of the Far West, about which no books have been written by persons who were on the ground in person, and saw the happenings of the time with their own eyes. I allude to the rise, growth and culmination of the silver-mining fever in Nevada – a curious episode, in some respects; the only one, of its peculiar kind, that has occurred in the land; and the only one, indeed, that is likely to occur in it.

Yes, take it all around, there is quite a good deal of information in the book. I regret this very much; but really it could not be helped: information appears to stew out of me naturally, like the precious ottar of roses out of the otter. Sometimes it has seemed to me that I would give worlds if I could retain my facts; but it cannot be. The more I calk up the sources, and the tighter I get, the more I leak wisdom. Therefore, I can only claim indulgence at the hands of the reader, not justification.

THE AUTHOR

CHAPTER I

MY BROTHER HAD just been appointed Secretary of Nevada Territory – an office of such majesty that it concentrated in itself the duties and dignities of Treasurer, Comptroller, Secretary of State, and Acting Governor in the Governor's absence. A salary of eighteen hundred dollars a year and the title of "Mr. Secretary," gave to the great position an air of wild and imposing grandeur. I was young and ignorant, and I envied my brother. I coveted his distinction and his financial splendor, but particularly and especially the long, strange journey he was going to make, and the curious new world he was going to explore. He was going to travel! I never had been away from home, and that word "travel" had a seductive charm for me. Pretty soon he would be hundreds and hundreds of miles away on the great plains and deserts, and among the mountains of the Far West, and would see buffaloes and Indians, and prairie dogs, and antelopes, and have all kinds of adventures, and may be get hanged or scalped, and have ever such a fine time, and write home and tell us all about it, and be a hero. And he would see the gold mines and the silver mines, and maybe go about of an afternoon when his work was done, and pick up two or three pailfuls of shining slugs, and nuggets of gold and silver on the hill-side. And by and by he would become very rich, and return home by sea, and be able to talk as calmly about San Francisco and the ocean, and "the isthmus" as if it was nothing of any consequence to have seen those marvels face to face. What I suffered in contemplating his happiness, pen cannot describe. And so, when he offered me, in cold blood, the sublime position of private secretary under him, it appeared to me that the heavens and the earth passed away, and the firmament was rolled together as a scroll! I had nothing more to desire. My contentment was complete. At the end of an hour or two I was ready for the journey. Not much packing up was necessary, because we were going in the overland stage from the Missouri frontier to Nevada, and passengers were only allowed a small quantity of baggage apiece. There was no Pacific railroad in those fine times of ten or twelve years ago – not a single rail of it.

I only proposed to stay in Nevada three months – I had no thought of staying longer than that. I meant to see all I could that was new and strange, and then hurry home to business. I little thought that I would not see the end of that three-month pleasure excursion for six or seven uncommonly long years!

I dreamed all night about Indians, deserts, and silver bars, and in due time, next day, we took shipping at the St. Louis wharf on board a steamboat bound up the Missouri River.

We were six days going from St. Louis to "St. Jo." – a trip that was so dull, and sleepy, and eventless that it has left no more impression on my memory than if its duration had been six minutes instead of that many days. No record is left in my mind, now, concerning it, but a confused jumble of savage-looking snags, which we deliberately walked over with one wheel or the other; and of reefs which we butted and butted, and then retired from and climbed over in some softer place; and of sand-bars which we roosted on occasionally, and rested, and then got out our crutches and sparred over. In fact, the boat might almost as well have gone to St. Jo. by land, for she was walking most of the time, anyhow – climbing over reefs and clambering over snags patiently and laboriously all day long. The captain said she was a "bully" boat, and all she wanted was more "shear" and a bigger wheel. I thought she wanted a pair of stilts, but I had the deep sagacity not to say so.

CHAPTER II

THE FIRST THING we did on that glad evening that landed us at St. Joseph was to hunt up the stage-office, and pay a hundred and fifty dollars apiece for tickets per overland coach to Carson City, Nevada.

The next morning, bright and early, we took a hasty breakfast, and hurried to the starting-place. Then an inconvenience presented itself which we had not properly appreciated before, namely, that one cannot make a heavy traveling trunk stand for twenty-five pounds of baggage – because it weighs a good deal more. But that was all we could take – twenty-five pounds each. So we had to snatch our trunks open, and make a selection in a good deal of hurry. We put our lawful twenty-five pounds apiece all in one valise, and shipped the trunks back to St. Louis again. It was a sad parting, for now we had no swallow-tail coats and white kid gloves to wear at Pawnee receptions in the Rocky Mountains, and no stove-pipe hats nor patent-leather boots, nor anything else necessary to make life calm and peaceful. We were reduced to a war footing. Each of us put on a rough, heavy suit of clothing, woolen army shirt and "stogy" boots included; and into the valise we crowded a few white shirts, some under-clothing and such things. My brother, the Secretary, took along about four pounds of United States statutes and six pounds of Unabridged Dictionary; for we did not know – poor innocents – that such things could be bought in San Francisco on one day and received in Carson City the next. I was armed to the teeth with a pitiful little Smith & Wesson's seven-shooter, which carried a ball like a homoepathic pill, and it took the whole seven to make a dose for an adult. But I thought it was grand. It appeared to me to be a dangerous weapon. It only had one fault – you could not hit anything with it. One of our "conductors" practiced awhile on a cow with it, and as long as she stood still and behaved herself she was safe; but as soon as she went to moving about, and he got to shooting at other things, she came to grief. The Secretary had a small-sized Colt's revolver strapped around him for protection against the Indians, and to guard against accidents he carried it uncapped. Mr. George Bemis was dismally formidable. George Bemis was our fellow-traveler. We had never seen him before. He wore in his belt an old original "Allen" revolver, such as irreverent people called a "pepper-box." Simply drawing the trigger back, cocked and fired the pistol. As the trigger came back, the hammer would begin to rise and the barrel to turn over, and presently down would drop the hammer, and away would speed the ball. To aim along the turning barrel and hit the thing aimed at was a feat which was probably never done with an "Allen" in the world. But George's was a reliable weapon, nevertheless, because, as one of the stage-drivers afterward said, "If she didn't get what she went after, she would fetch something else." And so she did. She went after a deuce of spades nailed against a tree, once, and fetched a mule standing about thirty yards to the left of it. Bemis did not want the mule; but the owner came out with a double-barreled shotgun and persuaded him to buy it, anyhow. It was a cheerful weapon – the "Allen." Sometimes all its six barrels would go off at once, and then there was no safe place in all the region round about, but behind it.

We took two or three blankets for protection against frosty weather in the mountains. In the matter of luxuries we were modest – we took none along but some pipes and five pounds of smoking-tobacco. We had two large canteens to carry water in, between stations on the Plains, and we also took with us a little shot-bag of silver coin for daily expenses in the way of breakfasts and dinners.

By eight o'clock everything was ready, and we were on the other side of the river. We jumped into the stage, the driver cracked his whip, and we bowled away and left "the States" behind us. It was a superb summer morning, and all the landscape was brilliant with sunshine. There was a freshness and breeziness, too, and an exhilarating sense of emancipation from all sorts of cares and responsibilities, that almost made us feel that the years we had spent in the close, hot city, toiling and slaving, had been wasted and thrown away. We were spinning along through Kansas, and in the course of an hour and a half we were fairly abroad on the great Plains. Just here the land was rolling – a grand sweep of regular elevations and depressions as far as the eye could reach – like the stately heave and swell of the ocean's bosom after a storm. And everywhere were cornfields, accenting with squares of deeper green, this limitless expanse of grassy land. But presently this sea upon dry ground was to lose its "rolling" character and stretch away for seven hundred miles as level as a floor!

Our coach was a great swinging and swaying stage, of the most sumptuous description – an imposing cradle on wheels. It was drawn by six handsome horses, and by the side of the driver sat the "conductor," the legitimate captain of the craft; for it was his business to take charge and care of the mails, baggage, express matter, and passengers. We three were the only passengers, this trip. We sat on the back seat, inside. About all the rest of the coach was full of mail bags – for we had three days' delayed mails with us. Almost touching our knees, a perpendicular wall of mail matter rose up to the roof. There was a great pile of it strapped on top of the stage, and both the fore and hind boots were full. We had twenty-seven hundred pounds of it aboard, the driver said – "a little for Brigham, and Carson, and 'Frisco, but the heft of it for the Injuns, which is powerful troublesome 'thout they get plenty of truck to read." But as he just then got up a fearful convulsion of his countenance which was suggestive of a wink being swallowed by an earthquake, we guessed that his remark was intended to be facetious, and to mean that we would unload the most of our mail matter somewhere on the Plains and leave it to the Indians, or whosoever wanted it.

We changed horses every ten miles, all day long, and fairly flew over the hard, level road. We jumped out and stretched our legs every time the coach stopped, and so the night found us still vivacious and unfatigued.

After supper a woman got in, who lived about fifty miles further on, and we three had to take turns at sitting outside with the driver and conductor. Apparently she was not a talkative woman. She would sit there in the gathering twilight and fasten her steadfast eyes on a mosquito rooting into her arm, and slowly she would raise her other hand till she had got his range, and then she would launch a slap at him that would have jolted a cow; and after that she would sit and contemplate the corpse with tranquil satisfaction – for she never missed her mosquito; she was a dead shot at short range. She never removed a carcase, but left them there for bait. I sat by this grim Sphynx and watched her kill thirty or forty mosquitoes – watched her, and waited for her to say something, but she never did. So I finally opened the conversation myself. I said:

"The mosquitoes are pretty bad, about here, madam."

"You bet!"

"What did I understand you to say, madam?"

"You bet!"

Then she cheered up, and faced around and said:

"Danged if I didn't begin to think you fellers was deef and dumb. I did, b'gosh. Here I've sot, and sot, and sot, a-bust'n muskeeters and wonderin' what was ailin' ye. Fust I thot you was deef and dumb, then I thot you was sick or crazy, or suthin', and then by and by I begin to reckon you was a passel of sickly fools that couldn't think of nothing to say. Wher'd ye come from?"

The Sphynx was a Sphynx no more! The fountains of her great deep were broken up, and she rained the nine parts of speech forty days and forty nights, metaphorically speaking, and buried us under a desolating deluge of trivial gossip that left not a crag or pinnacle of rejoinder projecting above the tossing waste of dislocated grammar and decomposed pronunciation!

How we suffered, suffered, suffered! She went on, hour after hour, till I was sorry I ever opened the mosquito question and gave her a start. She never did stop again until she got to her journey's end toward daylight; and then she stirred us up as she was leaving the stage (for we were nodding, by that time), and said:

"Now you git out at Cottonwood, you fellers, and lay over a couple o'days, and I'll be along some time tonight, and if I can do ye any good by edgin' in a word now and then, I'm right thar. Folks'll tell you't I've always ben kind o' offish and partic'lar for a gal that's raised in the woods, and I *am*, with the rag-tag and bobtail, and a gal *has* to be, if she wants to *be* anything, but when people comes along which is my equals, I reckon I'm a pretty sociable heifer after all."

We resolved not to "lay by at Cottonwood."

CHAPTER V

ANOTHER NIGHT OF alternate tranquillity and turmoil. But morning came, by and by. It was another glad awakening to fresh breezes, vast expanses of level greensward, bright sunlight, an impressive solitude utterly without visible human beings or human habitations, and an atmosphere of such amazing magnifying properties that trees that seemed close at hand were more than three miles away. We resumed undress uniform, climbed a-top of the flying coach, dangled our legs over the side, shouted occasionally at our frantic mules, merely to see them lay their ears back and scamper faster, tied our hats on to keep our hair from blowing away, and leveled an outlook over the world-wide carpet about us for things new and strange to gaze at. Even at this day it thrills me through and through to think of the life, the gladness and the wild sense of freedom that used to make the blood dance in my veins on those fine overland mornings!

Along about an hour after breakfast we saw the first prairie-dog villages, the first antelope, and the first wolf. If I remember rightly, this latter was the regular *cayote* (pronounced ky-*o*-te) of the farther deserts. And if it *was*, he was not a pretty creature or respectable either, for I got well acquainted with his race afterward, and can speak with confidence. The cayote is a long, slim, sick and sorry-looking skeleton, with a gray wolf-skin stretched over it, a tolerably bushy tail that forever sags down with a despairing expression of forsakenness and misery, a furtive and evil eye, and a long, sharp face, with slightly lifted lip and exposed teeth. He has a general slinking expression all over. The cayote is a living, breathing allegory of Want. He is *always* hungry. He is always poor, out of luck and friendless. The meanest creatures despise him, and even the fleas would desert him for a velocipede. He is so spiritless and cowardly that even while his exposed teeth are pretending a threat, the rest of his face is apologizing for it. And he is *so* homely! – so scrawny, and ribby, and coarse-haired, and pitiful. When he sees you he lifts his lip and lets a flash of his teeth out, and then turns a little out of the course he was pursuing, depresses his head a bit, and strikes a long, soft-footed trot through the sage-brush, glancing over his shoulder at you, from time to time, till he is about out of easy pistol range, and then he stops and takes a deliberate survey of you; he will trot fifty yards and stop again – another fifty and stop again; and finally the gray of his gliding body blends with the gray of the sage-brush, and he disappears. All this is when you make no demonstration against him; but if you do, he develops a livelier interest in his journey, and instantly electrifies his heels and puts such a deal of real estate between himself and your weapon, that by the time you have raised the hammer you see that you need a minie rifle, and by the time you have got him in line you need a rifled cannon, and by the time you have "drawn a bead" on him you see well enough that nothing but an unusually long-winded streak of lightning could reach him where he is now. But if you start a swift-footed dog after him, you will enjoy it ever so much – especially if it is a dog that has a good opinion of himself, and has been brought up to think he knows something about speed. The cayote will go swinging gently off on that deceitful trot of his, and every little while he will smile a fraudful smile over his shoulder that will fill that dog entirely full of encouragement and worldly ambition, and make him lay his head still lower to the ground, and stretch his neck further to the front, and pant more fiercely, and stick his tail out straighter behind, and move his furious legs with a yet wilder frenzy, and leave a broader and broader, and higher and denser cloud of desert sand smoking behind, and marking his long wake across the level plain! And all this time the dog is only a short twenty feet behind the cayote, and to save the soul of him he cannot understand why it is that he can not get perceptibly closer; and he begins to get aggravated, and it makes him madder and madder to see how gently the cayote glides along and never pants or sweats or ceases to smile; and he grows still more and more incensed to see how shamefully he has been taken in by an entire stranger, and what an ignoble swindle that long, calm, soft-footed trot is; and next he notices that he is getting fagged, and that the cayote actually has to slacken speed a little to keep from running away from him – and *then* that town-dog is mad in earnest, and he begins to strain and weep and swear, and paw the sand higher than ever, and reach for the cayote with concentrated and desperate energy. This "spurt" finds him six feet behind the gliding enemy, and two miles from his friends. And then, in the instant that a wild new hope is lighting up his face, the cayote turns and smiles blandly upon him once more, and with a something about it which seems to say: "Well, I shall have to tear myself away from you, bub – business is business, and it will not do for me to be fooling along this way all day" – and forthwith there is a rushing sound, and the sudden splitting of a long crack through the atmosphere, and behold that dog is solitary and alone in the midst of a vast solitude!

It makes his head swim. He stops, and looks all around; climbs the nearest sand-mound, and gazes into the distance; shakes his head reflectively, and then, without a word, he turns and jogs along back to his train, and takes up a humble position under the hindmost wagon, and feels unspeakably mean, and looks ashamed, and hangs his tail at half-mast for a week. And for as much as a year after that, whenever there is a great hue and cry after a cayote, that dog will merely glance in that direction without emotion, and apparently observe to himself, "I believe I do not wish any of the pie."

The cayote lives chiefly in the most desolate and forbidding deserts, along with the lizard, the jackass-rabbit and the raven, and gets an uncertain and precarious living, and earns it. He seems to subsist almost wholly on the carcases of oxen, mules and horses that have dropped out of emigrant trains and died, and upon windfalls of carrion, and occasional legacies of offal bequeathed to him by white men who have been opulent enough to have something better to butcher than condemned army bacon. He will eat anything in the world that his first cousins, the desert-frequenting tribes of Indians will, and they will eat anything they can bite. It is a curious fact that these latter are the only creatures known to history who will eat nitro-glycerine and ask for more if they survive.

The cayote of the deserts beyond the Rocky Mountains has a peculiarly hard time of it, owing to the fact that his relations, the Indians, are just as apt to be the first to detect a seductive scent on the desert breeze, and follow the fragrance to the late ox it emanated from, as he is himself; and when this occurs he has to content himself with sitting off at a little distance watching those people strip off and dig out everything edible, and walk off with it. Then he and the waiting ravens explore the skeleton and polish the bones. It is considered that the cayote, and the obscene bird, and the Indian of the desert, testify their blood kinship with each other in that they live together in the waste places of the earth on terms of perfect confidence and friendship, while hating all other creatures and yearning to assist at their funerals. He does not mind going a hundred miles to breakfast, and a hundred and fifty to dinner, because he is sure to have three or four days between meals, and he can just as well be traveling and looking at the scenery as lying around doing nothing and adding to the burdens of his parents.

We soon learned to recognize the sharp, vicious bark of the cayote as it came across the murky plain at night to disturb our dreams among the mail-sacks; and remembering his forlorn aspect and his hard fortune, made shift to wish him the blessed novelty of a long day's good luck and a limitless larder the morrow.

CHAPTER VIII

IN A LITTLE while all interest was taken up in stretching our necks and watching for the "pony-rider" – the fleet messenger who sped across the continent from St. Joe to Sacramento, carrying letters nineteen hundred miles in eight days! Think of that for perishable horse and human flesh and blood to do! The pony-rider was usually a little bit of a man, brimful of spirit and endurance. No matter what time of the day or night his watch came on, and no matter whether it was winter or summer, raining, snowing, hailing, or sleeting, or whether his "beat" was a level straight road or a crazy trail over mountain crags and precipices, or whether it led through peaceful regions or regions that swarmed with hostile Indians, he must be always ready to leap into the saddle and be off like the wind! There was no idling-time for a pony-rider on duty. He rode fifty miles without stopping, by daylight, moonlight, starlight, or through the blackness of darkness – just as it happened. He rode a splendid horse that was born for a racer and fed and lodged like a gentleman; kept him at his utmost speed for ten miles, and then, as he came crashing up to the station where stood two men holding fast a fresh, impatient steed, the transfer of rider and mail bag was made in the twinkling of an eye, and away flew the eager pair and were out of sight before the spectator could get hardly the ghost of a look. Both rider and horse went "flying light." The rider's dress was thin, and fitted close; he wore a "round-about," and a skull-cap, and tucked his pantaloons into his boot-tops like a race-rider. He carried no arms – he carried nothing that was not absolutely necessary, for even the postage on his literary freight was worth *five dollars a letter*. He got but little frivolous correspondence to carry – his bag had business letters in it, mostly. His horse was stripped of all unnecessary weight, too. He wore a little wafer of a racing-saddle, and no visible blanket. He wore light shoes, or none at all. The little flat mail-pockets strapped under the rider's thighs would each hold about the bulk of a child's primer. They held many and many an important business chapter and newspaper letter, but these were written on paper as airy and thin as gold-leaf, nearly, and thus bulk and weight were economized. The stage-coach traveled about a hundred to a hundred and twenty-five miles a day (twenty-four hours), the pony-rider about two hundred and fifty. There were about eighty pony-riders in the saddle all the time, night and day, stretching in a long, scattering procession from Missouri to California, forty flying eastward, and forty toward the west, and among them making four hundred gallant horses earn a stirring livelihood and see a deal of scenery every single day in the year.

We had had a consuming desire, from the beginning, to see a pony-rider, but somehow or other all that passed us and all that met us managed to streak by in the night, and so we heard only a whiz and a hail, and the swift phantom of the desert was gone before we could get our heads out of the windows. But now we were expecting one along every moment, and would see him in broad daylight. Presently the driver exclaims:

"Here he comes!"

Every neck is stretched further, and every eye strained wider. Away across the endless dead level of the prairie a black speck appears against the sky, and it is plain that it moves. Well, I should think so! In a second or two it becomes a horse and rider, rising and falling, rising and falling – sweeping toward us nearer and nearer – growing more and more distinct, more and more sharply defined – nearer and still nearer, and the flutter of the hoofs comes faintly to the ear – another instant a whoop and a hurrah from our upper deck, a wave of the rider's hand, but no reply, and man and horse burst past our excited faces, and go winging away like a belated fragment of a storm!

So sudden is it all, and so like a flash of unreal fancy, that but for the flake of white foam left quivering and perishing on a mail-sack after the vision had flashed by and disappeared, we might have doubted whether we had seen any actual horse and man at all, maybe.

We rattled through Scott's Bluffs Pass, by and by. It was along here somewhere that we first came across genuine and unmistakable alkali water in the road, and we cordially hailed it as a first-class curiosity, and a thing to be mentioned with eclat in letters to the ignorant at home. This water gave the road a soapy appearance, and in many places the ground looked as if it had been white-washed. I think the strange alkali water excited us as much as any wonder we had come upon yet, and I know we felt very complacent and conceited, and better satisfied with life after we had added it to our list of things which *we* had seen and some other people had not. In a small way we were the same sort of simpletons as those who climb unnecessarily the perilous peaks of Mont Blanc and the Matterhorn, and derive no pleasure from it except the reflection that it isn't a common experience. But once in a while one of those parties trips and comes darting down the long mountain-crags in a sitting posture, making the crusted snow smoke behind him, flitting from bench to bench, and from terrace to terrace, jarring the earth where he strikes, and still glancing and flitting on again, sticking an iceberg into himself every now and then, and tearing his clothes, snatching at things to save himself, taking hold of trees and fetching them along with him, roots and all, starting little rocks now and then,

then big boulders, then acres of ice and snow and patches of forest, gathering and still gathering as he goes, adding and still adding to his massed and sweeping grandeur as he nears a three-thousand-foot precipice, till at last he waves his hat magnificently and rides into eternity on the back of a raging and tossing avalanche!

This is all very fine, but let us not be carried away by excitement, but ask calmly, how does this person feel about it in his cooler moments next day, with six or seven thousand feet of snow and stuff on top of him?

We crossed the sand hills near the scene of the Indian mail robbery and massacre of 1856, wherein the driver and conductor perished, and also all the passengers but one, it was supposed; but this must have been a mistake, for at different times afterward on the Pacific coast I was personally acquainted with a hundred and thirty-three or 1-four people who were wounded during that massacre, and barely escaped with their lives. There was no doubt of the truth of it – I had it from their own lips. One of these parties told me that he kept coming across arrow-heads in his system for nearly seven years after the massacre; and another of them told me that he was stuck so literally full of arrows that after the Indians were gone and he could raise up and examine himself, he could not restrain his tears, for his clothes were completely ruined.

The most trustworthy tradition avers, however, that only one man, a person named Babbitt, survived the massacre, and he was desperately wounded. He dragged himself on his hands and knee (for one leg was broken) to a station several miles away. He did it during portions of two nights, lying concealed one day and part of another, and for more than forty hours suffering unimaginable anguish from hunger, thirst and bodily pain. The Indians robbed the coach of everything it contained, including quite an amount of treasure.

CHAPTER IX

WE PASSED FORT Laramie in the night, and on the seventh morning out we found ourselves in the Black Hills, with Laramie Peak at our elbow (apparently) looming vast and solitary – a deep, dark, rich indigo blue in hue, so portentously did the old colossus frown under his beetling brows of storm-cloud. He was thirty or forty miles away, in reality, but he only seemed removed a little beyond the low ridge at our right. We breakfasted at Horse-Shoe Station, six hundred and seventy-six miles out from St. Joseph. We had now reached a hostile Indian country, and during the afternoon we passed Laparelle Station, and enjoyed great discomfort all the time we were in the neighborhood, being aware that many of the trees we dashed by at arm's length concealed a lurking Indian or two. During the preceding night an ambushed savage had sent a bullet through the pony-rider's jacket, but he had ridden on, just the same, because pony-riders were not allowed to stop and inquire into such things except when killed. As long as they had life enough left in them they had to stick to the horse and ride, even if the Indians had been waiting for them a week, and were entirely out of patience. About two hours and a half before we arrived at Laparelle Station, the keeper in charge of it had fired four times at an Indian, but he said with an injured air that the Indian had "skipped around so's to spile everything – and ammunition's blamed skurse, too." The most natural inference conveyed by his manner of speaking was, that in "skipping around," the Indian had taken an unfair advantage. The coach we were in had a neat hole through its front – a reminiscence of its last trip through this region. The bullet that made it wounded the driver slightly, but he did not mind it much. He said the place to keep a man "huffy" was down on the Southern Overland, among the Apaches, before the company moved the stage-line up on the northern route. He said the Apaches used to annoy him all the time down there, and that he came as near as anything to starving to death in the midst of abundance, because they kept him so leaky with bullet holes that he "couldn't hold his vittles." This person's statements were not generally believed.

We shut the blinds down very tightly that first night in the hostile Indian country, and lay on our arms. We slept on them some, but most of the time we only lay on them. We did not talk much, but kept quiet and listened. It was an inky-black night, and occasionally rainy. We were among woods and rocks, hills and gorges – so shut in, in fact, that when we peeped through a chink in a curtain, we could discern nothing. The driver and conductor on top were still, too, or only spoke at long intervals, in low tones, as is the way of men in the midst of invisible dangers. We listened to rain-drops pattering on the roof; and the grinding of the wheels through the muddy gravel; and the low wailing of the wind; and all the time we had that absurd sense upon us, inseparable from travel at night in a close-curtained vehicle, the sense of remaining perfectly still in one place, notwithstanding the jolting and swaying of the vehicle, the trampling of the horses, and the grinding of the wheels. We listened a long time, with intent faculties and bated breath; every time one of us would relax, and draw a long sigh of relief and start to say something, a comrade would be sure to utter a sudden "Hark!" and instantly the experimenter was rigid and listening again. So the tiresome minutes and decades of minutes dragged away, until at last our tense forms filmed over with a dulled consciousness, and we slept, if one might call such a condition by so strong a name – for it was a sleep set with a hair-trigger. It was a sleep seething and teeming with a weird and distressful confusion of shreds and fag-ends of dreams – a sleep that was a chaos. Presently, dreams and sleep and the sullen hush of the night were startled by a ringing report, and cloven by *such* a long, wild, agonizing shriek! Then we heard – ten steps from the stage –

"Help! help! help!" [It was our driver's voice.]

"Kill him! Kill him like a dog!"

"I'm being murdered! Will no man lend me a pistol?"

"Look out! head him off! head him off!"

[Two pistol shots; a confusion of voices and the trampling of many feet, as if a crowd were closing and surging together around some object; several heavy, dull blows, as with a club; a voice that said appealingly, "Don't, gentlemen, please don't – I'm a dead man!" Then a fainter groan, and another blow, and away sped the stage into the darkness, and left the grisly mystery behind us.]

What a startle it was! Eight seconds would amply cover the time it occupied – maybe even five would do it. We only had time to plunge at a curtain and unbuckle and unbutton part of it in an awkward and hindering flurry, when our whip cracked sharply overhead, and we went rumbling and thundering away, down a mountain "grade."

We fed on that mystery the rest of the night – what was left of it, for it was waning fast. It had to remain a present mystery, for all we could get from the conductor in answer to our hails was something that sounded, through the clatter of the wheels, like "Tell you in the morning!"

So we lit our pipes and opened the corner of a curtain for a chimney, and lay there in the dark, listening to each other's story of how he first felt and how many thousand Indians he first thought had hurled themselves upon us, and what his remembrance of the subsequent sounds was, and the order of their occurrence. And we theorized, too, but there was never a theory that would account for our driver's voice being out there, nor yet account for his Indian murderers talking such good English, if they *were* Indians.

So we chatted and smoked the rest of the night comfortably away, our boding anxiety being somehow marvelously dissipated by the real presence of something to be anxious *about.*

We never did get much satisfaction about that dark occurrence. All that we could make out of the odds and ends of the information we gathered in the morning, was that the disturbance occurred at a station; that we changed drivers there, and that the driver that got off there had been talking roughly about some of the outlaws that infested the region ("for there wasn't a man around there but had a price on his head and didn't dare show himself in the settlements," the conductor said); he had talked roughly about these characters, and ought to have "drove up there with his pistol cocked and ready on the seat alongside of him, and begun business himself, because any softy would know they would be laying for him."

That was all we could gather, and we could see that neither the conductor nor the new driver were much concerned about the matter. They plainly had little respect for a man who would deliver offensive opinions of people and then be so simple as to come into their presence unprepared to "back his judgment," as they pleasantly phrased the killing of any fellow-being who did not like said opinions. And likewise they plainly had a contempt for the man's poor discretion in venturing to rouse the wrath of such utterly reckless wild beasts as those outlaws – and the conductor added:

"I tell you it's as much as Slade himself wants to do!"

This remark created an entire revolution in my curiosity. I cared nothing now about the Indians, and even lost interest in the murdered driver. There was such magic in that name, SLADE! Day or night, now, I stood always ready to drop any subject in hand, to listen to something new about Slade and his ghastly exploits. Even before we got to Overland City, we had begun to hear about Slade and his "division" (for he was a "division-agent") on the Overland; and from the hour we had left Overland City we had heard drivers and conductors talk about only three things – "Californy," the Nevada silver mines, and this desperado Slade. And a deal the most of the talk was about Slade. We had gradually come to have a realizing sense of the fact that Slade was a man whose heart and hands and soul were steeped in the blood of offenders against his dignity;

a man who awfully avenged all injuries, affronts, insults or slights, of whatever kind – on the spot if he could, years afterward if lack of earlier opportunity compelled it; a man whose hate tortured him day and night till vengeance appeased it – and not an ordinary vengeance either, but his enemy's absolute death – nothing less; a man whose face would light up with a terrible joy when he surprised a foe and had him at a disadvantage. A high and efficient servant of the Overland, an outlaw among outlaws and yet their relentless scourge, Slade was at once the most bloody, the most dangerous and the most valuable citizen that inhabited the savage fastnesses of the mountains.

CHAPTER X

REALLY AND TRULY, two-thirds of the talk of drivers and conductors had been about this man Slade, ever since the day before we reached Julesburg. In order that the eastern reader may have a clear conception of what a Rocky Mountain desperado is, in his highest state of development, I will reduce all this mass of overland gossip to one straightforward narrative, and present it in the following shape:

Slade was born in Illinois, of good parentage. At about twenty-six years of age he killed a man in a quarrel and fled the country. At St. Joseph, Missouri, he joined one of the early California-bound emigrant trains, and was given the post of train-master. One day on the plains he had an angry dispute with one of his wagon-drivers, and both drew their revolvers. But the driver was the quicker artist, and had his weapon cocked first. So Slade said it was a pity to waste life on so small a matter, and proposed that the pistols be thrown on the ground and the quarrel settled by a fist-fight. The unsuspecting driver agreed, and threw down his pistol – whereupon Slade laughed at his simplicity, and shot him dead!

He made his escape, and lived a wild life for awhile, dividing his time between fighting Indians and avoiding an Illinois sheriff, who had been sent to arrest him for his first murder. It is said that in one Indian battle he killed three savages with his own hand, and afterward cut their ears off and sent them, with his compliments, to the chief of the tribe.

Slade soon gained a name for fearless resolution, and this was sufficient merit to procure for him the important post of overland division-agent at Julesburg, in place of Mr. Jules, removed. For some time previously, the company's horses had been frequently stolen, and the coaches delayed, by gangs of outlaws, who were wont to laugh at the idea of any man's having the temerity to resent such outrages. Slade resented them promptly. The outlaws soon found that the new agent was a man who did not fear anything that breathed the breath of life. He made short work of all offenders. The result was that delays ceased, the company's property was let alone, and no matter what happened or who suffered, Slade's coaches went through, every time! True, in order to bring about this wholesome change, Slade had to kill several men – some say three, others say four, and others six – but the world was the richer for their loss. The first prominent difficulty he had was with the ex-agent Jules, who bore the reputation of being a reckless and desperate man himself. Jules hated Slade for supplanting him, and a good fair occasion for a fight was all he was waiting for. By and by Slade dared to employ a man whom Jules had once discharged. Next, Slade seized a team of stage-horses which he accused Jules of having driven off and hidden somewhere for his own use. War was declared, and for a day or two the two men walked warily about the streets, seeking each other, Jules armed with a double-barreled shotgun, and Slade with his history-creating revolver. Finally, as Slade stepped into a store, Jules poured the contents of his gun into him from behind the door. Slade was pluck, and Jules got several bad pistol wounds in return. Then both men fell, and were carried to their respective lodgings, both swearing that better aim should do deadlier work next time. Both were bedridden a long time, but Jules got on his feet first, and gathering his possessions together, packed them on a couple of mules, and fled to the Rocky Mountains to gather strength in safety against the day of reckoning. For many months he was not seen or heard of, and was gradually dropped out of the remembrance of all save Slade himself. But Slade was not the man to forget him. On the contrary, common report said that Slade kept a reward standing for his capture, dead or alive!

After awhile, seeing that Slade's energetic administration had restored peace and order to one of the worst divisions of the road, the overland stage company transferred him to the Rocky Ridge division in the Rocky Mountains, to see if he could perform a like miracle there. It was the very paradise of outlaws and desperadoes. There was absolutely no semblance of law there. Violence was the rule. Force was the only recognized authority. The commonest misunderstandings were settled on the spot with the revolver or the knife. Murders were done in open day, and with sparkling frequency, and nobody thought of inquiring into them. It was considered that the parties who did the killing had their private reasons for it; for other people to meddle would have been looked upon as indelicate. After a murder, all that Rocky Mountain etiquette required of a spectator was, that he should help the gentleman bury his game – otherwise his churlishness would surely be remembered against him the first time he killed a man himself and needed a neighborly turn in interring him.

Slade took up his residence sweetly and peacefully in the midst of this hive of horse-thieves and assassins, and the very first time one of them aired his insolent swaggerings in his presence he shot him dead! He began a raid on the outlaws, and in a singularly short space of time he had completely stopped their depredations on the stage stock, recovered a large number of stolen horses, killed several of the worst desperadoes of the district, and gained such a dread ascendancy over the rest that they respected him, admired him, feared him, obeyed him! He wrought the same marvelous change in the ways of the community that had marked his administration at Overland City. He captured two men who had stolen overland stock, and with his own hands he hanged them. He was supreme judge in his district, and he was jury and executioner likewise – and not only in the case of offences against his employers, but against passing emigrants as well. On one occasion some emigrants had their stock lost or stolen, and told Slade, who chanced to visit their camp. With a single companion he rode to a ranch, the owners of which he suspected, and opening the door, commenced firing, killing three, and wounding the fourth.

From a bloodthirstily interesting little Montana book* I take this paragraph:

> While on the road, Slade held absolute sway. He would ride down to a station, get into a quarrel, turn the house out of windows, and maltreat the occupants most cruelly. The unfortunates had no means of redress, and were compelled to

* "The Vigilantes of Montana," by Prof. Thos. J. Dimsdale.

recuperate as best they could. On one of these occasions, it is said he killed the father of the fine little half-breed boy Jemmy, whom he adopted, and who lived with his widow after his execution. Stories of Slade's hanging men, and of innumerable assaults, shootings, stabbings and beatings, in which he was a principal actor, form part of the legends of the stage line. As for minor quarrels and shootings, it is absolutely certain that a minute history of Slade's life would be one long record of such practices.

Slade was a matchless marksman with a navy revolver. The legends say that one morning at Rocky Ridge, when he was feeling comfortable, he saw a man approaching who had offended him some days before – observe the fine memory he had for matters like that – and, "Gentlemen," said Slade, drawing, "it is a good twenty-yard shot – I'll clip the third button on his coat!" Which he did. The bystanders all admired it. And they all attended the funeral, too.

On one occasion a man who kept a little whiskey-shelf at the station did something which angered Slade – and went and made his will. A day or two afterward Slade came in and called for some brandy. The man reached under the counter (ostensibly to get a bottle – possibly to get something else), but Slade smiled upon him that peculiarly bland and satisfied smile of his which the neighbors had long ago learned to recognize as a death-warrant in disguise, and told him to "none of that! – pass out the high-priced article." So the poor bar-keeper had to turn his back and get the high-priced brandy from the shelf; and when he faced around again he was looking into the muzzle of Slade's pistol. "And the next instant," added my informant, impressively, "he was one of the deadest men that ever lived."

The stage-drivers and conductors told us that sometimes Slade would leave a hated enemy wholly unmolested, unnoticed and unmentioned, for weeks together – had done it once or twice at any rate. And some said they believed he did it in order to lull the victims into unwatchfulness, so that he could get the advantage of them, and others said they believed he saved up an enemy that way, just as a schoolboy saves up a cake, and made the pleasure go as far as it would by gloating over the anticipation. One of these cases was that of a Frenchman who had offended Slade. To the surprise of everybody Slade did not kill him on the spot, but let him alone for a considerable time. Finally, however, he went to the Frenchman's house very late one night, knocked, and when his enemy opened the door, shot him dead – pushed the corpse inside the door with his foot, set the house on fire and burned up the dead man, his widow and three children! I heard this story from several different people, and they evidently believed what they were saying. It may be true, and it may not. "Give a dog a bad name," etc.

Slade was captured, once, by a party of men who intended to lynch him. They disarmed him, and shut him up in a strong log-house, and placed a guard over him. He prevailed on his captors to send for his wife, so that he might have a last interview with her. She was a brave, loving, spirited woman. She jumped on a horse and rode for life and death. When she arrived they let her in without searching her, and before the door could be closed she whipped out a couple of revolvers, and she and her lord marched forth defying the party. And then, under a brisk fire, they mounted double and galloped away unharmed!

In the fullness of time Slade's myrmidons captured his ancient enemy Jules, whom they found in a well-chosen hiding-place in the remote fastnesses of the mountains, gaining a precarious livelihood with his rifle. They brought him to Rocky Ridge, bound hand and foot, and deposited him in the middle of the cattle-yard with his back against a post. It is said that the pleasure that lit Slade's face when he heard of it was something fearful to contemplate. He examined his enemy to see that he was securely tied, and then went to bed, content to wait till morning before enjoying the luxury of killing him. Jules spent the night in the cattle-yard, and it is a region where warm nights are never known. In the morning Slade practiced on him with his revolver, nipping the flesh here and there, and occasionally clipping off a finger, while Jules begged him to kill him outright and put him out of his misery. Finally Slade reloaded, and walking up close to his victim, made some characteristic remarks and then dispatched him. The body lay there half a day, nobody venturing to touch it without orders, and then Slade detailed a party and assisted at the burial himself. But he first cut off the dead man's ears and put them in his vest pocket, where he carried them for some time with great satisfaction. That is the story as I have frequently heard it told and seen it in print in California newspapers. It is doubtless correct in all essential particulars.

In due time we rattled up to a stage-station, and sat down to breakfast with a half-savage, half-civilized company of armed and bearded mountaineers, ranchmen and station employees. The most gentlemanly-appearing, quiet and affable officer we had yet found along the road in the Overland Company's service was the person who sat at the head of the table, at my elbow. Never youth stared and shivered as I did when I heard them call him SLADE!

Here was romance, and I sitting face to face with it! – looking upon it – touching it – hobnobbing with it, as it were! Here, right by my side, was the actual ogre who, in fights and brawls and various ways, *had taken the lives of twenty-six human beings*, or all men lied about him! I suppose I was the proudest stripling that ever traveled to see strange lands and wonderful people.

He was so friendly and so gentle-spoken that I warmed to him in spite of his awful history. It was hardly possible to realize that this pleasant person was the pitiless scourge of the outlaws, the raw-head-and-bloody-bones the nursing mothers of the mountains terrified their children with. And to this day I can remember nothing remarkable about Slade except that his face was rather broad across the cheek bones, and that the cheek bones were low and the lips peculiarly thin and straight. But that was enough to leave something of an effect upon me, for since then I seldom see a face possessing those characteristics without fancying that the owner of it is a dangerous man.

The coffee ran out. At least it was reduced to one tin-cupful, and Slade was about to take it when he saw that my cup was empty. He politely offered to fill it, but although I wanted it, I politely declined. I was afraid he had not killed anybody that morning, and might be needing diversion. But still with firm politeness he insisted on filling my cup, and said I had traveled all night and better deserved it than he – and while he talked he placidly poured the fluid, to the last drop. I thanked him and drank it, but it gave me no comfort, for I could not feel sure that he would not be sorry, presently, that he had given it away, and proceed to kill me to distract his thoughts from the loss. But nothing of the kind occurred. We left him with only twenty-six dead people to account for, and I felt a tranquil satisfaction in the thought that in so judiciously taking care of No. 1 at that breakfast-table I had pleasantly escaped being No. 27. Slade came out to the coach and saw us off, first ordering certain reärrangements of the mail bags for our comfort, and then we took leave of him, satisfied that we should hear of him again, some day, and wondering in what connection.

CHAPTER XI

AND SURE ENOUGH, two or three years afterward, we did hear of him again. News came to the Pacific coast that the Vigilance Committee in Montana (whither Slade had removed from Rocky Ridge) had hanged him. I find an account of the affair in the thrilling little book I quoted a paragraph from in the last chapter – "The Vigilantes of Montana; being a Reliable Account of the Capture, Trial and Execution of Henry Plummer's Notorious Road Agent Band: By Prof. Thos. J. Dimsdale, Virginia City, M. T." Mr. Dimsdale's chapter is well worth reading, as a specimen of how the people of the frontier deal with criminals when the courts of law prove inefficient. Mr. Dimsdale makes two remarks about Slade, both of which are accurately descriptive, and one of which is exceedingly picturesque: "Those who saw him in his natural state only, would pronounce him to be a kind husband, a most hospitable host and a courteous gentleman; on the contrary, those who met him when maddened with liquor and surrounded by a gang of armed roughs, would pronounce him a fiend incarnate." And this: "From Fort Kearney, west, he was feared *a great deal more than the Almighty*." For compactness, simplicity and vigor of expression, I will "back" that sentence against anything in literature. Mr. Dimsdale's narrative is as follows. In all places where italics occur, they are mine:

> After the execution of the five men on the 14th of January, the Vigilantes considered that their work was nearly ended. They had freed the country of highwaymen and murderers to a great extent, and they determined that in the absence of the regular civil authority they would establish a People's Court where all offenders should be tried by judge and jury. This was the nearest approach to social order that the circumstances permitted, and, though strict legal authority was wanting, yet the people were firmly determined to maintain its efficiency, and to enforce its decrees. It may here be mentioned that the overt act which was the last round on the fatal ladder to the scaffold on which Slade perished, *was the tearing in pieces and stamping upon a writ of this court, followed by his arrest of the Judge, Alex. Davis, by authority of a presented Derringer, and with his own hands.*

J. A. Slade was himself, we have been informed, a Vigilante; he openly boasted of it, and said he knew all that they knew. He was never accused, or even suspected, of either murder or robbery, committed in this Territory (the latter crime was never laid to his charge, in any place); but that he had killed several men in other localities was notorious, and his bad reputation in this respect was a most powerful argument in determining his fate, when he was finally arrested for the offence above mentioned. On returning from Milk River he became more and more addicted to drinking, until at last it was a common feat for him and his friends to "take the town." He and a couple of his dependents might often be seen on one horse, galloping through the streets, shouting and yelling, firing revolvers, etc. On many occasions he would ride his horse into stores, break up bars, toss the scales out of doors and use most insulting language to parties present. Just previous to the day of his arrest, he had given a fearful beating to one of his followers; but such was his influence over them that the man wept bitterly at the gallows, and begged for his life with all his power. *It had become quite common, when Slade was on a spree, for the shopkeepers and citizens to close the stores and put out all the lights;* being fearful of some outrage at his hands. For his wanton destruction of goods and furniture, he was always ready to pay, when sober, if he had money; but there were not a few who regarded payment as small satisfaction for the outrage, and these men were his personal enemies.

From time to time Slade received warnings from men that he well knew would not deceive him, of the certain end of his conduct. There was not a moment, for weeks previous to his arrest, in which the public did not expect to hear of some bloody outrage. The dread of his very name, and the presence of the armed band of hangers-on who followed him alone prevented a resistance which must certainly have ended in the instant murder or mutilation of the opposing party.

Slade was frequently arrested by order of the court whose organization we have described, and had treated it with respect by paying one or two fines and promising to pay the rest when he had money; but in the transaction that occurred at this crisis, he forgot even this caution, and goaded by passion and the hatred of restraint, he sprang into the embrace of death.

Slade had been drunk and "cutting up" all night. He and his companions had made the town a perfect hell. In the morning, J. M. Fox, the sheriff, met him, arrested him, took him into court and commenced reading a warrant that he had for his arrest, by way of arraignment. He became uncontrollably furious, and *seizing the writ, he tore it up, threw it on the ground and stamped upon it.* The clicking of the locks of his companions' revolvers was instantly heard, and a crisis was expected. The sheriff did not attempt his retention; but being at least as prudent as he was valiant, he succumbed, leaving Slade the *master of the situation and the conqueror and ruler of the courts, law and law-makers.* This was a declaration of war, and was so accepted. The Vigilance Committee now felt that the question of social order and the preponderance of the law-abiding citizens had then and there to be decided. They knew the character of Slade, and they were well aware that they must submit to his rule without murmur, or else that he must be dealt with in such fashion as would prevent his being able to wreak his vengeance on the committee, who could never have hoped to live in the Territory secure from outrage or death, and who could never leave it without encountering his friends, whom his victory would have emboldened and stimulated to a pitch that would have rendered them reckless of consequences. The day previous he had ridden into Dorris's store, and on being requested to leave, he drew his revolver and threatened to kill the gentleman who spoke to him. Another saloon he had led his horse into, and buying a bottle of wine, he tried to make the animal drink it. This was not considered an uncommon performance, as he had often entered saloons and commenced firing at the lamps, causing a wild stampede.

A leading member of the committee met Slade, and informed him in the quiet, earnest manner of one who feels the importance of what he is saying: "Slade, get your horse at once, and go home, or there will be —— to pay." Slade started and took a long look, with his dark and piercing eyes, at the gentleman. "What do you mean?" said he. "You have no right to ask me what I mean," was the quiet reply, "get your horse at once, and remember what I tell you." After a short pause he promised to do so, and actually got into the saddle; but, being still intoxicated, he began calling aloud to one after another of his friends, and at last seemed to have forgotten the warning he had received and became again uproarious, shouting the name of a well-known courtezan in company with those of two men whom he considered heads of the committee, as a sort of a challenge; perhaps, however, as a simple act of bravado. It seems probable that the intimation of personal danger he had received had not been forgotten entirely; though fatally for him, he took a foolish way of showing his remembrance of it. He sought out Alexander Davis, the Judge of the Court, and drawing a cocked Derringer, he presented it at his head, and told him that he should hold him as a hostage for his own safety. As the judge stood perfectly quiet, and offered no resistance to his captor, no further outrage followed on this score. Previous to this, on account of the critical state of affairs, the committee had met, and at last resolved to arrest him. His execution had not been agreed upon, and, at that time, would have been negatived, most assuredly. A messenger rode down to Nevada to inform the leading men of what was on hand, as it was desirable to show that there was a feeling of unanimity on the subject, all along the gulch.

The miners turned out almost *en masse*, leaving their work and forming in solid column, about six hundred strong, armed to the teeth, they marched up to Virginia. The leader of the body well knew the temper of his men on the subject. He spurred on ahead of them, and hastily calling a meeting of the executive, he told them plainly that the miners meant "business," and that, if they came up, they would not stand in the street to be shot down by Slade's friends; but that they would take him and hang him. The meeting was small, as the Virginia men were loath to act at all. This momentous announcement of the feeling of the Lower Town was made to a cluster of men, who were deliberating behind a wagon, at the rear of a store on Main street.

The committee were most unwilling to proceed to extremities. All the duty they had ever performed seemed as nothing to the task before them; but they had to decide, and that quickly. It was finally agreed that if the whole body of miners were of the opinion that he should be hanged, that the committee left it in their hands to deal with him. Off, at hot speed, rode the leader of the Nevada men to join his command.

Slade had found out what was intended, and the news sobered him instantly. He went into P. S. Pfouts' store, where Davis was, and apologized for his conduct, saying that he would take it all back.

The head of the column now wheeled into Wallace street and marched up at quick time. Halting in front of the store, the executive officer of the committee stepped forward and arrested Slade, who was at once informed of his doom, and inquiry was made as to whether he had any business to settle. Several parties spoke to him on the subject; but to all such inquiries he turned a deaf ear, being entirely absorbed in the terrifying reflections on his own awful position. He never ceased his entreaties for life, and to see his dear wife. The unfortunate lady referred to, between whom and Slade there existed a warm affection, was at this time living at their ranch on the Madison. She was possessed of considerable personal attractions; tall, well-formed, of graceful carriage, pleasing manners, and was, withal, an accomplished horsewoman.

A messenger from Slade rode at full speed to inform her of her husband's arrest. In an instant she was in the saddle, and with all the energy that love and despair could lend to an ardent temperament and a strong physique, she urged her fleet charger over the twelve miles of rough and rocky ground that intervened between her and the object of her passionate devotion.

Meanwhile a party of volunteers had made the necessary preparations for the execution, in the valley traversed by the branch. Beneath the site of Pfouts and Russell's stone building there was a corral, the gate-posts of which were strong and high. Across the top was laid a beam, to which the rope was fastened, and a dry-goods box served for the platform. To this place Slade was marched, surrounded by a guard, composing the best-armed and most numerous force that has ever appeared in Montana Territory.

The doomed man had so exhausted himself by tears, prayers and lamentations, that he had scarcely strength left to stand under the fatal beam. He repeatedly exclaimed, "My God! my God! must I die? Oh, my dear wife!"

On the return of the fatigue party, they encountered some friends of Slade, staunch and reliable citizens and members of the committee, but who were personally attached to the condemned. On hearing of his sentence, one of them, a stout-hearted man, pulled out his handkerchief and walked away, weeping like a child. Slade still begged to see his wife, most piteously, and it seemed hard to deny his request; but the bloody consequences that were sure to follow the inevitable attempt at a rescue, that her presence and entreaties would have certainly incited, forbade the granting of his request. Several gentlemen were sent for to see him, in his last moment, one of whom (Judge Davis) made a short address to the people; but in such low tones as to be inaudible, save to a few in his immediate vicinity. One of his friends, after exhausting his powers of entreaty, threw off his coat and declared that the prisoner could not be hanged until he himself was killed. A hundred guns were instantly leveled at him; whereupon he turned and fled; but, being brought back, he was compelled to resume his coat, and to give a promise of future peaceable demeanor.

Scarcely a leading man in Virginia could be found, though numbers of the citizens joined the ranks of the guard when the arrest was made. All lamented the stern necessity which dictated the execution.

Everything being ready, the command was given, "Men, do your duty," and the box being instantly slipped from beneath his feet, he died almost instantaneously.

The body was cut down and carried to the Virginia Hotel, where, in a darkened room, it was scarcely laid out, when the unfortunate and bereaved companion of the deceased arrived, at headlong speed, to find that all was over, and that she was a widow. Her grief and heart-piercing cries were terrible evidences of the depth of her attachment for her lost husband, and a considerable period elapsed before she could regain the command of her excited feelings.

There is something about the desperado-nature that is wholly unaccountable – at least it looks unaccountable. It is this. The true desperado is gifted with splendid courage, and yet he will take the most infamous advantage of his enemy; armed and free, he will stand up before a host and fight until he is shot all to pieces, and yet when he is under the gallows and helpless he will cry and plead like a child. Words are cheap, and it is easy to call Slade a coward (all executed men who do not "die game" are promptly called cowards by unreflecting people), and when we read of Slade that he "had so exhausted himself by tears, prayers and lamentations, that he had scarcely strength left to stand under the fatal beam," the disgraceful word suggests itself in a moment – yet in frequently defying and inviting the vengeance of banded Rocky Mountain cutthroats by shooting down their comrades and leaders, and never offering to hide or fly, Slade showed that he was a man of peerless bravery. No coward would dare that. Many a notorious coward, many a chicken-livered poltroon, coarse, brutal, degraded, has made his dying speech without a quaver in his voice and been swung into eternity with what looked like the calmest fortitude, and so we are justified in believing, from the low intellect of such a creature, that it was not *moral* courage that enabled him to do it. Then, if moral courage is not the requisite quality, what could it have been that this stout-hearted Slade lacked? – this bloody, desperate, kindly-mannered, urbane gentleman, who never hesitated to warn his most ruffianly enemies that he would kill them whenever or wherever he came across them next! I think it is a conundrum worth investigating.

CHAPTER XVII

AT THE END of our two days' sojourn, we left Great Salt Lake City hearty and well fed and happy – physically superb but not so very much wiser, as regards the "Mormon question," than we were when we arrived, perhaps. We had a deal more "information" than we had before, of course, but we did not know what portion of it was reliable and what was not – for it all came from acquaintances of a day – strangers, strictly speaking. We were told, for instance, that the dreadful "Mountain Meadows Massacre" was the work of the Indians entirely, and that the Gentiles had meanly tried to fasten it upon the Mormons; we were told, likewise, that the Indians were to blame, partly, and partly the Mormons; and we were told, likewise, and just as positively, that the Mormons were almost if not wholly and completely responsible for that most treacherous and pitiless butchery. We got the story in all these different shapes, but it was not till several years afterward that Mrs. Waite's book, "The Mormon Prophet," came out with Judge Cradlebaugh's trial of the accused parties in it and revealed the truth that the latter version was the correct one and that the Mormons *were* the assassins. All our "information" had three sides to it, and so I gave up the idea that I could settle the "Mormon question" in two days. Still I have seen newspaper correspondents do it in one.

I left Great Salt Lake a good deal confused as to what state of things existed there – and sometimes even questioning in my own mind whether a state of things existed there at all or not. But presently I remembered with a lightening sense of relief that we had learned two or three trivial things there which we could be certain of; and so the two days were not wholly lost. For instance, we had learned that we were at last in a pioneer land, in absolute and tangible reality. The high prices charged for trifles were eloquent of high freights and bewildering distances of freightage. In the east, in those days, the smallest moneyed denomination was a penny and it represented the smallest purchasable quantity of any commodity. West of Cincinnati the smallest coin in use was the silver five-cent piece and no smaller quantity of an article could be bought than "five cents' worth." In Overland City the lowest coin appeared to be the ten-cent piece; but in Salt Lake there did not seem to be any money in circulation smaller than a quarter, or any smaller quantity purchasable of any commodity than twenty-five cents' worth. We had always been used to half dimes and "five cents' worth" as the minimum of financial negotiations; but in Salt Lake if one wanted a cigar, it was a quarter; if he wanted a chalk pipe, it was a quarter; if he wanted a peach, or a candle, or a newspaper, or a shave, or a little Gentile whiskey to rub on his corns to arrest indigestion and keep him from having the toothache, twenty-five cents was the price, every time. When we looked at the shot-bag of silver, now and then, we seemed to be wasting our substance in riotous living, but if we referred to the expense account we could see that we had not been doing anything of the kind. But people easily get reconciled to big money and big prices, and fond and vain of both – it is a descent to little coins and cheap prices that is hardest to bear and slowest to take hold upon one's toleration. After a month's acquaintance with the twenty-five-cent minimum, the average human being is ready to blush every time he thinks of his despicable five-cent days. How sun-burnt with blushes I used to get in gaudy Nevada, every time I thought of my first financial experience in Salt Lake. It was on this wise (which is a favorite expression of great authors, and a very neat one, too, but I never hear anybody *say* on this wise when they are talking). A young half-breed with a complexion like a yellow-jacket asked me if I would have my boots blacked. It was at the Salt Lake House the morning after we arrived. I said yes, and he blacked them. Then I handed him a silver five-cent piece, with the benevolent air of a person who is conferring wealth and blessedness upon poverty and suffering. The yellow-jacket took it with what I judged to be suppressed emotion, and laid it reverently down in the middle of his broad hand. Then he began to contemplate it, much as a philosopher contemplates a gnat's ear in the ample field of his microscope. Several mountaineers, teamsters, stage-drivers, etc., drew near and dropped into the tableau and fell to surveying the money with that attractive indifference to formality which is noticeable in the hardy pioneer. Presently the yellow-jacket handed the half dime back to me and told me I ought to keep my money in my pocket-book instead of in my soul, and then I wouldn't get it cramped and shriveled up so!

What a roar of vulgar laughter there was! I destroyed the mongrel reptile on the spot, but I smiled and smiled all the time I was detaching his scalp, for the remark he made *was* good for an "Injun."

Yes, we had learned in Salt Lake to be charged great prices without letting the inward shudder appear on the surface – for even already we had overheard and noted the tenor of conversations among drivers, conductors, and hostlers, and finally among citizens of Salt Lake, until we were well aware that these superior beings despised "emigrants." We permitted no tell-tale shudders and winces in our countenances, for we wanted to seem pioneers, or Mormons, half-breeds, teamsters, stage-drivers, Mountain Meadow assassins – anything in the world that the plains and Utah respected and admired – but we were wretchedly ashamed of being "emigrants," and sorry enough that we had white shirts and could not swear in the presence of ladies without looking the other way.

And many a time in Nevada, afterwards, we had occasion to remember with humiliation that we were "emigrants," and consequently a low and inferior sort of creatures. Perhaps the reader has visited Utah, Nevada, or California, even in these latter days, and while communing with himself upon the sorrowful banishment of those countries from what he considers "the world," has had his wings clipped by finding that *he* is the one to be pitied, and that there are entire populations around him ready and willing to do it for him – yea, who are complacently doing it for him already, wherever he steps his foot. Poor thing, they are making fun of his hat; and the cut of his New York coat; and his conscientiousness about his grammar; and his feeble profanity; and his consumingly ludicrous ignorance of ores, shafts, tunnels, and other things which he never saw before, and never felt enough interest in to read about. And all the time that he is thinking what a sad fate it is to be exiled to that far country, that lonely land, the citizens around him are looking down on him with a blighting compassion because he is an "emigrant" instead of that proudest and blessedest creature that exists on all the earth, a "FORTY-NINER."

The accustomed coach life began again, now, and by midnight it almost seemed as if we never had been out of our snuggery among the mail-sacks at all. We had made one alteration, however. We had provided enough bread, boiled ham and hard-boiled eggs to last double the six hundred miles of staging we had still to do.

And it was comfort in those succeeding days to sit up and contemplate the majestic panorama of mountains and valleys spread out below us and eat ham and hard-boiled eggs while our spiritual natures reveled alternately in rainbows, thunderstorms, and peerless sunsets. Nothing helps scenery like ham and eggs. Ham and eggs, and after these a pipe – an old, rank, delicious pipe – ham and eggs and scenery, a "down grade," a flying coach, a fragrant pipe and a contented heart – these make happiness. It is what all the ages have struggled for.

CHAPTER XVIII

AT EIGHT IN the morning we reached the remnant and ruin of what had been the important military station of "Camp Floyd," some forty-five or fifty miles from Salt Lake City. At four P.M. we had doubled our distance and were ninety or a hundred miles from Salt Lake. And now we entered upon one of that species of deserts whose concentrated hideousness shames the diffused and diluted horrors of Sahara – an "*alkali*" desert. For sixty-eight miles there was but one break in it. I do not remember that this was really a break; indeed it seems to me that it was nothing but a watering depot *in the midst* of the stretch of sixty-eight miles. If my memory serves me, there was no well or spring at this place, but the water was hauled there by mule and ox teams from the further side of the desert. There was a stage-station there. It was forty-five miles from the beginning of the desert, and twenty-three from the end of it.

We plowed and dragged and groped along, the whole live-long night, and at the end of this uncomfortable twelve hours we finished the forty-five-mile part of the desert and got to the stage-station where the imported water was. The sun was just rising. It was easy enough to cross a desert in the night while we were asleep; and it was pleasant to reflect, in the morning, that we in actual person *had* encountered an absolute desert and could always speak knowingly of deserts in presence of the ignorant thenceforward. And it was pleasant also to reflect that this was not an obscure, back-country desert, but a very celebrated one, the metropolis itself, as you may say. All this was very well and very comfortable and satisfactory – but now we were to cross a desert in *daylight*. This was fine – novel – romantic – dramatically adventurous – *this*, indeed, was worth living for, worth traveling for! We would write home all about it.

This enthusiasm, this stern thirst for adventure, wilted under the sultry August sun and did not last above one hour. One poor little hour – and then we were ashamed that we had "gushed" so. The poetry was all in the anticipation – there is none in the reality. Imagine a vast, waveless ocean stricken dead and turned to ashes; imagine this solemn waste tufted with ash-dusted sage-bushes; imagine the lifeless silence and solitude that belong to such a place; imagine a coach, creeping like a bug through the midst of this shoreless level, and sending up tumbled volumes of dust as if it were a bug that went by steam; imagine this aching monotony of toiling and plowing kept up hour after hour, and the shore still as far away as ever, apparently; imagine team, driver, coach and passengers so deeply coated with ashes that they are all one colorless color; imagine ash-drifts roosting above moustaches and eyebrows like snow accumulations on boughs and bushes. This is the reality of it.

The sun beats down with dead, blistering, relentless malignity; the perspiration is welling from every pore in man and beast, but scarcely a sign of it finds its way to the surface – it is absorbed before it gets there; there is not the faintest breath of air stirring; there is not a merciful shred of cloud in all the brilliant firmament; there is not a living creature visible in any direction whither one searches the blank level that stretches its monotonous miles on every hand; there is not a sound – not a sigh – not a whisper – not a buzz, or a whir of wings, or distant pipe of bird – not even a sob from the lost souls that doubtless people that dead air. And so the occasional sneezing of the resting mules, and the champing of the bits, grate harshly on the grim stillness, not dissipating the spell but accenting it and making one feel more lonesome and forsaken than before.

The mules, under violent swearing, coaxing and whip-cracking, would make at stated intervals a "spurt," and drag the coach a hundred or may be two hundred yards, stirring up a billowy cloud of dust that rolled back, enveloping the vehicle to the wheel-tops or higher, and making it seem afloat in a fog. Then a rest followed, with the usual sneezing and bit-champing. Then another "spurt" of a hundred yards and another rest at the end of it. All day long we kept this up, without water for the mules and without ever changing the team. At least we kept it up ten hours, which, I take it, is a day, and a pretty honest one, in an alkali desert. It was from four in the morning till two in the afternoon. And it was so hot! and so close! and our water canteens went dry in the middle of the day and we got so thirsty! It was so stupid and tiresome and dull! and the tedious hours did lag and drag and limp along with such a cruel deliberation! It was so trying to give one's watch a good long undisturbed spell and then take it out and find that it had been fooling away the time and not trying to get ahead any! The alkali dust cut through our lips, it persecuted our eyes, it ate through the delicate membranes and made our noses bleed and *kept* them bleeding – and truly and seriously the romance all faded far away and disappeared, and left the desert trip nothing but a harsh reality – a thirsty, sweltering, longing, hateful reality!

Two miles and a quarter an hour for ten hours – that was what we accomplished. It was hard to bring the comprehension away down to such a snail-pace as that, when we had been used to making eight and ten miles an hour. When we reached the station on the farther verge of the desert, we were glad, for the first time, that the dictionary was along, because we never could have found language to tell how glad we were, in any sort of dictionary but an unabridged one with pictures in it. But there could not have been found in a whole library of dictionaries language sufficient to tell how tired those mules were after their twenty-three-mile pull. To try to give the reader an idea of how *thirsty* they were, would be to "gild refined gold or paint the lily."

Somehow, now that it is there, the quotation does not seem to fit – but no matter, let it stay, any how. I think it is a graceful and attractive thing, and therefore have tried time and time again to work it in where it *would* fit, but could not succeed. These efforts have kept my mind distracted and ill at ease, and made my narrative seem broken and disjointed, in places. Under these circumstances it seems to me best to leave it in, as above, since this will afford at least a temporary respite from the wear and tear of trying to "lead up" to this really apt and beautiful quotation.

CHAPTER XIX

ON THE MORNING of the sixteenth day out from St. Joseph we arrived at the entrance of Rocky Canyon, two hundred and fifty miles from Salt Lake. It was along in this wild country somewhere, and far from any habitation of white men, except the stage-stations, that we came across the wretchedest type of mankind I have ever seen, up to this writing. I refer to the Goshoot Indians. From what we could see and all we could learn, they are very considerably inferior to even the despised Digger Indians of California; inferior to all races of savages on our continent; inferior to even the Terra del Fuegans; inferior to the Hottentots, and actually inferior in some respects to the Kytches of Africa. Indeed, I have been obliged to look the bulky volumes of Wood's "Uncivilized Races of Men" clear through in order to find a savage tribe degraded enough to take rank with the Goshoots. I find but one people fairly open to that shameful verdict. It is the Bosjesmans (bushmen) of South Africa. Such of the Goshoots as we saw, along the road and hanging about the stations, were small, lean, "scrawny" creatures; in complexion a dull black like the ordinary American negro; their faces and hands bearing dirt which they had been hoarding and accumulating for months, years, and even generations, according to the age of the proprietor; a silent, sneaking, treacherous-looking race; taking note of everything, covertly, like all the other "Noble Red Men" that we (do not) read about, and betraying no sign in their countenances; indolent, everlastingly patient and tireless, like all other Indians; prideless beggars – for if the beggar instinct were left out of an Indian he would not "go," any more than a clock without a pendulum; hungry, always hungry, and yet never refusing any thing that a hog would eat, though often eating what a hog would decline; hunters, but having no higher ambition than to kill and eat jackass-rabbits, crickets and grasshoppers, and embezzle carrion from the buzzards and cayotes; savages who, when asked if they have the common Indian belief in a Great Spirit show a something which almost amounts to emotion, thinking whiskey is referred to; a thin, scattering race of almost naked black children, these Goshoots are, who produce nothing at all, and have no villages, and no gatherings together into strictly defined tribal communities – a people whose only shelter is a rag cast on a bush to keep off a portion of the snow, and yet who inhabit one of the most rocky, wintry, repulsive wastes that our country or any other can exhibit.

The Bushmen and our Goshoots are manifestly descended from the self-same gorilla, or kangaroo, or Norway rat, whichever animal-Adam the Darwinians trace them to.

One would as soon expect the rabbits to fight as the Goshoots, and yet they used to live off the offal and refuse of the stations a few months and then come some dark night when no mischief was expected, and burn down the buildings and kill the men from ambush as they rushed out. And once, in the night, they attacked the stage-coach when a District Judge, of Nevada Territory, was the only passenger, and with their first volley of arrows (and a bullet or two) they riddled the stage curtains, wounded a horse or two and mortally wounded the driver. The latter was full of pluck, and so was his passenger. At the driver's call Judge Mott swung himself out, clambered to the box and seized the reins of the team, and away they plunged, through the racing mob of skeletons and under a hurtling storm of missiles. The stricken driver had sunk down on the boot as soon as he was wounded, but had held on to the reins and said he would manage to keep hold of them until relieved. And after they were taken from his relaxing grasp, he lay with his head between Judge Mott's feet, and tranquilly gave directions about the road; he said he believed he could live till the miscreants were outrun and left behind, and that if he managed that, the main difficulty would be at an end, and then if the Judge drove so and so (giving directions about bad places in the road, and general course) he would reach the next station without trouble. The Judge distanced the enemy and at last rattled up to the station and knew that the night's perils were done; but there was no comrade-in-arms for him to rejoice with, for the soldierly driver was dead.

Let us forget that we have been saying harsh things about the Overland drivers, now. The disgust which the Goshoots gave me, a disciple of Cooper and a worshiper of the Red Man – even of the scholarly savages in the "Last of the Mohicans" who are fittingly associated with backwoodsmen who divide each sentence into two equal parts: one part critically grammatical, refined and choice of language, and the other part just such an attempt to talk like a hunter or a mountaineer, as a Broadway clerk might make after eating an edition of Emerson Bennett's works and studying frontier life at the Bowery Theatre a couple of weeks – I say that the nausea which the Goshoots gave me, an Indian worshiper, set me to examining authorities, to see if perchance I had been over-estimating the Red Man while viewing him through the mellow moonshine of romance. The revelations that came were disenchanting. It was curious to see how quickly the paint and tinsel fell away from him and left him treacherous, filthy and repulsive – and how quickly the evidences accumulated that wherever one finds an Indian tribe he has only found Goshoots more or less modified by circumstances and surroundings – but Goshoots, after all. They deserve pity, poor creatures; and they can have mine – at this distance. Nearer by, they never get anybody's.

There is an impression abroad that the Baltimore and Washington Railroad Company and many of its employés are Goshoots; but it is an error. There is only a plausible resemblance, which, while it is apt enough to mislead the ignorant, cannot deceive parties who have contemplated both tribes. But seriously, it was not only poor wit, but very wrong to start the report referred to above; for however innocent the motive may have been, the necessary effect was to injure the reputation of a class who have a hard enough time of it in the pitiless deserts of the Rocky Mountains, Heaven knows! If we cannot find it in our hearts to give those poor naked creatures our Christian sympathy and compassion, in God's name let us at least not throw mud at them.

CHAPTER XXI

WE WERE APPROACHING the end of our long journey. It was the morning of the twentieth day. At noon we would reach Carson City, the capital of Nevada Territory. We were not glad, but sorry. It had been a fine pleasure-trip; we had fed fat on wonders every day; we were now well accustomed to stage life, and very fond of it; so the idea of coming to a stand-still and settling down to a humdrum existence in a village was not agreeable, but on the contrary depressing.

Visibly our new home was a desert, walled in by barren, snow-clad mountains. There was not a tree in sight. There was no vegetation but the endless sage-brush and grease wood. All nature was gray with it. We were plowing through great deeps of powdery alkali dust that rose in thick clouds and floated across the plain like smoke from a burning house. We were coated with it like millers; so were the coach, the mules, the mail bags, the driver – we and the sage-brush and the other scenery were all one monotonous color.

Long trains of freight wagons in the distance enveloped in ascending masses of dust suggested pictures of prairies on fire. These teams and their masters were the only life we saw. Otherwise we moved in the midst of solitude, silence and desolation. Every twenty steps we passed the skeleton of some dead beast of burthen, with its dust-coated skin stretched tightly over its empty ribs. Frequently a solemn raven sat upon the skull or the hips and contemplated the passing coach with meditative serenity.

By and by Carson City was pointed out to us. It nestled in the edge of a great plain and was a sufficient number of miles away to look like an assemblage of mere white spots in the shadow of a grim range of mountains overlooking it, whose summits seemed lifted clear out of companionship and consciousness of earthly things.

We arrived, disembarked, and the stage went on. It was a "wooden" town; its population two thousand souls. The main street consisted of four or five blocks of little white frame stores which were too high to sit down on, but not too high for various other purposes; in fact, hardly high enough. They were packed close together, side by side, as if room were scarce in that mighty plain. The sidewalk was of boards that were more or less loose and inclined to rattle when walked upon. In the middle of the town, opposite the stores, was the "plaza" which is native to all towns beyond the Rocky Mountains – a large, unfenced, level vacancy, with a liberty pole in it, and very useful as a place for public auctions, horse trades, and mass-meetings, and likewise for teamsters to camp in. Two other sides of the plaza were faced by stores, offices and stables. The rest of Carson City was pretty scattering.

We were introduced to several citizens, at the stage-office and on the way up to the Governor's from the hotel – among others, to a Mr. Harris, who was on horseback; he began to say something, but interrupted himself with the remark:

"I'll have to get you to excuse me a minute; yonder is the witness that swore I helped to rob the California coach – a piece of impertinent intermeddling, sir, for I am not even acquainted with the man."

Then he rode over and began to rebuke the stranger with a six-shooter, and the stranger began to explain with another. When the pistols were emptied, the stranger resumed his work (mending a whip-lash), and Mr. Harris rode by with a polite nod, homeward bound, with a bullet through one of his lungs, and several in his hips; and from them issued little rivulets of blood that coursed down the horse's sides and made the animal look quite picturesque. I never saw Harris shoot a man after that but it recalled to mind that first day in Carson.

This was all we saw that day, for it was two o'clock, now, and according to custom the daily "Washoe Zephyr" set in; a soaring dust-drift about the size of the United States set up edgewise came with it, and the capital of Nevada Territory disappeared from view. Still, there were sights to be seen which were not wholly uninteresting to new comers; for the vast dust cloud was thickly freckled with things strange to the upper air – things living and dead, that flitted hither and thither, going and coming, appearing and disappearing among the rolling billows of dust – hats, chickens and parasols sailing in the remote heavens; blankets, tin signs, sage-brush and shingles a shade lower; door-mats and buffalo robes lower still; shovels and coal scuttles on the next grade; glass doors, cats and little children on the next; disrupted lumber yards, light buggies and wheelbarrows on the next; and down only thirty or forty feet above ground was a skurrying storm of emigrating roofs and vacant lots.

It was something to see that much. I could have seen more, if I could have kept the dust out of my eyes.

But seriously a Washoe wind is by no means a trifling matter. It blows flimsy houses down, lifts shingle roofs occasionally, rolls up tin ones like sheet music, now and then blows a stage-coach over and spills the passengers; and tradition says the reason there are so many bald people there, is, that the wind blows the hair off their heads while they are looking skyward after their hats. Carson streets seldom look inactive on summer afternoons, because there are so many citizens skipping around their escaping hats, like chambermaids trying to head off a spider.

The "Washoe Zephyr" (Washoe is a pet nickname for Nevada) is a peculiarly Scriptural wind, in that no man knoweth "whence it cometh." That is to say, where it *originates*. It comes right over the mountains from the West, but when one crosses the ridge he does not find any of it on the other side! It probably is manufactured on the mountain top for the occasion, and starts from there. It is a pretty regular wind, in the summer time. Its office hours are from two in the afternoon till two the next morning; and anybody venturing abroad during those twelve hours needs to allow for the wind or he will bring up a mile or two to leeward of the point he is aiming at. And yet the first complaint a Washoe visitor to San Francisco makes, is that the sea winds blow so, there! There is a good deal of human nature in that.

We found the state palace of the Governor of Nevada Territory to consist of a white frame one-story house with two small rooms in it and a stanchion supported shed in front – for grandeur – it compelled the respect of the citizen and inspired the Indians with awe. The newly arrived Chief and Associate Justices of the Territory, and other machinery of the government, were domiciled with less splendor. They were boarding around privately, and had their offices in their bed-rooms.

The Secretary and I took quarters in the "ranch" of a worthy French lady by the name of Bridget O'Flannigan, a camp-follower of his Excellency the Governor. She had known him in his prosperity as commander-in-chief of the Metropolitan Police of New York, and she would not desert him in his adversity as Governor of Nevada. Our room was on the lower floor, facing the plaza, and when we had got our bed, a small table, two chairs, the government fire-proof safe, and the Unabridged Dictionary into it, there was still room enough left for a visitor – may be two, but not without straining the walls. But the walls could stand it – at least the partitions could, for they consisted simply of one thickness of white "cotton domestic" stretched from corner to corner of the room. This was the rule in Carson – any other kind of partition was the rare exception. And if you stood in a dark room and your neighbors in the next had lights, the shadows on your canvas told queer secrets sometimes! Very often these partitions were made of old flour sacks basted together; and then the difference between the common herd and the aristocracy was, that the common herd had unornamented sacks, while the walls of the aristocrat were overpowering with rudimental fresco – *i.e.*, red and blue mill brands on the flour sacks. Occasionally, also, the better classes embellished their canvas by pasting pictures from *Harper's Weekly* on them. In many cases, too, the wealthy and the cultured rose to spittoons and other evidences of a sumptuous and luxurious taste.* We had a carpet and a genuine queen's-ware wash-bowl. Consequently we were hated without reserve by the other tenants of the O'Flannigan "ranch." When we added a painted oilcloth window curtain, we simply took our lives into our own hands. To prevent bloodshed I removed up stairs and

* Washoe people take a joke so hard that I must explain that the above description was only the rule; there were many honorable exceptions in Carson – plastered ceilings and houses that had considerable furniture in them. – M. T.

took up quarters with the untitled plebeians in one of the fourteen white pine cot-bedsteads that stood in two long ranks in the one sole room of which the second story consisted.

It was a jolly company, the fourteen. They were principally voluntary camp-followers of the Governor, who had joined his retinue by their own election at New York and San Francisco and came along, feeling that in the scuffle for little territorial crumbs and offices they could not make their condition more precarious than it was, and might reasonably expect to make it better. They were popularly known as the "Irish Brigade," though there were only four or five Irishmen among all the Governor's retainers. His good-natured Excellency was much annoyed at the gossip his henchmen created – especially when there arose a rumor that they were paid assassins of his, brought along to quietly reduce the democratic vote when desirable!

Mrs. O'Flannigan was boarding and lodging them at ten dollars a week apiece, and they were cheerfully giving their notes for it. They were perfectly satisfied, but Bridget presently found that notes that could not be discounted were but a feeble constitution for a Carson boarding-house. So she began to harry the Governor to find employment for the "Brigade." Her importunities and theirs together drove him to a gentle desperation at last, and he finally summoned the Brigade to the presence. Then, said he:

"Gentlemen, I have planned a lucrative and useful service for you – a service which will provide you with recreation amid noble landscapes, and afford you never ceasing opportunities for enriching your minds by observation and study. I want you to survey a railroad from Carson City westward to a certain point! When the legislature meets I will have the necessary bill passed and the remuneration arranged."

"What, a railroad over the Sierra Nevada Mountains?"

"Well, then, survey it eastward to a certain point!"

He converted them into surveyors, chain-bearers and so on, and turned them loose in the desert. It was "recreation" with a vengeance! Recreation on foot, lugging chains through sand and sagebrush, under a sultry sun and among cattle bones, cayotes and tarantulas. "Romantic adventure" could go no further. They surveyed very slowly, very deliberately, very carefully. They returned every night during the first week, dusty, footsore, tired, and hungry, but very jolly. They brought in great store of prodigious hairy spiders –

tarantulas – and imprisoned them in covered tumblers up stairs in the "ranch." After the first week, they had to camp on the field, for they were getting well eastward. They made a good many inquiries as to the location of that indefinite "certain point," but got no information. At last, to a peculiarly urgent inquiry of "How far eastward?" Governor Nye telegraphed back:

"To the Atlantic Ocean, blast you! – and then bridge it and go on!"

This brought back the dusty toilers, who sent in a report and ceased from their labors. The Governor was always comfortable about it; he said Mrs. O'Flannigan would hold him for the Brigade's board any how, and he intended to get what entertainment he could out of the boys; he said, with his old-time pleasant twinkle, that he meant to survey them into Utah and then telegraph Brigham to hang them for trespass!

The surveyors brought back more tarantulas with them, and so we had quite a menagerie arranged along the shelves of the room. Some of these spiders could straddle over a common saucer with their hairy, muscular legs, and when their feelings were hurt, or their dignity offended, they were the wickedest-looking desperadoes the animal world can furnish. If their glass prison-houses were touched ever so lightly they were up and spoiling for a fight in a minute. Starchy? – proud? Indeed, they would take up a straw and pick their teeth like a member of Congress. There was as usual a furious "zephyr" blowing the first night of the Brigade's return, and about midnight the roof of an adjoining stable blew off, and a corner of it came crashing through the side of our ranch. There was a simultaneous awakening, and a tumultuous muster of the Brigade in the dark, and a general tumbling and sprawling over each other in the narrow aisle between the bed-rows. In the midst of the turmoil, Bob H—— sprung up out of a sound sleep, and knocked down a shelf with his head. Instantly he shouted:

"Turn out, boys – the tarantulas is loose!"

No warning ever sounded so dreadful. Nobody tried, any longer, to leave the room, lest he might step on a tarantula. Every man groped for a trunk or a bed, and jumped on it. Then followed the strangest silence – a silence of grisly suspense it was, too – waiting, expectancy, fear. It was as dark as pitch, and one had to imagine the spectacle of those fourteen scant-clad men roosting gingerly on trunks and beds, for not a thing could be seen. Then came occasional little interruptions of the silence, and one could recognize a man and tell his locality by his voice, or locate any other sound a sufferer made by his gropings or changes of position. The occasional voices were not given to much speaking – you simply heard a gentle ejaculation of "Ow!" followed by a solid thump, and you knew the gentleman had felt a hairy blanket or something touch his bare skin and had skipped from a bed to the floor. Another silence. Presently you would hear a gasping voice say:

"Su-su-something's crawling up the back of my neck!"

Every now and then you could hear a little subdued scramble and a sorrowful "O Lord!" and then you knew that somebody was getting away from something he took for a tarantula, and not losing any time about it, either. Directly a voice in the corner rang out wild and clear:

"I've got him! I've got him!" [Pause, and probable change of circumstances.] "No, he's got me! Oh, ain't they *never* going to fetch a lantern!"

The lantern came at that moment, in the hands of Mrs. O'Flannigan, whose anxiety to know the amount of damage done by the assaulting roof had not prevented her waiting a judicious interval, after getting out of bed and lighting up, to see if the wind was done, now, up stairs, or had a larger contract.

The landscape presented when the lantern flashed into the room was picturesque, and might have been funny to some people, but was not to us. Although we were perched so strangely upon boxes, trunks and beds, and so strangely attired, too, we were too earnestly distressed and too genuinely miserable to see any fun about it, and there was not the semblance of a smile anywhere visible. I know I am not capable of suffering more than I did during those few minutes of suspense in the dark, surrounded by those creeping, bloody-minded tarantulas. I had skipped from bed to bed and from box to box in a cold agony, and every time I touched anything that was furzy I fancied I felt the fangs. I had rather go to war than live that episode over again. Nobody was hurt. The man who thought a tarantula had "got him" was mistaken – only a crack in a box had caught his finger. Not one of those escaped tarantulas was ever seen again. There were ten or twelve of them. We took candles and hunted the place high and low for them, but with no success. Did we go back to bed then? We did nothing of the kind. We sat up the rest of the night playing cribbage and keeping a sharp lookout for the enemy.

CHAPTER XXII

IT WAS THE end of August, and the skies were cloudless and the weather superb. In two or three weeks I had grown wonderfully fascinated with the curious new country, and concluded to put off my return to "the States" awhile. I had grown well accustomed to wearing a damaged slouch hat, blue woolen shirt, and pants crammed into boot-tops, and gloried in the absence of coat, vest and braces. I felt rowdyish and "bully," (as the historian Josephus phrases it, in his fine chapter upon the destruction of the Temple). It seemed to me that nothing could be so fine and so romantic. I had become an officer of the government, but that was for mere sublimity. The office was an unique sinecure. I had nothing to do and no salary. I was private Secretary to his majesty the Secretary and there was not yet writing enough for two of us. So Johnny K—— and I devoted our time to amusement. He was the young son of an Ohio nabob and was out there for recreation. He got it. We had heard a world of talk about the marvelous beauty of Lake Tahoe, and finally curiosity drove us thither to see it. Three or four members of the Brigade had been there and located some timber lands on its shores and stored up a quantity of provisions in their camp. We strapped a couple of blankets on our shoulders and took an ax apiece and started – for we intended to take up a wood ranch or so ourselves and become wealthy. We were on foot. The reader will find it advantageous to go horse-back. We were told that the distance was eleven miles. We tramped a long time on level ground, and then toiled laboriously up a mountain about a thousand miles high and looked over. No lake there. We descended on the other side, crossed the valley and toiled up another mountain three or four thousand miles high, apparently, and looked over again. No lake yet. We sat down tired and perspiring, and hired a couple of Chinamen to curse those people who had beguiled us. Thus refreshed, we presently resumed the march with renewed vigor and determination. We plodded on, two or three hours longer, and at last the lake burst upon us – a noble sheet of blue water lifted six thousand three hundred feet above the level of the sea, and walled in by a rim of snow-clad mountain peaks that towered aloft full three thousand feet higher still! It was a vast oval, and one would have to use up eighty or a hundred good miles in traveling around it. As it lay there with the shadows of the mountains brilliantly photographed upon its still surface I thought it must surely be the fairest picture the whole earth affords.

We found the small skiff belonging to the Brigade boys, and without loss of time set out across a deep bend of the lake toward the landmarks that signified the locality of the camp. I got Johnny to row – not because I mind exertion myself, but because it makes me sick to ride backwards when I am at work. But I steered. A three-mile pull brought us to the camp just as the night fell, and we stepped ashore very tired and wolfishly hungry. In a "cache" among the rocks we found the provisions and the cooking utensils, and then, all fatigued as I was, I sat down on a boulder and superintended while Johnny gathered wood and cooked supper. Many a man who had gone through what I had, would have wanted to rest.

It was a delicious supper – hot bread, fried bacon, and black coffee. It was a delicious solitude we were in, too. Three miles away was a saw-mill and some workmen, but there were not fifteen other human beings throughout the wide circumference of the lake. As the darkness closed down and the stars came out and spangled the great mirror with jewels, we smoked meditatively in the solemn hush and forgot our troubles and our pains. In due time we spread our blankets in the warm sand between two large boulders and soon fell asleep, careless of the procession of ants that passed in through rents in our clothing and explored our persons. Nothing could disturb the sleep that fettered us, for it had been fairly earned, and if our consciences had any sins on them they had to adjourn court for that night, any way. The wind rose just as we were losing consciousness, and we were lulled to sleep by the beating of the surf upon the shore.

It is always very cold on that lake shore in the night, but we had plenty of blankets and were warm enough. We never moved a muscle all night, but waked at early dawn in the original positions, and got up at once, thoroughly refreshed, free from soreness, and brim full of friskiness. There is no end of wholesome medicine in such an experience. That morning we could have whipped ten such people as we were the day before – sick ones at any rate. But the world is slow, and people will go to "water cures" and "movement cures" and to foreign lands for health. Three months of camp life on Lake Tahoe would restore an Egyptian mummy to his pristine vigor, and give him an appetite like an alligator. I do not mean the oldest and dryest mummies, of course, but the fresher ones. The air up there in the clouds is very pure and fine, bracing and delicious. And why shouldn't it be? – it is the same the angels breathe. I think that hardly any amount of fatigue can be gathered together that a man cannot sleep off in one night on the sand by its side. Not under a roof, but under the sky; it seldom or never rains there in the summer time. I know a man who went there to die. But he made a failure of it. He was a skeleton when he came, and could barely stand. He had no appetite, and did nothing but read tracts and reflect on the future. Three months later he was sleeping out of doors regularly, eating all he could hold, three times a day, and chasing game over mountains three thousand feet high for recreation. And he was a skeleton no longer, but weighed part of a ton. This is no fancy sketch, but the truth. His disease was consumption. I confidently commend his experience to other skeletons.

I superintended again, and as soon as we had eaten breakfast we got in the boat and skirted along the lake shore about three miles and disembarked. We liked the appearance of the place, and so we claimed some three hundred acres of it and stuck our "notices" on a tree. It was yellow pine timber land – a dense forest of trees a hundred feet high and from one to five feet through at the butt. It was necessary to fence our property or we could not hold it. That is to say, it was necessary to cut down trees here and there and make them fall in such a way as to form a sort of enclosure (with pretty wide gaps in it). We cut down three trees apiece, and found it such heart-breaking work that we decided to "rest our case" on those; if they held the property, well and good; if they didn't, let the property spill out through the gaps and go; it was no use to work ourselves to death merely to save a few acres of land. Next day we came back to build a house – for a house was also necessary, in order to hold the property. We decided to build a substantial log-house and excite the envy of the Brigade boys; but by the time we had cut and trimmed the first log it seemed unnecessary to be so elaborate, and so we concluded to build it of saplings. However, two saplings, duly cut and trimmed, compelled recognition of the fact that a still modester architecture would satisfy the law, and so we concluded to build a "brush" house. We devoted the next day to this work, but we did so much "sitting around" and discussing, that by the middle of the afternoon we had achieved only a half-way sort of affair which one of us had to watch while the other cut brush, lest if both turned our backs we might not be able to find it again, it had such a strong family resemblance to the surrounding vegetation. But we were satisfied with it.

We were land owners now, duly seized and possessed, and within the protection of the law. Therefore we decided to take up our residence on our own domain and enjoy that large sense of independence which only such an experience can bring. Late the next afternoon, after a good long rest, we sailed away from the Brigade camp with all the provisions and cooking utensils we could carry off – borrow is the more accurate word – and just as the night was falling we beached the boat at our own landing.

CHAPTER XXIII

IF THERE IS any life that is happier than the life we led on our timber ranch for the next two or three weeks, it must be a sort of life which I have not read of in books or experienced in person. We did not see a human being but ourselves during the time, or hear any sounds but those that were made by the wind and the waves, the sighing of the pines, and now and then the far-off thunder of an avalanche. The forest about us was dense and cool, the sky above us was cloudless and brilliant with sunshine, the broad lake before us was glassy and clear, or rippled and breezy, or black and storm-tossed, according to Nature's mood; and its circling border of mountain domes, clothed with forests, scarred with land-slides, cloven by canons and valleys, and helmeted with glittering snow, fitly framed and finished the noble picture. The view was always fascinating, bewitching, entrancing. The eye was never tired of gazing, night or day, in calm or storm; it suffered but one grief, and that was that it could not look always, but must close sometimes in sleep.

We slept in the sand close to the water's edge, between two protecting boulders, which took care of the stormy night-winds for us. We never took any paregoric to make us sleep. At the first break of dawn we were always up and running foot-races to tone down excess of physical vigor and exuberance of spirits. That is, Johnny was – but I held his hat. While smoking the pipe of peace after breakfast we watched the sentinel peaks put on the glory of the sun, and followed the conquering light as it swept down among the shadows, and set the captive crags and forests free. We watched the tinted pictures grow and brighten upon the water till every little detail of forest, precipice and pinnacle was wrought in and finished, and the miracle of the enchanter complete. Then to "business."

That is, drifting around in the boat. We were on the north shore. There, the rocks on the bottom are sometimes gray, sometimes white. This gives the marvelous transparency of the water a fuller advantage than it has elsewhere on the lake. We usually pushed out a hundred yards or so from shore, and then lay down on the thwarts, in the sun, and let the boat drift by the hour whither it would. We seldom talked. It interrupted the Sabbath stillness, and marred the dreams the luxurious rest and indolence brought. The shore all along was indented with deep, curved bays and coves, bordered by narrow sand-beaches; and where the sand ended, the steep mountain sides rose right up aloft into space – rose up like a vast wall a little out of the perpendicular, and thickly wooded with tall pines.

So singularly clear was the water, that where it was only twenty or thirty feet deep the bottom was so perfectly distinct that the boat seemed floating in the air! Yes, where it was even *eighty* feet deep. Every little pebble was distinct, every speckled trout, every hand's breadth of sand. Often, as we lay on our faces, a granite boulder, as large as a village church, would start out of the bottom apparently, and seem climbing up rapidly to the surface, till presently it threatened to touch our faces, and we could not resist the impulse to seize an oar and avert the danger. But the boat would float on, and the boulder descend again, and then we could see that when we had been exactly above it, it must still have been twenty or thirty feet below the surface. Down through the transparency of these great depths, the water was not *merely* transparent, but dazzlingly, brilliantly so. All objects seen through it had a bright, strong vividness, not only of outline, but of every minute detail, which they would not have had when seen simply through the same depth of atmosphere. So empty and airy did all spaces seem below us, and so strong was the sense of floating high aloft in mid-nothingness, that we called these boat-excursions "balloon-voyages."

We fished a good deal, but we did not average one fish a week. We could see trout by the thousand winging about in the emptiness under us, or sleeping in shoals on the bottom, but they would not bite – they could see the line too plainly, perhaps. We frequently selected the trout we wanted, and rested the bait patiently and persistently on the end of his nose at a depth of eighty feet, but he would only shake it off with an annoyed manner, and shift his position.

We bathed occasionally, but the water was rather chilly, for all it looked so sunny. Sometimes we rowed out to the "blue water," a mile or two from shore. It was as dead blue as indigo there, because of the immense depth. By official measurement the lake in its centre is one thousand five hundred and twenty-five feet deep!

Sometimes, on lazy afternoons, we lolled on the sand in camp, and smoked pipes and read some old well-worn novels. At night, by the camp fire, we played euchre and seven-up to strengthen the mind – and played them with cards so greasy and defaced that only a whole summer's acquaintance with them could enable the student to tell the ace of clubs from the jack of diamonds.

We never slept in our "house." It never recurred to us, for one thing; and besides, it was built to hold the ground, and that was enough. We did not wish to strain it.

By and by our provisions began to run short, and we went back to the old camp and laid in a new supply. We were gone all day, and reached home again about night-fall, pretty tired and hungry. While Johnny was carrying the main bulk of the provisions up to our "house" for future use, I took the loaf of bread, some slices of bacon, and the coffee-pot, ashore, set them down by a tree, lit a fire, and went back to the boat to get the frying-pan. While I was at this, I heard a shout from Johnny, and looking up I saw that my fire was galloping all over the premises!

Johnny was on the other side of it. He had to run through the flames to get to the lake shore, and then we stood helpless and watched the devastation.

The ground was deeply carpeted with dry pine needles, and the fire touched them off as if they were gunpowder. It was wonderful to see with what fierce speed the tall sheet of flame traveled! My coffee-pot was gone, and everything with it. In a minute and a half the fire seized upon a dense growth of dry manzanita chapparal six or eight feet high, and then the roaring and popping and crackling was something terrific. We were driven to the boat by the intense heat, and there we remained, spell-bound.

Within half an hour all before us was a tossing, blinding tempest of flame! It went surging up adjacent ridges – surmounted them and disappeared in the canons beyond – burst into view upon higher and farther ridges, presently – shed a grander illumination abroad, and dove again – flamed out again, directly, higher and still higher up the mountain side – threw out skirmishing parties of fire here and there, and sent them trailing their crimson spirals away among remote ramparts and ribs and gorges, till as far as the eye could reach the lofty mountain-fronts were webbed as it were with a tangled network of red lava streams. Away across the water the crags and domes were lit with a ruddy glare, and the firmament above was a reflected hell!

Every feature of the spectacle was repeated in the glowing mirror of the lake! Both pictures were sublime, both were beautiful; but that in the lake had a bewildering richness about it that enchanted the eye and held it with the stronger fascination.

We sat absorbed and motionless through four long hours. We never thought of supper, and never felt fatigue. But at eleven o'clock the conflagration had traveled beyond our range of vision, and then darkness stole down upon the landscape again.

Hunger asserted itself now, but there was nothing to eat. The provisions were all cooked, no doubt, but we did not go to see. We were homeless wanderers again, without any property. Our fence was gone, our house burned down; no insurance. Our pine forest was well scorched, the dead trees all burned up, and our broad acres of manzanita swept away. Our blankets were on our usual sand-bed, however, and so we lay down and went to sleep. The next morning we started back to the old camp, but while out a long way from shore, so great a storm came up that we dared not try to land. So I baled out the seas we shipped, and Johnny pulled heavily through the billows till we had reached a point three or four miles beyond the camp. The storm was increasing, and it became evident that it was better to take the hazard of beaching the boat than go down in a hundred fathoms of water; so we ran in, with tall white-caps following, and I sat down in the stern-sheets and pointed her head-on to the shore. The instant the bow struck, a wave came over the stern that washed crew and cargo ashore, and saved a deal of trouble. We shivered in the lee of a boulder all the rest of the day, and froze all the night through. In the morning the tempest had gone down, and we paddled down to the camp without any unnecessary delay. We were so starved that we ate up the rest of the Brigade's provisions, and then set out to Carson to tell them about it and ask their forgiveness. It was accorded, upon payment of damages.

We made many trips to the lake after that, and had many a hair-breadth escape and blood-curdling adventure which will never be recorded in any history.

CHAPTER XXIV

I RESOLVED TO have a horse to ride. I had never seen such wild, free, magnificent horsemanship outside of a circus as these picturesquely-clad Mexicans, Californians and Mexicanized Americans displayed in Carson streets every day. How they rode! Leaning just gently forward out of the perpendicular, easy and nonchalant, with broad slouch-hat brim blown square up in front, and long *riata* swinging above the head, they swept through the town like the wind! The next minute they were only a sailing puff of dust on the far desert. If they trotted, they sat up gallantly and gracefully, and seemed part of the horse; did not go jiggering up and down after the silly Miss-Nancy fashion of the riding-schools. I had quickly learned to tell a horse from a cow, and was full of anxiety to learn more. I was resolved to buy a horse.

While the thought was rankling in my mind, the auctioneer came skurrying through the plaza on a black beast that had as many humps and corners on him as a dromedary, and was necessarily uncomely; but he was "going, going, at twenty-two! – horse, saddle and bridle at twenty-two dollars, gentlemen!" and I could hardly resist.

A man whom I did not know (he turned out to be the auctioneer's brother) noticed the wistful look in my eye, and observed that that was a very remarkable horse to be going at such a price; and added that the saddle alone was worth the money. It was a Spanish saddle, with ponderous *tapidaros*, and furnished with the ungainly sole-leather covering with the unspellable name. I said I had half a notion to bid. Then this keen-eyed person appeared to me to be "taking my measure"; but I dismissed the suspicion when he spoke, for his manner was full of guileless candor and truthfulness. Said he:

"I know that horse – know him well. You are a stranger, I take it, and so you might think he was an American horse, may be, but I assure you he is not. He is nothing of the kind; but – excuse my speaking in a low voice, other people being near – he is, without the shadow of a doubt, a Genuine Mexican Plug!"

I did not know what a Genuine Mexican Plug was, but there was something about this man's way of saying it, that made me swear inwardly that I would own a Genuine Mexican Plug, or die.

"Has he any other – er – advantages?" I inquired, suppressing what eagerness I could.

He hooked his forefinger in the pocket of my army-shirt, led me to one side and breathed in my ear impressively these words:

"He can out-buck anything in America!"

"Going, going, going – at *twent–ty*-four dollars and a half, gen—"

"Twenty-seven!" I shouted, in a frenzy.

"And sold!" said the auctioneer, and passed over the Genuine Mexican Plug to me.

I could scarcely contain my exultation. I paid the money, and put the animal in a neighboring livery-stable to dine and rest himself.

In the afternoon I brought the creature into the plaza, and certain citizens held him by the head, and others by the tail, while I mounted him. As soon as they let go, he placed all his feet in a bunch together, lowered his back, and then suddenly arched it upward, and shot me straight into the air a matter of three or four feet! I came as straight down again, lit in the saddle, went instantly up again, came down almost on the high pommel, shot up again, and came down on the horse's neck – all in the space of three or four seconds. Then he rose and stood almost straight up on his hind feet, and I, clasping his lean neck desperately, slid back into the saddle, and held on. He came down, and immediately hoisted his heels into the air, delivering a vicious kick at the sky, and stood on his forefeet. And then down he came once more, and began the original exercise of shooting me straight up again. The third time I went up I heard a stranger say:

"Oh, *don't* he buck, though!"

While I was up, somebody struck the horse a sounding thwack with a leathern strap, and when I arrived again the Genuine Mexican Plug was not there. A Californian youth chased him up and caught him, and asked if he might have a ride. I granted him that luxury. He mounted the Genuine, got lifted into the air once, but sent his spurs home as he descended, and the horse darted away like a telegram. He soared over three fences like a bird and disappeared on the road toward the Washoe Valley.

I sat down on a stone, with a sigh, and by a natural impulse one of my hands sought my forehead, and the other the base of my stomach. I believe I never appreciated, till then, the poverty of the human machinery – for I still needed a hand or two to place elsewhere. Pen can not describe how I was jolted up. Imagination can not conceive how disjointed I was – how internally, externally and universally I was unsettled, mixed up and ruptured. There was a sympathetic crowd around me, though.

One elderly-looking comforter said:

"Stranger, you've been taken in. Everybody in this camp knows that horse. Any child, any Injun, could have told you that he'd buck; he is the very worst devil to buck on the continent of America. You hear *me*. I'm Curry. *Old* Curry. Old *Abe* Curry. And moreover, he is a simon-pure, out-and-out, genuine d——d Mexican Plug, and an uncommon mean one at that, too. Why, you turnip, if you had laid low and kept dark, there's chances to buy an *American* horse for mighty little more than you paid for that bloody old foreign relic."

I gave no sign; but I made up my mind that if the auctioneer's brother's funeral took place while I was in the Territory I would postpone all other recreations and attend it.

After a gallop of sixteen miles the Californian youth and the Genuine Mexican Plug came tearing into town again, shedding foam-flakes like the spume-spray that drives before a typhoon, and, with one final skip over a wheelbarrow and a Chinaman, cast anchor in front of the "ranch."

Such panting and blowing! Such spreading and contracting of the red equine nostrils, and glaring of the wild equine eye! But was the imperial beast subjugated? Indeed he was not. His lordship the Speaker of the House thought he was, and mounted him to go down to the Capitol; but the first dash the creature made was over a pile of telegraph poles half as high as a church; and his time to the Capitol – one mile and three-quarters – remains unbeaten to this day. But then he took an advantage – he left out the mile, and only did the three-quarters. That is to say, he made a straight cut across lots, preferring fences and ditches to a crooked road; and when the Speaker got to the Capitol he said he had been in the air so much he felt as if he had made the trip on a comet.

In the evening the Speaker came home afoot for exercise, and got the Genuine towed back behind a quartz wagon. The next day I loaned the animal to the Clerk of the House to go down to the Dana silver mine, six miles, and *he* walked back for exercise, and got the horse towed. Everybody I loaned him to always walked back; they never could get enough exercise any other way. Still, I continued to loan him to anybody who was willing to borrow him, my idea being to get him crippled, and throw him on the borrower's hands, or killed, and make the borrower pay for him. But somehow nothing ever happened to him. He took chances that no other horse ever took and survived, but he always came out safe. It was his daily habit to try experiments that had always before been considered impossible, but he always got through. Sometimes he miscalculated a little, and did not get his rider through intact, but *he* always got through himself. Of course I had tried to sell him; but that was a stretch of simplicity which met with little sympathy. The auctioneer stormed up and down the streets on him for four days, dispersing the populace, interrupting business, and destroying children, and never got a bid – at least never any but the eighteen-dollar one he hired a notoriously substanceless bummer to make. The people only smiled pleasantly, and restrained their desire to buy, if they had any. Then the auctioneer brought in his bill, and I withdrew the horse from the market. We tried to trade him off at private vendue next, offering him at a sacrifice for second-hand tombstones, old iron, temperance tracts – any kind of property. But holders were stiff, and we retired from the market again. I never tried to ride the horse any more. Walking was good enough exercise for a man like me, that had nothing the matter with him except ruptures, internal injuries, and such things. Finally I tried to *give* him away. But it was a failure. Parties said earthquakes were handy enough on the Pacific coast – they did not wish to own one. As a last resort I offered him to the Governor for the use of the "Brigade." His face lit up eagerly at first, but toned down again, and he said the thing would be too palpable.

Just then the livery-stable man brought in his bill for six weeks' keeping – stall-room for the horse, fifteen dollars; hay for the horse, two hundred and fifty! The Genuine Mexican Plug had eaten a ton of the article, and the man said he would have eaten a hundred if he had let him.

I will remark here, in all seriousness, that the regular price of hay during that year and a part of the next was really two hundred and fifty dollars a ton. During a part of the previous year it had sold at five hundred a ton, in gold, and during the winter before that there was such scarcity of the article that in several instances small quantities had brought eight hundred dollars a ton in coin! The consequence might be guessed without my telling it; people turned their stock loose to starve, and before the spring arrived Carson and Eagle valleys were almost literally carpeted with their carcases! Any old settler there will verify these statements.

I managed to pay the livery bill, and that same day I gave the Genuine Mexican Plug to a passing Arkansas emigrant whom fortune delivered into my hand. If this ever meets his eye, he will doubtless remember the donation.

Now whoever has had the luck to ride a real Mexican Plug will recognize the animal depicted in this chapter, and hardly consider him exaggerated – but the uninitiated will feel justified in regarding his portrait as a fancy sketch, perhaps.

CHAPTER XXV

ORIGINALLY, NEVADA WAS a part of Utah and was called Carson county; and a pretty large county it was, too. Certain of its valleys produced no end of hay, and this attracted small colonies of Mormon stock-raisers and farmers to them. A few orthodox Americans straggled in from California, but no love was lost between the two classes of colonists. There was little or no friendly intercourse; each party staid to itself. The Mormons were largely in the majority, and had the additional advantage of being peculiarly under the protection of the Mormon government of the Territory. Therefore they could afford to be distant, and even peremptory toward their neighbors. One of the traditions of Carson Valley illustrates the condition of things that prevailed at the time I speak of. The hired girl of one of the American families was Irish, and a Catholic; yet it was noted with surprise that she was the only person outside of the Mormon ring who could get favors from the Mormons. She asked kindnesses of them often, and always got them. It was a mystery to every body. But one day as she was passing out at the door, a large bowie knife dropped from under her apron, and when her mistress asked for an explanation she observed that she was going out to "borry a wash-tub from the Mormons!"

In 1858 silver lodes were discovered in "Carson County," and then the aspect of things changed. Californians began to flock in, and the American element was soon in the majority. Allegiance to Brigham Young and Utah was renounced, and a temporary territorial government for "Washoe" was instituted by the citizens. Governor Roop was the first and only chief magistrate of it. In due course of time Congress passed a bill to organize "Nevada Territory," and President Lincoln sent out Governor Nye to supplant Roop.

At this time the population of the Territory was about twelve or fifteen thousand, and rapidly increasing. Silver mines were being vigorously developed and silver mills erected. Business of all kinds was active and prosperous and growing more so day by day.

The people were glad to have a legitimately constituted government, but did not particularly enjoy having strangers from distant States put in authority over them – a sentiment that was natural enough. They thought the officials should have been chosen from among themselves – from among prominent citizens who had earned a right to such promotion, and who would be in sympathy with the populace and likewise thoroughly acquainted with the needs of the Territory. They were right in viewing the matter thus, without doubt. The new officers were "emigrants," and that was no title to anybody's affection or admiration either.

The new government was received with considerable coolness. It was not only a foreign intruder, but a poor one. It was not even worth plucking – except by the smallest of small fry office-seekers and such. Every body knew that Congress had appropriated only twenty thousand dollars a year in greenbacks for its support – about money enough to run a quartz mill a month. And every body knew, also, that the first year's money was still in Washington, and that the getting hold of it would be a tedious and difficult process. Carson City was too wary and too wise to open up a credit account with the imported bantling with anything like indecent haste.

There is something solemnly funny about the struggles of a new-born Territorial government to get a start in this world. Ours had a trying time of it. The Organic Act and the "instructions" from the State Department commanded that a legislature should be elected at such-and-such a time, and its sittings inaugurated at such-and-such a date. It was easy to get legislators, even at three dollars a day, although board was four dollars and fifty cents, for distinction has its charm in Nevada as well as elsewhere, and there were plenty of patriotic souls out of employment; but to get a legislative hall for them to meet in was another matter altogether. Carson blandly declined to give a room rent-free, or let one to the government on credit.

But when Curry heard of the difficulty, he came forward, solitary and alone, and shouldered the Ship of State over the bar and got her afloat again. I refer to "Curry – *Old* Curry – Old *Abe* Curry." But for him the legislature would have been obliged to sit in the desert. He offered his large stone building just outside the capital limits, rent-free, and it was gladly accepted. Then he built a horse-railroad from town to the capitol, and carried the legislators gratis. He also furnished pine benches and chairs for the legislature, and covered the floors with clean saw-dust by way of carpet and spit-toon combined. But for Curry the government would have died in its tender infancy. A canvas partition to separate the Senate from the House of Representatives was put up by the Secretary, at a cost of three dollars and forty cents, but the United States declined to pay for it. Upon being reminded that the "instructions" permitted the payment of a liberal rent for a legislative hall, and that that money was saved to the country by Mr. Curry's generosity, the United States said that did not alter the matter, and the three dollars and forty cents would be subtracted from the Secretary's eighteen-hundred-dollar salary – and it *was!*

The matter of printing was from the beginning an interesting feature of the new government's difficulties. The Secretary was sworn to obey his volume of written "instructions," and these commanded him to do two certain things without fail, viz.:

1. Get the House and Senate journals printed; and,
2. For this work, pay one dollar and fifty cents per "thousand" for composition, and one dollar and fifty cents per "token" for press-work, in greenbacks.

It was easy to swear to do these two things, but it was entirely impossible to do more than one of them. When greenbacks had gone down to forty cents on the dollar, the prices regularly charged every-body by printing establishments were one dollar and fifty cents per "thousand" and one dollar and fifty cents per "token," in *gold*. The "instructions" commanded that the Secretary regard a paper dollar issued by the government as equal to any other dollar issued by the government. Hence the printing of the journals was discontinued. Then the United States sternly rebuked the Secretary for disregarding the "instructions," and warned him to correct his ways. Wherefore he got some printing done, forwarded the bill to Washington with full exhibits of the high prices of things in the Territory, and called attention to a printed market report wherein it would be observed that even hay was two hundred and fifty dollars a ton. The United States responded by subtracting the printing-bill from the Secretary's suffering salary – and moreover remarked with dense gravity that he would find nothing in his "instructions" requiring him to purchase hay!

Nothing in this world is palled in such impenetrable obscurity as a U. S. Treasury Comptroller's understanding. The very fires of the hereafter could get up nothing more than a fitful glimmer in it. In the days I speak of he never could be made to comprehend why it was that twenty thousand dollars would not go as far in Nevada, where all commodities ranged at an enormous figure, as it would in the other Territories, where exceeding cheapness was the rule. He was an officer who looked out for the little expenses all the time. The Secretary of the Territory kept his office in his bed-room, as

I before remarked; and he charged the United States no rent, although his "instructions" provided for that item and he could have justly taken advantage of it (a thing which I would have done with more than lightning promptness if I had been Secretary myself). But the United States never applauded this devotion. Indeed, I think my country was ashamed to have so improvident a person in its employ.

Those "instructions" (we used to read a chapter from them every morning, as intellectual gymnastics, and a couple of chapters in Sunday School every Sabbath, for they treated of all subjects under the sun and had much valuable religious matter in them along with the other statistics) those "instructions" commanded that penknives, envelopes, pens and writing-paper be furnished the members of the legislature. So the Secretary made the purchase and the distribution. The knives cost three dollars apiece. There was one too many, and the Secretary gave it to the Clerk of the House of Representatives. The United States said the Clerk of the House was not a "member" of the legislature, and took that three dollars out of the Secretary's salary, as usual.

White men charged three or four dollars a "load" for sawing up stove-wood. The Secretary was sagacious enough to know that the United States would never pay any such price as that; so he got an Indian to saw up a load of office wood at one dollar and a half. He made out the usual voucher, but signed no name to it – simply appended a note explaining that an Indian had done the work, and had done it in a very capable and satisfactory way, but could not sign the voucher owing to lack of ability in the necessary direction. The Secretary had to pay that dollar and a half. He thought the United States would admire both his economy and his honesty in getting the work done at half price and not putting a pretended Indian's signature to the voucher, but the United States did not see it in that light. The United States was too much accustomed to employing dollar-and-a-half thieves in all manner of official capacities to regard his explanation of the voucher as having any foundation in fact.

But the next time the Indian sawed wood for us I taught him to make a cross at the bottom of the voucher – it looked like a cross that had been drunk a year – and then I "witnessed" it and it went through all right. The United States never said a word. I was sorry I had not made the voucher for a thousand loads of wood instead of one. The government of my country snubs honest simplicity but fondles artistic villainy, and I think I might have developed into a very capable pickpocket if I had remained in the public service a year or two.

That was a fine collection of sovereigns, that first Nevada legislature. They levied taxes to the amount of thirty or forty thousand dollars and ordered expenditures to the extent of about a million. Yet they had their little periodical explosions of economy like all other bodies of the kind. A member proposed to save three dollars a day to the nation by dispensing with the Chaplain. And yet that short-sighted man needed the Chaplain more than any other member, perhaps, for he generally sat with his feet on his desk, eating raw turnips, during the morning prayer.

The legislature sat sixty days, and passed private toll-road franchises all the time. When they adjourned it was estimated that every citizen owned about three franchises, and it was believed that unless Congress gave the territory another degree of longitude there would not be room enough to accommodate the toll-roads. The ends of them were hanging over the boundary line every where like a fringe.

The fact is, the freighting business had grown to such important proportions that there was nearly as much excitement over suddenly acquired toll-road fortunes as over the wonderful silver mines.

CHAPTER XXVI

BY AND BY I was smitten with the silver fever. "Prospecting parties" were leaving for the mountains every day, and discovering and taking possession of rich silver-bearing lodes and ledges of quartz. Plainly this was the road to fortune. The great "Gould and Curry" mine was held at three or four hundred dollars a foot when we arrived; but in two months it had sprung up to eight hundred. The "Ophir" had been worth only a mere trifle, a year gone by, and now it was selling at nearly *four thousand dollars a foot!* Not a mine could be named that had not experienced an astonishing advance in value within a short time. Every body was talking about these marvels. Go where you would, you heard nothing else, from morning till far into the night. Tom So-and-So had sold out of the "Amanda Smith" for $40,000 – hadn't a cent when he "took up" the ledge six months ago. John Jones had sold half his interest in the "Bald Eagle and Mary Ann" for $65,000, gold coin, and gone to the States for his family. The widow Brewster had "struck it rich" in the "Golden Fleece" and sold ten feet for $18,000 – hadn't money enough to buy a crape bonnet when Sing-Sing Tommy killed her husband at Baldy Johnson's wake last spring. The "Last Chance" had found a "clay casing" and knew they were "right on the ledge" – consequence, "feet" that went begging yesterday were worth a brick house apiece today, and seedy owners who could not get trusted for a drink at any bar in the country yesterday were roaring drunk on champagne today and had hosts of warm personal friends in a town where they had forgotten how to bow or shake hands from long-continued want of practice. Johnny Morgan, a common loafer, had gone to sleep in the gutter and waked up worth a hundred thousand dollars, in consequence of the decision in the "Lady Franklin and Rough and Ready" lawsuit. And so on – day in and day out the talk pelted our ears and the excitement waxed hotter and hotter around us.

I would have been more or less than human if I had not gone mad like the rest. Cart-loads of solid silver bricks, as large as pigs of lead, were arriving from the mills every day, and such sights as that gave substance to the wild talk about me. I succumbed and grew as frenzied as the craziest.

Every few days news would come of the discovery of a bran-new mining region; immediately the papers would teem with accounts of its richness, and away the surplus population would scamper to take possession. By the time I was fairly inoculated with the disease, "Esmeralda" had just had a run and "Humboldt" was beginning to shriek for attention. "Humboldt! Humboldt!" was the new cry, and straightway Humboldt, the newest of the new, the richest of the rich, the most marvelous of the marvelous discoveries in silver-land, was occupying two columns of the public prints to "Esmeralda's" one. I was just on the point of starting to Esmeralda, but turned with the tide and got ready for Humboldt. That the reader may see what moved me, and what would as surely have moved him had he been there, I insert here one of the newspaper letters of the day. It and several other letters from the same calm hand were the main means of converting me. I shall not garble the extract, but put it in just as it appeared in the *Daily Territorial Enterprise:*

> But what about our mines? I shall be candid with you. I shall express an honest opinion, based upon a thorough examination.

> Humboldt county is the richest mineral region upon God's footstool. Each mountain range is gorged with the precious ores. Humboldt is the true Golconda.
>
> The other day an assay of mere *croppings* yielded exceeding *four thousand dollars to the ton.* A week or two ago an assay of just such surface developments made returns of *seven thousand* dollars to the ton. Our mountains are full of rambling prospectors. Each day and almost every hour reveals new and more startling evidences of the profuse and intensified wealth of our favored county. The metal is not silver alone. There are distinct ledges of auriferous ore. A late discovery plainly evinces cinnabar. The coarser metals are in gross abundance. Lately evidences of bituminous coal have been detected. My theory has ever been that coal is a ligneous formation. I told Col. Whitman, in times past, that the neighborhood of Dayton (Nevada) betrayed no present or previous manifestations of a ligneous foundation, and that hence I had no confidence in his lauded coal mines. I repeated the same doctrine to the exultant coal discoverers of Humboldt. I talked with my friend Captain Burch on the subject. My pyrhanism vanished upon his statement that in the very region referred to he had seen petrified trees of the length of two hundred feet. Then is the fact established that huge forests once cast their grim shadows over this remote section. I am firm in the coal faith. Have no fears of the mineral resources of Humboldt county. They are immense – incalculable.

Let me state one or two things which will help the reader to better comprehend certain items in the above. At this time, our near neighbor, Gold Hill, was the most successful silver mining locality in Nevada. It was from there that more than half the daily shipments of silver bricks came. "Very rich" (and scarce) Gold Hill ore yielded from $100 to $400 to the ton; but the usual yield was only $20 to $40 per ton – that is to say, each hundred pounds of ore yielded from one dollar to two dollars. But the reader will perceive by the above extract, that in Humboldt from one fourth to nearly half the mass was silver! That is to say, every one hundred pounds of the ore had from *two hundred* dollars up to about *three hundred and fifty* in it. Some days later this same correspondent wrote:

> I have spoken of the vast and almost fabulous wealth of this region – it is incredible. The intestines of our mountains are

gorged with precious ore to plethora. I have said that nature has so shaped our mountains as to furnish most excellent facilities for the working of our mines. I have also told you that the country about here is pregnant with the finest mill sites in the world. But what is the mining history of Humboldt? The Sheba mine is in the hands of energetic San Francisco capitalists. It would seem that the ore is combined with metals that render it difficult of reduction with our imperfect mountain machinery. The proprietors have combined the capital and labor hinted at in my exordium. They are toiling and probing. Their tunnel has reached the length of one hundred feet. From primal assays alone, coupled with the development of the mine and public confidence in the continuance of effort, the stock had reared itself to eight hundred dollars market value. I do not know that one ton of the ore has been converted into current metal. I do know that there are many lodes in this section that surpass the Sheba in primal assay value. Listen a moment to the calculations of the Sheba operators. They purpose transporting the ore concentrated to Europe. The conveyance from Star City (its locality) to Virginia City will cost seventy dollars per ton; from Virginia to San Francisco, forty dollars per ton; from thence to Liverpool, its destination, ten dollars per ton. Their idea is that its conglomerate metals will reimburse them their cost of original extraction, the price of transportation, and the expense of reduction, and that then a ton of the raw ore will net them twelve hundred dollars. The estimate may be extravagant. Cut it in twain, and the product is enormous, far transcending any previous developments of our racy Territory.

A very common calculation is that many of our mines will yield five hundred dollars to the ton. Such fecundity throws the Gould & Curry, the Ophir and the Mexican, of your neighborhood, in the darkest shadow. I have given you the estimate of the value of a single developed mine. Its richness is indexed by its market valuation. The people of Humboldt county are *feet* crazy. As I write, our towns are near deserted. They look as languid as a consumptive girl. What has become of our sinewy and athletic fellow-citizens? They are coursing through ravines and over mountain tops. Their tracks are visible in every direction. Occasionally a horseman will dash among us. His steed betrays hard usage. He alights before his

> adobe dwelling, hastily exchanges courtesies with his townsmen, hurries to an assay office and from thence to the District Recorder's. In the morning, having renewed his provisional supplies, he is off again on his wild and unbeaten route. Why, the fellow numbers already his feet by the thousands. He is the horse-leech. He has the craving stomach of the shark or anaconda. He would conquer metallic worlds.

This was enough. The instant we had finished reading the above article, four of us decided to go to Humboldt. We commenced getting ready at once. And we also commenced upbraiding ourselves for not deciding sooner – for we were in terror lest all the rich mines would be found and secured before we got there, and we might have to put up with ledges that would not yield more than two or three hundred dollars a ton, maybe. An hour before, I would have felt opulent if I had owned ten feet in a Gold Hill mine whose ore produced twenty-five dollars to the ton; now I was already annoyed at the prospect of having to put up with mines the poorest of which would be a marvel in Gold Hill.

CHAPTER XXVII

HURRY, WAS THE word! We wasted no time. Our party consisted of four persons – a blacksmith sixty years of age, two young lawyers, and myself. We bought a wagon and two miserable old horses. We put eighteen hundred pounds of provisions and mining tools in the wagon and drove out of Carson on a chilly December afternoon. The horses were so weak and old that we soon found that it would be better if one or two of us got out and walked. It was an improvement. Next, we found that it would be better if a third man got out. That was an improvement also. It was at this time that I volunteered to drive, although I had never driven a harnessed horse before and many a man in such a position would have felt fairly excused from such a responsibility. But in a little while it was found that it would be a fine thing if the driver got out and walked also. It was at this time that I resigned the position of driver, and never resumed it again. Within that hour, we found that it would not only be better, but was absolutely necessary, that we four, taking turns, two at a time, should put our hands against the end of the wagon and push it through the sand, leaving the feeble horses little to do but keep out of the way and hold up the tongue. Perhaps it is well for one to know his fate at first, and get reconciled to it. We had learned ours in one afternoon. It was plain that we had to walk through the sand and shove that wagon and those horses two hundred miles. So we accepted the situation, and from that time forth we never rode. More than that, we stood regular and nearly constant watches pushing up behind.

We made seven miles, and camped in the desert. Young Clagett (now member of Congress from Montana) unharnessed and fed and watered the horses; Oliphant and I cut sage-brush, built the fire and brought water to cook with; and old Mr. Ballou the blacksmith did the cooking. This division of labor, and this appointment was adhered to throughout the journey. We had no tent, and so we slept under our blankets in the open plain. We were so tired that we slept soundly.

We were fifteen days making the trip – two hundred miles; thirteen, rather, for we lay by a couple of days, in one place, to let the horses rest. We could really have accomplished the journey in ten days if we had towed the horses behind the wagon, but we did not think of that until it was too late, and so went on shoving the horses and the wagon too when we might have saved half the labor. Parties who met us, occasionally, advised us to put the horses *in* the wagon, but Mr. Ballou, through whose iron-clad earnestness no sarcasm could pierce, said that that would not do, because the provisions were exposed and would suffer, the horses being "bituminous from long deprivation." The reader will excuse me from translating. What Mr. Ballou customarily meant when he used a long word, was a secret between himself and his Maker. He was one of the best and kindest-hearted men that ever graced a humble sphere of life. He was gentleness and simplicity itself – and unselfishness, too. Although he was more than twice as old as the eldest of us he never gave himself any airs, privileges, or exemptions on that account. He did a *young* man's share of the work; and did his share of conversation and entertaining from the general stand-point of *any* age – not from the arrogant, overawing summit-height of sixty years. His one striking peculiarity was his Partingtonian fashion of loving and using big words *for their own sakes*, and independent of any bearing they might have upon the thought he was purposing to convey. He always let his ponderous syllables fall with an easy unconsciousness that left them wholly without offensiveness. In truth his air was so natural and so simple that one was always catching himself accepting his stately sentences as meaning something, when they really meant nothing in the world. If a word was long and grand and resonant, that was sufficient to win the old man's love, and he would drop that word into the most out-of-the-way place in a sentence or a subject, and be as pleased with it as if it were perfectly luminous with meaning.

We four always spread our common stock of blankets together on the frozen ground, and slept side by side; and finding that our foolish, long-legged hound pup had a deal of animal heat in him, Oliphant got to admitting him to the bed, between himself and Mr. Ballou, hugging the dog's warm back to his breast and finding great comfort in it. But in the night the pup would get stretchy and brace his feet against the old man's back and shove, grunting complacently the while; and now and then, being warm and snug, grateful and happy, he would paw the old man's back simply in excess of comfort; and at yet other times he would dream of the chase and in his sleep tug at the old man's back hair and bark in his ear. The old gentleman complained mildly about these familiarities, at last, and when he got through with his statement he said that such a dog as that was not a proper animal to admit to bed with tired men, because he was "so meretricious in his movements and so organic in his emotions." We turned the dog out.

It was a hard, wearing, toilsome journey, but it had its bright side; for after each day was done and our wolfish hunger appeased with a hot supper of fried bacon, bread, molasses and black coffee, the pipe-smoking, song-singing and yarn-spinning around the evening camp fire in the still solitudes of the desert was a happy, care-free sort of recreation that seemed the very summit and culmination of earthly luxury. It is a kind of life that has a potent charm for all men, whether city- or country-bred. We are descended from desert-lounging Arabs, and countless ages of growth toward perfect civilization have failed to root out of us the nomadic instinct. We all confess to a gratified thrill at the thought of "camping out."

Once we made twenty-five miles in a day, and once we made forty miles (through the Great American Desert), and ten miles beyond – fifty in all – in twenty-three hours, without halting to eat, drink or rest. To stretch out and go to sleep, even on stony and frozen ground, after pushing a wagon and two horses fifty miles, is a delight so supreme that for the moment it almost seems cheap at the price.

We camped two days in the neighborhood of the "Sink of the Humboldt." We tried to use the strong alkaline water of the Sink, but it would not answer. It was like drinking lye, and not weak lye, either. It left a taste in the mouth, bitter and every way execrable, and a burning in the stomach that was very uncomfortable. We put molasses in it, but that helped it very little; we added a pickle, yet the alkali was the prominent taste, and so it was unfit for drinking. The coffee we made of this water was the meanest compound man has yet invented. It was really viler to the taste than the unameliorated water itself. Mr. Ballou, being the architect and builder of the beverage felt constrained to endorse and uphold it, and so drank half a cup, by little sips, making shift to praise it faintly the while, but finally threw out the remainder, and said frankly it was "too technical for *him.*"

But presently we found a spring of fresh water, convenient, and then, with nothing to mar our enjoyment, and no stragglers to interrupt it, we entered into our rest.

CHAPTER XXVIII

AFTER LEAVING THE Sink, we traveled along the Humboldt river a little way. People accustomed to the monster mile-wide Mississippi, grow accustomed to associating the term "river" with a high degree of watery grandeur. Consequently, such people feel rather disappointed when they stand on the shores of the Humboldt or the Carson and find that a "river" in Nevada is a sickly rivulet which is just the counterpart of the Erie canal in all respects save that the canal is twice as long and four times as deep. One of the pleasantest and most invigorating exercises one can contrive is to run and jump across the Humboldt river till he is overheated, and then drink it dry.

On the fifteenth day we completed our march of two hundred miles and entered Unionville, Humboldt county, in the midst of a driving snow-storm. Unionville consisted of eleven cabins and a liberty pole. Six of the cabins were strung along one side of a deep canyon, and the other five faced them. The rest of the landscape was made up of bleak mountain walls that rose so high into the sky from both sides of the canon that the village was left, as it were, far down in the bottom of the crevice. It was always daylight on the mountain tops a long time before the darkness lifted and revealed Unionville.

We built a small, rude cabin in the side of the crevice and roofed it with canvas leaving a corner open to serve as a chimney, through which the cattle used to tumble occasionally, at night, and mash our furniture and interrupt our sleep. It was very cold weather and fuel was scarce. Indians brought brush and bushes several miles on their backs; and when we could catch a laden Indian it was well – and when we could not (which was the rule, not the exception), we shivered and bore it.

I confess, without shame, that I expected to find masses of silver lying all about the ground. I expected to see it glittering in the sun on the mountain summits. I said nothing about this, for some instinct told me that I might possibly have an exaggerated idea about it, and so if I betrayed my thought I might bring derision upon myself. Yet I was as perfectly satisfied in my own mind as I could be of anything, that I was going to gather up, in a day or two, or at furthest a week or two, silver enough to make me satisfactorily wealthy – and so my fancy was already busy with plans for spending this money. The first opportunity that offered, I sauntered carelessly away from the cabin, keeping an eye on the other boys, and stopping and contemplating the sky when they seemed to be observing me; but as soon as the coast was manifestly clear, I fled away as guiltily as a thief might have done and never halted till I was far beyond sight and call. Then I began my search with a feverish excitement that was brimful of expectation – almost of certainty. I crawled about the ground, seizing and examining bits of stone, blowing the dust from them or rubbing them on my clothes, and then peering at them with anxious hope. Presently I found a bright fragment and my heart bounded! I hid behind a boulder and polished it and scrutinized it with a nervous eagerness and a delight that was more pronounced than absolute certainty itself could have afforded. The more I examined the fragment the more I was convinced that I had found the door to fortune. I marked the spot and carried away my specimen. Up and down the rugged mountain side I searched, with always increasing interest and always augmenting gratitude that I had come to Humboldt and come in time. Of all the experiences of my life, this secret search among the hidden treasures of silver-land was the nearest to unmarred ecstasy. It was a delirious revel. By and by, in the bed of a shallow rivulet, I found a deposit of shining yellow scales, and my breath almost forsook me! A gold mine, and in my simplicity I had been content with vulgar silver! I was so excited that I half believed my overwrought imagination was deceiving me. Then a fear came upon me that people might be observing me and would guess my secret. Moved by this thought, I made a circuit of the place, and ascended a knoll to reconnoiter. Solitude. No creature was near. Then I returned to my mine, fortifying myself against possible disappointment, but my fears were groundless – the shining scales were still there. I set about scooping them out, and for an hour I toiled down the windings of the stream and robbed its bed. But at last the descending sun warned me to give up the quest, and I turned homeward laden with wealth. As I walked along I could not help smiling at the thought of my being so excited over my fragment of silver when a nobler metal was almost under my nose. In this little time the former had so fallen in my estimation that once or twice I was on the point of throwing it away.

The boys were as hungry as usual, but I could eat nothing. Neither could I talk. I was full of dreams and far away. Their conversation interrupted the flow of my fancy somewhat, and annoyed me a little, too. I despised the sordid and commonplace things they talked about. But as they proceeded, it began to amuse me. It grew to be rare fun to hear them planning their poor little economies and sighing over possible privations and distresses when a gold mine, all our own, lay within sight of the cabin and I could point it out at any moment. Smothered hilarity began to oppress me, presently. It was hard to resist the impulse to burst out with exultation and reveal everything; but I did resist. I said within myself that I would filter the great news through my lips calmly and be serene as a summer morning while I watched its effect in their faces. I said:

"Where have you all been?"

"Prospecting."

"What did you find?"

"Nothing."

"Nothing? What do you think of the country?"

"Can't tell, yet," said Mr. Ballou, who was an old gold miner, and had likewise had considerable experience among the silver mines.

"Well, haven't you formed any sort of opinion?"

"Yes, a sort of a one. It's fair enough here, may be, but overrated. Several-thousand-dollar ledges are scarce, though. That Sheba may be rich enough, but we don't own it; and besides, the rock is so full of base metals that all the science in the world can't work it. We'll not starve, here, but we'll not get rich, I'm afraid."

"So you think the prospect is pretty poor?"

"No name for it!"

"Well, we'd better go back, hadn't we?"

"Oh, not yet – of course not. We'll try it a riffle, first."

"Suppose, now – this is merely a supposition, you know – suppose you could find a ledge that would yield, say, a hundred and fifty dollars a ton – would that satisfy you?"

"Try us once!" from the whole party.

"Or suppose – merely a supposition, of course – suppose you were to find a ledge that would yield two thousand dollars a ton – would *that* satisfy you?"

"Here – what do you mean? What are you coming at? Is there some mystery behind all this?"

"Never mind. I am not saying any thing. You know perfectly well there are no rich mines here – of course you do. Because you have been around and examined for yourselves. Anybody would know that, that had been around. But just for the sake of argument, suppose – in a kind of general way – suppose some person were to tell you that two-thousand-dollar ledges were simply contemptible – contemptible, understand – and that right yonder in sight of this very cabin there were piles of pure gold and pure silver – oceans of it – enough to make you all rich in twenty-four hours! Come!"

"I should say he was as crazy as a loon!" said old Ballou, but wild with excitement, nevertheless.

"Gentlemen," said I, "I don't say anything – *I* haven't been around, you know, and of course don't know anything – but all I ask of you is to cast your eye on *that*, for instance, and tell me what you think of it!" and I tossed my treasure before them.

There was an eager scramble for it, and a closing of heads together over it under the candle-light. Then old Ballou said:

"Think of it? I think it is nothing but a lot of granite rubbish and nasty glittering mica that isn't worth ten cents an acre!"

So vanished my dream. So melted my wealth away. So toppled my airy castle to the earth and left me stricken and forlorn.

Moralizing, I observed, then, that "all that glitters is not gold."

Mr. Ballou said I could go further than that, and lay it up among my treasures of knowledge, that *nothing* that glitters is gold. So I learned then, once for all, that gold in its native state is but dull, unornamental stuff, and that only low-born metals excite the admiration of the ignorant with an ostentatious glitter. However, like the rest of the world, I still go on underrating men of gold and glorifying men of mica. Commonplace human nature cannot rise above that.

CHAPTER XXIX

TRUE KNOWLEDGE OF the nature of silver mining came fast enough. We went out "prospecting" with Mr. Ballou. We climbed the mountain sides, and clambered among sage-brush, rocks and snow till we were ready to drop with exhaustion, but found no silver – nor yet any gold. Day after day we did this. Now and then we came upon holes burrowed a few feet into the declivities and apparently abandoned; and now and then we found one or two listless men still burrowing. But there was no appearance of silver. These holes were the beginnings of tunnels, and the purpose was to drive them hundreds of feet into the mountain, and some day tap the hidden ledge where the silver was. Some day! It seemed far enough away, and very hopeless and dreary. Day after day we toiled, and climbed and searched, and we younger partners grew sicker and still sicker of the promise-less toil. At last we halted under a beetling rampart of rock which projected from the earth high upon the mountain. Mr. Ballou broke off some fragments with a hammer, and examined them long and attentively with a small eye-glass; threw them away and broke off more; said this rock was quartz, and quartz was the sort of rock that contained silver. *Contained* it! I had thought that at least it would be caked on the outside of it like a kind of veneering. He still broke off pieces and critically examined them, now and then wetting the piece with his tongue and applying the glass. At last he exclaimed:

"We've got it!"

We were full of anxiety in a moment. The rock was clean and white, where it was broken, and across it ran a ragged thread of blue. He said that that little thread had silver in it, mixed with base metals, such as lead and antimony, and other rubbish, and that there was a speck or two of gold visible. After a great deal of effort we managed to discern some little fine yellow specks, and judged that a couple of tons of them massed together might make a gold dollar, possibly. We were not jubilant, but Mr. Ballou said there were worse ledges in the world than that. He saved what he called the "richest" piece of the rock, in order to determine its value by the process called the "fire-assay." Then we named the mine "Monarch of the Mountains" (modesty of nomenclature is not a prominent feature in the mines), and Mr. Ballou wrote out and stuck up the following "notice," preserving a copy to be entered upon the books in the mining recorder's office in the town.

"NOTICE"

> "We the undersigned claim three claims, of three hundred feet each [and one for discovery], on this silver-bearing quartz lead or lode, extending north and south from this notice, with all its dips, spurs, and angles, variations and sinuosities, together with fifty feet of ground on either side for working the same."

We put our names to it and tried to feel that our fortunes were made. But when we talked the matter all over with Mr. Ballou, we felt depressed and dubious. He said that this surface quartz was not all there was of our mine; but that the wall or ledge of rock called the "Monarch of the Mountains," extended down hundreds and hundreds of feet into the earth – he illustrated by saying it was like a curbstone, and maintained a nearly uniform thickness – say twenty feet – away down into the bowels of the earth, and was perfectly distinct from the casing rock on each side of it; and that it kept to itself, and maintained its distinctive character always, no matter how deep it extended into the earth or how far it stretched itself through and across the hills and valleys. He said it might be a mile deep and ten miles long, for all we knew; and that wherever we bored into it above ground or below, we would find gold and silver in it, but no gold or silver in the meaner rock it was cased between. And he said that down in the great depths of the ledge was its richness, and the deeper it went the richer it grew. Therefore, instead of working here on the surface, we must either bore down into the rock with a shaft till we came to where it was rich – say a hundred feet or so – or else we must go down into the valley and bore a long tunnel into the mountain side and tap the ledge far under the earth. To do either was plainly the labor of months; for we could blast and bore only a few feet a day – some five or six. But this was not all. He said that after we got the ore out it must be hauled in wagons to a distant silver-mill, ground up, and the silver extracted by a tedious and costly process. Our fortune seemed a century away!

But we went to work. We decided to sink a shaft. So, for a week we climbed the mountain, laden with picks, drills, gads, crowbars, shovels, cans of blasting-powder and coils of fuse and strove with might and main. At first the rock was broken and loose and we dug it up with picks and threw it out with shovels, and the hole progressed very well. But the rock became more compact, presently, and gads and crowbars came into play. But shortly nothing could make an impression but blasting-powder. That was the weariest work! One of us held the iron drill in its place and another would strike with an eight-pound sledge – it was like driving nails on a large scale. In the course of an hour or two the drill would reach a depth of two or three feet, making a hole a couple of inches in diameter. We would put in a charge of powder, insert half a yard of fuse, pour in sand and gravel and ram it down, then light the fuse and run. When the explosion came and the rocks and smoke shot into the air, we would go back and find about a bushel of that hard, rebellious quartz jolted out. Nothing more. One week of this satisfied me. I resigned. Clagget and Oliphant followed. Our shaft was only twelve feet deep. We decided that a tunnel was the thing we wanted.

So we went down the mountain side and worked a week; at the end of which time we had blasted a tunnel about deep enough to hide a hogshead in, and judged that about nine hundred feet more of it would reach the ledge. I resigned again, and the other boys only held out one day longer. We decided that a tunnel was not what we wanted. We wanted a ledge that was already "developed." There were none in the camp.

We dropped the "Monarch" for the time being.

Meantime the camp was filling up with people, and there was a constantly growing excitement about our Humboldt mines. We fell victims to the epidemic and strained every nerve to acquire more "feet." We prospected and took up new claims, put "notices" on them and gave them grandiloquent names. We traded some of our "feet" for "feet" in other people's claims. In a little while we owned largely in the "Gray Eagle," the "Columbiana," the "Branch Mint," the "Maria Jane," the "Universe," the "Root-Hog-or-Die," the "Samson and Delilah," the "Treasure Trove," the "Golconda," the "Sultana," the "Boomerang," the "Great Republic," the "Grand Mogul," and fifty other "mines" that had never been molested by a shovel or scratched with a pick. We had not less than thirty thousand "feet" apiece in the "richest mines on earth" as the frenzied cant phrased it – and were in debt to the butcher. We were stark mad with excitement – drunk with happiness – smothered under mountains of prospective wealth – arrogantly compassionate toward the plodding millions who knew not our marvelous canon – but our credit was not good at the grocer's.

It was the strangest phase of life one can imagine. It was a beggars' revel. There was nothing doing in the district – no mining – no milling – no productive effort – no income – and not enough money in the entire camp to buy a corner lot in an eastern village, hardly; and yet a stranger would have supposed he was walking among bloated millionaires. Prospecting parties swarmed out of town with the first flush of dawn, and swarmed in again at night-fall laden with spoil – rocks. Nothing but rocks. Every man's pockets were full of them; the floor of his cabin was littered with them; they were disposed in labeled rows on his shelves.

CHAPTER XXX

I MET MEN at every turn who owned from one thousand to thirty thousand "feet" in undeveloped silver mines, every single foot of which they believed would shortly be worth from fifty to a thousand dollars – and as often as any other way they were men who had not twenty-five dollars in the world. Every man you met had his new mine to boast of, and his "specimens" ready; and if the opportunity offered, he would infallibly back you into a corner and offer as a favor to *you*, not to *him*, to part with just a few feet in the "Golden Age," or the "Sarah Jane," or some other unknown stack of croppings, for money enough to get a "square meal" with, as the phrase went. And you were never to reveal that he had made you the offer at such a ruinous price, for it was only out of friendship for you that he was willing to make the sacrifice. Then he would fish a piece of rock out of his pocket, and after looking mysteriously around as if he feared he might be waylaid and robbed if caught with such wealth in his possession, he would dab the rock against his tongue, clap an eye-glass to it, and exclaim:

"Look at that! Right there in that red dirt! See it? See the specks of gold? And the streak of silver? That's from the 'Uncle Abe.' There's a hundred thousand tons like that in sight! Right in sight, mind you! And when we get down on it and the ledge comes in solid, it will be the richest thing in the world! Look at the assay! I don't want you to believe *me* – look at the assay!"

Then he would get out a greasy sheet of paper which showed that the portion of rock assayed had given evidence of containing silver and gold in the proportion of so many hundreds or thousands of dollars to the ton. I little knew, then, that the custom was to hunt out the *richest* piece of rock and get it assayed! Very often, that piece, the size of a filbert, was the only fragment in a ton that had a particle of metal in it – and yet the assay made it pretend to represent the average value of the ton of rubbish it came from!

On such a system of assaying as that, the Humboldt world had gone crazy. On the authority of such assays its newspaper correspondents were frothing about rock worth four and seven thousand dollars a ton!

And does the reader remember, a few pages back, the calculations, of a quoted correspondent, whereby the ore is to be mined and shipped all the way to England, the metals extracted, and the gold and silver contents received back by the miners as clear profit, the copper, antimony and other things in the ore being sufficient to pay all the expenses incurred? Everybody's head was full of such "calculations" as those – such raving insanity, rather. Few people took *work* into their calculations – or outlay of money either; except the work and expenditures of other people.

We never touched our tunnel or our shaft again. Why? Because we judged that we had learned the *real* secret of success in silver mining – which was, *not* to mine the silver ourselves by the sweat of our brows and the labor of our hands, but to *sell* the ledges to the dull slaves of toil and let them do the mining!

Before leaving Carson, the Secretary and I had purchased "feet" from various Esmeralda stragglers. We had expected immediate returns of bullion, but were only afflicted with regular and constant "assessments" instead – demands for money wherewith to develop the said mines. These assessments had grown so oppressive that it seemed necessary to look into the matter personally. Therefore I projected a pilgrimage to Carson and thence to Esmeralda. I bought a horse and started, in company with Mr. Ballou and a gentleman named Ollendorff, a Prussian – not the party who has inflicted so much suffering on the world with his wretched foreign grammars, with their interminable repetitions of questions which never have occurred and are never likely to occur in any conversation among human beings. We rode through a snow-storm for two or three days, and arrived at "Honey Lake Smith's," a sort of isolated inn on the Carson river. It was a two-story log-house situated on a small knoll in the midst of the vast basin or desert through which the sickly Carson winds its melancholy way. Close to the house were the Overland stage stables, built of sun-dried bricks. There was not another building within several leagues of the place. Towards sunset about twenty hay-wagons arrived and camped around the house and all the teamsters came in to supper – a very, very rough set. There were one or two Overland stage-drivers there also, and half a dozen vagabonds and stragglers; consequently the house was well crowded.

We walked out, after supper, and visited a small Indian camp in the vicinity. The Indians were in a great hurry about something, and were packing up and getting away as fast as they could. In their broken English they said, "By'm-by, heap water!" and by the help of signs made us understand that in their opinion a flood was coming. The weather was perfectly clear and this was not the rainy season. There was about a foot of water in the insignificant river – or maybe two feet; the stream was not wider than a back alley in a village, and its banks were scarcely higher than a man's head. So, where was the flood to come from? We canvassed the subject awhile and then concluded it was a ruse, and that the Indians had some better reason for leaving in a hurry than fears of a flood in such an exceedingly dry time.

At seven in the evening we went to bed in the second story – with our clothes on, as usual, and all three in the same bed, for every available space on the floors, chairs, etc., was in request, and even then there was barely room for the housing of the inn's guests. An hour later we were awakened by a great turmoil, and springing out of bed we picked our way nimbly among the ranks of snoring teamsters on the floor and got to the front windows of the long room. A glance revealed a strange spectacle, under the moonlight. The crooked Carson was full to the brim, and its waters were raging and foaming in the wildest way – sweeping around the sharp bends at a furious speed, and bearing on their surface a chaos of logs, brush and all sorts of rubbish. A depression, where its bed had once been, in other times, was already filling, and in one or two places the water was beginning to wash over the main bank. Men were flying hither and thither, bringing cattle and wagons close up to the house, for the spot of high ground on which it stood extended only some thirty feet in front and about a hundred in the rear. Close to the old river bed just spoken of, stood a little log stable, and in this our horses were lodged. While we looked, the waters increased so fast in this place that in a few minutes a torrent was roaring by the little stable and its margin encroaching steadily on the logs. We suddenly realized that this flood was not a mere holiday spectacle but meant damage – and not only to the small log stable but to the Overland buildings close to the main river, for the waves had now come ashore and were creeping about the foundations and invading the great hay-corral adjoining. We ran down and joined the crowd of excited men and frightened animals. We waded knee-deep into the log stable, unfastened the horses and waded out almost *waist*-deep, so fast the waters increased. Then the crowd rushed in a body to the hay-corral and began to tumble down the huge stacks of baled hay and roll the bales up on the high ground by the house. Meantime it was discovered that Owens, an Overland driver, was missing, and a man ran to the large stable, and wading in, boot-top deep, discovered him asleep in his bed, awoke him, and waded out again. But Owens was drowsy and resumed his nap; but only for a minute or two, for presently he turned in his bed, his hand dropped over the side and came in contact with the cold water! It was up level with the mattress! He waded out, breast-deep, almost, and the next moment the sun-burned bricks melted down like sugar and the big building crumbled to a ruin and was washed away in a twinkling.

At eleven o'clock only the roof of the little log stable was out of water, and our inn was on an island in mid-ocean. As far as the eye could reach, in the moonlight, there was no desert visible but only a level waste of shining water. The Indians were true prophets, but how did they get their information? I am not able to answer the question.

We remained cooped up eight days and nights with that curious crew. Swearing, drinking and card playing were the order of the day, and occasionally a fight was thrown in for variety. Dirt and vermin – but let us forget those features; their profusion is simply inconceivable – it is better that they remain so.

There were two men – however, this chapter is long enough.

CHAPTER XXXI

THERE WERE TWO men in the company who caused me particular discomfort. One was a little Swede, about twenty-five years old, who knew only one song, and he was forever singing it. By day we were all crowded into one small, stifling barroom, and so there was no escaping this person's music. Through all the profanity, whiskey-guzzling, "old sledge" and quarreling, his monotonous song meandered with never a variation in its tiresome sameness, and it seemed to me, at last, that I would be content to die, in order to be rid of the torture. The other man was a stalwart ruffian called "Arkansas," who carried two revolvers in his belt and a bowie knife projecting from his boot, and who was always drunk and always suffering for a fight. But he was so feared, that nobody would accommodate him. He would try all manner of little wary ruses to entrap somebody into an offensive remark, and his face would light up now and then when he fancied he was fairly on the scent of a fight, but invariably his victim would elude his toils and then he would show a disappointment that was almost pathetic. The landlord, Johnson, was a meek, well-meaning fellow, and Arkansas fastened on him early, as a promising subject, and gave him no rest day or night, for awhile. On the fourth morning, Arkansas got drunk and sat himself down to wait for an opportunity. Presently Johnson came in, just comfortably sociable with whiskey, and said:

"I reckon the Pennsylvania 'lection—"

Arkansas raised his finger impressively and Johnson stopped. Arkansas rose unsteadily and confronted him. Said he:

"Wha-what do you know a-about Pennsylvania? Answer me that. Wha-what do you know 'bout Pennsylvania?"

"I was only goin' to say—"

"You was only going to *say*. *You* was! You was only goin' to say – *what* was you goin' to say? That's it! That's what *I* want to know. *I* want to know wha-what you (*'ic*) what you know about Pennsylvania, since you're makin' yourself so d——d free. Answer me that!"

"Mr. Arkansas, if you'd only let me—"

"Who's a henderin' you? Don't you insinuate nothing agin me! – don't you do it. Don't you come in here bullyin' around, and cussin' and goin' on like a lunatic – don't you do it. 'Coz *I* won't *stand* it. If fight's what you want, out with it! I'm your man! Out with it!"

Said Johnson, backing into a corner, Arkansas following, menacingly:

"Why, *I* never said nothing, Mr. Arkansas. You don't give a man no chance. I was only goin' to say that Pennsylvania was goin' to have an election next week – that was all – that was everything I was goin' to say – I wish I may never stir if it wasn't."

"Well then why d'n't you say it? What did you come swellin' around that way for, and tryin' to raise trouble?"

"Why *I* didn't come swellin' around, Mr. Arkansas – I just—"

"I'm a liar am I! Ger-reat Caesar's ghost—"

"Oh, please, Mr. Arkansas, I never meant such a thing as that, I wish I may die if I did. All the boys will tell you that I've always spoke well of you, and respected you more'n any man in the house. Ask Smith. Ain't it so, Smith? Didn't I say, no longer ago than last night, that for a man that was a gentleman *all* the time and every way you took him, give me Arkansas? I'll leave it to any gentleman here if them warn't the very words I used. Come, now, Mr. Arkansas, le's take a drink – le's shake hands and take a drink. Come up – every body! It's my treat. Come up, Bill, Tom, Bob, Scotty – come up. I want you all to take a drink with me and Arkansas – *old* Arkansas, I call him – bully old Arkansas. Gimme your hand agin. Look at him, boys – just take a *look* at him. Thar stands the whitest man in America! – and the man that denies it has got to fight *me*, that's all. Gimme that old flipper agin!"

They embraced, with drunken affection on the landlord's part and unresponsive toleration on the part of Arkansas, who, bribed by a drink, was disappointed of his prey once more. But the foolish landlord was so happy to have escaped butchery, that he went on talking when he ought to have marched himself out of danger. The consequence was that Arkansas shortly began to glower upon him dangerously, and presently said:

"Lan'lord, will you p-please make that remark over agin if you please?"

"I was a-sayin' to Scotty that my father was up'ards of eighty year old when he died."

"Was that *all* that you said?"

"Yes, that was all."

"Didn't say nothing but that?"

"No – nothing."

Then an uncomfortable silence.

Arkansas played with his glass a moment, lolling on his elbows on the counter. Then he meditatively scratched his left shin with his right boot, while the awkward silence continued. But presently he loafed away toward the stove, looking dissatisfied; roughly shouldered two or three men out of a comfortable position; occupied it himself, gave a sleeping dog a kick that sent him howling under a bench, then spread his long legs and his blanket-coat tails apart and proceeded to warm his back. In a little while he fell to grumbling to himself, and soon he slouched back to the bar and said:

"Lan'lord, what's your idea for rakin' up old personalities and blowin' about your father? Ain't this company agreeable to you? Ain't it? If this company ain't agreeable to you, p'r'aps we'd better leave. Is that your idea? Is that what you're coming at?"

"Why bless your soul, Arkansas, I warn't thinking of such a thing. My father and my mother—"

"Lan'lord, *don't* crowd a man! Don't do it. If nothing'll do you but a disturbance, out with it like a man (*'ic*) – but *don't* rake up old bygones and fling 'em in the teeth of a passel of people that wants to be peaceable if they could git a chance. What's the matter with you this mornin', anyway? I never see a man carry on so."

"Arkansas, I reely didn't mean no harm, and I won't go on with it if it's onpleasant to you. I reckon my licker's got into my head, and what with the flood, and havin' so many to feed and look out for—"

"So *that's* what's a-ranklin' in your heart, is it? You want us to leave do you? There's too many on us. You want us to pack up and swim. Is that it? Come!"

"Please be reasonable, Arkansas. Now *you* know that I ain't the man to—"

"Are you a threatenin' me? Are you? By George, the man don't live that can skeer me! Don't you try to come that game, my chicken – 'cuz I can stand a good deal, but I won't stand that. Come out from behind that bar till I clean you! You want to drive us out, do you, you sneakin' underhanded hound! Come out from behind that bar! *I'll* learn you to bully and badger and browbeat a gentleman that's forever trying to befriend you and keep you out of trouble!"

"Please, Arkansas, please don't shoot! If there's got to be bloodshed—"

"Do you hear that, gentlemen? Do you hear him talk about bloodshed? So it's blood you want, is it, you ravin' desperado! You'd made up your mind to murder somebody this mornin' – I knowed it perfectly well. I'm the man, am I? It's me you're goin' to murder, is it? But you can't do it 'thout I get one chance first, you thievin' black-hearted, white-livered son of a nigger! Draw your weepon!"

With that, Arkansas began to shoot, and the landlord to clamber over benches, men and every sort of obstacle in a frantic desire to escape. In the midst of the wild hubbub the landlord crashed through a glass door, and as Arkansas charged after him the landlord's wife suddenly appeared in the doorway and confronted the desperado with a pair of scissors! Her fury was magnificent. With head erect and flashing eye she stood a moment and then advanced, with her weapon raised. The astonished ruffian hesitated, and then fell back a step. She followed. She backed him step by step into the middle of the barroom, and then, while the wondering crowd closed up and gazed, she gave him such another tongue-lashing as never a cowed and shamefaced braggart got before, perhaps! As she finished and retired victorious, a roar of applause shook the house, and every man ordered "drinks for the crowd" in one and the same breath.

The lesson was entirely sufficient. The reign of terror was over, and the Arkansas domination broken for good. During the rest of the season of island captivity, there was one man who sat apart in a state of permanent humiliation, never mixing in any quarrel or uttering a boast, and never resenting the insults the once cringing crew now constantly leveled at him, and that man was "Arkansas."

By the fifth or sixth morning the waters had subsided from the land, but the stream in the old river bed was still high and swift and there was no possibility of crossing it. On the eighth it was still too high for an entirely safe passage, but life in the inn had become next to insupportable by reason of the dirt, drunkenness, fighting, etc., and so we made an effort to get away. In the midst of a heavy snow-storm we embarked in a canoe, taking our saddles aboard and towing our horses after us by their halters. The Prussian, Ollendorff, was in the bow, with a paddle, Ballou paddled in the middle, and I sat in the stern holding the halters. When the horses lost their footing and began to swim, Ollendorff got frightened, for there was great danger that the horses would make our aim uncertain, and it was plain that if we failed to land at a certain spot the current would throw us off and almost surely cast us into the main Carson, which was a boiling torrent, now. Such a catastrophe would be death, in all probability, for we would be swept to sea in the "Sink" or overturned and drowned. We warned Ollendorff to keep his wits about him and handle himself carefully, but it was useless; the moment the bow touched the bank, he made a spring and the canoe whirled upside down in ten-foot water. Ollendorff seized some brush and dragged himself ashore, but Ballou and I had to swim for it encumbered with our overcoats. But we held on to the canoe, and although we were washed down nearly to the Carson, we managed to push the boat ashore and make a safe landing. We were cold and water-soaked, but safe. The horses made a landing too, but our saddles were gone, of course. We tied the animals in the sage-brush and there they had to stay for twenty-four hours. We baled out the canoe and ferried over some food and blankets for them, but we slept one more night in the inn before making another venture on our journey.

The next morning it was still snowing furiously when we got away with our new stock of saddles and accoutrements. We mounted and started. The snow lay so deep on the ground that there was no sign of a road perceptible, and the snow-fall was so thick that we could not see more than a hundred yards ahead, else we could have guided our course by the mountain ranges. The case looked dubious, but Ollendorff said his instinct was as sensitive as any compass, and that he could "strike a bee-line" for Carson city and never diverge from it. He said that if he were to straggle a single point out of the true line his instinct would assail him like an outraged conscience. Consequently we dropped into his wake happy and content. For half an hour we poked along warily enough, but at the end of that time we came upon a fresh trail, and Ollendorff shouted proudly:

"I knew I was as dead certain as a compass, boys! Here we are, right in somebody's tracks that will hunt the way for us without any trouble. Let's hurry up and join company with the party."

So we put the horses into as much of a trot as the deep snow would allow, and before long it was evident that we were gaining on our predecessors, for the tracks grew more distinct. We hurried along, and at the end of an hour the tracks looked still newer and fresher – but what surprised us was, that the *number* of travelers in advance of us seemed to steadily increase. We wondered how so large a party came to be traveling at such a time and in such a solitude. Somebody suggested that it must be a company of soldiers from the fort, and so we accepted that solution and jogged along a little faster still, for they could not be far off now. But the tracks still multiplied, and we began to think the platoon of soldiers was miraculously expanding into a regiment – Ballou said they had already increased to five hundred! Presently he stopped his horse and said:

"Boys, these are our own tracks, and we've actually been circussing round and round in a circle for more than two hours out here in this blind desert! By George this is perfectly hydraulic!"

Then the old man waxed wroth and abusive. He called Ollendorff all manner of hard names – said he never saw such a lurid fool as he was, and ended with the peculiarly venomous opinion that he "did not know as much as a logarythm!"

We certainly had been following our own tracks. Ollendorff and his "mental compass" were in disgrace from that moment. After all our hard travel, here we were on the bank of the stream again, with the inn beyond dimly outlined through the driving snow-fall. While we were considering what to do, the young Swede landed from the canoe and took his pedestrian way Carson-wards, singing his same tiresome song about his "sister and his brother" and "the child in the grave with its mother," and in a short minute faded and disappeared in the white oblivion. He was never heard of again. He no doubt got bewildered and lost, and Fatigue delivered him over to Sleep and Sleep betrayed him to Death. Possibly he followed our treacherous tracks till he became exhausted and dropped.

Presently the Overland stage forded the now fast receding stream and started toward Carson on its first trip since the flood came. We hesitated no longer, now, but took up our march in its wake, and trotted merrily along, for we had good confidence in the driver's bump of locality. But our horses were no match for the fresh stage team. We were soon left out of sight; but it was no matter, for we had the deep ruts the wheels made for a guide. By this time it was three in the afternoon, and consequently it was not very long before night came – and not with a lingering twilight, but with a sudden shutting down like a cellar door, as is its habit in that country. The snow-fall was still as thick as ever, and of course we could not see fifteen steps before us; but all about us the white glare of the snow-bed enabled us to discern the smooth sugar-loaf mounds made by the covered sage-bushes, and just in front of us the two faint grooves which we knew were the steadily filling and slowly disappearing wheel-tracks.

Now those sage-bushes were all about the same height – three or four feet; they stood just about seven feet apart, all over the vast desert; each of them was a mere snow-mound, now; in *any* direction that you proceeded (the same as in a well-laid-out orchard) you would find yourself moving down a distinctly defined avenue, with a row of these snow-mounds on either side of it – an avenue the customary width of a road, nice and level in its breadth, and rising at the sides in the most natural way, by reason of the mounds. But we had not thought of this. Then imagine the chilly thrill that shot through us when it finally occurred to us, far in the night, that since the last faint trace of the wheel-tracks had long ago been buried from sight, we might now be wandering down a mere sage-brush avenue, miles away from the road and diverging further and further away from it all the time. Having a cake of ice slipped down one's back is placid comfort compared to it. There was a sudden leap and stir of blood that had been asleep for an hour, and as sudden a rousing of all the drowsing activities in our minds and bodies. We were alive and awake at once – and shaking and quaking with consternation, too. There was an instant halting and dismounting, a bending low and an anxious scanning of the road-bed. Useless, of course;

for if a faint depression could not be discerned from an altitude of four or five feet above it, it certainly could not with one's nose nearly against it.

CHAPTER XXXII

WE SEEMED TO be in a road, but that was no proof. We tested this by walking off in various directions – the regular snow-mounds and the regular avenues between them convinced each man that *he* had found the true road, and that the others had found only false ones. Plainly the situation was desperate. We were cold and stiff and the horses were tired. We decided to build a sage-brush fire and camp out till morning. This was wise, because if we were wandering from the right road and the snow-storm continued another day our case would be the next thing to hopeless if we kept on.

All agreed that a camp fire was what would come nearest to saving us, now, and so we set about building it. We could find no matches, and so we tried to make shift with the pistols. Not a man in the party had ever tried to do such a thing before, but not a man in the party doubted that it *could* be done, and without any trouble – because every man in the party had read about it in books many a time and had naturally come to believe it, with trusting simplicity, just as he had long ago accepted and believed *that other* common book-fraud about Indians and lost hunters making a fire by rubbing two dry sticks together.

We huddled together on our knees in the deep snow, and the horses put their noses together and bowed their patient heads over us; and while the feathery flakes eddied down and turned us into a group of white statuary, we proceeded with the momentous experiment. We broke twigs from a sage-bush and piled them on a little cleared place in the shelter of our bodies. In the course of ten or fifteen minutes all was ready, and then, while conversation ceased and our pulses beat low with anxious suspense, Ollendorff applied his revolver, pulled the trigger and blew the pile clear out of the county! It was the flattest failure that ever was.

This was distressing, but it paled before a greater horror – the horses were gone! I had been appointed to hold the bridles, but in my absorbing anxiety over the pistol experiment I had unconsciously dropped them and the released animals had walked off in the storm. It was useless to try to follow them, for their foot falls could make no sound, and one could pass within two yards of the creatures and never see them. We gave them up without an effort at recovering them, and cursed the lying books that said horses would stay by their masters for protection and companionship in a distressful time like ours.

We were miserable enough, before; we felt still more forlorn, now. Patiently, but with blighted hope, we broke more sticks and piled them, and once more the Prussian shot them into annihilation. Plainly, to light a fire with a pistol was an art requiring practice and experience, and the middle of a desert at midnight in a snow-storm was not a good place or time for the acquiring of the accomplishment. We gave it up and tried the other. Each man took a couple of sticks and fell to chafing them together. At the end of half an hour we were thoroughly chilled, and so were the sticks. We bitterly execrated the Indians, the hunters and the books that had betrayed us with the silly device, and wondered dismally what was next to be done. At this critical moment Mr. Ballou fished out four matches from the rubbish of an overlooked pocket. To have found four gold bars would have seemed poor and cheap good luck compared to this. One cannot think how good a match looks under such circumstances – or how lovable and precious, and sacredly beautiful to the eye. This time we gathered sticks with high hopes; and when Mr. Ballou prepared to light the first match, there was an amount of interest centred upon him that pages of writing could not describe. The match burned hopefully a moment, and then went out. It could not have carried more regret with it if it had been a human life. The next match simply flashed and died. The wind puffed the third one out just as it was on the imminent verge of success. We gathered together closer than ever, and developed a solicitude that was rapt and painful, as Mr. Ballou scratched our last hope on his leg. It lit, burned blue and sickly, and then budded into a robust flame. Shading it with his hands, the old gentleman bent gradually down and every heart went with him – every body, too, for that matter – and blood and breath stood still. The flame touched the sticks at last, took gradual hold upon them – hesitated – took a stronger hold – hesitated again – held its breath five heart-breaking seconds, then gave a sort of human gasp and went out.

Nobody said a word for several minutes. It was a solemn sort of silence; even the wind put on a stealthy, sinister quiet and made no more noise than the falling flakes of snow. Finally a sad-voiced conversation began, and it was soon apparent that in each of our hearts lay the conviction that this was our last night with the living. I had so hoped that I was the only one who felt so. When the others calmly acknowledged their conviction, it sounded like the summons itself. Ollendorff said:

"Brothers, let us die together. And let us go without one hard feeling towards each other. Let us forget and forgive bygones. I know that you have felt hard towards me for turning over the canoe, and for knowing too much and leading you round and round in the snow – but I meant well; forgive me. I acknowledge freely that I have had hard feelings against Mr. Ballou for abusing me and calling me a logarythm, which is a thing I do not know what, but no doubt a thing considered disgraceful and unbecoming in America, and it has scarcely been out of my mind and has hurt me a great deal – but let it go; I forgive Mr. Ballou with all my heart and—"

Poor Ollendorff broke down and the tears came. He was not alone, for I was crying too, and so was Mr. Ballou. Ollendorff got his voice again and forgave me for things I had done and said. Then he got out his bottle of whiskey and said that whether he lived or died he would never touch another drop. He said he had given up all hope of life, and although ill-prepared, was ready to submit humbly to his fate; that he wished he could be spared a little longer, not for any selfish reason, but to make a thorough reform in his character, and by devoting himself to helping the poor, nursing the sick, and pleading with the people to guard themselves against the evils of intemperance, make his life a beneficent example to the young, and lay it down at last with the precious reflection that it had not been lived in vain. He ended by saying that his reform should begin at this moment, even here in the presence of death, since no longer time was to be vouchsafed wherein to prosecute it to men's help and benefit – and with that he threw away the bottle of whiskey.

Mr. Ballou made remarks of similar purport, and began the reform he could not live to continue, by throwing away the ancient pack of cards that had solaced our captivity during the flood and made it bearable. He said he never gambled, but still was satisfied that the meddling with cards in any way was immoral and injurious, and no man could be wholly pure and blemishless without eschewing them. "And therefore," continued he, "in doing this act I already feel more in sympathy with that spiritual saturnalia necessary to entire and obsolete reform." These rolling syllables touched him as no intelligible eloquence could have done, and the old man sobbed with a mournfulness not unmingled with satisfaction.

My own remarks were of the same tenor as those of my comrades, and I know that the feelings that prompted them were heartfelt and sincere. We were all sincere, and all deeply moved and earnest, for we were in the presence of death and without hope. I threw away my pipe, and in doing it felt that at last I was free of a hated vice and one that had ridden me like a tyrant all my days. While I yet talked, the thought of the good I might have done in the world and the still greater good I might *now* do, with these new incentives and higher and better aims to guide me if I could only be spared a few years longer, overcame me and the tears came again. We put our arms about each other's necks and awaited the warning drowsiness that precedes death by freezing.

It came stealing over us presently, and then we bade each other a last farewell. A delicious dreaminess wrought its web about my yielding senses, while the snowflakes wove a winding sheet about my conquered body. Oblivion came. The battle of life was done.

CHAPTER XXXIII

I DO NOT know how long I was in a state of forgetfulness, but it seemed an age. A vague consciousness grew upon me by degrees, and then came a gathering anguish of pain in my limbs and through all my body. I shuddered. The thought flitted through my brain, "this is death – this is the hereafter."

Then came a white upheaval at my side, and a voice said, with bitterness:

"Will some gentleman be so good as to kick me behind?"

It was Ballou – at least it was a towzled snow image in a sitting posture, with Ballou's voice.

I rose up, and there in the gray dawn, not fifteen steps from us, were the frame buildings of a stage-station, and under a shed stood our still saddled and bridled horses!

An arched snow-drift broke up, now, and Ollendorff emerged from it, and the three of us sat and stared at the houses without speaking a word. We really had nothing to say. We were like the profane man who could not "do the subject justice," the whole situation was so painfully ridiculous and humiliating that words were tame and we did not know where to commence any how.

The joy in our hearts at our deliverance was poisoned; well-nigh dissipated, indeed. We presently began to grow pettish by degrees, and sullen; and then, angry at each other, angry at ourselves, angry at everything in general, we moodily dusted the snow from our clothing and in unsociable single file plowed our way to the horses, unsaddled them, and sought shelter in the station.

I have scarcely exaggerated a detail of this curious and absurd adventure. It occurred almost exactly as I have stated it. We actually went into camp in a snow-drift in a desert, at midnight in a storm, forlorn and hopeless, within fifteen steps of a comfortable inn.

For two hours we sat apart in the station and ruminated in disgust. The mystery was gone, now, and it was plain enough why the horses had deserted us. Without a doubt they were under that shed a quarter of a minute after they had left us, and they must have overheard and enjoyed all our confessions and lamentations.

After breakfast we felt better, and the zest of life soon came back. The world looked bright again, and existence was as dear to us as ever. Presently an uneasiness came over me – grew upon me – assailed me without ceasing. Alas, my regeneration was not complete – I wanted to smoke! I resisted with all my strength, but the flesh was weak. I wandered away alone and wrestled with myself an hour. I recalled my promises of reform and preached to myself persuasively, upbraidingly, exhaustively. But it was all vain, I shortly found myself sneaking among the snow-drifts hunting for my pipe. I discovered it after a considerable search, and crept away to hide myself and enjoy it. I remained behind the barn a good while, asking myself how I would feel if my braver, stronger, truer comrades should catch me in my degradation. At last I lit the pipe, and no human being can feel meaner and baser than I did then. I was ashamed of being in my own pitiful company. Still dreading discovery, I felt that perhaps the further side of the barn would be somewhat safer, and so I turned the corner. As I turned the one corner, smoking, Ollendorff turned the other with his bottle to his lips, and between us sat unconscious Ballou deep in a game of "solitaire" with the old greasy cards!

Absurdity could go no farther. We shook hands and agreed to say no more about "reform" and "examples to the rising generation."

The station we were at was at the verge of the Twenty-six-Mile Desert. If we had approached it half an hour earlier the night before, we must have heard men shouting there and firing pistols; for they were expecting some sheep drovers and their flocks and knew that they would infallibly get lost and wander out of reach of help unless guided by sounds. While we remained at the station, three of the drovers arrived, nearly exhausted with their wanderings, but two others of their party were never heard of afterward.

We reached Carson in due time, and took a rest. This rest, together with preparations for the journey to Esmeralda, kept us there a week, and the delay gave us the opportunity to be present at the trial of the great landslide case of Hyde *vs.* Morgan – an episode which is famous in Nevada to this day. After a word or two of necessary explanation, I will set down the history of this singular affair just as it transpired.

CHAPTER XL

I NOW COME to a curious episode – the most curious, I think, that had yet accented my slothful, valueless, heedless career. Out of a hill-side toward the upper end of the town, projected a wall of reddish-looking quartz-croppings, the exposed comb of a silver-bearing ledge that extended deep down into the earth, of course. It was owned by a company entitled the "Wide West." There was a shaft sixty or seventy feet deep on the under side of the croppings, and every body was acquainted with the rock that came from it – and tolerably rich rock it was, too, but nothing extraordinary. I will remark here, that although to the inexperienced stranger all the quartz of a particular "district" looks about alike, an old resident of the camp can take a glance at a mixed pile of rock, separate the fragments and tell you which mine each came from, as easily as a confectioner can separate and classify the various kinds and qualities of candy in a mixed heap of the article.

All at once the town was thrown into a state of extraordinary excitement. In mining parlance the Wide West had "struck it rich!" Everybody went to see the new developments, and for some days there was such a crowd of people about the Wide West shaft that a stranger would have supposed there was a mass-meeting in session there. No other topic was discussed but the rich strike, and nobody thought or dreamed about any thing else. Every man brought away a specimen, ground it up in a hand mortar, washed it out in his horn spoon, and glared speechless upon the marvelous result. It was not hard rock, but black, decomposed stuff which could be crumbled in the hand like a baked potato, and when spread out on a paper exhibited a thick sprinkling of gold and particles of "native" silver. Higbie brought a handful to the cabin, and when he had washed it out his amazement was beyond description. Wide West stock soared skywards. It was said that repeated offers had been made for it at a thousand dollars a foot, and promptly refused. We have all had the "blues" – the mere sky-blues – but mine were indigo, now – because I did not own in the Wide West. The world seemed hollow to me, and existence a grief. I lost my appetite, and ceased to take an interest in anything. Still I had to stay, and listen to other people's rejoicings, because I had no money to get out of the camp with.

The Wide West company put a stop to the carrying away of "specimens," and well they might, for every handful of the ore was worth a sum of some consequence. To show the exceeding value of the ore, I will remark that a sixteen-hundred-pounds parcel of it was sold, just as it lay, at the mouth of the shaft, at *one dollar a pound;* and the man who bought it "packed" it on mules a hundred and fifty or two hundred miles, over the mountains, to San Francisco, satisfied that it would yield at a rate that would richly compensate him for his trouble. The Wide West people also commanded their foreman to refuse any but their own operatives permission to enter the mine at any time or for any purpose. I kept up my "blue" meditations and Higbie kept up a deal of thinking, too, but of a different sort. He puzzled over the "rock," examined it with a glass, inspected it in different lights and from different points of view, and after each experiment delivered himself, in soliloquy, of one and the same unvarying opinion in the same unvarying formula:

"It is *not* Wide West rock!"

He said once or twice that he meant to have a look into the Wide West shaft if he got shot for it. I was wretched, and did not care whether he got a look into it or not. He failed that day, and tried again at night; failed again; got up at dawn and tried, and failed again. Then he lay in ambush in the sage-brush hour after hour, waiting for the two or three hands to adjourn to the shade of a boulder for dinner; made a start once, but was premature – one of the men came back for some thing; tried it again, but when almost at the mouth of the shaft, another of the men rose up from behind the boulder as if to reconnoitre, and he dropped on the ground and lay quiet; presently he crawled on his hands and knees to the mouth of the shaft, gave a quick glance around, then seized the rope and slid down the shaft. He disappeared in the gloom of a "side drift" just as a head appeared in the mouth of the shaft and somebody shouted "Hello!" – which he did not answer. He was not disturbed any more. An hour later he entered the cabin, hot, red, and ready to burst with smothered excitement, and exclaimed in a stage whisper:

"I knew it! We are rich! IT'S A BLIND LEAD!"

I thought the very earth reeled under me. Doubt – conviction – doubt again – exultation – hope, amazement, belief, unbelief – every emotion imaginable swept in wild procession through my heart and brain, and I could not speak a word. After a moment or two of this mental fury, I shook myself to rights, and said:

"Say it again!"

"It's a blind lead!"

"Cal., let's – let's burn the house – or kill some body! Let's get out where there's room to hurrah! But what is the use? It is a hundred times too good to be true."

"It's a blind lead, for a million! – hanging wall – foot wall – clay casings – everything complete!" He swung his hat and gave three cheers, and I cast doubt to the winds and chimed in with a will. For I was worth a million dollars, and did not care "whether school kept or not!"

But perhaps I ought to explain. A "blind lead" is a lead or ledge that does not "crop out" above the surface. A miner does not know where to look for such leads, but they are often stumbled upon by accident in the course of driving a tunnel or sinking a shaft. Higbie knew the Wide West rock perfectly well, and the more he had examined the new developments the more he was satisfied that the ore could not have come from the Wide West vein. And so had it occurred to him alone, of all the camp, that there was a blind lead down in the shaft, and that even the Wide West people themselves did not suspect it. He was right. When he went down the shaft, he found that the blind lead held its independent way through the Wide West vein, cutting it diagonally, and that it was enclosed in its own well-defined casing-rocks and clay. Hence it was public property. Both leads being perfectly well defined, it was easy for any miner to see which one belonged to the Wide West and which did not.

We thought it well to have a strong friend, and therefore we brought the foreman of the Wide West to our cabin that night and revealed the great surprise to him. Higbie said:

"We are going to take possession of this blind lead, record it and establish ownership, and then forbid the Wide West company to take out any more of the rock. You cannot help your company in this matter – nobody can help them. I will go into the shaft with you and prove to your entire satisfaction that it *is* a blind lead. Now we propose to take you in with us, and claim the blind lead in our three names. What do you say?"

What could a man say who had an opportunity to simply stretch forth his hand and take possession of a fortune without risk of any kind and without wronging any one or attaching the least taint of dishonor to his name? He could only say, "Agreed."

The notice was put up that night, and duly spread upon the recorder's books before ten o'clock. We claimed two hundred feet each – six hundred feet in all – the smallest and compactest organization in the district, and the easiest to manage.

No one can be so thoughtless as to suppose that we slept, that night. Higbie and I went to bed at midnight, but it was only to lie broad awake and think, dream, scheme. The floorless, tumble-down cabin was a palace, the ragged gray blankets silk, the furniture rosewood and mahogany. Each new splendor that burst out of my visions of the future whirled me bodily over in bed or jerked me to a sitting posture just as if an electric battery had been applied to me. We shot fragments of conversation back and forth at each other. Once Higbie said:

"When are you going home – to the States?"

"To-morrow!" – with an evolution or two, ending with a sitting position. "Well – no – but next month, at furthest."

"We'll go in the same steamer."

"Agreed."

A pause.

"Steamer of the 10th?"

"Yes. No, the 1st."

"All right."

Another pause.

"Where are you going to live?" said Higbie.

"San Francisco."

"That's me!"

Pause.

"Too high – too much climbing" – from Higbie.

"What is?"

"I was thinking of Russian Hill – building a house up there."

"Too much climbing? Shan't you keep a carriage?"

"Of course. I forgot that."

Pause.

"Cal., what kind of a house are you going to build?"

"I was thinking about that. Three-story and an attic."

"But what *kind?*"

"Well, I don't hardly know. Brick, I suppose."

"Brick – bosh."

"Why? What is your idea?"

"Brown stone front – French plate glass – billiard-room off the dining-room – statuary and paintings – shrubbery and two-acre grass plat – greenhouse – iron dog on the front stoop – gray horses – landau, and a coachman with a bug on his hat!"

"By George!"

A long pause.

"Cal., when are you going to Europe?"

"Well – I hadn't thought of that. When are you?"

"In the spring."

"Going to be gone all summer?"

"All summer! I shall remain there three years."

"No – but are you in earnest?"

"Indeed I am."

"I will go along too."

"Why of course you will."

"What part of Europe shall you go to?"

"All parts, France, England, Germany – Spain, Italy, Switzerland, Syria, Greece, Palestine, Arabia, Persia, Egypt – all over – everywhere."

"I'm agreed."

"All right."

"Won't it be a swell trip!"

"We'll spend forty or fifty thousand dollars trying to make it one, any way."

Another long pause.

"Higbie, we owe the butcher six dollars, and he has been threatening to stop our—"

"Hang the butcher!"

"Amen."

And so it went on. By three o'clock we found it was no use, and so we got up and played cribbage and smoked pipes till sunrise. It was my week to cook. I always hated cooking – now, I abhorred it.

The news was all over town. The former excitement was great – this one was greater still. I walked the streets serene and happy. Higbie said the foreman had been offered two hundred thousand dollars for his third of the mine. I said I would like to see myself selling for any such price. My ideas were lofty. My figure was a million. Still, I honestly believe that if I had been offered it, it would have had no other effect than to make me hold off for more.

I found abundant enjoyment in being rich. A man offered me a three-hundred-dollar horse, and wanted to take my simple, unendorsed note for it. That brought the most realizing sense I had yet had that I was actually rich, beyond shadow of doubt. It was followed by numerous other evidences of a similar nature – among which I may mention the fact of the butcher leaving us a double supply of meat and saying nothing about money.

By the laws of the district, the "locators" or claimants of a ledge were obliged to do a fair and reasonable amount of work on their new property within ten days after the date of the location, or the property was forfeited, and anybody could go and seize it that chose. So we determined to go to work the next day. About the middle of the afternoon, as I was coming out of the post-office, I met a Mr. Gardiner, who told me that Capt. John Nye was lying dangerously ill at his place (the "Nine-Mile Ranch"), and that he and his wife were not able to give him nearly as much care and attention as his case demanded. I said if he would wait for me a moment, I would go down and help in the sick room. I ran to the cabin to tell Higbie. He was not there, but I left a note on the table for him, and a few minutes later I left town in Gardiner's wagon.

CHAPTER XLI

CAPTAIN NYE WAS very ill indeed, with spasmodic rheumatism. But the old gentleman was himself – which is to say, he was kind-hearted and agreeable when comfortable, but a singularly violent wild-cat when things did not go well. He would be smiling along pleasantly enough, when a sudden spasm of his disease would take him and he would go out of his smile into a perfect fury. He would groan and wail and howl with the anguish, and fill up the odd chinks with the most elaborate profanity that strong convictions and a fine fancy could contrive. With fair opportunity he could swear very well and handle his adjectives with considerable judgment; but when the spasm was on him it was painful to listen to him, he was so awkward. However, I had seen him nurse a sick man himself and put up patiently with the inconveniences of the situation, and consequently I was willing that he should have full license now that his own turn had come. He could not disturb me, with all his raving and ranting, for my mind had work on hand, and it labored on diligently, night and day, whether my hands were idle or employed. I was altering and amending the plans for my house, and thinking over the propriety of having the billiard-room in the attic, instead of on the same floor with the dining-room; also, I was trying to decide between green and blue for the upholstery of the drawing-room, for, although my preference was blue I feared it was a color that would be too easily damaged by dust and sunlight; likewise while I was content to put the coachman in a modest livery, I was uncertain about a footman – I needed one, and was even resolved to have one, but wished he could properly appear and perform his functions out of livery, for I somewhat dreaded so much show; and yet, inasmuch as my late grandfather had had a coachman and such things, but no liveries, I felt rather drawn to beat him; – or beat his ghost, at any rate; I was also systematizing the European trip, and managed to get it all laid out, as to route and length of time to be devoted to it – everything, with one exception – namely, whether to cross the desert from Cairo to Jerusalem per camel, or go by sea to Beirout, and thence down through the country per caravan. Meantime I was writing to the friends at home every day, instructing them concerning all my plans and intentions, and directing them to look up a handsome homestead for my mother and agree upon a price for it against my coming, and also directing them to sell my share of the Tennessee land and tender the proceeds to the widows' and orphans' fund of the typographical union of which I had long been a member in good standing. [This Tennessee land had been in the possession of the family many years, and promised to confer high fortune upon us some day; it still promises it, but in a less violent way.]

When I had been nursing the Captain nine days he was somewhat better, but very feeble. During the afternoon we lifted him into a chair and gave him an alcoholic vapor bath, and then set about putting him on the bed again. We had to be exceedingly careful, for the least jar produced pain. Gardiner had his shoulders and I his legs; in an unfortunate moment I stumbled and the patient fell heavily on the bed in an agony of torture. I never heard a man swear so in my life. He raved like a maniac, and tried to snatch a revolver from the table – but I got it. He ordered me out of the house, and swore a world of oaths that he would kill me wherever he caught me when he got on his feet again. It was simply a passing fury, and meant nothing. I knew he would forget it in an hour, and may be be sorry for it, too; but it angered me a little, at the moment. So much so, indeed, that I determined to go back to Esmeralda. I thought he was able to get along alone, now, since he was on the war path. I took supper, and as soon as the moon rose, began my nine-mile journey, on foot. Even millionaires needed no horses, in those days, for a mere nine-mile jaunt without baggage.

As I "raised the hill" overlooking the town, it lacked fifteen minutes of twelve. I glanced at the hill over beyond the canon, and in the bright moonlight saw what appeared to be about half the population of the village massed on and around the Wide West croppings. My heart gave an exulting bound, and I said to myself, "They have made a new strike to-night – and struck it richer than ever, no doubt." I started over there, but gave it up. I said the "strike" would keep, and I had climbed hills enough for one night. I went on down through the town, and as I was passing a little German bakery, a woman ran out and begged me to come in and help her. She said her husband had a fit. I went in, and judged she was right – he appeared to have a hundred of them, compressed into one. Two Germans were there, trying to hold him, and not making much of a success of it. I ran up the street half a block or so and routed out a sleeping doctor, brought him down half dressed, and we four wrestled with the maniac, and doctored, drenched and bled him, for more than an hour, and the poor German woman did the crying. He grew quiet, now, and the doctor and I withdrew and left him to his friends.

It was a little after one o'clock. As I entered the cabin door, tired but jolly, the dingy light of a tallow candle revealed Higbie, sitting by the pine table gazing stupidly at my note, which he held in his fingers, and looking pale, old, and haggard. I halted, and looked at him. He looked at me, stolidly. I said:

"Higbie, what – what is it?"

"We're ruined – we didn't do the work – THE BLIND LEAD'S RELOCATED!"

It was enough. I sat down sick, grieved – broken-hearted, indeed. A minute before, I was rich and brimful of vanity; I was a pauper now, and very meek. We sat still an hour, busy with thought, busy with vain and useless self-upbraidings, busy with "Why *didn't* I do this, and why *didn't* I do that," but neither spoke a word. Then we dropped into mutual explanations, and the mystery was cleared away. It came out that Higbie had depended on me, as I had on him, and as both of us had on the foreman. The folly of it! It was the first time that ever staid and steadfast Higbie had left an important matter to chance or failed to be true to his full share of a responsibility.

But he had never seen my note till this moment, and this moment was the first time he had been in the cabin since the day he had seen me last. He, also, had left a note for me, on that same fatal afternoon – had ridden up on horse-back, and looked through the window, and being in a hurry and not seeing me, had tossed the note into the cabin through a broken pane. Here it was, on the floor, where it had remained undisturbed for nine days:

> "Don't fail to do the work before the ten days expire. W. has passed through and given me notice. I am to join him at Mono Lake, and we shall go on from there to-night. He says he will find it this time, sure. CAL."

"W." meant Whiteman, of course. That thrice accursed "cement!"

That was the way of it. An old miner, like Higbie, could no more withstand the fascination of a mysterious mining excitement like this "cement" foolishness, than he could refrain from eating when he was famishing. Higbie had been dreaming about the marvelous cement for months; and now, against his better judgment, he had gone off and "taken the chances" on my keeping secure a mine worth a million undiscovered cement veins. They had not been followed this time. His riding out of town in broad daylight was such a commonplace thing to do that it had not attracted any attention. He said they prosecuted their search in the fastnesses of the mountains during nine days, without success; they could not find the cement. Then a ghastly fear came over him that something might have happened to prevent the doing of the necessary work to hold the blind lead (though indeed he thought such a thing hardly possible), and forthwith he started home with all speed. He would have reached Esmeralda in time, but his horse broke down and he had to walk a great part of the distance. And so it happened that as he came into Esmeralda by one road, I entered it by another. His was the superior energy, however, for he went straight to the Wide West, instead of turning aside as I had done – and he arrived there about five or ten minutes too late! The "notice" was already up, the "relocation" of our mine completed beyond recall, and the crowd rapidly dispersing. He learned some facts before he left the ground. The foreman had not been seen about the streets since the night we had located the mine – a telegram had called him to California on a matter of life and death, it was said. At any rate he had done no work and the watchful eyes of the community were taking note of the fact. At midnight of this woful tenth day, the ledge would be "relocatable," and by eleven o'clock the hill was black with men prepared to do the relocating. That was the crowd I had seen when I fancied a new "strike" had been made – idiot that I was. [We three had the same right to relocate the lead that other people had, provided we were quick enough.] As midnight was announced, fourteen men, duly armed and ready to back their proceedings, put up their "notice" and proclaimed their ownership of the blind lead, under the new name of the "Johnson." But A. D. Allen our partner (the foreman) put in a sudden appearance about that time, with a cocked revolver in his hand, and said his name must be added to the list, or he would "thin out the Johnson company some." He was a manly, splendid, determined fellow, and known to be as good as his word, and therefore a compromise was effected. They put in his name for a hundred feet, reserving to themselves the customary two hundred feet each. Such was the history of the night's events, as Higbie gathered from a friend on the way home.

Higbie and I cleared out on a new mining excitement the next morning, glad to get away from the scene of our sufferings, and after a month or two of hardship and disappointment, returned to Esmeralda once more. Then we learned that the Wide West and the Johnson companies had consolidated; that the stock, thus united, comprised five thousand feet, or shares; that the foreman, apprehending tiresome litigation, and considering such a huge concern unwieldly, had sold his hundred feet for ninety thousand dollars in gold and gone home to the States to enjoy it. If the stock was worth such a gallant figure, with five thousand shares in the corporation, it makes me dizzy to think what it would have been worth with only our original six hundred in it. It was the difference between six hundred men owning a house and five thousand owning it. We would have been millionaires if we had only worked with pick and spade one little day on our property and so secured our ownership!

It reads like a wild fancy sketch, but the evidence of many witnesses, and likewise that of the official records of Esmeralda District, is easily obtainable in proof that it is a true history. I can always have it to say that I was absolutely and unquestionably worth a million dollars, once, for ten days.

A year ago my esteemed and in every way estimable old millionaire partner, Higbie, wrote me from an obscure little mining camp in California that after nine or ten years of bufferings and hard striving, he was at last in a position where he could command twenty-five hundred dollars, and said he meant to go into the fruit business in a modest way. How such a thought would have insulted him the night we lay in our cabin planning European trips and brown stone houses on Russian Hill!

CHAPTER XLII

WHAT TO DO next?

It was a momentous question. I had gone out into the world to shift for myself, at the age of thirteen (for my father had endorsed for friends; and although he left us a sumptuous legacy of pride in his fine Virginian stock and its national distinction, I presently found that I could not live on that alone without occasional bread to wash it down with). I had gained a livelihood in various vocations, but had not dazzled anybody with my successes; still the list was before me, and the amplest liberty in the matter of choosing, provided I wanted to work – which I did not, after being so wealthy. I had once been a grocery clerk, for one day, but had consumed so much sugar in that time that I was relieved from further duty by the proprietor; said he wanted me outside, so that he could have my custom. I had studied law an entire week, and then given it up because it was so prosy and tiresome. I had engaged briefly in the study of blacksmithing, but wasted so much time trying to fix the bellows so that it would blow itself, that the master turned me adrift in disgrace, and told me I would come to no good. I had been a bookseller's clerk for awhile, but the customers bothered me so much I could not read with any comfort, and so the proprietor gave me a furlough and forgot to put a limit to it. I had clerked in a drug store part of a summer, but my prescriptions were unlucky, and we appeared to sell more stomach pumps than soda water. So I had to go. I had made of myself a tolerable printer, under the impression that I would be another Franklin some day, but somehow had missed the connection thus far. There was no berth open in the Esmeralda *Union*, and besides I had always been such a slow compositor that I looked with envy upon the achievements of apprentices of two years' standing; and when I took a "take," foremen were in the habit of suggesting that it would be wanted "some time during the year." I was a good average St. Louis and New Orleans pilot and by no means ashamed of my abilities in that line; wages were two hundred and fifty dollars a month and no board to pay, and I did long to stand behind a wheel again and never roam any more – but I had been making such an ass of myself lately in grandiloquent letters home about my blind lead and my European excursion that I did what many and many a poor disappointed miner had done before; said "It is all over with me now, and I will never go back home to be pitied – and snubbed." I had been a private secretary, a silver miner and a silver-mill operative, and amounted to less than nothing in each, and now –

What to do next?

I yielded to Higbie's appeals and consented to try the mining once more. We climbed far up on the mountain side and went to work on a little rubbishy claim of ours that had a shaft on it eight feet deep. Higbie descended into it and worked bravely with his pick till he had loosened up a deal of rock and dirt and then I went down with a long-handled shovel (the most awkward invention yet contrived by man) to throw it out. You must brace the shovel forward with the side of your knee till it is full, and then, with a skillful toss, throw it backward over your shoulder. I made the toss and landed the mess just on the edge of the shaft and it all came back on my head and down the back of my neck. I never said a word, but climbed out and walked home. I inwardly resolved that I would starve before I would make a target of myself and shoot rubbish at it with a long-handled shovel. I sat down, in the cabin, and gave myself up to solid misery – so to speak. Now in pleasanter days I had amused myself with writing letters to the chief paper of the

Territory, the Virginia *Daily Territorial Enterprise*, and had always been surprised when they appeared in print. My good opinion of the editors had steadily declined; for it seemed to me that they might have found something better to fill up with than my literature. I had found a letter in the post-office as I came home from the hill-side, and finally I opened it. Eureka! [I never did know what Eureka meant, but it seems to be as proper a word to heave in as any when no other that sounds pretty offers.] It was a deliberate offer to me of Twenty-Five Dollars a week to come up to Virginia and be city editor of the *Enterprise*.

I would have challenged the publisher in the "blind lead" days – I wanted to fall down and worship him, now. Twenty-Five Dollars a week – it looked like bloated luxury – a fortune – a sinful and lavish waste of money. But my transports cooled when I thought of my inexperience and consequent unfitness for the position – and straightway, on top of this, my long array of failures rose up before me. Yet if I refused this place I must presently become dependent upon somebody for my bread, a thing necessarily distasteful to a man who had never experienced such a humiliation since he was thirteen years old. Not much to be proud of, since it is so common – but then it was all I had to *be* proud of. So I was scared into being a city editor. I would have declined, otherwise. Necessity is the mother of "taking chances." I do not doubt that if, at that time, I had been offered a salary to translate the Talmud from the original Hebrew, I would have accepted – albeit with diffidence and some misgivings – and thrown as much variety into it as I could for the money.

I went up to Virginia and entered upon my new vocation. I was a rusty-looking city editor, I am free to confess – coatless, slouch hat, blue woolen shirt, pantaloons stuffed into boot-tops, whiskered half down to the waist, and the universal navy revolver slung to my belt. But I secured a more Christian costume and discarded the revolver. I had never had occasion to kill anybody, nor ever felt a desire to do so, but had worn the thing in deference to popular sentiment, and in order that I might not, by its absence, be offensively conspicuous, and a subject of remark. But the other editors, and all the printers, carried revolvers. I asked the chief editor and proprietor (Mr. Goodman, I will call him, since it describes him as well as any name could do) for some instructions with regard to my duties, and he told me to go all over town and ask all sorts of people all sorts of questions, make notes of the information gained, and write them out for publication. And he added:

"Never say, 'We learn' so-and-so, or 'It is reported,' or 'It is rumored,' or 'We understand' so-and-so, but go to headquarters and get the absolute facts, and then speak out and say 'It *is* so-and-so.' Otherwise, people will not put confidence in your news. Unassailable certainty is the thing that gives a newspaper the firmest and most valuable reputation."

It was the whole thing in a nut-shell; and to this day when I find a reporter commencing his article with "We understand," I gather a suspicion that he has not taken as much pains to inform himself as he ought to have done. I moralize well, but I did not always practice well when I was a city editor; I let fancy get the upper hand of fact too often when there was a dearth of news. I can never forget my first day's experience as a reporter. I wandered about town questioning every body, boring every body, and finding out that nobody knew any thing. At the end of five hours my notebook was still barren. I spoke to Mr. Goodman. He said:

"Dan used to make a good thing out of the hay-wagons in a dry time when there were no fires or inquests. Are there no hay-wagons in from the Truckee? If there are, you might speak of the renewed activity and all that sort of thing, in the hay business, you know. It isn't sensational or exciting, but it fills up and looks business-like."

I canvassed the city again and found one wretched old hay truck dragging in from the country. But I made affluent use of it. I multiplied it by sixteen, brought it into town from sixteen different directions, made sixteen separate items out of it, and got up such another sweat about hay as Virginia City had never seen in the world before.

This was encouraging. Two nonpareil columns had to be filled, and I was getting along. Presently, when things began to look dismal again, a desperado killed a man in a saloon and joy returned once more. I never was so glad over any mere trifle before in my life. I said to the murderer:

"Sir, you are a stranger to me, but you have done me a kindness this day which I can never forget. If whole years of gratitude can be to you any slight compensation, they shall be yours. I was in trouble and you have relieved me nobly and at a time when all seemed dark and drear. Count me your friend from this time forth, for I am not a man to forget a favor."

If I did not really say that to him I at least felt a sort of itching desire to do it. I wrote up the murder with a hungry attention to details, and when it was finished experienced but one regret – namely, that they had not hanged my benefactor on the spot, so that I could work him up too.

Next I discovered some emigrant wagons going into camp on the plaza and found that they had lately come through the hostile Indian country and had fared rather roughly. I made the best of the item that the circumstances permitted, and felt that if I were not confined within rigid limits by the presence of the reporters of the other papers I could add particulars that would make the article much more interesting. However, I found one wagon that was going on to California, and made some judicious inquiries of the proprietor. When I learned, through his short and surly answers to my cross-questioning, that he was certainly going on and would not be in the city next day to make trouble, I got ahead of the other papers, for I took down his list of names and added his party to the killed and wounded. Having more scope here, I put this wagon through an Indian fight that to this day has no parallel in history.

My two columns were filled. When I read them over in the morning I felt that I had found my legitimate occupation at last. I reasoned within myself that news, and stirring news, too, was what a paper needed, and I felt that I was peculiarly endowed with the ability to furnish it. Mr. Goodman said that I was as good a reporter as Dan. I desired no higher commendation. With encouragement like that, I felt that I could take my pen and murder all the immigrants on the plains if need be and the interests of the paper demanded it.

CHAPTER XLIII

HOWEVER, AS I grew better acquainted with the business and learned the run of the sources of information I ceased to require the aid of fancy to any large extent, and I became able to fill my columns without diverging noticeably from the domain of fact.

I struck up friendships with the reporters of the other journals, and we swapped "regulars" with each other and thus economized work. "Regulars" are permanent sources of news, like courts, bullion returns, "clean-ups" at the quartz mills, and inquests. Inasmuch as everybody went armed, we had an inquest about every day, and so this department was naturally set down among the "regulars." We had lively papers in those days. My great competitor among the reporters was Boggs of the *Union*. He was an excellent reporter. Once in three or four months he would get a little intoxicated, but as a general thing he was a wary and cautious drinker although always ready to tamper a little with the enemy. He had the advantage of me in one thing; he could get the monthly public school report and I could not, because the principal hated the *Enterprise*. One snowy night when the report was due, I started out sadly wondering how I was going to get it. Presently a few steps up the almost deserted street I stumbled on Boggs and asked him where he was going.

"After the school report."

"I'll go along with you."

"No, *sir*. I'll excuse you."

"Just as you say."

A saloon-keeper's boy passed by with a steaming pitcher of hot punch, and Boggs snuffed the fragrance gratefully. He gazed fondly after the boy and saw him start up the *Enterprise* stairs. I said:

"I wish you could help me get that school business, but since you can't, I must run up to the *Union* office and see if I can get them to let me have a proof of it after they have set it up, though I don't begin to suppose they will. Good night."

"Hold on a minute. I don't mind getting the report and sitting around with the boys a little, while you copy it, if you're willing to drop down to the principal's with me."

"Now you talk like a rational being. Come along."

We plowed a couple of blocks through the snow, got the report and returned to our office. It was a short document and soon copied. Meantime Boggs helped himself to the punch. I gave the manuscript back to him and we started out to get an inquest, for we heard pistol shots near by. We got the particulars with little loss of time, for it was only an inferior sort of barroom murder, and of little interest to the public, and then we separated. Away at three o'clock in the morning, when we had gone to press and were having a relaxing concert as usual – for some of the printers were good singers and others good performers on the guitar and on that atrocity the accordeon – the proprietor of the *Union* strode in and desired to know if anybody had heard anything of Boggs or the school report. We stated the case, and all turned out to help hunt for the delinquent. We found him standing on a table in a saloon, with an old tin lantern in one hand and the school report in the other, haranguing a gang of intoxicated Cornish miners on the iniquity of squandering the public moneys on education "when hundreds and hundreds of honest hard-working men are literally starving for whiskey." [Riotous applause.] He had been assisting in a regal spree with those parties for hours. We dragged him away and put him to bed.

Of course there was no school report in the *Union*, and Boggs held me accountable, though I was innocent of any intention or desire to compass its absence from that paper and was as sorry as any one that the misfortune had occurred.

But we were perfectly friendly. The day that the school report was next due, the proprietor of the "Genessee" mine furnished us a buggy and asked us to go down and write something about the property – a very common request and one always gladly acceded to when people furnished buggies, for we were as fond of pleasure excursions as other people. In due time we arrived at the "mine" – nothing but a hole in the ground ninety feet deep, and no way of getting down into it but by holding on to a rope and being lowered with a windlass. The workmen had just gone off somewhere to dinner. I was not strong enough to lower Boggs's bulk; so I took an unlighted candle in my teeth, made a loop for my foot in the end of the rope, implored Boggs not to go to sleep or let the windlass get the start of him, and then swung out over the shaft. I reached the bottom muddy and bruised about the elbows, but safe. I lit the candle, made an examination of the rock, selected some specimens and shouted to Boggs to hoist away. No answer. Presently a head appeared in the circle of daylight away aloft, and a voice came down:

"Are you all set?"

"All set – hoist away."

"Are you comfortable?"

"Perfectly."

"Could you wait a little?"

"Oh certainly – no particular hurry."

"Well – good-bye."

"Why? Where are you going?"

"After the school report!"

And he did. I staid down there an hour, and surprised the workmen when they hauled up and found a man on the rope instead of a bucket of rock. I walked home, too – five miles – up hill. We had no school report next morning; but the *Union* had.

Six months after my entry into journalism the grand "flush times" of Silverland began, and they continued with unabated splendor for three years. All difficulty about filling up the "local department" ceased, and the only trouble now was how to make the lengthened columns hold the world of incidents and happenings that came to our literary net every day. Virginia had grown to be the "livest" town, for its age and population, that America had ever produced. The sidewalks swarmed with people – to such an extent, indeed, that it was generally no easy matter to stem the human tide. The streets themselves were just as crowded with quartz wagons, freight teams and other vehicles. The procession was endless. So great was the pack, that buggies frequently had to wait half an hour for an opportunity to cross the principal street. Joy sat on every countenance, and there was a glad, almost fierce, intensity in every eye, that told of the money-getting schemes that were seething in every brain and the high hope that held sway in every heart. Money was as plenty as dust; every individual considered himself wealthy, and a melancholy countenance was nowhere to be seen. There were military companies, fire companies, brass bands, banks, hotels, theatres, "hurdy-gurdy houses," wide-open gambling palaces, political pow-wows, civic processions, street fights, murders, inquests, riots, a whiskey mill every fifteen steps, a Board of Aldermen, a Mayor, a City Surveyor, a City Engineer, a Chief of the Fire Department, with First, Second and Third Assistants, a Chief of Police, City Marshal and a large police force, two Boards of Mining Brokers, a dozen breweries and half a dozen jails and station-houses in full operation, and some talk of building a church. The "flush times" were in magnificent flower! Large fireproof brick buildings were going up in the principal streets, and the wooden suburbs were spreading out in all directions. Town lots soared up to prices that were amazing.

The great "Comstock lode" stretched its opulent length straight through the town from north to south, and every mine on it was in diligent process of development. One of these mines alone employed six hundred and seventy-five men, and in the matter of elections the adage was, "as the 'Gould and Curry' goes, so goes the city." Laboring men's wages were four and six dollars a day, and they worked in three "shifts" or gangs, and the blasting and picking and shoveling went on without ceasing, night and day.

The "city" of Virginia roosted royally midway up the steep side of Mount Davidson, seven thousand two hundred feet above the level of the sea, and in the clear Nevada atmosphere was visible from a distance of fifty miles! It claimed a population of fifteen thousand to eighteen thousand, and all day long half of this little army swarmed the streets like bees and the other half swarmed among the drifts and tunnels of the "Comstock," hundreds of feet down in the earth directly under those same streets. Often we felt our chairs jar, and heard the faint boom of a blast down in the bowels of the earth under the office.

The mountain side was so steep that the entire town had a slant to it like a roof. Each street was a terrace, and from each to the next street below the descent was forty or fifty feet. The fronts of the houses were level with the street they faced, but their rear first floors were propped on lofty stilts; a man could stand at a rear first-floor window of a C street house and look down the chimneys of the row of houses below him facing D street. It was a laborious climb, in that thin atmosphere, to ascend from D to A street, and you were panting and out of breath when you got there; but you could turn around and go down again like a house a-fire – so to speak. The atmosphere was so rarefied, on account of the great altitude, that one's blood lay near the surface always, and the scratch of a pin was a disaster worth worrying about, for the chances were that a grievous erysipelas would ensue. But to offset this, the thin atmosphere seemed to carry healing to gunshot wounds, and therefore, to simply shoot your adversary through both lungs was a thing not likely to afford you any permanent satisfaction, for he would be nearly certain to be around looking for you within the month, and not with an opera glass, either.

From Virginia's airy situation one could look over a vast, far-reaching panorama of mountain ranges and deserts; and whether the day was bright or overcast, whether the sun was rising or setting, or flaming in the zenith, or whether night and the moon held sway, the spectacle was always impressive and beautiful. Over your head Mount Davidson lifted its gray dome, and before and below you a rugged canon clove the battlemented hills, making a sombre gateway through which a soft-tinted desert was glimpsed, with the silver thread of a river winding through it, bordered with trees which many miles of distance diminished to a delicate fringe; and still further away the snowy mountains rose up and stretched their long barrier to the filmy horizon – far enough beyond a lake that burned in the desert like a fallen sun, though that, itself, lay fifty miles removed. Look from your window where you would, there was fascination in the picture. At rare intervals – but very rare – there were clouds in our skies, and then the setting sun would gild and flush and glorify this mighty expanse of scenery with a bewildering pomp of color that held the eye like a spell and moved the spirit like music.

CHAPTER XLVI

THERE WERE NABOBS in those days – in the "flush times," I mean. Every rich strike in the mines created one or two. I call to mind several of these. They were careless, easy-going fellows, as a general thing, and the community at large was as much benefited by their riches as they were themselves – possibly more, in some cases.

Two cousins, teamsters, did some hauling for a man and had to take a small segregated portion of a silver mine in lieu of $300 cash. They gave an outsider a third to open the mine, and they went on teaming. But not long. Ten months afterward the mine was out of debt and paying each owner $8,000 to $10,000 a month – say $100,000 a year.

One of the earliest nabobs that Nevada was delivered of wore $6,000 worth of diamonds in his bosom, and swore he was unhappy because he could not spend his money as fast as he made it.

Another Nevada nabob boasted an income that often reached $16,000 a month; and he used to love to tell how he had worked in the very mine that yielded it, for five dollars a day, when he first came to the country.

The silver and sage-brush State has knowledge of another of these pets of fortune – lifted from actual poverty to affluence almost in a single night – who was able to offer $100,000 for a position of high official distinction, shortly afterward, and did offer it – but failed to get it, his politics not being as sound as his bank account.

Then there was John Smith. He was a good, honest, kind-hearted soul, born and reared in the lower ranks of life, and miraculously ignorant. He drove a team, and owned a small ranch – a ranch that paid him a comfortable living, for although it yielded but little hay, what little it did yield was worth from $250 to $300 in gold per ton in the market. Presently Smith traded a few acres of the ranch for a small undeveloped silver mine in Gold Hill. He opened the mine and built a little unpretending ten-stamp mill. Eighteen months afterward he retired from the hay business, for his mining income had reached a most comfortable figure. Some people said it was $30,000 a month, and others said it was $60,000. Smith was very rich at any rate.

And then he went to Europe and traveled. And when he came back he was never tired of telling about the fine hogs he had seen in England, and the gorgeous sheep he had seen in Spain, and the fine cattle he had noticed in the vicinity of Rome. He was full of the wonders of the old world, and advised everybody to travel. He said a man never imagined what surprising things there were in the world till he had traveled.

One day, on board ship, the passengers made up a pool of $500, which was to be the property of the man who should come nearest to guessing the run of the vessel for the next twenty-four hours. Next day, toward noon, the figures were all in the purser's hands in sealed envelopes. Smith was serene and happy, for he had been bribing the engineer. But another party won the prize! Smith said:

"Here, that won't do! He guessed two miles wider of the mark than I did."

The pursuer said, "Mr. Smith, you missed it further than any man on board. We traveled two hundred and eight miles yesterday."

"Well, sir," said Smith, "that's just where I've got you, for I guessed two hundred and nine. If you'll look at my figgers again you'll find a 2 and two 00's, which stands for 200, don't it? – and after 'em you find a 9 (2009), which stands for two hundred and nine. I reckon I'll take that money, if you please."

The Gould & Curry claim comprised twelve hundred feet, and it all belonged originally to the two men whose names it bears. Mr. Curry owned two-thirds of it – and he said that he sold it out for twenty-five hundred dollars in cash, and an old plug horse that ate up his market value in hay and barley in seventeen days by the watch. And he said that Gould sold out for a pair of second-hand government blankets and a bottle of whiskey that killed nine men in three hours, and that an unoffending stranger that smelt the cork was disabled for life. Four years afterward the mine thus disposed of was worth in the San Francisco market seven millions six hundred thousand dollars in gold coin.

In the early days a poverty-stricken Mexican who lived in a canon directly back of Virginia City, had a stream of water as large as a man's wrist trickling from the hill-side on his premises. The Ophir Company segregated a hundred feet of their mine and traded it to him for the stream of water. The hundred feet proved to be the richest part of the entire mine; four years after the swap, its market value (including its mill) was $1,500,000.

An individual who owned twenty feet in the Ophir mine before its great riches were revealed to men, traded it for a horse, and a very sorry-looking brute he was, too. A year or so afterward, when Ophir stock went up to $3,000 a foot, this man, who had not a cent, used to say he was the most startling example of magnificence and misery the world had ever seen – because he was able to ride a sixty-thousand-dollar horse – yet could not scrape up cash enough to buy a saddle, and was obliged to borrow one or ride bareback. He said if fortune were to give him another sixty-thousand-dollar horse it would ruin him.

A youth of nineteen, who was a telegraph operator in Virginia on a salary of a hundred dollars a month, and who, when he could not make out German names in the list of San Francisco steamer arrivals, used to ingeniously select and supply substitutes for them out of an old Berlin city directory, made himself rich by watching the mining telegrams that passed through his hands and buying and selling stocks accordingly, through a friend in San Francisco. Once when a private dispatch was sent from Virginia announcing a rich strike in a prominent mine and advising that the matter be kept secret till a large amount of the stock could be secured, he bought forty "feet" of the stock at twenty dollars a foot, and afterward sold half of it at eight hundred dollars a foot and the rest at double that figure. Within three months he was worth $150,000, and had resigned his telegraphic position.

Another telegraph operator who had been discharged by the company for divulging the secrets of the office, agreed with a moneyed man in San Francisco to furnish him the result of a great Virginia mining lawsuit within an hour after its private reception by the parties to it in San Francisco. For this he was to have a large per centage of the profits on purchase and sales made on it by his fellow-conspirator. So he went, disguised as a teamster, to a little wayside telegraph office in the mountains, got acquainted with the operator, and sat in the office day after day, smoking his pipe, complaining that his team was fagged out and unable to travel – and meantime listening to the dispatches as they passed clicking through the machine from Virginia. Finally the private dispatch announcing the result of the lawsuit sped over the wires, and as soon as he heard it he telegraphed his friend in San Francisco.

"Am tired waiting. Shall sell the team and go home."

It was the signal agreed upon. The word "waiting" left out, would have signified that the suit had gone the other way. The mock teamster's friend picked up a deal of the mining stock, at low figures, before the news became public, and a fortune was the result.

For a long time after one of the great Virginia mines had been incorporated, about fifty feet of the original location were still in the hands of a man who had never signed the incorporation papers. The stock became very valuable, and every effort was made to find this man, but he had disappeared. Once it was heard that he was in New York, and one or two speculators went east but failed to find him. Once the news came that he was in the Bermudas, and straightway a speculator or two hurried east and sailed for Bermuda – but he was not there. Finally he was heard of in Mexico, and a friend of his, a bar-keeper on a salary, scraped together a little money and sought him out, bought his "feet" for a hundred dollars, returned and sold the property for $75,000.

But why go on? The traditions of Silverland are filled with instances like these, and I would never get through enumerating them were I to attempt to do it. I only desired to give the reader an idea of a peculiarity of the "flush times" which I could not present so strikingly in any other way, and which some mention of was necessary to a realizing comprehension of the time and the country.

I was personally acquainted with the majority of the nabobs I have referred to, and so, for old acquaintance sake, I have shifted their occupations and experiences around in such a way as to keep the Pacific public from recognizing these once notorious men. No longer notorious, for the majority of them have drifted back into poverty and obscurity again.

In Nevada there used to be current the story of an adventure of two of her nabobs, which may or may not have occurred. I give it for what it is worth:

Col. Jim had seen somewhat of the world, and knew more or less of its ways; but Col. Jack was from the back settlements of the States, had led a life of arduous toil, and had never seen a city. These two, blessed with sudden wealth, projected a visit to New York, – Col. Jack to see the sights, and Col. Jim to guard his unsophistication from misfortune. They reached San Francisco in the night, and sailed in the morning. Arrived in New York, Col. Jack said:

"I've heard tell of carriages all my life, and now I mean to have a ride in one; I don't care what it costs. Come along."

They stepped out on the sidewalk, and Col. Jim called a stylish barouche. But Col. Jack said:

"*No*, sir! None of your cheap-John turn-outs for me. I'm here to have a good time, and money ain't any object. I mean to have the nobbiest rig that's going. Now here comes the very trick. Stop that yaller one with the pictures on it – don't you fret – I'll stand all the expenses myself."

So Col. Jim stopped an empty omnibus, and they got in. Said Col. Jack:

"Ain't it gay, though? Oh, no, I reckon not! Cushions, and windows, and pictures, till you can't rest. What would the boys say if they could see us cutting a swell like this in New York? By George, I wish they *could* see us."

Then he put his head out of the window, and shouted to the driver:

"Say, Johnny, this suits *me!* – suits yours truly, you bet, you! I want this shebang all day. I'm *on* it, old man! Let 'em out! Make 'em go! We'll make it all right with *you*, sonny!"

The driver passed his hand through the strap-hole, and tapped for his fare – it was before the gongs came into common use. Col. Jack took the hand, and shook it cordially. He said:

"You twig me, old pard! All right between gents. Smell of *that*, and see how you like it!"

And he put a twenty-dollar gold piece in the driver's hand. After a moment the driver said he could not make change.

"Bother the change! Ride it out. Put it in your pocket."

Then to Col. Jim, with a sounding slap on his thigh:

"*Ain't* it style, though? Hanged if I don't hire this thing every day for a week."

The omnibus stopped, and a young lady got in. Col. Jack stared a moment, then nudged Col. Jim with his elbow.

"Don't say a word," he whispered. "Let her ride, if she wants to. Gracious, there's room enough."

The young lady got out her porte-monnaie, and handed her fare to Col. Jack.

"What's this for?" said he.

"Give it to the driver, please."

"Take back your money, madam. We can't allow it. You're welcome to ride here as long as you please, but this shebang's chartered, and we can't let you pay a cent."

The girl shrunk into a corner, bewildered. An old lady with a basket climbed in, and proffered her fare.

"Excuse me," said Col. Jack. "You're perfectly welcome here, madam, but we can't allow you to pay. Set right down there, mum, and don't you be the least uneasy. Make yourself just as free as if you was in your turn-out."

Within two minutes, three gentlemen, two fat women, and a couple of children, entered.

"Come right along, friends," said Col. Jack; "don't mind *us*. This is a free blow-out." Then he whispered to Col. Jim, "New York ain't no sociable place, I don't reckon – it ain't no *name* for it!"

He resisted every effort to pass fares to the driver, and made everybody cordially welcome. The situation dawned on the people, and they pocketed their money, and delivered themselves up to covert enjoyment of the episode. Half a dozen more passengers entered.

"Oh, there's *plenty* of room," said Col. Jack. "Walk right in, and make yourselves at home. A blow-out ain't worth anything *as* a blow-out, unless a body has company." Then in a whisper to Col. Jim: "But *ain't* these New Yorkers friendly? And ain't they cool about it, too? Icebergs ain't anywhere. I reckon they'd tackle a hearse, if it was going their way."

More passengers got in; more yet, and still more. Both seats were filled, and a file of men were standing up, holding on to the cleats overhead. Parties with baskets and bundles were climbing up on the roof. Half-suppressed laughter rippled up from all sides.

"Well, for clean, out-and-out cheek, if this don't bang anything that ever I saw, I'm an Injun!" whispered Col. Jack.

A Chinaman crowded his way in.

"I weaken!" said Col. Jack. "Hold on, driver! Keep your seats, ladies and gents. Just make yourselves free – everything's paid for. Driver, rustle these folks around as long as they're a mind to go – friends of ours, you know. Take them everywheres – and if you want more money, come to the St. Nicholas, and we'll make it all right. Pleasant journey to you, ladies and gents – go it just as long as you please – it shan't cost you a cent!"

The two comrades got out, and Col. Jack said:

"Jimmy, it's the sociablest place *I* ever saw. The Chinaman waltzed in as comfortable as anybody. If we'd staid awhile, I reckon we'd had some niggers. B' George, we'll have to barricade our doors to-night, or some of these ducks will be trying to sleep with us."

CHAPTER XLVII

SOME BODY HAS said that in order to know a community, one must observe the style of its funerals and know what manner of men they bury with most ceremony. I can not say which class we buried with most eclat in our "flush times," the distinguished public benefactor or the distinguished rough – possibly the two chief grades or grand divisions of society honored their illustrious dead about equally; and hence, no doubt the philosopher I have quoted from would have needed to see two representative funerals in Virginia before forming his estimate of the people.

There was a grand time over Buck Fanshaw when he died. He was a representative citizen. He had "killed his man" – not in his own quarrel, it is true, but in defense of a stranger unfairly beset by numbers. He had kept a sumptuous saloon. He had been the proprietor of a dashing helpmeet whom he could have discarded without the formality of a divorce. He had a held a high position in the fire department and been a very Warwick in politics. When he died there was great lamentation throughout the town, but especially in the vast bottom-stratum of society.

On the inquest it was shown that Buck Fanshaw, in the delirium of a wasting typhoid fever, had taken arsenic, shot himself through the body, cut his throat, and jumped out of a four-story window and broken his neck – and after due deliberation, the jury, sad and tearful, but with intelligence unblinded by its sorrow, brought in a verdict of death "by the visitation of God." What could the world do without juries?

Prodigious preparations were made for the funeral. All the vehicles in town were hired, all the saloons put in mourning, all the municipal and fire-company flags hung at half-mast, and all the firemen ordered to muster in uniform and bring their machines duly draped in black. Now – let us remark in parenthesis – as all the peoples of the earth had representative adventurers in the Silverland, and as each adventurer had brought the slang of his nation or his locality with him, the combination made the slang of Nevada the richest and the most infinitely varied and copious that had ever existed anywhere in the world, perhaps, except in the mines of California in the "early days." Slang was the language of Nevada. It was hard to preach a sermon without it, and be understood. Such phrases as "You bet!" "Oh, no, I reckon not!" "No Irish need apply," and a hundred others, became so common as to fall from the lips of a speaker unconsciously – and very often when they did not touch the subject under discussion and consequently failed to mean any thing.

After Buck Fanshaw's inquest, a meeting of the short-haired brotherhood was held, for nothing can be done on the Pacific coast without a public meeting and an expression of sentiment. Regretful resolutions were passed and various committees appointed; among others, a committee of one was deputed to call on the minister, a fragile, gentle, spirituel new fledgling from an Eastern theological seminary, and as yet unacquainted with the ways of the mines. The committeeman, "Scotty" Briggs, made his visit; and in after days it was worth something to hear the minister tell about it. Scotty was a stalwart rough, whose customary suit, when on weighty official business, like committee work, was a fire helmet, flaming red flannel shirt, patent-leather belt with spanner and revolver attached, coat hung over arm, and pants stuffed into boot-tops. He formed something of a contrast to the pale theological student. It is fair to say of Scotty, however, in passing, that he had a warm heart, and a strong love for his friends, and never entered into a quarrel when he could reasonably keep out of it. Indeed, it was commonly said that whenever one of Scotty's fights was investigated, it always turned out that it had originally been no affair of his, but that out of native goodheartedness he had dropped in of his own accord to help the man who was getting the worst of it. He and Buck Fanshaw were bosom friends, for years, and had often taken adventurous "pot-luck" together. On one occasion, they had thrown off their coats and taken the weaker side in a fight among strangers, and after gaining a hard-earned victory, turned and found that the men they were helping had deserted early, and not only that, but had stolen their coats and made off with them! But to return to Scotty's visit to the minister. He was on a sorrowful mission, now, and his face was the picture of woe. Being admitted to the presence he sat down before the clergyman, placed his fire-hat on an unfinished manuscript sermon under the minister's nose, took from it a red silk handkerchief, wiped his brow and heaved a sigh of dismal impressiveness, explanatory of his business. He choked, and even shed tears; but with an effort he mastered his voice and said in lugubrious tones:

"Are you the duck that runs the gospel-mill next door?"

"Am I the – pardon me, I believe I do not understand?"

With another sigh and a half-sob, Scotty rejoined:

"Why you see we are in a bit of trouble, and the boys thought maybe you would give us a lift, if we'd tackle you – that is, if I've got the rights of it and you are the head clerk of the doxology-works next door."

"I am the shepherd in charge of the flock whose fold is next door."

"The which?"

"The spiritual adviser of the little company of believers whose sanctuary adjoins these premises."

Scotty scratched his head, reflected a moment, and then said:

"You ruther hold over me, pard. I reckon I can't call that hand. Ante and pass the buck."

"How? I beg pardon. What did I understand you to say?"

"Well, you've ruther got the bulge on me. Or maybe we've both got the bulge, somehow. You don't smoke me and I don't smoke you. You see, one of the boys has passed in his checks and we want to give him a good send-off, and so the thing I'm on now is to roust out somebody to jerk a little chin-music for us and waltz him through handsome."

"My friend, I seem to grow more and more bewildered. Your observations are wholly incomprehensible to me. Cannot you simplify them in some way? At first I thought perhaps I understood you, but I grope now. Would it not expedite matters if you restricted yourself to categorical statements of fact unencumbered with obstructing accumulations of metaphor and allegory?"

Another pause, and more reflection. Then, said Scotty:

"I'll have to pass, I judge."

"How?"

"You've raised me out, pard."

"I still fail to catch your meaning."

"Why, that last lead of yourn is too many for me – that's the idea. I can't neither trump nor follow suit."

The clergyman sank back in his chair perplexed. Scotty leaned his head on his hand and gave himself up to thought. Presently his face came up, sorrowful but confident.

"I've got it now, so's you can savvy," he said. "What we want is a gospel-sharp. See?"

"A what?"

"Gospel-sharp, Parson."

"Oh! Why did you not say so before? I am a clergyman – a parson."

"Now you talk! You see my blind and straddle it like a man. Put it there!" – extending a brawny paw, which closed over the minister's small hand and gave it a shake indicative of fraternal sympathy and fervent gratification.

"Now we're all right, pard. Let's start fresh. Don't you mind my snuffling a little – becuz we're in a power of trouble. You see, one of the boys has gone up the flume—"

"Gone where?"

"Up the flume – throwed up the sponge, you understand."

"Thrown up the sponge?"

"Yes – kicked the bucket—"

"Ah – has departed to that mysterious country from whose bourne no traveler returns."

"Return! I reckon not. Why pard, he's *dead!*"

"Yes, I understand."

"Oh, you do? Well I thought maybe you might be getting tangled some more. Yes, you see he's dead again—"

"*Again?* Why, has he ever been dead before?"

"Dead before? No! Do you reckon a man has got as many lives as a cat? But you bet you he's awful dead now, poor old boy, and I wish I'd never seen this day. I don't want no better friend than Buck Fanshaw. I knowed him by the back; and when I know a man and like him, I freeze to him – you hear *me.* Take him all round, pard, there never was a bullier man in the mines. No man ever knowed Buck Fanshaw to go back on a friend. But it's all up, you know, it's all up. It ain't no use. They've scooped him."

"Scooped him?"

"Yes – death has. Well, well, well, we've got to give him up. Yes indeed. It's a kind of a hard world, after all, *ain't* it? But pard, he was a rustler! You ought to seen him get started once. He was a bully boy with a glass eye! Just spit in his face and give him room according to his strength, and it was just beautiful to see him peel and go in. He was the worst son of a thief that ever drawed breath. Pard, he was *on* it! He was on it bigger than an Injun!"

"On it? On what?"

"On the shoot. On the shoulder. On the fight, you understand. *He* didn't give a continental for *any*body. *Beg* your pardon, friend, for coming so near saying a cuss-word – but you see I'm on an awful strain, in this palaver, on account of having to cramp down and draw everything so mild. But we've got to give him up. There ain't any getting around that, I don't reckon. Now if we can get you to help plant him—"

"Preach the funeral discourse? Assist at the obsequies?"

"Obs'quies is good. Yes. That's it – that's our little game. We are going to get the thing up regardless, you know. He was always nifty himself, and so you bet you his funeral ain't going to be no slouch – solid silver door-plate on his coffin, six plumes on the hearse, and a nigger on the box in a biled shirt and a plug hat – how's that for high? And we'll take care of *you*, pard. We'll fix you all right. There'll be a kerridge for you; and whatever you want, you just 'scape out and we'll 'tend to it. We've got a shebang fixed up for you to stand behind, in No. 1's house, and don't you be afraid. Just go in and toot your horn, if you don't sell a clam. Put Buck through as bully as you can, pard, for anybody that knowed him will tell you that he was one of the whitest men that was ever in the mines. You can't draw it too strong. He never could stand it to see things going wrong. He's done more to make this town quiet and peaceable than any man in it. I've seen him lick four Greasers in eleven minutes, myself. If a thing wanted regulating, *he* warn't a man to go browsing around after some body to do it, but he would prance in and regulate it himself. He warn't a Catholic. Scasely. He was down on 'em. His word was, 'No Irish need apply!' But it didn't make no difference about that when it came down to what a man's rights was – and so, when some roughs jumped the Catholic bone-yard and started in to stake out town-lots in it he *went* for 'em! And he *cleaned* 'em, too! I was there, pard, and I seen it myself."

"That was very well indeed – at least the impulse was – whether the act was strictly defensible or not. Had deceased any religious convictions? That is to say, did he feel a dependence upon, or acknowledge allegiance to a higher power?"

More reflection.

"I reckon you've stumped me again, pard. Could you say it over once more, and say it slow?"

"Well, to simplify it somewhat, was he, or rather had he ever been connected with any organization sequestered from secular concerns and devoted to self-sacrifice in the interests of morality?"

"All down but nine – set 'em up on the other alley, pard."

"What did I understand you to say?"

"Why, you're most too many for me, you know. When you get in with your left I hunt grass every time. Every time you draw, you fill; but I don't seem to have any luck. Let's have a new deal."

"How? Begin again?"

"That's it."

"Very well. Was he a good man, and—"

"There – I see that; don't put up another chip till I look at my hand. A good man, says you? Pard, it ain't no name for it. He was the best man that ever – pard, you would have doted on that man. He could lam any galoot of his inches in America. It was him that put down the riot last election before it got a start; and every body said he was the only man that could have done it. He waltzed in with a spanner in one hand and a trumpet in the other, and sent fourteen men home on a shutter in less than three minutes. He had that riot all broke up and prevented nice before anybody ever got a chance to strike a blow. He was always for peace, and he would *have* peace – he could not stand disturbances. Pard, he was a great loss to this town. It would please the boys if you could chip in some thing like that and do him justice. Here once when the Micks got to throwing stones through the Methodis' Sunday School windows, Buck Fanshaw, all of his own notion, shut up his saloon and took a couple of six-shooters and mounted guard over the Sunday School. Says he, 'No Irish need apply!' And they didn't. He was the bulliest man in the mountains, pard! He could run faster, jump higher, hit harder, and hold more tangle-foot whiskey without spilling it than any man in seventeen counties. Put that in, pard – it'll please the boys more than anything you could say. And you can say, pard, that he never shook his mother."

"Never shook his mother?"

"That's it – any of the boys will tell you so."

"Well, but why *should* he shake her?"

"That's what *I* say – but some people does."

"Not people of any repute?"

"Well, some that averages pretty so-so."

"In my opinion the man that would offer personal violence to his own mother, ought to—"

"Cheese it, pard; you've banked your ball clean outside the string. What I was a drivin' at, was, that he never *throwed off* on his mother – don't you see? No indeedy. He give her a house to live in, and town-lots, and plenty of money; and he looked after her and took care of her all the time; and when she was down with the small-pox I'm d——d if he didn't set up nights and nuss her himself! *Beg* your pardon for saying it, but it hopped out too quick for yours truly. You've treated me like a gentleman, pard, and I ain't the man to hurt your feelings intentional. I think you're white. I think you're a square man, pard. I like you, and I'll lick any man that don't. I'll lick him till he can't tell himself from a last year's corpse! Put it *there!*" [Another fraternal handshake – and exit.]

The obsequies were all that "the boys" could desire. Such a marvel of funeral pomp had never been seen in Virginia. The plumed hearse, the dirge-breathing brass bands, the closed marts of business, the flags drooping at half-mast, the long, plodding procession of uniformed secret societies, military battalions and fire companies, draped engines, carriages of officials, and citizens in vehicles and on foot, attracted multitudes of spectators to the sidewalks, roofs and windows; and for years afterward, the degree of grandeur attained by any civic display in Virginia was determined by comparison with Buck Fanshaw's funeral.

Scotty Briggs, as a pall-bearer and a mourner, occupied a prominent place at the funeral, and when the sermon was finished and the last sentence of the prayer for the dead man's soul ascended, he responded, in a low voice, but with feeling:

"AMEN. No Irish need apply."

As the bulk of the response was without apparent relevancy, it was probably nothing more than a humble tribute to the memory of the friend that was gone; for, as Scotty had once said, it was "his word."

Scotty Briggs, in after days, achieved the distinction of becoming the only convert to religion that was ever gathered from the Virginia roughs; and it transpired that the man who had it in him to espouse the quarrel of the weak out of inborn nobility of spirit was no mean timber whereof to construct a Christian. The making him one did not warp his generosity or diminish his courage; on the contrary it gave intelligent direction to the one and a broader field to the other. If his Sunday School class progressed faster than the other classes, was it matter for wonder? I think not. He talked to his pioneer small-fry in a language they understood! It was my large privilege, a month before he died, to hear him tell the beautiful story of Joseph and his brethren to his class "without looking at the book." I leave it to the reader to fancy what it was like, as it fell, riddled with slang, from the lips of that grave, earnest teacher, and was listened to by his little learners with a consuming interest that showed that they were as unconscious as he was that any violence was being done to the sacred proprieties!

CHAPTER LI

VICE FLOURISHED LUXURIANTLY during the hey-day of our "flush times." The saloons were overburdened with custom; so were the police courts, the gambling dens, the brothels and the jails – unfailing signs of high prosperity in a mining region – in any region for that matter. Is it not so? A crowded police court docket is the surest of all signs that trade is brisk and money plenty. Still, there is one other sign; it comes last, but when it does come it establishes beyond cavil that the "flush times" are at the flood. This is the birth of the "literary" paper. The *Weekly Occidental*, "devoted to literature," made its appearance in Virginia. All the literary people were engaged to write for it. Mr. F. was to edit it. He was a felicitous skirmisher with a pen, and a man who could say happy things in a crisp, neat way. Once, while editor of the *Union*, he had disposed of a labored, incoherent, two-column attack made upon him by a contemporary, with a single line, which, at first glance, seemed to contain a solemn and tremendous compliment – viz: "THE LOGIC OF OUR ADVERSARY RESEMBLES THE PEACE OF GOD," – and left it to the reader's memory and after-thought to invest the remark with another and "more different" meaning by supplying for himself and at his own leisure the rest of the Scripture – "*in that it passeth understanding*." He once said of a little, half-starved, wayside community that had no subsistence except what they could get by preying upon chance passengers who stopped over with them a day when traveling by the overland stage, that in their church service they had altered the Lord's Prayer to read: "Give us this day our daily stranger!"

We expected great things of the *Occidental*. Of course it could not get along without an original novel, and so we made arrangements to hurl into the work the full strength of the company. Mrs. F. was an able romancist of the ineffable school – I know no other name to apply to a school whose heroes are all dainty and all perfect. She wrote the opening chapter, and introduced a lovely blonde simpleton who talked nothing but pearls and poetry and who was virtuous to the verge of eccentricity. She also introduced a young French Duke of aggravated refinement, in love with the blonde. Mr. F. followed next week, with a brilliant lawyer who set about getting the Duke's estates into trouble, and a sparkling young lady of high society who fell to fascinating the Duke and impairing the appetite of the blonde. Mr. D., a dark and bloody editor of one of the dailies, followed Mr. F., the third week, introducing a mysterious Roscicrucian who transmuted metals, held consultations with the devil in a cave at dead of night, and cast the horoscope of several heroes and heroines in such a way as to provide plenty of trouble for their future careers and breed a solemn and awful public interest in the novel. He also introduced a cloaked and masked melodramatic miscreant, put him on a salary and set him on the midnight track of the Duke with a poisoned dagger. He also created an Irish coachman with a rich brogue and placed him in the service of the society-young-lady with an ulterior mission to carry billet-doux to the Duke.

About this time there arrived in Virginia a dissolute stranger with a literary turn of mind – rather seedy he was, but very quiet and unassuming; almost diffident, indeed. He was so gentle, and his manners were so pleasing and kindly, whether he was sober or intoxicated, that he made friends of all who came in contact with him. He applied for literary work, offered conclusive evidence that he wielded an easy and practiced pen, and so Mr. F. engaged him at once to help write the novel. His chapter was to follow Mr. D.'s, and mine was to come next. Now what does this fellow do but go off and get drunk and then proceed to his quarters and set to work with his imagination in a state of chaos, and that chaos in a condition of extravagant activity. The result may be guessed. He scanned the chapters of his predecessors, found plenty of heroes and heroines already created, and was satisfied with them; he decided to introduce no more, with all the confidence that whiskey inspires and all the easy complacency it gives to its servant, he then launched himself lovingly into his work: he married the coachman to the society-young-lady for the sake of the scandal; married the Duke to the blonde's stepmother, for the sake of the sensation; stopped the desperado's salary; created a misunderstanding between the devil and the Roscicrucian; threw the Duke's property into the wicked lawyer's hands; made the lawyer's upbraiding conscience drive him to drink, thence to *delirium tremens*, thence to suicide; broke the coachman's neck; let his widow succumb to contumely, neglect, poverty and consumption; caused the blonde to drown herself, leaving her clothes on the bank with the customary note pinned to them forgiving the Duke and hoping he would be happy; revealed to the Duke, by means of the usual strawberry mark on left arm, that he had married his own long-lost mother and destroyed his long-lost sister, instituted the proper and necessary suicide of the Duke and the Duchess in order to compass poetical justice; opened the earth and let the Roscicrucian through, accompanied with the accustomed smoke and thunder and smell of brimstone, and finished with the promise that in the next chapter, after holding a general inquest, he would take up the surviving character of the novel and tell what became of the devil!

It read with singular smoothness, and with a "dead" earnestness that was funny enough to suffocate a body. But there was war when it came in. The other novelists were furious. The mild stranger, not yet more than half sober, stood there, under a scathing fire of vituperation, meek and bewildered, looking from one to another of his assailants, and wondering what he could have done to invoke such a storm. When a lull came at last, he said his say gently and appealingly – said he did not rightly remember what he had written, but was sure he had tried to do the best he could, and knew his object had been to make the novel not only pleasant and plausible but instructive and –

The bombardment began again. The novelists assailed his ill-chosen adjectives and demolished them with a storm of denunciation and ridicule. And so the siege went on. Every time the stranger tried to appease the enemy he only made matters worse. Finally he offered to rewrite the chapter. This arrested hostilities. The indignation gradually quieted down, peace reigned again and the sufferer retired in safety and got him to his own citadel.

But on the way thither the evil angel tempted him and he got drunk again. And again his imagination went mad. He led the heroes and heroines a wilder dance than ever; and yet all through it ran that same convincing air of honesty and earnestness that had marked his first work. He got the characters into the most extraordinary situations, put them through the most surprising performances, and made them talk the strangest talk! But the chapter cannot be described. It was symmetrically crazy; it was artistically absurd; and it had explanatory footnotes that were fully as curious as the text. I remember one of the "situations," and will offer it as an example of the whole. He altered the character of the brilliant lawyer, and made him a great-hearted, splendid fellow; gave him fame and riches, and set his age at thirty-three years. Then he made the blonde discover, through the help of the Roscicrucian and the melodramatic miscreant, that while the Duke loved her money ardently and wanted it, he secretly felt a sort of leaning toward the society-young-lady. Stung to the quick, she tore her affections from him and bestowed them with tenfold power upon the lawyer, who responded with consuming zeal. But the parents would none of it. What they wanted in the family was a Duke; and a Duke they were determined to have; though they confessed that next to the Duke the lawyer had their preference. Necessarily the blonde now went into a decline. The parents were alarmed. They pleaded with her to marry the Duke, but she steadfastly refused, and pined on. Then they laid a plan. They told her to wait a year and a day, and if at the end of that time she still felt that she could not marry the Duke, she might marry the lawyer with their full consent. The result was as they had foreseen: gladness came again, and the flush of returning health. Then the parents took the next step in their scheme. They had the family physician recommend a long sea-voyage and much land travel for the thorough restoration of the blonde's strength; and they invited the Duke to be of the party. They judged that the Duke's constant presence and the lawyer's protracted absence would do the rest – for they did not invite the lawyer.

So they set sail in a steamer for America – and the third day out, when their seasickness called truce and permitted them to take their first meal at the public table, behold there sat the lawyer! The Duke and party made the best of an awkward situation; the voyage progressed, and the vessel neared America. But, by and by two hundred miles off New Bedford, the ship took fire; she burned to the water's edge; of all her crew and passengers, only thirty were saved. They floated about the sea half an afternoon and all night long. Among them were our friends. The lawyer, by superhuman exertions, had saved the blonde and her parents, swimming back and forth two hundred yards and bringing one each time – (the girl first). The Duke had saved himself. In the morning two whale ships arrived on the scene and sent their boats. The weather was stormy and the embarkation was attended with much confusion and excitement. The lawyer did his duty like a man; helped his exhausted and insensible blonde, her parents and some others into a boat (the Duke helped himself in); then a child fell overboard at the other end of the raft and the lawyer rushed thither and helped half a dozen people fish it out, under the stimulus of its mother's screams. Then he ran back – a few seconds too late – the blonde's boat was under way. So he had to take the other boat, and go to the other ship. The storm increased and drove the vessels out of sight of each other – drove them whither it would. When it calmed, at the end of three days, the blonde's ship was seven hundred miles north of Boston and the other about seven hundred south of that port. The blonde's captain was bound on a whaling cruise in the North Atlantic and could not go back such a distance or make a port without orders; such being nautical law. The lawyer's captain was to cruise in the North Pacific, and *he* could not go back or make a port without orders. All the lawyer's money and baggage were in the blonde's boat and went to the blonde's ship – so his captain made him work his passage as a common sailor. When both ships had been cruising nearly a year, the one was off the coast of Greenland and the other in Behring's Strait. The blonde had long ago been well-nigh persuaded that her lawyer had been washed overboard and lost just before the whale ships reached the raft, and now, under the pleadings of her parents and the Duke she was at last beginning to nerve herself for the doom of the covenant, and prepare for the hated marriage. But she would not yield a day before the date set. The weeks dragged on, the time narrowed, orders were given to deck the ship for the wedding – a wedding at sea among icebergs and walruses. Five days more and all would be over. So the blonde reflected, with a sigh and a tear. Oh where was her true love – and why, why did he not come and save her? At that moment he was lifting his harpoon to strike a whale in Behring's Strait, five thousand miles away, by the way of the Arctic Ocean, or twenty thousand by the way of the Horn – that was the reason. He struck, but not with perfect aim – his foot slipped and he fell in the whale's mouth and went down his throat. He was insensible five days. Then he came to himself and heard voices; daylight was streaming through a hole cut in the whale's roof. He climbed out and astonished the sailors who were hoisting blubber up a ship's side. He recognized the vessel, flew aboard, surprised the wedding party at the altar and exclaimed:

"Stop the proceedings – I'm here! Come to my arms, my own!"

There were footnotes to this extravagant piece of literature wherein the author endeavored to show that the whole thing was within the possibilities; he said he got the incident of the whale traveling from Behring's Strait to the coast of Greenland, five thousand miles in five days, through the Arctic Ocean, from Charles Reade's "Love Me Little Love Me Long," and considered that that established the fact that the thing could be done; and he instanced Jonah's adventure as proof that a man could live in a whale's belly, and added that if a preacher could stand it three days a lawyer could surely stand it five!

There was a fiercer storm than ever in the editorial sanctum now, and the stranger was peremptorily discharged, and his manuscript flung at his head. But he had already delayed things so much that there was not time for some one else to rewrite the chapter, and so the paper came out without any novel in it. It was but a feeble, struggling, stupid journal, and the absence of the novel probably shook public confidence; at any rate, before the first side of the next issue went to press, the *Weekly Occidental* died as peacefully as an infant.

An effort was made to resurrect it, with the proposed advantage of a telling new title, and Mr. F. said that *The Phenix* would be just the name for it, because it would give the idea of a resurrection from its dead ashes in a new and undreamed-of condition of splendor; but some low-priced smarty on one of the dailies suggested that we call it the *Lazarus;* and inasmuch as the people were not profound in Scriptural matters but thought the resurrected Lazarus and the dilapidated mendicant that begged in the rich man's gateway were one and the same person, the name became the laughing stock of the town, and killed the paper for good and all.

I was sorry enough, for I was very proud of being connected with a literary paper – prouder than I have ever been of any thing since, perhaps. I had written some rhymes for it – poetry I considered it – and it was a great grief to me that the production was on the "first side" of the issue that was not completed, and hence did not see the light. But time brings its revenges – I can put it in here; it will answer in place of a tear dropped to the memory of the lost *Occidental.* The idea (not the chief idea, but the vehicle that bears it) was probably suggested by the old song called "The Raging Canal," but I cannot remember now. I do remember, though, that at that time I thought my doggerel was one of the ablest poems of the age:

THE AGED PILOT MAN

On the Erie Canal, it was,
  All on a summer's day,
I sailed forth with my parents
  Far away to Albany.

From out the clouds at noon that day
  There came a dreadful storm,
That piled the billows high about,
  And filled us with alarm.

A man came rushing from a house,
  Saying, "Snub up* your boat I pray,

*The customary canal technicality for "tie up."

Snub up your boat, snub up, alas,
  Snub up while yet you may."

Our captain cast one glance astern,
  Then forward glancèd he,
And said, "My wife and little ones
  I never more shall see."

Said Dollinger the pilot man,
  In noble words, but few, –
"Fear not, but lean on Dollinger,
  And he will fetch you through."

The boat drove on, the frightened mules
  Tore through the rain and wind,
And bravely still, in danger's post,
  The whip-boy strode behind.

"Come 'board, come 'board," the captain cried,
  "Nor tempt so wild a storm;"
But still the raging mules advanced,
  And still the boy strode on.

Then said the captain to us all,
  "Alas, 'tis plain to me,
The greater danger is not there,
  But here upon the sea.

So let us strive, while life remains,
  To save all souls on board,
And then if die at last we must,
  Let. . . . I *cannot* speak the word!"

Said Dollinger the pilot man,
  Tow'ring above the crew,
"Fear not, but trust in Dollinger,
  And he will fetch you through."

"Low bridge! low bridge!" all heads went down,
  The laboring bark sped on;
A mill we passed, we passed a church,
  Hamlets, and fields of corn;
And all the world came out to see,
  And chased along the shore

Crying, "Alas, alas, the sheeted rain,
  The wind, the tempest's roar!
Alas, the gallant ship and crew,
  Can *nothing* help them more?"

And from our deck sad eyes looked out
  Across the stormy scene:
The tossing wake of billows aft,
  The bending forests green,

The chickens sheltered under carts
  In lee of barn the cows,
The skurrying swine with straw in mouth,
  The wild spray from our bows!

          "She balances!
          She wavers!
Now let her go about!
  If she misses stays and broaches to,
We're all" – [then with a shout,]
        "Huray! huray!
        Avast! belay!
        Take in more sail!
        Lord, what a gale!
Ho, boy, haul taut on the hind mule's tail!

"Ho! lighten ship! ho! man the pump!
  Ho, hostler, heave the lead!
And count ye all, both great and small,
  As numbered with the dead!
For mariner for forty year,
  On Erie, boy and man,
I never yet saw such a storm,
  Or one 't with it began!"

So overboard a keg of nails
  And anvils three we threw,
Likewise four bales of gunny-sacks
  Two hundred pounds of glue,
Two sacks of corn, four ditto wheat,
  A box of books, a cow,
A violin, Lord Byron's works,
  A rip-saw and a sow.

A curve! a curve! the dangers grow!
  "Labbord! – stabbord – s-t-e-a-d-y! – so! –
Hard-a-port, Dol! – hellum-a-lee!
  Haw the head mule! – the aft one gee!
Luff! – bring her to the wind!"

"A quarter-three! – 'tis shoaling fast!
  Three feet large! – t-h-r-e-e- feet! –
Three feet scant!" I cried in fright
  "Oh, is there *no* retreat?"

Said Dollinger, the pilot man,
  As on the vessel flew,
"Fear not, but trust in Dollinger,
  And he will fetch you through."

A panic struck the bravest hearts,
  The boldest cheek turned pale;
For plain to all, this shoaling said
A leak had burst the ditch's bed!
And, straight as bolt from crossbow sped,
Our ship swept on, with shoaling lead,
  Before the fearful gale!
"Sever the tow-line! Cripple the mules!"
  Too late! ..... There comes a shock!

* * *

Another length, and the fated craft
  Would have swum in the saving lock!

Then gathered together the shipwrecked crew
  And took one last embrace,
While sorrowful tears from despairing eyes
  Ran down each hopeless face;
And some did think of their little ones
  Whom they never more might see,
And others of waiting wives at home,
  And mothers that grieved would be.

But of all the children of misery there
  On that poor sinking frame,
But one spake words of hope and faith,
  And I worshipped as they came:

Said Dollinger the pilot man, –
(O brave heart, strong and true!) –
"Fear not, but trust in Dollinger,
For he will fetch you through."

Lo! scarce the words have passed his lips
The dauntless prophet say'th,
When every soul about him seeth
A wonder crown his faith!
For straight a farmer brought a plank, –
(Mysteriously inspired) –
And laying it unto the ship,
In silent awe retired.

Then every sufferer stood amazed
That pilot man before;
A moment stood. Then wondering turned,
And speechless walked ashore.

CHAPTER LIII

EVERY NOW AND then, in these days, the boys used to tell me I ought to get one Jim Blaine to tell me the stirring story of his grandfather's old ram – but they always added that I must not mention the matter unless Jim was drunk at the time – just comfortably and sociably drunk. They kept this up until my curiosity was on the rack to hear the story. I got to haunting Blaine; but it was of no use, the boys always found fault with his condition; he was often moderately but never satisfactorily drunk. I never watched a man's condition with such absorbing interest, such anxious solicitude; I never so pined to see a man uncompromisingly drunk before. At last, one evening I hurried to his cabin, for I learned that this time his situation was such that even the most fastidious could find no fault with it – he was tranquilly, serenely, symmetrically drunk – not a hiccup to mar his voice, not a cloud upon his brain thick enough to obscure his memory. As I entered, he was sitting upon an empty powder-keg, with a clay pipe in one hand and the other raised to command silence. His face was round, red, and very serious; his throat was bare and his hair tumbled; in general appearance and costume he was a stalwart miner of the period. On the pine table stood a candle, and its dim light revealed "the boys" sitting here and there on bunks, candle-boxes, powder-kegs, etc. They said:

"Sh—! Don't speak – he's going to commence."

THE STORY OF THE OLD RAM

I found a seat at once, and Blaine said:

"I don't reckon them times will ever come again. There never was a more bullier old ram than what he was. Grandfather fetched him from Illinois – got him of a man by the name of Yates – Bill Yates – maybe you might have heard of him; his father was a deacon – Baptist – and he was a rustler, too; a man had to get up ruther early to get the start of old Thankful Yates; it was him that put the Greens up to jining teams with my grandfather when he moved west. Seth Green was prob'ly the pick of the flock; he married a Wilkerson – Sarah Wilkerson – good cretur, she was – one of the likeliest heifers that was ever raised in old Stoddard, every body said that knowed her. She could heft a bar'l of flour as easy as I can flirt a flapjack. And spin? Don't mention it! Independent? Humph! When Sile Hawkins come a browsing around her, she let him know that for all his tin he couldn't trot in harness alongside of *her*. You see, Sile Hawkins was – no, it warn't Sile Hawkins, after all – it was a galoot by the name of Filkins – I disremember his first name; but he *was* a stump – come into pra'r meeting drunk, one night, hooraying for Nixon, becuz he thought it was a primary; and old deacon Ferguson up and scooted him through the window and he lit on old Miss Jefferson's head, poor old filly. She was a good soul – had a glass eye and used to lend it to old Miss Wagner, that hadn't any, to receive company in; it warn't big enough, and when Miss Wagner warn't noticing, it would get twisted around in the socket, and look up, maybe, or out to one side, and every which way, while t' other one was looking as straight ahead as a spy-glass. Grown people didn't mind it, but it most always made the children cry, it was so sort of scary. She tried packing it in raw cotton, but it wouldn't work, somehow – the cotton would get loose and stick out and look so kind of awful that the children couldn't stand it no way. She was always dropping it out, and turning up her old dead-light on the company empty, and making them oncomfortable, becuz *she* never could tell when it hopped out, being blind on that side, you see. So some body would have to hunch her and say, "Your game eye has fetched loose, Miss Wagner dear" – and then all of them would have to sit and wait till she jammed it in again – wrong side before, as a general thing, and green as a bird's egg, being a bashful cretur and easy sot back before company. But being wrong side before warn't much difference, anyway, becuz her own eye was sky-blue and the glass one was yaller on the front side, so whichever way she turned it it didn't match nohow. Old Miss Wagner was considerable on the borrow, she was. When she had a quilting, or Dorcas S'iety at her house she gen'ally borrowed Miss Higgins's wooden leg to stump around on; it was considerable shorter than her other pin, but much *she* minded that. She said she couldn't abide crutches when she had company, becuz they were so slow; said when she had company and things had to be done, she wanted to get up and hump herself. She was as bald as a jug, and so she used to borrow Miss Jacops's wig – Miss Jacops was the coffin-peddler's wife – a ratty old buzzard, he was, that used to go roosting around where people was sick, waiting for 'em; and there that old rip would sit all day, in the shade, on a coffin that he judged would fit the can'idate; and if it was a slow customer and kind of uncertain, he'd fetch his rations and a blanket along and sleep in the coffin nights. He was anchored out that way, in frosty weather, for about three weeks, once, before old Robbins's place, waiting for him; and after that, for as much as two years, Jacops was not on speaking terms with the old man, on account of his disapp'inting him. He got one of his feet froze, and lost money, too, becuz old Robbins took a favorable turn and got well. The next time Robbins got sick, Jacops tried to make up with him, and varnished up the same old coffin and fetched it along; but old Robbins was too many for him; he had him in, and 'peared to be powerful weak; he bought the coffin for ten dollars and Jacops was to pay it back and twenty-five more besides if Robbins didn't like the coffin after he'd tried it. And then Robbins died, and at the funeral he bursted off the lid and riz up in his shroud and told the parson to let up on the performances, becuz he could *not* stand such a coffin as that. You see he had been in a trance once before, when he was young, and he took the chances on another, cal'lating that if he made the trip it was money in his pocket, and if he missed fire he couldn't lose a cent. And by George he sued Jacops for the rhino and got jedgment; and he set up the coffin in his back parlor and said he 'lowed to take his time, now. It was always an aggravation to Jacops, the way that miserable old thing acted. He moved back to Indiany pretty soon – went to Wellsville – Wellsville was the place the Hogadorns was from. Mighty fine family. Old Maryland stock. Old Squire Hogadorn could carry around more mixed licker, and cuss better than most any man I ever see. His second wife was the widder Billings – she that was Becky Martin; her dam was deacon Dunlap's first wife. Her oldest child, Maria, married a missionary and died in grace – et up by the savages. They et *him*, too, poor feller – biled him. It warn't the custom, so they say, but they explained to friends of his'n that went down there to bring away his things, that they'd tried missionaries every other way and never could get any good out of 'em – and so it annoyed all his relations to find out that that man's life was fooled away just out of a dern'd experiment, so to speak. But mind you, there ain't any thing ever reely lost; everything that people can't understand and don't see the reason of does good if you only hold on and give it a fair shake; Prov'dence don't fire no blank ca'tridges, boys. That there missionary's substance, unbeknowns to himself, actu'ly converted every last one of them heathens that took a chance at the barbacue. Nothing ever fetched them but that. Don't tell *me* it was an accident that he was biled. There ain't no such thing as an accident. When my uncle Lem was leaning up agin a scaffolding once, sick, or drunk, or suthin, an Irishman with a hod full of bricks fell on him out of the third story and broke the old man's back in two places. People said it was an accident. Much accident there was about that. He didn't know what he was there for, but he was there for a good object. If he hadn't been there the Irishman would have been killed. Nobody can ever make me believe anything different from that. Uncle Lem's dog was there. Why didn't the Irishman fall on the dog? Becuz the dog would a seen him a coming and stood from under. That's the reason the dog warn't appinted. A dog can't be depended on to carry out a special providence. Mark my words it was a put-up thing. Accidents don't happen, boys. Uncle Lem's dog – I wish you could a seen that dog. He was a reglar shepherd – or ruther he was part bull and part shepherd – splendid animal; belonged to parson Hagar before Uncle Lem got him. Parson Hagar belonged to the Western Reserve Hagars; prime family; his mother was a Watson; one of his sisters married a Wheeler; they settled in Morgan county, and he got nipped by the machinery in a carpet factory and went through in less than a quarter of a minute; his widder bought the piece of carpet that had his remains wove in, and people come a hundred mile to 'tend the funeral. There was fourteen yards in the piece. She wouldn't let them roll him up, but planted him just so – full length. The church was middling small where they preached the funeral, and they had to let one end of the coffin stick out of the window. They didn't bury him – they planted one end, and let him stand up, same as a monument. And they nailed a sign on it and put – put on – put on it – sacred to – the m-e-m-o-r-y – of fourteen y-a-r-d-s – of three-ply – car - - - pet – containing all that was – m-o-r-t-a-l – of – of – W-i-l-l-i-a-m – W-h-e—"

Jim Blaine had been growing gradually drowsy and drowsier – his head nodded, once, twice, three times – dropped peacefully upon his breast, and he fell tranquilly asleep. The tears were running down the boys' cheeks – they were suffocating with suppressed laughter – and had been from the start, though I had never noticed it. I perceived that I was "sold." I learned then that Jim Blaine's peculiarity was that whenever he reached a certain stage of intoxication, no human power could keep him from setting out, with impressive unction, to tell about a wonderful adventure which he had once had with his grandfather's old ram – and the mention of the ram in the first sentence was as far as any man had ever heard him get, concerning it. He always maundered off, interminably, from one thing to another, till his whiskey got the best of him and he fell asleep. What the thing was that happened to him and his grandfather's old ram is a dark mystery to this day, for nobody has ever yet found out.

CHAPTER LIV

OF COURSE THERE was a large Chinese population in Virginia – it is the case with every town and city on the Pacific coast. They are a harmless race when white men either let them alone or treat them no worse than dogs; in fact they are almost entirely harmless any how, for they seldom think of resenting the vilest insults or the cruelest injuries. They are quiet, peaceable, tractable, free from drunkenness, and they are as industrious as the day is long. A disorderly Chinaman is rare, and a lazy one does not exist. So long as a Chinaman has strength to use his hands he needs no support from anybody; white men often complain of want of work, but a Chinaman offers no such complaint; he always manages to find some thing to do. He is a great convenience to every body – even to the worst class of white men, for he bears the most of their sins, suffering fines for their petty thefts, imprisonment for their robberies, and death for their murders. Any white man can swear a Chinaman's life away in the courts, but no Chinaman can testify against a white man. Ours is the "land of the free" – nobody denies that – nobody challenges it. [May be it is because we won't let other people testify.] As I write, news comes that in broad daylight in San Francisco, some boys have stoned an inoffensive Chinaman to death, and that although a large crowd witnessed the shameful deed, no one interfered.

There are seventy thousand (and possibly one hundred thousand) Chinamen on the Pacific coast. There were about a thousand in Virginia. They were penned into a "Chinese quarter" – a thing which they do not particularly object to, as they are fond of herding together. Their buildings were of wood; usually only one story high, and set thickly together along streets scarcely wide enough for a wagon to pass through. Their quarter was a little removed from the rest of the town. The chief employment of Chinamen in towns is to wash clothing. They always send a bill, like this below, pinned to the clothes. It is mere ceremony, for it does not enlighten the customer much. Their price for washing was $2.50 per dozen – rather cheaper than white people could afford to wash for at that time. A very common sign on the Chinese houses was: "See Yup, Washer and Ironer"; "Hong Wo, Washer"; "Sam Sing & Ah Hop, Washing." The house servants, cooks, etc., in California and Nevada, were chiefly Chinamen. There were few white servants and no Chinawomen so employed. Chinamen make good house servants, being quick, obedient, patient, quick to learn and tirelessly industrious. They do not need to be taught a thing twice, as a general thing. They are imitative. If a Chinaman were to see his master break up a centre table, in a passion, and kindle a fire with it, that Chinaman would be likely to resort to the furniture for fuel forever afterward.

All Chinamen can read, write and cipher with easy facility – pity but all our petted *voters* could. In California they rent little patches of ground and do a deal of gardening. They will raise surprising crops of vegetables on a sand pile. They waste nothing. What is rubbish to a Christian, a Chinaman carefully preserves and makes useful in one way or another. He gathers up all the old oyster and sardine cans that white people throw away, and procures marketable tin and solder from them by melting. He gathers up old bones and turns them into manure. In California he gets a living out of old mining claims that white men have abandoned as exhausted and worthless – and then the officers come down on him once a month with an exorbitant swindle to which the legislature has given the broad, general name of "foreign" mining tax, but it is usually inflicted on no foreigners but Chinamen. This swindle has in some cases been repeated once or twice on the same victim in the course of the same month – but the public treasury was not additionally enriched by it, probably.

Chinamen hold their dead in great reverence – they worship their departed ancestors, in fact. Hence, in China, a man's front yard, back yard, or any other part of his premises, is made his family burying ground, in order that he may visit the graves at any and all times. Therefore that huge empire is one mighty cemetery; it is ridged and wringled from its centre to its circumference with graves – and inasmuch as every foot of ground must be made to do its utmost, in China, lest the swarming population suffer for food, the very graves are cultivated and yield a harvest, custom holding this to be no dishonor to the dead. Since the departed are held in such worshipful reverence, a Chinaman cannot bear that any indignity be offered the places where they sleep. Mr. Burlingame said that herein lay China's bitter opposition to railroads; a road could not be built anywhere in the empire without disturbing the graves of their ancestors or friends.

A Chinaman hardly believes he could enjoy the hereafter except his body lay in his beloved China; also, he desires to receive, himself, after death, that worship with which he has honored his dead that preceded him. Therefore, if he visits a foreign country, he makes arrangements to have his bones returned to China in case he dies; if he hires to go to a foreign country on a labor contract, there is always a stipulation that his body shall be taken back to China if he dies; if the government sells a gang of Coolies to a foreigner for the usual five-year term, it is specified in the contract that their bodies shall be restored to China in case of death. On the Pacific coast the Chinamen all belong to one or another of several great companies or organizations, and these companies keep track of their members, register their names, and ship their bodies home when they die. The See Yup Company is held to be the largest of these. The Ning Yeong

Company is next, and numbers eighteen thousand members on the coast. Its headquarters are at San Francisco, where it has a costly temple, several great officers (one of whom keeps regal state in seclusion and cannot be approached by common humanity), and a numerous priesthood. In it I was shown a register of its members, with the dead and the date of their shipment to China duly marked. Every ship that sails from San Francisco carries away a heavy freight of Chinese corpses – or did, at least, until the legislature, with an ingenious refinement of Christian cruelty, forbade the shipments, as a neat underhanded way of deterring Chinese immigration. The bill was offered, whether it passed or not. It is my impression that it passed. There was another bill – it became a law – compelling every incoming Chinaman to be vaccinated on the wharf and pay a duly appointed quack (no decent doctor would defile himself with such legalized robbery) ten dollars for it. As few importers of Chinese would want to go to an expense like that, the law-makers thought this would be another heavy blow to Chinese immigration.

What the Chinese quarter of Virginia was like – or indeed, what the Chinese quarter of any Pacific coast town was and is like – may be gathered from this item which I printed in the *Enterprise* while reporting for that paper:

> CHINATOWN. – Accompanied by a fellow-reporter, we made a trip through our Chinese quarter the other night. The Chinese have built their portion of the city to suit themselves; and as they keep neither carriages nor wagons, their streets are not wide enough, as a general thing, to admit of the passage of vehicles. At ten o'clock at night the Chinaman may be seen in all his glory. In every little cooped-up, dingy cavern of a hut, faint with the odor of burning Josh-lights and with nothing to see the gloom by save the sickly, guttering tallow candle, were two or three yellow, long-tailed vagabonds, coiled up on a sort of short truckle-bed, smoking opium, motionless and with their lustreless eyes turned inward from excess of satisfaction – or rather the recent smoker looks thus, immediately after having passed the pipe to his neighbor – for opium-smoking is a comfortless operation, and requires constant attention. A lamp sits on the bed, the length of the long pipe-stem from the smoker's mouth; he puts a pellet of opium on the end of a wire, sets it on fire, and plasters it into the pipe much as a Christian would fill a hole with putty; then he applies the bowl to the lamp and

proceeds to smoke – and the stewing and frying of the drug and the gurgling of the juices in the stem would well-nigh turn the stomach of a statue. John likes it, though; it soothes him, he takes about two dozen whiffs, and then rolls over to dream, Heaven only knows what, for we could not imagine by looking at the soggy creature. Possibly in his visions he travels far away from the gross world and his regular washing, and feasts on succulent rats and birds'-nests in Paradise.

Mr. Ah Sing keeps a general grocery and provision store at No. 13 Wang street. He lavished his hospitality upon our party in the friendliest way. He had various kinds of colored and colorless wines and brandies, with unpronounceable names, imported from China in little crockery jugs, and which he offered to us in dainty little miniature wash-basins of porcelain. He offered us a mess of birds'-nests; also, small, neat sausages, of which we could have swallowed several yards if we had chosen to try, but we suspected that each link contained the corpse of a mouse, and therefore refrained. Mr. Sing had in his store a thousand articles of merchandise, curious to behold, impossible to imagine the uses of, and beyond our ability to describe.

His ducks, however, and his eggs, we could understand; the former were split open and flattened out like codfish, and came from China in that shape, and the latter were plastered over with some kind of paste which kept them fresh and palatable through the long voyage.

We found Mr. Hong Wo, No. 37 Chow-chow street, making up a lottery scheme – in fact we found a dozen others occupied in the same way in various parts of the quarter, for about every third Chinaman runs a lottery, and the balance of the tribe "buck" at it. "Tom," who speaks faultless English, and used to be chief and only cook to the *Territorial Enterprise*, when the establishment kept bachelor's hall two years ago, said that "Sometime Chinaman buy ticket one dollar hap, ketch um two tree hundred, sometime no ketch um anyting; lottery like one man fight um seventy – may-be he whip, may-be he get whip heself, welly good." However, the per centage being sixty-nine against him, the chances are, as a general thing, that "he get whip heself." We could not see that these lotteries differed in any respect from our own, save that the figures being Chinese, no ignorant white man might ever hope to succeed in telling "t'other from which;" the manner of drawing is similar to ours.

Mr. See Yup keeps a fancy store on Live Fox street. He sold us fans of white feathers, gorgeously ornamented; perfumery that smelled like Limburger cheese, Chinese pens, and watch-charms made of a stone unscratchable with steel instruments, yet polished and tinted like the inner coat of a sea-shell.* As tokens of his esteem, See Yup presented the party with gaudy plumes made of gold tinsel and trimmed with peacocks' feathers.

We ate chow-chow with chop-sticks in the celestial restaurants; our comrade chided the moon-eyed damsels in front of the houses for their want of feminine reserve; we received protecting Josh-lights from our hosts and "dickered" for a pagan God or two. Finally, we were impressed with the genius of a Chinese book-keeper; he figured up his accounts on a machine like a gridiron with buttons strung on its bars; the different rows represented units, tens, hundreds and thousands. He fingered them with incredible rapidity – in fact, he pushed them from place to place as fast as a musical professor's fingers travel over the keys of a piano.

They are a kindly disposed, well-meaning race, and are respected and well treated by the upper classes, all over the Pacific coast. No Californian *gentleman or lady* ever abuses or oppresses a Chinaman, under any circumstances, an explanation that seems to be much needed in the East. Only the scum of the population do it – they and their children; they, and, naturally and consistently, the policemen and politicians, likewise, for these are the dust-licking pimps and slaves of the scum, there as well as elsewhere in America.

CHAPTER LV

I BEGAN TO get tired of staying in one place so long. There was no longer satisfying variety in going down to Carson to report the proceedings of the legislature once a year, and horse-races and pumpkin-shows once in three months; (they had got to raising pumpkins and potatoes in Washoe Valley, and of course one of the first achievements of the legislature was to institute a ten-thousand-dollar Agricultural Fair to show off forty dollars' worth of those

*A peculiar species of the "jade-stone" – to a Chinaman peculiarly precious.

pumpkins in – however, the territorial legislature was usually spoken of as the "asylum"). I wanted to see San Francisco. I wanted to go somewhere. I wanted – I did not know *what* I wanted. I had the "spring fever" and wanted a change, principally, no doubt. Besides, a convention had framed a State Constitution; nine men out of every ten wanted an office; I believed that these gentlemen would "treat" the moneyless and the irresponsible among the population into adopting the constitution and thus well-nigh killing the country (it could not well carry such a load as a State government, since it had nothing to tax that could stand a tax, for undeveloped mines could not, and there were not fifty developed ones in the land, there was but little realty to tax, and it did seem as if nobody was ever going to think of the simple salvation of inflicting a money penalty on murder). I believed that a State government would destroy the "flush times," and I wanted to get away. I believed that the mining stocks I had on hand would soon be worth $100,000, and thought if they reached that before the Constitution was adopted, I would sell out and make myself secure from the crash the change of government was going to bring. I considered $100,000 sufficient to go home with decently, though it was but a small amount compared to what I had been expecting to return with. I felt rather down-hearted about it, but I tried to comfort myself with the reflection that with such a sum I could not fall into want. About this time a schoolmate of mine whom I had not seen since boyhood, came tramping in on foot from Reese River, a very allegory of Poverty. The son of wealthy parents, here he was, in a strange land, hungry, bootless, mantled in an ancient horse-blanket, roofed with a brimless hat, and so generally and so extravagantly dilapidated that he could have "taken the shine out of the Prodigal Son himself," as he pleasantly remarked. He wanted to borrow forty-six dollars – twenty-six to take him to San Francisco, and twenty for something else; to buy some soap with, may be, for he needed it. I found I had but little more than the amount wanted, in my pocket; so I stepped in and borrowed forty-six dollars of a banker (on twenty days' time, without the formality of a note), and gave it him, rather than walk half a block to the office, where I had some specie laid up. If anybody had told me that it would take me two years to pay back that forty-six dollars to the banker (for I did not expect it of the Prodigal, and was not disappointed), I would have felt injured. And so would the banker.

I wanted a change. I wanted variety of some kind. It came. Mr. Goodman went away for a week and left me the post of chief editor. It destroyed me. The first day, I wrote my "leader" in the forenoon.

The second day, I had no subject and put it off till the afternoon. The third day I put it off till evening, and then copied an elaborate editorial out of the "American Cyclopedia," that steadfast friend of the editor, all over this land. The fourth day I "fooled around" till midnight, and then fell back on the Cyclopedia again. The fifth day I cudgeled my brain till midnight, and then kept the press waiting while I penned some bitter personalities on six different people. The sixth day I labored in anguish till far into the night and brought forth – nothing. The paper went to press without an editorial. The seventh day I resigned. On the eighth, Mr. Goodman returned and found six duels on his hands – my personalities had borne fruit.

Nobody, except he has tried it, knows what it is to be an editor. It is easy to scribble local rubbish, with the facts all before you; it is easy to clip selections from other papers; it is easy to string out a correspondence from any locality; but it is unspeakable hardship to write editorials. *Subjects* are the trouble – the dreary lack of them, I mean. Every day, it is drag, drag, drag – think, and worry and suffer – all the world is a dull blank, and yet the editorial columns *must* be filled. Only give the editor a *subject*, and his work is done – it is no trouble to write it up; but fancy how you would feel if you had to pump your brains dry every day in the week, fifty-two weeks in the year. It makes one low-spirited simply to think of it. The matter that each editor of a daily paper in America writes in the course of a year would fill from four to eight bulky volumes like this book! Fancy what a library an editor's work would make, after twenty or thirty years' service. Yet people often marvel that Dickens, Scott, Bulwer, Dumas, etc., have been able to produce so many books. If these authors had wrought as voluminously as newspaper editors do, the result would be something to marvel at, indeed. How editors can continue this tremendous labor, this exhausting consumption of brain fibre (for their work is creative, and not a mere mechanical laying-up of facts, like reporting), day after day and year after year, is incomprehensible. Preachers take two months' holiday in midsummer, for they find that to produce two sermons a week is wearing, in the long run. In truth it must be so, and is so; and therefore, how an editor can take from ten to twenty texts and build upon them from ten to twenty painstaking editorials a week and keep it up all the year round, is farther beyond comprehension than ever. Ever since I survived my week as editor, I have found at least one pleasure in any newspaper that comes to my hand; it is in admiring the long columns of editorial, and wondering to myself how in the mischief he did it!

Mr. Goodman's return relieved me of employment, unless I chose to become a reporter again. I could not do that; I could not serve in the ranks after being General of the army. So I thought I would depart and go abroad into the world somewhere. Just at this juncture, Dan, my associate in the reportorial department, told me, casually, that two citizens had been trying to persuade him to go with them to New York and aid in selling a rich silver mine which they had discovered and secured in a new mining district in our neighborhood. He said they offered to pay his expenses and give him one third of the proceeds of the sale. He had refused to go. It was the very opportunity I wanted. I abused him for keeping so quiet about it, and not mentioning it sooner. He said it had not occurred to him that I would like to go, and so he had recommended them to apply to Marshall, the reporter of the other paper. I asked Dan if it was a good, honest mine, and no swindle. He said the men had shown him nine tons of the rock, which they had got out to take to New York, and he could cheerfully say that he had seen but little rock in Nevada that was richer; and moreover, he said that they had secured a tract of valuable timber and a mill-site, near the mine. My first idea was to kill Dan. But I changed my mind, notwithstanding I was so angry, for I thought may be the chance was not yet lost. Dan said it was by no means lost; that the men were absent at the mine again, and would not be in Virginia to leave for the East for some ten days; that they had requested him to do the talking to Marshall, and he had promised that he would either secure Marshall or some body else for them by the time they got back; he would now say nothing to anybody till they returned, and then fulfil his promise by furnishing me to them.

It was splendid. I went to bed all on fire with excitement; for nobody had yet gone East to sell a Nevada silver mine, and the field was white for the sickle. I felt that such a mine as the one described by Dan would bring a princely sum in New York, and sell without delay or difficulty. I could not sleep, my fancy so rioted through its castles in the air. It was the "blind lead" come again.

Next day I got away, on the coach, with the usual eclat attending departures of old citizens, – for if you have only half a dozen friends out there they will make noise for a hundred rather than let you seem to go away neglected and unregretted – and Dan promised to keep strict watch for the men that had the mine to sell.

The trip was signalized but by one little incident, and that occurred just as we were about to start. A very seedy-looking vagabond passenger got out of the stage a moment to wait till the usual ballast of silver bricks was thrown in. He was standing on the pavement, when an awkward express employé, carrying a brick weighing a hundred pounds, stumbled and let it fall on the bummer's foot. He instantly dropped on the ground and began to howl in the most heart-breaking way. A sympathizing crowd gathered around and were going to pull his boot off; but he screamed louder than ever and they desisted; then he fell to gasping, and between the gasps ejaculated "Brandy! for Heaven's sake, brandy!" They poured half a pint down him, and it wonderfully restored and comforted him. Then he begged the people to assist him to the stage, which was done. The express people urged him to have a doctor at their expense, but he declined, and said that if he only had a little brandy to take along with him, to soothe his paroxysms of pain when they came on, he would be grateful and content. He was quickly supplied with two bottles, and we drove off. He was so smiling and happy after that, that I could not refrain from asking him how he could possibly be so comfortable with a crushed foot.

"Well," said he, "I hadn't had a drink for twelve hours, and hadn't a cent to my name. I was most perishing – and so, when that duffer dropped that hundred-pounder on my foot, I see my chance. Got a cork leg, you know!" and he pulled up his pantaloons and proved it.

He was as drunk as a lord all day long, and full of chuckles over his timely ingenuity.

One drunken man necessarily reminds one of another. I once heard a gentleman tell about an incident which he witnessed in a Californian barroom. He entitled it "Ye Modest Man Taketh a Drink." It was nothing but a bit of acting, but it seemed to me a perfect rendering, and worthy of Toodles himself. The modest man, tolerably far gone with beer and other matters, enters a saloon (twenty-five cents is the price for any thing and every thing, and specie the only money used) and lays down a half dollar; calls for whiskey and drinks it; the bar-keeper makes change and lays the quarter in a wet place on the counter; the modest man fumbles at it with nerveless fingers, but it slips and the water holds it; he contemplates it, and tries again; same result; observes that people are interested in what he is at, blushes; fumbles at the quarter again – blushes – puts his forefinger carefully, slowly down, to make sure of his aim – pushes the coin toward the bar-keeper, and says with a sigh:

"('ic!) Gimme a cigar!"

Naturally, another gentleman present told about another drunken man. He said he reeled toward home late at night; made a mistake and entered the wrong gate; thought he saw a dog on the stoop; and it was – an iron one. He stopped and considered; wondered if it was a dangerous dog; ventured to say "Be (hic) begone!" No effect. Then he approached warily, and adopted conciliation; pursed up his lips and tried to whistle, but failed; still approached, saying, "Poor dog! – doggy, doggy, doggy! – poor doggy-dog!" Got up on the stoop, still petting with fond names; still master of the advantages; then exclaimed, "Leave, you thief!" – planted a vindictive kick in his ribs, and went head-over-heels overboard, of course. A pause; a sigh or two of pain, and then a remark in a reflective voice:

"Awful solid dog. What could he ben eating? ('ic!) Rocks, p'raps. Such animals is dangerous. 'At's what *I* say – they're dangerous. If a man – ('ic!) – if a man wants to feed a dog on rocks, let him *feed* him on rocks; 'at's all right; but let him keep him at *home* – not have him layin' round promiscuous, where ('ic!) where people's liable to stumble over him when they ain't noticin'!"

It was not without regret that I took a last look at the tiny flag (it was thirty-five feet long and ten feet wide) fluttering like a lady's handkerchief from the topmost peak of Mount Davidson, two thousand feet above Virginia's roofs, and felt that doubtless I was bidding a permanent farewell to a city which had afforded me the most vigorous enjoyment of life I had ever experienced. And this reminds me of an incident which the dullest memory Virginia could boast at the time it happened must vividly recall, at times, till its possessor dies. Late one summer afternoon we had a rain shower. That was astonishing enough, in itself, to set the whole town buzzing, for it only rains (during a week or two weeks) in the winter in Nevada, and even then not enough at a time to make it worth while for any merchant to keep umbrellas for sale. But the rain was not the chief wonder. It only lasted five or ten minutes; while the people were still talking about it all the heavens gathered to themselves a dense blackness as of midnight. All the vast eastern front of Mount Davidson, overlooking the city, put on such a funereal gloom that only the nearness and solidity of the mountain made its outlines even faintly distinguishable from the dead blackness of the heavens they rested against. This unaccustomed sight turned all eyes toward the mountain; and as they looked, a little tongue of rich golden flame was seen waving and quivering in the heart of the midnight, away up on the extreme summit! In a few minutes the streets were packed with people, gazing with hardly an uttered word, at the one brilliant mote in the brooding world of darkness. It flicked like a candle-flame, and looked no larger; but with such a background it was wonderfully bright, small as it was. It was the flag! – though no one suspected it at first, it seemed so like a supernatural visitor of some kind – a mysterious messenger of good tidings, some were fain to believe. It was the nation's emblem transfigured by the departing rays of a sun that was entirely palled from view; and on no other object did the glory fall, in all the broad panorama of mountain ranges and deserts. Not even upon the staff of the flag – for that, a needle in the distance at any time, was now untouched by the light and undistinguishable in the gloom. For a whole hour the weird visitor winked and burned in its lofty solitude, and still the thousands of uplifted eyes watched it with fascinated interest. How the people were wrought up! The superstition grew apace that this was a mystic courier come with great news from the war – the poetry of the idea excusing and commending it – and on it spread, from heart to heart, from lip to lip and from street to street, till there was a general impulse to have out the military and welcome the bright waif with a salvo of artillery!

And all that time one sorely tried man, the telegraph operator sworn to official secrecy, had to lock his lips and chain his tongue with a silence that was like to rend them; for he, and he only, of all the speculating multitude, knew the great things this sinking sun had seen that day in the east – Vicksburg fallen, and the Union arms victorious at Gettysburg!

But for the journalistic monopoly that forbade the slightest revealment of eastern news till a day after its publication in the California papers, the glorified flag on Mount Davidson would have been saluted and re-saluted, that memorable evening, as long as there was a charge of powder to thunder with; the city would have been illuminated, and every man that had any respect for himself would have got drunk, – as was the custom of the country on all occasions of public moment. Even at this distant day I cannot think of this needlessly marred supreme opportunity without regret. What a time we might have had!

CHAPTER LVI

WE RUMBLED OVER the plains and valleys, climbed the Sierras to the clouds, and looked down upon summer-clad California. And

I will remark here, in passing, that all scenery in California requires *distance* to give it its highest charm. The mountains are imposing in their sublimity and their majesty of form and altitude, from any point of view – but one must have distance to soften their ruggedness and enrich their tintings; a Californian forest is best at a little distance, for there is a sad poverty of variety in species, the trees being chiefly of one monotonous family – redwood, pine, spruce, fir – and so, at a near view there is a wearisome sameness of attitude in their rigid arms, stretched downward and outward in one continued and reiterated appeal to all men to "Sh! – don't say a word! – you might disturb somebody!" Close at hand, too, there is a reliefless and relentless smell of pitch and turpentine; there is a ceaseless melancholy in their sighing and complaining foliage; one walks over a soundless carpet of beaten yellow bark and dead spines of the foliage till he feels like a wandering spirit bereft of a foot fall; he tires of the endless tufts of needles and yearns for substantial, shapely leaves; he looks for moss and grass to loll upon, and finds none, for where there is no bark there is naked clay and dirt, enemies to pensive musing and clean apparel. Often a grassy plain in California, is what it should be, but often, too, it is best contemplated at a distance, because although its grass blades are tall, they stand up vindictively straight and self-sufficient, and are unsociably wide apart, with uncomely spots of barren sand between.

One of the queerest things I know of, is to hear tourists from "the States" go into ecstasies over the loveliness of "ever-blooming California." And they always do go into that sort of ecstasies. But perhaps they would modify them if they knew how old Californians, with the memory full upon them of the dust-covered and questionable summer greens of Californian "verdure," stand astonished, and filled with worshiping admiration, in the presence of the lavish richness, the brilliant green, the infinite freshness, the spendthrift variety of form and species and foliage that make an Eastern landscape a vision of Paradise itself. The idea of a man falling into raptures over grave and sombre California, when that man has seen New England's meadow-expanses and her maples, oaks and cathedral-windowed elms decked in summer attire, or the opaline splendors of autumn descending upon her forests, comes very near being funny – would be, in fact, but that it is so pathetic. No land with an unvarying climate can be very beautiful. The tropics are not, for all the sentiment that is wasted on them. They seem beautiful at first, but sameness impairs the charm by and by. *Change* is the handmaiden

Nature requires to do her miracles with. The land that has four well-defined seasons, cannot lack beauty, or pall with monotony. Each season brings a world of enjoyment and interest in the watching of its unfolding, its gradual, harmonious development, its culminating graces – and just as one begins to tire of it, it passes away and a radical change comes, with new witcheries and new glories in its train. And I think that to one in sympathy with nature, each season, in its turn, seems the loveliest.

San Francisco, a truly fascinating city to live in, is stately and handsome at a fair distance, but close at hand one notes that the architecture is mostly old-fashioned, many streets are made up of decaying, smoke-grimed, wooden houses, and the barren sand hills toward the outskirts obtrude themselves too prominently. Even the kindly climate is sometimes pleasanter when read about than personally experienced, for a lovely, cloudless sky wears out its welcome by and by, and then when the longed-for rain does come it *stays*. Even the playful earthquake is better contemplated at a dis—

However there are varying opinions about that.

The climate of San Francisco is mild and singularly equable. The thermometer stands at about seventy degrees the year round. It hardly changes at all. You sleep under one or two light blankets summer and winter, and never use a mosquito bar. Nobody ever wears summer clothing. You wear black broadcloth – if you have it – in August and January, just the same. It is no colder, and no warmer, in the one month than the other. You do not use overcoats and you do not use fans. It is as pleasant a climate as could well be contrived, take it all around, and is doubtless the most unvarying in the whole world. The wind blows there a good deal in the summer months, but then you can go over to Oakland, if you choose – three or four miles away – it does not blow there. It has only snowed twice in San Francisco in nineteen years, and then it only remained on the ground long enough to astonish the children, and set them to wondering what the feathery stuff was.

During eight months of the year, straight along, the skies are bright and cloudless, and never a drop of rain falls. But when the other four months come along, you will need to go and steal an umbrella. Because you will require it. Not just one day, but one hundred and twenty days in hardly varying succession. When you want to go visiting, or attend church, or the theatre, you never look up at the clouds to see whether it is likely to rain or not – you look at the almanac. If it is winter, it will *rain* – and if it is summer, it *won't* rain, and you cannot help it. You never need a lightning-rod, because it never thunders and it never lightens. And after you have listened for six or eight weeks, every night, to the dismal monotony of those quiet rains, you will wish in your heart the thunder *would* leap and crash and roar along those drowsy skies once, and make everything alive – you will wish the prisoned lightnings *would* cleave the dull firmament asunder and light it with a blinding glare for *one* little instant. You would give *any thing* to hear the old familiar thunder again and see the lightning strike some body. And along in the summer, when you have suffered about four months of lustrous, pitiless sunshine, you are ready to go down on your knees and plead for rain – hail – snow – thunder and lightning – anything to break the monotony – you will take an earthquake, if you cannot do any better. And the chances are that you'll get it, too.

San Francisco is built on sand hills, but they are prolific sand hills. They yield a generous vegetation. All the rare flowers which people in "the States" rear with such patient care in parlor flower-pots and green-houses, flourish luxuriantly in the open air there all the year round. Calla lilies, all sorts of geraniums, passion flowers, moss roses – I do not know the names of a tenth part of them. I only know that while New Yorkers are burdened with banks and drifts of snow, Californians are burdened with banks and drifts of flowers, if they only keep their hands off and let them grow. And I have heard that they have also that rarest and most curious of all the flowers, the beautiful *Espiritu Santo*, as the Spaniards call it – or flower of the Holy Spirit – though I thought it grew only in Central America – down on the Isthmus. In its cup is the daintiest little fac-simile of a dove, as pure as snow. The Spaniards have a superstitious reverence for it. The blossom has been conveyed to the States, submerged in ether; and the bulb has been taken thither also, but every attempt to make it bloom after it arrived, has failed.

I have elsewhere spoken of the endless Winter of Mono, California, and but this moment of the eternal Spring of San Francisco. Now if we travel a hundred miles in a straight line, we come to the eternal Summer of Sacramento. One never sees summer-clothing or mosquitoes in San Francisco – but they can be found in Sacramento. Not always and unvaryingly, but about one hundred and forty-three months out of twelve years, perhaps. Flowers bloom there, always, the reader can easily believe – people suffer and sweat, and swear, morning, noon and night, and wear out their stanchest energies fanning themselves. It gets hot there, but if you go down to Fort Yuma you will find it hotter. Fort Yuma is probably the hottest place on earth. The thermometer stays at one hundred and twenty in the shade there all the time – except when it varies and goes higher. It is a U. S. military post, and its occupants get so used to the terrific heat that they suffer without it. There is a tradition (attributed to John Phenix*) that a very, very wicked soldier died there, once, and of course, went straight to the hottest corner of perdition, – and the next day he *telegraphed back for his blankets*. There is no doubt about the truth of this statement – there can be no doubt about it. I have seen the place where that soldier used to board. In Sacramento it is fiery summer always, and you can gather roses, and eat strawberries and ice-cream, and wear white linen clothes, and pant and perspire, at eight or nine o'clock in the morning, and then take the cars, and at noon put on your furs and your skates, and go skimming over frozen Donner Lake, seven thousand feet above the valley, among snow banks fifteen feet deep, and in the shadow of grand mountain peaks that lift their frosty crags ten thousand feet above the level of the sea. There is a transition for you! Where will you find another like it in the Western hemisphere? And some of us have swept around snow-walled curves of the Pacific Railroad in that vicinity, six thousand feet above the sea, and looked down as the birds do, upon the deathless summer of the Sacramento Valley, with its fruitful fields, its feathery foliage, its silver streams, all slumbering in the mellow haze of its enchanted atmosphere, and all infinitely softened and spiritualized by distance – a dreamy, exquisite glimpse of fairy-land, made all the more charming and striking that it was caught through a forbidden gateway of ice and snow, and savage crags and precipices.

CHAPTER LIX

FOR A TIME I WROTE literary screeds for the *Golden Era*. C. H. Webb had established a very excellent literary weekly called the *Californian*, but high merit was no guaranty of success; it languished, and he sold out to three printers, and Bret Harte became editor at $20 a week, and I was

*It has been purloined by fifty different scribblers who were too poor to invent a fancy but not ashamed to steal one. – M. T.

employed to contribute an article a week at $12. But the journal still languished, and the printers sold out to Captain Ogden, a rich man and a pleasant gentleman who chose to amuse himself with such an expensive luxury without much caring about the cost of it. When he grew tired of the novelty, he re-sold to the printers, the paper presently died a peaceful death, and I was out of work again. I would not mention these things but for the fact that they so aptly illustrate the ups and downs that characterize life on the Pacific coast. A man could hardly stumble into such a variety of queer vicissitudes in any other country.

For two months my sole occupation was avoiding acquaintances; for during that time I did not earn a penny, or buy an article of any kind, or pay my board. I became a very adept at "slinking." I slunk from back street to back street, I slunk away from approaching faces that looked familiar, I slunk to my meals, ate them humbly and with a mute apology for every mouthful I robbed my generous landlady of, and at midnight, after wanderings that were but slinkings away from cheerfulness and light, I slunk to my bed. I felt meaner, and lowlier and more despicable than the worms. During all this time I had but one piece of money – a silver ten-cent piece – and I held to it and would not spend it on any account, lest the consciousness coming strong upon me that I was *entirely* penniless, might suggest suicide. I had pawned every thing but the clothes I had on; so I clung to my dime desperately, till it was smooth with handling.

However, I am forgetting. I did have one other occupation beside that of "slinking." It was the entertaining of a collector (and being entertained by him,) who had in his hands the Virginia banker's bill for the forty-six dollars which I had loaned my schoolmate, the "Prodigal." This man used to call regularly once a week and dun me, and sometimes oftener. He did it from sheer force of habit, for he knew he could get nothing. He would get out his bill, calculate the interest for me, at five per cent. A month, and show me clearly that there was no attempt at fraud in it and no mistakes; and then plead, and argue and dun with all his might for any sum – any little trifle – even a dollar – even half a dollar, on account. Then his duty was accomplished and his conscience free. He immediately dropped the subject there always; got out a couple of cigars and divided, put his feet in the window, and then we would have a long, luxurious talk about every thing and every body, and he would furnish me a world of curious dunning adventures out of the ample store in his memory. By and by he would clap his hat on his head, shake hands and say briskly:

"Well, business is business – can't stay with you always!" – and was off in a second.

The idea of pining for a dun! And yet I used to long for him to come, and would get as uneasy as any mother if the day went by without his visit, when I was expecting him. But he never collected that bill, at last nor any part of it. I lived to pay it to the banker myself.

Misery loves company. Now and then at night, in out-of-the-way, dimly lighted places, I found myself happening on another child of misfortune. He looked so seedy and forlorn, so homeless and friendless and forsaken, that I yearned toward him as a brother. I wanted to claim kinship with him and go about and enjoy our wretchedness together. The drawing toward each other must have been mutual; at any rate we got to falling together oftener, though still seemingly by accident; and although we did not speak or evince any recognition, I think the dull anxiety passed out of both of us when we saw each other, and then for several hours we would idle along contentedly, wide apart, and glancing furtively in at home lights and fireside gatherings, out of the night shadows, and very much enjoying our dumb companionship.

Finally we spoke, and were inseparable after that. For our woes were identical, almost. He had been a reporter too, and lost his berth, and this was his experience, as nearly as I can recollect it. After losing his berth, he had gone down, down, down, with never a halt: from a boarding-house on Russian Hill to a boarding-house in Kearney street; from thence to Dupont; from thence to a low sailor den; and from thence to lodgings in goods boxes and empty hogsheads near the wharves. Then, for a while, he had gained a meagre living by sewing up bursted sacks of grain on the piers; when that failed he had found food here and there as chance threw it in his way. He had ceased to show his face in daylight, now, for a reporter knows every body, rich and poor, high and low, and cannot well avoid familiar faces in the broad light of day.

This mendicant Blucher – I call him that for convenience – was a splendid creature. He was full of hope, pluck and philosophy; he was well read and a man of cultivated taste; he had a bright wit and was a master of satire; his kindliness and his generous spirit made him royal in my eyes and changed his curbstone seat to a throne and his damaged hat to a crown.

He had an adventure, once, which sticks fast in my memory as the most pleasantly grotesque that ever touched my sympathies. He had been without a penny for two months. He had shirked about obscure streets, among friendly dim lights, till the thing had become second nature to him. But at last he was driven abroad in daylight. The cause was sufficient; *he had not tasted food for forty-eight hours*, and he could not endure the misery of his hunger in idle hiding. He came along a back street, glowering at the loaves in bake-shop windows, and feeling that he could trade his life away for a morsel to eat. The sight of the bread doubled his hunger; but it was good to look at it, any how, and imagine what one might do if one only had it. Presently, in the middle of the street he saw a shining spot – looked again – did not, and could not, believe his eyes – turned away, to try them, then looked again. It was a verity – no vain, hunger-inspired delusion – it was a silver dime! He snatched it – gloated over it; doubted it – bit it – found it genuine – choked his heart down, and smothered a halleluiah. Then he looked around – saw that nobody was looking at him – threw the dime down where it was before – walked away a few steps, and approached again, pretending he did not know it was there, so that he could re-enjoy the luxury of finding it. He walked around it, viewing it from different points; then sauntered about with his hands in his pockets, looking up at the signs and now and then glancing at it and feeling the old thrill again. Finally he took it up, and went away, fondling it in his pocket. He idled through unfrequented streets, stopping in doorways and corners to take it out and look at it. By and by he went home to his lodgings – an empty queensware hogshead, – and employed himself till night trying to make up his mind what to buy with it. But it was hard to do. To get the most for it was the idea. He knew that at the Miner's Restaurant he could get a plate of beans and a piece of bread for ten cents; or a fish-ball and some few trifles, but they gave "no bread with one fish-ball" there. At French Pete's he could get a veal cutlet, plain, and some radishes and bread, for ten cents; or a cup of coffee – a pint at least – and a slice of bread; but the slice was not thick enough by the eighth of an inch, and sometimes they were still more criminal than that in the cutting of it. At seven o'clock his hunger was wolfish; and still his mind was not made up. He turned out and went up Merchant street, still ciphering; and chewing a bit of stick, as is the way of starving men. He passed before the lights of Martin's restaurant, the most aristocratic in the city, and stopped. It was a place where he had often dined, in better days, and Martin knew him well. Standing aside, just out of the range of the light, he worshiped the quails and steaks in the show window, and imagined that may be the fairy times were not gone yet and some prince in disguise would come along presently and tell him to go in there and take whatever he wanted. He chewed his stick with a hungry interest as he warmed to his subject. Just at this juncture he was conscious of some one at his side, sure enough; and then a finger touched his arm. He looked up, over his shoulder, and saw an apparition – a very allegory of Hunger! It was a man six feet high, gaunt, unshaven, hung with rags; with a haggard face and sunken cheeks, and eyes that pleaded piteously. This phantom said:

"Come with me – please."

He locked his arm in Blucher's and walked up the street to where the passengers were few and the light not strong, and then facing about, put out his hands in a beseeching way, and said:

"Friend – stranger – look at me! Life is easy to you – you go about, placid and content, as I did once, in my day – you have been in there, and eaten your sumptuous supper, and picked your teeth, and hummed your tune, and thought your pleasant thoughts, and said to yourself it is a good world – but you've never *suffered!* You don't know what trouble is – you don't know what misery is – nor hunger! Look at me! Stranger have pity on a poor friendless, homeless dog! As God is my judge, I have not tasted food for eight and forty hours! – look in my eyes and see if I lie! Give me the least trifle in the world to keep me from starving – anything – twenty-five cents! Do it, stranger – do it, *please.* It will be nothing to you, but life to me. Do it, and I will go down on my knees and lick the dust before you! I will kiss your footprints – I will worship the very ground you walk on! Only twenty-five cents! I am famishing – perishing – starving by inches! For God's sake don't desert me!"

Blucher was bewildered – and touched, too – stirred to the depths. He reflected. Thought again. Then an idea struck him, and he said:

"Come with me."

He took the outcast's arm, walked him down to Martin's restaurant, seated him at a marble table, placed the bill of fare before him, and said:

"Order what you want, friend. Charge it to me, Mr. Martin."

"All right, Mr. Blucher," said Martin.

Then Blucher stepped back and leaned against the counter and watched the man stow away cargo after cargo of buckwheat cakes at seventy-five cents a plate; cup after cup of coffee, and porter house steaks worth two dollars apiece; and when six dollars and a half's worth of destruction had been accomplished, and the stranger's hunger appeased, Blucher went down to French Pete's, bought a veal cutlet plain, a slice of bread, and three radishes, with his dime, and set to and feasted like a king!

Take the episode all around, it was as odd as any that can be culled from the myriad curiosities of Californian life, perhaps.

CHAPTER LXII

AFTER A THREE months' absence, I found myself in San Francisco again, without a cent. When my credit was about exhausted, (for I had become too mean and lazy, now, to work on a morning paper, and there were no vacancies on the evening journals,) I was created San Francisco correspondent of the *Enterprise*, and at the end of five months I was out of debt, but my interest in my work was gone; for my correspondence being a daily one, without rest or respite, I got unspeakably tired of it. I wanted another change. The vagabond instinct was strong upon me. Fortune favored and I got a new berth and a delightful one. It was to go down to the Sandwich Islands and write some letters for the Sacramento *Union*, an excellent journal and liberal with employés.

We sailed in the propeller *Ajax*, in the middle of winter. The almanac called it winter, distinctly enough, but the weather was a compromise between spring and summer. Six days out of port, it became summer altogether. We had some thirty passengers; among them a cheerful soul by the name of Williams, and three sea-worn old whale-ship captains going down to join their vessels. These latter played euchre in the smoking room day and night, drank astonishing quantities of raw whiskey without being in the least affected by it, and were the happiest people I think I ever saw. And then there was "the old Admiral – " a retired whaleman. He was a roaring, terrific combination of wind and lightning and thunder, and earnest, whole-souled profanity. But nevertheless he was tender-hearted as a girl. He was a raving, deafening, devastating typhoon, laying waste the cowering seas but with an unvexed refuge in the centre where all comers were safe and at rest. Nobody could know the "Admiral" without liking him; and in a sudden and dire emergency I think no friend of his would know which to choose – to be cursed by him or prayed for by a less efficient person.

His title of "Admiral" was more strictly "official" than any ever worn by a naval officer before or since, perhaps – for it was the voluntary offering of a whole nation, and came direct from the *people* themselves without any intermediate red tape – the people of the Sandwich Islands. It was a title that came to him freighted with affection, and honor, and appreciation of his unpretending merit. And in testimony of the genuineness of the title it was publicly ordained that an exclusive flag should be devised for him and used solely to welcome his coming and wave him God-speed in his going. From that time forth, whenever his ship was signaled in the offing, or he catted his anchor and stood out to sea, that ensign streamed from the royal halliards on the parliament house and the nation lifted their hats to it with spontaneous accord.

Yet he had never fired a gun or fought a battle in his life. When I knew him on board the *Ajax*, he was seventy-two years old and had plowed the salt water sixty-one of them. For sixteen years he had gone in and out of the harbor of Honolulu in command of a whale ship, and for sixteen more had been captain of a San Francisco and Sandwich Island passenger packet and had never had an accident or lost a vessel. The simple natives knew him for a friend who never failed them, and regarded him as children regard a father. It was a dangerous thing to oppress them when the roaring Admiral was around.

Two years before I knew the Admiral, he had retired from the sea on a competence, and had sworn a colossal nine-jointed oath that he would "never go within *smelling* distance of the salt water again as long as he lived." And he had conscientiously kept it. That is to say, *he* considered he had kept it, and it would have been more than dangerous to suggest to him, even in the gentlest way, that making eleven long sea-voyages, as a passenger, during the two years that had transpired since he "retired," was only keeping the general spirit of it and not the strict letter.

The Admiral knew only one narrow line of conduct to pursue in any and all cases where there was a fight, and that was to shoulder his way straight in without an inquiry as to the rights or the merits of it, and take the part of the weaker side. – And this was the reason why he was always sure to be present at the trial of any universally execrated criminal to oppress and intimidate the jury with a vindictive pantomime of what he would do to them if he ever caught them out of the box. And this was why harried cats and outlawed dogs that knew him confidently took sanctuary under his chair in time of trouble. In the beginning he was the most frantic and bloodthirsty Union man that drew breath in the shadow of the Flag; but the instant the Southerners began to go down before the sweep of the Northern armies, he ran up the Confederate colors and from that time till the end was a rampant and inexorable secessionist.

He hated intemperance with a more uncompromising animosity than any individual I have ever met, of either sex; and he was never tired of storming against it and beseeching friends and strangers alike to be wary and drink with moderation. And yet if any creature had been guileless enough to intimate that his absorbing nine gallons of "straight" whiskey during our voyage was any fraction short of rigid or inflexible abstemiousness, in that self-same moment the old man would have spun him to the uttermost parts of the earth in the whirlwind of his wrath. Mind, I am not saying his whiskey ever affected his head or his legs, for it did not, in even the slightest degree. He was a capacious container, but he did not hold enough for that. He took a level tumblerful of whiskey every morning before he put his clothes on – "to sweeten his bilgewater," he said. – He took another after he got the most of his clothes on, "to settle his mind and give him his bearings." He then shaved, and put on a clean shirt; after which he recited the Lord's Prayer in a fervent, thundering bass that shook the ship to her kelson and suspended all conversation in the main cabin. Then, at this stage, being invariably "by the head," or "by the stern," or "listed to port or starboard," he took one more to "put him on an even keel so that he would mind his hellum and not miss stays and go about, every time he came up in the wind." – And now, his state-room door swung open and the sun of his benignant face beamed redly out upon men and women and children, and he roared his "Shipmets a'hoy!" in a way that was calculated to wake the dead and precipitate the final resurrection; and forth he strode, a picture to look at and a presence to enforce attention. Stalwart and portly; not a gray hair; broad-brimmed slouch hat; semi-sailor toggery of blue navy flannel – roomy and ample; a stately expanse of shirt-front and a liberal amount of black silk neck-cloth tied with a sailor knot; large chain and imposing seals impending from his fob; awe-inspiring feet, and "a hand like the hand of Providence," as his whaling brethren expressed it; wrist-bands and sleeves pushed back half way to the elbow, out of respect for the warm weather, and exposing hairy arms, gaudy with red and blue anchors, ships, and goddesses of liberty tattooed in India ink. But these details were only secondary matters – his face was the lodestone that chained the eye. It was a sultry disk, glowing determinedly out through a weather-beaten mask of mahogany, and studded with warts, seamed with scars, "blazed" all over with unfailing fresh slips of the razor; and with cheery eyes, under shaggy brows, contemplating the world from over the back of a gnarled crag of a nose that loomed vast and lonely out of the undulating immensity that spread away from its foundations. At his heels frisked the darling of his bachelor estate, his terrier "Fan," a creature no larger than a squirrel. The main part of his daily life was occupied in looking after "Fan," in a motherly way, and doctoring her for a hundred ailments which existed only in his imagination.

The Admiral seldom read newspapers; and when he did he never believed anything they said. He read nothing, and believed in nothing, but "The Old Guard," a secession periodical published in New York. He carried a dozen copies of it with him, always, and referred to them for all required information. If it was not there, he supplied it himself, out of a bountiful fancy, inventing history, names, dates, and every thing else necessary to make his point good in an argument. Consequently he was a formidable antagonist in a dispute. Whenever he swung clear of the record and began to create history, the enemy was helpless and had to surrender. Indeed, the enemy could not keep from betraying some little spark of indignation at his manufactured history – and when it came to indignation, that was the Admiral's very "best hold." He was always ready for a political argument, and if nobody started one he would do it himself. With his third retort his temper would begin to rise, and within five minutes he would be blowing a gale, and within fifteen his smoking-room audience would be utterly stormed away and the old man left solitary and alone, banging the table with his fist, kicking the chairs, and roaring a hurricane of profanity. It got so, after a while, that whenever the Admiral approached, with politics in his eye, the passengers would drop out with quiet accord, afraid to meet him; and he would camp on a deserted field.

But he found his match at last, and before a full company. At one time or another, everybody had entered the lists against him and been routed, except the quiet passenger Williams. He had never been able to get an expression of opinion out of him on politics. But now, just as the Admiral drew near the door and the company were about to slip out, Williams said:

"Admiral, are you *certain* about that circumstance concerning the clergymen you mentioned the other day?" – referring to a piece of the Admiral's manufactured history.

Everyone was amazed at the man's rashness. The idea of deliberately inviting annihilation was a thing incomprehensible. The retreat came to a halt; then every body sat down again wondering, to await the upshot of it. The Admiral himself was as surprised as any one. He paused in the door, with his red handkerchief half raised to his sweating face, and contemplated the daring reptile in the corner.

"*Certain* of it? Am I *certain* of it? Do you think I've been lying about it? What do you take me for? Anybody that don't know that circumstance, don't know any thing; a child ought to know it. Read up your history! Read it up ——— ——— ——— ———, and don't come asking a man if he's *certain* about a bit of A B C stuff that the very southern niggers know all about."

Here the Admiral's fires began to wax hot, the atmosphere thickened, the coming earthquake rumbled, he began to thunder and lighten. Within three minutes his volcano was in full irruption and he was discharging flames and ashes of indignation, belching black volumes of foul history aloft, and vomiting red-hot torrents of profanity from his crater. Meantime Williams sat silent, and apparently deeply and earnestly interested in what the old man was saying. By and by, when the lull came, he said in the most deferential way, and with the gratified air of a man who has had a mystery cleared up which had been puzzling him uncomfortably:

"*Now* I understand it. I always thought I knew that piece of history well enough, but was still afraid to trust it, because there was not that convincing particularity about it that one likes to have in history; but when you mentioned every name, the other day, and every date, and every little circumstance, in their just order and sequence, I said to myself, *this* sounds something like – *this* is history – *this* is putting it in a shape that gives a man confidence; and I said to myself afterward, I will just ask the Admiral if he is perfectly certain about the details, and if he is I will come out and thank him for clearing this matter up for me. And that is what I want to do now – for until you set that matter right it was nothing but just a confusion in my mind, without head or tail to it."

Nobody ever saw the Admiral look so mollified before, and so pleased. Nobody had ever received his bogus history as gospel before; its genuineness had always been called in question either by words or looks; but here was a man that not only swallowed it all down, but was grateful for the dose. He was taken aback; he hardly knew what to say; even his profanity failed him. Now, Williams continued, modestly and earnestly:

"But Admiral, in saying that this was the first stone thrown, and that this precipitated the war, you have overlooked a circumstance which you are perfectly familiar with, but which has escaped your memory. Now I grant you that what you have stated is correct in every detail – to wit: that on the 16th of October, 1860, two Massachusetts clergymen, named Waite and Granger, went in disguise to the house of John Moody, in Rockport, at dead of night, and dragged forth two southern women and their two little children, and after tarring and feathering them conveyed them to Boston and burned them alive in the State House square; and I also grant your proposition that this deed is what led to the secession of South Carolina on the 20th of December following. Very well." [Here the company were pleasantly surprised to hear Williams proceed to come back at the Admiral with his own invincible weapon – clean, pure, *manufactured history*, without a word of truth in it.] "Very well, I say. But Admiral, why overlook the Willis and Morgan case in South Carolina? You are too well informed a man not to know all about that circumstance. Your arguments and your conversations have shown you to be intimately conversant with every detail of this national quarrel. You develop matters of history every day that show plainly that you are no smatterer in it, content to nibble about the surface, but a man who has searched the depths and possessed yourself of everything that has a bearing upon the great question. Therefore, let me just recall to your mind that Willis and Morgan case – though I see by your face that the whole thing is already passing through your memory at this moment. On the 12th of August, 1860, *two months* before the Waite and Granger affair, two South Carolina clergymen, named John H. Morgan and Winthrop L. Willis, one a Methodist and the other an Old School Baptist, disguised themselves, and went at midnight to the house of a planter named Thompson – Archibald F. Thompson, Vice President under Thomas Jefferson, – and took thence, at midnight, his widowed aunt, (a Northern woman,) and her adopted child, an orphan named Mortimer Highie, afflicted with epilepsy and suffering at the time from white swelling on one of his legs, and compelled to walk on crutches in consequence; and the two ministers, in spite of the pleadings of the victims, dragged them to the bush, tarred and feathered them, and afterward burned them at the stake in the city of Charleston. You remember perfectly well what a stir it made; you remember perfectly well that even the Charleston *Courier* stigmatized the act as being unpleasant, of questionable propriety, and scarcely justifiable, and likewise that it would not be matter of surprise if retaliation ensued. And you remember also, that this thing was the *cause* of the Massachusetts outrage. Who, indeed, were the two Massachusetts ministers? and who were the two Southern women they burned? I do not need to remind *you*, Admiral, with your intimate knowledge of history, that Waite was the nephew of the woman burned in Charleston; that Granger was her cousin in the second degree, and that the woman they burned in Boston was the wife of John H. Morgan, and the still loved but divorced wife of Winthrop L. Willis. Now, Admiral, it is only fair that you should acknowledge that the first provocation came from the Southern preachers and that the Northern ones were justified in retaliating. In your arguments you never yet have shown the least disposition to withhold a just verdict or be in anywise unfair, when authoritative history condemned your position, and therefore I have no hesitation in asking you to take the original blame from the Massachusetts ministers, in this matter, and transfer it to the South Carolina clergymen where it justly belongs."

The Admiral was conquered. This sweet-spoken creature who swallowed his fraudulent history as if it were the bread of life; basked in his furious blasphemy as if it were generous sunshine; found only calm, even-handed justice in his rampant partisanship; and flooded him with invented history so sugar-coated with flattery and deference that there was no rejecting it, was "too many" for him. He stammered some awkward, profane sentences about the —— —— —— —— Willis and Morgan business having escaped his memory, but that he "remembered it now," and then, under pretence of giving Fan some medicine for an imaginary cough, drew out of the battle and went away, a vanquished man. Then cheers and laughter went up, and Williams, the ship's benefactor was a hero. The news went about the vessel, champagne was ordered, an enthusiastic reception instituted in the smoking room, and everybody flocked thither to shake hands with the conqueror. The wheelsman said afterward, that the Admiral stood up behind the pilot-house and "ripped and cursed all to himself" till he loosened the smoke-stack guys and becalmed the mainsail.

The Admiral's power was broken. After that, if he began an argument, somebody would bring Williams, and the old man would grow weak and begin to quiet down at once. And as soon as he was done, Williams in his dulcet, insinuating way, would invent some history (referring for proof, to the old man's own excellent memory and to copies of "The Old Guard" known not to be in his possession) that would turn the tables completely and leave the Admiral all abroad and helpless. By and by he came to so dread Williams and his gilded tongue that he would stop talking when he saw him approach, and finally ceased to mention politics altogether, and from that time forward there was entire peace and serenity in the ship.

CHAPTER LXIII

ON A CERTAIN bright morning the Islands hove in sight, lying low on the lonely sea, and every body climbed to the upper deck to look. After two thousand miles of watery solitude the vision was a welcome one. As we approached, the imposing promontory of Diamond Head rose up out of the ocean, its rugged front softened by the hazy distance, and presently the details of the land began to make themselves manifest: first the line of beach; then the plumed cocoanut trees of the tropics; then cabins of the natives; then the white town of Honolulu, said to contain between twelve and fifteen thousand inhabitants spread over a dead level; with streets from twenty to thirty feet wide, solid and level as a floor, most of them straight as a line and few as crooked as a corkscrew.

The further I traveled through the town the better I liked it. Every step revealed a new contrast – disclosed something I was unaccustomed to. In place of the grand mud-colored brown fronts of San Francisco, I saw dwellings built of straw, adobies, and cream-colored pebble-and-shell-conglomerated coral, cut into oblong blocks and laid in cement; also a great number of neat white cottages, with green window-shutters; in place of front yards like billiard-tables with iron fences around them, I saw these homes surrounded by ample yards, thickly clad with green grass, and shaded by tall trees, through whose dense foliage the sun could scarcely penetrate; in place of the customary geranium, calla lily, etc., languishing in dust and general debility, I saw luxurious banks and thickets of flowers, fresh as a meadow after a rain, and glowing with the richest dyes; in place of the dingy horrors of San Francisco's pleasure grove, the "Willows," I saw huge-bodied, wide-spreading forest trees, with strange names and stranger appearance – trees that cast a shadow like a thunder-cloud, and were able to stand alone without being tied to green poles; in place of gold fish, wiggling around in glass globes, assuming countless shades and degrees of distortion through the magnifying and diminishing qualities of their transparent prison-houses, I saw cats – Tom-cats, Mary Ann cats, long-tailed cats, bob-tailed cats, blind cats, one-eyed cats, wall-eyed cats, cross-eyed cats, gray cats, black cats, white cats, yellow cats, striped cats, spotted cats, tame cats, wild cats, singed cats, individual cats, groups of cats, platoons of cats, companies of cats, regiments of cats, armies of cats, multitudes of cats, millions of cats, and all of them sleek, fat, lazy and sound asleep.

I looked on a multitude of people, some white, in white coats, vests, pantaloons, even white cloth shoes, made snowy with chalk duly laid on every morning; but the majority of the people were almost as dark as negroes – women with comely features, fine black eyes, rounded forms, inclining to the voluptuous, clad in a single bright red or white garment that fell free and unconfined from shoulder to heel, long black hair falling loose, gypsy hats, encircled with wreaths of natural flowers of a brilliant carmine tint; plenty of dark men in various costumes, and some with nothing on but a battered stove-pipe hat tilted on the nose, and a very scant breech-clout; – certain smoke-dried children were clothed in nothing but sunshine – a very neat fitting and picturesque apparel indeed.

In place of roughs and rowdies staring and blackguarding on the corners, I saw long-haired, saddle-colored Sandwich Island maidens sitting on the ground in the shade of corner houses, gazing indolently at whatever or whoever happened along; instead of wretched cobble-stone pavements, I walked on a firm foundation of coral, built up from the bottom of the sea by the absurd but persevering insect of that name, with a light layer of lava and cinders overlying the coral, belched up out of fathomless perdition long ago through the seared and blackened crater that stands dead and harmless in the distance now; instead of cramped and crowded street cars, I met dusky native women sweeping by, free as the wind, on fleet horses and astride, with gaudy riding-sashes, streaming like banners behind them; instead of the combined stenches of Chinadom and Brannan street slaughter-houses, I breathed the balmy fragrance of jessamine, oleander, and the Pride of India; in place of the hurry and bustle and noisy confusion of San Francisco,

I moved in the midst of a summer calm as tranquil as dawn in the Garden of Eden; in place of the Golden City's skirting sand hills and the placid bay, I saw on the one side a frame-work of tall, precipitous mountains close at hand, clad in refreshing green, and cleft by deep, cool, chasm-like valleys – and in front the grand sweep of the ocean: a brilliant, transparent green near the shore, bound and bordered by a long white line of foamy spray dashing against the reef, and further out the dead blue water of the deep sea, flecked with "white caps," and in the far horizon a single, lonely sail – a mere accent-mark to emphasize a slumberous calm and a solitude that were without sound or limit. When the sun sunk down – the one intruder from other realms and persistent in suggestions of them – it was tranced luxury to sit in the perfumed air and forget that there was any world but these enchanted islands.

It was such ecstasy to dream, and dream – till you got a bite. A scorpion bite. Then the first duty was to get up out of the grass and kill the scorpion; and the next to bathe the bitten place with alcohol or brandy; and the next to resolve to keep out of the grass in future. Then came an adjournment to the bed-chamber and the pastime of writing up the day's journal with one hand and the destruction of mosquitoes with the other – a whole community of them at a slap. Then, observing an enemy approaching, – a hairy tarantula on stilts – why not set the spittoon on him? It is done, and the projecting ends of his paws give a luminous idea of the magnitude of his reach. Then to bed and become a promenade for a centipede with forty-two legs on a side and every foot hot enough to burn a hole through a raw-hide. More soaking with alcohol, and a resolution to examine the bed before entering it, in future. Then wait, and suffer, till all the mosquitoes in the neighborhood have crawled in under the bar, then slip out quickly, shut them in and sleep peacefully on the floor till morning. Meantime it is comforting to curse the tropics in occasional wakeful intervals.

We had an abundance of fruit in Honolulu, of course. Oranges, pine-apples, bananas, strawberries, lemons, limes, mangoes, guavas, melons, and a rare and curious luxury called the chirimoya, which is deliciousness itself. Then there is the tamarind. I thought tamarinds were made to eat, but that was probably not the idea. I ate several, and it seemed to me that they were rather sour that year. They pursed up my lips, till they resembled the stem-end of a tomato, and I had to take my sustenance through a quill for twenty-four hours. They sharpened my teeth till I could have shaved with them, and gave them a "wire edge" that I was afraid would stay; but a citizen said "no, it will come off when the enamel does" – which was comforting, at any rate. I found, afterward, that only strangers eat tamarinds – but they only eat them once.

CHAPTER LXIV

IN MY DIARY of our third day in Honolulu, I find this: I am probably the most sensitive man in Hawaii tonight – especially about sitting down in the presence of my betters. I have ridden fifteen or twenty miles on horse-back since 5 P.M. and to tell the honest truth, I have a delicacy about sitting down at all.

An excursion to Diamond Head and the King's Cocoanut Grove was planned to-day – time, 4:30 P.M. – the party to consist of half a dozen gentlemen and three ladies. They all started at the appointed hour except myself. I was at the Government prison, (with Captain Fish and another whale ship skipper, Captain Phillips,) and got so interested in its examination that I did not notice how quickly the time was passing. Somebody remarked that it was twenty minutes past five o'clock, and that woke me up. It was a fortunate circumstance that Captain Phillips was along with his "turn-out," as he calls a top-buggy that Captain Cook brought here in 1778, and a horse that was here when Captain Cook came. Captain Phillips takes a just pride in his driving and in the speed of his horse, and to his passion for displaying them I owe it that we were only sixteen minutes coming from the prison to the American Hotel – a distance which has been estimated to be over half a mile. But it took some fearful driving. The Captain's whip came down fast, and the blows started so much dust out of the horse's hide that during the last half of the journey we rode through an impenetrable fog, and ran by a pocket compass in the hands of Captain Fish, a whaler of twenty-six years experience, who sat there through the perilous voyage as self-possessed as if he had been on the euchre-deck of his own ship, and calmly said, "Port your helm – port," from time to time, and "Hold her a little free – steady – so-o," and "Luff – hard down to starboard!" and never once lost his presence of mind or betrayed the least anxiety by voice or manner. When we came to anchor at last, and Captain Phillips looked at his watch and said, "Sixteen minutes – I told you it was in her! that's over three miles an hour!" I could see he felt entitled to a compliment, and so I said I had never seen lightning go like that horse. And I never had.

The landlord of the American said the party had been gone nearly an hour, but that he could give me my choice of several horses that could overtake them. I said, never mind – I preferred a safe horse to a fast one – I would like to have an excessively gentle horse – a horse with no spirit whatever – a lame one, if he had such a thing. Inside of five minutes I was mounted, and perfectly satisfied with my outfit. I had no time to label him "This is a horse," and so if the public took him for a sheep I cannot help it. I was satisfied, and that was the main thing. I could see that he had as many fine points as any man's horse, and so I hung my hat on one of them, behind the saddle, and swabbed the perspiration from my face and started. I named him after this island, "Oahu" (pronounced O-waw-hee). The first gate he came to he started in; I had neither whip nor spur, and so I simply argued the case with him. He resisted argument, but ultimately yielded to insult and abuse. He backed out of that gate and steered for another one on the other side of the street. I triumphed by my former process. Within the next six hundred yards he crossed the street fourteen times and attempted thirteen gates, and in the meantime the tropical sun was beating down and threatening to cave the top of my head in, and I was literally dripping with perspiration. He abandoned the gate business after that and went along peaceably enough, but absorbed in meditation. I noticed this latter circumstance, and it soon began to fill me with apprehension. I said to myself, this creature is planning some new outrage, some fresh deviltry or other – no horse ever thought over a subject so profoundly as this one is doing just for nothing. The more this thing preyed upon my mind the more uneasy I became, until the suspense became almost unbearable and I dismounted to see if there was anything wild in his eye – for I had heard that the eye of this noblest of our domestic animals is very expressive. I cannot describe what a load of anxiety was lifted from my mind when I found that he was only asleep. I woke him up and started him into a faster walk, and then the villainy of his nature came out again. He tried to climb over a stone wall, five or six feet high. I saw that I must apply force to this horse, and that I might as well begin first as last. I plucked a stout switch from a tamarind tree, and the moment he saw it, he surrendered. He broke into a convulsive sort of a canter, which had three short steps in it and one long one, and reminded me alternately of the clattering shake of the great earthquake, and the sweeping plunging of the Ajax in a storm.

And now there can be no fitter occasion than the present to pronounce a left-handed blessing upon the man who invented the American saddle. There is no seat to speak of about it – one might as well sit in a shovel – and the stirrups are nothing but an ornamental nuisance. If I were to write down here all the abuse I expended on those stirrups, it would make a large book, even without pictures. Sometimes I got one foot so far through, that the stirrup partook of the nature of an anklet; sometimes both feet were through, and I was handcuffed by the legs; and sometimes my feet got clear out and left the stirrups wildly dangling about my shins. Even when I was in proper position and carefully balanced upon the balls of my feet, there was no comfort in it, on account of my nervous dread that they were going to slip one way or the other in a moment. But the subject is too exasperating to write about.

A mile and a half from town, I came to a grove of tall cocoanut trees, with clean, branchless stems reaching straight up sixty or seventy feet and topped with a spray of green foliage sheltering clusters of cocoanuts – not more picturesque than a forest of colossal ragged parasols, with bunches of magnified grapes under them, would be. I once heard a grouty northern invalid say that a cocoanut tree might be poetical, possibly it was; but it looked like a feather-duster struck by lightning. I think that describes it better than a picture – and yet, without any question, there is something fascinating about a cocoanut tree – and graceful, too.

About a dozen cottages, some frame and the others of native grass, nestled sleepily in the shade here and there. The grass cabins are of a grayish color, are shaped much like our own cottages, only with higher and steeper roofs usually, and are made of some kind of weed strongly bound together in bundles. The roofs are very thick, and so are the walls; the latter have square holes in them for windows. At a little distance these cabins have a furry appearance, as if they might be made of bear skins. They are very cool and pleasant inside. The King's flag was flying from the roof of one of the cottages, and His Majesty was probably within. He owns the whole concern thereabouts, and passes his time there frequently, on sultry days "laying off." The spot is called "The King's Grove."

Near by is an interesting ruin – the meagre remains of an ancient heathen temple – a place where human sacrifices were offered up in those old bygone days when the simple child of nature, yielding momentarily to sin when sorely tempted, acknowledged his error when calm reflection had shown it to him, and came forward with noble frankness and offered up his grandmother as an atoning sacrifice – in those old days when the luckless sinner could keep on cleansing his conscience and achieving periodical happiness as long as his relations held out; long, long before the missionaries braved a thousand privations to come and make them permanently miserable by telling them how beautiful and how blissful a place heaven is, and how nearly impossible it is to get there; and showed the poor native how dreary a place perdition is and what unnecessarily liberal facilities there are for going to it; showed him how, in his ignorance he had gone and fooled away all his kinfolks to no purpose; showed him what rapture it is to work all day long for fifty cents to buy food for next day with, as compared with fishing for pastime and lolling in the shade through eternal summer, and eating of the bounty that nobody labored to provide but Nature. How sad it is to think of the multitudes who have gone to their graves in this beautiful island and never knew there was a hell!

This ancient temple was built of rough blocks of lava, and was simply a roofless inclosure a hundred and thirty feet long and seventy wide – nothing but naked walls, very thick, but not much higher than a man's head. They will last for ages no doubt, if left unmolested. Its three altars and other sacred appurtenances have crumbled and passed away years ago. It is said that in the old times thousands of human beings were slaughtered here, in the presence of naked and howling savages. If these mute stones could speak, what tales they could tell, what pictures they could describe, of fettered victims writhing under the knife; of massed forms straining forward out of the gloom, with ferocious faces lit up by the sacrificial fires; of the background of ghostly trees; of the dark pyramid of Diamond Head standing sentinel over the uncanny scene, and the peaceful moon looking down upon it through rifts in the cloud-rack!

When Kamehameha (pronounced Ka-may-ha-may-ah) the Great – who was a sort of a Napoleon in military genius and uniform success – invaded this island of Oahu three-quarters of a century ago, and exterminated the army sent to oppose him, and took full and final possession of the country, he searched out the dead body of the King of Oahu, and those of the principal chiefs, and impaled their heads on the walls of this temple.

Those were savage times when this old slaughter-house was in its prime. The King and the chiefs ruled the common herd with a rod of iron; made them gather all the provisions the masters needed; build all the houses and temples; stand all the expenses, of whatever kind; take kicks and cuffs for thanks; drag out lives well flavored with misery, and then suffer death for trifling offenses or yield up their lives on the sacrificial altars to purchase favors from the gods for their hard rulers. The missionaries have clothed them, educated them, broken up the tyrannous authority of their chiefs, and given them freedom and the right to enjoy whatever their hands and brains produce with equal laws for all, and punishment for all alike who transgress them. The contrast is so strong – the benefit conferred upon this people by the missionaries is so prominent, so palpable and so unquestionable, that the frankest compliment I can pay them, and the best, is simply to point to the condition of the Sandwich Islanders of Captain Cook's time, and their condition to-day. Their work speaks for itself.

CHAPTER LXV

BY AND BY, after a rugged climb, we halted on the summit of a hill which commanded a far-reaching view. The moon rose and flooded mountain and valley and ocean with a mellow radiance, and out of the shadows of the foliage the distant lights of Honolulu glinted like an encampment of fire-flies. The air was heavy with the fragrance of flowers. The halt was brief. – Gayly laughing and talking, the party galloped on, and I clung to the pommel and cantered after. Presently we came to a place where no grass grew – a wide expanse of deep sand. They said it was an old battle-ground. All around every where, not three feet apart, the bleached bones of men gleamed white in the moonlight. We picked up a lot of them for mementoes. I got quite a number of arm bones and leg bones – of great chiefs, may be, who had fought savagely in that fearful battle in the old days, when blood flowed like wine where we now stood – and wore the choicest of them out on Oahu afterward, trying to make him go. All sorts of bones could be found except skulls; but a citizen said, irreverently, that there had been an unusual number of "skull-hunters" there lately – a species of sportsmen I had never heard of before.

Nothing whatever is known about this place – its story is a secret that will never be revealed. The oldest natives make no pretense of being possessed of its history. They say these bones were here when they were children. They were here when their grandfathers were children – but how they came here, they can only conjecture. Many people believe this spot to be an ancient battle-ground, and it is usual to call it so; and they believe that these skeletons have lain for ages just where their proprietors fell in the great fight. Other people believe that Kamehameha I. fought his first battle here. On this point, I have heard a story, which may have been taken from one of the numerous books which have been written concerning these islands – I do not know where the narrator got it. He said that when Kamehameha (who was at first merely a subordinate chief on the island of Hawaii), landed here, he brought a large army with him, and encamped at Waikiki. The Oahuans marched against him, and so confident were they of success that they readily acceded to a demand of their priests that they should draw a line where these bones now lie, and take an oath that, if forced to retreat at all, they would never retreat beyond this boundary. The priests told them that death and everlasting punishment would overtake any who violated the oath, and the march was resumed. Kamehameha drove them back step by step; the priests fought in the front rank and exhorted them both by voice and inspiriting example to remember their oath – to die, if need be, but never cross the fatal line. The struggle was manfully maintained, but at last the chief priest fell, pierced to the heart with a spear, and the unlucky omen fell like a blight upon the brave souls at his back, with a triumphant shout the invaders pressed forward – the line was crossed – the offended gods deserted the despairing army, and, accepting the doom their perjury had brought upon them, they broke and fled over the plain where Honolulu stands now – up the beautiful Nuuanu Valley – paused a moment, hemmed in by precipitous mountains on either hand and the frightful precipice of the Pari in front, and then were driven over – a sheer plunge of six hundred feet!

The story is pretty enough, but Mr. Jarves' excellent history says the Oahuans were intrenched in Nuuanu Valley; that Kamehameha ousted them, routed them, pursued them up the valley and drove them over the precipice. He makes no mention of our bone-yard at all in his book.

Impressed by the profound silence and repose that rested over the beautiful landscape, and being, as usual, in the rear, I gave voice to my thoughts. I said:

"What a picture is here slumbering in the solemn glory of the moon! How strong the rugged outlines of the dead volcano stand out against the clear sky! What a snowy fringe marks the bursting of the surf over the long, curved reef! How calmly the dim city sleeps yonder in the plain! How soft the shadows lie upon the stately mountains that border the dream-haunted Mauoa Valley! What a grand pyramid of billowy clouds towers above the storied Pari! How the grim warriors of the past seem flocking in ghostly squadrons to their ancient battle-field again – how the wails of the dying well up from the—"

At this point the horse called Oahu sat down in the sand. Sat down to listen, I suppose. Never mind what he heard, I stopped apostrophizing and convinced him that I was not a man to allow contempt of court on the part of a horse. I broke the back-bone of a Chief over his rump and set out to join the cavalcade again.

Very considerably fagged out we arrived in town at 9 o'clock at night, myself in the lead – for when my horse finally came to understand that he was homeward bound and hadn't far to go, he turned his attention strictly to business.

This is a good time to drop in a paragraph of information. There is no regular livery-stable in Honolulu, or, indeed, in any part of the kingdom of Hawaii; therefore unless you are acquainted with wealthy residents (who all have good horses), you must hire animals of the wretchedest description from the Kanakas. (*i.e.* natives.) Any horse you hire, even though it be from a white man, is not often of much account, because it will be brought in for you from some ranch, and has necessarily been leading a hard life. If the Kanakas who have been caring for him (inveterate riders they are) have not ridden him half to death every day themselves, you can depend upon it they have been doing the same thing by proxy, by clandestinely hiring him out. At least, so I am informed. The result is, that no horse has a chance to eat, drink, rest, recuperate, or look well or feel well, and so strangers go about the Islands mounted as I was today.

In hiring a horse from a Kanaka, you must have all your eyes about you, because you can rest satisfied that you are dealing with a shrewd unprincipled rascal. You may leave your door open and your trunk unlocked as long as you please, and he will not meddle with your property; he has no important vices and no inclination to commit robbery on a large scale; but if he can get ahead of you in the horse business, he will take a genuine delight in doing it. This trait is characteristic of horse-jockeys, the world over, is it not? He will overcharge you if he can; he will hire you a fine-looking horse at night (anybody's – may be the King's, if the royal steed be in convenient view), and bring you the mate to my Oahu in the morning, and contend that it is the same animal. If you make trouble, he will get out by saying it was not himself who made the bargain with you, but his brother, "who went out in the country this morning." They have always got a "brother" to shift the responsibility upon. A victim said to one of these fellows one day:

"But I know I hired the horse of you, because I noticed that scar on your cheek."

The reply was not bad: "Oh, yes – yes – my brother all same – we twins!"

A friend of mine, J. Smith, hired a horse yesterday, the Kanaka warranting him to be in excellent condition. Smith had a saddle and blanket of his own, and he ordered the Kanaka to put these on the horse. The Kanaka protested that he was perfectly willing to trust the gentleman with the saddle that was already on the animal, but Smith refused to use it. The change was made; then Smith noticed that the Kanaka had only changed the saddles, and had left the original blanket on the horse; he said he forgot to change the blankets, and so, to cut the bother short, Smith mounted and rode away. The horse went lame a mile from town, and afterward got to cutting up some extraordinary capers. Smith got down and took off the saddle, but the blanket stuck fast to the horse – glued to a procession of raw places. The Kanaka's mysterious conduct stood explained.

Another friend of mine bought a pretty good horse from a native, a day or two ago, after a tolerably thorough examination of the animal. He discovered to-day that the horse was as blind as a bat, in one eye. He meant to have examined that eye, and came home with a general notion that he had done it; but he remembers now that every time he made the attempt his attention was called to something else by his victimizer.

One more instance, and then I will pass to something else. I am informed that when a certain Mr. L., a visiting stranger, was here, he bought a pair of very respectable-looking match horses from a native. They were in a stable with a partition through the middle of it – one horse in each apartment. Mr. L. examined one of them critically through a window (the Kanaka's "brother" having gone to the country with the key), and then went around the house and examined the other through a window on the other side. He said it was the neatest match he had ever seen, and paid for the horses on the spot. Whereupon the Kanaka departed to join his brother in the country. The fellow had shamefully swindled L. There was only one "match" horse, and he had examined his starboard side through one window and his port side through another! I decline to believe this story, but I give it because it is worth something as a fanciful illustration of a fixed fact – namely, that the Kanaka horse-jockey is fertile in invention and elastic in conscience.

You can buy a pretty good horse for forty or fifty dollars, and a good enough horse for all practical purposes for two dollars and a half. I estimate "Oahu" to be worth somewhere in the neighborhood of thirty-five cents. A good deal better animal than he is was sold here day before yesterday for a dollar and seventy-five cents, and sold again to-day for two dollars and twenty-five cents; Williams bought a handsome and lively little pony yesterday for ten dollars; and about the best common horse on the island (and he is a really good one) sold yesterday, with Mexican saddle and bridle, for seventy dollars – a horse which is well and widely known, and greatly respected for his speed, good disposition and everlasting bottom. You give your horse a little grain once a day; it comes from San Francisco, and is worth about two cents a pound; and you give him as much hay as he wants; it is cut and brought to the market by natives, and is not very good; it is baled into long, round bundles, about the size of a large man; one of them is stuck by the middle on each end of a six-foot pole, and the Kanaka shoulders the pole and walks about the streets between the upright bales in search of customers. These hay bales, thus carried, have a general resemblance to a colossal capital H.

The hay-bundles cost twenty-five cents apiece, and one will last a horse about a day. You can get a horse for a song, a week's hay for another song, and you can turn your animal loose among the luxuriant grass in your neighbor's broad front yard without a song at all – you do it at midnight, and stable the beast again before morning. You have been at no expense thus far, but when you come to buy a saddle and bridle they will cost you from twenty to thirty-five dollars. You can hire a horse, saddle and bridle at from seven to ten dollars a week, and the owner will take care of them at his own expense.

It is time to close this day's record – bed time. As I prepare for sleep, a rich voice rises out of the still night, and, far as this ocean rock is toward the ends of the earth, I recognize a familiar home air. But the words seem somewhat out of joint:

"Waikiki lantoni œ Kaa hooly hooly wawhoo."

Translated, that means, "When we were marching through Georgia."

CHAPTER XLVI

PASSING THROUGH THE marketplace we saw that feature of Honolulu under its most favorable auspices – that is, in the full glory of Saturday afternoon, which is a festive day with the natives. The native girls by twos and threes and parties of a dozen, and sometimes in whole platoons and companies, went cantering up and down the neighboring streets astride of fleet but homely horses, and with their gaudy riding habits streaming like banners behind them. Such a troop of free and easy riders, in their natural home, the saddle, makes a gay and graceful spectacle. The riding habit I speak of is simply a long, broad scarf, like a tavern table-cloth brilliantly colored, wrapped around the loins once, then apparently passed between the limbs and each end thrown backward over the same, and floating and flapping behind on both sides beyond the horse's tail like a couple of fancy flags; then, slipping the stirrup-irons between her toes, the girl throws her chest forward, sits up like a Major General and goes sweeping by like the wind.

The girls put on all the finery they can on Saturday afternoon – fine black silk robes; flowing red ones that nearly put your eyes out; others as white as snow; still others that discount the rainbow; and they wear their hair in nets, and trim their jaunty hats with fresh flowers, and encircle their dusky throats with home-made necklaces of the brilliant vermillion-tinted blossom of the *ohia;* and they fill the markets and the adjacent streets with their bright presences, and smell like a rag factory on fire with their offensive cocoanut oil.

Occasionally you see a heathen from the sunny isles away down in the South Seas, with his face and neck tattooed till he looks like the customary mendicant from Washoe who has been blown up in a mine. Some are tattooed a dead blue color down to the upper lip – masked, as it were – leaving the natural light yellow skin of Micronesia unstained from thence down; some with broad marks drawn down from hair to neck, on both sides of the face and a strip of the original yellow skin, two inches wide, down the centre – a gridiron with a spoke broken out; and some with the entire face discolored with the popular mortification tint, relieved only by one or two thin, wavy threads of natural yellow running across the face from ear to ear, and eyes twinkling out of this darkness, from under shadowing hat-brims, like stars in the dark of the moon.

Moving among the stirring crowds, you come to the poi merchants, squatting in the shade on their hams, in true native fashion, and surrounded by purchasers. (The Sandwich Islanders always squat on their hams, and who knows but they may be the old original "ham sandwiches?" The thought is pregnant with interest.) The poi looks like common flour paste, and is kept in large bowls formed of a species of gourd, and capable of holding from one to three or four gallons. Poi is the chief article of food among the natives, and is prepared from the *taro* plant. The taro root looks like a thick, or, if you please, a corpulent sweet potato, in shape, but is of a light purple color when boiled. When boiled it answers as a passable substitute for bread. The buck Kanakas bake it under ground, then mash it up well with a heavy lava pestle, mix water with it until it becomes a paste, set it aside and let it ferment, and then it is poi – and an unseductive mixture it is, almost tasteless before it ferments and too sour for a luxury afterward. But nothing is more nutritious. When solely used, however, it produces acrid humors, a fact which sufficiently accounts for the humorous character of the Kanakas. I think there must be as much of a knack in handling poi as there is in eating with chop-sticks. The forefinger is thrust into the mess and stirred quickly round several times and drawn as quickly out, thickly coated, just as if it were poulticed; the head is thrown back, the finger inserted in the mouth and the delicacy stripped off and swallowed – the eye closing gently, meanwhile, in a languid sort of ecstasy. Many a different finger goes into the same bowl and many a different kind of dirt and shade and quality of flavor is added to the virtues of its contents.

Around a small shanty was collected a crowd of natives buying the *awa* root. It is said that but for the use of this root the destruction of the people in former times by certain imported diseases would have been far greater than it was, and by others it is said that this is merely a fancy. All agree that poi will rejuvenate a man who is used up and his vitality almost annihilated by hard drinking, and that in some kinds of diseases it will restore health after all medicines have failed; but all are not willing to allow to the *awa* the virtues claimed for it. The natives manufacture an intoxicating drink from it which is fearful in its effects when persistently indulged in. It covers the body with dry, white scales, inflames the eyes, and causes premature decrepitude. Although the man before whose establishment we stopped has to pay a Government license of eight hundred dollars a year for the exclusive right to sell *awa* root, it is said that he makes a small fortune every twelve-month; while saloon-keepers, who pay a thousand dollars a year for the privilege of retailing whiskey, etc., only make a bare living.

We found the fish market crowded; for the native is very fond of fish, and *eats the article raw and alive!* Let us change the subject.

In old times here Saturday was a grand gala day indeed. All the native population of the town forsook their labors, and those of the surrounding country journeyed to the city. Then the white folks had to stay indoors, for every street was so packed with charging cavaliers and cavalieresses that it was next to impossible to thread one's way through the cavalcades without getting crippled.

At night they feasted and the girls danced the lascivious *hula hula* – a dance that is said to exhibit the very perfection of educated motion of limb and arm, hand, head and body, and the exactest uniformity of movement and accuracy of "time." It was performed by a circle of girls with no raiment on them to speak of, who went through an infinite variety of motions and figures without prompting, and yet so true was their "time," and in such perfect concert did they move that when they were placed in a straight line, hands, arms, bodies, limbs and heads waved, swayed, gesticulated, bowed, stooped, whirled, squirmed, twisted and undulated as if they were part and parcel of a single individual; and it was difficult to believe they were not moved in a body by some exquisite piece of mechanism.

Of late years, however, Saturday has lost most of its quondam gala features. This weekly stampede of the natives interfered too much with labor and the interests of the white folks, and by sticking in a law here, and preaching a sermon there, and by various other means, they gradually broke it up. The demoralizing *hula hula* was forbidden to be performed, save at night, with closed doors, in presence of few spectators, and only by permission duly procured from the authorities and the payment of ten dollars for the same. There are few girls now-a-days able to dance this ancient national dance in the highest perfection of the art.

The missionaries have christianized and educated all the natives. They all belong to the Church, and there is not one of them, above the age of eight years, but can read and write with facility in the native tongue. It is the most universally educated race of people outside of China. They have any quantity of books, printed in the Kanaka language, and all the natives are fond of reading. They are inveterate church-goers – nothing can keep them away. All this ameliorating cultivation has at last built up in the native women a profound respect for chastity – in other people. Perhaps that is enough to say on that head. The national sin will die out when the race does, but perhaps not earlier. – But doubtless this purifying is not far off, when we reflect that contact with civilization and the whites has reduced the native population from *four hundred thousand* (Captain Cook's estimate,) to *fifty-five thousand* in something over eighty years!

Society is a queer medley in this notable missionary, whaling and governmental centre. If you get into conversation with a stranger and experience that natural desire to know what sort of ground you are treading on by finding out what manner of man your stranger is, strike out boldly and address him as "Captain." Watch him narrowly, and if you see by his countenance that you are on the wrong tack, ask him where he preaches. It is a safe bet that he is either a missionary or captain of a whaler. I am now personally acquainted with seventy-two captains and ninety-six missionaries. The captains and ministers form one-half of the population; the third fourth is composed of common Kanakas and mercantile foreigners and their families, and the final fourth is made up of high officers of the Hawaiian Government. And there are just about cats enough for three apiece all around.

A solemn stranger met me in the suburbs the other day, and said:

"Good-morning, your reverence. Preach in the stone church yonder, no doubt?"

"No, I don't. I'm not a preacher."

"Really, I beg your pardon, Captain. I trust you had a good season. How much oil—"

"Oil? What do you take me for? I'm not a whaler."

"Oh, I beg a thousand pardons, your Excellency. Major General in the household troops, no doubt? Minister of the Interior, likely? Secretary of War? First Gentleman of the Bed-chamber? Commissioner of the Royal—"

"Stuff! I'm no official. I'm not connected in any way with the Government."

"Bless my life! Then, who the mischief are you? what the mischief are you? and how the mischief did you get here, and where in thunder did you come from?"

"I'm only a private personage – an unassuming stranger – lately arrived from America."

"No? Not a missionary! Not a whaler! not a member of his Majesty's Government! not even Secretary of the Navy! Ah, Heaven! it is too blissful to be true; alas, I do but dream. And yet that noble, honest countenance – those oblique, ingenuous eyes – that massive head, incapable of – of – anything; your hand; give me your hand, bright waif. Excuse these tears. For sixteen weary years I have yearned for a moment like this, and—"

Here his feelings were too much for him, and he swooned away. I pitied this poor creature from the bottom of my heart. I was deeply moved. I shed a few tears on him and kissed him for his mother. I then took what small change he had and "shoved."

CHAPTER LXVII

I STILL QUOTE from my journal:

I found the national Legislature to consist of half a dozen white men and some thirty or forty natives. It was a dark assemblage. The nobles and Ministers (about a dozen of them altogether) occupied the extreme left of the hall, with David Kalakaua (the King's Chamberlain) and Prince William at the head. The President of the Assembly, His Royal Highness M. Kekuanaoa,* and the Vice President (the latter a white man,) sat in the pulpit, if I may so term it.

The President is the King's father. He is an erect, strongly built, massive-featured, white-haired, tawny old gentleman of eighty years of age or thereabouts. He was simply but well dressed, in a blue cloth coat and white vest, and white pantaloons, without spot, dust or blemish upon them. He bears himself with a calm, stately dignity, and is a man of noble presence. He was a young man and a distinguished warrior under that terrific fighter, Kamehameha I., more than half a century ago. A knowledge of his career suggested some such thought as this: "This man, naked as the day he was born, and war-club and spear in hand, has charged at the head of a horde of savages against other hordes of savages more than a generation and a half ago, and reveled in slaughter and carnage; has worshiped

*Since dead.

wooden images on his devout knees; has seen hundreds of his race offered up in heathen temples as sacrifices to wooden idols, at a time when no missionary's foot had ever pressed this soil, and he had never heard of the white man's God; has believed his enemy could secretly pray him to death; has seen the day, in his childhood, when it was a crime punishable by death for a man to eat with his wife, or for a plebeian to let his shadow fall upon the King – and now look at him; an educated Christian; neatly and handsomely dressed; a high-minded, elegant gentleman; a traveler, in some degree, and one who has been the honored guest of royalty in Europe; a man practiced in holding the reins of an enlightened government, and well versed in the politics of his country and in general, practical information. Look at him, sitting there presiding over the deliberations of a legislative body, among whom are white men – a grave, dignified, statesmanlike personage, and as seemingly natural and fitted to the place as if he had been born in it and had never been out of it in his life time. How the experiences of this old man's eventful life shame the cheap inventions of romance!"

Kekuanaoa is not of the blood royal. He derives his princely rank from his wife, who was a daughter of Kamehameha the Great. Under other monarchies the male line takes precedence of the female in tracing genealogies, but here the opposite is the case – the female line takes precedence. Their reason for this is exceedingly sensible, and I recommend it to the aristocracy of Europe: They say it is easy to know who a man's mother was, but, etc., etc.

The christianizing of the natives has hardly even weakened some of their barbarian superstitions, much less destroyed them. I have just referred to one of these. It is still a popular belief that if your enemy can get hold of any article belonging to you he can get down on his knees over it and *pray you to death.* Therefore many a native gives up and dies merely because he *imagines* that some enemy is putting him through a course of damaging prayer. This praying an individual to death seems absurd enough at a first glance, but then when we call to mind some of the pulpit efforts of certain of our own ministers the thing looks plausible.

In former times, among the Islanders, not only a plurality of wives was customary, but a *plurality of husbands* likewise. Some native women of noble rank had as many as six husbands. A woman thus supplied did not reside with all her husbands at once, but lived several months with each in turn. An understood sign hung at her door during these months. When the sign was taken down, it meant "NEXT."

In those days woman was rigidly taught to "know her place." Her place was to do all the work, take all the cuffs, provide all the food, and content herself with what was left after her lord had finished his dinner. She was not only forbidden, by ancient law, and under penalty of death, to eat with her husband or enter a canoe, but was debarred, under the same penalty, from eating bananas, pine-apples, oranges and other choice fruits at any time or in any place. She had to confine herself pretty strictly to "poi" and hard work. These poor ignorant heathen seem to have had a sort of groping idea of what came of women eating fruit in the garden of Eden, and they did not choose to take any more chances. But the missionaries broke up this satisfactory arrangement of things. They liberated woman and made her the equal of man.

The natives had a romantic fashion of burying some of their children alive when the family became larger than necessary. The missionaries interfered in this matter too, and stopped it.

To this day the natives are able to *lie down and die whenever they want to*, whether there is any thing the matter with them or not. If a Kanaka takes a notion to die, that is the end of him; nobody can persuade him to hold on; all the doctors in the world could not save him.

A luxury which they enjoy more than any thing else, is a large funeral. If a person wants to get rid of a troublesome native, it is only necessary to promise him a fine funeral and name the hour and he will be on hand to the minute – at least his remains will.

All the natives are Christians, now, but many of them still desert to the Great Shark God for temporary succor in time of trouble. An irruption of the great volcano of Kilauea, or an earthquake, always brings a deal of latent loyalty to the Great Shark God to the surface. It is common report that the King, educated, cultivated and refined Christian gentleman as he undoubtedly is, still turns to the idols of his fathers for help when disaster threatens. A planter caught a shark, and one of his christianized natives testified his emancipation from the thrall of ancient superstition by assisting to dissect the shark after a fashion forbidden by his abandoned creed. But remorse shortly began to torture him. He grew moody and sought solitude; brooded over his sin, refused food, and finally said he must die and ought to die, for he had sinned against the Great Shark God and could never know peace any more. He was proof against persuasion and ridicule, and in the course of a day or two took to his bed and died, although he showed no symptom of disease. His young daughter followed his lead and suffered a like fate within the week. Superstition is ingrained in the native blood and bone and it is only natural that it should crop out in time of distress. Wherever one goes in the Islands, he will find small piles of stones by the wayside, covered with leafy offerings, placed there by the natives to appease evil spirits or honor local deities belonging to the mythology of former days.

In the rural districts of any of the Islands, the traveler hourly comes upon parties of dusky maidens bathing in the streams or in the sea without any clothing on and exhibiting no very intemperate zeal in the matter of hiding their nakedness. When the missionaries first took up their residence in Honolulu, the native women would pay their families frequent friendly visits, day by day, not even clothed with a blush. It was found a hard matter to convince them that this was rather indelicate. Finally the missionaries provided them with long, loose calico robes, and that ended the difficulty – for the women would troop through the town, stark naked, with their robes folded under their arms, march to the missionary houses and then proceed to dress! – The natives soon manifested a strong proclivity for clothing, but it was shortly apparent that they only wanted it for grandeur. The missionaries imported a quantity of hats, bonnets, and other male and female wearing apparel, instituted a general distribution, and begged the people not to come to church naked, next Sunday, as usual. And they did not; but the national spirit of unselfishness led them to divide up with neighbors who were not at the distribution, and next Sabbath the poor preachers could hardly keep countenance before their vast congregations. In the midst of the reading of a hymn a brown, stately dame would sweep up the aisle with a world of airs, with nothing in the world on but a "stove-pipe" hat and a pair of cheap gloves; another dame would follow, tricked out in a man's shirt, and nothing else; another one would enter with a flourish, with simply the sleeves of a bright calico dress tied around her waist and the rest of the garment dragging behind like a peacock's tail off duty; a stately "buck" Kanaka would stalk in with a woman's bonnet on, wrong side before – only this, and nothing more; after him would stride his fellow, with the legs of a pair of pantaloons tied around his neck, the rest of his person untrammeled; in his rear would come another gentleman simply gotten up in a fiery neck-tie and a striped vest. The poor creatures were beaming with complacency and wholly unconscious of any absurdity in their appearance. They gazed at each other with happy admiration, and it was plain to see that the young girls were taking note of what each other had on, as naturally as if they had always lived in a land of Bibles and knew what churches were made for; here was the evidence of a dawning civilization. The spectacle which the congregation presented was so extraordinary and withal so moving, that the missionaries found it difficult to keep to the text and go on with the services; and by and by when the simple children of the sun began a general swapping of garments in open meeting and produced some irresistibly grotesque effects in the course of re-dressing, there was nothing for it but to cut the thing short with the benediction and dismiss the fantastic assemblage.

In our country, children play "keep house;" and in the same high-sounding but miniature way the grown folk here, with the poor little material of slender territory and meagre population, play "empire." There is his royal Majesty the King, with a New York detective's income of thirty or thirty-five thousand dollars a year from the "royal civil list" and the "royal domain." He lives in a two-story frame "palace."

And there is the "royal family" – the customary hive of royal brothers, sisters, cousins and other noble drones and vagrants usual to monarchy, – all with a spoon in the national pap-dish, and all bearing such titles as His or Her Royal Highness the Prince or Princess So-and-so. Few of them can carry their royal splendors far enough to ride in carriages, however; they sport the economical Kanaka horse or "hoof it"* with the plebeians.

Then there is his Excellency the "royal Chamberlain" – a sinecure, for His Majesty dresses himself with his own hands, except when he is ruralizing at Waikiki and then he requires no dressing.

Next we have his Excellency the Commander-in-chief of the Household Troops, whose forces consist of about the number of soldiers usually placed under a corporal in other lands.

Next comes the royal Steward and the Grand Equerry in Waiting – high dignitaries with modest salaries and little to do.

Then we have his Excellency the First Gentleman of the Bedchamber – an office as easy as it is magnificent.

Next we come to his Excellency the Prime Minister, a renegade American from New Hampshire, all jaw, vanity, bombast and ignorance, a lawyer of "shyster" calibre, a fraud by nature, a humble worshiper of the sceptre above him, a reptile never tired of

*Missionary phrase.

sneering at the land of his birth or glorifying the ten-acre kingdom that has adopted him – salary, $4,000 a year, vast consequence, and no perquisites.

Then we have his Excellency the Imperial Minister of Finance, who handles a million dollars of public money a year, sends in his annual "budget" with great ceremony, talks prodigiously of "finance," suggests imposing schemes for paying off the "national debt" (of $150,000,) and does it all for $4,000 a year and unimaginable glory.

Next we have his Excellency the Minister of War, who holds sway over the royal armies – they consist of two hundred and thirty uniformed Kanakas, mostly Brigadier Generals, and if the country ever gets into trouble with a foreign power we shall probably hear from them. I knew an American whose copper-plate visiting card bore this impressive legend: "Lieutenant-Colonel in the Royal Infantry." To say that he was proud of this distinction is stating it but tamely. The Minister of War has also in his charge some venerable swivels on Punch-Bowl Hill wherewith royal salutes are fired when foreign vessels of war enter the port.

Next comes his Excellency the Minister of the Navy – a nabob who rules the "royal fleet," (a steam-tug and a sixty-ton schooner.)

And next comes his Grace the Lord Bishop of Honolulu, the chief dignitary of the "Established Church" – for when the American Presbyterian missionaries had completed the reduction of the nation to a compact condition of Christianity, native royalty stepped in and erected the grand dignity of an "Established (Episcopal) Church" over it, and imported a cheap ready-made Bishop from England to take charge. The chagrin of the missionaries has never been comprehensively expressed, to this day, profanity not being admissible.

Next comes his Excellency the Minister of Public Instruction.

Next, their Excellencies the Governors of Oahu, Hawaii, etc., and after them a string of High Sheriffs and other small fry too numerous for computation.

Then there are their Excellencies the Envoy Extraordinary and Minister Plenipotentiary of his Imperial Majesty the Emperor of the French; her British Majesty's Minister; the Minister Resident, of the United States; and some six or eight representatives of other foreign nations, all with sounding titles, imposing dignity and prodigious but economical state.

Imagine all this grandeur in a play-house "kingdom" whose population falls absolutely short of sixty thousand souls!

The people are so accustomed to nine-jointed titles and colossal magnates that a foreign prince makes very little more stir in Honolulu than a Western Congressman does in New York.

And let it be borne in mind that there is a strictly defined "court costume" of so "stunning" a nature that it would make the clown in a circus look tame and commonplace by comparison; and each Hawaiian official dignitary has a gorgeous vari-colored, gold-laced uniform peculiar to his office – no two of them are alike, and it is hard to tell which one is the "loudest." The King has a "drawing-room" at stated intervals, like other monarchs, and when these varied uniforms congregate there weak-eyed people have to contemplate the spectacle through smoked glass. Is there not a gratifying contrast between this latter-day exhibition and the one the ancestors of some of these magnates afforded the missionaries the Sunday after the old-time distribution of clothing? Behold what religion and civilization have wrought!

CHAPTER LXIX

BOUND FOR HAWAII (a hundred and fifty miles distant,) to visit the great volcano and behold the other notable things which distinguish that island above the remainder of the group, we sailed from Honolulu on a certain Saturday afternoon, in the good schooner Boomerang.

The Boomerang was about as long as two street cars, and about as wide as one. She was so small (though she was larger than the majority of the inter-island coasters) that when I stood on her deck I felt but little smaller than the Colossus of Rhodes must have felt when he had a man-of-war under him. I could reach the water when she lay over under a strong breeze. When the Captain and my comrade (a Mr. Billings), myself and four other persons were all assembled on the little after portion of the deck which is sacred to the cabin passengers, it was full – there was not room for any more quality folks. Another section of the deck, twice as large as ours, was full of natives of both sexes, with their customary dogs, mats, blankets, pipes, calabashes of poi, fleas, and other luxuries and baggage of minor importance. As soon as we set sail the natives all lay down on the deck as thick as negroes in a slave-pen, and smoked, conversed, and spit on each other, and were truly sociable.

The little low-ceiled cabin below was rather larger than a hearse, and as dark as a vault. It had two coffins on each side – I mean two bunks. A small table, capable of accommodating three persons at dinner, stood against the forward bulkhead, and over it hung the dingiest whale-oil lantern that ever peopled the obscurity of a dungeon with ghostly shapes. The floor room unoccupied was not extensive. One might swing a cat in it, perhaps, but not a long cat. The hold forward of the bulkhead had but little freight in it, and from morning till night a portly old rooster, with a voice like Baalam's ass, and the same disposition to use it, strutted up and down in that part of the vessel and crowed. He usually took dinner at six o'clock, and then, after an hour devoted to meditation, he mounted a barrel and crowed a good part of the night. He got hoarser and hoarser all the time, but he scorned to allow any personal consideration to interfere with his duty, and kept up his labors in defiance of threatened diphtheria.

Sleeping was out of the question when he was on watch. He was a source of genuine aggravation and annoyance. It was worse than useless to shout at him or apply offensive epithets to him – he only took these things for applause, and strained himself to make more noise. Occasionally, during the day, I threw potatoes at him through an aperture in the bulkhead, but he only dodged and went on crowing.

The first night, as I lay in my coffin, idly watching the dim lamp swinging to the rolling of the ship, and snuffing the nauseous odors of bilgewater, I felt something gallop over me. I turned out promptly. However, I turned in again when I found it was only a rat. Presently something galloped over me once more. I knew it was not a rat this time, and I thought it might be a centipede, because the Captain had killed one on deck in the afternoon. I turned out. The first glance at the pillow showed me a repulsive sentinel perched upon each end of it – cockroaches as large as peach leaves – fellows with long, quivering antennæ and fiery, malignant eyes. They were grating their teeth like tobacco worms, and appeared to be dissatisfied about something. I had often heard that these reptiles were in the habit of eating off sleeping sailors' toe-nails down to the quick, and I would not get in the bunk anymore. I lay down on the floor. But a rat came and bothered me, and shortly afterward a procession of cockroaches arrived and camped in my hair. In a few moments the rooster was crowing with uncommon spirit and a party of fleas were throwing double somersaults about my person in the wildest disorder, and taking a bite every time they struck. I was beginning to feel really annoyed. I got up and put my clothes on and went on deck.

The above is not overdrawn; it is a truthful sketch of inter-island schooner life. There is no such thing as keeping a vessel in elegant condition, when she carried molasses and Kanakas.

It was compensation for my sufferings to come unexpectedly upon so beautiful a scene as met my eye – to step suddenly out of the sepulchral gloom of the cabin and stand under the strong light of the moon – in the centre, as it were, of a glittering sea of liquid silver – to see the broad sails straining in the gale, the ship keeled over on her side, the angry foam hissing past her lee bulwarks, and sparkling sheets of spray dashing high over her bows and raining upon her decks; to brace myself and hang fast to the first object that presented itself, with hat jammed down and coat-tails whipping in the breeze, and feel that exhilaration that thrills in one's hair and quivers down his back-bone when he knows that every inch of canvas is drawing and the vessel cleaving through the waves at her utmost speed. There was no darkness, no dimness, no obscurity there. All was brightness, every object was vividly defined. Every prostrate Kanaka; every coil of rope; every calabash of poi; every puppy; every seam in the flooring; every bolthead; every object, however minute, showed sharp and distinct in its every outline; and the shadow of the broad mainsail lay black as a pall upon the deck, leaving Billings's white upturned face glorified and his body in a total eclipse.

Monday morning we were close to the island of Hawaii. Two of its high mountains were in view – Mauna Loa and Hualaiai. The latter is an imposing peak, but being only ten thousand feet high is seldom mentioned or heard of. Mauna Loa is said to be sixteen thousand feet high. The rays of glittering snow and ice, that clasped its summit like a claw, looked refreshing when viewed from the blistering climate we were in. One could stand on that mountain (wrapped up in blankets and furs to keep warm), and while he nibbled a snowball or an icicle to quench his thirst he could look down the long sweep of its sides and see spots where plants are growing that grow only where the bitter cold of winter prevails; lower down he could see sections devoted to productions that thrive in the temperate zone alone; and at the bottom of the mountain he could see the home of the tufted cocoa palms and other species of vegetation that grow only in the sultry atmosphere of eternal summer. He could see all the climes of the world at a single glance of the eye, and that glance would only pass over a distance of four or five miles as the bird flies!

By and by we took boat and went ashore at Kailua, designing to ride horse-back through the pleasant orange and coffee region of Kona, and rejoin the vessel at a point some leagues distant. This journey is well worth taking. The trail passes along on high ground – say a thousand feet above sea level – and usually about a mile distant from the ocean, which is always in sight, save that occasionally you find yourself buried in the forest in the midst of a rank tropical vegetation and a dense growth of trees, whose great bows overarch the road and shut out sun and sea and everything, and leave you in a dim, shady tunnel, haunted with invisible singing birds and fragrant with the odor of flowers. It was pleasant to ride occasionally in the warm sun, and feast the eye upon the ever-changing panorama of the forest (beyond and below us), with its many tints, its softened lights and shadows, its billowy undulations sweeping gently down from the mountain to the sea. It was pleasant also, at intervals, to leave the sultry sun and pass into the cool, green depths of this forest and indulge in sentimental reflections under the inspiration of its brooding twilight and its whispering foliage.

We rode through one orange grove that had ten thousand trees in it! They were all laden with fruit.

At one farmhouse we got some large peaches of excellent flavor. This fruit, as a general thing, does not do well in the Sandwich Islands. It takes a sort of almond shape, and is small and bitter. It needs frost, they say, and perhaps it does; if this be so, it will have a good opportunity to go on needing it, as it will not be likely to get it. The trees from which the fine fruit I have spoken of, came, had been planted and replanted *sixteen times*, and to this treatment the proprietor of the orchard attributed his success.

We passed several sugar plantations – new ones and not very extensive. The crops were, in most cases, third rattoons. [Note. – The first crop is called "plant cane;" subsequent crops which spring from the original roots, without replanting, are called "rattoons."] Almost every where on the island of Hawaii sugar-cane matures in twelve months, both rattoons and plant, and although it ought to be taken off as soon as it tassels, no doubt, it is not absolutely necessary to do it until about four months afterward. In Kona, the average yield of an acre of ground is *two tons* of sugar, they say. This is only a moderate yield for these islands, but would be astounding for Louisiana and most other sugar-growing countries. The plantations in Kona being on pretty high ground – up among the light and frequent rains – no irrigation whatever is required.

CHAPTER LXXI

AT FOUR O'CLOCK in the afternoon we were winding down a mountain of dreary and desolate lava to the sea, and closing our pleasant land journey. This lava is the accumulation of ages; one torrent of fire after another has rolled down here in old times, and built up the island structure higher and higher. Underneath, it is honey-combed with caves; it would be of no use to dig wells in such a place; they would not hold water – you would not find any for them to hold, for that matter. Consequently, the planters depend upon cisterns.

The last lava flow occurred here so long ago that there are none now living who witnessed it. In one place it enclosed and burned down a grove of cocoanut trees, and the holes in the lava where the trunks stood are still visible; their sides retain the impression of the bark; the trees fell upon the burning river, and becoming partly submerged, left in it the perfect counterpart of every knot and branch and leaf, and even nut, for curiosity-seekers of a long distant day to gaze upon and wonder at.

There were doubtless plenty of Kanaka sentinels on guard hereabouts at that time, but they did not leave casts of their figures in the lava as the Roman sentinels at Herculaneum and Pompeii did. It is a pity it is so, because such things are so interesting; but so it is. They probably went away. They went away early, perhaps. However, they had their merits; the Romans exhibited the higher pluck, but the Kanakas showed the sounder judgment.

Shortly we came in sight of that spot whose history is so familiar to every schoolboy in the wide world – Kealakekua Bay – the place where Captain Cook, the great circumnavigator, was killed by the natives, nearly a hundred years ago. The setting sun was flaming upon it, a summer shower was falling, and it was spanned by two magnificent rainbows. Two men who were in advance of us rode through one of these and for a moment their garments shone with a more than regal splendor. Why did not Captain Cook have taste enough to call his great discovery the Rainbow Islands? These charming spectacles are present to you at every turn, they are common in all the islands; they are visible every day, and frequently at night also – not the silvery bow we see once in an age in the States, by moonlight, but barred with all bright and beautiful colors, like the children of the sun and rain. I saw one of them a few nights ago. What the sailors call "rain dogs" – little patches of rainbow – are often seen drifting about the heavens in these latitudes, like stained cathedral windows.

Kealakekua Bay is a little curve like the last kink of a snail-shell, winding deep into the land, seemingly not more than a mile wide from shore to shore. It is bounded on one side – where the murder was done – by a little flat plain, on which stands a cocoanut grove and some ruined houses; a steep wall of lava, a thousand feet high at the upper end and three or four hundred at the lower, comes down from the mountain and bounds the inner extremity of it. From this wall the place takes its name, *Kealakekua*, which in the native tongue signifies "The Pathway of the Gods." They say, (and still believe, in spite of their liberal education in Christianity), that the great god *Lono*, who used to live upon the hill-side, always traveled that causeway when urgent business connected with heavenly affairs called him down to the seas-hore in a hurry.

As the red sun looked across the placid ocean through the tall, clean stems of the cocoanut trees, like a blooming whiskey bloat through the bars of a city prison, I went and stood in the edge of the water on the flat rock pressed by Captain Cook's feet when the blow was dealt which took away his life, and tried to picture in my mind the doomed man struggling in the midst of the multitude of exasperated savages – the men in the ship crowding to the vessel's side and gazing in anxious dismay toward the shore – the – but I discovered that I could not do it.

It was growing dark, the rain began to fall, we could see that the distant Boomerang was helplessly becalmed at sea, and so I adjourned to the cheerless little box of a warehouse and sat down to smoke and think, and wish the ship would make the land – for we had not eaten much for ten hours and were viciously hungry.

Plain unvarnished history takes the romance out of Captain Cook's assassination, and renders a deliberate verdict of justifiable homicide. Wherever he went among the islands, he was cordially received and welcomed by the inhabitants, and his ships lavishly supplied with all manner of food. He returned these kindnesses with insult and ill-treatment. Perceiving that the people took him for the long vanished and lamented god Lono, he encouraged them in the delusion for the sake of the limitless power it gave him; but during the famous disturbance at this spot, and while he and his comrades were surrounded by fifteen thousand maddened savages, he received a hurt and betrayed his earthly origin with a groan. It was his death-warrant. Instantly a shout went up: "He groans! – he is not a god!" So they closed in upon him and dispatched him.

His flesh was stripped from the bones and burned (except nine pounds of it which were sent on board the ships). The heart was hung up in a native hut, where it was found and eaten by three children, who mistook it for the heart of a dog. One of these children grew to be a very old man, and died in Honolulu a few years ago. Some of Cook's bones were recovered and consigned to the deep by the officers of the ships.

Small blame should attach to the natives for the killing of Cook. They treated him well. In return, he abused them. He and his men inflicted bodily injury upon many of them at different times, and killed at least three of them before they offered any proportionate retaliation.

Near the shore we found "Cook's Monument" – only a cocoanut stump, four feet high and about a foot in diameter at the butt. It had lava boulders piled around its base to hold it up and keep it in its place, and it was entirely sheathed over, from top to bottom, with rough, discolored sheets of copper, such as ships' bottoms are coppered with. Each sheet had a rude inscription scratched upon it – with a nail, apparently – and in every case the execution was wretched. Most of these merely recorded the visits of British naval commanders to the spot, but one of them bore this legend:

"Near this spot fell
CAPTAIN JAMES COOK,
The Distinguished Circumnavigator, who Discovered these
Islands A. D. 1778.

After Cook's murder, his second in command, on board the ship, opened fire upon the swarms of natives on the beach, and one of his cannon balls cut this cocoanut tree short off and left this monumental stump standing. It looked sad and lonely enough to us, out there in the rainy twilight. But there is no other monument to Captain Cook. True, up on the mountain side we had passed by a large inclosure like an ample hog-pen, built of lava blocks, which marks the spot where Cook's flesh was stripped from his bones and burned; but this is not properly a monument, since it was erected by the natives themselves, and less to do honor to the circumnavigator than for the sake of convenience in roasting him. A thing like a guide-board was elevated above this pen on a tall pole, and formerly there was an inscription upon it describing the memorable occurrence that had there taken place; but the sun and the wind have long ago so defaced it as to render it illegible.

Toward midnight a fine breeze sprang up and the schooner soon worked herself into the bay and cast anchor. The boat came ashore for us, and in a little while the clouds and the rain were all gone. The moon was beaming tranquilly down on land and sea, and we two were stretched upon the deck sleeping the refreshing sleep and dreaming the happy dreams that are only vouchsafed to the weary and the innocent.

CHAPTER LXXIV

WE GOT BACK to the schooner in good time, and then sailed down to Kau, where we disembarked and took final leave of the vessel. Next day we bought horses and bent our way over the summer-clad mountain-terraces, toward the great volcano of Kilauea (Ke-low-way-ah). We made nearly a two days' journey of it, but that was on account of laziness. Toward sunset on the second day, we reached an elevation of some four thousand feet above sea level, and as we picked our careful way through billowy wastes of lava long generations ago stricken dead and cold in the climax of its tossing fury, we began to come upon signs of the near presence of the volcano – signs in the nature of ragged fissures that discharged jets of sulphurous vapor into the air, hot from the molten ocean down in the bowels of the mountain.

Shortly the crater came into view. I have seen Vesuvius since, but it was a mere toy, a child's volcano, a soup-kettle, compared to this. Mount Vesuvius is a shapely cone thirty-six hundred feet high; its crater an inverted cone only three hundred feet deep, and not more than a thousand feet in diameter, if as much as that; its fires meagre, modest, and docile. – But here was a vast, perpendicular, walled cellar, nine hundred feet deep in some places, thirteen hundred in others, level-floored, and *ten miles in circumference!* Here was a yawning pit upon whose floor the armies of Russia could camp, and have room to spare.

Perched upon the edge of the crater, at the opposite end from where we stood, was a small lookout-house – say three miles away. It assisted us, by comparison, to comprehend and appreciate the great depth of the basin – it looked like a tiny martin-box clinging at the eaves of a cathedral. After some little time spent in resting and looking and ciphering, we hurried on to the hotel.

By the path it is a half a mile from the Volcano House to the lookout-house. After a hearty supper we waited until it was thoroughly dark and then started to the crater. The first glance in that direction revealed a scene of wild beauty. There was a heavy fog over the crater and it was splendidly illuminated by the glare from the fires below. The illumination was two miles wide and a mile high, perhaps; and if you ever, on a dark night and at a distance beheld the light from thirty or forty blocks of distant buildings all on fire at once, reflected strongly against overhanging clouds, you can form a fair idea of what this looked like.

A colossal column of cloud towered to a great height in the air immediately above the crater, and the outer swell of every one of its vast folds was dyed with a rich crimson luster, which was subdued to a pale rose tint in the depressions between. It glowed like a muffled torch and stretched upward to a dizzy height toward the zenith. I thought it just possible that its like had not been seen since the children of Israel wandered on their long march through the desert so many centuries ago over a path illuminated by the mysterious "pillar of fire." And I was sure that I now had a vivid conception of what the majestic "pillar of fire" was like, which almost amounted to a revelation.

Arrived at the little thatched lookout-house, we rested our elbows on the railing in front and looked abroad over the wide crater and down over the sheer precipice at the seething fires beneath us. The view was a startling improvement on my daylight experience. I turned to see the effect on the balance of the company and found the reddest-faced set of men I almost ever saw. In the strong light every countenance glowed like red-hot iron, every shoulder was suffused with crimson and shaded rearward into dingy, shapeless obscurity! The place below looked like the infernal regions and these men like half-cooled devils just come up on a furlough.

I turned my eyes upon the volcano again. The "cellar" was tolerably well lighted up. For a mile and a half in front of us and half a mile on either side, the floor of the abyss was magnificently illuminated; beyond these limits the mists hung down their gauzy curtains and cast a deceptive gloom over all that made the twinkling fires in the remote corners of the crater seem countless leagues removed – made them seem like the camp fires of a great army far away. Here was room for the imagination to work! You could imagine those lights the width of a continent away – and that hidden under the intervening darkness were hills, and winding rivers, and weary wastes of plain and desert – and even then the tremendous vista stretched on, and on, and on! – to the fires and far beyond! You could not compass it – it was the idea of eternity made tangible – and the longest end of it made visible to the naked eye!

The greater part of the vast floor of the desert under us was as black as ink, and apparently smooth and level; but over a mile square of it was ringed and streaked and striped with a thousand branching streams of liquid and gorgeously brilliant fire! It looked like a colossal railroad map of the State of Massachusetts done in chain lightning on a midnight sky. Imagine it – imagine a coal-black sky shivered into a tangled net-work of angry fire!

Here and there were gleaming holes a hundred feet in diameter, broken in the dark crust, and in them the melted lava – the color a dazzling white just tinged with yellow – was boiling and surging furiously; and from these holes branched numberless bright torrents in many directions, like the spokes of a wheel, and kept a tolerably straight course for a while and then swept round in huge rainbow curves, or made a long succession of sharp worm-fence angles, which looked precisely like the fiercest jagged lightning. These streams met other streams, and they mingled with and crossed and recrossed each other in every conceivable direction, like skate tracks on a popular skating ground. Sometimes streams twenty or thirty feet wide flowed from the holes to some distance without dividing – and through the opera glasses we could see that they ran down small, steep hills and were genuine cataracts of fire, white at their source, but soon cooling and turning to the richest red, grained with alternate lines of black and gold. Every now and then masses of the dark crust broke away and floated slowly down these streams like rafts down a river. Occasionally the molten lava flowing under the superincumbent crust broke through – split a dazzling streak, from five hundred to a thousand feet long, like a sudden flash of lightning, and then acre after acre of the cold lava parted into fragments, turned up edgewise like cakes of ice when a great river breaks up, plunged downward and were swallowed in the crimson cauldron. Then the wide expanse of the "thaw" maintained a ruddy glow for a while, but shortly cooled and became black and level again. During a "thaw," every dismembered cake was marked by a glittering white border which was superbly shaded inward by aurora borealis rays, which were a flaming yellow where they joined the white border, and from thence toward their points tapered into glowing crimson, then into a rich, pale carmine, and finally into a faint blush that held its own a moment and then dimmed and turned black. Some of the streams preferred to mingle together in a tangle of fantastic circles, and then they looked something like the confusion of ropes one sees on a ship's deck when she has just taken in sail and dropped anchor – provided one can imagine those ropes on fire.

Through the glasses, the little fountains scattered about looked very beautiful. They boiled, and coughed, and spluttered, and discharged sprays of stringy red fire – of about the consistency of mush, for instance – from ten to fifteen feet into the air, along with a shower of brilliant white sparks – a quaint and unnatural mingling of gouts of blood and snowflakes!

We had circles and serpents and streaks of lightning all twined and wreathed and tied together, without a break throughout an area more than a mile square (that amount of ground was covered, though it was not strictly "square"), and it was with a feeling of placid exultation that we reflected that many years had elapsed since any visitor had seen such a splendid display – since any visitor had seen anything more than the now snubbed and insignificant "North" and "South" lakes in action. We had been reading old files of Hawaiian newspapers and the "Record Book" at the Volcano House, and were posted.

I could see the North Lake lying out on the black floor away off in the outer edge of our panorama, and knitted to it by a web-work of lava streams. In its individual capacity it looked very little more respectable than a schoolhouse on fire. True, it was about nine hundred feet long and two or three hundred wide, but then, under the present circumstances, it necessarily appeared rather insignificant, and besides it was so distant from us.

I forgot to say that the noise made by the bubbling lava is not great, heard as we heard it from our lofty perch. It makes three distinct sounds – a rushing, a hissing, and a coughing or puffing sound; and if you stand on the brink and close your eyes it is no trick at all to imagine that you are sweeping down a river on a large low-pressure steamer, and that you hear the hissing of the steam about her boilers, the puffing from her escape-pipes and the churning rush of the water abaft her wheels. The smell of sulphur is strong, but not unpleasant to a sinner.

We left the lookout-house at ten o'clock in a half-cooked condition, because of the heat from Pele's furnaces, and wrapping up in blankets, for the night was cold, we returned to our hotel.

CHAPTER LXXVI

WE RODE HORSE-BACK all around the island of Hawaii (the crooked road making the distance two hundred miles), and enjoyed the journey very much. We were more than a week making the trip, because our Kanaka horses would not go by a house or a hut without stopping – whip and spur could not alter their minds about it, and so we finally found that it economized time to let them have their way. Upon inquiry the mystery was explained: the natives are such thorough-going gossips that they never pass a house without stopping to swap news, and consequently their horses learn to regard that sort of thing as an essential part of the whole duty of man, and his salvation not to be compassed without it. However, at a former crisis of my life I had once taken an aristocratic young lady out driving, behind a horse that had just retired from a long and honorable career as the moving impulse of a milk wagon, and so this present experience awoke a reminiscent sadness in me in place of the exasperation more natural to the occasion. I remembered how helpless I was that day, and how humiliated; how ashamed I was of having intimated to the girl that I had always owned the horse and was accustomed to grandeur; how hard I tried to appear easy, and even vivacious, under suffering that was consuming my vitals; how placidly and maliciously the girl smiled, and kept on smiling, while my hot blushes baked themselves into a permanent blood-pudding in my face; how the horse ambled from one side of the street to the other and waited complacently before every third house two minutes and a quarter while I belabored his back and reviled him in my heart; how I tried to keep him from turning corners, and failed; how I moved heaven and earth to get him out of town, and did not succeed; how he traversed the entire settlement and delivered imaginary milk at a hundred and sixty-two different domiciles, and how he finally brought up at a dairy depot and refused to budge further, thus rounding and completing the revealment of what the plebeian service of his life had been; how, in eloquent silence, I walked the girl home, and how, when I took leave of her, her parting remark scorched my soul and appeared to blister me all over: she said that my horse was a fine, capable animal, and I must have taken great comfort in him in my time – but that if I would take along some milk-tickets next time, and appear to deliver them at the various halting places, it might expedite his movements a little. There was a coolness between us after that.

In one place in the island of Hawaii, we saw a laced and ruffled cataract of limpid water leaping from a sheer precipice fifteen hundred feet high; but that sort of scenery finds its stanchest ally in the arithmetic rather than in spectacular effect. If one desires to be so stirred by a poem of Nature wrought in the happily commingled graces of picturesque rocks, glimpsed distances, foliage, color, shifting lights and shadows, and falling water, that the tears almost come into his eyes so potent is the charm exerted, he need not go away from America to enjoy such an experience. The Rainbow Fall, in Watkins Glen (N. Y.), on the Erie railway, is an example. It would recede into pitiable insignificance if the callous tourist drew an arithmetic on it; but left to compete for the honors simply on scenic grace and beauty – the grand, the august and the sublime being barred the contest – it could challenge the old world and the new to produce its peer.

In one locality, on our journey, we saw some horses that had been born and reared on top of the mountains, above the range of running water, and consequently they had never drank that fluid in their lives, but had been always accustomed to quenching their thirst by eating dew-laden or shower-wetted leaves. And now it was destructively funny to see them sniff suspiciously at a pail of water, and then put in their noses and try to take a *bite* out of the fluid, as if it were a solid. Finding it liquid, they would snatch away their heads and fall to trembling, snorting and showing other evidences of fright. When they became convinced at last that the water was friendly and harmless, they thrust in their noses up to their eyes, brought out a mouthful of the water, and proceeded to *chew* it complacently. We saw a man coax, kick and spur one of them five or ten minutes before he could make it cross a running stream. It spread its nostrils, distended its eyes and trembled all over, just as horses customarily do in the presence of a serpent – and for aught I know it thought the crawling stream *was* a serpent.

In due course of time our journey came to an end at Kawaehae (usually pronounced To-a-*hi* – and before we find fault with this elaborate orthographical method of arriving at such an unostentatious result, let us lop off the *ugh* from our word "though"). I made this horse-back trip on a mule. I paid ten dollars for him at Kau (Kah-oo), added four to get him shod, rode him two hundred miles, and then sold him for fifteen dollars. I mark the circumstance with a white stone (in the absence of chalk – for I never saw a white stone that a body could mark anything with, though out of respect for the ancients I have tried it often enough); for up to that day and date it was the first strictly commercial transaction I had ever entered into, and come out winner. We returned to Honolulu, and from thence sailed to the island of Maui, and spent several weeks there very pleasantly. I still remember, with a sense of indolent luxury, a picnicking excursion up a romantic gorge there, called the Iao Valley. The trail lay along the edge of a brawling stream in the bottom of a gorge – a shady route, for it was well roofed with the verdant domes of forest trees. Through openings in the foliage we glimpsed picturesque scenery that revealed ceaseless changes and new charms with every step of our progress. Perpendicular walls from one to three thousand feet high guarded the way, and were sumptuously plumed with varied foliage, in places, and in places swathed in waving ferns. Passing shreds of cloud trailed their shadows across these shining fronts, mottling them with blots; billowy masses of white vapor hid the turreted summits, and far above the vapor swelled a background of gleaming green crags and cones that came and went, through the veiling mists, like islands drifting in a fog; sometimes the cloudy curtain descended till half the canon wall was hidden, then shredded gradually away till only airy glimpses of the ferny front appeared through it – then swept aloft and left it glorified in the sun again. Now and then, as our position changed, rocky bastions swung out from the wall, a mimic ruin of castellated ramparts and crumbling towers clothed with mosses and hung with garlands of swaying vines, and as we moved on they swung back again and hid themselves once more in the foliage. Presently a verdure-clad needle of stone, a thousand feet high, stepped out from behind a corner, and mounted guard over the mysteries of the valley. It seemed to me that if Captain Cook needed a monument, here was one ready made – therefore, why not put up his sign here, and sell out the venerable cocoanut stump?

But the chief pride of Maui is her dead volcano of Haleakala – which means, translated, "the house of the sun." We climbed a thousand feet up the side of this isolated colossus one afternoon; then camped, and next day climbed the remaining nine thousand feet, and anchored on the summit, where we built a fire and froze and roasted by turns, all night. With the first pallor of dawn we got up and saw things that were new to us. Mounted on a commanding pinnacle, we watched Nature work her silent wonders. The sea was spread abroad on every hand, its tumbled surface seeming only wrinkled and dimpled in the distance. A broad valley below appeared like an ample checker-board, its velvety green sugar plantations alternating with dun squares of barrenness and groves of trees diminished to mossy tufts. Beyond the valley were mountains picturesquely grouped together; but bear in mind, we fancied that we were looking *up* at these things – not down. We seemed to sit in the bottom of a symmetrical bowl ten thousand feet deep, with the valley and the skirting sea lifted away into the sky above us! It was curious; and not only curious, but aggravating; for it was having our trouble all for nothing, to climb ten thousand feet toward heaven and then have to look *up* at our scenery. However, we had to be content with it and make the best of it; for, all we could do we could not coax our landscape down out of the clouds. Formerly, when I had read an article in which Poe treated of this singular fraud perpetrated upon the eye by isolated great altitudes, I had looked upon the matter as an invention of his own fancy.

I have spoken of the outside view – but we had an inside one, too. That was the yawning dead crater, into which we now and then tumbled rocks, half as large as a barrel, from our perch, and saw them go careering down the almost perpendicular sides, bounding three hundred feet at a jump; kicking up dust clouds wherever they struck; diminishing to our view as they sped farther into distance; growing invisible, finally, and only betraying their course by faint little puffs of dust; and coming to a halt at last in the bottom of the abyss, two thousand five hundred feet down from where they started! It was magnificent sport. We wore ourselves out at it.

The crater of Vesuvius, as I have before remarked, is a modest pit about a thousand feet deep and three thousand in circumference; that of Kilauea is somewhat deeper, and *ten miles* in circumference. But what are either of them compared to the vacant stomach of Haleakala? I will not offer any figures of my own, but give official ones – those of Commander Wilkes, U. S. N., who surveyed it and testifies that it is *twenty-seven miles in circumference!* If it had a level bottom it would make a fine site for a city like London. It must have afforded a spectacle worth contemplating in the old days when its furnaces gave full rein to their anger.

Presently vagrant white clouds came drifting along, high over the sea and the valley; then they came in couples and groups; then in imposing squadrons; gradually joining their forces, they banked themselves solidly together, a thousand feet under us, and *totally shut out land and ocean* – not a vestige of *any thing* was left in view but just a little of the rim of the crater, circling away from the pinnacle whereon we sat (for a ghostly procession of wanderers from the filmy hosts without had drifted through a chasm in the crater wall and filed round and round, and gathered and sunk and blended together till the abyss was stored to the brim with a fleecy fog). Thus banked, motion ceased, and silence reigned. Clear to the horizon, league on league, the snowy floor stretched without a break – not level, but in rounded folds, with shallow creases between, and with here and there stately piles of vapory architecture lifting themselves aloft out of the common plain – some near at hand, some in the middle distances, and others relieving the monotony of the remote solitudes. There was little conversation, for the impressive scene overawed speech. I felt like the Last Man, neglected of the judgment, and left pinnacled in mid-heaven, a forgotten relic of a vanished world.

While the hush yet brooded, the messengers of the coming resurrection appeared in the east. A growing warmth suffused the horizon, and soon the sun emerged and looked out over the cloud-waste, flinging bars of ruddy light across it, staining its folds and billow-caps with blushes, purpling the shaded troughs between, and glorifying the massy vapor-palaces and cathedrals with a wasteful splendor of all blendings and combinations of rich coloring.

It was the sublimest spectacle I ever witnessed, and I think the memory of it will remain with me always.

CHAPTER LXXVIII

AFTER HALF A year's luxurious vagrancy in the islands, I took shipping in a sailing vessel, and regretfully returned to San Francisco – a voyage in every way delightful, but without an incident: unless lying two long weeks in a dead calm, eighteen hundred miles from the nearest land, may rank as an incident. Schools of whales grew so tame that day after day they played about the ship among the porpoises and the sharks without the least apparent fear of us, and we pelted them with empty bottles for lack of better sport. Twenty-four hours afterward these bottles would be still lying on the glassy water under our noses, showing that the ship had not moved out of her place in all that time. The calm was absolutely breathless, and the surface of the sea absolutely without a wrinkle. For a whole day and part of a night we lay so close to another ship that had drifted to our vicinity, that we carried on conversations with her passengers, introduced each other by name, and became pretty intimately acquainted with people we had never heard of before, and have never heard of since. This was the only vessel we saw during the whole lonely voyage. We had fifteen passengers, and to show how hard pressed they were at last for occupation and amusement, I will mention that the gentlemen gave a good part of their time every day, during the calm, to trying to sit on an empty champagne bottle (lying on its side), and thread a needle without touching their heels to the deck, or falling over; and the ladies sat in the shade of the mainsail, and watched the enterprise with absorbing interest. We were at sea five Sundays; and yet, but for the almanac, we never would have known but that all the other days were Sundays too.

I was home again, in San Francisco, without means and without employment. I tortured my brain for a saving scheme of some kind, and at last a public lecture occurred to me! I sat down and wrote one, in a fever of hopeful anticipation. I showed it to several friends, but they all shook their heads. They said nobody would come to hear me, and I would make a humiliating failure of it. They said that as I had never spoken in public, I would break down in the delivery, anyhow. I was disconsolate now. But at last an editor slapped me on the back and told me to "go ahead." He said, "Take the largest house in town, and charge a dollar a ticket." The audacity of the proposition was charming; it seemed fraught with practical worldly wisdom, however. The proprietor of the several theatres endorsed the advice, and said I might have his handsome new opera-house at half price – fifty dollars. In sheer desperation I took it – on credit, for sufficient reasons. In three days I did a hundred and fifty dollars' worth of printing and advertising, and was the most distressed and frightened creature on the Pacific coast. I could not sleep – who could, under such circumstances? For other people there was facetiousness in the last line of my posters, but to me it was plaintive with a pang when I wrote it:

"Doors open at 7½. The trouble will begin at 8."

That line has done good service since. Showmen have borrowed it frequently. I have even seen it appended to a newspaper advertisement reminding school pupils in vacation what time next term would begin. As those three days of suspense dragged by, I grew more and more unhappy. I had sold two hundred tickets among my personal friends, but I feared they might not come. My lecture, which had seemed "humorous" to me, at first, grew steadily more and more dreary, till not a vestige of fun seemed left, and I grieved that I could not bring a coffin on the stage and turn the thing into a funeral. I was so panic-stricken, at last, that I went to three old friends, giants in stature, cordial by nature, and stormy-voiced, and said:

"This thing is going to be a failure; the jokes in it are so dim that nobody will ever see them; I would like to have you sit in the parquette, and help me through."

They said they would. Then I went to the wife of a popular citizen, and said that if she was willing to do me a very great kindness, I would be glad if she and her husband would sit prominently in the left-hand stage-box, where the whole house could see them. I explained that I should need help, and would turn toward her and smile, as a signal, when I had been delivered of an obscure joke – "and then," I added, "don't wait to investigate, but *respond!*"

She promised. Down the street I met a man I never had seen before. He had been drinking, and was beaming with smiles and good nature. He said:

"My name's Sawyer. You don't know me, but that don't matter. I haven't got a cent, but if you knew how bad I wanted to laugh, you'd give me a ticket. Come, now, what do you say?"

"Is your laugh hung on a hair-trigger? – that is, is it critical, or can you get it off *easy?*"

My drawling infirmity of speech so affected him that he laughed a specimen or two that struck me as being about the article I wanted, and I gave him a ticket, and appointed him to sit in the second circle, in the centre, and be responsible for that division of the house. I gave him minute instructions about how to detect indistinct jokes, and then went away, and left him chuckling placidly over the novelty of the idea.

I ate nothing on the last of the three eventful days – I only suffered. I had advertised that on this third day the box-office would be opened for the sale of reserved seats. I crept down to the theatre at four in the afternoon to see if any sales had been made. The ticket seller was gone, the box-office was locked up. I had to swallow suddenly, or my heart would have got out. "No sales," I said to myself; "I might have known it." I thought of suicide, pretended illness, flight. I thought of these things in earnest, for I was very miserable and scared. But of course I had to drive them away, and prepare to meet my fate. I could not wait for half-past seven – I wanted to face the horror, and end it – the feeling of many a man doomed to hang, no doubt. I went down back streets at six o'clock, and entered the theatre by the back door. I stumbled my way in the dark among the ranks of canvas scenery, and stood on the stage. The house was gloomy and silent, and its emptiness depressing. I went into the dark among the scenes again, and for an hour and a half gave myself up to the horrors, wholly unconscious of everything else. Then I heard a murmur; it rose higher and higher, and ended in a crash, mingled with cheers. It made my hair raise, it was so close to me, and so loud. There was a pause, and then another; presently came a third, and before I well knew what I was about, I was in the middle of the stage, staring at a sea of faces, bewildered by the fierce glare of the lights, and quaking in every limb with a terror that seemed like to take my life away. The house was full, aisles and all!

The tumult in my heart and brain and legs continued a full minute before I could gain any command over myself. Then I recognized the charity and the friendliness in the faces before me, and little by little my fright melted away, and I began to talk. Within three or four minutes I was comfortable, and even content. My three chief allies, with three auxiliaries, were on hand, in the parquette, all sitting together, all armed with bludgeons, and all ready to make an onslaught upon the feeblest joke that might show its head. And whenever a joke did fall, their bludgeons came down and their faces seemed to split from ear to ear; Sawyer, whose hearty countenance was seen looming redly in the centre of the second circle, took it up, and the house was carried handsomely. Inferior jokes never fared so royally before. Presently I delivered a bit of serious matter with impressive unction (it was my pet), and the audience listened with an absorbed hush that gratified me more than any applause; and as I dropped the last word of the clause, I happened to turn and catch Mrs. ——'s intent and waiting eye; my conversation with her flashed upon me, and in spite of all I could do I smiled. She took it for the signal, and promptly delivered a mellow laugh that touched off the whole audience; and the explosion that followed was the triumph of the evening. I thought that that honest man Sawyer would choke himself; and as for the bludgeons, they performed like pile-drivers. But my poor little morsel of pathos was ruined. It was taken in good faith as an intentional joke, and the prize one of the entertainment, and I wisely let it go at that.

All the papers were kind in the morning; my appetite returned; I had abundance of money. All's well that ends well.

CHAPTER LXXIX

I LAUNCHED OUT as a lecturer, now, with great boldness. I had the field all to myself, for public lectures were almost an unknown commodity in the Pacific market. They are not so rare, now, I suppose. I took an old personal friend along to play agent for me, and for two or three weeks we roamed through Nevada and California and had a very cheerful time of it. Two days before I lectured in Virginia City, two stage-coaches were robbed within two miles of the town. The daring act was committed just at dawn, by six masked men, who sprang up alongside the coaches, presented revolvers at the heads of the drivers and passengers, and commanded a general dismount. Every body climbed down, and the robbers took their watches and every cent they had. Then they took gunpowder and blew up the express specie boxes and got their contents. The leader of the robbers was a small, quick-spoken man, and the fame of his vigorous manner and his intrepidity was in every body's mouth when we arrived.

The night after instructing Virginia, I walked over the desolate "divide" and down to Gold Hill, and lectured there. The lecture done, I stopped to talk with a friend, and did not start back till eleven. The "divide" was high, unoccupied ground, between the towns, the scene of twenty midnight murders and a hundred robberies. As we climbed up and stepped out on this eminence, the Gold Hill lights dropped out of sight at our backs, and the night closed down gloomy and dismal. A sharp wind swept the place, too, and chilled our perspiring bodies through.

"I tell you I don't like this place at night," said Mike the agent.

"Well, don't speak so loud," I said. "You needn't remind anybody that we are here."

Just then a dim figure approached me from the direction of Virginia – a man, evidently. He came straight at me, and I stepped aside to let him pass; he stepped in the way and confronted me again. Then I saw that he had a mask on and was holding something in my face – I heard a click-click and recognized a revolver in dim outline. I pushed the barrel aside with my hand and said:

"Don't!"

He ejaculated sharply:

"Your watch! Your money!"

I said:

"You can have them with pleasure – but take the pistol away from my face, please. It makes me shiver."

"No remarks! Hand out your money!"

"Certainly – I—"

"Put up your hands! Don't you go for a weapon! Put 'em up! Higher!"

I held them above my head.

A pause. Then:

"Are you going to hand out your money or not?"

I dropped my hands to my pockets and said:

"Certainly! I—"

"Put up your *hands!* Do you want your head blown off? Higher!"

I put them above my head again.

Another pause.

"*Are* you going to hand out your money or *not?* Ah-ah – again? Put up your hands! By George, you want the head shot off you awful bad!"

"Well, friend, I'm trying my best to please you. You tell me to give up my money, and when I reach for it you tell me to put up my hands. If you would only – Oh, now – don't! All six of you at me! That other man will get away while. – Now please take some of those revolvers out of my face – *do*, if you *please!* Every time one of them clicks, my liver comes up into my throat! If you have a mother – any of you – or if any of you have ever *had* a mother – or a – grandmother – or a—"

"Cheese it! *Will* you give up your money, or have we got to – There-there – none of that! Put up your *hands!*"

"Gentlemen – I know you are gentlemen by your—"

"Silence! If you want to be facetious, young man, there are times and places more fitting. *This* is a serious business."

"You prick the marrow of my opinion. The funerals I have attended in my time were comedies compared to it. Now *I* think—"

"Curse your palaver! Your money! – your money! – your money! Hold! – put up your hands!"

"Gentlemen, listen to reason. You *see* how I am situated – now *don't* put those pistols so close – I smell the powder. You see how I am situated. If I had four hands – so that I could hold up two and—"

"Throttle him! Gag him! Kill him!"

"Gentlemen, *don't!* Nobody's watching the other fellow. Why don't some of you—Ouch! Take it away, please! Gentlemen, you see that I've got to hold up my hands; and so I can't take out my money – but if you'll be so kind as to take it out for me, I will do as much for you some—"

"Search him Beauregard – and stop his jaw with a bullet, quick, if he wags it again. Help Beauregard, Stonewall."

Then three of them, with the small, spry leader, adjourned to Mike and fell to searching him. I was so excited that my lawless fancy tortured me to ask my two men all manner of facetious questions about their rebel brother-generals of the South, but, considering the order they had received, it was but common prudence to keep still. When everything had been taken from me, – watch, money, and a multitude of trifles of small value, – I supposed I was free, and forthwith put my cold hands into my empty pockets and began an inoffensive jig to warm my feet and stir up some latent courage – but instantly all pistols were at my head, and the order came again:

"Be still! Put up your hands! And *keep* them up!"

They stood Mike up alongside of me, with strict orders to keep his hands above his head, too, and then the chief highwayman said:

"Beauregard, hide behind that boulder; Phil Sheridan, you hide behind that other one; Stonewall Jackson, put yourself behind that sage-bush there. Keep your pistols bearing on these fellows, and if they take down their hands within ten minutes, or move a single peg, let them have it!"

Then three disappeared in the gloom toward the several ambushes, and the other three disappeared down the road toward Virginia.

It was depressingly still, and miserably cold. Now this whole thing was a practical joke, and the robbers were personal friends of ours in disguise, and twenty more lay hidden within ten feet of us during the whole operation, listening. Mike knew all this, and was in the joke, but I suspected nothing of it. To me it was most uncomfortably genuine.

When we had stood there in the middle of the road five minutes, like a couple of idiots, with our hands aloft, freezing to death by inches, Mike's interest in the joke began to wane. He said:

"The time's up, now, ain't it?"

"No, you keep still. Do you want to take any chances with those bloody savages?"

Presently Mike said:

"*Now* the time's up, any way. I'm freezing."

"Well freeze. Better freeze than carry your brains home in a basket. Maybe the time *is* up, but how do *we* know? – got no watch to tell by. I mean to give them good measure. I calculate to stand here fifteen minutes or die. Don't you move."

So, without knowing it, I was making one joker very sick of his contract. When we took our arms down at last, they were aching with cold and fatigue, and when we went sneaking off, the dread I was in that the time might not yet be up and that we would feel bullets in a moment, was not sufficient to draw all my attention from the misery that racked my stiffened body.

The joke of these highwaymen friends of ours was mainly a joke upon themselves; for they had waited for me on the cold hill-top two full hours before I came, and there was very little fun in that; they were so chilled that it took them a couple of weeks to get warm again. Moreover, I never had a thought that they would kill me to get money which it was so perfectly easy to get without any such folly, and so they did not really frighten me bad enough to make their enjoyment worth the trouble they had taken. I was only afraid that their weapons would go off accidentally. Their very numbers inspired me with confidence that no blood would be intentionally spilled. They were not smart; they ought to have sent only *one* highwayman, with a double-barrelled shotgun, if they desired to see the author of this volume climb a tree.

However, I suppose that in the long run I got the largest share of the joke at last; and in a shape not foreseen by the highwaymen; for the chilly exposure on the "divide" while I was in a perspiration gave me a cold which developed itself into a troublesome disease and kept my hands idle some three months, besides costing me quite a sum in doctor's bills. Since then I play no practical jokes on people and generally lose my temper when one is played upon me.

When I returned to San Francisco I projected a pleasure journey to Japan and thence westward around the world; but a desire to see home again changed my mind, and I took a berth in the steamship, bade good-bye to the friendliest land and livest, heartiest community on our continent, and came by the way of the Isthmus to New York – a trip that was not much of a picnic excursion, for the cholera broke out among us on the passage and we buried two or three bodies at sea every day. I found home a dreary place after my long absence; for half the children I had known were now wearing whiskers or waterfalls, and few of the grown people I had been acquainted with remained at their hearthstones prosperous and happy – some of them had wandered to other scenes, some were in jail, and the rest had been hanged. These changes touched me deeply, and I went away and joined the famous Quaker City European Excursion and carried my tears to foreign lands.

Thus, after seven years of vicissitudes, ended a "pleasure-trip" to the silver mines of Nevada which had originally been intended to occupy only three months. However, I usually miss my calculations further than that.

MORAL

If the reader thinks he is done, now, and that this book has no moral to it, he is in error. The moral of it is this: If you are of any account, stay at home and make your way by faithful diligence; but if you are "no account," go away from home, and then you will *have* to work, whether you want to or not. Thus you become a blessing to your friends by ceasing to be a nuisance to them – if the people you go among suffer by the operation.

From

A TRAMP ABROAD

1880

Yrs Truly
Mark Twain

CHAPTER I

ONE DAY IT occurred to me that it had been many years since the world had been afforded the spectacle of a man adventurous enough to undertake a journey through Europe on foot. After much thought, I decided that I was a person fitted to furnish to mankind this spectacle. So I determined to do it. This was in March, 1878.

I looked about me for the right sort of person to accompany me in the capacity of agent, and finally hired a Mr. Harris for this service.

It was also my purpose to study art while in Europe. Mr. Harris was in sympathy with me in this. He was as much of an enthusiast in art as I was, and not less anxious to learn to paint. I desired to learn the German language; so did Harris.

Toward the middle of April we sailed in the *Holsatia*, Capt. Brandt, and had a very pleasant trip indeed.

After a brief rest at Hamburg, we made preparations for a long pedestrian trip southward in the soft spring weather, but at the last moment we changed the program, for private reasons, and took the express train.

We made a short halt at Frankfort-on-the-Main, and found it an interesting city. I would have liked to visit the birthplace of Guttenberg, but it could not be done, as no memorandum of the site of the house has been kept. So we spent an hour in the Goethe mansion instead. The city permits this house to belong to private parties, instead of gracing and dignifying herself with the honor of possessing and protecting it.

Frankfort is one of the sixteen cities which have the distinction of being the place where the following incident occurred. Charlemagne, while chasing the Saxons, (as *he* said,) or being chased by them, (as *they* said,) arrived at the bank of the river at dawn, in a fog. The enemy were either before him or behind him; but in any case he wanted to get across, very badly. He would have given anything for a guide, but none was to be had. Presently he saw a deer, followed by her young, approach the water. He watched her, judging that she would seek a ford, and he was right. She waded over, and the army followed. So a great Frankish victory or defeat was gained or avoided; and in order to commemorate the episode, Charlemagne commanded a city to be built there, which he named Frankfort, – the ford of the Franks. None of the other cities where this event happened were named from it. This is good evidence that Frankfort was the first place it occurred at.

Frankfort has another distinction, – it is the birthplace of the German alphabet: or at least of the German word for alphabet, – *Buchstaben.* They say that the first movable types were made on birch sticks, – *Buchstabe,* – hence the name.

I was taught a lesson in political economy in Frankfort. I had brought from home a box containing a thousand very cheap cigars. By way of experiment, I stepped into a little shop in a queer old back street, took four gaily decorated boxes of wax matches and three cigars, and laid down a silver piece worth 48 cents. The man gave me 43 cents change.

In Frankfort every body wears clean clothes, and I think we noticed that this strange thing was the case in Hamburg too, and in the villages along the road. Even in the narrowest and poorest and most ancient quarters of Frankfort neat and clean clothes were the rule. The little children of both sexes were nearly always nice enough to take into a body's lap. And as for the uniforms of the soldiers, they were newness and brightness carried to perfection. One could never detect a smirch or a grain of dust upon them. The street car conductors and drivers wore pretty uniforms which seemed to be just out of the bandbox, and their manners were as fine as their clothes.

In one of the shops I had the luck to stumble upon a book which has charmed me nearly to death. It is entitled "The Legends of the Rhine from Basle to Rotterdam, by F. J. Kiefer; Translated by L. W. Garnham, B. A."

All tourists *mention* the Rhine legends, – in that sort of way which quietly pretends that the mentioner has been familiar with them all his life, and that the reader cannot possibly be ignorant of them, – but no tourist ever *tells* them. So this little book fed me in a very hungry place; and I, in my turn, intend to feed my reader, with one or two little lunches from the same larder. I shall not mar Garnham's translation by meddling with its English; for the most toothsome thing about it is its quaint fashion of building English sentences on the German plan, – and punctuating them according to no plan at all.

In the chapter devoted to "Legends of Frankfort," I find the following:

THE KNAVE OF BERGEN

In Frankfort at the Romer was a great mask-ball, at the coronation festival, and in the illuminated saloon, the clanging music invited to dance, and splendidly appeared the rich toilets and charms of the ladies, and the festively costumed Princes and Knights. All seemed pleasure, joy, and roguish gayety, only one of the numerous guests had a gloomy exterior; but exactly the black armor in which he walked about excited general attention, and his tall figure, as well as the noble propriety of his movements, attracted especially the regards of the ladies. Who the Knight was? Nobody could guess, for his Vizier was well closed, and nothing made him recognizable. Proud and yet modest he advanced to the Empress; bowed on one knee before her seat, and begged for the favor of a waltz with the Queen of the festival. And she allowed his request. With light and graceful steps he danced through the long saloon, with the sovereign who thought never to have found a more dexterous and excellent dancer. But also by the grace of his manner, and fine conversation he knew to win the Queen, and she graciously accorded him a second dance for which he begged, a third, and a fourth, as well as others were not refused him. How all regarded the happy dancer, how many envied him the high favor; how increased curiosity, who the masked knight could be.

Also the Emperor became more and more excited with curiosity, and with great suspense one awaited the hour, when according to mask-law, each masked guest must make himself known. This moment came, but although all others had unmasked; the secret knight still refused to allow his features to be seen, till at last the Queen driven by curiosity, and vexed at the obstinate refusal; commanded him to open his Vizier. He opened it, and none of the high ladies and knights knew him. But from the crowded spectators, 2 officials advanced, who recognized the black dancer, and horror and terror spread in the saloon, as they said who the supposed knight was. It was the executioner of Bergen. But glowing with rage, the King commanded to seize the criminal and lead him to death, who had ventured to dance, with the queen; so disgraced the Empress, and insulted the crown. The culpable threw himself at the feet of the Emperor, and said, –

"Indeed I have heavily sinned against all noble guests assembled here, but most heavily against you my sovereign and my queen. The

Queen is insulted by my haughtiness equal to treason, but no punishment even blood, will not be able to wash out the disgrace, which you have suffered by me. Therefore oh King! allow me to propose a remedy, to efface the shame, and to render it as if not done. Draw your sword and knight me, then I will throw down my gauntlet, to every one who dares to speak disrespectfully of my king."

The Emperor was surprised at this bold proposal, however it appeared the wisest to him; "You are a knave," he replied after a moment's consideration, "however your advice is good, and displays prudence, as your offense shows adventurous courage. Well then," and gave him the knight-stroke, "so I raise you to nobility, who begged for grace for your offense now kneels before me, rise as knight; knavish you have acted, and Knave of Bergen shall you be called henceforth," and gladly the Black Knight rose; three cheers were given in honor of the Emperor, and loud cries of joy testified the approbation with which the Queen danced still once with the Knave of Bergen.

CHAPTER II

HEIDELBERG

WE STOPPED AT a hotel by the railway station. Next morning, as we sat in my room waiting for breakfast to come up, we got a good deal interested in some thing which was going on over the way, in front of another hotel. First, the personage who is called the *portier*, (who is not the *porter*, but is a sort of first-mate of a hotel,)* appeared at the door in a spick and span new blue cloth uniform, decorated with shining brass buttons, and with bands of gold lace around his cap and wrist-bands; and he wore white gloves, too. He shed an official glance upon the situation, and then began to give orders. Two women servants came out with pails and brooms and brushes, and gave the sidewalk a thorough scrubbing; meanwhile two others scrubbed the four marble steps which led up to the door; beyond these we could see some men-servants taking up the carpet of the grand staircase. This carpet was carried away and the last grain of

*See Appendix A, p.586.

dust beaten and banged and swept out of it; then brought back and put down again. The brass stair rods received an exhaustive polishing and were returned to their places. Now a troop of servants brought pots and tubs of blooming plants and formed them into a beautiful jungle about the door and the base of the staircase. Other servants adorned all the balconies of the various stories with flowers and banners; others ascended to the roof and hoisted a great flag on a staff there. Now came some more chamber-maids and retouched the sidewalk, and afterwards wiped the marble steps with damp cloths and finished by dusting them off with feather brushes. Now a broad black carpet was brought out and laid down the marble steps and out across the sidewalk to the curbstone. The *portier* cast his eye along it, and found it was not absolutely straight; he commanded it to be straightened; the servants made the effort, – made several efforts, in fact, – but the *portier* was not satisfied. He finally had it taken up, and then he put it down himself and got it right.

At this stage of the proceedings, a narrow bright red carpet was unrolled and stretched from the top of the marble steps to the curbstone, along the centre of the black carpet. This red path cost the *portier* more trouble than even the black one had done. But he patiently fixed and refixed it until it was exactly right and lay precisely in the middle of the black carpet. In New York these performances would have gathered a mighty crowd of curious and intensely interested spectators; but here it only captured an audience of half-a-dozen little boys, who stood in a row across the pavement, some with their school knapsacks on their backs and their hands in their pockets, others with arms full of bundles, and all absorbed in the show. Occasionally one of them skipped irreverently over the carpet and took up a position on the other side. This always visibly annoyed the *portier*.

Now came a waiting interval. The landlord, in plain clothes, and bare-headed, placed himself on the bottom marble step, abreast the *portier*, who stood on the other end of the same steps; six or eight waiters, gloved, bare-headed, and wearing their whitest linen, their whitest cravats, and their finest swallow-tails, grouped themselves about these chiefs, but leaving the carpet-way clear. Nobody moved or spoke any more but only waited.

In a short time the shrill piping of a coming train was heard, and immediately groups of people began to gather in the street. Two or three open carriages arrived, and deposited some maids of honor and some male officials at the hotel. Presently another open carriage brought the Grand Duke of Baden, a stately man in uniform, who wore the handsome brass-mounted, steel-spiked helmet of the army on his head. Last came the Empress of Germany and the Grand Duchess of Baden in a close carriage; these passed through the low-bowing groups of servants and disappeared in the hotel, exhibiting to us only the backs of their heads, and then the show was over.

It appears to be as difficult to land a monarch as it is to launch a ship.

But as to Heidelberg. The weather was growing pretty warm, – very warm, in fact. So we left the valley and took quarters at the Schloss Hotel, on the hill, above the Castle.

Heidelberg lies at the mouth of a narrow gorge – a gorge the shape of a shepherd's crook; if one looks up it he perceives that it is about straight, for a mile and a half, then makes a sharp curve to the right and disappears. This gorge, – along whose bottom pours the swift Neckar, – is confined between (or cloven through) a couple of long, steep ridges, a thousand feet high and densely wooded clear to their summits, with the exception of one section which has been shaved and put under cultivation. These ridges are chopped off at the mouth of the gorge and form two bold and conspicuous headlands, with Heidelberg nestling between them; from their bases spreads away the vast dim expanse of the Rhine valley, and into this expanse the Neckar goes wandering in shining curves and is presently lost to view.

Now if one turns and looks up the gorge once more, he will see the Schloss hotel on the right, perched on a precipice overlooking the Neckar, – a precipice which is so sumptuously cushioned and draped with foliage that no glimpse of the rock appears. The building seems very airily situated. It has the appearance of being on a shelf half way up the wooded mountain side; and as it is remote and isolated, and very white, it makes a strong mark against the lofty leafy rampart at its back.

This hotel had a feature which was a decided novelty; and one which might be adopted with advantage by any house which is perched in a commanding situation. This feature may be described as a series of glass-enclosed parlors *clinging to the outside of the house*, one against each and every bed-chamber and drawing-room. They are like long, narrow, high-ceiled bird-cages hung against the building.

My room was a corner room, and had two of these things, a north one and a west one.

From the north cage one looks up the Neckar gorge; from the west one he looks down it. This last affords the most extensive view, and it is one of the loveliest that can be imagined, too. Out of a billowy upheaval of vivid green foliage, a rifle-shot removed, rises the huge ruin of Heidelberg Castle,* with empty window arches, ivy-mailed battlements, moldering towers – the Lear of inanimate nature, – deserted, discrowned, beaten by the storms, but royal still, and beautiful. It is a fine sight to see the evening sunlight suddenly strike the leafy declivity at the Castle's base and dash up it and drench it as with a luminous spray, while the adjacent groves are in deep shadow.

Behind the Castle swells a great dome-shaped hill, forest-clad, and beyond that a nobler and loftier one. The Castle looks down upon the compact brown-roofed town; and from the town two picturesque old bridges span the river. Now the view broadens; through the gateway of the sentinel headlands you gaze out over the wide Rhine plain, which stretches away, softly and richly tinted, grows gradually and dreamily indistinct, and finally melts imperceptibly into the remote horizon.

I have never enjoyed a view which had such a serene and satisfying charm about it as this one gives.

The first night we were there, we went to bed and to sleep early; but I awoke at the end of two or three hours, and lay a comfortable while listening to the soothing patter of the rain against the balcony windows. I took it to be rain, but it turned out to be only the murmur of the restless Neckar, tumbling over her dikes and dams far below, in the gorge. I got up and went into the west balcony and saw a wonderful sight. Away down on the level, under the black mass of the Castle, the town lay, stretched along the river, its intricate cobweb of streets jeweled with twinkling lights; there were rows of lights on the bridges; these flung lances of light upon the water, in the black shadows of the arches; and away at the extremity of all this fairy spectacle blinked and glowed a massed multitude of gas-jets which seemed to cover acres of ground; it was as if all the diamonds in the world had been spread out there. I did not know before, that a half mile of sextuple railway tracks could be made such an adornment.

*See Appendix B, p.590.

One thinks Heidelberg by day – with its surroundings – is the last possibility of the beautiful; but when he sees Heidelberg by night, a fallen Milky Way, with that glittering railway constellation pinned to the border, he requires time to consider upon the verdict.

One never tires of poking about in the dense woods that clothe all these lofty Neckar hills to their tops. The great deeps of a boundless forest have a beguiling and impressive charm in any country; but German legends and fairy tales have given these an added charm. They have peopled all that region with gnomes, and dwarfs, and all sorts of mysterious and uncanny creatures. At the time I am writing of, I had been reading so much of this literature that sometimes I was not sure but I was beginning to believe in the gnomes and fairies as realities.

One afternoon I got lost in the woods about a mile from the hotel, and presently fell into a train of dreamy thought about animals which talk, and kobolds, and enchanted folk, and the rest of the pleasant legendary stuff; and so, by stimulating my fancy, I finally got to imagining I glimpsed small flitting shapes here and there down the columned aisles of the forest. It was a place which was peculiarly meet for the occasion. It was a pine wood, with so thick and soft a carpet of brown needles that one's foot fall made no more sound than if he was treading on wool; the tree-trunks were as round and straight and smooth as pillars, and stood close together; they were bare of branches to a point about twenty-five feet above ground, and from there upward so thick with boughs that not a ray of sunlight could pierce through. The world was bright with sunshine outside, but a deep and mellow twilight reigned in there, and also a silence so profound that I seemed to hear my own breathings.

When I had stood ten minutes, thinking and imagining, and getting my spirit in tune with the place, and in the right mood to enjoy the supernatural, a raven suddenly uttered a hoarse croak over my head. It made me start; and then I was angry because I started. I looked up, and the creature was sitting on a limb right over me, looking down at me. I felt something of the same sense of humiliation and injury which one feels when he finds that a human stranger has been clandestinely inspecting him in his privacy and mentally commenting upon him. I eyed the raven, and the raven eyed me. Nothing was said during some seconds. Then the bird stepped a little way along his limb to get a better point of observation, lifted his wings, stuck his head far down below his shoulders toward me, and croaked again – a croak with a distinctly insulting expression about it. If he had spoken in English he could not have said any more plainly than he did say in raven, "Well, what do *you* want here?" I felt as foolish as if I had been caught in some mean act by a responsible being, and reproved for it. However, I made no reply; I would not bandy words with a raven. The adversary waited a while, with his shoulders still lifted, his head thrust down between them, and his keen bright eye fixed on me; then he threw out two or three more insults, which I could not understand, further than that I knew a portion of them consisted of language not used in church.

I still made no reply. Now the adversary raised his head and called. There was an answering croak from a little distance in the wood, – evidently a croak of inquiry. The adversary explained with enthusiasm, and the other raven dropped everything and came. The two sat side by side on the limb and discussed me as freely and offensively as two great naturalists might discuss a new kind of bug. The thing became more and more embarrassing. They called in another friend. This was too much. I saw that they had the advantage of me, and so I concluded to get out of the scrape by walking out of it. They enjoyed my defeat as much as any low white people could have done. They craned their necks and laughed at me, (for a raven *can* laugh, just like a man,) they squalled insulting remarks after me as long as they could see me. They were nothing but ravens – I knew that, – what they thought about me could be a matter of no consequence, – and yet when even a raven shouts after you, "What a hat!" "O, pull down your vest!" and that sort of thing, it hurts you and humiliates you, and there is no getting around it with fine reasoning and pretty arguments.

Animals talk to each other, of course. There can be no question about that; but I suppose there are very few people who can understand them. I never knew but one man who could. I knew he could, however, because he told me so himself. He was a middle-aged, simple-hearted miner who had lived in a lonely corner of California, among the woods and mountains, a good many years, and had studied the ways of his only neighbors, the beasts and the birds, until he believed he could accurately translate any remark which they made. This was Jim Baker. According to Jim Baker, some animals have only a limited education, and use only very simple words, and scarcely ever a comparison or a flowery figure; whereas, certain other animals have a large vocabulary, a fine command of language and a ready and fluent delivery; consequently these latter talk a great deal; they like it; they are conscious of their talent, and they enjoy "showing off." Baker said, that after long and careful observation, he had come to the conclusion that the blue-jays were the best talkers he had found among birds and beasts. Said he: –

"There's more *to* a blue-jay than any other creature. He has got more moods, and more different kinds of feelings than other creatures; and mind you, whatever a blue-jay feels, he can put into language. And no mere commonplace language, either, but rattling, out-and-out book-talk – and bristling with metaphor, too – just bristling! And as for command of language – why *you* never see a blue-jay get stuck for a word. No man ever did. They just boil out of him! And another thing: I've noticed a good deal, and there's no bird, or cow, or any thing that uses as good grammar as a blue-jay. You may say a cat uses good grammar. Well, a cat does – but you let a cat get excited, once; you let a cat get to pulling fur with another cat on a shed, nights, and you'll hear grammar that will give you the lock-jaw. Ignorant people think it's the *noise* which fighting cats make that is so aggravating, but it ain't so; it's the sickening grammar they use. Now I've never heard a jay use bad grammar but very seldom; and when they do, they are as ashamed as a human; they shut right down and leave.

"You may call a jay a bird. Well, so he is, in a measure – because he's got feathers on him, and don't belong to no church, perhaps; but otherwise he is just as much a human as you be. And I'll tell you for why. A jay's gifts, and instincts, and feelings, and interests, cover the whole ground. A jay hasn't got any more principle than a Congressman. A jay will lie, a jay will steal, a jay will deceive, a jay will betray; and four times out of five, a jay will go back on his solemnest promise. The sacredness of an obligation is a thing which you can't cram into no blue-jay's head. Now on top of all this, there's another thing: a jay can out-swear any gentleman in the mines. You think a cat can swear. Well, a cat can; but you give a blue-jay a subject that calls for his reserve-powers, and where is your cat? Don't talk to *me* – I know too much about this thing. And there's yet another thing: in the one little particular of scolding – just good, clean, out-and-out scolding – a blue-jay can lay over any thing, human or divine. Yes, sir, a jay is everything that a man is. A jay can cry, a jay can laugh, a jay can feel shame, a jay can reason and plan and discuss, a jay likes gossip and scandal, a jay has got a sense of humor, a jay knows when he is an ass just as well as you do – maybe better. If a jay ain't human, he better take in his sign, that's all. Now I'm going to tell you a perfectly true fact about some blue-jays."

CHAPTER III

BAKER'S BLUE-JAY YARN

"WHEN I FIRST begun to understand jay language correctly, there was a little incident happened here. Seven years ago, the last man in this region but me, moved away. There stands his house, – been empty ever since; a log-house, with a plank roof – just one big room, and no more; no ceiling – nothing between the rafters and the floor. Well, one Sunday morning I was sitting out here in front of my cabin, with my cat, taking the sun, and looking at the blue hills, and listening to the leaves rustling so lonely in the trees, and thinking of the home away yonder in the States, that I hadn't heard from in thirteen years, when a blue-jay lit on that house, with an acorn in his mouth, and says, 'Hello, I reckon I've struck something.' When he spoke, the acorn dropped out of his mouth and rolled down the roof, of course, but he didn't care; his mind was all on the thing he had struck. It was a knot-hole in the roof. He cocked his head to one side, shut one eye and put the other one to the hole, like a 'possum looking down a jug; then he glanced up with his bright eyes, gave a wink or two with his wings – which signifies gratification, you understand, – and says, 'It looks like a hole, it's located like a hole, – blamed if I don't believe it *is* a hole!'

"Then he cocked his head down and took another look; he glances up perfectly joyful, this time; winks his wings and his tail both, and says, 'O, no, this ain't no fat thing, I reckon! If I ain't in luck! – why it's a perfectly elegant hole!' So he flew down and got that acorn, and fetched it up and dropped it in, and was just tilting his head back, with the heavenliest smile on his face, when all of a sudden he was paralyzed into a listening attitude and that smile faded gradually out of his countenance like breath off'n a razor, and the queerest look of surprise took its place. Then he says, 'Why I didn't hear it fall!' He cocked his eye at the hole again, and took a long look; raised up and shook his head; stepped around to the other side of the hole and took another look from that side; shook his head again. He studied a while, then he just went into the *de*tails – walked round and round the hole and spied into it from every point of the compass. No use. Now he took a thinking attitude on the comb of the roof and scratched the back of his head with his right foot a minute, and finally says, 'Well, it's too many for *me*, that's certain; must be a mighty long hole; however, I ain't got no time to fool around here, I got to ’tend to business; I reckon it’s all right – chance it, anyway.’

“So he flew off and fetched another acorn and dropped it in, and tried to flirt his eye to the hole quick enough to see what become of it, but he was too late. He held his eye there as much as a minute; then he raised up and sighed, and says, ‘Confound it, I don’t seem to understand this thing, no way; however, I’ll tackle her again.’ He fetched another acorn, and done his level best to see what become of it, but he couldn’t. He says, ‘Well, *I* never struck no such a hole as this, before; I’m of the opinion it’s a totally new kind of a hole.’ Then he begun to get mad. He held in for a spell, walking up and down the comb of the roof and shaking his head and muttering to himself; but his feelings got the upper hand of him, presently, and he broke loose and cussed himself black in the face. I never see a bird take on so about a little thing. When he got through he walks to the hole and looks in again for half a minute; then he says, ‘Well, you’re a long hole, and a deep hole, and a mighty singular hole altogether – but I’ve started in to fill you, and I’m d—d if I *don’t* fill you, if it takes a hundred years!’

“And with that, away he went. You never see a bird work so since you was born. He laid into his work like a nigger, and the way he hove acorns into that hole for about two hours and a half was one of the most exciting and astonishing spectacles I ever struck. He never stopped to take a look anymore – he just hove ’em in and went for more. Well at last he could hardly flop his wings, he was so tuckered out. He comes a-drooping down, once more, sweating like an ice-pitcher, drops his acorn in and says, ‘*Now* I guess I’ve got the bulge on you by this time!’ So he bent down for a look. If you’ll believe me, when his head come up again he was just pale with rage. He says, ‘I’ve shoveled acorns enough in there to keep the family thirty years, and if I can see a sign of one of ’em I wish I may land in a museum with a belly full of sawdust in two minutes!’

“He just had strength enough to crawl up on to the comb and lean his back agin the chimbly, and then he collected his impressions and begun to free his mind. I see in a second that what I had mistook for profanity in the mines was only just the rudiments, as you may say.

“Another jay was going by, and heard him doing his devotions, and stops to inquire what was up. The sufferer told him the whole circumstance, and says, 'Now yonder's the hole, and if you don't believe me, go and look for yourself.' So this fellow went and looked, and comes back and says, 'How many did you say you put in there?' 'Not any less than two tons,' says the sufferer. The other jay went and looked again. He couldn't seem to make it out, so he raised a yell, and three more jays come. They all examined the hole, they all made the sufferer tell it over again, then they all discussed it, and got off as many leather-headed opinions about it as an average crowd of humans could have done.

"They called in more jays; then more and more, till pretty soon this whole region 'peared to have a blue flush about it. There must have been five thousand of them; and such another jawing and disputing and ripping and cussing, you never heard. Every jay in the whole lot put his eye to the hole and delivered a more chuckle-headed opinion about the mystery than the jay that went there before him. They examined the house all over, too. The door was standing half open, and at last one old jay happened to go and light on it and look in. Of course that knocked the mystery galley-west in a second. There lay the acorns, scattered all over the floor. He flopped his wings and raised a whoop. 'Come here!' he says, 'Come here, everybody; hang'd if this fool hasn't been trying to fill up a house with acorns!' They all came a-swooping down like a blue cloud, and as each fellow lit on the door and took a glance, the whole absurdity of the contract that that first jay had tackled hit him home and he fell over backwards suffocating with laughter, and the next jay took his place and done the same.

"Well, sir, they roosted around here on the house-top and the trees for an hour, and guffawed over that thing like human beings. It ain't any use to tell me a blue-jay hasn't got a sense of humor, because I know better. And memory, too. They brought jays here from all over the United States to look down that hole, every summer for three years. Other birds too. And they could all see the point, except an owl that come from Nova Scotia to visit the Yo Semite, and he took this thing in on his way back. He said he couldn't see any thing funny in it. But then he was a good deal disappointed about Yo Semite, too."

CHAPTER VIII
THE GREAT FRENCH DUEL

MUCH AS THE modern French duel is ridiculed by certain smart people, it is in reality one of the most dangerous institutions of our day. Since it is always fought in the open air the combatants are nearly sure to catch cold. M. Paul de Cassagnac, the most inveterate of the French duelists, has suffered so often in this way that he is at last a confirmed invalid; and the best physician in Paris has expressed the opinion that if he goes on dueling for fifteen or twenty years more, – unless he forms the habit of fighting in a comfortable room where damps and draughts cannot intrude, – he will eventually endanger his life. This ought to moderate the talk of those people who are so stubborn in maintaining that the French duel is the most health-giving of recreations because of the open-air exercise it affords. And it ought also to moderate that foolish talk about French duelists and socialist-hated monarchs being the only people who are immortal.

But it is time to get at my subject. As soon as I heard of the late fiery outbreak between M. Gambetta and M. Fourtou in the French Assembly, I knew that trouble must follow. I knew it because a long personal friendship with M. Gambetta had revealed to me the desperate and implacable nature of the man. Vast as are his physical proportions, I knew that the thirst for revenge would penetrate to the remotest frontiers of his person.

I did not wait for him to call on me, but went at once to him. As I expected, I found the brave fellow steeped in a profound French calm. I say French calm, because French calmness and English calmness have points of difference. He was moving swiftly back and forth among the *débris* of his furniture, now and then staving chance fragments of it across the room with his foot; grinding a constant grist of curses through his set teeth; and halting every little while to deposit another handful of his hair on the pile which he had been building of it on the table.

He threw his arms around my neck, bent me over his stomach to his breast, kissed me on both cheeks, hugged me four or five times, and then placed me in his own arm-chair. As soon as I had got well again, we began business at once.

I said I supposed he would wish me to act as his second, and he said, "Of course." I said I must be allowed to act under a French name, so that I might be shielded from obloquy in my country, in case of fatal results. He winced here, probably at the suggestion that dueling was not regarded with respect in America. However, he agreed to my requirement. This accounts for the fact that in all the newspaper reports M. Gambetta's second was apparently a Frenchman.

First, we drew up my principal's will. I insisted upon this, and stuck to my point. I said I had never heard of a man in his right mind going out to fight a duel without first making his will. He said he had never heard of a man in his right mind doing any thing of the kind. When he had finished the will, he wished to proceed to a choice of his "last words." He wanted to know how the following words, as a dying exclamation, struck me: –

"I die for my God, for my country, for freedom of speech, for progress, and the universal brotherhood of man!"

I objected that this would require too lingering a death; it was a good speech for a consumptive, but not suited to the exigencies of the field of honor. We wrangled over a good many ante-mortem outbursts, but I finally got him to cut his obituary down to this, which he copied into his memorandum book, purposing to get it by heart: –

"I DIE THAT FRANCE MAY LIVE."

I said that this remark seemed to lack relevancy; but he said relevancy was a matter of no consequence in last words, what you wanted was thrill.

The next thing in order was the choice of weapons. My principal said he was not feeling well, and would leave that and the other details of the proposed meeting to me. Therefore I wrote the following note and carried it to M. Fourtou's friend: –

SIR:

M. Gambetta accepts M. Fourtou's challenge, and authorizes me to propose Plessis-Piquet as the place of meeting; to-morrow morning at daybreak as the time; and axes as the weapons. I am, sir, with great respect,

MARK TWAIN

M. Fourtou's friend read this note, and shuddered. Then he turned to me, and said, with a suggestion of severity in his tone: –

"Have you considered, sir, what would be the inevitable result of such a meeting as this?"

"Well, for instance, what *would* it be?"

"Bloodshed!"

"That's about the size of it," I said. "Now, if it is a fair question, what was your side proposing to shed?"

I had him, there. He saw he had made a blunder, so he hastened to explain it away. He said he had spoken jestingly. Then he added that he and his principal would enjoy axes, and indeed prefer them, but such weapons were barred by the French code, and so I must change my proposal.

I walked the floor, turning the thing over in my mind, and finally it occurred to me that Gatling guns at fifteen paces would be a likely way to get a verdict on the field of honor. So I framed this idea into a proposition.

But it was not accepted. The code was in the way again. I proposed rifles; then double-barreled shotguns; then, Colt's navy revolvers. These being all rejected, I reflected a while, and sarcastically suggested brick-bats at three-quarters of a mile. I always hate to fool away a humorous thing on a person who has no perception of humor; and it filled me with bitterness when this man went soberly away to submit the last proposition to his principal.

He came back presently and said his principal was charmed with the idea of brick-bats at three-quarters of a mile, but must decline on account of the danger to disinterested parties passing between. Then I said: –

"Well, I am at the end of my string, now. Perhaps *you* would be good enough to suggest a weapon? Perhaps you have even had one in your mind all the time?"

His countenance brightened, and he said with alacrity, –

"Oh, without doubt, monsieur!"

So he fell to hunting in his pockets, – pocket after pocket, and he had plenty of them, – muttering all the while, "Now, what could I have done with them?"

At last he was successful. He fished out of his vest pocket a couple of little things which I carried to the light and ascertained to be pistols. They were single-barreled and silver-mounted, and very dainty and pretty. I was not able to speak for emotion. I silently hung one of them on my watch chain, and returned the other. My companion in crime now unrolled a postage-stamp containing several cartridges, and gave me one of them. I asked if he meant to signify by this that our men were to be allowed but one shot apiece. He replied that the French code permitted no more. I then begged him to go on and suggest a distance, for my mind was growing weak and confused under the strain which had been put upon it. He named sixty-five yards. I nearly lost my patience. I said, –

"Sixty-five yards, with these instruments? Squirt-guns would be deadlier at fifty. Consider, my friend, you and I are banded together to destroy life, not make it eternal."

But with all my persuasions, all my arguments, I was only able to get him to reduce the distance to thirty-five yards; and even this concession he made with reluctance, and said with a sigh, –

"I wash my hands of this slaughter; on your head be it."

There was nothing for me but to go home to my old lion-heart and tell my humiliating story. When I entered, M. Gambetta was laying his last lock of hair upon the altar. He sprang toward me, exclaiming,

"You have made the fatal arrangements, – I see it in your eye!"

"I have."

His face paled a trifle, and he leaned upon the table for support. He breathed thick and heavily for a moment or two, so tumultuous were his feelings; then he hoarsely whispered, –

"The weapon, the weapon! Quick! what is the weapon?"

"This!" and I displayed that silver-mounted thing. He cast but one glance at it, then swooned ponderously to the floor.

When he came to, he said mournfully, –

"The unnatural calm to which I have subjected myself has told upon my nerves. But away with weakness! I will confront my fate like a man and a Frenchman."

He rose to his feet, and assumed an attitude which for sublimity has never been approached by man, and has seldom been surpassed by statues. Then he said, in his deep bass tones, –

"Behold, I am calm, I am ready; reveal to me the distance."

"Thirty-five yards."

I could not lift him up, of course; but I rolled him over, and poured water down his back. He presently came to, and said, –

"Thirty-five yards, – without a rest? But why ask? Since murder was that man's intention, why should he palter with small details? But mark you one thing: in my fall the world shall see how the chivalry of France meets death."

After a long silence he asked, –

"Was nothing said about that man's family standing up with him, as an offset to my bulk? But no matter; I would not stoop to make such a suggestion; if he is not noble enough to suggest it himself, he is welcome to this advantage, which no honorable man would take."

He now sank into a sort of stupor of reflection, which lasted some minutes; after which he broke silence with, –

"The hour, – what is the hour fixed for the collision?"

"Dawn, to-morrow."

He seemed greatly surprised, and immediately said, –

"Insanity! I never heard of such a thing. Nobody is abroad at such an hour."

"That is the reason I named it. Do you mean to say you want an audience?"

"It is no time to bandy words. I am astonished that M. Fourtou should ever have agreed to so strange an innovation. Go at once and require a later hour."

I ran down stairs, threw open the front door, and almost plunged into the arms of M. Fourtou's second. He said, –

"I have the honor to say that my principal strenuously objects to the hour chosen, and begs you will consent to change it to half-past nine."

"Any courtesy, sir, which it is in our power to extend is at the service of your excellent principal. We agree to the proposed change of time."

"I beg you to accept the thanks of my client." Then he turned to a person behind him, and said, "You hear M. Noir, the hour is altered to half-past nine." Whereupon M. Noir bowed, expressed his thanks, and went away. My accomplice continued: –

"If agreeable to you, your chief surgeons and ours shall proceed to the field in the same carriage, as is customary."

"It is entirely agreeable to me, and I am obliged to you for mentioning the surgeons, for I am afraid I should not have thought of them. How many shall I want? I suppose two or three will be enough?"

"Two is the customary number for each party. I refer to 'chief' surgeons; but considering the exalted positions occupied by our clients, it will be well and decorous that each of us appoint several consulting surgeons, from among the highest in the profession. These will come in their own private carriages. Have you engaged a hearse?"

"Bless my stupidity, I never thought of it! I will attend to it right away. I must seem very ignorant to you; but you must try to overlook that, because I have never had any experience of such a swell duel as this before. I have had a good deal to do with duels on the Pacific coast, but I see now that they were crude affairs. A hearse, – sho! we used to leave the elected lying around loose, and let anybody cord them up and cart them off that wanted to. Have you anything further to suggest?"

"Nothing, except that the head undertakers shall ride together, as is usual. The subordinates and mutes will go on foot, as is also usual. I will see you at eight o'clock in the morning, and we will then arrange the order of the procession. I have the honor to bid you a good day."

I returned to my client, who said, "Very well; at what hour is the engagement to begin?"

"Half-past nine."

"Very good indeed. Have you sent the fact to the newspapers?"

"*Sir!* If after our long and intimate friendship you can for a moment deem me capable of so base a treachery—"

"Tut, tut! What words are these, my dear friend? Have I wounded you? Ah, forgive me; I am overloading you with labor. Therefore go on with the other details, and drop this one from your list. The bloody-minded Fourtou will be sure to attend to it. Or I myself – yes, to make certain, I will drop a note to my journalistic friend, M. Noir—"

"Oh, come to think, you may save yourself the trouble; that other second has informed M. Noir."

"H'm! I might have known it. It is just like that Fourtou, who always wants to make a display."

At half-past nine in the morning the procession approached the field of Plessis-Piquet in the following order: first came our carriage, – nobody in it but M. Gambetta and myself; then a carriage containing M. Fourtou and his second; then a carriage containing two poet-orators who did not believe in God, and these had MS. funeral orations projecting from their breast pockets; then a carriage containing the head surgeons and their cases of instruments; then eight private carriages containing consulting surgeons; then a hack containing a coroner; then the two hearses; then a carriage containing the head undertakers; then a train of assistants and mutes on foot; and after these came plodding through the fog a long procession of camp-followers, police, and citizens generally. It was a noble turn-out, and would have made a fine display if we had had thinner weather.

There was no conversation. I spoke several times to my principal, but I judge he was not aware of it, for he always referred to his note-book and muttered absently, "I die that France may live."

Arrived on the field, my fellow-second and I paced off the thirty-five yards, and then drew lots for choice of position. This latter was but an ornamental ceremony, for all choices were alike in such weather. These preliminaries being ended, I went to my principal and asked him if he was ready. He spread himself out to his full width, and said in a stern voice, "Ready! Let the batteries be charged."

The loading was done in the presence of duly constituted witnesses. We considered it best to perform this delicate service with the assistance of a lantern, on account of the state of the weather. We now placed our men.

At this point the police noticed that the public had massed themselves together on the right and left of the field; they therefore begged a delay, while they should put these poor people in a place of safety. The request was granted.

The police having ordered the two multitudes to take positions behind the duelists, we were once more ready. The weather growing still more opaque, it was agreed between myself and the other second that before giving the fatal signal we should each deliver a loud whoop to enable the combatants to ascertain each other's whereabouts.

I now returned to my principal, and was distressed to observe that he had lost a good deal of his spirit. I tried my best to hearten him. I said, "Indeed, sir, things are not as bad as they seem. Considering the character of the weapons, the limited number of shots allowed, the generous distance, the impenetrable solidity of the fog, and the added fact that one of the combatants is one-eyed and the other cross-eyed and near-sighted, it seems to me that this conflict need not necessarily be fatal. There are chances that both of you may survive. Therefore, cheer up; do not be down-hearted."

This speech had so good an effect that my principal immediately stretched forth his hand and said, "I am myself again; give me the weapon."

I laid it, all lonely and forlorn, in the centre of the vast solitude of his palm. He gazed at it and shuddered. And still mournfully contemplating it, he murmured, in a broken voice, –

"Alas, it is not death I dread but mutilation."

I heartened him once more, and with such success that he presently said, "Let the tragedy begin. Stand at my back; do not desert me in this solemn hour, my friend."

I gave him my promise. I now assisted him to point his pistol toward the spot where I judged his adversary to be standing, and cautioned him to listen well and further guide himself by my fellow-second's whoop. Then I propped myself against M. Gambetta's back, and raised a rousing "Whoop-ee!" This was answered from out the far distances of the fog, and I immediately shouted, –

"One, – two, – three, – *fire!*"

Two little sounds like *spit! spit!* broke upon my ear, and in the same instant I was crushed to the earth under a mountain of flesh. Bruised as I was, I was still able to catch a faint accent from above, to this effect, –

"I die for...for...perdition take it, what *is* it I die for?...oh, yes, – FRANCE! I die that France may live!"

The surgeons swarmed around with their probes in their hands, and applied their microscopes to the whole area of M. Gambetta's person, with the happy result of finding nothing in the nature of a wound. Then a scene ensued which was in every way gratifying and inspiriting.

The two gladiators fell upon each other's necks, with floods of proud and happy tears; that other second embraced me; the surgeons, the orators, the undertakers, the police, every body embraced, every body congratulated, every body cried, and the whole atmosphere was filled with praise and with joy unspeakable.

It seemed to me then that I would rather be a hero of a French duel than a crowned and sceptred monarch.

When the commotion had somewhat subsided, the body of surgeons held a consultation, and after a good deal of debate decided that with proper care and nursing there was reason to believe that I would survive my injuries. My internal hurts were deemed the most serious, since it was apparent that a broken rib had penetrated my left lung, and that many of my organs had been pressed out so far to one side or the other of where they belonged, that it was doubtful if they would ever learn to perform their functions in such remote and unaccustomed localities. They then set my left arm in two places, pulled my right hip into its socket again, and re-elevated my nose. I was an object of great interest, and even admiration; and many sincere and warm-hearted persons had themselves introduced to me, and said they were proud to know the only man who had been hurt in a French duel in forty years.

I was placed in an ambulance at the very head of the procession; and thus with gratifying *éclat* I was marched into Paris, the most conspicuous figure in that great spectacle, and deposited at the hospital.

The cross of the Legion of Honor has been conferred upon me. However, few escape that distinction.

Such is the true version of the most memorable private conflict of the age.

I have no complaints to make against any one. I acted for myself, and I can stand the consequences. Without boasting, I think I may say I am not afraid to stand before a modern French duelist, but as long as I keep in my right mind I will never consent to stand behind one again.

CHAPTER IX

ONE DAY WE took the train and went down to Mannheim to see King Lear played in German. It was a mistake. We sat in our seats three whole hours and never understood any thing but the thunder and lightning; and even that was reversed to suit German ideas, for the thunder came first and the lightning followed after.

The behavior of the audience was perfect. There were no rustlings, or whisperings, or other little disturbances; each act was listened to in silence, and the applauding was done after the curtain was down. The doors opened at half-past four, the play began promptly at half-past five, and within two minutes afterward all who were coming were in their seats, and quiet reigned. A German gentleman in the train had said that a Shakespearian play was an appreciated treat in Germany and that we should find the house filled. It was true; all the six tiers were filled, and remained so to the end, – which suggested that it is not only balcony people who like Shakespeare in Germany, but those of the pit and the gallery, too.

Another time, we went to Mannheim and attended a shivaree, – otherwise an opera, – the one called Lohengrin. The banging and slamming and booming and crashing were something beyond belief. The racking and pitiless pain of it remains stored up in my memory alongside the memory of the time that I had my teeth fixed. There were circumstances which made it necessary for me to stay through the four hours to the end, and I staid; but the recollection of that long, dragging, relentless season of suffering is indestructible. To have to endure it in silence, and sitting still, made it all the harder. I was in a railed compartment with eight or ten strangers, of the two sexes, and this compelled repression; yet at times the pain was so exquisite that I could hardly keep the tears back. At those times, as the howlings and wailings and shriekings of the singers, and the ragings and roarings and explosions of the vast orchestra rose higher and higher, and wilder and wilder, and fiercer and fiercer, I could have cried if I had been alone. Those strangers would not have been surprised to see a man do such a thing who was being gradually skinned, but they would have marveled at it here, and made remarks about it no doubt, whereas there was nothing in the present case which was an advantage over being skinned. There was a wait of half an hour at the end of the first act, and I could have gone out and rested during that time, but I could not trust myself to do it, for I felt that I should desert and stay out. There was another wait of half an hour toward nine o'clock, but I had gone through so much by that time that I had no spirit left, and so had no desire but to be let alone.

I do not wish to suggest that the rest of the people there were like me, for indeed they were not. Whether it was that they naturally liked that noise, or whether it was that they had learned to like it by getting used to it, I did not at that time know; but they did like it, – this was plain enough. While it was going on they sat and looked as rapt and grateful as cats do when one strokes their backs; and whenever the curtain fell they rose to their feet, in one solid mighty multitude, and the air was snowed thick with waving handkerchiefs, and hurricanes of applause swept the place. This was not comprehensible to me. Of course there were many people there who were not under compulsion to stay; yet the tiers were as full at the close as they had been at the beginning. This showed that the people liked it.

It was a curious sort of a play. In the matter of costumes and scenery it was fine and showy enough; but there was not much action. That is to say, there was not much really done, it was only talked about; and always violently. It was what one might call a narrative play. Everybody had a narrative and a grievance, and none were reasonable about it but all in an offensive and ungovernable state. There was little of that sort of customary thing where the tenor and the soprano stand down by the footlights, warbling, with blended voices, and keep holding out their arms toward each other and drawing them back and spreading both hands over first one breast and then the other with a shake and a pressure, – no, it was every rioter for himself and no blending. Each sang his indictive narrative in turn, accompanied by the whole orchestra of sixty instruments, and when this had continued for some time, and one was hoping they might come to an understanding and modify the noise, a great chorus composed entirely of maniacs would suddenly break forth, and then during two minutes, and sometimes three, I lived over again all that I had suffered the time the orphan asylum burned down.

We only had one brief little season of heaven and heaven's sweet ecstasy and peace during all this long and diligent and acrimonious reproduction of the other place. This was while a gorgeous procession of people marched around and around, in the third act, and sang the Wedding Chorus. To my untutored ear that was music, – almost divine music. While my seared soul was steeped in the healing balm of those gracious sounds, it seemed to me that I could almost re-suffer the torments which had gone before, in order to be so healed again. There is where the deep ingenuity of the operatic idea is betrayed. It deals so largely in pain that its scattered delights are prodigiously augmented by the contrasts. A pretty air in an opera is prettier there than it could be anywhere else, I suppose, just as an honest man in politics shines more than he would elsewhere.

I have since found out that there is nothing the Germans like so much as an opera. They like it, not in a mild and moderate way, but with their whole hearts. This is a legitimate result of habit and education. Our nation will like the opera, too, by and by, no doubt. One in fifty of those who attend our operas likes it already, perhaps, but I think a good many of the other forty-nine go in order to learn to like it, and the rest in order to be able to talk knowingly about it. The latter usually hum the airs while they are being sung, so that their neighbors may perceive that they have been to operas before. The funerals of these do not occur often enough.

A gentle, old-maidish person and a sweet young girl of seventeen sat right in front of us that night at the Mannheim opera. These people talked, between the acts, and I understood them, though I understood nothing that was uttered on the distant stage. At first they were guarded in their talk, but after they had heard my agent and me conversing in English they dropped their reserve and I picked up many of their little confidences; no, I mean many of *her* little confidences, – meaning the elder party, – for the young girl only listened, and gave assenting nods, but never said a word. How pretty she was, and how sweet she was! I wished she would speak. But evidently she was absorbed in her own thoughts, her own young-girl dreams, and found a dearer pleasure in silence. But she was not dreaming sleepy dreams, – no, she was awake, alive, alert, she could not sit still a moment. She was an enchanting study. Her gown was of a soft white silky stuff that clung to her round young figure like a fish's skin, and it was rippled over with the gracefullest little fringy films of lace; she had deep, tender eyes, with long, curved lashes; and she had peachy cheeks, and a dimpled chin, and such a dear little dewy rose-bud of a mouth; and she was so dove-like, so pure, and so gracious, so sweet and bewitching. For long hours I did mightily wish she would speak. And at last she did; the red lips parted, and out leaped her thought, – and with such a guileless and pretty enthusiasm, too: "Auntie, I just *know* I've got five hundred fleas on me!"

That was probably over the average. Yes, it must have been very much over the average. The average at that time in the Grand Duchy of Baden was forty-five to a young person, (when alone,) according to the official estimate of the Home Secretary for that year; the average for older people was shifty and indeterminable, for whenever a wholesome young girl came into the presence of her elders she immediately lowered their average and raised her own. She became a sort of contribution box. This dear young thing in the theatre had been sitting there unconsciously taking up a collection. Many a skinny old being in our neighborhood was the happier and the restfuller for her coming.

In that large audience, that night, there were eight very conspicuous people. These were ladies who had their hats or bonnets on. What a blessed thing it would be if a lady could make herself conspicuous in our theatres by wearing her hat. It is not usual in Europe to allow ladies and gentlemen to take bonnets, hats, over coats, canes or umbrellas into the auditorium, but in Mannheim this rule was not enforced because the audiences were largely made up of people from a distance, and among these were always a few timid ladies who were afraid that if they had to go into an ante-room to get their things when the play was over, they would miss their train. But the great mass of those who came from a distance always ran the risk and took the chances, preferring the loss of the train to a breach of good manners and the discomfort of being unpleasantly conspicuous during a stretch of three or four hours.

CHAPTER X

THREE OR FOUR hours. That is a long time to sit in one place, whether one be conspicuous or not, yet some of Wagner's operas bang along for six whole hours on a stretch! But the people sit there and enjoy it all, and wish it would last longer. A German lady in Munich told me that a person could not like Wagner's music at first, but must go through the deliberate process of learning to like it, – then he would have his sure reward; for when he had learned to like it he would hunger for it and never be able to get enough of it. She said that six hours of Wagner was by no means too much. She said that this composer had made a complete revolution in music and was burying the old masters one by one. And she said that Wagner's operas differed from all others in one notable respect, and that was that they were not merely spotted with music here and there, but were *all* music, from the first strain to the last. This surprised me. I said I had attended one of his insurrections, and found hardly *any* music in it except the Wedding Chorus. She said Lohengrin was noisier than Wagner's other operas, but that if I would keep on going to see it I would find by and by that it was all music, and therefore would then enjoy it. I *could* have said, "But would you advise a person to deliberately practice having the toothache in the pit of his stomach for a couple of years in order that he might then come to enjoy it?" But I reserved that remark.

This lady was full of the praises of the head-tenor who had performed in a Wagner opera the night before, and went on to enlarge upon his old and prodigious fame, and how many honors had been lavished upon him by the princely houses of Germany. Here was another surprise. I had attended that very opera, in the person of my agent, and had made close and accurate observations. So I said: –

"Why madam, *my* experience warrants me in stating that that tenor's voice is not a voice at all, but only a shriek, – the shriek of a hyena."

"That is very true," she said; "he cannot sing now; it is already many years that he has lost his voice, but in other times he sang, yes, divinely! So whenever he comes, now, you shall see, yes, that the theatre will not hold the people. *Jawohl bei Gott!* his voice is *wunderschön* in that past time."

I said she was discovering to me a kindly trait in the Germans which was worth emulating. I said that over the water we were not quite so generous; that with us, when a singer had lost his voice and a jumper had lost his legs, these parties ceased to draw. I said I had been to the opera in Hanover, once, and in Mannheim once, and in Munich, (through my authorized agent,) once, and this large experience had nearly persuaded me that the Germans *preferred* singers who couldn't sing. This was not such a very extravagant speech, either, for that burly Mannheim tenor's praises had been the talk of all Heidelberg for a week before his performance took place, – yet his voice was like the distressing noise which a nail makes when you screech it across a window pane. I said so to Heidelberg friends the next day, and they said, in the calmest and simplest way, that that was very true, but that in earlier times his voice *had* been wonderfully fine. And the tenor in Hanover was just another example of this sort. The English-speaking German gentleman who went with me to the opera there was brimming with enthusiasm over that tenor. He said: –

"*Ach Gott!* a great man! You shall see him. He is so celebrate in all Germany, – and he has a pension, yes, from the government. He not obliged to sing, now, only twice every year; but if he not sing twice each year they take him his pension away."

Very well, we went. When the renowned old tenor appeared, I got a nudge and an excited whisper: –

"Now you see him!"

But the "celebrate" was an astonishing disappointment to me. If he had been behind a screen I should have supposed they were performing a surgical operation on him. I looked at my friend, – to my great surprise he seemed intoxicated with pleasure, his eyes were dancing with eager delight. When the curtain at last fell, he burst into the stormiest applause, and kept it up, – as did the whole house, – until the afflictive tenor had come three times before the curtain to make his bow. While the glowing enthusiast was swabbing the perspiration from his face, I said: –

"I don't mean the least harm, but really, now, do you think he can sing?"

"Him? *No! Gott im Himmel, aber*, how he has been able to sing twenty-five years ago?" [Then pensively.]"*Ach*, no, *now* he not sing any more, he only cry. When he think he sing, now, he not sing at all, no, he only make like a cat which is unwell."

Where and how did we get the idea that the Germans are a stolid, phlegmatic race? In truth they are widely removed from that. They are warm-hearted, emotional, impulsive, enthusiastic, their tears come at the mildest touch, and it is not hard to move them to laughter. They are the very children of impulse. We are cold and self-contained, compared to the Germans. They hug and kiss and cry and shout and dance and sing; and where we use one loving, petting expression they pour out a score. Their language is full of endearing diminutives; nothing that they love escapes the application of a petting diminutive, – neither the house, nor the dog, nor the horse, nor the grandmother, nor any other creature, animate or inanimate.

In the theatres at Hanover, Hamburg, and Mannheim, they had a wise custom. The moment the curtain went up, the lights in the body of the house went down. The audience sat in the cool gloom of a deep twilight, which greatly enhanced the glowing splendors of the stage. It saved gas, too, and people were not sweated to death.

When I saw King Lear played, nobody was allowed to see a scene shifted; if there was nothing to be done but slide a forest out of the way and expose a temple beyond, one did not see that forest split itself in the middle and go shrieking away, with the accompanying disenchanting spectacle of the hands and heels of the impelling impulse, – no, the curtain was always dropped for an instant, – one heard not the least movement behind it, – but when it went up, the next instant, the forest was gone. Even when the stage was being entirely re-set, one heard no noise. During the whole time that King Lear was playing, the curtain was never down two minutes at any one time. The orchestra played until the curtain was ready to go up for the first time, then they departed for the evening. Where the stage-waits never reach two minutes, there is no occasion for music. I had never seen this two-minute business between acts but once before, and that was when the "Shaughran" was played at Wallack's.

I was at a concert in Munich one night, the people were streaming in, the clock-hand pointed to seven, the music struck up, and instantly all movement in the body of the house ceased, – nobody was standing, or walking up the aisles or fumbling with a seat, the stream of incomers had suddenly dried up at its source. I listened undisturbed to a piece of music that was fifteen minutes long, – always expecting some tardy ticket-holders to come crowding past my knees, and being continuously and pleasantly disappointed, – but when the last note was struck, here came the stream again. You see, they had made those late comers wait in the comfortable waiting-parlor from the time the music had begun until it was ended.

It was the first time I had ever seen this sort of criminals denied the privilege of destroying the comfort of a house full of their betters. Some of these were pretty fine birds, but no matter, they had to tarry outside in the long parlor under the inspection of a double rank of liveried footmen and waiting-maids who supported the two walls with their backs and held the wraps and traps of their masters and mistresses on their arms.

We had no footmen to hold our things, and it was not permissible to take them into the concert room; but there were some men and women to take charge of them for us. They gave us checks for them and charged a fixed price, payable in advance, – five cents.

In Germany they always hear one thing at an opera which has never yet been heard in America, perhaps, – I mean the closing strain of a fine solo or duet. We always smash into it with an earthquake of applause. The result is that we rob ourselves of the sweetest part of the treat; we get the whiskey, but we don't get the sugar in the bottom of the glass.

Our way of scattering applause along through an act seems to me to be better than the Mannheim way of saving it all up till the act is ended. I do not see how an actor can forget himself and portray hot passion before a cold still audience. I should think he would feel foolish. It is a pain to me to this day, to remember how that old German Lear raged and wept and howled around the stage, with never a response from that hushed house, never a single outburst till the act was ended. To me there was something unspeakably uncomfortable in the solemn dead silences that always followed this old person's tremendous outpourings of his feelings. I could not help putting myself in his place, – I thought I knew how sick and flat he felt during those silences, because I remembered a case which came under my observation once, and which, – but I will tell the incident:

One evening on board a Mississippi steamboat, a boy of ten years lay asleep in a berth, – a long, slim-legged boy, he was, encased in quite a short shirt; it was the first time he had ever made a trip on a steamboat, and so he was troubled, and scared, and had gone to bed with his head filled with impending snaggings, and explosions, and conflagrations, and sudden death. About ten o'clock some twenty ladies were sitting around about the ladies' saloon, quietly reading, sewing, embroidering, and so on, and among them sat a sweet, benignant old dame with round spectacles on her nose and her busy knitting-needles in her hands. Now all of a sudden, into the midst of this peaceful scene burst that slim-shanked boy in the brief shirt, wild-eyed, erect-haired, and shouting, "Fire, fire! *jump and run, the boat's afire and there ain't a minute to lose!*" All those ladies looked sweetly up and smiled, nobody stirred, the old lady pulled her spectacles down, looked over them, and said, gently, –

"But you mustn't catch cold, child. Run and put on your breast-pin, and then come and tell us all about it."

It was a cruel chill to give to a poor little devil's gushing vehemence. He was expecting to be a sort of hero – the creator of a wild panic – and here every body sat and smiled a mocking smile, and an old woman made fun of his bugbear. I turned and crept humbly away – for I was that boy – and never even cared to discover whether I had dreamed the fire or actually seen it.

I am told that in a German concert or opera, they hardly ever encore a song; that though they may be dying to hear it again, their good breeding usually preserves them against requiring the repetition.

Kings may encore; that is quite another matter; it delights every body to see that the king is pleased; and as to the actor encored, his pride and gratification are simply boundless. Still, there are circumstances in which even a royal encore –

But it is better to illustrate. The King of Bavaria is a poet, and has a poet's eccentricities – with the advantage over all other poets of being able to gratify them, no matter what form they may take. He is fond of the opera, but not fond of sitting in the presence of an audience; therefore, it has sometimes occurred, in Munich, that when an opera has been concluded and the players were getting off their paint and finery, a command has come to them to get their paint and finery on again. Presently the King would arrive, solitary and alone, and the players would begin at the beginning and do the entire opera over again with only that one individual in the vast solemn theatre for audience. Once he took an odd freak into his head. High up and out of sight, over the prodigious stage of the court theatre is a maze of interlacing water-pipes, so pierced that in case of fire, innumerable little thread-like streams of water can be caused to descend; and in case of need, this discharge can be augmented to a pouring flood. American managers might make a note of that. The King was sole audience. The opera proceeded, it was a piece with a storm in it; the mimic thunder began to mutter, the mimic wind began to wail and sough, and the mimic rain to patter. The King's interest rose higher and higher; it developed into enthusiasm. He cried out, –

"It is good, very good indeed! But I will have real rain! Turn on the water!"

The manager pleaded for a reversal of the command; said it would ruin the costly scenery and the splendid costumes, but the King cried, –

"No matter, no matter, I will have real rain! Turn on the water!"

So the real rain was turned on and began to descend in gossamer lances to the mimic flower-beds and gravel walks of the stage. The richly-dressed actresses and actors tripped about singing bravely and pretending not to mind it. The King was delighted, – his enthusiasm grew higher. He cried out, –

"Bravo, bravo! More thunder! more lightning! turn on more rain!"

The thunder boomed, the lightning glared, the storm-winds raged, the deluge poured down. The mimic royalty on the stage, with their soaked satins clinging to their bodies, slopped around ankle deep in water, warbling their sweetest and best, the fiddlers under the eaves of the stage sawed away for dear life, with the cold overflow spouting down the backs of their necks, and the dry and happy King sat in his lofty box and wore his gloves to ribbons applauding.

"More yet!" cried the King; "more yet, – let loose all the thunder, turn on all the water! I will hang the man that raises an umbrella!"

When this most tremendous and effective storm that had ever been produced in any theatre was at last over, the King's approbation was measureless. He cried, –

"Magnificent, magnificent! *Encore!* Do it again!"

But the manager succeeded in persuading him to recall the encore, and said the company would feel sufficiently rewarded and complimented in the mere fact that the encore was desired by his Majesty, without fatiguing him with a repetition to gratify their own vanity.

During the remainder of the act the lucky performers were those whose parts required changes of dress; the others were a soaked, bedraggled and uncomfortable lot, but in the last degree picturesque.

The stage scenery was ruined, trap-doors were so swollen that they wouldn't work for a week afterward, the fine costumes were spoiled, and no end of minor damages were done by that remarkable storm.

It was a royal idea – that storm – and royally carried out. But observe the moderation of the King: he did not insist upon his encore. If he had been a gladsome, unreflecting American opera-audience, he probably would have had his storm repeated and repeated until he drowned all those people.

CHAPTER XI

THE SUMMER DAYS passed pleasantly in Heidelberg. We had a skilled trainer, and under his instructions we were getting our legs in the right condition for the contemplated pedestrian tours; we were well satisfied with the progress which we had made in the German language,* and more than satisfied with what we had accomplished in Art. We had had the best instructors in drawing and painting in Germany, – Hämmerling, Vogel, Müller, Dietz and Schumann. Hämmerling taught us landscape painting, Vogel taught us figure drawing, Müller taught us to do still-life, and Dietz and Schumann gave us a finishing course in two specialties, – battle-pieces and shipwrecks. Whatever I am in Art I owe to these men. I have some thing of the manner of each and all of them; but they all said that I had also a manner of my own, and that it was conspicuous. They said there was a marked individuality about my style, – insomuch that if I ever painted the commonest type of a dog, I should be sure to throw a something into the aspect of that dog which would keep him from being mistaken for the creation of any other artist. Secretly I wanted to believe all these kind sayings, but I could not; I was afraid that my masters' partiality for me, and pride in me, biased their judgment. So I resolved to make a test. Privately, and unknown to any one, I painted my great picture, "Heidelberg Castle Illuminated," – my first really important work in oils, – and had it hung up in the midst of a wilderness of oil pictures in the Art Exhibition, with no name attached to it. To my great gratification it

*See Appendix D, p.595, for information concerning this fearful tongue.

was instantly recognized as mine. All the town flocked to see it, and people even came from neighboring localities to visit it. It made more stir than any other work in the Exhibition. But the most gratifying thing of all, was, that chance strangers, passing through, who had not heard of my picture, were not only drawn to it, as by a lodestone, the moment they entered the gallery, but always took it for a "Turner."

Mr. Harris was graduated in Art about the same time with myself, and we took a studio together. We waited awhile for some orders; then as time began to drag a little, we concluded to make a pedestrian tour. After much consideration, we determined on a trip up the shores of the beautiful Neckar to Heilbronn. Apparently nobody had ever done that. There were ruined castles on the overhanging cliffs and crags all the way; these were said to have their legends, like those on the Rhine, and what was better still, they had never been in print. There was nothing in the books about that lovely region; it had been neglected by the tourist, it was virgin soil for the literary pioneer.

Meantime the knapsacks, the rough walking suits and the stout walking shoes which we had ordered, were finished and brought to us. A Mr. X. and a young Mr. Z. had agreed to go with us. We went around, one evening and bade good-bye to our friends, and afterwards had a little farewell banquet at the hotel. We got to bed early, for we wanted to make an early start, so as to take advantage of the cool of the morning.

We were out of bed at break of day, feeling fresh and vigorous, and took a hearty breakfast, then plunged down through the leafy arcades of the Castle grounds, toward the town. What a glorious summer morning it was, and how the flowers did pour out their fragrance, and how the birds did sing! It was just the time for a tramp through the woods and mountains.

We were all dressed alike: broad slouch hats, to keep the sun off; gray knapsacks; blue army shirts; blue overalls; leathern gaiters buttoned tight from knee down to ankle; high-quarter coarse shoes snugly laced. Each man had an opera glass, a canteen, and a guide-book case slung over his shoulder, and carried an alpenstock in one hand and a sun umbrella in the other. Around our hats were wound many folds of soft white muslin, with the ends hanging and flapping down our backs, – an idea brought from the Orient and used by tourists all over Europe. Harris carried the little watch-like machine called a "pedometer," whose office is to keep count of a man's steps and tell how far he has walked. Every body stopped to admire our costumes and give us a hearty: "Pleasant march to you!"

When we got down town I found that we could go by rail to within five miles of Heilbronn. The train was just starting, so we jumped aboard and went tearing away in splendid spirits. It was agreed all around that we had done wisely, because it would be just as enjoyable to walk *down* the Neckar as up it, and it could not be needful to walk both ways. There were some nice German people in our compartment. I got to talking some pretty private matters presently, and Harris became nervous; so he nudged me and said, –

"Speak in German, – these Germans may understand English."

I did so, and it was well I did; for it turned out that there was not a German in that party who did not understand English perfectly. It is curious how wide-spread our language is in Germany. After a while some of those folks got out and a German gentleman and his two young daughters got in. I spoke in German to one of the latter several times, but without result. Finally she said, –

"Ich verstehe nur Deutch und Englische," – or words to that effect. That is, "I don't understand any language but German and English."

And sure enough, not only she but her father and sister spoke English. So after that we had all the talk we wanted; and we wanted a good deal, for they were very agreeable people. They were greatly interested in our costumes; especially the alpenstocks, for they had not seen any before. They said that the Neckar road was perfectly level, so we must be going to Switzerland or some other rugged country; and asked us if we did not find the walking pretty fatiguing in such warm weather. But we said no.

We reached Wimpfen, – I think it was Wimpfen, – in about three hours, and got out, not the least tired; found a good hotel and ordered beer and dinner, – then took a stroll through the venerable old village. It was very picturesque and tumble-down, and dirty and interesting. It had queer houses five hundred years old in it, and a military tower, 115 feet high, which had stood there more than ten centuries. I made a little sketch of it. I kept a copy, but gave the original to the Burgomaster. I think the original was better than the copy, because it had more windows in it and the grass stood up better and had a brisker look. There was none around the tower though; I composed the grass myself, from studies I made in a field by Heidelberg in Hämmerling's time. The man on top, looking at the view, is apparently too large, but I found he could not be made smaller, conveniently. I wanted him there, and I wanted him visible, so I thought out a way to manage it; I composed the picture from two points of view; the spectator is to observe the man from about where that flag is, and he must observe the tower itself from the ground. This harmonizes the seeming discrepancy.

Near an old Cathedral, under a shed, were three crosses of stone, – mouldy and damaged things, bearing life-size stone figures. The two thieves were dressed in the fanciful court costumes of the middle of the sixteenth century, while the Saviour was nude, with the exception of a cloth around the loins.

We had dinner under the green trees in a garden belonging to the hotel and overlooking the Neckar; then, after a smoke, we went to bed. We had a refreshing nap, then got up about three in the afternoon and put on our panoply. As we tramped gaily out at the gate of the town, we overtook a peasant's cart, partly laden with odds and ends of cabbages and similar vegetable rubbish, and drawn by a small cow and a smaller donkey yoked together. It was a pretty slow concern, but it got us into Heilbronn before dark, – five miles, or possibly it was seven.

We stopped at the very same inn which the famous old robber knight and rough fighter, Götz von Berlichingen, abode in after he got out of captivity in the Square Tower of Heilbronn between three hundred and fifty and four hundred years ago. Harris and I occupied the same room which he had occupied and the same paper had not all peeled off the walls yet. The furniture was quaint old carved stuff, full four hundred years old, and some of the smells were over a thousand. There was a hook in the wall, which the landlord said the terrific old Götz used to hang his iron hand on when he took it off to go to bed. This room was very large, – it might be called immense, – and it was on the first floor; which means it was in the second story, for in Europe the houses are so high that they do not count the first story, else they would get tired climbing before they got to the top. The wall paper was a fiery red, with huge gold figures in it, well smirched by time, and it covered all the doors. These doors fitted so snugly and continued the figures of the paper so unbrokenly, that when they were closed one had to go feeling and searching along the wall to find them. There was a stove in the corner, – one of those tall, square, stately white porcelain things that looks like a monument and keeps you thinking of death when you ought to be enjoying your travels. The windows looked out on a little alley, and over that into a stable and some poultry and pig yards in the rear of some tenement houses. There were the customary two beds in the room, one in one end of it, the other in the other, about an old-fashioned brass-mounted, single-barreled pistol shot apart. They were fully as narrow as the usual German bed, too, and had the German bed's ineradicable habit of spilling the blankets on the floor every time you forgot yourself and went to sleep.

A round-table as large as King Arthur's stood in the centre of the room; while the waiters were getting ready to serve our dinner on it we all went out to see the renowned clock on the front of the municipal buildings.

CHAPTER XIII

WHEN WE GOT back to the hotel I wound and set the pedometer and put it in my pocket, for I was to carry it next day and keep record of the miles we made. The work which we had given the instrument to do during the day which had just closed, had not fatigued it perceptibly.

We were in bed by ten, for we wanted to be up and away on our tramp homeward with the dawn. I hung fire, but Harris went to sleep at once. I hate a man who goes to sleep at once; there is a sort of indefinable something about it which is not exactly an insult, and yet is an insolence; and one which is hard to bear, too. I lay there fretting over this injury, and trying to go to sleep; but the harder I tried, the wider awake I grew. I got to feeling very lonely in the dark, with no company but an undigested dinner. My mind got a start by and by, and began to consider the beginning of every subject which has ever been thought of; but it never went further than the beginning; it was touch and go; it fled from topic to topic with a frantic speed. At the end of an hour my head was in a perfect whirl and I was dead tired, fagged out.

The fatigue was so great that it presently began to make some head against the nervous excitement; while imagining myself wide awake, I would really doze into momentary unconsciousnesses, and come suddenly out of them with a physical jerk which nearly wrenched my joints apart, – the delusion of the instant being that I was tumbling backwards over a precipice. After I had fallen over eight or nine precipices and thus found out that one half of my brain had been asleep eight or nine times without the wide-awake, hard-working other half suspecting it, the periodical unconsciousnesses began to extend their spell gradually over more of my brain-territory, and at last I sank into a drowse which grew deeper and deeper and was doubtless just on the very point of becoming a solid, blessed, dreamless stupor, when, – what was that?

My dulled faculties dragged themselves partly back to life and took a receptive attitude. Now out of an immense, a limitless distance, came a something which grew and grew, and approached, and presently was recognizable as a sound, – it had rather seemed to be a feeling, before. This sound was a mile away, now – perhaps it was the murmur of a storm; and now it was nearer, – not a quarter of a mile away; was it the muffled rasping and grinding of distant machinery? No, it came still nearer; was it the measured tramp of a marching troop? But it came nearer still, and still nearer, – and at last it was right in the room: it was merely a mouse gnawing the wood-work. So I had held my breath all that time for such a trifle.

Well, what was done could not be helped; I would go to sleep at once and make up the lost time. That was a thoughtless thought. Without intending it, – hardly knowing it, – I fell to listening intently to that sound, and even unconsciously counting the strokes of the mouse's nutmeg-grater. Presently I was deriving exquisite suffering from this employment, yet maybe I could have endured it if the mouse had attended steadily to his work; but he did not do that; he stopped every now and then, and I suffered more while waiting and listening for him to begin again than I did while he was gnawing. Along at first I was mentally offering a reward of five, – six, – seven, – ten – dollars for that mouse; but toward the last I was offering rewards which were entirely beyond my means. I close-reefed my ears, – that is to say, I bent the flaps of them down and furled them into five or six folds, and pressed them against the hearing-orifice, – but it did no good: the faculty was so sharpened by nervous excitement that it was become a microphone and could hear through the overlays without trouble.

My anger grew to a frenzy. I finally did what all persons before me have done, clear back to Adam, – resolved to throw something. I reached down and got my walking shoes, then sat up in bed and listened, in order to exactly locate the noise. But I couldn't do it; it was as unlocatable as a cricket's noise; and where one thinks that

that is, is always the very place where it isn't. So I presently hurled a shoe at random, and with a vicious vigor. It struck the wall over Harris's head and fell down on him; I had not imagined I could throw so far. It woke Harris, and I was glad of it until I found he was not angry; then I was sorry. He soon went to sleep again, which pleased me; but straightway the mouse began again, which roused my temper once more. I did not want to wake Harris a second time, but the gnawing continued until I was compelled to throw the other shoe. This time I broke a mirror, – there were two in the room, – I got the largest one, of course. Harris woke again, but did not complain, and I was sorrier than ever. I resolved that I would suffer all possible torture before I would disturb him a third time.

The mouse eventually retired, and by and by I was sinking to sleep, when a clock began to strike; I counted, till it was done, and was about to drowse again when another clock began; I counted; then the two great Rathhaus clock angels began to send forth soft, rich, melodious blasts from their long trumpets. I had never heard any thing that was so lovely, or weird, or mysterious, – but when they got to blowing the quarter-hours, they seemed to me to be overdoing the thing. Every time I dropped off for a moment, a new noise woke me. Each time I woke I missed my coverlet, and had to reach down to the floor and get it again.

At last all sleepiness forsook me. I recognized the fact that I was hopelessly and permanently wide-awake. Wide-awake, and feverish and thirsty. When I had lain tossing there as long as I could endure it, it occurred to me that it would be a good idea to dress and go out in the great square and take a refreshing wash in the fountain, and smoke and reflect there until the remnant of the night was gone.

I believed I could dress in the dark without waking Harris. I had banished my shoes after the mouse, but my slippers would do for a summer night. So I rose softly, and gradually got on everything, – down to one sock. I couldn't seem to get on the track of that sock, any way I could fix it. But I had to have it; so I went down on my hands and knees, with one slipper on and the other in my hand, and began to paw gently around and rake the floor, but with no success. I enlarged my circle, and went on pawing and raking. With every pressure of my knee, how the floor creaked! and every time I chanced to rake against any article, it seemed to give out thirty-five or thirty-six times more noise than it would have done in the day time. In those cases I always stopped and held my breath till I was sure Harris had not awakened, – then I crept along again.

I moved on and on, but I could not find the sock; I could not seem to find anything but furniture. I could not remember that there was much furniture in the room when I went to bed, but the place was alive with it now, – especially chairs, – chairs every where, – had a couple of families moved in, in the meantime? And I never could seem to *glance* on one of those chairs, but always struck it full and square with my head. My temper rose, by steady and sure degrees, and as I pawed on and on, I fell to making vicious comments under my breath.

Finally, with a venomous access of irritation, I said I would leave without the sock; so I rose up and made straight for the door, – as I supposed, – and suddenly confronted my dim spectral image in the unbroken mirror. It startled the breath out of me, for an instant; it also showed me that I was lost, and had no sort of idea where I was. When I realized this, I was so angry that I had to sit down on the floor and take hold of something to keep from lifting the roof off with an explosion of opinion. If there had been only one mirror, it might possibly have helped to locate me; but there were two, and two were as bad as a thousand; besides these were on opposite sides of the room. I could see the dim blur of the windows, but in my turned-around condition they were exactly where they ought not to be, and so they only confused me instead of helping me.

I started to get up, and knocked down an umbrella; it made a noise like a pistol shot when it struck that hard, slick carpetless floor; I grated my teeth and held my breath, – Harris did not stir. I set the umbrella slowly and carefully on end against the wall, but as soon as I took my hand away, its heel slipped from under it, and down it came again with another bang. I shrunk together and listened a moment in silent fury, – no harm done, everything quiet. With the most painstaking care and nicety I stood the umbrella up once more, took my hand away, and down it came again.

I have been strictly reared, but if it had not been so dark and solemn and awful there in that lonely vast room, I do believe I should have said some thing then which could not be put into a Sunday School book without injuring the sale of it. If my reasoning powers had not been already sapped dry by my harassments, I would have known better than to try to set an umbrella on end on one of those glassy German floors in the dark; it can't be done in the day time without four failures to one success. I had one comfort, though, – Harris was yet still and silent, – he had not stirred.

The umbrella could not locate me, – there were four standing around the room, and all alike. I thought I would feel along the wall and find the door in that way. I rose up and began this operation, but raked down a picture. It was not a large one, but it made noise enough for a panorama. Harris gave out no sound, but I felt that if I experimented any further with the pictures I should be sure to wake him. Better give up trying to get out. Yes, I would find King Arthur's Round Table once more, – I had already found it several times, – and use it for a base of departure on an exploring tour for my bed; if I could find my bed I could then find my water pitcher; I would quench my raging thirst and turn in. So I started on my hands and knees, because I could go faster that way, and with more confidence, too, and not knock down things. By and by I found the table, – with my head, – rubbed the bruise a little, then rose up and started, with hands abroad and fingers spread, to balance myself. I found a chair; then the wall; then another chair; then a sofa; then an alpenstock, then another sofa; this confounded me, for I had thought there was only one sofa. I hunted up the table again and took a fresh start; found some more chairs.

It occurred to me, now, as it ought to have done before, that as the table was round, it was therefore of no value as a base to aim from; so I moved off once more, and at random among the wilderness of chairs and sofas, – wandered off into unfamiliar regions, and presently knocked a candlestick off a mantel-piece; grabbed at the candlestick and knocked off a lamp; grabbed at the lamp and knocked off a water pitcher with a rattling crash, and thought to myself, "I've found you at last, – I judged I was close upon you." Harris shouted "murder," and "thieves," and finished with "I'm absolutely drowned."

The crash had roused the house. Mr. X. pranced in, in his long night garment, with a candle, young Z. after him with another candle; a procession swept in at another door, with candles and lanterns, – landlord and two German guests in their nightgowns, and a chamber-maid in hers.

I looked around; I was at Harris's bed, a Sabbath day's journey from my own. There was only one sofa; it was against the wall; there was only one chair where a body could get at it, – I had been revolving around it like a planet, and colliding with it like a comet half the night.

I explained how I had been employing myself, and why. Then the landlord's party left, and the rest of us set about our preparations for breakfast, for the dawn was ready to break. I glanced furtively at my pedometer, and found I had made 47 miles. But I did not care, for I had come out for a pedestrian tour any way.

CHAPTER XIV

WHEN THE LANDLORD learned that I and my agent were artists, our party rose perceptibly in his esteem; we rose still higher when he learned that we were making a pedestrian tour of Europe.

He told us all about the Heidelberg road, and which were the best places to avoid and which the best ones to tarry at; he charged me less than cost for the things I broke in the night; he put up a fine luncheon for us and added to it a quantity of great light-green plums, the pleasantest fruit in Germany; he was so anxious to do us honor that he would not allow us to walk out of Heilbronn, but called up Götz von Berlichingen's horse and cab and made us ride.

I made a sketch of the turn-out. It is not a Work, it is only what artists call a "study" – a thing to make a finished picture from. This sketch has several blemishes in it; for instance, the wagon is not traveling as fast as the horse is. This is wrong. Again, the person trying to get out of the way is too small; he is out of perspective, as we say. The two upper lines are not the horse's back, they are the reins; – there seems to be a wheel missing – this would be corrected in a finished Work, of course. That thing flying out behind is not a flag, it is a curtain. That other thing up there is the sun, but I didn't get enough distance on it. I do not remember, now, what that thing is that is in front of the man who is running, but I think it is a haystack or a woman. This study was exhibited in the Paris Salon of 1879, but did not take any medal; they do not give medals for studies.

We discharged the carriage at the bridge. The river was full of logs, – long, slender, barkless pine logs, – and we leaned on the rails of the bridge and watched the men put them together into rafts. These rafts were of a shape and construction to suit the crookedness and extreme narrowness of the Neckar. They were from 50 to 100 yards long, and they gradually tapered from a 9-log breadth at their sterns, to a 3-log breadth at their bow-ends. The main part of the steering is done at the bow, with a pole; the 3-log breadth there furnishes room for only the steersman, for these little logs are not larger around than an average young lady's waist. The connections of the several sections of the raft are slack and pliant, so that the raft may be readily bent into any sort of curve required by the shape of the river.

The Neckar is in many places so narrow that a person can throw a dog across it, if he has one; when it is also sharply curved in such places, the raftsman has to do some pretty nice snug piloting to make the turns. The river is not always allowed to spread over its whole bed, – which is as much as 30, and sometimes 40, yards wide, – but is split into three equal bodies of water, by stone dikes which throw the main volume, depth, and current, into the central one. In low water these neat narrow-edged dikes project four or five inches above the surface, like the comb of a submerged roof, but in high water they are overflowed. A hatful of rain makes high water in the Neckar, and a basketful produces an overflow.

There are dikes abreast the Schloss Hotel, and the current is violently swift at that point. I used to sit for hours in my glass cage, watching the long, narrow rafts slip along through the central channel, grazing the right-bank dike and aiming carefully for the middle arch of the stone bridge below; I watched them in this way, and lost all this time hoping to see one of them hit the bridge-pier and wreck itself sometime or other, but was always disappointed. One was smashed there one morning, but I had just stepped into my room a moment to light a pipe, so I lost it.

While I was looking down upon the rafts that morning in Heilbronn, the dare-devil spirit of adventure came suddenly upon me, and I said to my comrades, –

"*I* am going to Heidelberg on a raft. Will you venture with me?"

Their faces paled a little, but they assented with as good a grace as they could. Harris wanted to cable his mother, – thought it his duty to do that, as he was all she had in this world, – so, while he attended to this, I went down to the longest and finest raft and hailed the captain with a hearty "Ahoy, shipmate!" which put us upon pleasant terms at once, and we entered upon business. I said we were on a pedestrian tour to Heidelberg, and would like to take passage with him. I said this partly through young Z., who spoke German very well, and partly through Mr. X., who spoke it peculiarly. I can *understand* German as well as the maniac that invented it, but I *talk* it best through an interpreter.

The captain hitched up his trowsers, then shifted his quid thoughtfully. Presently he said just what I was expecting he would say, – that he had no license to carry passengers, and therefore was afraid the law would be after him in case the matter got noised about or any accident happened. So I *chartered* the raft and the crew and took all the responsibilities on myself.

With a rattling song the starboard watch bent to their work and hove the cable short, then got the anchor home, and our bark moved off with a stately stride, and soon was bowling along at about two knots an hour.

Our party were grouped amidships. At first the talk was a little gloomy, and ran mainly upon the shortness of life, the uncertainty of it, the perils which beset it, and the need and wisdom of being always prepared for the worst; this shaded off into low-voiced references to the dangers of the deep, and kindred matters; but as the gray east began to redden and the mysterious solemnity and silence of the dawn to give place to the joy-songs of the birds, the talk took a cheerier tone, and our spirits began to rise steadily.

Germany, in the summer, is the perfection of the beautiful, but nobody has understood, and realized, and enjoyed the utmost possibilities of this soft and peaceful beauty unless he has voyaged down the Neckar on a raft. The motion of a raft is the needful motion; it is gentle, and gliding, and smooth, and noiseless; it calms down all feverish activities, it soothes to sleep all nervous hurry and impatience; under its restful influence all the troubles and vexations and sorrows that harass the mind vanish away, and existence becomes a dream, a charm, a deep and tranquil ecstasy. How it contrasts with hot and perspiring pedestrianism, and dusty and deafening railroad rush, and tedious jolting behind tired horses over blinding white roads!

We went slipping silently along, between the green and fragrant banks, with a sense of pleasure and contentment that grew, and grew, all the time. Sometimes the banks were over-hung with thick masses of willows that wholly hid the ground behind; sometimes we had noble hills on one hand, clothed densely with foliage to their tops, and on the other hand open levels blazing with poppies, or clothed in the rich blue of the corn-flower; sometimes we drifted in the shadow of forests, and sometimes along the margin of long stretches of velvety grass, fresh and green and bright, a tireless charm to the eye. And the birds! – they were every where; they swept back and forth across the river constantly, and their jubilant music was never stilled.

It was a deep and satisfying pleasure to see the sun create the new morning, and gradually, patiently, lovingly, clothe it on with splendor after splendor, and glory after glory, till the miracle was complete. How different is this marvel observed from a raft, from what it is when one observes it through the dingy windows of a railway station in some wretched village while he munches a petrified sandwich and waits for the train.

CHAPTER XV
DOWN THE RIVER

MEN AND WOMEN and cattle were at work in the dewy fields by this time. The people often stepped aboard the raft, as we glided along the grassy shores, and gossiped with us and with the crew for a hundred yards or so, then stepped ashore again, refreshed by the ride.

Only the men did this; the women were too busy. The women do all kinds of work on the continent. They dig, they hoe, they reap, they sow, they bear monstrous burdens on their backs, they shove similar ones long distances on wheelbarrows, they drag the cart when there is no dog or lean cow to drag it, – and when there is, they assist the dog or cow. Age is no matter, – the older the woman, the stronger she is, apparently. On the farm a woman's duties are not defined, – she does a little of everything; but in the towns it is different, there she only does certain things, the men do the rest. For instance, a hotel chamber-maid has nothing to do but make beds and fires in fifty or sixty rooms, bring towels and candles, and fetch several tons of water up several flights of stairs, a hundred pounds at a time, in prodigious metal pitchers. She does not have to work more than eighteen or twenty hours a day, and she can always get down on her knees and scrub the floors of halls and closets when she is tired and needs a rest.

As the morning advanced and the weather grew hot, we took off our outside clothing and sat in a row along the edge of the raft and enjoyed the scenery, with our sun umbrellas over our heads and our legs dangling in the water. Every now and then we plunged in and had a swim. Every projecting grassy cape had its joyous group of naked children, the boys to themselves and the girls to themselves, the latter usually in care of some motherly dame who sat in the shade of a tree with her knitting. The little boys swam out to us, sometimes, but the little maids stood knee deep in the water and stopped their splashing and frolicking to inspect the raft with their innocent eyes as it drifted by. Once we turned a corner suddenly and surprised a slender girl of twelve years or upwards, just stepping into the water. She had not time to run, but she did what answered just as well; she promptly drew a lithe young willow bough athwart her white body with one hand, and then contemplated us with a simple and untroubled interest. Thus she stood while we glided by. She was a pretty creature, and she and her willow bough made a very pretty picture, and one which could not offend the modesty of the most fastidious spectator. Her white skin had a low bank of fresh green willows for background and effective contrast, – for she stood against them, – and above and out of them projected the eager faces and white shoulders of two smaller girls.

Towards noon we heard the inspiriting cry, –

"Sail ho!"

"Where away?" shouted the captain.

"Three points off the weather bow!"

We ran forward to see the vessel. It proved to be a steamboat, – for they had begun to run a steamer up the Neckar, for the first time in May. She was a tug, and one of very peculiar build and aspect. I had often watched her from the hotel, and wondered how she propelled herself, for apparently she had no propeller or paddles. She came churning along, now, making a deal of noise of one kind and another, and aggravating it every now and then by blowing a hoarse whistle. She had nine keel-boats hitched on behind and following after her in a long, slender rank. We met her in a narrow place, between dikes, and there was hardly room for us both in the cramped passage. As she went grinding and groaning by, we perceived the secret of her moving impulse. She did not drive herself up the river with paddles or propeller, she pulled herself by hauling on a great chain. This chain is laid in the bed of the river and is only fastened at the two ends. It is seventy miles long. It comes in over the boat's bow, passes around a drum, and is payed out astern. She pulls on that chain, and so drags herself up the river or down it. She has neither bow nor stern, strictly speaking, for she has a long-bladed rudder on each end and she never turns around. She uses both rudders all the time, and they are powerful enough to enable her to turn to the right or the left and steer around curves, in spite of the strong resistance of the chain. I would not have believed that that impossible thing could be done; but I saw it done, and therefore I know that there is one impossible thing which *can* be done. What miracle will man attempt next?

We met many big keel-boats on their way up, using sails, mule power, and profanity – a tedious and laborious business. A wire rope led from the foretop mast to the file of mules on the tow-path a hundred yards ahead, and by dint of much banging and swearing and urging, the detachment of drivers managed to get a speed of two or three miles an hour out of the mules against the stiff current. The Neckar has always been used as a canal, and thus has given employment to a great many men and animals; but now that this steamboat is able, with a small crew and a bushel or so of coal, to take nine keel-boats farther up the river in one hour than thirty men and thirty mules can do it in two, it is believed that the old-fashioned towing industry is on its death-bed. A second steamboat began work in the Neckar three months after the first one was put in service.

At noon we stepped ashore and bought some bottled beer and got some chickens cooked, while the raft waited; then we immediately put to sea again, and had our dinner while the beer was cold and the chickens hot. There is no pleasanter place for such a meal than a raft that is gliding down the winding Neckar past green meadows and wooded hills, and slumbering villages, and craggy heights graced with crumbling towers and battlements.

In one place we saw a nicely dressed German gentleman without any spectacles. Before I could come to anchor he had got away. It was a great pity. I so wanted to make a sketch of him. The captain comforted me for my loss, however, by saying that the man was without any doubt a fraud who had spectacles, but kept them in his pocket in order to make himself conspicuous.

Below Hassmersheim we passed Hornberg, Götz von Berlichingen's old castle. It stands on a bold elevation 200 feet above the surface of the river; it has high vine-clad walls enclosing trees, and a peaked tower about 75 feet high. The steep hill-side, from the castle clear down to the water's edge, is terraced, and clothed thick with grape-vines. This is like farming a mansard roof. All the steeps along that part of the river which furnish the proper exposure, are given up to the grape. That region is a great producer of Rhine wines. The Germans are exceedingly fond of Rhine wines; they are put up in tall, slender bottles, and are considered a pleasant beverage. One tells them from vinegar by the label.

The Hornberg hill is to be tunneled, and the new railway will pass under the castle.

THE CAVE OF THE SPECTRE

Two miles below Hornberg castle is a cave in a low cliff, which the captain of the raft said had once been occupied by a beautiful heiress of Hornberg, – the Lady Gertrude, – in the old times. It was seven hundred years ago. She had a number of rich and noble lovers and one poor and obscure one, Sir Wendel Lobenfeld. With the native chuckle-headedness of the heroine of romance, she preferred the poor and obscure lover. With the native sound judgment of the father of a heroine of romance, the von Berlichingen of that day shut his daughter up in his donjon keep, or his oubliette, or his culverin, or some such place, and resolved that she should stay there until she selected a husband from among her rich and noble lovers. The latter visited her and persecuted her with their supplications, but without effect, for her heart was true to her poor despised Crusader, who was fighting in the Holy Land. Finally she resolved that she would endure the attentions of the rich lovers no longer; so one stormy night she escaped and went down the river and hid herself in the cave on the other side. Her father ransacked the country for her, but found not a trace of her. As the days went by, and still no tidings of her came, his conscience began to torture him, and he caused proclamation to be made that if she were yet living and would return, he would oppose her no longer, she might marry whom she would. The months dragged on, all hope forsook the old man, he ceased from his customary pursuits and pleasures, he devoted himself to pious works, and longed for the deliverance of death.

Now just at midnight, every night, the lost heiress stood in the mouth of her cave, arrayed in white robes, and sang a little love ballad which her Crusader had made for her. She judged that if he came home alive the superstitious peasants would tell him about the ghost that sang in the cave, and that as soon as they described the ballad he would know that none but he and she knew that song, therefore he would suspect that she was alive, and would come and find her. As time went on, the people of the region became sorely distressed about the Spectre of the Haunted Cave. It was said that ill luck of one kind or another always overtook any one who had the misfortune to hear that song. Eventually, every calamity that happened thereabouts was laid at the door of that music. Consequently no boatman would consent to pass the cave at night; the peasants shunned the place, even in the day time.

But the faithful girl sang on, night after night, month after month, and patiently waited; her reward must come at last. Five years dragged by, and still, every night at midnight, the plaintive tones floated out over the silent land, while the distant boatmen and peasants thrust their fingers into their ears and shuddered out a prayer.

And now came the Crusader home, bronzed and battle-scarred, but bringing a great and splendid fame to lay at the feet of his bride. The old lord of Hornberg received him as a son, and wanted him to stay by him and be the comfort and blessing of his age; but the tale of that young girl's devotion to him and its pathetic consequences, made a changed man of the knight. He could not enjoy his well-earned rest. He said his heart was broken, he would give the remnant of his life to high deeds in the cause of humanity, and so find a worthy death and a blessed reunion with the brave true heart whose love had more honored him than all his victories in war.

When the people heard this resolve of his, they came and told him there was a pitiless dragon in human disguise in the Haunted Cave, a dread creature which no knight had yet been bold enough to face, and begged him to rid the land of its desolating presence. He said he would do it. They told him about the song, and when he asked what song it was, they said the memory of it was gone, for nobody had been hardy enough to listen to it for the past four years and more.

Towards midnight the Crusader came floating down the river in a boat, with his trusty cross-bow in his hands. He drifted silently through the dim reflections of the crags and trees, with his intent eyes fixed upon the low cliff which he was approaching. As he drew nearer, he discerned the black mouth of the cave. Now, – is that a white figure? Yes. The plaintive song begins to well forth and float away over meadow and river, – the cross-bow is slowly raised to position, a steady aim is taken, the bolt flies straight to the mark, – the figure sinks down, still singing, the knight takes the wool out of his ears, and recognizes the old ballad, – too late! Ah, if he had only not put the wool in his ears!

The Crusader went away to the wars again, and presently fell in battle, fighting for the Cross. Tradition says that during several centuries the spirit of the unfortunate girl sang nightly from the cave at midnight, but the music carried no curse with it; and although many listened for the mysterious sounds, few were favored, since only those could hear them who had never failed in a trust. It is believed that the singing still continues, but it is known that nobody has heard it during the present century.

CHAPTER XXI

BADEN-BADEN SITS IN the lap of the hills, and the natural and artificial beauties of the surroundings are combined effectively and charmingly. The level strip of ground which stretches through and beyond the town is laid out in handsome pleasure grounds, shaded by noble trees and adorned at intervals with lofty and sparkling fountain-jets. Thrice a day a fine band makes music in the public promenade before the Conversation-House, and in the afternoon and evenings that locality is populous with fashionably dressed people of both sexes, who march back and forth past the great music stand and look very much bored, though they make a show of feeling otherwise. It seems like a rather aimless and stupid existence. A good many of these people are there for a real purpose, however; they are racked with rheumatism, and they are there to stew it out in the hot baths. These invalids looked melancholy enough, limping about on their canes and crutches, and apparently brooding over all sorts of cheerless things. People say that Germany, with her damp stone houses, is the home of rheumatism. If that is so, Providence must have foreseen that it would be so, and therefore filled the land with these healing baths. Perhaps no other country is so generously supplied with medicinal springs as Germany. Some of these baths are good for one ailment, some for another; and again, peculiar ailments are conquered by combining the individual virtues of several different baths. For instance, for some forms of disease, the patient drinks the native hot water of Baden-Baden, with a spoonful of salt from the Carlsbad springs dissolved in it. That is not a dose to be forgotten right away.

They don't *sell* this hot water; no, you go into the great Trinkhalle, and stand around, first on one foot and then on the other, while two or three young girls sit pottering at some sort of lady-like sewing work in your neighborhood and can't seem to see you, – polite as three-dollar clerks in government offices.

By and by one of these rises painfully, and "stretches"; – stretches fists and body heavenward till she raises her heels from the floor, at the same time refreshing herself with a yawn of such comprehensiveness that the bulk of her face disappears behind her upper lip and one is able to see how she is constructed inside, – then she slowly closes her cavern, brings down her fists and her heels, comes languidly forward, contemplates you contemptuously, draws you a glass of hot water and sets it down where you can get it by reaching for it. You take it and say, –

"How much?" – and she returns you, with elaborate indifference, a beggar's answer, –

"*Nach Beliebe*," (what you please.)

This thing of using the common beggar's trick and the common beggar's shibboleth to put you on your liberality when you were expecting a simple straight-forward commercial transaction, adds a little to your prospering sense of irritation. You ignore her reply, and ask again, –

"How much?"

– and she calmly, indifferently, repeats, –

"*Nach Beliebe.*"

You are getting angry, but you are trying not to show it; you resolve to keep on asking your question till she changes her answer, or at least her annoyingly indifferent manner. Therefore, if your case be like mine, you two fools stand there, and without perceptible emotion of any kind, or any emphasis on any syllable, you look blandly into each other's eyes, and hold the following idiotic conversation, –

"How much?"

"Nach Beliebe."

"How much?"

"Nach Beliebe."

"How much?"

"Nach Beliebe."

"How much?"

"Nach Beliebe."

"How much?"

"Nach Beliebe."

"How much?"

"Nach Beliebe."

I do not know what another person would have done, but at this point I gave it up; that cast-iron indifference, that tranquil contemptuousness, conquered me, and I struck my colors. Now I knew she was used to receiving about a penny from manly people who care nothing about the opinions of scullery maids, and about tuppence from moral cowards; but I laid a silver twenty-five-cent piece within her reach and tried to shrivel her up with this sarcastic speech, –

"If it isn't enough, will you stoop sufficiently from your official dignity to say so?"

She did not shrivel. Without deigning to look at me at all, she languidly lifted the coin and bit it! – to see if it was good. Then she turned her back and placidly waddled to her former roost again, tossing the money into an open till as she went along. She was victor to the last, you see.

I have enlarged upon the ways of this girl because they are typical; her manners are the manners of a goodly number of the Baden-Baden shopkeepers. The shopkeeper there swindles you if he can, and insults you whether he succeeds in swindling you or not. The keepers of baths also take great and patient pains to insult you. The frowsy woman who sat at the desk in the lobby of the great Friēderichsbad and sold bath tickets, not only insulted me twice every day, with rigid fidelity to her great trust, but she took trouble enough to cheat me out of a shilling, one day, to have fairly entitled her to ten. Baden-Baden's splendid gamblers are gone, only her microscopic knaves remain.

An English gentleman who had been living there several years, said, –

"If you could disguise your nationality, you would not find any insolence here. These shopkeepers detest the English and despise the Americans; they are rude to both, more especially to ladies of your nationality and mine. If these go shopping without a gentleman or a man-servant, they are tolerably sure to be subjected to petty insolences, – insolences of manner and tone, rather than word, though words that are hard to bear are not always wanting. I know of an instance where a shopkeeper tossed a coin back to an American lady with the remark, snappishly uttered, 'We don't take French money here.' – And I know of a case where an English lady said to one of these shopkeepers, 'Don't you think you ask too much for this article?' and he replied with the question, 'Do you think you are obliged to buy it?' However, these people are not impolite to Russians or Germans. And as to rank, they worship that, for they have long been used to generals and nobles. If you wish to see to what abysses servility can descend, present yourself before a Baden-Baden shopkeeper in the character of a Russian prince."

It is an inane town, filled with sham, and petty fraud, and snobbery, but the baths are good. I spoke with many people, and they were all agreed in that. I had had twinges of rheumatism unceasingly during three years, but the last one departed after a fortnight's bathing there, and I have never had one since. I fully believe I left my rheumatism in Baden-Baden. Baden-Baden is welcome to it. It was little, but it was all I had to give. I would have preferred to leave something that was catching, but it was not in my power.

There are several hot springs there, and during two thousand years they have poured forth a never diminishing abundance of the healing water. This water is conducted in pipes to the numerous bath-houses, and is reduced to an endurable temperature by the addition of cold water. The new Frīēderichsbad is a very large and beautiful building, and in it one may have any sort of bath that has ever been invented, and with all the additions of herbs and drugs that his ailment may need or that the physician of the establishment may consider a useful thing to put into the water. You go there, enter the great door, get a bow graduated to your style and clothes from the gorgeous portier, and a bath ticket and an insult from the frowsy woman for a quarter, she strikes a bell and a serving man conducts you down a long hall and shuts you into a commodious room which has a washstand, a mirror, a bootjack and a sofa in it, and there you undress at your leisure.

The room is divided by a great curtain; you draw this curtain aside, and find a large white marble bath-tub, with its rim sunk to the level of the floor, and with three white marble steps leading down into it. This tub is full of water which is as clear as crystal, and is tempered to 28° Reaumur, (about 95° Fahrenheit.) Sunk into the floor, by the tub, is a covered copper box which contains some warm towels and a sheet. You look fully as white as an angel when you are stretched out in that limpid bath. You remain in it ten minutes, the first time, and afterwards increase the duration from day to day, till you reach twenty-five or thirty minutes. There you stop. The appointments of the place are so luxurious, the benefit so marked, the price so moderate, and the insults so sure, that you very soon find yourself adoring the Frīēderichsbad and infesting it.

We had a plain, simple, unpretending, good hotel, in Baden-Baden, – the Hotel de France, – and alongside my room I had a giggling, cackling, chattering family who always went to bed just two hours after me and always got up just two hours ahead of me. But that is common in German hotels; the people generally go to bed long after eleven and get up long before eight. The partitions convey sound like a drum-head, and every body knows it; but no matter, a German family who are all kindness and consideration in the day time make apparently no effort to moderate their noises for your benefit at night. They will sing, laugh and talk loudly, and bang furniture around in the most pitiless way. If you knock on your wall appealingly, they will quiet down and discuss the matter softly amongst themselves for a moment, – then, like the mice, they fall to persecuting you again, and as vigorously as before. They keep cruelly late and early hours, for such noisy folk.

Of course when one begins to find fault with foreign people's ways, he is very likely to get a reminder to look nearer home, before he gets far with it. I open my notebook to see if I can find some more information of a valuable nature about Baden-Baden, and the first thing I fall upon is this:

Baden-Baden, (no date.) Lot of vociferous Americans at breakfast this morning. Talking *at* every body, while pretending to talk among themselves. On their first travels, manifestly. Showing off. The usual signs, – airy, easy-going references to grand distances and foreign places. "Well, *good*-bye, old fellow, – if I don't run across you in Italy, you hunt me up in London before you sail."

The next item which I find in my notebook is this one:

"The fact that a band of 6,000 Indians are now murdering our frontiersmen at their impudent leisure, and that we are only able to send 1,200 soldiers against them, is utilized here to discourage emigration to America. The common people think the Indians are in New Jersey."

This is a new and peculiar argument against keeping our army down to a ridiculous figure in the matter of numbers. It is rather a striking one, too. I have not distorted the truth in saying that the facts in the above item, about the army and the Indians, are made use of to discourage emigration to America. That the common people should be rather foggy in their geography, and foggy as to the location of the Indians, is matter for amusement, may be, but not of surprise.

There is an interesting old cemetery in Baden-Baden, and we spent several pleasant hours in wandering through it and spelling out the inscriptions on the aged tombstones. Apparently after a man has lain there a century or two, and has had a good many people buried on top of him, it is considered that his tombstone is not needed by him any longer. I judge so from the fact that hundreds of old gravestones have been removed from the graves and placed against the inner walls of the cemetery. What artists they had in the old times! They chiseled angels and cherubs and devils and skeletons on the tombstones in the most lavish and generous way, – as to supply, – but curiously grotesque and outlandish as to form. It is not always easy to tell which of the figures belong among the blest and which of them among the opposite party. But there was an inscription, in French, on one of those old stones, which was quaint and pretty, and was plainly not the work of any other than a poet. It was to this effect:

HERE
REPOSES IN GOD,
CAROLINE DE CLERY,
A RELIGIEUSE OF ST. DENIS,
AGED 83 YEARS, – AND BLIND.
THE LIGHT WAS RESTORED TO HER
IN BADEN THE 5TH OF JANUARY,
1839.

We made several excursions on foot to the neighboring villages, over winding and beautiful roads and through enchanting woodland scenery. The woods and roads were similar to those at Heidelberg, but not so bewitching. I suppose that roads and woods which are up to the Heidelberg mark are rare in the world.

Once we wandered clear away to La Favorita Palace, which is several miles from Baden-Baden. The grounds about the palace were fine; the palace was a curiosity. It was built by a Margravine in 1725, and remains as she left it at her death. We wandered through a great many of its rooms, and they all had striking peculiarities of decoration. For instance, the walls of one room were pretty completely covered with small pictures of the Margravine in all conceivable varieties of fanciful costumes, some of them male.

The walls of another room were covered with grotesquely and elaborately figured hand-wrought tapestry. The musty ancient beds remained in the chambers, and their quilts and curtains and canopies were decorated with curious hand-work, and the walls and ceilings frescoed with historical and mythological scenes in glaring colors. There was enough crazy and rotten rubbish in the building to make the true brick-a-bracker green with envy. A painting in the dining hall verged upon the indelicate, – but then the Margravine was herself a trifle indelicate.

It is in every way a wildly and picturesquely decorated house, and brim full of interest as a reflection of the character and tastes of that rude bygone time.

In the grounds, a few rods from the palace, stands the Margravine's chapel, just as she left it, – a coarse wooden structure, wholly barren of ornament. It is said that the Margravine would give herself up to debauchery and exceedingly fast living for several months at a time, and then retire to this miserable wooden den and spend a few months in repenting and getting ready for another good time. She was a devoted Catholic, and was perhaps quite a model sort of a Christian as Christians went then, in high life.

Tradition says she spent the last two years of her life in the strange den I have been speaking of, after having indulged herself in one final, triumphant and satisfying spree. She shut herself up there, without company, and without even a servant, and so abjured and forsook the world. In her little bit of a kitchen she did her own cooking; she wore a hair shirt next the skin, and castigated herself with whips, – these aids to grace are exhibited there yet. She prayed and told her beads, in another little room before a waxen Virgin niched in a little box against the wall; she bedded herself like a slave.

In another small room is an unpainted wooden table, and behind it sit half-life-size waxen figures of the Holy Family, made by the very worst artist that ever lived, perhaps, and clothed in gaudy, flimsy drapery.* The Margravine used to bring her meals to this table and *dine with the Holy Family*. What an idea that was! What a grisly spectacle it must have been! Imagine it: Those rigid, shock-headed figures, with corpsy complexions and fishy glass eyes, occupying one side of the table in the constrained attitudes and dead fixedness that distinguish all men that are born of wax, and this wrinkled, smouldering old fire-eater occupying the other side, mumbling her prayers and munching her sausages in the ghostly stillness and shadowy indistinctness of a winter twilight. It makes one feel crawly even to think of it.

In this sordid place, and clothed, bedded and fed like a pauper, this strange princess lived and worshiped during two years, and in it

*The Saviour was represented as a lad of about 15 years of age. This figure had lost one eye.

she died. Two or three hundred years ago, this would have made the poor den holy ground; and the church would have set up a miracle-factory there and made plenty of money out of it. The den could be moved into some portions of France and made a good property even now.

CHAPTER XXII

FROM BADEN-BADEN WE made the customary trip into the Black Forest. We were on foot most of the time. One cannot describe those noble woods, nor the feeling with which they inspire him. A feature of the feeling, however, is a deep sense of contentment; another feature of it is a buoyant, boyish gladness; and a third and very conspicuous feature of it is one's sense of the remoteness of the work-day world and his entire emancipation from it and its affairs.

Those woods stretch unbroken over a vast region; and every where they are such dense woods, and so still, and so piney and fragrant. The stems of the trees are trim and straight, and in many places all the ground is hidden for miles under a thick cushion of moss of a vivid green color, with not a decayed or ragged spot in its surface, and not a fallen leaf or twig to mar its immaculate tidiness. A rich cathedral gloom pervades the pillared aisles; so the stray flecks of sunlight that strike a trunk here and a bough yonder are strongly accented, and when they strike the moss they fairly seem to burn. But the weirdest effect, and the most enchanting, is that produced by the diffused light of the low afternoon sun; no single ray is able to pierce its way in, then, but the diffused light takes color from moss and foliage, and pervades the place like a faint, green-tinted mist, the theatrical fire of fairy-land. The suggestion of mystery and the supernatural which haunts the forest at all times, is intensified by this unearthly glow.

We found the Black Forest farmhouses and villages all that the Black Forest stories have pictured them. The first genuine specimen which we came upon was the mansion of a rich farmer and member of the Common Council of the parish or district. He was an important personage in the land and so was his wife also, of course. His daughter was the "catch" of the region, and she may be already entering into immortality as the heroine of one of Auerbach's novels for all I know. We shall see, for if he puts her in I shall recognize her by her Black Forest clothes, and her burned complexion, her plump figure, her fat hands, her dull expression, her gentle spirit, her generous feet, her bonnetless head, and the plaited tails of hemp-colored hair hanging down her back.

The house was big enough for a hotel; it was a hundred feet long and fifty wide, and ten feet high, from ground to eaves; but from the eaves to the comb of the mighty roof was as much as forty feet, or maybe even more. This roof was of ancient mud-colored straw thatch a foot thick, and was covered all over, except in a few trifling spots, with a thriving and luxurious growth of green vegetation, mainly moss. The mossless spots were places where repairs had been made by the insertion of bright new masses of yellow straw. The eaves projected far down, like sheltering, hospitable wings. Across the gable that fronted the road, and about ten feet above the ground, ran a narrow porch, with a wooden railing; a row of small windows filled with very small panes looked upon the porch. Above were two or three other little windows, one clear up under the sharp apex of the roof. Before the ground-floor door was a huge pile of manure. The door of a second-story room on the side of the house was open, and occupied by the rear elevation of a cow. Was this probably the drawing-room? All of the front half of the house from the ground up seemed to be occupied by the people, the cows and the chickens, and all the rear half by draft animals and hay. But the chief feature, all around this house was the big heaps of manure.

We became very familiar with the fertilizer in the Forest. We fell unconsciously into the habit of judging of a man's station in life by this outward and eloquent sign. Sometimes we said "Here is a poor devil, this is manifest." When we saw a stately accumulation, we said, "Here is a banker." When we encountered a country seat surrounded by an Alpine pomp of manure, we said, "Doubtless a Duke lives here."

The importance of this feature has not been properly magnified in the Black Forest stories. Manure is evidently the Black Forester's main treasure, – his coin, his jewel, his pride, his Old Master, his keramics, his bric-a-brac, his darling, his title to public consideration, envy, veneration, and his first solicitude when he gets ready to make his will. The true Black Forest novel, if it is ever written, will be skeletoned somewhat in this way:

SKELETON FOR BLACK FOREST NOVEL

Rich old farmer, named Huss. Has inherited great wealth of manure, and by diligence has added to it. It is double-starred in Baedeker.* The Black Forest artist paints it – his masterpiece. The king comes to see it. Gretchen Huss, daughter and heiress. Paul Hoch, young neighbor, suitor for Gretchen's hand, – ostensibly; he really wants the manure. Hoch has a good many cart-loads of the Black Forest currency himself, and therefore is a good catch; but he is sordid, mean, and without sentiment, whereas Gretchen is all sentiment and poetry. Hans Schmidt, young neighbor, full of sentiment, full of poetry, loves Gretchen, Gretchen loves him. But he has no manure. Old Huss forbids him the house. His heart breaks, he goes away to die in the woods, far from the cruel world, – for he says, bitterly, "What is man, without manure?"

[Interval of six months.]

Paul Hoch comes to old Huss and says, "I am at last as rich as you required, – come and view the pile." Old Huss views it and says, "It is sufficient – take her and be happy," – meaning Gretchen.

[Interval of two weeks.]

Wedding party assembled in old Huss's drawing-room; Hoch placid and content, Gretchen weeping over her hard fate. Enter old Huss's head book-keeper. Huss says fiercely, "I gave you three weeks to find out why your books don't balance, and to prove that you are not a defaulter; the time is up, – find me the missing property or you go to prison as a thief." Book-keeper: "I have found it." "Where?" Book-keeper: sternly, – tragically: "In the bridegroom's pile! – behold the thief – see him blench and tremble!" [Sensation.] Paul Hoch: "Lost, lost!" – falls over the cow in a swoon and is handcuffed. Gretchen: "Saved!" Falls over the calf in a swoon of joy, but is caught in the arms of Hans Schmidt, who springs in at that moment. Old Huss: "What, you here, varlet? unhand the maid and quit the place." Hans: still supporting the insensible girl: "Never! Cruel old man, know that I come with claims which even you can not despise."

Huss: "What, *you?* name them."

Hans: "Then listen. The world had forsaken me, I forsook the world. I wandered in the solitude of the forest, longing for death

*When Baedeker's guide-books mention a thing and put two stars ** after it, it means "well worth visiting." M. T.

but finding none. I fed upon roots, and in my bitterness I dug for the bitterest, loathing the sweeter kind. Digging, three days agone, I struck a manure mine! – a Golconda, a limitless Bonanza, of solid manure! I can buy you *all*, and have mountain ranges of manure left! Ha-ha, *now* thou smilest a smile!" [Immense sensation.] Exhibition of specimens from the mine. Old Huss, enthusiastically: "Wake her up, shake her up, noble young man, she is yours!" Wedding takes place on the spot; book-keeper restored to his office and emoluments; Paul Hoch led off to jail. The Bonanza king of the Black Forest lives to a good old age, blessed with the love of his wife and of his twenty-seven children, and the still sweeter envy of every body around.

We took our noon meal of fried trout one day at the Plow Inn, in a very pretty village, (Ottenhöfen,) and then went into the public room to rest and smoke. There we found nine or ten Black Forest grandees assembled around a table. They were the Common Council of the parish. They had gathered there at 8 o'clock that morning to elect a new member, and they had now been drinking beer four hours at the new member's expense. They were men of fifty or sixty years of age, with grave good-natured faces, and were all dressed in the costume made familiar to us by the Black Forest stories: broad, round-topped black felt hats with the brims curled up all around; long red waistcoats with large metal buttons, black alpaca coats with the waists up between the shoulders. There were no speeches, there was but little talk, there were no frivolities; the Council filled themselves gradually, steadily, but surely, with beer, and conducted themselves with sedate decorum, as became men of position, men of influence, men of manure.

We had a hot afternoon tramp up the valley, along the grassy bank of a rushing stream of clear water, past farmhouses, water mills, and no end of wayside crucifixes and saints and Virgins. These crucifixes, etc., are set up in memory of departed friends by survivors, and are almost as frequent as telegraph poles are in other lands.

We followed the carriage road, and had our usual luck: we traveled under a beating sun, and always saw the shade leave the shady places before we could get to them. In all our wanderings we seldom managed to strike a piece of road at its time for being shady. We had a particularly hot time of it on that particular afternoon, and with no comfort but what we could get out of the fact that the peasants at work away up on the steep mountain sides above our heads were even worse off than we were. By and by it became impossible to endure the intolerable glare and heat any longer; so we struck across the ravine and entered the deep cool twilight of the forest, to hunt for what the guide-book called the "old road."

We found an old road, and it proved eventually to be the right one, though we followed it at the time with the conviction that it was the wrong one. If it was the wrong one there could be no use in hurrying, therefore we did not hurry, but sat down frequently on the soft moss and enjoyed the restful quiet and shade of the forest solitudes. There had been distractions in the carriage road, – school children, peasants, wagons, troops of pedestrianizing students from all over Germany, – but we had the old road all to ourselves.

Now and then, while we rested, we watched the laborious ant at his work. I found nothing new in him, – certainly nothing to change my opinion of him. It seems to me that in the matter of intellect the ant must be a strangely overrated bird. During many summers, now, I have watched him, when I ought to have been in better business, and I have not yet come across a living ant that seemed to have any more sense than a dead one. I refer to the ordinary ant, of course; I have had no experience of those wonderful Swiss and African ones which vote, keep drilled armies, hold slaves, and dispute about religion. Those particular ants may be all that the naturalist paints them, but I am persuaded that the average ant is a sham. I admire his industry, of course; he is the hardest-working creature in the world, – when anybody is looking, – but his leather-headedness is the point I make against him. He goes out foraging, he makes a capture, and then what does he do? Go home? No, – he goes anywhere but home. He doesn't know where home is. His home may be only three feet away, – no matter, he can't find it. He makes his capture, as I have said; it is generally some thing which can be of no sort of use to himself or anybody else; it is usually seven times bigger than it ought to be; he hunts out the awkwardest place to take hold of it; he lifts it bodily up in the air by main force, and starts: not toward home, but in the opposite direction; not calmly and wisely, but with a frantic haste which is wasteful of his strength; he fetches up against a pebble, and instead of going around it, he climbs over it backwards dragging his booty after him, tumbles down on the other side, jumps up in a passion, kicks the dust off his clothes, moistens his hands, grabs his property viciously, yanks it this way then that, shoves it ahead of him a moment, turns tail and lugs it after him another moment, gets madder and madder, then presently hoists it into the air and goes tearing away in an entirely new direction; comes to a weed; it never occurs to him to go around it; no, he must climb it; and he does climb it, dragging his worthless property to the top – which is as bright a thing to do as it would be for me to carry a sack of flour from Heidelberg to Paris by way of Strasburg steeple; when he gets up there he finds that that is not the place; takes a cursory glance at the scenery and either climbs down again or tumbles down, and starts off once more – as usual, in a new direction. At the end of half an hour, he fetches up within six inches of the place he started from and lays his burden down; meantime he has been over all the ground for two yards around, and climbed all the weeds and pebbles he came across. Now he wipes the sweat from his brow, strokes his limbs, and then marches aimlessly off, in as violent a hurry as ever. He traverses a good deal of zig-zag country, and by and by stumbles on his same booty again. He does not remember to have ever seen it before; he looks around to see which is not the way home, grabs his bundle and starts; he goes through the same adventures he had before; finally stops to rest, and a friend comes along. Evidently the friend remarks that a last year's grasshopper leg is a very noble acquisition, and inquires where he got it. Evidently the proprietor does not remember exactly where he did get it, but thinks he got it "around here somewhere." Evidently the friend contracts to help him freight it home. Then, with a judgment peculiarly antic, (pun not intentional,) they take hold of opposite ends of that grasshopper leg and begin to tug with all their might in opposite directions. Presently they take a rest and confer together. They decide that something is wrong, they can't make out what. Then they go at it again, just as before. Same result. Mutual recriminations follow. Evidently each accuses the other of being an obstructionist. They warm up, and the dispute ends in a fight. They lock themselves together and chew each other's jaws for a while; then they roll and tumble on the ground till one loses a horn or a leg and has to haul off for repairs. They make up and go to work again in the same old insane way, but the crippled ant is at a disadvantage; tug as he may, the other one drags off the booty and him at the end of it. Instead of giving up, he hangs on, and gets his shins bruised against every obstruction that comes in the way. By and by, when that grasshopper leg has been dragged all over the same old ground once more, it is finally dumped at about the spot where it originally lay, the two perspiring ants inspect it thoughtfully and decide that dried grasshopper legs are a poor sort of property after all, and then each starts off in a different direction to see if he can't find an old nail or something else that is heavy enough to afford entertainment and at the same time valueness enough to make an ant want to own it.

There in the Black Forest, on the mountain side, I saw an ant go through with such a performance as this with a dead spider of fully ten times his own weight. The spider was not quite dead, but too far gone to resist. He had a round body the size of a pea. The little ant – observing that I was noticing – turned him on his back, sunk his fangs into his throat, lifted him into the air and started vigorously off with him, stumbling over little pebbles, stepping on the spider's legs and tripping himself up, dragging him backwards, shoving him bodily ahead, dragging him up stones six inches high instead of going around them, climbing weeds twenty times his own height and jumping from their summits, – and finally leaving him in the middle of the road to be confiscated by any other fool of an ant that wanted him. I measured the ground which this ass traversed, and arrived at the conclusion that what he had accomplished inside of twenty minutes would constitute some such job as this, – relatively speaking, – for a man; to-wit: to strap two eight-hundred-pound horses together, carry them eighteen hundred feet, mainly over (not around) boulders averaging six feet high, and in the course of the journey climb up and jump from the top of one precipice like Niagara, and three steeples, each a hundred and twenty feet high; and then put the horses down, in an exposed place, without anybody to watch them, and go off to indulge in some other idiotic miracle for vanity's sake.

Science has recently discovered that the ant does not lay up any thing for winter use. This will knock him out of literature, to some extent. He does not work, except when people are looking, and only then when the observer has a green, naturalistic look, and seems to be taking notes. This amounts to deception, and will injure him for the Sunday Schools. He has not judgment enough to know what is good to eat from what isn't. This amounts to ignorance, and will impair the world's respect for him. He cannot stroll around a stump and find his way home again. This amounts to idiotcy, and once the damaging fact is established, thoughtful people will cease to look up to him, the sentimental will cease to fondle him. His vaunted industry is but a vanity and of no effect, since he never gets home with any thing he starts with. This disposes of the last remnant of his reputation and wholly destroys his main usefulness as a moral agent, since it will make the sluggard hesitate to go to him anymore. It is strange beyond comprehension, that so manifest a humbug as the ant has been able to fool so many nations and keep it up so many ages without being found out.

The ant is strong, but we saw another strong thing, where we had not suspected the presence of much muscular power before. A toadstool – that vegetable which springs to full growth in a single night – had torn loose and lifted a matted mass of pine needles and dirt of twice its own bulk into the air, and supported it there, like a column supporting a shed. Ten thousand toadstools, with the right purchase, could lift a man, I suppose. But what good would it do?

All our afternoon's progress had been up hill. About five or half-past we reached the summit, and all of a sudden the dense curtain of the forest parted and we looked down into a deep and beautiful gorge and out over a wide panorama of wooded mountains with their summits shining in the sun and their glade-furrowed sides dimmed with purple shade. The gorge under our feet – called Allerheiligen, – afforded room in the grassy level at its head for a cosy and delightful human nest, shut away from the world and its botherations, and consequently the monks of the old times had not failed to spy it out; and here were the brown and comely ruins of their church and convent to prove that priests had as fine an instinct seven hundred years ago in ferreting out the choicest nooks and corners in a land as priests have to-day.

A big hotel crowds the ruins a little, now, and drives a brisk trade with summer tourists. We descended into the gorge and had a supper which would have been very satisfactory if the trout had not been boiled. The Germans are pretty sure to boil a trout or any thing else if left to their own devices. This is an argument of some value in support of the theory that they were the original colonists of the wild islands off the coast of Scotland. A schooner laden with oranges was wrecked upon one of those islands a few years ago, and the gentle savages rendered the captain such willing assistance that he gave them as many oranges as they wanted. Next day he asked them how they liked them. They shook their heads and said, –

"Baked, they were tough; and even boiled, they warn't things for a hungry man to hanker after."

We went down the glen after supper. It is beautiful, – a mixture of sylvan loveliness and craggy wildness. A limpid torrent goes whistling down the glen, and toward the foot of it winds through a narrow cleft between lofty precipices and hurls itself over a succession of falls. After one passes the last of these he has a backward glimpse at the falls which is very pleasing, – they rise in a seven-stepped stairway of foamy and glittering cascades, and make a picture which is as charming as it is unusual.

CHAPTER XXV

NEXT MORNING WE left in the train for Switzerland, and reached Lucerne about ten o'clock at night. The first discovery I made was that the beauty of the lake had not been exaggerated. Within a day or two I made another discovery. This was, that the lauded chamois is not a wild goat; that it is not a horned animal; that it is not shy; that it does not avoid human society; and that there is no peril in hunting it. The chamois is a black or brown creature no bigger than a mustard seed; you do not have to go after it, it comes after you; it arrives in vast herds and skips and scampers all over your body, inside your clothes; thus it is not shy, but extremely sociable; it is not afraid of man, on the contrary it will attack him; its bite is not dangerous, but neither is it pleasant; its activity has not been overstated, – if you try to put your finger on it, it will skip a thousand times its own length at one jump, and no eye is sharp enough to see where it lights. A great deal of romantic nonsense has been written about the Swiss chamois and the perils of hunting it, whereas the truth is that even women and children hunt it, and fearlessly; indeed, every body hunts it; the hunting is going on all the time, day and night, in bed and out of it. It is poetic foolishness to hunt it with a gun; very few people do that; there is not one man in a million who can hit it with a gun. It is much easier to catch it than it is to shoot it, and only the experienced chamois hunter can do either. Another common piece of exaggeration is that about the "scarcity" of the chamois. It is the reverse of scarce. Droves of 100,000,000 chamois are not unusual in the Swiss hotels. Indeed they are so numerous as to be a great pest. The romancers always dress up the chamois hunter, in a fanciful and picturesque costume, whereas the best way to hunt this game is to do it without any costume at all. The article of commerce called chamois-skin is another fraud; nobody could skin a chamois, it is too small. The creature is a humbug in every way, and everything which has been written about it is sentimental exaggeration.

It was no pleasure to me to find the chamois out, for he had been one of my pet illusions; all my life it had been my dream to see him in his native wilds some day, and engage in the adventurous sport of chasing him from cliff to cliff. It is no pleasure to me to expose him, now, and destroy the reader's delight in him and respect for him, but still it must be done, for when an honest writer discovers an imposition it is his simple duty to strip it bare and hurl it down from its place of honor, no matter who suffers by it; any other course would render him unworthy of the public confidence.

Lucerne is a charming place. It begins at the water's edge, with a fringe of hotels, and scrambles up and spreads itself over two or three sharp hills in a crowded, disorderly, but picturesque way, offering to the eye a heaped-up confusion of red roofs, quaint gables, dormer windows, toothpick steeples, with here and there a bit of ancient embattled wall bending itself over the ridges, worm-fashion, and here and there an old square tower of heavy masonry. And also here and there a town clock with only one hand, – a hand which stretches straight across the dial and has no joint in it; such a clock helps out the picture, but you cannot tell the time of day by it. Between the curving line of hotels and the lake is a broad avenue with lamps and a double rank of low shade trees. The lake front is walled with masonry like a pier, and has a railing, to keep people from walking overboard. All day long the vehicles dash along the avenue, and nurses, children and tourists sit in the shade of the trees, or lean on the railing and watch the schools of fishes darting about in the clear water or gaze out over the lake at the stately border of snow-hooded mountain peaks. Little pleasure-steamers, black with people, are coming and going all the time; and every where one sees young girls and young men paddling about in fanciful row-boats, or skimming along by the help of sails when there is any wind. The front rooms of the hotels have little railed balconies, where one may take his private luncheon in calm cool comfort and look down upon this busy and pretty scene and enjoy it without having to do any of the work connected with it.

Most of the people, both male and female, are in walking costume, and carry alpenstocks. Evidently it is not considered safe to go about in Switzerland, even in town, without an alpenstock. If the tourist forgets, and comes down to breakfast without his alpenstock, he goes back and gets it, and stands it up in the corner. When his touring in Switzerland is finished, he does not throw that broomstick away, but lugs it home with him, to the far corners of the earth, although this costs him more trouble and bother than a baby or a courier could. You see, the alpenstock is his trophy; his name is burned upon it; and if he has climbed a hill, or jumped a brook, or traversed a brickyard with it, he has the names of those places burned upon it, too. Thus it is his regimental flag, so to speak, and bears the record of his achievements. It is worth three francs when he buys it, but a bonanza could not purchase it after his great deeds have been inscribed upon it. There are artisans all about Switzerland whose trade it is to burn these things upon the alpenstock of the tourist. And observe, a man is respected in Switzerland according to his alpenstock. I found I could get no attention there, while I carried an unbranded one. However, branding is not expensive, so I soon remedied that. The effect upon the next detachment of tourists was very marked. I felt repaid for my trouble.

Half of the summer horde in Switzerland is made up of English people; the other half is made up of many nationalities, the Germans leading and the Americans coming next. The Americans were not as numerous as I had expected they would be.

The 7.30 table d'hote at the great Schweitzerhof furnished a mighty array and variety of nationalities, but it offered a better opportunity to observe costumes than people, for the multitude sat at immensely long tables, and therefore the faces were mainly seen in perspective; but the breakfasts were served at small round tables, and then if one had the fortune to get a table in the midst of the assemblage he could have as many faces to study as he could desire. We used to try to guess out the nationalities, and generally succeeded tolerably well. Sometimes we tried to guess people's names; but that was a failure; that is a thing which probably requires a good deal of practice. We presently dropped it and gave our efforts to less difficult particulars. One morning I said, –

"There is an American party."

Harris said, –

"Yes, – but name the State."

I named one State, Harris named another. We agreed upon one thing, however, – that the young girl with the party was very beautiful, and very tastefully dressed. But we disagreed as to her age. I said she was eighteen, Harris said she was twenty. The dispute between us waxed warm and I finally said, with a pretense of being in earnest, –

"Well, there is one way to settle the matter, – I will go and ask her."

Harris said, sarcastically, "Certainly, that is the thing to do. All you need to do is to use the common formula over here: go and say, 'I'm an American!' Of course she will be glad to see you."

Then he hinted that perhaps there was no great danger of my venturing to speak to her.

I said, "I was only talking, – I didn't intend to approach her, but I see that you do not know what an intrepid person I am. I am not afraid of any woman that walks. I will go and speak to this young girl."

The thing I had in my mind was not difficult. I meant to address her in the most respectful way and ask her to pardon me if her strong resemblance to a former acquaintance of mine was deceiving me; and when she should reply that the name I mentioned was not the name she bore, I meant to beg pardon again, most respectfully, and retire. There would be no harm done. I walked to her table, bowed to the gentleman, then turned to her and was about to begin my little speech when she exclaimed, –

"I *knew* I wasn't mistaken, – I told John it was you! John said it probably wasn't, but I knew I was right. I said you would recognize me presently and come over; and I'm glad you did, for I shouldn't have felt much flattered if you had gone out of this room without recognizing me. Sit down, sit down, – how odd it is, – you are the last person I was ever expecting to see again."

This was a stupefying surprise. It took my wits clear away, for an instant. However, we shook hands cordially all around, and I sat down. But truly this was the tightest place I ever was in. I seemed to vaguely remember the girl's face, now, but I had no idea where I had seen it before, or what name belonged with it. I immediately tried to get up a diversion about Swiss scenery, to keep her from launching into topics that might betray that I did not know her, but it was of no use, she went right along upon matters which interested her more:

"O dear, what a night that was, when the sea washed the forward boats away, – do you remember it?"

"O, *don't* I!" said I, – but I didn't. I wished the sea had washed the rudder and the smoke-stack and the captain away, – then I could have located this questioner.

"And don't you remember how frightened poor Mary was, and how she cried?"

"Indeed I do!" said I. "Dear me, how it all comes back!"

I fervently wished it *would* come back, – but my memory was a blank. The wise way would have been to frankly own up; but I could not bring myself to do that, after the young girl had praised me so for recognizing her; so I went on, deeper and deeper into the mire, hoping for a chance clue but never getting one. The Unrecognizable continued, with vivacity, –

"Do you know, George married Mary, after all?"

"Why, no! Did he?"

"Indeed he did. He said he did not believe she was half as much to blame as her father was, and I thought he was right. Didn't you?"

"Of course he was. It was a perfectly plain case. I always said so."

"Why no you didn't! – at least that summer."

"Oh, no, not that summer. No, you are perfectly right about that. It was the following winter that I said it."

"Well, as it turned out, Mary was not in the least to blame, – it was all her father's fault, – at least his and old Darley's."

It was necessary to say some thing, – so I said, –

"I always regarded Darley as a troublesome old thing."

"So he was, but then they always had a great affection for him, although he had so many eccentricities. You remember that when the weather was the least cold, he would try to come into the house."

I was rather afraid to proceed. Evidently Darley was not a man, – he must be some other kind of animal, – possibly a dog, maybe an elephant. However, tails are common to all animals, so I ventured to say, –

"And what a tail he had!"

"*One!* He had a thousand!"

This was bewildering. I did not quite know what to say, so I only said, –

"Yes, he *was* rather well fixed in the matter of tails."

"For a negro, and a crazy one at that, I should say he was," said she.

It was getting pretty sultry for me. I said to myself, "Is it possible she is going to stop there, and wait for me to speak? If she does, the conversation is blocked. A negro with a thousand tails is a topic which a person cannot talk upon fluently and instructively without more or less preparation. As to diving rashly into such a vast subject,—"

But here, to my gratitude, she interrupted my thought by saying, –

"Yes, when it came to tales of his crazy woes, there was simply no end to them if anybody would listen. His own quarters were comfortable enough, but when the weather was cold, the family were sure to have his company, – nothing could keep him out of the house. But they always bore it kindly because he had saved Tom's life, years before. You remember Tom?"

"O, perfectly. Fine fellow he was, too."

"Yes he was. And what a pretty little thing his child was!"

"You may well say that. I never saw a prettier child."

"I used to delight to pet it and dandle it and play with it."

"So did I."

"You named it. What *was* that name? I can't call it to mind."

It appeared to me that the ice was getting pretty thin, here. I would have given some thing to know what the child's sex was. However, I had the good luck to think of a name that would fit either sex, – so I brought it out, –

"I named it Frances."

"From a relative, I suppose? But you named the one that died, too, – one that I never saw. What did you call that one?"

I was out of neutral names, but as the child was dead and she had never seen it, I thought I might risk a name for it and trust to luck. Therefore I said, –

"I called that one Thomas Henry."

She said, musingly, –

"That is very singular... very singular."

I sat still and let the cold sweat run down. I was in a good deal of trouble, but I believed I could worry through if she wouldn't ask me to name any more children. I wondered where the lightning was going to strike next. She was still ruminating over that last child's title, but presently she said, –

"I have always been sorry you were away at the time, – I would have had you name my child."

"*Your* child! Are you married?"

"I have been married thirteen years."

"Christened, you mean."

"No, married. The youth by your side is my son."

"It seems incredible, – even impossible. I do not mean any harm by it, but would you mind telling me if you are any over eighteen? – that is to say, will you tell me how old you are?"

"I was just nineteen the day of the storm we were talking about. That was my birth-day."

That did not help matters much, as I did not know the date of the storm. I tried to think of some non-committal thing to say, to keep up my end of the talk and render my poverty in the matter of reminiscences as little noticeable as possible, but I seemed to be about out of non-committal things. I was about to say, "You haven't changed a bit since then," – but that was risky. I thought of saying "You have improved ever so much since then," – but that wouldn't answer, of course. I was about to try a shy at the weather, for a saving change, when the girl slipped in ahead of me and said, –

"How I have enjoyed this talk over those happy old times, – haven't you?"

"I never have spent such a half-hour in all my life before!" said I, with emotion; and I could have added, with a near approach to truth, "and I would rather be scalped than spend another one like it." I was holily grateful to be through with the ordeal, and was about to make my good-byes and get out, when the girl said, –

"But there is one thing that is ever so puzzling to me."

"Why what is that?"

"That dead child's name. What did you say it was?"

Here was another balmy place to be in: I had forgotten the child's name; I hadn't imagined it would be needed again. However, I had to pretend to know, any way, so I said, –

"Joseph William."

The youth at my side corrected me, and said, –

"No, – Thomas Henry."

I thanked him, – in words, – and said, with trepidation, –

"O yes, – I was thinking of another child that I named, – I have named a great many, and I get them confused, – this one *was* named Henry Thompson,—"

"Thomas Henry," calmly interposed the boy.

I thanked him again, – strictly in words, – and stammered out, –

"Thomas Henry, – yes, Thomas Henry was the poor child's name. I named him for Thomas, – er, – Thomas Carlyle, the great author, you know, – and Henry – er, – er, – Henry the Eighth. The parents were very grateful to have a child named Thomas Henry."

"That makes it more singular than ever," murmured my beautiful friend.

"Does it? Why?"

"Because when the parents speak of that child now, they always call it Susan Amelia."

That spiked my gun. I could not say any thing. I was entirely out of verbal obliquities; to go further would be to lie, and that I would not do; so I simply sat still and suffered, – sat mutely and resignedly there, and sizzled, – for I was being slowly fried to death in my own blushes. Presently the enemy laughed a happy laugh and said, –

"I *have* enjoyed this talk over old times, but you have not. I saw very soon that you were only pretending to know me, and so as I had wasted a compliment on you in the beginning, I made up my mind to punish you. And I have succeeded pretty well. I was glad to see that you knew George and Tom and Darley, for I had never heard of them before and therefore could not be sure that you had; and I was glad to learn the names of those imaginary children, too. One can get quite a fund of information out of you if one goes at it cleverly. Mary and the storm, and the sweeping away of the forward boats, were facts – all the rest was fiction. Mary was my sister; her full name was Mary ——. *Now* do you remember me?"

"Yes," I said, "I do remember you now; and you are as hard-hearted as you were thirteen years ago in that ship, else you wouldn't have punished me so. You haven't changed your nature nor your person, in any way at all; you look just as young as you did then, you are just as beautiful as you were then, and you have transmitted a deal of your comeliness to this fine boy. There, – if that speech moves you any, let's fly the flag of truce, with the understanding that I am conquered and confess it."

All of which was agreed to and accomplished, on the spot. When I went back to Harris, I said, –

"Now you see what a person with talent and address can do."

"Excuse me, I see what a person of colossal ignorance and simplicity can do. The idea of your going and intruding on a party of strangers, that way, and talking for half an hour; why I never heard of a man in his right mind doing such a thing before. What did you say to them?"

"I never said any harm. I merely asked the girl what her name was."

"I don't doubt it. Upon my word I don't. I think you were capable of it. It was stupid in me to let you go over there and make such an exhibition of yourself. But you know I couldn't really believe you would do such an inexcusable thing. What will those people think of us? But how did you say it? – I mean the manner of it. I hope you were not abrupt."

"No, I was careful about that. I said 'My friend and I would like to know what your name is, if you don't mind.'"

"No, that was not abrupt. There is a polish about it that does you infinite credit. And I am glad you put me in; that was a delicate attention which I appreciate at its full value. What did she do?"

"She didn't do any thing in particular. She told me her name."

"Simply told you her name. Do you mean to say she did not show any surprise?"

"Well, now I come to think, she did show some thing; may be it was surprise; I hadn't thought of that, – I took it for gratification."

"O, undoubtedly you were right; it must have been gratification; it could not be otherwise than gratifying to be assaulted by a stranger with such a question as that. Then what did you do?"

"I offered my hand and the party gave me a shake."

"I saw it! I did not believe my own eyes, at the time. Did the gentleman say any thing about cutting your throat?"

"No, they all seemed glad to see me, as far as I could judge."

"And do you know, I believe they were. I think they said to themselves, 'Doubtless this curiosity has got away from his keeper – let us amuse ourselves with him.' There is no other way of accounting for their facile docility. You sat down. Did they *ask* you to sit down?"

"No, they did not ask me, but I supposed they did not think of it."

"You have an unerring instinct. What else did you do? What did you talk about?"

"Well, I asked the girl how old she was."

"*Un*doubtedly. Your delicacy is beyond praise. Go on, go on, – don't mind my apparent misery, – I always look so when I am steeped in a profound and reverent joy. Go on, – she told you her age?"

"Yes, she told me her age, and all about her mother, and her grandmother, and her other relations, and all about herself."

"Did she volunteer these statistics?"

"No, not exactly that. I asked the questions and she answered them."

"This is divine. Go on, – it is not possible that you forgot to inquire into her politics?"

"No, I thought of that. She is a democrat, her husband is a republican, and both of them are Baptists."

"Her husband? Is that child married?"

"She is not a child. She is married, and that is her husband who is there with her."

"Has she any children?"

"Yes, – seven and a half."

"That is impossible."

"No, she has them. She told me herself."

"Well, but seven and a *half*? How do you make out the half? Where does the half come in?"

"That is a child which she had by another husband, – not this one but another one, – so it is a step-child, and they do not count it full measure."

"Another husband? Has she had another husband?"

"Yes, four. This one is number four."

"I do not believe a word of it. It is impossible, upon its face. Is that boy there her brother?"

"No, that is her son. He is her youngest. He is not as old as he looks; he is only eleven and a half."

"These things are all manifestly impossible. This is a wretched business. It is a plain case: they simply took your measure, and concluded to fill you up. They seem to have succeeded. I am glad I am not in the mess; they may at least be charitable enough to think there ain't a pair of us. Are they going to stay here long?"

"No, they leave before noon."

"There is one man who is deeply grateful for that. How did you find out? You asked, I suppose?"

"No, along at first I inquired into their plans, in a general way, and they said they were going to be here a week, and make trips round about; but toward the end of the interview, when I said you and I would tour around with them with pleasure, and offered to bring you over and introduce you, they hesitated a little, and asked if you were from the same establishment that I was. I said you were, and then they said they had changed their mind and considered it necessary to start at once and visit a sick relative in Siberia."

"Ah me, you struck the summit! You struck the loftiest altitude of stupidity that human effort has ever reached. You shall have a monument of jackasses, skulls as high as the Strasburg spire if you die before I do. They wanted to know if I was from the same 'establishment' that you hail from, did they? What did they mean by 'establishment'?"

"I don't know; it never occurred to me to ask."

"Well *I* know. They meant an asylum – an *idiot* asylum, do you understand? So they *do* think there's a pair of us, after all. Now what do you think of yourself?"

"Well I don't know. I didn't know I was doing any harm; I didn't *mean* to do any harm. They were very nice people, and they seemed to like me."

Harris made some rude remarks and left for his bed-room, – to break some furniture, he said. He was a singularly irascible man; any little thing would disturb his temper.

I had been well scorched by the young woman, but no matter, I took it out of Harris. One should always "get even" in some way, else the sore place will go on hurting.

CHAPTER XXVII

CLOSE BY THE Lion of Lucerne is what they call the "Glacier Garden," – and it is the only one in the world. It is on high ground. Four or five years ago, some workmen who were digging foundations for a house came upon this interesting relic of a long departed age. Scientific men perceived in it a confirmation of their theories concerning the glacial period; so through their persuasions the little tract of ground was bought and permanently protected against being built upon. The soil was removed, and there lay the rasped and guttered track which the ancient glacier had made as it moved along upon its slow and tedious journey. This track was perforated by huge pot-shaped holes in the bed-rock, formed by the furious washing-around in them of boulders by the turbulent torrent which flows beneath all glaciers. These huge round boulders still remain in the holes; they and the walls of the holes are worn smooth by the long continued chafing which they gave each other in those old days. It took a mighty force to churn these big lumps of stone around in that vigorous way. The neighboring country had a very different shape, at that time, – the valleys have risen up and become hills, since, and the hills have become valleys. The boulders discovered in the pots had traveled a great distance, for there is no rock like them nearer than the distant Rhone Glacier.

For some days we were content to enjoy looking at the blue lake Lucerne and at the piled-up masses of snow mountains that border it all around, – an enticing spectacle, this last, for there is a strange and fascinating beauty and charm about a majestic snow-peak with the sun blazing upon it or the moonlight softly enriching it, – but finally we concluded to try a bit of excursioning around on a steamboat, and a dash on foot at the Rigi. Very well, we had a delightful trip to Fluelen, on a breezy, sunny day. Every body sat on the upper deck, on benches, under an awning; every body talked, laughed, and exclaimed at the wonderful scenery; in truth, a trip on that lake is almost the perfection of pleasuring. The mountains were a never ceasing marvel. Sometimes they rose straight up out of the lake, and towered aloft and overshadowed our pigmy steamer with their prodigious bulk in the most impressive way. Not snow-clad mountains, these, yet they climbed high enough toward the sky to meet the clouds and veil their foreheads in them. They were not barren and repulsive, but clothed in green, and restful and pleasant to the eye. And they were so almost straight-up-and-down, sometimes, that one could not imagine a man being able to keep his footing upon such a surface, yet there are paths, and the Swiss people go up and down them every day.

Sometimes one of these monster precipices had the slight inclination of the huge ship-houses in dock-yards, – then high aloft, toward the sky, it took a little stronger inclination, like that of a mansard roof, – and perched on this dizzy mansard one's eye detected little things like martin-boxes, and presently perceived that these were the dwellings of peasants, – an airy place for a home, truly. And suppose a peasant should walk in his sleep, or his child should fall out of the front yard? – the friends would have a tedious long journey down out of those cloud-heights before they found the remains. And yet those far-away homes looked ever so seductive, they were so remote from the troubled world, they dozed in such an atmosphere of peace and dreams, – surely no one who had learned to live up there would ever want to live on a meaner level.

We swept through the prettiest little curving arms of the lake, among these colossal green walls, enjoying new delights, always, as the stately panorama unfolded itself before us and re-rolled and hid itself behind us; and now and then we had the thrilling surprise of bursting suddenly upon a tremendous white mass like the distant and dominating Jungfrau, or some kindred giant, looming head and shoulders above a tumbled waste of lesser Alps.

Once, while I was hungrily taking in one of these surprises, and doing my best to get all I possibly could of it while it should last, I was interrupted by a young and care-free voice,

"You're an American, I think, – so'm I."

He was about eighteen, or possibly nineteen; slender and of medium height; open, frank, happy face; a restless but independent eye; a snub nose, which had the air of drawing back with a decent reserve from the silky new-born moustache below it until it should be introduced; a loosely hung jaw, calculated to work easily in the sockets. He wore a low-crowned, narrow-brimmed straw hat, with a broad blue ribbon around it which had a white anchor embroidered on it in front; nobby short-tailed coat, pantaloons, vest, all trim and neat and up with the fashion; red-striped stockings, very low-quarter patent leather shoes, tied with black ribbon; blue ribbon around his neck, wide-open collar; tiny diamond studs; wrinkleless kids; projecting cuffs, fastened with large oxydized silver sleeve-buttons, bearing the device of a dog's face, – English pug. He carried a slim cane, surmounted with an English pug's head with red glass eyes. Under his arm he carried a German Grammar, – Otto's. His hair was short, straight and smooth, and presently when he turned his head a moment, I saw that it was nicely parted behind. He took a cigarette out of a dainty box, stuck it into a meerschaum holder which he carried in a morocco case, and reached for my cigar. While he was lighting, I said, –

"Yes, – I am an American."

"I knew it, – I can always tell them. What ship did you come over in?"

"Holsatia."

"We came in the Batavia, – Cunard, you know. What kind of a passage did you have?"

"Tolerably rough."

"So did we. Captain said he'd hardly ever seen it rougher. Where are you from?"

"New England."

"So'm I. I'm from New Bloomfield. Anybody with you?"

"Yes, – a friend."

"Our whole family's along. It's awful slow, going around alone, – don't you think so?"

"Rather slow."

"Ever been over here before?"

"Yes."

"I haven't. My first trip. But we've been all around, – Paris and every where. I'm to enter Harvard next year. Studying German all the time, now. Can't enter till I know German. I know considerable French, – I get along pretty well in Paris, or anywhere where they speak French. What hotel are you stopping at?"

"Schweitzerhof."

"No! is that so? I never see you in the reception room. I go to the reception room a good deal of the time, because there's so many Americans there. I make lots of acquaintances. I know an American as soon as I see him, – and so I speak to him and make his acquaintance. I like to be always making acquaintances, – don't you?"

"Lord, yes!"

"You see it breaks up a trip like this, first rate. I never get bored on a trip like this, if I can make acquaintances and have some body to talk to. But I think a trip like this would be an awful bore, if a body couldn't find anybody to get acquainted with and talk to on a trip like this. I'm fond of talking, ain't you?"

"Passionately."

"Have you felt bored, on this trip?"

"Not all the time, part of it."

"That's it! – you see you ought to go around and get acquainted, and talk. That's my way. That's the way I always do, – I just go 'round, 'round, 'round, and talk, talk, talk, – I never get bored. You been up the Rigi yet?"

"No."

"Going?"

"I think so."

"What hotel you going to stop at?"

"I don't know. Is there more than one?"

"Three. You stop at the Schreiber – you'll find it full of Americans. What ship did you say you came over in?"

"City of Antwerp."

"German, I guess. You going to Geneva?"

"Yes."

"What hotel you going to stop at?"

"Hotel de l'Ecu de Genève."

"Don't you do it! No Americans there? You stop at one of those big hotels over the bridge, – they're packed full of Americans."

"But I want to practice my Arabic."

"Good gracious, do you speak Arabic?"

"Yes, – well enough to get along."

"Why, hang it, you won't get along in Geneva, – *they* don't speak Arabic, they speak French. What hotel are you stopping at here?"

"Hotel Pension-Beaurivage."

"Sho, you ought to stop at the Schweitzerhof. Didn't you know the Schweitzerhof was the best hotel in Switzerland? – look at your Baedecker."

"Yes, I know, – but I had an idea there warn't any Americans there."

"No Americans! Why bless your soul it's just alive with them! I'm in the great reception room most all the time. I make lots of acquaintances there. Not as many as I did at first, because now only the new ones stop in there, – the others go right along through. Where are you from?"

"Arkansaw."

"Is that so? I'm from New England, – New Bloomfield's my town when I'm at home. I'm having a mighty good time to-day, ain't you?"

"Divine."

"That's what I call it. I like this knocking around, loose and easy, and making acquaintances and talking. I know an American, soon as I see him; so I go and speak to him and make his acquaintance. I ain't ever bored, on a trip like this, if I can make new acquaintances and talk. I'm awful fond of talking when I can get hold of the right kind of a person, ain't you?"

"I prefer it to any other dissipation."

"That's my notion, too. Now some people like to take a book and sit down and read, and read, and read, or moon around yawping at the lake or these mountains and things, but that ain't my way; no, sir, if they like it, let 'em do it, I don't object; but as for me, talking's what *I* like. You been up the Rigi?"

"Yes."

"What hotel did you stop at?"

"Schreiber."

"That's the place! – I stopped there too. *Full* of Americans, *wasn't* it? It always is, – always is. That's what they say. Every body says that. What ship did you come over in?"

"Ville de Paris."

"French, I reckon. What kind of a passage did...excuse me a minute, there's some Americans I haven't seen before."

And away he went. He went uninjured, too, – I had the murderous impulse to harpoon him in the back with my alpenstock, but as I raised the weapon the disposition left me; I found I hadn't the heart to kill him, he was such a joyous, innocent, good-natured numskull.

Half an hour later I was sitting on a bench inspecting, with strong interest, a noble monolith which we were skimming by, – a monolith not shaped by man, but by Nature's free great hand, – a massy pyramidal rock eighty feet high, devised by Nature ten million years ago against the day when a man worthy of it should need it for his monument. The time came at last, and now this grand remembrancer bears Schiller's name in huge letters upon its face. Curiously enough, this rock was not degraded or defiled in any way. It is said that two years ago a stranger let himself down from the top of it with ropes and pulleys, and painted all over it, in blue letters bigger than those in Schiller's name, these words:

TRY SOZODONT;
BUY SUN STOVE POLISH;
HELMBOLD'S BUCHU;
TRY BENZALINE FOR THE BLOOD.

He was captured, and it turned out that he was an American. Upon his trial the judge said to him, –

"You are from a land where any insolent that wants to, is privileged to profane and insult Nature, and through her, Nature's God, if by so doing he can put a sordid penny in his pocket. But here the case is different. Because you are a foreigner and ignorant, I will make your sentence light; if you were a native I would deal strenuously with you. – Hear and obey: You will immediately remove every trace of your offensive work from the Schiller monument; you pay a fine of ten thousand francs; you will suffer two years' imprisonment at hard labor; you will then be horsewhipped, tarred and feathered, deprived of your ears, ridden on a rail to the confines of the canton, and banished forever. The severer penalties are omitted in your case, – not as a grace to you, but to that great republic which had the misfortune to give you birth."

The steamer's benches were ranged back to back across the deck. My back hair was mingling innocently with the back hair of a couple of ladies. Presently they were addressed by some one and I overheard this conversation:

"You are Americans, I think? So'm I."

"Yes, – we are Americans."

"I knew it, – I can always tell them. What ship did you come over in?"

"City of Chester."

"O yes, – Inman line. We came in the Batavia, – Cunard, you know. What kind of a passage did you have?"

"Pretty fair."

"That was luck. We had it awful rough. Captain said he'd hardly ever seen it rougher. Where are you from?"

"New Jersey."

"So'm I. No – I didn't mean that; I'm from New England. New Bloomfield's my place. These your children? – belong to both of you?"

"Only to one of us; they are mine; my friend is not married."

"Single, I reckon? So'm I. Are you two ladies traveling alone?"

"No, – my husband is with us."

"Our whole family's along. It's awful slow, going around alone, – don't you think so?"

"I suppose it must be."

"Hi, there's Mount Pilatus coming in sight again. Named after Pontius Pilate, you know, that shot the apple off of William Tell's head. Guide-book tells all about it, they say. I didn't read it – an American told me. I don't read when I'm knocking around like this, having a good time. Did you ever see the chapel where William Tell used to preach?"

"I did not know he ever preached there."

"O, yes he did. That American told me so. He don't ever shut up his guide-book. He knows more about this lake than the fishes in it. Besides, they *call* it 'Tell's Chapel' – you know that yourself. You ever been over here before?"

"Yes."

"I haven't. It's my first trip. But we've been all around, – Paris and every where. I'm to enter Harvard next year. – Studying German all the time now. Can't enter till I know German. This book's Otto's Grammar. It's a mighty good book to get the *ich habe gehabt haben's* out of. But I don't really study when I'm knocking around this way. If the notion takes me, I just run over my little old *ich habe gehabt, du hast gehabt, er hat gehabt, wir haben gehabt, ihr habet gehabt, sie haben gehabt*, – kind of 'Now-I-lay-me-down-to-sleep' fashion, you know, and after that, maybe I don't buckle to it again for three days. It's awful undermining to the intellect, German is; you want to take it in small doses, or first you know your brains all run together, and you feel them sloshing around in your head same as so much drawn butter. But French is different; *French* ain't any thing. I ain't any more afraid of French than a tramp's afraid of pie; I can rattle off my little *j'aì, tu as, il a*, and the rest of it, just as easy as a-b-c. I get along pretty well in Paris, or anywhere where they speak French. What hotel you stopping at?"

"The Schweitzerhof."

"No! is that so? I never see you in the big reception room. I go in there a good deal of the time, because there's so many Americans there. I make lots of acquaintances. You been up the Rigi yet?"

"No."

"Going?"

"We think of it."

"What hotel you going to stop at?"

"I don't know."

"Well, then, you stop at the Schreiber, – it's full of Americans. What ship did you come over in?"

"City of Chester."

"O, yes, I remember I asked you that before. But I always ask every body what ship they came over in, and so sometimes I forget and ask again. You going to Geneva?"

"Yes."

"What hotel you going to stop at?"

"We expect to stop in a pension."

"I don't hardly believe you'll like that: there's very few Americans in the pensions. What hotel are you stopping at here?"

"The Schweitzerhof."

"O, yes, I asked you that before, too. But I always ask every body what hotel they're stopping at, and so I've got my head all mixed up with hotels. But it makes talk, and I love to talk. It refreshes me up so, – don't it you – on a trip like this?"

"Yes, – sometimes."

"Well, it does me, too. As long as I'm talking I never feel bored, – ain't that the way with you?"

"Yes – generally. But there are exceptions to the rule."

"O, of course. *I* don't care to talk to every body, *myself*. If a person starts in to jabber-jabber-jabber about scenery, and history, and pictures, and all sorts of tiresome things, I get the fan-tods mighty soon. I say 'Well, I must be going now, – hope I'll see you again' – and then I take a walk. Where you from?"

"New Jersey."

"Why, bother it all, I asked you *that* before, too. Have you seen the Lion of Lucerne?"

"Not yet."

"Nor I, either. But the man who told me about Mount Pilatus says it's one of the things to see. It's twenty-eight feet long. It don't seem reasonable, but he said so, any way. He saw it yesterday; said it was dying, then, so I reckon it's dead by this time. But that ain't any matter, of course they'll stuff it. Did you say the children are yours, – or *hers*?"

"Mine."

"O, so you did. Are you going up the ... no, I asked you that. What ship ... no, I asked you that, too. What hotel are you ... no, you told me that. Let me see ... um ... O, what kind of a voy ... no, we've been over that ground, too. Um...um...well, I believe that is all. *Bonjour* – I am very glad to have made your acquaintance, ladies. *Guten Tag.*"

CHAPTER XXVIII

THE RIGI-KULM IS an imposing Alpine mass, 6,000 feet high, which stands by itself, and commands a mighty prospect of blue lakes, green valleys, and snowy mountains – a compact and magnificent picture three hundred miles in circumference. The ascent is made by rail, or horse-back, or on foot, as one may prefer. I and my agent panoplied ourselves in walking costume, one bright morning, and started down the lake on the steamboat; we got ashore at the village of Wäggis, three-quarters of an hour distant from Lucerne. This village is at the foot of the mountain.

We were soon tramping leisurely up the leafy mule-path, and then the talk began to flow, as usual. It was twelve o'clock noon, and a breezy, cloudless day; the ascent was gradual, and the glimpses, from under the curtaining boughs, of blue water, and tiny sail boats, and beetling cliffs, were as charming as glimpses of dreamland. All the circumstances were perfect – and the anticipations, too, for we should soon be enjoying, for the first time, that wonderful spectacle, an Alpine sunrise – the object of our journey. There was (apparently) no real need to hurry, for the guide-book made the walking distance from Wäggis to the summit only three hours and a quarter. I say "apparently," because the guide-book had already fooled us once, – about the distance from Allerheiligen to Oppenau, – and for aught I knew it might be getting ready to fool us again. We were only certain as to the altitudes, – we calculated to find out for ourselves how many hours it is from the bottom to the top. The summit is 6,000 feet above the sea, but only 4,500 feet above the lake. When we had walked half an hour, we were fairly into the swing and humor of the undertaking, so we cleared for action; that is to say, we got a boy whom we met to carry our alpenstocks and satchels and over coats and things for us; that left us free for business.

I suppose we must have stopped oftener to stretch out on the grass in the shade and take a bit of a smoke than this boy was used to, for presently he asked if it had been our idea to hire him by the job, or by the year? We told him he could move along if he was in a hurry. He said he wasn't in such a very particular hurry, but he wanted to get to the top while he was young. We told him to clear out, then, and leave the things at the uppermost hotel and say we should be along presently. He said he would secure us a hotel if he could, but if they were all full he would ask them to build another one and hurry up and get the paint and plaster dry against we arrived. Still gently chaffing us he pushed ahead, up the trail, and soon disappeared. By six o'clock we were pretty high up in the air, and the view of lake and mountains had greatly grown in breadth and interest. We halted a while at a little public house, where we had bread and cheese and a quart or two of fresh milk, out on the porch, with the big panorama all before us, – and then moved on again.

Ten minutes afterward we met a hot, red-faced man plunging down the mountain, with mighty strides, swinging his alpenstock ahead of him and taking a grip on the ground with its iron point to support these big strides. He stopped, fanned himself with his hat, swabbed the perspiration from his face and neck with a red handkerchief, panted a moment or two, and asked how far it was to Wäggis. I said three hours. He looked surprised, and said, –

"Why, it seems as if I could toss a biscuit into the lake from here, it's so close by. Is that an inn, there?"

I said it was.

"Well," said he, "I can't stand another three hours, I've had enough for to-day; I'll take a bed there."

I asked, –

"Are we nearly to the top?"

"Nearly to the *top!* Why, bless your soul, you haven't really started, yet."

I said we would put up at the inn, too. So we turned back and ordered a hot supper, and had quite a jolly evening of it with this Englishman.

The German landlady gave us neat rooms and nice beds, and when I and my agent turned in, it was with the resolution to be up early and make the utmost of our first Alpine sunrise. But of course we were dead tired, and slept like policemen; so when we awoke in the morning and ran to the window it was already too late, because it was half-past eleven. It was a sharp disappointment. However, we ordered breakfast and told the landlady to call the Englishman, but she said he was already up and off at daybreak, – and swearing mad about some thing or other. We could not find out what the matter was. He had asked the landlady the altitude of her place above the level of the lake, and she had told him fourteen hundred and ninety-five feet. That was all that was said; then he lost his temper. He said that between —— fools and guide-books, a man could acquire ignorance enough in twenty-four hours in a country like this to last him a year. Harris believed our boy had been loading him up with misinformation; and this was probably the case, for his epithet described that boy to a dot.

We got under way about the turn of noon, and pulled out for the summit again, with a fresh and vigorous step. When we had gone about two hundred yards, and stopped to rest, I glanced to the left while I was lighting my pipe, and in the distance detected a long worm of black smoke crawling lazily up the steep mountain. Of course that was the locomotive. We propped ourselves on our elbows at once, to gaze, for we had never seen a mountain railway yet. Presently we could make out the train. It seemed incredible that that thing should creep straight up a sharp slant like the roof of a house, – but there it was, and it was doing that very miracle.

In the course of a couple of hours we reached a fine breezy altitude where the little shepherd-huts had big stones all over their roofs to hold them down to the earth when the great storms rage. The country was wild and rocky about here, but there were plenty of trees, plenty of moss, and grass.

Away off on the opposite shore of the lake we could see some villages, and now for the first time we could observe the real difference between their proportions and those of the giant mountains at whose feet they slept. When one is in one of those villages it seems spacious, and its houses seem high and not out of proportion to the mountain that overhangs them – but from our altitude, what a change! The mountains were bigger and grander than ever, as they stood there thinking their solemn thoughts with their heads in the drifting clouds, but the villages at their feet, – when the painstaking eye could trace them up and find them, – were so reduced, so almost invisible, and lay so flat against the ground, that the exactest simile I can devise is to compare them to ant-deposits of granulated dirt over-shadowed by the huge bulk of a cathedral. The steamboats skimming along under the stupendous precipices were diminished by distance to the daintiest little toys, the sail boats and row-boats to shallops proper for fairies that keep house in the cups of lilies and ride to court on the backs of bumble-bees.

Presently we came upon half a dozen sheep nibbling grass in the spray of a stream of clear water that sprang from a rock wall a hundred feet high, and all at once our ears were startled with a melodious "Lul ... l...l...lul-lul-*la*hee-o-o-o!" pealing joyously from a near but invisible source, and recognized that we were hearing for the first time the famous Alpine *jodel* in its own native wilds. And we recognized, also, that it was that sort of quaint commingling of baritone and falsetto which at home we call "Tyrolese warbling."

The jodling (pronounced y*o*dling, – emphasis on the o,) continued, and was very pleasant and inspiriting to hear. Now the jodler appeared, – a shepherd boy of sixteen, – and in our gladness and gratitude we gave him a franc to jodel some more, so he jodeled, and we listened. We moved on, presently, and he generously jodeled us out of sight. After about fifteen minutes we came across another shepherd boy who was jodling, and gave him half a franc to keep it up. He also jodled us out of sight. After that, we found a jodler every ten minutes; we gave the first one eight cents, the second one six cents, the third one four, the fourth one a penny, contributed nothing to Nos. 5, 6, and 7, and during the remainder of the day hired the rest of the jodlers, at a franc apiece, not to jodel anymore. There is somewhat too much of this jodling in the Alps.

About the middle of the afternoon we passed through a prodigious natural gateway called the Felsenthor, formed by two enormous upright rocks, with a third lying across the top. There was a very attractive little hotel close by, but our energies were not conquered yet, so we went on.

Three hours afterward we came to the railway track. It was planted straight up the mountain with the slant of a ladder that leans against a house, and it seemed to us that a man would need good nerves who proposed to travel up it or down it either.

During the latter part of the afternoon we cooled our roasting interiors with ice-cold water from clear streams, the only really satisfying water we had tasted since we left home, for at the hotels on the continent they merely give you a tumbler of ice to soak your water in, and that only modifies its hotness, doesn't make it cold. Water can only be made cold enough for summer comfort by being prepared in a refrigerator or a closed ice-pitcher. Europeans say ice-water impairs digestion. How do they know? – they never drink any.

At ten minutes past six we reached the Kaltbad station, where there is a spacious hotel with great verandahs which command a majestic expanse of lake and mountain scenery. We were pretty well fagged out, now, but as we did not wish to miss the Alpine sunrise, we got through with our dinner as quickly as possible and hurried off to bed. It was unspeakably comfortable to stretch our weary limbs between the cool damp sheets. And how we did sleep! – for there is no opiate like Alpine pedestrianism.

In the morning we both awoke and leaped out of bed at the same instant and ran and stripped aside the window curtains; but we suffered a bitter disappointment again: it was already half-past three in the afternoon.

We dressed sullenly and in ill spirits, each accusing the other of over-sleeping. Harris said if we had brought the courier along, as we ought to have done, we should not have missed these sunrises. I said he knew very well that one of us would have had to sit up and wake the courier; and I added that we were having trouble enough to take care of ourselves, on this climb, without having to take care of a courier besides.

During breakfast our spirits came up a little, since we found by the guide-book that in the hotels on the summit the tourist is not left to trust to luck for his sunrise, but is roused betimes by a man who goes through the halls with a great Alpine horn, blowing blasts that would raise the dead. And there was another consoling thing: the guide-book said that up there on the summit the guests did not wait to dress much, but seized a red bed-blanket and sailed out arrayed like an Indian. This was good; this would be romantic; two hundred and fifty people grouped on the windy summit, with their hair flying and their red blankets flapping, in the solemn presence of the snowy ranges and the messenger splendors of the coming sun, would be a striking and memorable spectacle. So it was good luck, not ill luck, that we had missed those other sunrises.

We were informed by the guide-book that we were now 3,228 feet above the level of the lake, – therefore full two-thirds of our journey had been accomplished. We got away at a quarter-past four, P.M.; a hundred yards above the hotel the railway divided; one track went straight up the steep hill, the other one turned square off to the right, with a very slight grade. We took the latter, and followed it more than a mile, turned a rocky corner and came in sight of a handsome new hotel. If we had gone on, we should have arrived at the summit, but Harris preferred to ask a lot of questions, – as usual, of a man who didn't know anything, – and he told us to go back and follow the other route. We did so. We could ill afford this loss of time.

We climbed, and climbed; and we kept on climbing; we reached about forty summits but there was always another one just ahead. It came on to rain, and it rained in dead earnest. We were soaked through, and it was bitter cold. Next a smoky fog of clouds covered the whole region densely, and we took to the railway ties to keep from getting lost. Sometimes we slopped along in a narrow path on the left-hand side of the track, but by and by when the fog blew aside a little and we saw that we were treading the rampart of a precipice and that our left elbows were projecting over a perfectly boundless and bottomless vacancy, we gasped, and jumped for the ties again.

The night shut down, dark and drizzly and cold. About eight in the evening the fog lifted and showed us a well-worn path which led up a very steep rise to the left. We took it and as soon as we had got far enough from the railway to render the finding it again an impossibility, the fog shut down on us once more.

We were in a bleak unsheltered place, now, and had to trudge right along, in order to keep warm, though we rather expected to go over a precipice sooner or later. About nine o'clock we made an important discovery, – that we were not in any path. We groped around a while on our hands and knees, but could not find it; so we sat down in the mud and the wet scant grass to wait. We were terrified into this by being suddenly confronted with a vast body which showed itself vaguely for an instant and in the next instant was smothered in the fog again. It was really the hotel we were after, monstrously magnified by the fog, but we took it for the face of a precipice and decided not to try to claw up it.

We sat there an hour, with chattering teeth and quivering bodies, and quarreled over all sorts of trifles, but gave most of our attention to abusing each other for the stupidity of deserting the railway track. We sat with our backs to that precipice, because what little wind there was came from that quarter. At some time or other the fog thinned a little; we did not know when, for we were facing the empty universe and the thinness could not show; but at last Harris happened to look around, and there stood a huge, dim, spectral hotel where the precipice had been. One could faintly discern the windows and chimneys, and a dull blur of lights. Our first emotion was deep, unutterable gratitude, our next was a foolish rage, born of the suspicion that possibly the hotel had been visible three-quarters of an hour while we sat there in those cold puddles quarreling.

Yes, it was the Rigi-Kulm hotel – the one that occupies the extreme summit, and whose remote little sparkle of lights we had often seen glinting high aloft among the stars from our balcony away down yonder in Lucerne. The crusty portier and the crusty clerks gave us the surly reception which their kind deal in in prosperous times, but by mollifying them with an extra display of obsequiousness and servility we finally got them to show us to the room which our boy had engaged for us.

We got into some dry clothing, and while our supper was preparing we loafed forsakenly through a couple of vast cavernous drawing-rooms, one of which had a stove in it. This stove was in a corner, and densely walled around with people. We could not get near the fire, so we moved at large in the arctic spaces, among a multitude of people who sat silent, smileless, forlorn and shivering, – thinking what fools they were to come, perhaps. There were some Americans, and some Germans, but one could see that the great majority were English.

We lounged into an apartment where there was a great crowd, to see what was going on. It was a memento-magazine. The tourists were eagerly buying all sorts and styles of paper-cutters, marked "Souvenir of the Rigi," with handles made of the little curved horn of the ostensible chamois; there were all manner of wooden goblets and such things, similarly marked. I was going to buy a paper-cutter, but I believed I could remember the cold comfort of the Rigi-Kulm without it, so I smothered the impulse.

Supper warmed us, and we went immediately to bed, – but first, as Mr. Baedeker requests all tourists to call his attention to any errors which they may find in his guide-books, I dropped him a line to inform him that when he said the foot-journey from Wäggis to the summit was only three hours and a quarter, he missed it by just about three days. I had previously informed him of his mistake about the distance from Allerheiligen to Oppenau, and had also informed the Ordnance Department of the German government of the same error in the imperial maps. I will add, here, that I never got any answer to these letters, or any thanks from either of those sources; and what is still more discourteous, these corrections have not been made, either in the maps or the guide-books. But I will write again when I get time, for my letters may have miscarried.

We curled up in the clammy beds, and went to sleep without rocking. We were so sodden with fatigue that we never stirred nor turned over till the booming blasts of the Alpine horn aroused us. It may well be imagined that we did not lose any time. We snatched on a few odds and ends of clothing, cocooned ourselves in the proper red blankets, and plunged along the halls and out into the whistling wind bare-headed. We saw a tall wooden scaffolding on the very peak of the summit, a hundred yards away, and made for it. We rushed up the stairs to the top of this scaffolding, and stood there, above the vast outlying world, with hair flying and ruddy blankets waving and cracking in the fierce breeze.

"Fifteen minutes too late, at last!" said Harris, in a vexed voice. "The sun is clear above the horizon."

"No matter," I said, "it is a most magnificent spectacle, and we will see it do the rest of its rising, any way."

In a moment we were deeply absorbed in the marvel before us, and dead to everything else. The great cloud-barred disk of the sun stood just above a limitless expanse of tossing white-caps, – so to speak, – a billowy chaos of massy mountain domes and peaks draped in imperishable snow, and flooded with an opaline glory of changing and dissolving splendors, whilst through rifts in a black cloud-bank above the sun, radiating lances of diamond dust shot to the zenith. The cloven valleys of the lower world swam in a tinted mist which veiled the ruggedness of their crags and ribs and ragged forests, and turned all the forbidding region into a soft and rich and sensuous paradise.

We could not speak. We could hardly breathe. We could only gaze in drunken ecstasy and drink it in. Presently Harris exclaimed, –

"Why – nation, it's going *down*!"

Perfectly true. We had missed the *morning* horn-blow, and slept all day. This was stupefying. Harris said, –

"Look here, the sun isn't the spectacle, – it's *us*, – stacked up here on top of this gallows, in these idiotic blankets, and two hundred and fifty well-dressed men and women down here gawking up at us and not caring a straw whether the sun rises or sets, as long as they've got such a ridiculous spectacle as this to set down in their memorandum-books. They seem to be laughing their ribs loose, and there's one girl there that appears to be going all to pieces. I never saw such a man as you before. I think you are the very last possibility in the way of an ass."

"What have *I* done?" I answered with heat.

"What have you done? You've got up at half-past seven o'clock in the evening to see the sun rise, that's what you've done."

"And have you done any better, I'd like to know? I always used to get up with the lark, till I came under the petrifying influence of your turgid intellect."

"*You* used to get up with the lark, – O, no doubt, – you'll get up with the hangman one of these days. But you ought to be ashamed to be jawing here like this, in a red blanket, on a forty-foot scaffold on top of the Alps. And no end of people down here to boot; this isn't any place for an exhibition of temper."

And so the customary quarrel went on. When the sun was fairly down, we slipped back to the hotel in the charitable gloaming, and went to bed again. We had encountered the horn-blower on the way, and he had tried to collect compensation, not only for announcing the sunset, which we did see, but for the sunrise, which we had totally missed; but we said no, we only took our solar rations on the "European plan" – pay for what you get. He promised to make us hear his horn in the morning, if we were alive.

CHAPTER XXIX

HE KEPT HIS word. We heard his horn and instantly got up. It was dark and cold and wretched. As I fumbled around for the matches, knocking things down with my quaking hands, I wished the sun would rise in the middle of the day, when it was warm and bright and cheerful, and one wasn't sleepy. We proceeded to dress by the gloom of a couple of sickly candles, but we could hardly button any thing, our hands shook so. I thought of how many happy people there were in Europe, Asia and America, and every where, who were sleeping peacefully in their beds and did not have to get up and see the Rigi sunrise, – people who did not appreciate their advantage, as like as not, but would get up in the morning wanting more boons of Providence. While thinking these thoughts I yawned, in a rather ample way, and my upper teeth got hitched on a nail over the door, and whilst I was mounting a chair to free myself, Harris drew the window curtain and said, –

"O, this is luck! We shan't have to go out at all, – yonder are the mountains, in full view."

That was glad news, indeed. It made us cheerful right away. One could see the grand Alpine masses dimly outlined against the black firmament, and one or two faint stars blinking through rifts in the night. Fully clothed, and wrapped in blankets, we huddled ourselves up, by the window, with lighted pipes, and fell into chat, while we waited in exceeding comfort to see how an Alpine sunrise was going to look by candle-light. By and by a delicate, spiritual sort of effulgence spread itself by imperceptible degrees over the loftiest altitudes of the snowy wastes, – but there the effort seemed to stop. I said, presently, –

"There is a hitch about this sunrise somewhere. It doesn't seem to go. What do you reckon is the matter with it?"

"I don't know. It appears to hang fire somewhere. I never saw a sunrise act like that before. Can it be that the hotel is playing any thing on us?"

"Of course not. The hotel merely has a property interest in the sun, it has nothing to do with the management of it. It is a precarious kind of property, too; a succession of total eclipses would probably ruin this tavern. Now what can be the matter with this sunrise?"

Harris jumped up and said, –

"I've got it! I know what's the matter with it! We've been looking at the place where the sun *set* last night!"

"It is perfectly true! Why couldn't you have thought of that sooner? Now we've lost another one! And all through your blundering. It was exactly like you to light a pipe and sit down to wait for the sun to rise in the west."

"It was exactly like me to find out the mistake, too. You never would have found it out. I find out all the mistakes."

"You make them all, too, else your most valuable faculty would be wasted on you. But don't stop to quarrel, now, – maybe we are not too late yet."

But we were. The sun was well up when we got to the exhibition ground.

On our way up we met the crowd returning – men and women dressed in all sorts of queer costumes, and exhibiting all degrees of cold and wretchedness in their gaits and countenances. A dozen still remained on the ground when we reached there, huddled together about the scaffold with their backs to the bitter wind. They had their red guide-books open at the diagram of the view, and were painfully picking out the several mountains and trying to impress their names and positions on their memories. It was one of the saddest sights I ever saw.

Two sides of this place were guarded by railings, to keep people from being blown over the precipices. The view, looking sheer down into the broad valley, eastward, from this great elevation, –

almost a perpendicular mile, – was very quaint and curious. Counties, towns, hilly ribs and ridges, wide stretches of green meadow, great forest tracts, winding streams, a dozen blue lakes, a flock of busy steamboats – we saw all this little world in unique circumstantiality of detail – saw it just as the birds see it – and all reduced to the smallest of scales and as sharply worked out and finished as a steel engraving. The numerous toy villages, with tiny spires projecting out of them, were just as the children might have left them when done with play the day before; the forest tracts were diminished to cushions of moss; one or two big lakes were dwarfed to ponds, the smaller ones to puddles, – though they did not look like puddles, but like blue ear drops which had fallen and lodged in slight depressions, conformable to their shapes, among the moss-beds and the smooth levels of dainty green farm-land; the microscopic steamboats glided along, as in a city reservoir, taking a mighty time to cover the distance between ports which seemed only a yard apart; and the isthmus which separated two lakes looked as if one might stretch out on it and lie with both elbows in the water, yet we knew invisible wagons were toiling across it and finding the distance a tedious one. This beautiful miniature world had exactly the appearance of those "relief maps" which reproduce nature precisely, with the heights and depressions and other details graduated to a reduced scale, and with the rocks, trees, lakes, etc., colored after nature.

I believed we could walk down to Wäggis or Vitznau in a day, but I knew we could go down by rail in about an hour, so I chose the latter method. I wanted to see what it was like, any way. The train came along about the middle of the forenoon, and an odd thing it was. The locomotive boiler stood on end, and it and the whole locomotive were tilted sharply backward. There were two passenger cars, roofed, but wide open all around. These cars were not tilted back, but the seats were; this enables the passenger to sit level while going down a steep incline.

There are three railway tracks; the central one is cogged; the "lantern wheel" of the engine grips its way along these cogs, and pulls the train up the hill or retards its motion on the down trip. About the same speed, – three miles an hour, – is maintained both ways. Whether going up or down, the locomotive is always at the lower end of the train. It pushes, in the one case, braces back in the other. The passenger rides backward, going up, and faces forward going down.

We got front seats, and while the train moved along about fifty yards on level ground, I was not the least frightened; but now it started abruptly down stairs, and I caught my breath. And I, like my neighbors, unconsciously held back all I could, and threw my weight to the rear, but of course that did no particular good. I had slidden down the balusters when I was a boy, and thought nothing of it, but to slide down the balusters in a railway train is a thing to make one's flesh creep. Sometimes we had as much as ten yards of almost level ground, and this gave us a few full breaths in comfort; but straightway we would turn a corner and see a long steep line of rails stretching down below us, and the comfort was at an end. One expected to see the locomotive pause, or slack up a little, and approach this plunge cautiously, but it did nothing of the kind; it went calmly on, and when it reached the jumping-off place it made a sudden bow, and went gliding smoothly down stairs, untroubled by the circumstances.

It was wildly exhilarating to slide along the edge of the precipices, after this grisly fashion, and look straight down upon that far-off valley which I was describing a while ago.

There was no level ground at the Kaltbad station; the railbed was as steep as a roof; I was curious to see how the stop was going to be managed. But it was very simple: the train came sliding down, and when it reached the right spot it just stopped – that was all there was "to it" – stopped on the steep incline, and when the exchange of passengers and baggage had been made, it moved off and went sliding down again. The train can be stopped anywhere, at a moment's notice.

There was one curious effect, which I need not take the trouble to describe, – because I can scissor a description of it out of the railway company's advertising pamphlet, and save my ink:

"On the whole tour, particularly at the Descent, we undergo an optical illusion which often seems to be incredible. All the shrubs, fir trees, stables, houses, etc., seem to be bent in a slanting direction, as by an immense pressure of air. They are all standing awry, so much awry that the chalets and cottages of the peasants seem to be tumbling down. It is the consequence of the steep inclination of the line. Those who are seated in the carriage do not observe that they are going down a declivity of 20 to 25° (their seats being adapted to this course of proceeding and being bent down at their backs.) They mistake their carriage and its horizontal lines for a proper measure of the normal plain, and therefore all the objects outside which really are in a horizontal position, must show a disproportion of 20 to 25° declivity, in regard to the mountain."

By the time one reaches Kaltbad, he has acquired confidence in the railway, and he now ceases to try to ease the locomotive by holding back. Thenceforward he smokes his pipe in serenity, and gazes out upon the magnificent picture below and about him with unfettered enjoyment. There is nothing to interrupt the view or the breeze; it is like inspecting the world on the wing. However, – to be exact, – there is one place where the serenity lapses for a while: this is while one is crossing the Schnurrtobel Bridge, a frail structure which swings its gossamer frame down through the dizzy air, over a gorge, like a vagrant spider-strand.

One has no difficulty in remembering his sins while the train is creeping down this bridge; and he repents of them, too; though he sees, when he gets to Vitznau, that he need not have done it, the bridge was perfectly safe.

So ends the eventful trip which we made to the Rigi-Kulm to see an Alpine sunrise.

CHAPTER XXI

THE BEAUTIFUL GIESBACH Fall is near Interlaken, on the other side of the lake of Brienz, and is illuminated every night with those gorgeous theatrical fires whose name I cannot call just at this moment. This was said to be a spectacle which the tourist ought by no means to miss. I was strongly tempted, but I could not go there with propriety, because one goes in a boat. The task which I had set myself was to walk over Europe on foot, not skim over it in a boat. I had made a tacit contract with myself; it was my duty to abide by it. I was willing to make boat trips for pleasure, but I could not conscientiously make them in the way of business.

It cost me something of a pang to lose that fine sight, but I lived down the desire, and gained in my self-respect through the triumph. I had a finer and a grander sight, however, where I was. This was the mighty dome of the Jungfrau softly outlined against the sky and faintly silvered by the starlight. There was something subduing in the influence of that silent and solemn and awful presence; one seemed to meet the immutable, the indestructible, the eternal, face to face, and to feel the trivial and fleeting nature of his own existence the more sharply by the contrast. One had the sense of being under the brooding contemplation of a spirit, not an inert mass of rocks and ice, – a spirit which had looked down, through the slow drift of the ages, upon a million vanished races of men, and judged them; and would judge a million more, – and still be there, watching, unchanged and unchangeable, after all life should be gone and the earth have become a vacant desolation.

While I was feeling these things, I was groping, without knowing it, toward an understanding of what the spell is which people find in the Alps, and in no other mountains, – that strange, deep, nameless influence, which, once felt, cannot be forgotten, – once felt, leaves always behind it a restless longing to feel it again, – a longing which is like homesickness; a grieving, haunting yearning, which will plead, implore, and persecute till it has its will. I met dozens of people, imaginative and unimaginative, cultivated and uncultivated, who had come from far countries and roamed through the Swiss Alps year after year, – they could not explain why. They had come first, they said, out of idle curiosity, because every body talked about it; they had come since because they could not help it, and they should keep on coming, while they lived, for the same reason; they had tried to break their chains and stay away, but it was futile; now, they had no desire to break them. Others came nearer formulating what they felt: they said they could find perfect rest and peace nowhere else when they were troubled: all frets and worries and chafings sank to sleep in the presence of the benignant serenity of the Alps; the Great Spirit of the Mountain breathed his own peace upon their hurt minds and sore hearts, and healed them; they could not think base thoughts or do mean and sordid things here, before the visible throne of God.

Down the road a piece was a Kursaal, – whatever that may be, – and we joined the human tide to see what sort of enjoyment it might afford. It was the usual open-air concert, in an ornamental garden, with wines, beer, milk, whey, grapes, etc., – the whey and the grapes being necessaries of life to certain invalids whom physicians cannot repair, and who only continue to exist by the grace of whey or grapes. One of these departed spirits told me, in a sad and lifeless way, that there was no way for him to live but by whey; never drank any thing, now, but whey, and dearly, dearly loved whey, he didn't know whey he did, but he did. After making this pun he died, – that is the whey it served him.

Some other remains, preserved from decomposition by the grape system, told me that the grapes were of a peculiar breed, highly medicinal in their nature, and that they were counted out and administered by the grape-doctors as methodically as if they were pills. The new patient, if very feeble, began with one grape before breakfast, took three during breakfast, a couple between meals, five at luncheon, three in the afternoon, seven at dinner, four for supper, and part of a grape just before going to bed, by way of a general regulator. The quantity was gradually and regularly increased, according to the needs and capacities of the patient, until by and by you would find him disposing of his one grape per second all the day long, and his regular barrel per day.

He said that men cured in this way, and enabled to discard the grape system, never afterward got over the habit of talking as if they were dictating to a slow amanuensis, because they always made a pause between each two words while they sucked the substance out of an imaginary grape. He said these were tedious people to talk with. He said that men who had been cured by the other process were easily distinguished from the rest of mankind because they always tilted their heads back, between every two words, and swallowed a swig of imaginary whey. He said it was an impressive thing to observe two men, who had been cured by the two processes, engaged in conversation, – said their pauses and accompanying movements were so continuous and regular that a stranger would think himself in the presence of a couple of automatic machines. One finds out a great many wonderful things, by traveling, if he stumbles upon the right person.

I did not remain long at the Kursaal; the music was good enough, but it seemed rather tame after the cyclone of that Arkansaw expert. Besides, my adventurous spirit had conceived a formidable enterprise – nothing less than a trip from Interlaken, by the Gemmi and Visp, clear to Zermatt, on foot! So it was necessary to plan the details, and get ready for an early start. The courier (this was not the one I have just been speaking of,) thought that the portier of the hotel would be able to tell us how to find our way. And so it turned out. He showed us the whole thing, on a relief-map, and we could see our route, with all its elevations and depressions, its villages and its rivers, as clearly as if we were sailing over it in a balloon. A relief-map is a great thing. The portier also wrote down each day's journey and the nightly hotel on a piece of paper, and made our course so plain that we should never be able to get lost without high-priced outside help.

I put the courier in the care of a gentleman who was going to Lausanne, and then we went to bed, after laying out the walking costumes and putting them into condition for instant occupation in the morning.

However, when we came down to breakfast at 8 A.M., it looked so much like rain that I hired a two-horse top-buggy for the first third of the journey. For two or three hours we jogged along the level road which skirts the beautiful lake of Thun, with a dim and dream-like picture of watery expanses and spectral Alpine forms always before us, veiled in a mellowing mist. Then a steady down-pour set in, and hid everything but the nearest objects. We kept the rain out of our faces with umbrellas, and away from our bodies with the leather apron of the buggy; but the driver sat unsheltered and placidly soaked the weather in and seemed to like it. We had the road all to ourselves, and I never had a pleasanter excursion.

The weather began to clear while we were driving up a valley called the Kienthal, and presently a vast black cloud-bank in front of us dissolved away and uncurtained the grand proportions and the soaring loftinesses of the Blumis Alp. It was a sort of breath-taking surprise; for we had not supposed there was any thing behind that low-hung blanket of sable cloud but level valley. What we had been mistaking for fleeting glimpses of sky away aloft there, were really patches of the Blumis's snowy crest caught through shredded rents in the drifting pall of vapor.

We dined in the inn at Frutigen, and our driver ought to have dined there, too, but he would not have had time to dine and get drunk both, so he gave his mind to making a masterpiece of the latter, and succeeded. A German gentleman and his two young lady daughters had been taking their nooning at the inn, and when they left, just ahead of us, it was plain that their driver was as drunk as ours, and as happy and good-natured, too, which was saying a good deal. These rascals overflowed with attentions and information for their guests, and with brotherly love for each other. They tied their reins, and took off their coats and hats, so that they might be able to give unencumbered attention to conversation and to the gestures necessary for its illustration.

The road was smooth; it led up and over and down a continual succession of hills; but it was narrow, the horses were used to it, and could not well get out of it any how; so why shouldn't the drivers entertain themselves and us? The noses of our horses projected sociably into the rear of the forward carriage, and as we toiled up the long hills our driver stood up and talked to his friend, and his friend stood up and talked back to him, with his rear to the scenery. When the top was reached and we went flying down the other side, there was no change in the program. I carry in my memory yet, the picture of that forward driver, on his knees on his high seat, resting his elbows on its back, and beaming down on his passengers, with happy eye, and flying hair, and jolly red face, and offering his card to the old German gentleman while he praised his hack and horses and both teams were whizzing down a long hill with nobody in a position to tell whether we were bound to destruction or an undeserved safety.

Toward sunset we entered a beautiful green valley dotted with chalets, a cosy little domain hidden away from the busy world in a cloistered nook among giant precipices topped with snowy peaks that seemed to float like islands above the curling surf of the sea of vapor that severed them from the lower world. Down from vague and vaporous heights, little ruffled zig-zag milky currents came crawling, and found their way to the verge of one of those tremendous overhanging walls, whence they plunged, a shaft of silver, shivered to atoms in mid-descent and turned to an airy puff of luminous dust. Here and there, in grooved depressions among the snowy desolations of the upper altitudes, one glimpsed the extremity of a glacier, with its sea-green and honey-combed battlements of ice.

Up the valley, under a dizzy precipice, nestled the village of Kandersteg, our halting place for the night. We were soon there, and housed in the hotel. But the waning day had such an inviting influence that we did not remain housed many moments, but struck out and followed a roaring torrent of ice-water up to its far source in a sort of little grass-carpeted parlor, walled in all around by vast precipices and overlooked by clustering summits of ice. This was the snuggest little croquet ground imaginable; it was perfectly level, and not more than a mile long by half a mile wide. The walls around it were so gigantic, and everything about it was on so mighty a scale that it was belittled, by contrast, to what I have likened it to, – a cosy and carpeted parlor. It was so high above the Kandersteg valley that there was nothing between it and the snow-peaks. I had never been in such intimate relations with the high altitudes before; the snow-peaks had always been remote and unapproachable grandeurs, hitherto, but now we were hob-a-nob, – if one may use such a seemingly irreverent expression about creations so august as these.

We could see the streams which fed the torrent we had followed issuing from under the greenish ramparts of glaciers; but two or three of these, instead of flowing over the precipices, sank down into the rock and sprang in big jets out of holes in the mid-face of the walls.

The green nook which I have been describing is called the Gasternthal. The glacier streams gather and flow through it in a broad and rushing brook to a narrow cleft between lofty precipices; here the rushing brook becomes a mad torrent and goes booming and thundering down toward Kandersteg, lashing and thrashing its way over and among monster boulders, and hurling chance roots and logs about like straws. There was no lack of cascades along this route. The path by the side of the torrent was so narrow that one had to look sharp, when he heard a cow bell, and hunt for a place that was wide enough to accommodate a cow and a Christian side by side, and such places were not always to be had at an instant's notice. The cows wear church bells, and that is a good idea in the cows, for where that torrent is, you couldn't hear an ordinary cow bell any further than you could hear the ticking of a watch.

I needed exercise, so I employed my agent in setting stranded logs and dead trees adrift, and I sat on a boulder and watched them go whirling and leaping head over heels down the boiling torrent. It was a wonderfully exhilarating spectacle. When I had had exercise enough, I made the agent take some, by running a race with one of those logs. I made a trifle by betting on the log.

After dinner we had a walk up and down the quiet Kandersteg valley, in the soft gloaming, with the spectacle of the dying lights of day playing about the crests and pinnacles of the still and solemn upper realm for contrast, and text for talk. There were no sounds but the dulled complaining of the torrent and the occasional tinkling of a distant bell. The spirit of the place was a sense of deep, pervading peace; one might dream his life tranquilly away there, and not miss it or mind it when it was gone.

The summer departed with the sun, and winter came with the stars. It grew to be a bitter night in that little hotel, backed up against a precipice that had no visible top to it, but we kept warm, and woke in time in the morning to find that every body else had left for the Gemmi three hours before, – so our little plan of helping that German family (principally the old man,) over the Pass, was a blocked generosity.

CHAPTER XXXIV

WE HIRED THE only guide left, to lead us on our way. He was over seventy, but he could have given me nine-tenths of his strength and still had all his age entitled him to. He shouldered our satchels, overcoats, and alpen stocks, and we set out up the steep path. It was hot work. The old man soon begged us to hand over our coats and waistcoats to him to carry, too, and we did it: one could not refuse so little a thing to a poor old man like that; he should have had them if he had been a hundred and fifty.

When we began that ascent, we could see a microscopic chalet perched away up against heaven on what seemed to be the highest mountain near us. It was on our right, across the narrow head of the valley. But when we got up abreast it on its own level, mountains were towering high above on every hand, and we saw that its altitude was just about that of the little Gasternthal which we had visited the evening before. Still it seemed a long way up in the air, in that waste and lonely wilderness of rocks. It had an unfenced grass-plot in front of it which seemed about as big as a billiard-table, and this grass-plot slanted so sharply downwards, and was so brief, and ended so exceedingly soon at the verge of the absolute precipice, that it was a shuddery thing to think of a person's venturing to trust his foot on an incline so situated at all. Suppose a man stepped on an orange peel in that yard: there would be nothing for him to seize; nothing could keep him from rolling; five revolutions would bring him to the edge, and over he would go. What a frightful distance he would fall! – for there are very few birds that fly as high as his starting-point. He would strike and bounce, two or three times, on his way down, but this would be no advantage to him. I would as soon take an airing on the slant of a rainbow as in such a front yard. I would rather, in fact, for the distance down would be about the same, and it is pleasanter to slide than to bounce. I could not see how the peasants got up to that chalet, – the region seemed too steep for anything but a balloon.

As we strolled on climbing up higher and higher, we were continually bringing neighboring peaks into view and lofty prominence which had been hidden behind lower peaks before; so by and by, while standing before a group of these giants, we looked around for the chalet again: there it was, away down below us, apparently on an inconspicuous ridge in the valley! It was as far below us, now, as it had been above us when we were beginning the ascent.

After a while the path led us along a railed precipice, and we looked over – far beneath us was the snug parlor again, the little Gasternthal, with its water jets spouting from the face of its rock walls. We could have dropped a stone into it. We had been finding the top of the world all along – and always finding a still higher top stealing into view in a disappointing way just ahead: when we looked down into the Gasternthal we felt pretty sure that we had reached the genuine top at last, but it was not so; there were much higher altitudes to be scaled yet. We were still in the pleasant shade of forest trees, we were still in a region which was cushioned with beautiful mosses and aglow with the many-tinted lustre of innumerable wild flowers.

We found, indeed, more interest in the wild flowers than in any thing else. We gathered a specimen or two of every kind which we were unacquainted with; so we had sumptuous bouquets. But one of the chief interests lay in chasing the seasons of the year up the mountain, and determining them by the presence of flowers and berries which we were acquainted with. For instance, it was the end of August at the level of the sea; in the Kandersteg valley at the base of the Pass, we found flowers which would not be due at the sea level for two or three weeks; higher up, we entered October, and gathered fringed gentians. I made no notes, and have forgotten the details, but the construction of the floral calendar was very entertaining while it lasted.

In the high regions we found rich store of the splendid red flower called the Alpine rose, but we did not find any examples of the ugly Swiss favorite called *Edelweiss*. Its name seems to indicate that it is a noble flower and that it is white. It may be noble enough, but it is not attractive, and it is not white. The fuzzy blossom is the color of bad cigar ashes, and appears to be made of a cheap quality of gray plush. It has a noble and distant way of confining itself to the high altitudes, but that is probably on account of its looks; it apparently has no monopoly of those upper altitudes, however, for they are sometimes intruded upon by some of the loveliest of the valley families of wild flowers. Everybody in the Alps wears a sprig of Edelweiss in his hat. It is the native's pet, and also the tourist's.

All the morning, as we loafed along, having a good time, other pedestrians went staving by us with vigorous strides, and with the intent and determined look of men who were walking for a wager.

These wore loose knee-breeches, long yarn stockings, and hob-nailed high-laced walking shoes. They were gentlemen who would go home to England or Germany and tell how many miles they had beaten the guide-book every day. But I doubted if they ever had much real fun, outside of the mere magnificent exhilaration of the tramp through the green valleys and the breezy heights; for they were almost always alone, and even the finest scenery loses incalculably when there is no one to enjoy it with.

All the morning an endless double procession of mule-mounted tourists filed past us along the narrow path, – the one procession going, the other coming. We had taken a good deal of trouble to teach ourselves the kindly German custom of saluting all strangers with doffed hat, and we resolutely clung to it, that morning, although it kept us bare-headed most of the time and was not always responded to. Still we found an interest in the thing, because we naturally liked to know who were English and Americans among the passers-by. All continental natives responded, of course; so did some of the English and Americans, but as a general thing these two races gave no sign. Whenever a man or a woman showed us cold neglect, we spoke up confidently in our own tongue and asked for such information as we happened to need, and we always got a reply in the same language. The English and American folk are not less kindly than other races, they are only more reserved, and that comes of habit and education. In one dreary, rocky waste, away above the line of vegetation, we met a procession of twenty-five mounted young men, all from America. We got answering bows enough from these, of course, for they were of an age to learn to do in Rome as Rome does, without much effort.

At one extremity of this patch of desolation, overhung by bare and forbidding crags which husbanded drifts of everlasting snow in their shaded cavities, was a small stretch of thin and discouraged grass, and a man and a family of pigs were actually living here in some shanties. Consequently this place could be really reckoned as "property;" it had a money value, and was doubtless taxed. I think it must have marked the limit of real estate in this world. It would be hard to set a money value upon any piece of earth that lies between that spot and the empty realm of space. That man may claim the distinction of owning the end of the world, for if there is any definite end to the world he has certainly found it.

From here forward we moved through a storm-swept and smileless desolation. All about us rose gigantic masses, crags, and ramparts of bare and dreary rock, with not a vestige or semblance of plant or tree or flower anywhere, or glimpse of any creature that had life. The frost and the tempests of unnumbered ages had battered and hacked at these cliffs, with a deathless energy, destroying them piecemeal; so all the region about their bases was a tumbled chaos of great fragments which had been split off and hurled to the ground. Soiled and aged banks of snow lay close about our path. The ghastly desolation of the place was as tremendously complete as if Doré had furnished the working plans for it. But every now and then, through the stern gateways around us we caught a view of some neighboring majestic dome, sheathed with glittering ice, and displaying its white purity at an elevation compared to which ours was groveling and plebeian, and this spectacle always chained one's interest and admiration at once, and made him forget there was any thing ugly in the world.

I have just said that there was nothing but death and desolation in these hideous places, but I forgot. In the most forlorn and arid and dismal one of all, where the racked and splintered *débris* was thickest, where the ancient patches of snow lay against the very path, where the winds blew bitterest and the general aspect was mournfulest and dreariest, and furthest from any suggestion of cheer or hope, I found a solitary wee forget-me-not flourishing away, not a droop about it anywhere, but holding its bright blue star up with the prettiest and gallantest air in the world, the only happy spirit, the only smiling thing, in all that grisly desert. She seemed to say, "Cheer up! – as long as we are here, let us make the best of it." I judged she had earned a right to a more hospitable place; so I plucked her up and sent her to America to a friend who would respect her for the fight she had made, all by her small self, to make a whole vast despondent Alpine desolation stop breaking its heart over the unalterable, and hold up its head and look at the bright side of things for once.

We stopped for a nooning at a strongly built little inn called the Schwarenbach. It sits in a lonely spot among the peaks, where it is swept by the trailing fringes of the cloud-rack, and is rained on, snowed on, and pelted and persecuted by the storms, nearly every day of its life. It was the only habitation in the whole Gemmi Pass.

Close at hand, now, was a chance for a blood-curdling Alpine adventure. Close at hand was the snowy mass of the Great Altels cooling its top-knot in the sky and daring us to an ascent. I was fired with the idea, and immediately made up my mind to procure the necessary guides, ropes, etc., and undertake it. I instructed Harris to go to the landlord of the inn and set him about our preparations.

Meantime I went diligently to work to read up and find out what this much-talked-of mountain-climbing was like, and how one should go about it, – for in these matters I was ignorant. I opened Mr. Hinchliff's "Summer Months among the Alps," (published 1857,) and selected his account of his ascent of Monte Rosa. It began, –

"It is very difficult to free the mind from excitement on the evening before a grand expedition,—"

I saw that I was too calm; so I walked the room a while and worked myself into a high excitement; but the book's next remark, – that the adventurer must get up at two in the morning, – came as near as any thing to flatting it all out again. However, I reinforced it, and read on, about how Mr. Hinchliff dressed by candle-light and was "soon down among the guides, who were bustling about in the passage, packing provisions, and making every preparation for the start;" and how he glanced out into the cold clear night and saw that –

"The whole sky was blazing with stars, larger and brighter than they appear through the dense atmosphere breathed by inhabitants of the lower parts of the earth. They seemed actually suspended from the dark vault of heaven, and their gentle light shed a fairy like gleam over the snow-fields around the foot of the Matterhorn, which raised its stupendous pinnacle on high, penetrating to the heart of the Great Bear, and crowning itself with a diadem of his magnificent stars. Not a sound disturbed the deep tranquillity of the night, except the distant roar of streams which rush from the high plateau of the St. Theodule glacier, and fall headlong over precipitous rocks till they lose themselves in the mazes of the Gorner glacier."

He took his hot toast and coffee, and then about half-past three his caravan of ten men filed away from the Riffel Hotel, and began the steep climb. At half-past five he happened to turn around, and "beheld the glorious spectacle of the Matterhorn, just touched by the rosy-fingered morning, and looking like a huge pyramid of fire rising out of the barren ocean of ice and rock around it." Then the Breithorn and the Dent Blanche caught the radiant glow; but "the intervening mass of Monte Rosa made it necessary for us to climb many hours before we could hope to see the sun himself, yet the whole air soon grew warmer after the splendid birth of day."

He gazed at the lofty crown of Monte Rosa and the wastes of snow that guarded its steep approaches, and the chief guide delivered the opinion that no man could conquer their awful heights and put his foot upon that summit. But the adventurers moved steadily on, nevertheless.

They toiled up, and up, and still up; they passed the Grand Plateau; then toiled up a steep shoulder of the mountain, clinging like flies to its rugged face; and now they were confronted by a tremendous wall from which great blocks of ice and snow were evidently in the habit of falling. They turned aside to skirt this wall, and gradually ascended until their way was barred by a "maze of gigantic snow crevasses," – so they turned aside again, and "began a long climb of sufficient steepness to make a zig-zag course necessary."

Fatigue compelled them to halt frequently, for a moment or two. At one of these halts some body called out, "Look at Mont Blanc!" and "we were at once made aware of the very great height we had attained by actually seeing the monarch of the Alps and his attendant satellites right over the top of the Breithorn, itself at least 14,000 feet high!"

These people moved in single file, and were all tied to a strong rope, at regular distances apart, so that if one of them slipped, on those giddy heights, the others could brace themselves on their alpenstocks and save him from darting into the valley, thousands of feet below. By and by they came to an ice-coated ridge which was tilted up at a sharp angle, and had a precipice on one side of it. They had to climb this, so the guide in the lead cut steps in the ice with his hatchet, and as fast as he took his toes out of one of these slight holes, the toes of the man behind him occupied it.

"Slowly and steadily we kept on our way over this dangerous part of the ascent, and I daresay it was fortunate for some of us that attention was distracted from the head by the paramount necessity of looking after the feet; *for, while on the left the incline of ice was so steep that it would be impossible for any man to save himself in case of a slip, unless the others could hold him up, on the right we might drop a pebble from the hand over precipices of unknown extent down upon the tremendous glacier below.*

"Great caution, therefore, was absolutely necessary, and in this exposed situation we were attacked by all the fury of that grand enemy of aspirants to Monte Rosa – a severe and bitterly cold wind from the north. The fine powdery snow was driven past us in clouds, penetrating the interstices of our clothes, and the pieces of ice which flew from the blows of Peter's axe were whisked into the air, and then dashed over the precipice. We had quite enough to do to prevent ourselves from being served in the same ruthless fashion, and now and then, in the more violent gusts of wind, were glad to stick our alpenstocks into the ice and hold on hard."

Having surmounted this perilous steep, they sat down and took a brief rest with their backs against a sheltering rock and their heels dangling over a bottomless abyss; then they climbed to the base of another ridge, – a more difficult and dangerous one still:

"The whole of the ridge was exceedingly narrow, and the fall on each side desperately steep, but the ice in some of these intervals between the masses of rock assumed the form of a mere sharp edge, almost like a knife; these places, though not more than three or four short paces in length, looked uncommonly awkward; but, like the sword leading true believers to the gates of Paradise, they must needs be passed before we could attain to the summit of our ambition. These were in one or two places so narrow, that in stepping over them with toes well turned out for greater security, *one end of the foot projected over the awful precipice on the right, while the other was on the beginning of the icy slope on the left, which was scarcely less steep than the rocks.* On these occasions Peter would take my hand, and each of us stretching as far as we could, he was thus enabled to get a firm footing two paces or rather more from me, whence a spring would probably bring him to the rock on the other side; then, turning round, he called to me to come, and taking a couple of steps carefully, I was met at the third by his outstretched hand ready to clasp mine, and in a moment stood by his side. The others followed in much the same fashion. Once my right foot slipped on the side towards the precipice, but I threw out my left arm in a moment so that it caught the icy edge under my armpit as I fell, and supported me considerably; at the same instant I cast my eyes down the side on which I had slipped, and contrived to plant my right foot on a piece of rock as large as a cricket ball, which chanced to protrude through the ice, on the very edge of the precipice. Being thus anchored fore and aft, as it were, I believe I could easily have recovered myself, even if I had been alone, though it must be confessed the situation would have been an awful one; as it was, however, a jerk from Peter settled the matter very soon, and I was on my legs all right in an instant. The rope is an immense help in places of this kind."

Now they arrived at the base of a great knob or dome veneered with ice and powdered with snow – the utmost summit, the last bit of solidity between them and the hollow vault of heaven. They set to work with their hatchets, and were soon creeping, insect-like, up its surface, with their heels projecting over the thinnest kind of nothingness, thickened up a little with a few wandering shreds and films of cloud moving in lazy procession far below. Presently one man's toe-hold broke and he fell! There he dangled in mid-air at the end of the rope, like a spider, till his friends above hauled him into place again.

A little bit later, the party stood upon the wee pedestal of the very summit, in a driving wind, and looked out upon the vast green expanses of Italy and a shoreless ocean of billowy Alps.

When I had read thus far, Harris burst into the room in a noble excitement and said the ropes and the guides were secured, and asked if I was ready. I said I believed I wouldn't ascend the Altels this time. I said Alp-climbing was a different thing from what I had supposed it was, and so I judged we had better study its points a little more before we went definitely into it. But I told him to retain the guides and order them to follow us to Zermatt, because I meant to use them there. I said I could feel the spirit of adventure beginning to stir in me, and was sure that the fell fascination of Alp-climbing would soon be upon me. I said he could make up his mind to it that we would do a deed before we were a week older which would make the hair of the timid curl with fright.

This made Harris happy, and filled him with ambitious anticipations. He went at once to tell the guides to follow us to Zermatt and bring all their paraphernalia with them.

CHAPTER XXXV

A GREAT AND priceless thing is a new interest! How it takes possession of a man! how it clings to him, how it rides him! I strode onward from the Schwarenbach hostelry a changed man, a reorganized personality. I walked in a new world, I saw with new eyes. I had been looking aloft at the giant snow-peaks only as things to be worshiped for their grandeur and magnitude, and their unspeakable grace of form; I looked up at them now, as also things to be conquered and climbed. My sense of their grandeur and their noble beauty was neither lost nor impaired; I had gained a new interest in the mountains without losing the old ones. I followed the steep lines up, inch by inch, with my eye, and noted the possibility or impossibility of following them with my feet. When I saw a shining helmet of ice projecting above the clouds, I tried to imagine I saw files of black specks toiling up it roped together with a gossamer thread.

We skirted the lonely little lake called the Daubensee, and presently passed close by a glacier on the right, – a thing like a great river frozen solid in its flow and broken square off like a wall at its mouth. I had never been so near a glacier before.

Here we came upon a new board shanty, and found some men engaged in building a stone house; so the Schwarenbach was soon to have a rival. We bought a bottle or so of beer here; at any rate they called it beer, but I knew by the price that it was dissolved jewelry, and I perceived by the taste that dissolved jewelry is not good stuff to drink.

We were surrounded by a hideous desolation. We stepped forward to a sort of jumping-off place, and were confronted by a startling contrast: we seemed to look down into fairy-land. Two or three thousand feet below us was a bright green level, with a pretty town in its midst, and a silvery stream winding among the meadows; the charming spot was walled in on all sides by gigantic precipices clothed with pines; and over the pines, out of the softened distances, rose the snowy domes and peaks of the Monte Rosa region. How exquisitely green and beautiful that little valley down there was! The distance was not great enough to obliterate details, it only made them little, and mellow, and dainty, like landscapes and towns seen through the wrong end of a spy-glass.

Right under us a narrow ledge rose up out of the valley, with a green, slanting, bench-shaped top, and grouped about upon this green-baize bench were a lot of black and white sheep which looked merely like oversized worms. The bench seemed lifted well up into our neighborhood, but that was a deception, – it was a long way down to it.

We began our descent, now, by the most remarkable road I have ever seen. It wound in corkscrew curves down the face of the colossal precipice, – a narrow way, with always the solid rock wall at one elbow, and perpendicular nothingness at the other. We met an everlasting procession of guides, porters, mules, litters, and tourists climbing up this steep and muddy path, and there was no room to spare when you had to pass a tolerably fat mule. I always took the inside, when I heard or saw the mule coming, and flattened myself against the wall. I preferred the inside, of course, but I should have had to take it any how, because the mule prefers the outside. A mule's preference, – on a precipice – is a thing to be respected. Well, his choice is always the outside. His life is mostly devoted to carrying bulky paniers and packages which rest against his body, – therefore he is habituated to taking the outside edge of mountain paths, to keep his bundles from rubbing against rocks or banks on the other. When he goes into the passenger business he absurdly clings to his old habit, and keeps one leg of his passenger always dangling over the great deeps of the lower world while that passenger's heart is in the highlands, so to speak. More than once I saw a mule's hind foot cave over the outer edge and send earth and rubbish into the bottomless abyss; and I noticed that upon these occasions the rider, whether male or female, looked tolerably unwell.

There was one place where an 18-inch breadth of light masonry had been added to the verge of the path, and as there was a very sharp turn, here, a panel of fencing had been set up there at some ancient time, as a protection. This panel was old and gray and feeble, and the light masonry had been loosened by recent rains. A young American girl came along on a mule, and in making the turn the mule's hind foot caved all the loose masonry and one of the fence posts over board; the mule gave a violent lurch in board to save himself and succeeded in the effort, but that girl turned as white as the snows of Mont Blanc for a moment.

The path here was simply a groove cut into the face of the precipice; there was a four-foot breadth of solid rock under the traveler, and a four-foot breadth of solid rock just above his head, like the roof of a narrow porch; he could look out from this gallery and see a sheer summitless and bottomless wall of rock before him, across a gorge or crack a biscuit's toss in width, – but he could not see the bottom of his own precipice unless he lay down and projected his nose over the edge. I did not do this, because I did not wish to soil my clothes.

Every few hundred yards, at particularly bad places, one came across a panel or so of plank fencing; but they were always old and weak, and they generally leaned out over the chasm and did not make any rash promises to hold up people who might need support. There was one of these panels which had only its upper board left; a pedestrianizing English youth came tearing down the path, was seized with an impulse to look over the precipice, and without an instant's thought he threw his weight upon that crazy board. It bent outward a foot! I never made a gasp before that came so near suffocating me. The English youth's face simply showed a lively surprise, but nothing more. He went swinging along valleywards again, as if he did not know he had just swindled a coroner by the closest kind of a shave.

The Alpine litter is sometimes like a cushioned box made fast between the middles of two long poles, and sometimes it is a chair with a back to it and a support for the feet. It is carried by relays of strong porters. The motion is easier than that of any other conveyance. We met a few men and a great many ladies in litters; it seemed to me that most of the ladies looked pale and nauseated; their general aspect gave me the idea that they were patiently enduring a horrible suffering. As a rule, they looked at their laps, and left the scenery to take care of itself.

But the most frightened creature I saw, was a led horse that overtook us. Poor fellow, he had been born and reared in the grassy levels of the Kandersteg valley and had never seen any thing like this hideous place before. Every few steps he would stop short, glance wildly out from the dizzy height, and then spread his red nostrils wide and pant as violently as if he had been running a race; and all the while he quaked from head to heel as with a palsy. He was a handsome fellow, and he made a fine statuesque picture of terror, but it was pitiful to see him suffer so.

This dreadful path has had its tragedy. Baedeker, with his customary over-terseness, begins and ends the tale thus:

"The descent on horse-back should be avoided. In 1861 a Comtesse d' Herlincourt fell from her saddle over the precipice and was killed on the spot."

We looked over the precipice there, and saw the monument which commemorates the event. It stands in the bottom of the gorge, in a place which has been hollowed out of the rock to protect it from the torrent and the storms. Our old guide never spoke but when spoken to, and then limited himself to a syllable or two; but when we asked him about this tragedy he showed a strong interest in the matter. He said the Countess was very pretty, and very young, – hardly out of her girlhood, in fact. She was newly married, and was on her bridal tour. The young husband was riding a little in advance; one guide was leading the husband's horse, another was leading the bride's. The old man continued, –

"The guide that was leading the husband's horse happened to glance back, and there was that poor young thing sitting up staring out over the precipice; and her face began to bend downward a little, and she put up her two hands slowly and met it, – so, – and put them flat against her eyes, – so, – and then she sunk out of the saddle, with a sharp shriek, and one caught only the flash of a dress, and it was all over."

Then after a pause, –

"Ah yes, that guide saw these things, – yes, he saw them all. He saw them all, just as I have told you."

After another pause, –

"Ah yes, he saw them all. My God, that was *me*. I was that guide!"

This had been the one event of the old man's life; so one may be sure he had forgotten no detail connected with it. We listened to all he had to say about what was done and what happened and what was said after the sorrowful occurrence, and a painful story it was.

When we had wound down toward the valley until we were about on the last spiral of the corkscrew, Harris's hat blew over the last remaining bit of precipice, – a small cliff a hundred or a hundred and fifty feet high, – and sailed down towards a steep slant composed of rough chips and fragments which the weather had flaked away from the precipices. We went leisurely down there, expecting to find it without any trouble, but we had made a mistake, as to that. We hunted during a couple of hours, – not because the old straw hat was valuable, but out of curiosity to find out how such a thing could manage to conceal itself in open ground where there was nothing for it to hide behind. When one is reading in bed, and lays his paper-knife down, he cannot find it again if it is smaller than a sabre; that hat was as stubborn as any paper-knife could have been, and we finally had to give it up; but we found a fragment that had once belonged to an opera glass, and by digging around and turning over the rocks we gradually collected all the lenses and the cylinders and the various odds and ends that go to make up a complete opera glass. We afterwards had the thing reconstructed, and the owner can have his adventurous long-lost property by submitting proofs and paying costs of rehabilitation. We had hopes of finding the owner there, distributed around amongst the rocks, for it would have made an elegant paragraph; but we were disappointed. Still, we were far from being disheartened, for there was a considerable area which we had not thoroughly searched; we were satisfied he was there, somewhere, so we resolved to wait over a day at Leuk and come back and get him. Then we sat down to polish off the perspiration and arrange about what we would do with him when we got him. Harris was for contributing him to the British Museum; but I was for mailing him to his widow. That is the difference between Harris and me: Harris is all for display, I am all for the simple right, even though I lose money by it. Harris argued in favor of his proposition and against mine, I argued in favor of mine and against his. The discussion warmed into a dispute; the dispute warmed into a quarrel. I finally said, very decidedly, –

"My mind is made up. He goes to the widow."

Harris answered sharply, –

"And *my* mind is made up. He goes to the Museum."

I said, calmly, –

"The Museum may whistle when it gets him."

Harris retorted, –

"The widow may save herself the trouble of whistling, for I will see that she never gets him."

After some angry bandying of epithets, I said, –

"It seems to me that you are taking on a good many airs about these remains. I don't quite see what *you've* got to say about them?"

"*I?* I've got *all* to say about them. They'd never have been thought of if I hadn't found their opera glass. The corpse belongs to me, and I'll do as I please with him."

I was leader of the Expedition, and all discoveries achieved by it naturally belonged to me. I was entitled to these remains, and could have enforced my right; but rather than have bad blood about the matter, I said we would toss up for them. I threw heads and won, but it was a barren victory, for although we spent all the next day searching, we never found a bone. I cannot imagine what could ever have become of that fellow.

The town in the valley is called Leuk or Leukerbad, we pointed our course toward it, down a verdant slope which was adorned with fringed gentians and other flowers, and presently entered the narrow alleys of the outskirts and waded toward the middle of the town through liquid "fertilizer." They ought to either pave that village or organize a ferry.

Harris's body was simply a chamois-pasture; his person was populous with the little hungry pests; his skin, when he stripped, was splotched like a scarlet fever patient's; so, when we were about to enter one of the Leukerbad inns, and he noticed its sign, "Chamois Hotel," he refused to stop there. He said the chamois was plentiful enough, without hunting up hotels where they made a specialty of it. I was indifferent, for the chamois is a creature that will neither bite me nor abide with me: but to calm Harris, we went to the Hotel des Alpes.

At the table d'hote we had this, for an incident. A very grave man, – in fact his gravity amounted to solemnity, and almost to austerity, – sat opposite us and he was "tight," but doing his best to appear sober. He took up a *corked* bottle of wine, tilted it over his glass a while, then sat it out of the way, with a contented look, and went on with his dinner.

Presently he put his glass to his mouth, and of course found it empty. He looked puzzled, and glanced furtively and suspiciously out of the corner of his eye at a benignant and unconscious old lady who sat at his right. Shook his head, as much as to say, "No, she couldn't have done it." He tilted the corked bottle over his glass again, meantime searching around with his watery eye to see if anybody was watching him. He ate a few mouthfuls, raised his glass to his lips, and of course it was still empty. He bent an injured and accusing side gaze upon that unconscious old lady, which was a study to see. She went on eating and gave no sign. He took up his glass and his bottle, with a wise private nod of his head, and set them gravely on the left-hand side of his plate, – poured himself another imaginary drink, – went to work with his knife and fork once more, – presently lifted his glass with good confidence, and found it empty, as usual.

This was almost a petrifying surprise. He straightened himself up in his chair and deliberately and sorrowfully inspected the busy old ladies at his elbows, first one and then the other. At last he softly pushed his plate away, set his glass directly in front of him, held on to it with his left hand, and proceeded to pour with his right. This time he observed that nothing came. He turned the bottle clear upside down; still nothing issued from it; a plaintive look came into his face, and he said, as if to himself, "'*ic! They've got it all!*" Then he set the bottle down, resignedly, and took the rest of his dinner dry.

It was at that table d'hote, too, that I had under inspection the largest lady I have ever seen in private life. She was over seven feet high, and magnificently proportioned. What had first called my attention to her, was my stepping on an outlying flange of her foot, and hearing, from up toward the ceiling, a deep "Pardon, m'sieu, but you encroach!"

That was when we were coming through the hall, and the place was dim, and I could see her only vaguely. The thing which called my attention to her the second time, was, that at a table beyond ours were two very pretty girls, and this great lady came in and sat down between them and me and blotted out the view. She had a handsome face, and she was very finely formed, – perfectly formed,

I should say. But she made every body around her look trivial and commonplace. Ladies near her looked like children, and the men about her looked mean. They looked like failures; and they looked as if they felt so, too. She sat with her back to us. I never saw such a back in my life. I would have so liked to see the moon rise over it. The whole congregation waited, under one pretext or another, till she finished her dinner and went out; they wanted to see her at her full altitude, and they found it worth tarrying for. She filled one's idea of what an empress ought to be, when she rose up in her unapproachable grandeur and moved superbly out of that place.

We were not at Leuk in time to see her at her heaviest weight. She had suffered from corpulence and had come there to get rid of her extra flesh in the baths. Five weeks of soaking, – five uninterrupted hours of it every day, – had accomplished her purpose and reduced her to the right proportions.

Those baths remove fat, and also skin-diseases. The patients remain in the great tanks hours at a time. A dozen gentlemen and ladies occupy a tank together, and amuse themselves with rompings and various games. They have floating desks and tables, and they read or lunch or play chess in water that is breast deep. The tourist can step in and view this novel spectacle if he chooses. There's a poor-box, and he will have to contribute. There are several of these big bathing houses, and you can always tell when you are near one of them by the romping noises and shouts of laughter that proceed from it. The water is running water, and changes all the time, else a patient with a ringworm might take the bath with only a partial success, since while he was ridding himself of his ringworm, he might catch the itch.

The next morning we wandered back up the green valley, leisurely, with the curving walls of those bare and stupendous precipices rising into the clouds before us. I had never seen a clean, bare precipice stretching up five thousand feet above me before, and I never shall expect to see another one. They exist, perhaps, but not in places where one can easily get close to them. This pile of stone is peculiar. From its base to the soaring tops of its mighty towers, all its lines and all its details vaguely suggest human architecture. There are rudimentary bow windows, cornices, chimneys, demarcations of stories, etc. One could sit and stare up there and study the features and exquisite graces of this grand structure, bit by bit, and day after day, and never weary his interest. The termination, toward the town, observed in profile, is the perfection of shape.

It comes down out of the clouds in a succession of rounded, colossal, terrace-like projections, – a stairway for the gods; at its head spring several lofty storm-scarred towers, one above another, with faint films of vapor curling always about them like spectral banners. If there were a king whose realms included the whole world, here would be the palace meet and proper for such a monarch. He would only need to hollow it out and put in the electric light. He could give audience to a nation at a time under its roof.

Our search for those remains having failed, we inspected with a glass the dim and distant track of an old-time avalanche that once swept down from some pine-grown summits behind the town and swept away the houses and buried the people; then we struck down the road that leads toward the Rhone, to see the famous *Ladders*. These perilous things are built against the perpendicular face of a cliff two or three hundred feet high. The peasants, of both sexes, were climbing up and down them, with heavy loads on their backs. I ordered Harris to make the ascent, so I could put the thrill and horror of it in my book, and he accomplished the feat successfully, through a sub-agent for three francs, which I paid. It makes me shudder yet when I think of what I felt when I was clinging there between heaven and earth in the person of that proxy. At times the world swam around me, and I could hardly keep from letting go, so dizzying was the appalling danger. Many a person would have given up and descended, but I stuck to my task, and would not yield until I had accomplished it. I felt a just pride in my exploit, but I would not have repeated it for the wealth of the world. I shall break my neck yet with some such fool-hardy performance, for warnings never seem to have any lasting effect upon me. When the people of the hotel found that I had been climbing those crazy Ladders, it made me an object of considerable distinction.

Next morning, early, we drove to the Rhone valley and took the train for Visp. There we shouldered our knapsacks and things, and set out on foot, in a tremendous rain, up the winding gorge, toward Zermatt. Hour after hour we slopped along, by the roaring torrent, and under noble Lesser Alps which were clothed in rich velvety green all the way up and had little atomy Swiss homes perched upon grassy benches along their mist-dimmed heights.

The rain continued to pour and the torrent to boom, and we continued to enjoy both. At the one spot where this torrent tossed its white mane highest, and thundered loudest, and lashed the big boulders fiercest, the canton had done itself the honor to build the flimsiest wooden bridge that exists in the world. While we were walking over it, along with a party of horsemen, I noticed that even the larger rain-drops made it shake. I called Harris's attention to it, and he noticed it, too. It seemed to me that if I owned an elephant that was a keepsake, and I thought a good deal of him, I would think twice before I would ride him over that bridge.

We climbed up to the village of St. Nicholas, about half-past four in the afternoon, waded ankle deep through the fertilizer-juice, and stopped at a new and nice hotel close by the little church. We stripped and went to bed, and sent our clothes down to be baked. All the horde of soaked tourists did the same. That chaos of clothing got mixed in the kitchen, and there were consequences. I did not get back the same drawers I sent down, when our things came up at 6:15; I got a pair on a new plan. They were merely a pair of white ruffle-cuffed absurdities, hitched together at the top with a narrow band, and they did not come quite down to my knees. They were pretty enough, but they made me feel like two people, and disconnected at that. The man must have been an idiot that got himself up like that, to rough it in the Swiss mountains. The shirt they brought me was shorter than the drawers, and hadn't any sleeves to it, – at least it hadn't any thing more than what Mr. Darwin would call "rudimentary" sleeves; these had "edging" around them, but the bosom was ridiculously plain. The knit silk undershirt they brought me was on a new plan, and was really a sensible thing; it opened behind, and had pockets in it to put your shoulder blades in; but they did not seem to fit mine, and so I found it a sort of uncomfortable garment. They gave my bob-tail coat to some body else, and sent me an ulster suitable for a giraffe. I had to tie my collar on, because there was no button behind on that foolish little shirt which I described a while ago.

When I was dressed for dinner at 6.30, I was too loose in some places and too tight in others, and altogether I felt slovenly and ill conditioned. However, the people at the table d'hote were no better off than I was; they had everbody's clothes but their own on. A long stranger recognized his ulster as soon as he saw the tail of it following me in, but nobody claimed my shirts or my drawers, though I described them as well as I was able. I gave them to the chamber-maid that night when I went to bed, and she probably found the owner, for my own things were on a chair outside my door in the morning.

There was a lovable English clergyman who did not get to the table d'hote at all. His breeches had turned up missing, and without any equivalent. He said he was not more particular than other people, but he had noticed that a clergyman at dinner without any breeches was almost sure to excite remark.

CHAPTER XXXVI

WE DID NOT oversleep at St. Nicholas. The church bell began to ring at 4:30 in the morning, and from the length of time it continued to ring I judged that it takes the Swiss sinner a good while to get the invitation through his head. Most church bells in the world are of poor quality, and have a harsh and rasping sound which upsets the temper and produces much sin, but the St. Nicholas bell is a good deal the worst one that has been contrived yet, and is peculiarly maddening in its operation. Still, it may have its right and its excuse to exist, for the community is poor and not every citizen can afford a clock, perhaps; but there cannot be any excuse for our church bells at home, for there is no family in America without a clock, and consequently there is no fair pretext for the usual Sunday medley of dreadful sounds that issues from our steeples. There is much more profanity in America on Sunday than in all the other six days of the week put together, and it is of a more bitter and malignant character than the week-day profanity, too. It is produced by the cracked-pot clangor of the cheap church bells.

We build our churches almost without regard to cost; we rear an edifice which is an adornment to the town, and we gild it, and fresco it, and mortgage it, and do everything we can think of to perfect it, and then spoil it all by putting a bell on it which afflicts every body who hears it, giving some the headache, others St. Vitus's dance, and the rest the blind-staggers.

An American village at ten o'clock on a summer Sunday is the quietest and peacefulest and holiest thing in nature; but it is a pretty different thing half an hour later. Mr. Poe's poem of the "Bells" stands incomplete to this day; but it is well enough that it is so, for the public reciter or "reader" who goes around trying to imitate the sounds of the various sorts of bells with his voice would find himself "up a stump" when he got to the church bell – as Joseph Addison would say. The church is always trying to get other people to reform; it might not be a bad idea to reform itself a little, by way of example. It is still clinging to one or two things which were useful once, but which are not useful now, neither are they ornamental. One is the bell-ringing to remind a clock-caked town that it is church time, and another is the reading from the pulpit of a tedious list of "notices" which every body who is interested has already read in the newspaper. The clergyman even reads the hymn through, – a relic of an ancient time when hymn books were scarce and costly; but everybody has a hymn book, now, and so the public reading is no longer necessary. It is not merely unnecessary, it is generally painful; for the average clergyman could not fire into his congregation with a shotgun and hit a worse reader than himself, unless the weapon scattered shamefully. I am not meaning to be flippant and irreverent, I am only meaning to be truthful. The average clergyman, in all countries and of all denominations, is a very bad reader. One would think he would at least learn how to read the Lord's Prayer, by and by, but it is not so. He races through it as if he thought the quicker he got it in, the sooner it would be answered. A person who does not appreciate the exceeding value of pauses, and does not know how to measure their duration judiciously, can not render the grand simplicity and dignity of a composition like that effectively.

We took a tolerably early breakfast, and tramped off toward Zermatt through the reeking lanes of the village, glad to get away from that bell. By and by we had a fine spectacle on our right. It was the wall-like butt-end of a huge glacier, which looked down on us from an Alpine height which was well up in the blue sky. It was an astonishing amount of ice to be compacted together in one mass. We ciphered upon it and decided that it was not less than several hundred feet from the base of the wall of solid ice to the top of it, – Harris believed it was really twice that. We judged that if St. Paul's, St. Peter's, the Great Pyramid, the Strasburg Cathedral and the Capitol at Washington were clustered against that wall, a man sitting on its upper edge could not hang his hat on the top of any one of them without reaching down three or four hundred feet, – a thing which of course no man could do.

To me, that mighty glacier was very beautiful. I did not imagine that anybody could find fault with it; but I was mistaken. Harris had been snarling for several days. He was a rabid Protestant, and he was always saying, –

"In the Protestant cantons you never see such poverty and dirt and squalor as you do in this Catholic one; you never see the lanes and alleys flowing with foulness; you never see such wretched little sties of houses; you never see an inverted tin turnip on top of a church for a dome; and as for a church bell, why you never hear a church bell at all."

All this morning he had been finding fault, straight along. First it was with the mud. He said, "It ain't muddy in a Protestant canton when it rains." Then it was with the dogs: "They don't have those lop-eared dogs in a Protestant canton." Then it was with the roads: "They don't leave the roads to make themselves in a Protestant canton, the people make them, – and they make a road that *is* a road, too." Next it was the goats: "You never see a goat shedding tears in a Protestant canton – a goat, there, is one of the cheerfulest objects in nature." Next it was the chamois: "You never see a Protestant chamois act like one of these, – they take a bite or two and go; but these fellows camp with you and stay." Then it was the guide-boards: "In a Protestant canton you couldn't get lost if you wanted to, but you never see a guide-board in a Catholic canton." Next, "You never see any flower-boxes in the windows, here, – never any thing but now and then a cat, – a torpid one; but you take a Protestant canton: windows perfectly lovely with flowers, – and as for cats, there's just acres of them. These folks in this canton leave a road to make itself, and then fine you three francs if you 'trot' over it – as if a horse could trot over such a sarcasm of a road." Next about the goitre: "*They* talk about goitre! – I haven't seen a goitre in this whole canton that I couldn't put in a hat."

He had growled at everything, but I judged it would puzzle him to find any thing the matter with this majestic glacier. I intimated as much; but he was ready, and said with surly discontent, –

"You ought to see them in the Protestant cantons."

This irritated me. But I concealed the feeling, and asked,

"What is the matter with this one?"

"Matter? Why, it ain't in any kind of condition. They never take any care of a glacier here. The moraine has been spilling gravel around it, and got it all dirty."

"Why, man, *they* can't help that."

"*They?* You're right. That is, they *won't*. They could if they wanted to. You never see a speck of dirt on a Protestant glacier. Look at the Rhone glacier. It is fifteen miles long, and seven hundred feet thick. If this was a Protestant glacier you wouldn't see it looking like this, I can tell you."

"That is nonsense. What would they do with it?"

"They would white-wash it. They always do."

I did not believe a word of this, but rather than have trouble I let it go; for it is a waste of breath to argue with a bigot. I even doubted if the Rhone glacier *was* in a Protestant canton; but I did not know, so I could not make any thing by contradicting a man who would probably put me down at once with manufactured evidence.

About nine miles from St. Nicholas we crossed a bridge over the raging torrent of the Visp, and came to a long strip of flimsy fencing which was pretending to secure people from tumbling over a perpendicular wall forty feet high and into the river. Three children were approaching; one of them, a little girl about eight years old, was running; when pretty close to us she stumbled and fell, and her feet shot under the rail of the fence and for a moment projected over the stream. It gave us a sharp shock, for we thought she was gone, sure, for the ground slanted steeply, and to save herself seemed a sheer impossibility; but she managed to scramble up, and ran by us laughing.

We went forward and examined the place and saw the long tracks which her feet had made in the dirt when they darted over the verge. If she had finished her trip she would have struck some big rocks in the edge of the water, and then the torrent would have snatched her down stream among the half-covered boulders and she would have been pounded to pulp in two minutes. We had come exceedingly near witnessing her death.

And now Harris's contrary nature and inborn selfishness were strikingly manifested. He has no spirit of self-denial. He began straight off, and continued for an hour, to express his gratitude that the child was not destroyed. I never saw such a man. That was the kind of person he was; just so *he* was gratified, he never cared any thing about anybody else. I had noticed that trait in him, over and over again. Often, of course, it was mere heedlessness, mere want of reflection. Doubtless this may have been the case in most instances, but it was not the less hard to bear on that account, – and after all, its bottom, its groundwork, was selfishness. There is no avoiding that conclusion. In the instance under consideration, I did think the indecency of running on in that way might occur to him; but no, the child was saved and he was glad, that was sufficient, – he cared not a straw for *my* feelings, or my loss of such a literary plum, snatched from my very mouth at the instant it was ready to drop into it. His selfishness was sufficient to place his own gratification in being spared suffering clear before all concern for me, his friend. Apparently he did not once reflect upon the valuable details which would have fallen like a windfall to me: fishing the child out, – witnessing the surprise of the family and the stir the thing would have made among the peasants, – then a Swiss funeral, – then the roadside monument, to be paid for by us and have our names mentioned in it. And we should have gone into Baedeker and been immortal. I was silent. I was too much hurt to complain. If he could act so, and be so heedless and so frivolous at such a time, and actually seem to glory in it, after all I had done for him, I would have cut my hand off before I would let him see that I was wounded.

We were approaching Zermatt; consequently we were approaching the renowned Matterhorn. A month before, this mountain had been only a name to us, but latterly we had been moving through a steadily thickening double row of pictures of it, done in oil, water, chromo, wood, steel, copper, crayon, and photography, and so it had at length become a shape to us, – and a very distinct, decided, and familiar one, too. We were expecting to recognize that mountain whenever or wherever we should run across it. We were not deceived. The monarch was far away when we first saw him, but there was no such thing as mistaking him. He has the rare peculiarity of standing by himself; he is peculiarly steep, too, and is also most oddly shaped. He towers into the sky like a colossal wedge, with the upper third of its blade bent a little to the left. The broad base of this monster wedge is planted upon a grand glacier-paved Alpine platform whose elevation is ten thousand feet above sea level; as the wedge itself is some five thousand feet high, it follows that its apex is about fifteen thousand feet above sea level. So the whole bulk of this stately piece of rock, this sky-cleaving monolith, is above the line of eternal snow. Yet while all its giant neighbors have the look of being built of solid snow, from their waists up, the Matterhorn stands black and naked and forbidding, the year round, or merely powdered or streaked with white in places, for its sides are so steep that the snow cannot stay there. Its strange form, its august isolation, and its majestic unkinship with its own kind, make it, – so to speak, – the Napoleon of the mountain world. "Grand, gloomy, and peculiar," is a phrase which fits it as aptly as it fitted the great captain.

Think of a monument a mile high, standing on a pedestal two miles high! This is what the Matterhorn is, – a monument. Its office, henceforth, for all time, will be to keep watch and ward over the secret resting-place of the young Lord Douglas, who, in 1865, was precipitated from the summit over a precipice 4,000 feet high, and never seen again. No man ever had such a monument as this before; the most imposing of the world's other monuments are but atoms compared to it; and they will perish, and their places will pass from memory, but this will remain.*

A walk from St. Nicholas to Zermatt is a wonderful experience. Nature is built on a stupendous plan in that region. One marches continually between walls that are piled into the skies, with their upper heights broken into a confusion of sublime shapes that gleam white and cold against the background of blue; and here and there one sees a big glacier displaying its grandeurs on the top of a precipice, or a graceful cascade leaping and flashing down the green declivities. There is nothing tame, or cheap, or trivial, – it is all magnificent. That short valley is a picture gallery of a notable kind, for it contains no mediocrities; from end to end the Creator has hung it with His masterpieces.

We made Zermatt at 3 in the afternoon, nine hours out from St. Nicholas. Distance, by guide-book, 12 miles, by pedometer 72. We were in the heart and home of the mountain-climbers, now, as all visible things testified. The snow-peaks did not hold themselves aloof, in aristocratic reserve, they nestled close around, in a friendly, sociable way; guides, with the ropes and axes, and other implements of their fearful calling slung about their persons, roosted in a long line upon a stone wall in front of the hotel, and waited for customers; sun-burned climbers, in mountaineering costume, and followed by their guides and porters, arrived from time to time, from breakneck expeditions among the peaks and glaciers of the High Alps; male and female tourists, on mules, filed by, in a continuous procession, hotelward-bound from wild adventures which would grow in grandeur every time they were described at the English or American fireside, and at last outgrow the possible itself.

We were not dreaming; this was not a make-believe home of the Alp-climber, created by our heated imaginations: no, for here was Mr. Girdlestone himself, the famous Englishman who hunts his way to the most formidable Alpine summits without a guide. I was

*The accident which cost Lord Douglas his life also cost the lives of three other men. These three fell four-fifths of a mile, and their bodies were afterwards found, lying side by side, upon a glacier, whence they were borne to Zermatt and buried in the churchyard. The remains of Lord Douglas have never been found. The secret of his sepulture, like that of Moses, must remain a mystery always.

not equal to imagining a Girdlestone; it was all I could do to even realize him, while looking straight at him at short range. I would rather face whole Hyde Parks of artillery than the ghastly forms of death which he has faced among the peaks and precipices of the mountains. There is probably no pleasure equal to the pleasure of climbing a dangerous Alp; but it is a pleasure which is confined strictly to people who can find pleasure in it. I have not jumped to this conclusion; I have traveled to it per gravel train, so to speak. I have thought the thing all out, and am quite sure I am right. A born climber's appetite for climbing is hard to satisfy; when it comes upon him he is like a starving man with a feast before him; he may have other business on hand, but it must wait. Mr. Girdlestone had had his usual summer holiday in the Alps, and had spent it in his usual way, hunting for unique chances to break his neck; his vacation was over, and his luggage packed for England, but all of a sudden a hunger had come upon him to climb the tremendous Weisshorn once more, for he had heard of a new and utterly impossible route up it. His baggage was unpacked at once, and now he and a friend, laden with knapsacks, ice-axes, coils of rope, and canteens of milk, were just setting out. They would spend the night high up among the snows, somewhere, and get up at 2 in the morning and finish the enterprise. I had a strong desire to go with them, but forced it down, – a feat which Mr. Girdlestone, with all his fortitude, could not do.

Even ladies catch the climbing mania, and are unable to throw it off. A famous climber, of that sex, had attempted the Weisshorn a few days before our arrival, and she and her guides had lost their way in a snow-storm high up among the peaks and glaciers and been forced to wander around a good while before they could find a way down. When this lady reached the bottom, she had been on her feet twenty-three hours!

Our guides, hired on the Gemmi, were already at Zermatt when we reached there. So there was nothing to interfere with our getting up an adventure whenever we should choose the time and the object. I resolved to devote my first evening in Zermatt to studying up the subject of Alpine climbing, by way of preparation.

I read several books, and here are some of the things I found out. One's shoes must be strong and heavy, and have pointed hob-nails in them. The alpenstock must be of the best wood, for if it should break, loss of life might be the result. One should carry an ax, to cut steps in the ice with, on the great heights. There must be a ladder, for there are steep bits of rock which can be surmounted with this instrument, – or this utensil, – but could not be surmounted without it; such an obstruction has compelled the tourist to waste hours hunting another route, when a ladder would have saved him all trouble. One must have from 150 to 500 feet of strong rope, to be used in lowering the party down steep declivities which are too steep and smooth to be traversed in any other way. One must have a steel hook, on another rope, – a very useful thing; for when one is ascending and comes to a low bluff which is yet too high for the ladder, he swings this rope aloft like a lasso, the hook catches at the top of the bluff, and then the tourist climbs the rope, hand over hand, – being always particular to try and forget that if the hook gives way he will never stop falling till he arrives in some part of Switzerland where they are not expecting him. Another important thing – there must be a rope to tie the whole party together with, so that if one falls from a mountain or down a bottomless chasm in a glacier, the others may brace back on the rope and save him. One must have a silk veil, to protect his face from snow, sleet, hail and gale, and colored goggles to protect his eyes from that dangerous enemy, snow-blindness. Finally, there must be some porters, to carry provisions, wine and scientific instruments, and also blanket bags for the party to sleep in.

I closed my readings with a fearful adventure which Mr. Whymper once had on the Matterhorn when he was prowling around alone, 5,000 above the town of Breil. He was edging his way gingerly around the corner of a precipice where the upper edge of a sharp declivity of ice-glazed snow joined it. This declivity swept down a couple of hundred feet, into a gully which curved around and ended at a precipice 800 feet high, overlooking a glacier. His foot slipped, and he fell. He says:

"My knapsack brought my head down first, and I pitched into some rocks about a dozen feet below; they caught something, and tumbled me off the edge, head over heels, into the gully; the baton was dashed from my hands, and I whirled downwards in a series of bounds, each longer than the last; now over ice, now into rocks, striking my head four or five times, each time with increased force. The last bound sent me spinning through the air in a leap of fifty or sixty feet, from one side of the gully to the other, and I struck the rocks, luckily, with the whole of my left side. They caught my clothes for a moment, and I fell back on to the snow with motion arrested. My head fortunately came the right side up, and a few frantic catches brought me to a halt, in the neck of the gully and on the verge of the precipice. Baton, hat, and veil skimmed by and disappeared, and the crash of the rocks – which I had started – as they fell on to the glacier, told how narrow had been the escape from utter destruction. As it was, I fell nearly 200 feet in seven or eight bounds. Ten feet more would have taken me in one gigantic leap of 800 feet on to the glacier below.

"The situation was sufficiently serious. The rocks could not be let go for a moment, and the blood was spirting out of more than twenty cuts. The most serious ones were in the head, and I vainly tried to close them with one hand, whilst holding on with the other. It was useless; the blood gushed out in blinding jets at each pulsation. At last, in a moment of inspiration, I kicked out a big lump of snow and stuck it as plaster on my head. The idea was a happy one, and the flow of blood diminished. Then, scrambling up, I got, not a moment too soon, to a place of safety, and fainted away. The sun was setting when consciousness returned, and it was pitch dark before the Great Staircase was descended; but by a combination of luck and care, the whole 4,700 feet of descent to Breil was accomplished without a slip, or once missing the way."

His wounds kept him abed some days. Then he got up and climbed that mountain again. That is the way with a true Alp-climber; the more fun he has, the more he wants.

CHAPTER XLII

SWITZERLAND IS SIMPLY a large, humpy, solid rock, with a thin skin of grass stretched over it. Consequently, they do not dig graves, they blast them out with powder and fuse. They cannot afford to have large graveyards, the grass skin is too circumscribed and too valuable. It is all required for the support of the living.

The graveyard in Zermatt occupies only about one-eighth of an acre. The graves are sunk in the living rock, and are very permanent; but occupation of them is only temporary; the occupant can only stay till his grave is needed by a later subject, he is removed, then, for they do not bury one body on top of another. As I understand it, a family owns a grave, just as it owns a house. A man dies, and leaves his house to his son, – and at the same time, this dead father succeeds to his own father's grave. He moves out of the house and into the grave, and his predecessor moves out of the grave and into the cellar of the chapel. I saw a black box lying in the churchyard, with skull and cross-bones painted on it, and was told that this was used in transferring remains to the cellar.

In that cellar the bones and skulls of several hundreds of former citizens were compactly corded up. They made a pile 18 feet long, 7 feet high, and 8 feet wide. I was told that in some of the receptacles of this kind in the Swiss villages, the skulls were all marked, and if a man wished to find the skulls of his ancestors for several generations back, he could do it by these marks, preserved in the family records.

An English gentleman who had lived some years in this region, said it was the cradle of compulsory education. But he said that the English idea that compulsory education would reduce bastardy and intemperance was an error – it has not that effect. He said there was more seduction in the Protestant than in the Catholic cantons, because the confessional protected the girls. I wonder why it doesn't protect married women in France and Spain?

This gentleman said that among the poorer peasants in the Valaïs, it was common for the brothers in a family to cast lots to determine which of them should have the coveted privilege of marrying. Then the lucky one got married, and his brethren – doomed bachelors, – heroically banded themselves together to help support the new family.

We left Zermatt in a wagon – and in a rain storm, too, – for St. Nicholas about ten o'clock one morning. Again we passed between those grass-clad prodigious cliffs, specked with wee dwellings peeping over at us from velvety, green walls ten and twelve hundred feet high. It did not seem possible that the imaginary chamois even, could climb those precipices. Lovers on opposite cliffs probably kiss through a spy-glass, and correspond with a rifle.

In Switzerland the farmer's plow is a wide shovel, which scrapes up and turns over the thin earthy skin of his native rock – and there the man of the plow is a hero. Now here, by our St. Nicholas road, was a grave, and it had a tragic story. A plowman was skinning his farm one morning, – not the steepest part of it, but still a steep part – that is, he was not skinning the front of his farm, but the roof of it, near the eaves, – when he absentmindedly let go of the plow-handles to moisten his hands, in the usual way: he lost his balance and fell out of his farm backwards; poor fellow, he never touched any thing till he struck bottom, 1,500 feet below.* We throw a halo of heroism around the life of the soldier and the sailor, because of the deadly dangers they are facing all the time. But we are not used to looking upon farming as a heroic occupation. This is because we have not lived in Switzerland.

From St. Nicholas we struck out for Visp, – or Vispach – on foot. The rain storms had been at work during several days, and had done a deal of damage in Switzerland and Savoy. We came to one place where a stream had changed its course and plunged down the mountain in a new place, sweeping everything before it. Two poor but precious farms by the roadside were ruined. One was washed clear away, and the bed-rock exposed; the other was buried out of sight under a tumbled chaos of rocks, gravel, mud, and rubbish. The resistless might of water was well exemplified. Some saplings which had stood in the way were bent to the ground, stripped clean of their bark, and buried under rocky *débris*. The road had been swept away, too.

In another place, where the road was high up on the mountain's face, and its outside edge protected by flimsy masonry, we frequently came across spots where this masonry had caved off and left dangerous gaps for mules to get over; and with still more frequency we found the masonry slightly crumbled, and marked by mule-hoofs, thus showing that there had been danger of an accident to some body. When at last we came to a badly ruptured bit of masonry, with hoof-prints evidencing a desperate struggle to regain the lost foot-hold, I looked quite hopefully over the dizzy precipice. But there was nobody down there.

They take exceedingly good care of their rivers in Switzerland and other portions of Europe. They wall up both banks with slanting solid stone masonry – so that from end to end of these rivers the banks look like the wharves at St. Louis and other towns on the Mississippi river.

It was during this walk from St. Nicholas, in the shadow of the majestic Alps, that we came across some little children amusing themselves in what seemed, at first, a most odd and original way – but it wasn't: it was in simply a natural and characteristic way. They were roped together with a string, they had mimic alpenstocks and ice-axes, and were climbing a meek and lowly manure pile with a most blood-curdling amount of care and caution. The "guide" at the

* This was on a Sunday. M.T.

head of the line cut imaginary steps, in a laborious and painstaking way, and not a monkey budged till the step above him was vacated. If we had waited we should have witnessed an imaginary accident, no doubt; and we should have heard the intrepid band hurrah when they made the summit and looked around upon the "magnificent view," and seen them throw themselves down in exhausted attitudes for a rest in that commanding situation.

In Nevada I used to see the children play at silver mining. Of course the great thing was an accident in a mine, and there were two "star" parts: that of the man who fell down the mimic shaft, and that of the daring hero who was lowered into the depths to bring him up. I knew one small chap who always insisted on playing *both* of these parts, – and he carried his point. He would tumble into the shaft and die, and then come to the surface and go back after his own remains.

It is the smartest boy that gets the hero-part, every where: he is head guide in Switzerland, head miner in Nevada, head bull-fighter in Spain, etc., but I knew a preacher's son, seven years old, who once selected a part for himself compared to which those just mentioned are tame and unimpressive. Jimmy's father stopped him from driving imaginary horse-cars one Sunday – stopped him from playing captain of an imaginary steamboat next Sunday – stopped him from leading an imaginary army to battle the following Sunday – and so on. Finally the little fellow said, –

"I've tried everything, and they won't any of them do. What *can* I play?"

"I hardly know, Jimmy; but you *must* play only things that are suitable to the Sabbath day."

Next Sunday the preacher stepped softly to a back room door to see if the children were rightly employed. He peeped in. A chair occupied the middle of the room, and on the back of it hung Jimmy's cap; one of the little sisters took the cap down, nibbled at it, then passed it to another small sister and said, "Eat of this fruit, for it is good." The Reverend took in the situation – alas, they were playing the Expulsion from Eden! Yet he found one little crumb of comfort. He said to himself, "For once Jimmy has yielded the chief role – I have been wronging him, I did not believe there was so much modesty in him: I should have expected him to be either Adam or Eve." This crumb of comfort lasted but a very little while; he glanced around and discovered Jimmy standing in an imposing attitude in a corner, with a dark and deadly frown on his face. What that meant was very plain – *he was personating the Deity!* Think of the guileless sublimity of that idea.

We reached Vispach at 8 P.M., only about seven hours out from St. Nicholas. So we must have made fully a mile and a half an hour, and it was all down hill, too, and very muddy at that. We staid all night at the Hotel du Soleil; I remember it because the landlady, the portier, the waitress, and the chamber-maid, were not separate persons, but were all contained in one neat and chipper suit of spotless muslin, and she was the prettiest young creature I saw in all that region. She was the landlord's daughter. And I remember that the only native match to her I saw in all Europe was the young daughter of the landlord of a village inn in the Black Forest. Why don't more people in Europe marry and keep hotel?

Next morning we left with a family of English friends and went by train to Brevet, and thence by boat across the lake to Ouchy (Lausanne.)

Ouchy is memorable to me, not on account of its beautiful situation and lovely surroundings, – although these would make it stick long in one's memory, – but as the place where I caught the London *Times* dropping into humor. It was not aware of it, though. It did not do it on purpose. An English friend called my attention to this lapse, and cut out the reprehensible paragraph for me. Think of encountering a grin like this on the face of that grim journal:

> ERRATUM. – We are requested by Reuter's Telegram Company to correct an erroneous announcement made in their Brisbane telegram of the 2d inst., published in our impression of the 5th inst., stating that "Lady Kennedy had given birth to twins, the eldest being a son." The Company explain that the message they received contained the words "Governor of Queensland, *twins first son.*" Being, however, subsequently informed that Sir Arthur Kennedy was unmarried and that there must be some mistake, a telegraphic repetition was at once demanded. It has been received to-day (11th inst.) and shows that the words really telegraphed by Reuter's agent were "Governor Queensland *turns first sod,*" alluding to the Maryborough–Gympic Railway in course of construction. The words in italics were mutilated by the telegraph in transmission from Australia, and reaching the company in the form mentioned above gave rise to the mistake.

I had always had a deep and reverent compassion for the sufferings of the "prisoner of Chillon," whose story Byron has told in such moving verse; so I took the steamer and made pilgrimage to the dungeons of the Castle of Chillon, to see the place where poor Bonivard endured his dreary captivity 300 years ago. I am glad I did that, for it took away some of the pain I was feeling on the prisoner's account. His dungeon was a nice, cool, roomy place, and I can not see why he should have been so dissatisfied with it. If he had been imprisoned in a St. Nicholas private dwelling, where the fertilizer prevails, and the goat sleeps with the guest, and the chickens roost on him, and the cow comes in and bothers him when he wants to muse, it would have been another matter altogether; but he surely could not have had a very cheerless time of it in that pretty dungeon. It has romantic window-slits that let in generous bars of light, and it has tall, noble columns, carved apparently from the living rock; and what is more, they are written all over with thousands of names; some of them, – like Byron's and Victor Hugo's, – of the first celebrity. Why didn't he amuse himself reading these names? Then there are the couriers and tourists – swarms of them every day – what was to hinder him from having a good time with them? I think Bonivard's sufferings have been overrated.

Next, we took the train and went to Martigny, on the way to Mont Blanc. Next morning we started, about 8 o'clock, on foot. We had plenty of company, in the way of wagon-loads and mule-loads of tourists – and dust. This scattering procession of travelers was perhaps a mile long. The road was up hill – interminably up hill, – and tolerably steep. The weather was blistering hot, and the man or woman who had to sit on a creeping mule, or in a crawling wagon, and broil in the beating sun, was an object to be pitied. We could dodge among the bushes, and have the relief of shade, but those people could not. They paid for a conveyance, and to get their money's worth they rode.

We went by the way of the Tête Noire, and after we reached high ground there was no lack of fine scenery. In one place the road was tunneled through a shoulder of the mountain; from there one looked down into a gorge with a rushing torrent in it, and on every hand was a charming view of rocky buttresses and wooded heights. There was a liberal allowance of pretty water-falls, too, on the Tête Noire route.

About half an hour before we reached the village of Argentière a vast dome of snow with the sun blazing on it, drifted into view and framed itself in a strong V-shaped gateway of the mountains, and we recognized Mont Blanc, the "monarch of the Alps." With every step, after that, this stately dome rose higher and higher into the blue sky, and at last seemed to occupy the zenith.

Some of Mont Blanc's neighbors – bare, light-brown, steeple-like rocks, – were very peculiarly shaped. Some were whittled to a sharp point, and slightly bent at the upper end, like a lady's finger; one monster sugar-loaf resembled a bishop's hat; it was too steep to hold snow on its sides, but had some in the division.

While we were still on very high ground, and before the descent toward Argentière began, we looked up toward a neighboring mountain top, and saw exquisite prismatic colors playing about some white clouds which were so delicate as to almost resemble gossamer webs. The faint pinks and greens were peculiarly beautiful; none of the colors were deep, they were the lightest shades. They were bewitchingly commingled. We sat down to study and enjoy this singular spectacle. The tints remained during several minutes – flitting, changing, melting into each other; paling almost away, for a moment, then re-flushing, – a shifting, restless, unstable succession of soft opaline gleams, shimmering over that airy film of white cloud, and turning it into a fabric dainty enough to clothe an angel with.

By and by we perceived what those super-delicate colors, and their continuous play and movement, reminded us of: it is what one sees in a soap-bubble that is drifting along, catching changes of tint from the objects it passes. A soap-bubble is the most beautiful thing, and the most exquisite, in nature: that lovely phantom fabric in the sky was suggestive of a soap-bubble split open, and spread out in the sun. I wonder how much it would take to buy a soap-bubble, if there was only one in the world? One could buy a hat-full of Koh-i-Noors with the same money, no doubt.

We made the tramp from Martigny to Argentière in eight hours. We beat all the mules and wagons; we didn't usually do that. We hired a sort of open baggage-wagon for the trip down the valley to Chamonix, and then devoted an hour to dining. This gave the driver time to get drunk. He had a friend with him, and this friend also had had time to get drunk.

When we drove off, the driver said all the tourists had arrived and gone by while we were at dinner; "but," said he, impressively, "be not disturbed by that – remain tranquil – give yourselves no uneasiness – Their dust rises far before us, you shall see it fade and disappear far behind us – rest you tranquil, leave all to me – I am the king of drivers. Behold!"

Down came his whip, and away we clattered. I never had such a shaking up in my life. The recent flooding rains had washed the road clear away in places, but we never stopped, we never slowed down, for anything. We tore right along, over rocks, rubbish, gullies, open fields – sometimes with one or two wheels on the ground, but generally with none. Every now and then that calm, good-natured madman would bend a majestic look over his shoulder at us and say, "Ah, you perceive? It is as I have said – I am the king of drivers." Every time we just missed going to destruction, he would say, with tranquil happiness, "Enjoy it, gentlemen, it is very rare, it is very unusual – it is given to few to ride with the king of drivers – and observe, it is as I have said, *I* am he."

He spoke in French, and punctuated with hiccups. His friend was French, too, but spoke in German – using the same system of punctuation, however. The friend called himself the "Captain of Mont Blanc," and wanted us to make the ascent with him. He said he had made more ascents than any other man, – 47, – and his brother had made 37. His brother was the best guide in the world, except himself – but he, yes, observe him well, – he was the "Captain of Mont Blanc" – that title belonged to none other.

The "king" was as good as his word – he overtook that long procession of tourists and went by it like a hurricane. The result was that we got choicer rooms at the hotel in Chamonix than we should have done if his majesty had been a slower artist – or rather, if he hadn't most providentially got drunk before he left Argentière.

CHAPTER XLIII

EVERY BODY WAS OUT of doors; every body was in the principal street of the village, – not on the sidewalks, but all over the street; every body was lounging, loafing, chatting, waiting, alert, expectant, interested, – for it was train-time. That is to say, it was diligence-time – the half dozen big diligences would soon be arriving from Geneva, and the village was interested, in many ways, in knowing how many people were coming and what sort of folk they might be. It was altogether the livest-looking street we had seen in any village on the continent.

The hotel was by the side of a booming torrent, whose music was loud and strong; we could not see this torrent, for it was dark, now, but one could locate it without a light. There was a large enclosed yard in front of the hotel, and this was filled with groups of villagers waiting to see the diligences arrive, or to hire themselves to excursionists for the morrow. A telescope stood in the yard, with its huge barrel canted up toward the lustrous evening star. The long porch of the hotel was populous with tourists, who sat in shawls and wraps under the vast overshadowing bulk of Mont Blanc, and gossiped or meditated.

Never did a mountain seem so close; its big sides seemed at one's very elbow, and its majestic dome, and the lofty cluster of slender minarets that were its neighbors, seemed to be almost over one's head. It was night in the streets, and the lamps were sparkling every where; the broad bases and shoulders of the mountains were in a deep gloom, but their summits swam in a strange rich glow which was really daylight, and yet had a mellow something about it which was very different from the hard white glare of the kind of daylight I was used to. Its radiance was strong and clear, but at the same time it was singularly soft, and spiritual, and benignant. No, it was not our harsh, aggressive, realistic daylight; it seemed properer to an enchanted land – or to heaven.

I had seen moonlight and daylight together before, but I had not seen daylight and black night elbow to elbow before. At least I had not seen the daylight resting upon an object sufficiently close at hand, before, to make the contrast startling and at war with nature.

The daylight passed away. Presently the moon rose up behind some of those sky-piercing fingers or pinnacles of bare rock of which I have spoken – they were a little to the left of the crest of Mont Blanc, and right over our heads, – but she couldn't manage to climb high enough toward heaven to get entirely above them. She would show the glittering arch of her upper third, occasionally, and scrape it along behind the comb-like row; sometimes a pinnacle stood straight up, like a statuette of ebony, against that glittering white shield, then seemed to glide out of it by its own volition and power, and become a dim spectre, whilst the next pinnacle glided into its place and blotted the spotless disk with the black exclamation point of its presence. The top of one pinnacle took the shapely, clean-cut form of a rabbit's head, in the inkiest silhouette, while it rested against the moon. The unillumined peaks and minarets, hovering vague and phantom-like above us while the others were painfully white and strong with snow and moonlight, made a peculiar effect.

But when the moon, having passed the line of pinnacles, was hidden behind the stupendous white swell of Mont Blanc, the masterpiece of the evening was flung on the canvas. A rich greenish radiance sprang into the sky from behind the mountain, and in this some airy shreds and ribbons of vapor floated about, and being flushed with that strange tint, went waving to and fro like pale green flames. After a while, radiating bars, – vast broadening fan-shaped shadows, – grew up and stretched away to the zenith from behind the mountain. It was a spectacle to take one's breath, for the wonder of it, and the sublimity.

Indeed, those mighty bars of alternate light and shadow streaming up from behind that dark and prodigious form and occupying the half of the dull and opaque heavens, was the most imposing and impressive marvel I had ever looked upon. There is no simile for it, for nothing is like it. If a child had asked me what it was, I should have said, "Humble yourself, in this presence, it is the glory flowing from the hidden head of the Creator." One falls shorter of the truth than that, sometimes, in trying to explain mysteries to the little people. I could have found out the cause of this awe-compelling miracle by inquiring, for it is not infrequent at Mont Blanc, – but I did not wish to know. We have not the reverent feeling for the rainbow that a savage has, because we know how it is made. We have lost as much as we gained by prying into that matter.

We took a walk down street, a block or two, and at a place where four streets met and the principal shops were clustered, found the groups of men in the roadway thicker than ever – for this was the Exchange of Chamonix. These men were in the costumes of guides and porters, and were there to be hired.

The office of that great personage, the Guide-in-Chief of the Chamonix Guild of Guides, was near by. This guild is a close corporation, and is governed by strict laws. There are many excursion-routes, some dangerous and some not, some that can be made safely without a guide, and some that can not. The bureau determines these things. Where it decides that a guide is necessary, you are forbidden to go without one. Neither are you allowed to be a victim of extortion; the law states what you are to pay. The guides serve in rotation;

you cannot select the man who is to take your life into his hands, you must take the worst in the lot, if it is his turn.

A guide's fee ranges all the way up from a half dollar (for some trifling excursion of a few rods,) to twenty dollars, according to the distance traversed and the nature of the ground. A guide's fee for taking a person to the summit of Mont Blanc and back, is twenty dollars – and he earns it. The time employed is usually three days, and there is enough early rising in it to make a man far more "healthy and wealthy and wise" than any one man has any right to be. The porter's fee for the same trip is ten dollars. Several fools, – no, I mean several tourists, – usually go together, and divide up the expense, and thus make it light; for if only one f—tourist, I mean – went, he would have to have several guides and porters, and that would make the matter costly.

We went into the Chief's office. There were maps of mountains on the walls; also one or two lithographs of celebrated guides, and a portrait of the scientist De Saussure.

In glass cases were some labeled fragments of boots and batons, and other suggestive relics and remembrancers of casualties on Mont Blanc. In a book was a record of all the ascents which have ever been made, beginning with Nos. 1 and 2, – being those of Jacques Balmat and De Saussure, in 1787, and ending with No. 685, which wasn't cold yet. In fact No. 685 was standing by the official table waiting to receive the precious official diploma which should prove to his German household and to his descendants that he had once been indiscreet enough to climb to the top of Mont Blanc. He looked very happy when he got his document; in fact, he spoke up and said he *was* happy.

I tried to buy a diploma for an invalid friend at home who had never traveled, and whose desire all his life has been to ascend Mont Blanc, but the Guide-in-Chief rather insolently refused to sell me one. I was very much offended. I said I did not propose to be discriminated against on account of my nationality; that he had just sold a diploma to this German gentleman, and my money was as good as his; I would see to it that he couldn't keep shop for Germans and deny his produce to Americans; I would have his license taken away from him at the dropping of a handkerchief; if France refused to break him, I would make an international matter of it and bring on a war; the soil should be drenched with blood; and not only that, but I would set up an opposition shop and sell diplomas at half price.

For two cents I would have done these things, too; but nobody offered me the two cents. I tried to move that German's feelings, but it could not be done; he would not give me his diploma, neither would he sell it to me. I *told* him my friend was sick and could not come himself, but he said he did not care a verdammtes pfennig, he wanted his diploma for himself – did I suppose he was going to risk his neck for that thing and then give it to a sick stranger? Indeed he wouldn't, so he wouldn't. I resolved, then, that I would do all I could to injure Mont Blanc.

In the record book was a list of all the fatal accidents which had happened on the mountain. It began with the one in 1820 when the Russian Dr. Hamel's three guides were lost in a crevasse of the glacier, and it recorded the delivery of the remains in the valley by the slow-moving glacier 41 years later. The latest catastrophe bore date 1877.

We stepped out and roved about the village a while. In front of the little church was a monument to the memory of the bold guide Jacques Balmat, the first man who ever stood upon the summit of Mont Blanc. He made that wild trip solitary and alone. He accomplished the ascent a number of times afterward. A stretch of nearly half a century lay between his first ascent and his last one. At the ripe old age of 72 he was climbing around a corner of a lofty precipice of the Pic du Midi – nobody with him – when he slipped and fell. So he died in the harness.

He had grown very avaricious in his old age, and used to go off stealthily to hunt for non-existent and impossible gold among those perilous peaks and precipices. He was on a quest of that kind when he lost his life. There was a statue to him, and another to De Saussure, in the hall of our hotel, and a metal plate on the door of a room up stairs bore an inscription to the effect that that room had been occupied by Albert Smith. Balmat and De Saussure discovered Mont Blanc – so to speak – but it was Smith who made it a paying property. His articles in Blackwood and his lectures on Mont Blanc in London advertised it and made people as anxious to see it as if it owed them money.

As we strolled along the road we looked up and saw a red signal light glowing in the darkness of the mountain side. It seemed but a trifling way up, – perhaps a hundred yards, a climb of ten minutes. It was a lucky piece of sagacity in us that we concluded to stop a man whom we met and get a light for our pipes from him instead of continuing the climb to that lantern to get a light, as had been our purpose. The man said that that lantern was on the Grands Mulets, some

6,500 feet above the valley! I know by our Riffelberg experience, that it would have taken us a good part of a week to go up there. I would sooner not smoke at all, than take all that trouble for a light.

Even in the day time the foreshortening effect of the mountain's close proximity creates curious deceptions. For instance, one sees with the naked eye a cabin up there beside the glacier, and a little above and beyond he sees the spot where that red light was located; he thinks he could throw a stone from the one place to the other. But he couldn't, for the difference between the two altitudes is more than 3,000 feet. It looks impossible, from below, that this can be true, but it is true, nevertheless.

While strolling about, we kept the run of the moon all the time, and we still kept an eye on her after we got back to the hotel portico. I had a theory that the gravitation of refraction, being subsidiary to atmospheric compensation, the refrangibility of the earth's surface would emphasize this effect in regions where great mountain ranges occur, and possibly so even-handedly impact the odic and idyllic forces together, the one upon the other, as to prevent the moon from rising higher than 12,200 feet above sea level. This daring theory had been received with frantic scorn by some of my fellow-scientists, and with an eager silence by others. Among the former I may mention Prof. H——y; and among the latter Prof. T——l. Such is professional jealousy; a scientist will never show any kindness for a theory which he did not start himself. There is no feeling of brotherhood among these people. Indeed, they always resent it when I call them brother. To show how far their ungenerosity can carry them, I will state that I offered to let Prof. H——y publish my great theory as his own discovery; I even begged him to do it; I even proposed to print it myself as his theory. Instead of thanking me, he said that if I tried to fasten that theory on him he would sue me for slander. I was going to offer it to Mr. Darwin, whom I understood to be a man without prejudices, but it occurred to me that perhaps he would not be interested in it since it did not concern heraldry.

But I am glad, now, that I was forced to father my intrepid theory myself, for on the night of which I am writing, it was triumphantly justified and established. Mont Blanc is nearly 16,000 feet high; he hid the moon utterly; near him is a peak which is 12,216 feet high; the moon slid along behind the pinnacles, and when she approached that one I watched her with intense interest, for my reputation as a scientist must stand or fall by its decision. I cannot describe the emotions which surged like tidal waves through my breast when

I saw the moon glide behind that lofty needle and pass it by without exposing more than two feet four inches of her upper rim above it! I was secure, then. I knew she could rise no higher, and I was right. She sailed behind all the peaks and never succeeded in hoisting her disk above a single one of them.

While the moon was behind one of those sharp fingers, its shadow was flung athwart the vacant heavens – a long, slanting, clean-cut, dark ray – with a streaming and energetic suggestion of *force* about it, such as the ascending jet of water from a powerful fire engine affords. It was curious to see a good strong shadow of an earthly object cast upon so intangible a field as the atmosphere.

We went to bed, at last, and went quickly to sleep, but I woke up, after about three hours, with throbbing temples, and a head which was physically sore, outside and in. I was dazed, dreamy, wretched, seedy, unrefreshed. I recognized the occasion of all this; it was that torrent. In the mountain villages of Switzerland, and along the roads, one has always the roar of the torrent in his ears. He imagines it is music, and he thinks poetic things about it; he lies in his comfortable bed and is lulled to sleep by it. But by and by he begins to notice that his head is very sore – he cannot account for it; in solitudes where the profoundest silence reigns, he notices a sullen, distant, continuous roar in his ears, which is like what he would experience if he had sea-shells pressed against them – he can not account for it; he is drowsy and absentminded; there is no tenacity to his mind, he can not keep hold of a thought and follow it out; if he sits down to write, his vocabulary is empty, no suitable words will come, he forgets what he started to do, and remains there, pen in hand, head tilted up, eyes closed, listening painfully to the muffled roar of a distant train in his ears; in his soundest sleep, the strain continues, he goes on listening, always listening, intently, anxiously, and wakes at last, harrassed, irritable, unrefreshed. He can not manage to account for these things. Day after day he feels as if he had spent his nights in a sleeping car. It actually takes him weeks to find out that it is those persecuting torrents that have been making all the mischief. It is time for him to get out of Switzerland, then, for as soon as he has discovered the cause, the misery is magnified several fold. The roar of the torrent is maddening, then, for his imagination is assisting; the physical pain it inflicts is exquisite. When he finds he is approaching one of those streams, his dread is so lively that he is disposed to fly the track and avoid the implacable foe.

Eight or nine months after the distress of the torrents had departed from me, the roar and thunder of the streets of Paris brought it all back again. I moved to the sixth story of the hotel to hunt for peace. About midnight the noises dulled away, and I was sinking to sleep, when I heard a new and curious sound; I listened: evidently some joyous lunatic was softly dancing a "double shuffle" in the room over my head. I had to wait for him to get through, of course. Five long, long minutes he smoothly shuffled away – a pause followed, then something fell with a heavy thump on the floor. I said to myself "There – he is pulling off his boots – thank heavens he is done." Another slight pause – he went to shuffling again! I said to myself, "Is he trying to see what he can do with only one boot on?" Presently came another pause and another thump on the floor. I said "Good, he has pulled off his other boot – *now* he is done." But he wasn't. The next moment he was shuffling again. I said, "Confound him, he is at it in his slippers!" After a little came that same old pause, and right after it that thump on the floor once more. I said, "Hang him, he had on *two* pair of boots!" For an hour that magician went on shuffling and pulling off boots till he had shed as many as twenty-five pair, and I was hovering on the verge of lunacy. I got my gun and stole up there. The fellow was in the midst of an acre of sprawling boots, and he had a boot in his hand, shuffling it – no I mean *polishing* it. The mystery was explained. He hadn't been dancing. He was the "Boots" of the hotel, and was attending to business.

CHAPTER XLVII

WE SPENT A few pleasant restful days at Geneva, that delightful city where accurate time-pieces are made for all the rest of the world, but whose own clocks never give the correct time of day by any accident.

Geneva is filled with pretty little shops, and the shops are filled with the most enticing gimcrackery, but if one enters one of these places he is at once pounced upon, and followed up, and so persecuted to buy this, that, and the other thing, that he is very grateful to get out again, and is not at all apt to repeat his experiment. The shopkeepers of the smaller sort, in Geneva, are as troublesome and persistent as are the salesmen of that monster hive in

Paris, the Grands Magasins du Louvre – an establishment where ill-mannered pestering, pursuing and insistence have been reduced to a science.

In Geneva, prices in the smaller shops are very elastic – that is another bad feature. I was looking in at a window at a very pretty string of beads, suitable for a child. I was only admiring them; I had no use for them; I hardly ever wear beads. The shopwoman came out and offered them to me for 35 francs. I said it was cheap, but I did not need them.

"Ah, but monsieur, they are so beautiful!"

I confessed it, but said they were not suitable for one of my age and simplicity of character. She darted in and brought them out and tried to force them into my hands, saying, –

"Ah, but only see how lovely they are! Surely monsieur will take them; monsieur shall have them for 30 francs. There, I have said it – it is a loss, but one must live."

I dropped my hands, and tried to move her to respect my unprotected situation. But no, she dangled the beads in the sun before my face, exclaiming, "Ah, monsieur *can not* resist them!" She hung them on my coat button, folded her hands resignedly, and said, "Gone, – and for 30 francs, the lovely things – it is incredible! – but the good God will sanctify the sacrifice to me."

I removed them gently, returned them, and walked away, shaking my head and smiling a smile of silly embarrassment while the passers-by halted to observe. The woman leaned out of her door, shook the beads, and screamed after me, –

"Monsieur shall have them for 28!"

I shook my head.

"Twenty-seven! It is a cruel loss, it is ruin – but take them, only take them."

I still retreated, still wagging my head.

"Mon Dieu, they shall even go for 26! There, I have said it. Come!"

I wagged another negative. A nurse and a little English girl had been near me, and were following me, now. The shopwoman ran to the nurse, thrust the beads into her hands, and said, –

"Monsieur shall have them for 25! Take them to the hotel – he shall send me the money to-morrow – next day – when he likes." Then to the child: "When thy father sends me the money, come thou also, my angel, and thou shalt have something oh so pretty!"

I was thus providentially saved. The nurse refused the beads squarely and firmly, and that ended the matter.

The "sights" of Geneva are not numerous. I made one attempt to hunt up the houses once inhabited by those two disagreeable people, Rousseau and Calvin, but had no success. Then I concluded to go home. I found it was easier to propose to do that than to do it; for that town is a bewildering place. I got lost in a tangle of narrow and crooked streets, and staid lost for an hour or two. Finally I found a street which looked somewhat familiar, and said to myself, "Now I am at home, I judge." But I was wrong; this was "*Hell* street." Presently I found another place which had a familiar look, and said to myself, "Now I am at home, sure." It was another error. This was "*Purgatory* street." After a little I said, "*Now* I've got to the right place, anyway... no, this is '*Paradise* street;' I'm further from home than I was in the beginning." Those were queer names – Calvin was the author of them, likely. "Hell" and "Purgatory" fitted those two streets like a glove, but the "Paradise" appeared to be sarcastic.

I came out on the lake front, at last, and then I knew where I was. I was walking along before the glittering jewelry shops when I saw a curious performance. A lady passed by, and a trim dandy lounged across the walk in such an apparently carefully-timed way as to bring himself exactly in front of her when she got to him; he made no offer to step out of the way; he did not apologize; he did not even notice her. She had to stop still and let him lounge by. I wondered if he had done that piece of brutality purposely. He strolled to a chair and seated himself at a small table; two or three other males were sitting at similar tables sipping sweetened water. I waited; presently a youth came by, and this fellow got up and served him the same trick. Still, it did not seem possible that any one could do such a thing deliberately. To satisfy my curiosity I went around the block, and sure enough, as I approached, at a good round speed, he got up and lounged lazily across my path, fouling my course exactly at the right moment to receive all my weight. This proved that his previous performances had not been accidental, but intentional.

I saw that dandy's curious game played afterwards, in Paris, but not for amusement; not with a motive of any sort, indeed, but simply from a selfish indifference to other people's comfort and rights. One does not see it as frequently in Paris as he might expect to, for there the law says, in effect, "it is the business of the weak to get out of the way of the strong." We fine a cabman if he runs over a citizen; Paris fines the citizen for being run over. At least so every body says – but I saw some thing which caused me to doubt; I saw a horseman run over an old woman one day, – the police arrested him and took him away. That looked as if they meant to punish him.

It will not do for me to find merit in American manners – for are they not the standing butt for the jests of critical and polished Europe? Still I must venture to claim one little matter of superiority in our manners: a lady may traverse our streets all day, going and coming as she chooses, and she will never be molested by any man; but if a lady, unattended, walks abroad in the streets of London, even at noonday, she will be pretty likely to be accosted and insulted – and not by drunken sailors, but by men who carry the look and wear the dress of gentlemen. It is maintained that these people are not gentlemen, but are a lower sort, disguised as gentlemen. The case of Colonel Valentine Baker obstructs that argument, for a man can not become an officer in the British army except he hold the rank of gentleman. This person, finding himself alone in a railway compartment with an unprotected girl, – but it is an atrocious story, and doubtless the reader remembers it well enough. London must have been more or less accustomed to Bakers, and the ways of Bakers, else London would have been offended, and excited. Baker was "imprisoned" – in a parlor; and he could not have been more visited, or more overwhelmed with attentions, if he had committed six murders and then – while the gallows was preparing – "got religion" – after the manner of the holy Charles Peace, of saintly memory. Arkansaw – it seems a little indelicate to be trumpeting forth our own superiorities, and comparisons are always odious, but still – Arkansaw would certainly have hanged Baker. I do not say she would have tried him first, but she would have hanged him, any way.

Even the most degraded woman can walk our streets unmolested, her sex and her weakness being her sufficient protection. She will encounter less polish than she would in the old world, but she will run across enough humanity to make up for it.

The music of a donkey awoke us early in the morning, and we rose up and made ready for a pretty formidable walk – to Italy; but the road was so level that we took the train. We lost a good deal of time by this, but it was no matter, we were not in a hurry. We were four hours going to Chambery. The Swiss trains go upwards of three miles an hour, in places, but they are quite safe.

That aged French town of Chambery was as quaint and crooked as Heilbronn. A drowsy reposeful quiet reigned in the back streets which made strolling through them very pleasant, barring the almost unbearable heat of the sun. In one of these streets which was eight feet wide, gracefully curved, and built up with small antiquated houses, I saw three fat hogs lying asleep, and a boy (also asleep), taking care of them. From queer old-fashioned windows along the curve, projected boxes of bright flowers, and over the edge of one of these boxes hung the head and shoulders of a cat – asleep. The five sleeping creatures were the only living things visible in that street. There was not a sound; absolute stillness prevailed. It was Sunday; one is not used to such dreamy Sundays on the Continent. In our part of the town it was different that night. A regiment of brown and battered soldiers had arrived home from Algiers, and I judged they got thirsty on the way. They sang and drank till dawn, in the pleasant open air.

We left for Turin at 10 the next morning by a railway which was profusely decorated with tunnels. We forgot to take a lantern along, consequently we missed all the scenery. Our compartment was full. A ponderous tow-headed Swiss woman who put on many fine-lady airs, but was evidently more used to washing linen than wearing it, sat in a corner seat and put her legs across into the opposite one, propping them intermediately with her up-ended valise. In the seat thus pirated, sat two Americans, greatly incommoded by that woman's majestic coffin-clad feet. One of them begged her, politely, to remove them. She opened her wide eyes and gave him a stare, but answered nothing. By and by he preferred his request again, with great respectfulness. She said, in good English, and in a deeply offended tone, that she had paid her passage and was not going to be bullied out of her "rights" by ill-bred foreigners, even if she *was* alone and unprotected.

"But I have rights, also, madam. My ticket entitles me to a seat, but you are occupying half of it."

"I will not talk with you, sir. What right have you to speak to me? I do not know you. One would know you came from a land where there are no gentlemen. No *gentleman* would treat a lady as you have treated me."

"I come from a region where a lady would hardly give me the same provocation."

"You have insulted me, sir! You have intimated that I am not a lady – and I hope I am *not* one, after the pattern of your country."

"I beg that you will give yourself no alarm on that head, madam; but at the same time I must insist – always respectfully – that you let me have my seat."

Here the fragile laundress burst into tears and sobs.

"I never was so insulted before! Never, never! It is shameful, it is brutal, it is base, to bully and abuse an unprotected lady who has lost the use of her limbs and cannot put her feet to the floor without agony!"

"Good heavens, madam, why didn't you say that at first! I offer a thousand pardons. And I offer them most sincerely. I did not know – I *could* not know – that any thing was the matter. You are most welcome to the seat, and would have been from the first if I had only known. I am truly sorry it all happened, I do assure you."

But he couldn't get a word of forgiveness out of her. She simply sobbed and snuffled in a subdued but wholly unappeasable way for two long hours, meantime crowding the man more than ever with her undertaker-furniture and paying no sort of attention to his frequent and humble little efforts to do something for her comfort. Then the train halted at the Italian line and she hopped up and marched out of the car with as firm a leg as any washerwoman of all her tribe! And how sick I was, to see how she had fooled me.

Turin is a very fine city. In the matter of roominess it transcends any thing that was ever dreamed of before, I fancy. It sits in the midst of a vast dead-level, and one is obliged to imagine that land may be had for the asking, and no taxes to pay, so lavishly do they use it. The streets are extravagantly wide, the paved squares are prodigious, the houses are huge and handsome, and compacted into uniform blocks that stretch away as straight as an arrow, into the distance. The sidewalks are about as wide as ordinary European *streets*, and are covered over with a double arcade supported on great stone piers or columns. One walks from one end to the other of these spacious streets, under shelter all the time, and all his course is lined with the prettiest of shops and the most inviting dining-houses.

There is a wide and lengthy court, glittering with the most wickedly-enticing shops, which is roofed with glass, high aloft over head, and paved with soft-toned marbles laid in graceful figures; and at night when this place is brilliant with gas and populous with a sauntering and chatting and laughing multitude of pleasure seekers, it is a spectacle worth seeing.

Everything is on a large scale; the public buildings, for instance – and they are architecturally imposing, too, as well as large. The big squares have big bronze monuments in them. At the hotel they gave us rooms that were alarming, for size, and a parlor to match. It was well the weather required no fire in the parlor, for I think one might as well have tried to warm a park. The place would have a warm look, though, in any weather, for the window curtains were of red silk damask, and the walls were covered with the same fire-hued goods – so, also, were the four sofas and the brigade of chairs. The furniture, the ornaments, the chandeliers, the carpets, were all new and bright and costly. We did not need a parlor, at all, but they said it belonged to the two bedrooms and we might use it if we chose. Since it was to cost nothing, we were not averse from using it, of course.

Turin must surely read a good deal, for it has more book stores to the square rod than any other town I know of. And it has its own share of military folk. The Italian officers' uniforms are very much the most beautiful I have ever seen; and as a general thing the men in them were as handsome as the clothes. They were not large men, but they had fine forms, fine features, rich olive complexions and lustrous black eyes.

For several weeks I had been culling all the information I could about Italy, from tourists. The tourists were all agreed upon one thing – one must expect to be cheated at every turn by the Italians. I took an evening walk in Turin, and presently came across a little Punch and Judy show in one of the great squares. Twelve or fifteen people constituted the audience. This miniature theatre was not much bigger than a man's coffin stood on end; the upper part was open and displayed a tinseled parlor – a good-sized handkerchief would have answered for a drop-curtain; the footlights consisted of a couple of candle-ends an inch long; various manikins the size of dolls appeared on the stage and made long speeches at each other, gesticulating a good deal, and they generally had a fight before they got through. They were worked by strings from above, and the illusion was not perfect, for one saw not only the strings but the brawny hand that manipulated them – and the actors and actresses all talked in the same voice, too. The audience stood in front of the theatre, and seemed to enjoy the performance heartily.

When the play was done, a youth in his shirt-sleeves started around with a small copper saucer to make a collection. I did not know how much to put in, but thought I would be guided by my predecessors. Unluckily I only had two of these and they did not help me much because they did not put in any thing. I had no Italian money, so I put in a small Swiss coin worth about ten cents. The youth finished his collection-trip and emptied the result on the stage;

he had some very animated talk with the concealed manager, then he came working his way through the little crowd – seeking me, I thought. I had a mind to slip away, but concluded I wouldn't; I would stand my ground, and confront the villainy, whatever it was. The youth stood before me and held up that Swiss coin, sure enough, and said some thing. I did not understand him, but I judged he was requiring Italian money of me. The crowd gathered close, to listen. I was irritated, and said, – in English, of course, –

"I know it's Swiss, but you'll take that or none. I haven't any other."

He tried to put the coin in my hand, and spoke again. I drew my hand away, and said, –

"*No*, sir. I know all about you people. You can't play any of your fraudful tricks on me. If there is a discount on that coin, I am sorry, but I am not going to make it good. I noticed that some of the audience didn't pay you any thing at all. You let them go, without a word, but you come after me because you think I'm a stranger and will put up with an extortion rather than have a scene. But you are mistaken this time – you'll take that Swiss money or none."

The youth stood there with the coin in his fingers non-plussed, and bewildered; of course he had not understood a word. An English-speaking Italian spoke up, now, and said, –

"You are misunderstanding the boy. He does not mean any harm. He did not suppose you gave him so much money purposely, so he hurried back to return you the coin lest you might get away before you discovered your mistake. Take it, and give him a penny – that will make everything smooth again."

I probably blushed, then, for there was occasion. Through the interpreter I begged the boy's pardon, but I nobly refused to take back the ten cents. I said I was accustomed to squandering large sums in that way – it was the kind of person I was. Then I retired to make a note to the effect that in Italy, persons connected with the drama do not cheat.

The episode with the showman reminds me of a dark chapter in my history. I once robbed an aged and blind beggar-woman of four dollars – in a church. It happened in this way. When I was out with the Innocents Abroad, the ship stopped in the Russian port of Odessa, and I went ashore, with others, to view the town. I got separated from the rest, and wandered about, alone, until late in the afternoon, when I entered a Greek church to see what it was like. When I was ready to leave, I observed two wrinkled old women standing stiffly upright against the inner wall, near the door, with their brown palms open to receive alms. I contributed to the nearer one, and passed out. I had gone fifty yards, perhaps, when it occurred to me that I must remain ashore all night, as I had heard that the ship's business would carry her away at 4 o'clock and keep her away until morning. It was a little after 4, now. I had come ashore with only two pieces of money, both about the same size, but differing largely in value – one was a French gold piece worth four dollars, the other a Turkish coin worth two cents and a half. With a sudden and horrified misgiving, I put my hand in my pocket, now, and, sure enough, I fetched out that Turkish penny!

Here was a situation. A hotel would require pay in advance – I must walk the streets all night, and perhaps be arrested as a suspicious character. There was but one way out of the difficulty – I flew back to the church, and softly entered. There stood the old woman yet, and in the palm of the nearest one still lay my gold piece. I was grateful. I crept close, feeling unspeakably mean; I got my Turkish penny ready, and was extending a trembling hand to make the nefarious exchange, when I heard a cough behind me. I jumped back as if I had been accused, and stood quaking while a worshiper entered and passed up the aisle.

I was there a year trying to steal that money; that is, it seemed a year, though of course it must have been much less. The worshipers went and came; there were hardly ever three in the church at once, but there was always one or more. Every time I tried to commit my crime some body came in or some body started out, and I was prevented; but at last my opportunity came; for one moment there was nobody in the church but the two beggar-women and me. I whipped the gold piece out of the poor old pauper's palm and dropped my Turkish penny in its place. Poor old thing, she murmured her thanks – they smote me to the heart. Then I sped away in a guilty hurry, and even when I was a mile from the church I was still glancing back, every moment, to see if I was being pursued.

That experience has been of priceless value and benefit to me; for I resolved then, that as long as I lived I would never again rob a blind beggar-woman in a church; and I have always kept my word. The most permanent lessons in morals are those which come, not of booky teaching, but of experience.

CHAPTER XLVIII

IN MILAN WE spent most of our time in the vast and beautiful Arcade or Gallery, or whatever it is called. Blocks of tall new buildings of the most sumptuous sort, rich with decoration and graced with statues, the streets between these blocks roofed over with glass at a great height, the pavements all of smooth and variegated marble, arranged in tasteful patterns – little tables all over these marble streets, people sitting at them, eating, drinking, or smoking – crowds of other people strolling by – such is the Arcade. I should like to live in it all the time. The windows of the sumptuous restaurants stand open, and one breakfasts there and enjoys the passing show.

We wandered all over the town, enjoying whatever was going on in the streets. We took one omnibus ride, and as I did not speak Italian and could not ask the price, I held out some copper coins to the conductor, and he took two. Then he went and got his tariff-card and showed me that he had taken only the right sum. So I made a note – Italian omnibus conductors do not cheat.

Near the Cathedral I saw another instance of probity. An old man was peddling dolls and toy fans. Two small American children bought fans, and one gave the old man a franc and three copper coins, and both started away; but they were called back, and the franc and one of the coppers were restored to them. Hence it is plain that in Italy, parties connected with the drama and with the omnibus and toy interests do not cheat.

The stocks of goods in the shops were not extensive, generally. In the vestibule of what seemed to be a clothing store, we saw eight or ten wooden dummies grouped together, clothed in woolen business-suits and each suit marked with its price. One suit was marked 45 francs – nine dollars. Harris stepped in and said he wanted a suit like that. Nothing easier: the old merchant dragged in the dummy, brushed him off with a broom, stripped him, and shipped the clothes to the hotel. He said he did not keep two suits of the same kind in stock, but manufactured a second when it was needed to re-clothe the dummy.

In another quarter we found six Italians engaged in a violent quarrel. They danced fiercely about, gesticulating with their heads, their arms, their legs, their whole bodies; they would rush forward occasionally in a sudden access of passion and shake their fists in each other's very faces. We lost half an hour there, waiting to help cord up the dead, but they finally embraced each other affectionately, and the trouble was all over. The episode was interesting, but we could not have afforded all that time to it if we had known nothing was going to come of it but a reconciliation. Note made – in Italy, people who quarrel cheat the spectator.

We had another disappointment, afterward. We approached a deeply interested crowd, and in the midst of it found a fellow wildly chattering and gesticulating over a box on the ground which was covered with a piece of old blanket. Every little while he would bend down and take hold of the edge of the blanket with the extreme tips of his fingers, as if to show there was no deception – chattering away all the while, – but always, just as I was expecting to see a wonderful feat of legerdemain, he would let go the blanket and rise to explain further. However, at last he uncovered the box and got out a spoon with a liquid in it, and held it fair and frankly around, for people to see that it was all right and he was taking no advantage – his chatter became more excited than ever. I supposed he was going to set fire to the liquid and swallow it, so I was greatly wrought up and interested. I got a cent ready in one hand and a florin in the other, intending to give him the former if he survived and the latter if he killed himself – for his loss would be my gain in a literary way, and I was willing to pay a fair price for the item – but this impostor ended his intensely moving performance by simply adding some powder to the liquid and polishing the spoon! Then he held it aloft, and he could not have shown a wilder exultation if he had achieved an immortal miracle. The crowd applauded in a gratified way, and it seemed to me that history speaks the truth when it says these children of the south are easily entertained.

We spent an impressive hour in the noble cathedral, where long shafts of tinted light were cleaving through the solemn dimness from the lofty windows and falling on a pillar here, a picture there, and a kneeling worshiper yonder. The organ was muttering, censers were swinging, candles were glinting on the distant altar, and robed priests were filing silently past them; the scene was one to sweep all frivolous thoughts away and steep the soul in a holy calm. A trim young American lady paused a yard or two from me, fixed her eyes on the mellow sparks flecking the far-off altar, bent her head reverently a moment, then straightened up, kicked her train into the air with her heel, caught it deftly in her hand, and marched briskly out.

We visited the picture galleries and the other regulation "sights" of Milan – not because I wanted to write about them again, but to see if I had learned any thing in twelve years. I afterwards visited the great galleries of Rome and Florence for the same purpose. I found I had learned one thing. When I wrote about the Old Masters before, I said the copies were better than the originals. That was a mistake of large dimensions. The Old Masters were still unpleasing to me, but they were truly divine contrasted with the copies. The copy is to the original as the pallid, smart, inane new wax work-group is to the vigorous, earnest, dignified group of living men and women whom it professes to duplicate. There is a mellow richness, a subdued color, in the old pictures, which is to the eye what muffled and mellowed sound is to the ear. That is the merit which is most loudly praised in the old picture, and is the one which the copy most conspicuously lacks, and which the copyist must not hope to compass. It was generally conceded by the artists with whom I talked, that that subdued splendor, that mellow richness, is imparted to the picture by *age*. Then why should we worship the Old Master for it, who didn't impart it, instead of worshiping Old Time, who did? Perhaps the picture was a clanging bell, until Time muffled it and sweetened it.

In conversation with an artist in Venice, I asked, –

"What is it that people see in the Old Masters? I have been in the Doges' Palace and I saw several acres of very bad drawing, very bad perspective, and very incorrect proportions. Paul Veronese's dogs do not resemble dogs; all the horses look like bladders on legs; one man had a *right* leg on the left side of his body; in the large picture where the Emperor (Barbarossa?) is prostrate before the Pope, there are three men in the foreground who are over thirty feet high, if one may judge by the size of a kneeling little boy in the centre of the foreground; and according to the same scale, the Pope is 7 feet high and the Doge is a shriveled dwarf of 4 feet."

The artist said, –

"Yes, the Old Masters often drew badly; they did not care much for truth and exactness in minor details; but after all, in spite of bad drawing, bad perspective, bad proportions, and a choice of subjects which no longer appeal to people as strongly as they did three hundred years ago, there is a *something* about their pictures which is divine – a something which is above and beyond the art of any epoch since – a something which would be the despair of artists but that they never hope or expect to attain it, and therefore do not worry about it."

That is what he said – and he said what he believed; and not only believed, but felt.

Reasoning, – especially reasoning without technical knowledge, – must be put aside, in cases of this kind. It can not assist the inquirer. It will lead him, in the most logical progression, to what, in the eyes of artists, would be a most illogical conclusion. Thus: bad drawing, bad proportion, bad perspective, indifference to truthful detail, color which gets its merit from time, and not from the artist – these things constitute the Old Master; conclusion, the Old Master was a bad painter, the Old Master was not an Old Master at all, but an Old Apprentice. Your friend the artist will grant your premises, but deny your conclusion; he will maintain that notwithstanding this formidable list of confessed defects, there is still a something that is divine and unapproachable about the Old Master, and that there is no arguing the fact away by any system of reasoning whatever.

I can believe that. There are women who have an indefinable charm in their faces which makes them beautiful to their intimates; but a cold stranger who tried to reason the matter out and find this beauty would fail. He would say of one of these women: This chin is too short, this nose is too long, this forehead is too high, this hair is too red, this complexion is too pallid, the perspective of the entire composition is incorrect; conclusion, the woman is not beautiful. But her nearest friend might say, and say truly, "Your premises are right, your logic is faultless, but your conclusion is wrong, nevertheless; she is an Old Master – she is beautiful, but only to such as know her; it is a beauty which cannot be formulated, but it is there, just the same."

I found more pleasure in contemplating the Old Masters this time than I did when I was in Europe in former years, but still it was a calm pleasure; there was nothing overheated about it. When I was in Venice before, I think I found no picture which stirred me much, but this time there were two which enticed me to the Doges' Palace day after day, and kept me there hours at a time. One of these was Tintoretto's three-acre picture in the Great Council Chamber. When I saw it twelve years ago I was not strongly attracted to it – the guide told me it was an insurrection in heaven – but this was an error.

The movement of this great work is very fine. There are ten thousand figures, and they are all doing something. There is a wonderful "go" to the whole composition. Some of the figures are diving headlong downward, with clasped hands, others are swimming through the cloud-shoals, – some on their faces, some on their backs – great processions of bishops, martyrs and angels are pouring swiftly centrewards from various outlying directions – everywhere is enthusiastic joy, there is rushing movement every where. There are fifteen or twenty figures scattered here and there, with books, but they can not keep their attention on their reading – they offer the books to others, but no one wishes to read, now. The Lion of St. Mark is there with his book; St. Mark is there with his pen uplifted; he and the Lion are looking each other earnestly in the face, disputing about the way to spell a word – the Lion looks up in wrapt admiration while St. Mark spells. This is wonderfully interpreted by the artist. It is the master-stroke of this incomparable painting.

I visited the place daily, and never grew tired of looking at that grand picture. As I have intimated, the movement is almost unimaginably vigorous; the figures are singing, hosannahing, and many are blowing trumpets. So vividly is noise suggested, that spectators who become absorbed in the picture almost always fall to shouting comments in each other's ears, making ear-trumpets of their curved hands, fearing they may not otherwise be heard. One often sees a tourist, with the eloquent tears pouring down his cheeks, funnel his hands at his wife's ear, and hears him roar through them, "O, TO BE THERE AND AT REST!"

None but the supremely great in art can produce effects like these with the silent brush.

Twelve years ago I could not have appreciated this picture. One year ago I could not have appreciated it. My study of Art in Heidelberg has been a noble education to me. All that I am to-day in Art, I owe to that.

The other great work which fascinated me was Bassano's immortal Hair Trunk. This is in the Chamber of the Council of Ten. It is in one of the three forty-foot pictures which decorate the walls of the room. The composition of this picture is beyond praise. The Hair Trunk is not hurled at the stranger's head, – so to speak – as the chief feature of an immortal work so often is; no, it is carefully guarded from prominence, it is subordinated, it is restrained, it is most deftly and cleverly held in reserve, it is most cautiously and ingeniously led up to, by the master, and consequently when the spectator reaches it at last, he is taken unawares, he is unprepared, and it bursts upon him with a stupefying surprise.

One is lost in wonder at all the thought and care which this elaborate planning must have cost. A general glance at the picture could never suggest that there was a hair trunk in it; the Hair Trunk is not mentioned in the title even, – which is, "Pope Alexander III and the

Doge Ziani, the Conqueror of the Emperor Frederick Barbarossa;" you see, the title is actually utilized to help divert attention from the Trunk; thus, as I say, nothing suggests the presence of the Trunk, by any hint, yet everything studiedly leads up to it, step by step. Let us examine into this, and observe the exquisitely artful artlessness of the plan.

At the extreme left end of the picture are a couple of women, one of them with a child looking over her shoulder at a wounded man sitting with bandaged head on the ground. These people seem needless, but no, they are there for a purpose; one cannot look at them without seeing the gorgeous procession of grandees, bishops, halberdiers, and banner-bearers which is passing along behind them; one cannot see the procession without feeling a curiosity to follow it and learn whither it is going; it leads him to the Pope, in the centre of the picture, who is talking with the bonnetless Doge – talking tranquilly, too, although within 12 feet of them a man is beating a drum, and not far from the drummer two persons are blowing horns, and many horsemen are plunging and rioting about – indeed, 22 feet of this great work is all a deep and happy holiday serenity and Sunday School procession, and then we come suddenly upon 11½ feet of turmoil and racket and insubordination. This latter state of things is not an accident, it has its purpose. But for it, one would linger upon the Pope and the Doge, thinking them to be the motive and supreme feature of the picture; whereas one is drawn along, almost unconsciously, to see what the trouble is about. Now at the very *end* of this riot, within 4 feet of the end of the picture, and full 36 feet from the beginning of it, the Hair Trunk bursts with an electrifying suddenness upon the spectator, in all its matchless perfection, and the great master's triumph is sweeping and complete. From that moment no other thing in those forty feet of canvas has any charm; one sees the Hair Trunk, and the Hair Trunk only – and to see it is to worship it. Bassano even placed objects in the immediate vicinity of the Supreme Feature whose pretended purpose was to divert attention from it yet a little longer and thus delay and augment the surprise; for instance, to the right of it he has placed a stooping man with a cap so red that it is sure to hold the eye for a moment – to the left of it, some 6 feet away, he has placed a red-coated man on an inflated horse, and that coat plucks your eye to that locality the next moment – then, between the Trunk and the red horseman he has intruded a man, naked to his waist, who is carrying a fancy flour sack on the middle of his back instead of on his shoulder – this admirable feat interests you, of course – keeps you at bay a little longer, like a sock or a jacket thrown to the pursuing wolf – but at last, in spite of all distractions and detentions, the eye of even the most dull and heedless spectator is sure to fall upon the World's Masterpiece, and in that moment he totters to his chair or leans upon his guide for support.

Descriptions of such a work as this must necessarily be imperfect, yet they are of value. The top of the Trunk is arched; the arch is a perfect half circle, in the Roman style of architecture, for in the then rapid decadence of Greek art, the rising influence of Rome was already beginning to be felt in the art of the Republic. The Trunk is bound or bordered with leather all around where the lid joins the main body. Many critics consider this leather too cold in tone; but I consider this its highest merit, since it was evidently made so to emphasize by contrast the impassioned fervor of the hasp. The high lights in this part of the work are cleverly managed, the *motif* is admirably subordinated to the ground tints, and the *technique* is very fine. The brass nail-heads are in the purest style of the early Renaissance. The strokes, here, are very firm and bold – every nail-head is a portrait. The handle on the end of the Trunk has evidently been retouched – I think, with a piece of chalk – but one can still see the inspiration of the Old Master in the tranquil, almost too tranquil, hang of it. The hair of this Trunk is *real* hair – so to speak – white in patches, brown in patches. The details are finely worked out; the repose proper to hair in a recumbent and inactive attitude is charmingly expressed. There is a feeling about this part of the work which lifts it to the highest altitudes of art; the sense of sordid realism vanishes away – one recognizes that there is *soul* here. View this Trunk as you will, it is a gem, it is a marvel, it is a miracle. Some of the effects are very daring, approaching even to the boldest flights of the rococo, the sirocco, and the Byzantine schools – yet the master's hand never falters – it moves on, calm, majestic, confident, – and with that art which conceals art, it finally casts over the *tout ensemble*, by mysterious methods of its own, a subtle something which refines, subdues, etherealizes the arid components and endues them with the deep charm and gracious witchery of poesy.

Among the art treasures of Europe there are pictures which approach the Hair Trunk – there are two which may be said to equal it, possibly – but there is none that surpasses it. So perfect is the Hair Trunk that it moves even persons who ordinarily have no feeling for art. When an Erie baggage-master saw it two years ago, he could hardly keep from checking it; and once when a customs inspector was brought into its presence, he gazed upon it in silent rapture for some moments, then slowly and unconsciously placed one hand behind him with the palm uppermost, and got out his chalk with the other. These facts speak for themselves.

CHAPTER XLIX

ONE LINGERS ABOUT the Cathedral a good deal, in Venice. There is a strong fascination about it – partly because it is so old, and partly because it is so ugly. Too many of the world's famous buildings fail of one chief virtue – harmony; they are made up of a methodless mixture of the ugly and the beautiful; this is bad; it is confusing, it is unrestful. One has a sense of uneasiness, of distress, without knowing why. But one is calm before St. Mark, one is calm within it, one would be calm on top of it, calm in the cellar; for its details are masterfully ugly, no misplaced and impertinent beauties are intruded anywhere; and the consequent result is a grand harmonious whole, of soothing, entrancing, tranquilizing, soul-satisfying ugliness. One's admiration of a perfect thing always grows, never declines; and this is the surest evidence to him that it *is* perfect. St. Mark is perfect. To me it soon grew to be so nobly, so augustly ugly, that it was difficult to stay away from it, even for a little while. Every time its squat domes disappeared from my view, I had a despondent feeling; whenever they reappeared, I felt an honest rapture – I have not known any happier hours than those I daily spent in front of Florian's, looking across the Great Square at it. Propped on its long row of low thick-legged columns, its back knobbed with domes, it seemed like a vast warty bug taking a meditative walk.

St. Mark is not the oldest building in the world, of course, but it seems the oldest, and looks the oldest – especially inside. When the ancient mosaics in its walls become damaged, they are repaired but not altered; the grotesque old pattern is preserved. Antiquity has a charm of its own, and to smarten it up would only damage it. One day I was sitting on a red marble bench in the vestibule looking up at an ancient piece of apprentice-work, in mosaic, illustrative of the command to "multiply and replenish the earth." The Cathedral itself had seemed very old; but this picture was illustrating a period in history which made the building seem young by comparison. But I presently found an antique which was older than either the battered Cathedral or the date assigned to that piece of history; it was a spiral-shaped fossil as large as the crown of a hat; it was embedded in the marble bench, and had been sat upon by tourists until it was worn smooth. Contrasted with the inconceivable antiquity of this modest fossil, those other things were flippantly modern – jejune – mere matters of day-before-yesterday. The sense of the oldness of the Cathedral vanished away under the influence of this truly venerable presence.

St. Mark's is monumental; it is an imperishable remembrancer of the profound and simple piety of the Middle Ages. Whoever could ravish a column from a pagan temple, did it and contributed his swag to this Christian one. So this fane is upheld by several hundred acquisitions procured in that peculiar way. In our day it would be immoral to go on the highway to get bricks for a church, but it was no sin in the old times. St. Mark's was itself the victim of a curious robbery, once. The thing is set down in the history of Venice, but it might be smuggled into the Arabian Nights and not seem out of place there:

Nearly four hundred and fifty years ago, a Candian named Stammato, in the suite of a prince of the house of Este, was allowed to view the riches of St. Mark. His sinful eye was dazzled and he hid himself behind an altar, with an evil purpose in his heart, but a priest discovered him and turned him out. Afterward he got in again – by false keys, this time. He went there, night after night, and worked hard and patiently, all alone, overcoming difficulty after difficulty with his toil, and at last succeeded in removing a great block of the marble paneling which walled the lower part of the treasury; this block he fixed so that he could take it out and put it in at will. After that, for weeks, he spent all his midnights in his magnificent mine, inspecting it in security, gloating over its marvels at his leisure, and always slipping back to his obscure lodgings before dawn, with a duke's ransom under his cloak. He did not need to grab, haphazard, and run – there was no hurry. He could make deliberate and well-considered selections; he could consult his æsthetic tastes. One comprehends how undisturbed he was, and how safe from any danger of interruption, when it is stated that he even carried off a unicorn's horn – a mere curiosity – which would not pass through the egress entire, but had to be sawn in two – a bit of work which cost him hours of tedious labor. He continued to store up his treasures at home until his occupation lost the charm of novelty and became monotonous; then he ceased from it, contented. Well he might be; for his collection, raised to modern values, represented nearly $50,000,000!

He could have gone home much the richest citizen of his country, and it might have been years before the plunder was missed; but he was human – he could not enjoy his delight alone, he must have some body to talk about it with. So he exacted a solemn oath from a Candian noble named Crioni, then led him to his lodgings and nearly took his breath away with a sight of his glittering hoard. He detected a look in his friend's face which excited his suspicion, and was about to slip a stiletto into him when Crioni saved himself by explaining that that look was only an expression of supreme and happy astonishment. Stammato made Crioni a present of one of the State's principal jewels – a huge carbuncle, which afterward figured in the Ducal cap of state – and the pair parted. Crioni went at once to the palace, denounced the criminal, and handed over the carbuncle as evidence. Stammato was arrested, tried, and condemned, with the old-time Venetian promptness. He was hanged between the two great columns in the Piazza – with a gilded rope, out of compliment to his love of gold, perhaps. He got no good of his booty at all – it was *all* recovered.

In Venice we had a luxury which very seldom fell to our lot on the continent – a home dinner, with a private family. If one could always stop with private families, when traveling, Europe would have a charm which it now lacks. As it is, one must live in the hotels, of course, and that is a sorrowful business. A man accustomed to American food and American domestic cookery would not starve to death suddenly in Europe; but I think he would gradually waste away, and eventually die.

He would have to do without his accustomed morning meal. That is too formidable a change altogether; he would necessarily suffer from it. He could get the shadow, the sham, the base counterfeit of that meal; but that would do him no good, and money could not buy the reality.

To particularize: the average American's simplest and commonest form of breakfast consists of coffee and beefsteak; well, in Europe, coffee is an unknown beverage. You can get what the European hotel keeper thinks is coffee, but it resembles the real thing as hypocrisy resembles holiness. It is a feeble, characterless, uninspiring sort of stuff, and almost as undrinkable as if it had been made in an American hotel. The milk used for it is what the French call "Christian" milk, – milk which has been baptized.

After a few months' acquaintance with European "coffee," one's mind weakens, and his faith with it, and he begins to wonder if the rich beverage of home, with its clotted layer of yellow cream on top of it, is not a mere dream, after all, and a thing which never existed.

Next comes the European bread, – fair enough, good enough, after a fashion, but cold; cold and tough, and unsympathetic; and never any change, never any variety, – always the same tiresome thing.

Next, the butter, – the sham and tasteless butter; no salt in it, and made of goodness knows what.

Then there is the beefsteak. They have it in Europe, but they don't know how to cook it. Neither will they cut it right. It comes on the table in a small, round, pewter platter. It lies in the centre of this platter, in a bordering bed of grease-soaked potatoes; it is the size, shape, and thickness of a man's hand with the thumb and fingers cut off. It is a little overdone, is rather dry, it tastes pretty insipidly, it rouses no enthusiasm.

Imagine a poor exile contemplating that inert thing; and imagine an angel suddenly sweeping down out of a better land and setting before him a mighty porter house steak an inch and a half thick, hot and sputtering from the griddle; dusted with fragrant pepper; enriched with little melting bits of butter of the most unimpeachable freshness and genuineness; the precious juices of the meat trickling out and joining the gravy, archipelagoed with mushrooms; a township or two of tender, yellowish fat gracing an outlying district of this ample county of beefsteak; the long white bone which divides the sirloin from the tenderloin still in its place; and imagine that the angel also adds a great cup of American home-made coffee, with the cream a-froth on top, some real butter, firm and yellow and fresh, some smoking hot biscuits, a plate of hot buckwheat cakes, with transparent syrup, – could words describe the gratitude of this exile?

The European dinner is better than the European breakfast, but it has its faults and inferiorities, it does not satisfy. He comes to the table eager and hungry; he swallows his soup, – there is an undefinable lack about it somewhere; thinks the fish is going to be the thing he wants, – eats it and isn't sure; thinks the next dish is perhaps the one that will hit the hungry place, – tries it, and is conscious that there was a something wanting about it, also. And thus he goes on, from dish to dish, like a boy after a butterfly which just misses getting caught every time it alights, but somehow doesn't get caught after all; and at the end the exile and the boy have fared about alike: the one is full, but grievously unsatisfied, the other has had plenty of exercise, plenty of interest, and a fine lot of hopes, but he hasn't got any butterfly. There is here and there an American who will say he can remember rising from a European table d'hote perfectly satisfied; but we must not overlook the fact that there is also here and there an American who will lie.

The number of dishes is sufficient; but then it is such a monotonous variety of *unstriking* dishes. It is an inane dead level of "fair-to-middling." There is nothing to *accent* it. Perhaps if the roast of mutton or of beef, – a big generous one, – were brought on the table and carved in full view of the client, that might give the right sense of earnestness and reality to the thing; but they don't do that, they pass the sliced meat around on a dish, and so you are perfectly calm, it does not stir you in the least. Now a vast roast turkey, stretched on the broad of his back, with his heels in the air and the rich juices oozing from his fat sides. . . . but I may as well stop there, for they would not know how to cook him. They can't even cook a chicken respectably; and as for carving it, they do that with a hatchet.

This is about the customary table d'hote bill in summer:

Soup, (characterless.)
Fish – sole, salmon, or whiting – usually tolerably good.
Roast – mutton or beef – tasteless – and some last year's potatoes.
A pâté, or some other made-dish – usually good – "considering."
One vegetable – brought on in state, and all alone – usually insipid lentils, or string beans, or indifferent asparagus.
Roast chicken, as tasteless as paper.
Lettuce-salad – tolerably good.
Decayed strawberries or cherries.

Sometimes the apricots and figs are fresh, but this is no advantage, as these fruits are of no account any way.

The grapes are generally good, and sometimes there is a tolerably good peach, by mistake.

The variations of the above bill are trifling. After a fortnight one discovers that the variations are only apparent, not real; in the third week you get what you had the first, and in the fourth week you get what you had the second. Three or four months of this weary sameness will kill the robustest appetite.

It has now been many months, at the present writing, since I have had a nourishing meal, but I shall soon have one, – a modest, private affair, all to myself. I have selected a few dishes, and made out a little bill of fare, which will go home in the steamer that precedes me, and be hot when I arrive – as follows:

Radishes. Baked apples, with cream.
Fried oysters; stewed oysters. Frogs.
American coffee, with real cream.
American butter.
Fried chicken, Southern style.
Porter house steak.
Saratoga potatoes.
Broiled chicken, American style.
Hot biscuits, Southern style.
Hot wheat-bread, Southern style.
Hot buckwheat cakes.
American toast. Clear maple syrup.
Virginia bacon, broiled.
Blue points, on the half shell.
Cherry-stone clams.
San Francisco mussels, steamed.
Oyster soup. Clam soup.
Philadelphia Terrapin soup.
Bacon and greens, Southern style.

Oysters roasted in shell – Northern style.
Soft-shell crabs. Connecticut shad.
Baltimore perch.
Brook trout, from Sierra Nevadas.
Lake trout, from Tahoe.
Sheep-head and croakers, from New Orleans.
Black bass from the Mississippi.
American roast beef.
Roast turkey, Thanksgiving style.
Cranberry sauce. Celery.
Roast wild turkey. Woodcock.
Canvas-back-duck, from Baltimore.
Prairie hens, from Illinois.
Missouri partridges, broiled.
'Possum. Coon.
Boston bacon and beans.
Green corn, on the ear.

Hominy. Boiled onions. Turnips.
Pumpkin. Squash. Asparagus.
Butter beans. Sweet potatoes.
Lettuce. Succotash. String beans.
Mashed potatoes. Catsup.

Boiled potatoes, in their skins.
New potatoes, minus the skins.

Early rose potatoes, roasted in the ashes, Southern style, served hot.
Sliced tomatoes, with sugar or vinegar. Stewed tomatoes.
Green corn, cut from the ear and served with butter and pepper.

Hot corn-pone, with chitlings, Southern style.
Hot hoe-cake, Southern style.
Hot egg-bread, Southern style.
Hot light-bread, Southern style.
Buttermilk. Iced sweet milk.
Apple dumplings, with real cream.

Apple pie. Apple fritters.
Apple puffs, Southern style.

Peach cobbler, Southern style.
Peach pie. American mince pie.
Pumpkin pie. Squash pie.
All sorts of American pastry.

Fresh American fruits of all sorts, including strawberries which are not to be doled out as if they were jewelry, but in a more liberal way.
Ice-water – not prepared in the ineffectual goblet, but in the sincere and capable refrigerator.

Americans intending to spend a year or so in European hotels, will do well to copy this bill and carry it along. They will find it an excellent thing to get up an appetite with, in the dispiriting presence of the squalid table d'hote.

Foreigners cannot enjoy our food, I suppose, any more than we can enjoy theirs. It is not strange; for tastes are made, not born. I might glorify my bill of fare until I was tired; but after all, the Scotchman would shake his head and say, "Where's your haggis?" and the Fijian would sigh and say, "Where's your missionary?"

I have a neat talent in matters pertaining to nourishment. This has met with professional recognition. I have often furnished recipes for cook-books. Here are some designs for pies and things, which I recently prepared for a friend's projected cook-book, but as I forgot to furnish diagrams and perspectives, they had to be left out, of course:

Recipe for an Ash-Cake

Take a lot of water and add to it a lot of coarse Indian meal and about a quarter of a lot of salt. Mix well together, knead into the form of a "pone," and let the pone stand a while, – not on its edge, but the other way. Rake away a place among the embers, lay it there, and cover it an inch deep with hot ashes. When it is done, remove it; blow off all the ashes but one layer; butter that one and eat. N. B. No household should ever be without this talisman. It has been noticed that tramps never return for another ash-cake.

Recipe for New England Pie

To make this excellent breakfast dish, proceed as follows: Take a sufficiency of water and a sufficiency of flour, and construct a bullet-proof dough. Work this into the form of a disk, with the edges turned up some three-fourths of an inch. Toughen and kiln-dry it a couple of days in a mild but unvarying temperature. Construct a cover for this redoubt in the same way and of the same material. Fill with stewed dried apples; aggravate with cloves, lemon peel and slabs of citron; add two portions of New Orleans sugar, then solder on the lid and set in a safe place till it petrifies. Serve cold at breakfast and invite your enemy.

Recipe for German Coffee

Take a barrel of water and bring it to a boil; rub a chicory berry against a coffee berry, then convey the former into the water. Continue the boiling and evaporation until the intensity of the flavor and aroma of the coffee and chicory has been diminished to a proper degree; then set aside to cool. Now unharness the remains of a once cow from the plow, insert them in a hydraulic press, and when you shall have acquired a teaspoonful of that pale blue juice which a German superstition regards as milk, modify the malignity of its strength in a bucket of tepid water and ring up the breakfast. Mix the beverage in a cold cup, partake with moderation, and keep a wet rag around your head to guard against over-excitement.

To Carve Fowls in the German Fashion

Use a club, and avoid the joints.

CHAPTER L

I WONDER WHY some things are? For instance, Art is allowed as much indecent license to-day as in earlier times – but the privileges of Literature in this respect have been sharply curtailed within the past eighty or ninety years. Fielding and Smollett could portray the beastliness of their day in the beastliest language; we have plenty of foul subjects to deal with in our day, but we are not allowed to approach them very near, even with nice and guarded forms of speech. But not so with Art. The brush may still deal freely with any subject, however revolting or indelicate. It makes a body ooze sarcasm at every pore, to go about Rome and Florence and see what this last generation has been doing with the statues. These works, which had stood in innocent nakedness for ages, are all fig-leaved now. Yes, every one of them. Nobody noticed their nakedness before, perhaps; nobody can help noticing it now, the fig-leaf makes it so conspicuous. But the comical thing about it all, is, that the fig-leaf is confined to cold and pallid marble, which would be still cold and unsuggestive without this sham and ostentatious symbol of modesty, whereas warm-blooded paintings which do really need it have in no case been furnished with it.

At the door of the Ufizzi, in Florence, one is confronted by statues of a man and a woman, noseless, battered, black with accumulated grime, – they hardly suggest human beings – yet these ridiculous creatures have been thoughtfully and conscientiously fig-leaved by this fastidious generation. You enter, and proceed to that most-visited little gallery that exists in the world – the Tribune – and there, against the wall, without obstructing rag or leaf, you may look your fill upon the foulest, the vilest, the obscenest picture the world possesses – Titian's Venus. It isn't that she is naked and stretched out on a bed – no, it is the attitude of one of her arms and hand. If I ventured to describe that attitude, there would be a fine howl – but there the Venus lies, for anybody to gloat over that wants to – and there she has a right to lie, for she is a work of art, and Art has its privileges. I saw young girls stealing furtive glances at her; I saw young men gaze long and absorbedly at her; I saw aged, infirm men hang upon her charms with a pathetic interest. How I should like to describe her – just to see what a holy indignation I could stir up in the world – just to hear the unreflecting average man deliver himself about my grossness and coarseness, and all that. The world says that no worded description of a moving spectacle is a hundredth part as moving as the same spectacle seen with one's own eyes – yet the world is willing to let its son and its daughter and itself look at Titian's beast, but won't stand a description of it in words. Which shows that the world is not as consistent as it might be.

There are pictures of nude women which suggest no impure thought – I am well aware of that. I am not railing at such. What I am trying to emphasize is the fact that Titian's Venus is very far from being one of that sort. Without any question it was painted for a bagnio and it was probably refused because it was a trifle too strong. In truth it is too strong for any place but a public Art Gallery. Titian has two Venuses in the Tribune; persons who have seen them will easily remember which one I am referring to.

In every gallery in Europe there are hideous pictures of blood, carnage, oozing brains, putrefaction – pictures portraying intolerable suffering – pictures alive with every conceivable horror, wrought out in dreadful detail – and similar pictures are being put on the canvas every day and publicly exhibited – without a growl from anybody – for they are innocent, they are inoffensive, being works of art. But suppose a literary artist ventured to go into a pains-taking and elaborate description of one of these grisly things – the critics would skin him alive. Well, let it go, it cannot be helped; Art retains her privileges, Literature has lost hers. Some body else may cipher out the whys and the wherefores and the consistencies of it – I haven't got time.

Titian's Venus defiles and disgraces the Tribune, there is no softening that fact, but his "Moses" glorifies it. The simple truthfulness of this noble work wins the heart and the applause of every visitor, be he learned or ignorant. After wearying oneself with the acres of stuffy, sappy, expressionless babies that populate the canvases of the Old Masters in Italy, it is refreshing to stand before this peerless child and feel that thrill which tells you you are at last in the presence of the real thing. This is a human child, this is genuine. You have seen him a thousand times – you have seen him just as he is here – and you confess, without reserve, that Titian *was* a Master. The doll-faces of other painted babes may mean one thing, they may mean another, but with the "Moses" the case is different. The most famous of all the art critics has said, "There is no room for doubt, here – plainly this child is in trouble."

I consider that the "Moses" has no equal among the works of the Old Masters, except it be the divine Hair Trunk of Bassano. I feel sure that if all the other Old Masters were lost and only these two preserved, the world would be the gainer by it.

My sole purpose in going to Florence was to see this immortal "Moses," and by good fortune I was just in time, for they were already preparing to remove it to a more private and better protected place because a fashion of robbing the great galleries was prevailing in Europe at the time.

I got a capable artist to copy the picture; Pannemaker, the engraver of Doré's books, engraved it for me, and I have the pleasure of laying it before the reader in this volume [the 1880 edition].

We took a turn to Rome and some other Italian cities – then to Munich, and thence to Paris – partly for exercise, but mainly because these things were in our projected program, and it was only right that we should be faithful to it.

From Paris I branched out and walked through Holland and Belgium, procuring an occasional lift by rail or canal when tired, and I had a tolerably good time of it "by and large." I worked Spain and other regions through agents to save time and shoe leather.

We crossed to England, and then made the homeward passage in the Cunarder, *Gallia*, a very fine ship. I was glad to get home – immeasurably glad; so glad, in fact, that it did not seem possible that any thing could ever get me out of the country again. I had not enjoyed a pleasure abroad which seemed to me to compare with the pleasure I felt in seeing New York harbor again. Europe has many advantages which we have not, but they do not compensate for a good many still more valuable ones which exist nowhere but in our own country. Then we are such a homeless lot when we are over there! So are Europeans themselves, for that matter. They live in dark and chilly vast tombs, – costly enough, may be, but without conveniences. To be condemned to live as the average European family lives would make life a pretty heavy burden to the average American family.

On the whole, I think that short visits to Europe are better for us than long ones. The former preserve us from becoming Europeanized; they keep our pride of country intact, and at the same time they intensify our affection for our country and our people; whereas long visits have the effect of dulling those feelings, – at least in the majority of cases. I think that one who mixes much with Americans long resident abroad must arrive at this conclusion.

APPENDIX

A

THE PORTIER

Omar Khayam, the poet-prophet of Persia, writing more than eight hundred years ago, has said:

> In the four parts of the earth are many that are able to write learned books, many that are able to lead armies, and many also that are able to govern kingdoms and empires; but few there be that can keep hotel.

A word about the European hotel *portier*. He is a most admirable invention, a most valuable convenience. He always wears a conspicuous uniform; he can always be found when he is wanted, for he sticks closely to his post at the front door; he is as polite as a duke; he speaks from four to ten languages; he is your surest help and refuge in time of trouble or perplexity. He is not the clerk, he is not the landlord; he ranks above the clerk, and represents the landlord, who is seldom seen. Instead of going to the clerk for information, as we do at home, you go to the portier. It is the pride of our average hotel clerk to know nothing whatever; it is the pride of the portier to know everything. You ask the portier at what hours the trains leave, – he tells you instantly; or you ask him who is the best physician in town; or what is the hack tariff; or how many children the mayor has; or what days the galleries are open, and whether a permit is required, and where you are to get it, and what you must pay for it; or when the theatres open and close, what the plays are to be, and the price of seats; or what is the newest thing in hats; or how the bills of mortality average; or "who struck Billy Patterson." It does not matter what you ask him: in nine cases out of ten he knows, and in the tenth case he will find out for you before you can turn around three times. There is nothing he will not put his hand to. Suppose you tell him you wish to go from Hamburg to Peking by the way of Jericho, and are ignorant of routes and prices, – the next morning he will hand you a piece of paper with the whole thing worked out on it to the last detail. Before you have been long on European soil, you find yourself still *saying* you are relying on Providence, but when you come to look closer you will see that in reality you are relying on the portier. He discovers what is puzzling you, or what is troubling you, or what your need is, before you can get the half of it out, and he promptly says, "Leave that to me." Consequently you easily drift into the habit of leaving everything to him. There is a certain embarrassment about applying to the average American hotel clerk, a certain hesitancy, a sense of insecurity against rebuff; but you feel no embarrassment in your intercourse with the portier; he receives your propositions with an enthusiasm which cheers, and plunges into their accomplishment with an alacrity which almost inebriates. The more requirements you can pile upon him, the better he likes it. Of course the result is that you cease from doing any thing for yourself. He calls a hack when you want one; puts you into it; tells the driver whither to take you; receives you like a long-lost child when you return; sends you about your business, does all the quarreling with the hackman himself, and pays him his money out of his own pocket. He sends for your theatre tickets, and pays for them; he sends for any possible article you can require, be it a doctor, an elephant, or a postage-stamp; and when you leave, at last, you will find a subordinate seated with the cab driver who will put you in your railway compartment, buy your tickets, have your baggage weighed, bring you the printed tags, and tell you everything is in your bill and paid for. At home you get such elaborate, excellent, and willing service as this only in the best hotels of our large cities; but in Europe you get it in the mere back country towns just as well.

What is the secret of the portier's devotion? It is very simple: he gets *fees, and no salary*. His fee is pretty closely regulated, too. If you stay a week in the house, you give him five marks – a dollar and a quarter, or about eighteen cents a day. If you stay a month, you reduce this average somewhat. If you stay two or three months or longer, you cut it down half, or even more than half. If you stay only one day, you give the portier a mark.

The head waiter's fee is a shade less than the portier's; the Boots, who not only blacks your boots and brushes your clothes, but is usually the porter and handles your baggage, gets a somewhat smaller fee than the head waiter; the chamber-maid's fee ranks below that of the Boots. You fee only these four, and no one else. A German gentleman told me that when he remained a week in a hotel, he gave the portier five marks, the head waiter four, the Boots three, and the chamber-maid two; and if he staid three months he divided ninety marks among them, in about the above proportions. Ninety marks make $22.50.

None of these fees are ever payed until you leave the hotel, though it be a year, – except one of these four servants should go away in the meantime; in that case he will be sure to come and bid you good-bye and give you the opportunity to pay him what is fairly coming to him. It is considered very bad policy to fee a servant while you are still to remain longer in the hotel, because if you gave him too little he might neglect you afterward, and if you gave him too much he might neglect some body else to attend to you. It is considered best to keep his expectations "on a string" until your stay is concluded.

I do not know whether hotel servants in New York get any wages or not, but I do know that in some of the hotels there the feeing system in vogue is a heavy burden. The waiter expects a quarter at breakfast, – and gets it. You have a different waiter at luncheon, and so he gets a quarter. Your waiter at dinner is another stranger, – consequently he gets a quarter. The boy who carries your satchel to your room and lights your gas, fumbles around and hangs around significantly, and you fee him to get rid of him. Now you may ring for ice-water; and ten minutes later for a lemonade; and ten minutes afterwards, for a cigar; and by and by for a newspaper, – and what is the result? Why, a new boy has appeared every time and fooled and fumbled around until you have payed him something. Suppose you boldly put your foot down, and say it is the hotel's business to pay its servants? – and suppose you stand your ground and stop feeing? You will have to ring your bell ten or fifteen times before you get a servant there; and when he goes off to fill your order you will grow old and infirm before you see him again. You may struggle nobly for twenty-four hours, maybe, if you are an adamantine sort of person, but in the meantime you will have been so wretchedly served, and so insolently, that you will haul down your colors, and go to impoverishing yourself with fees.

It seems to me that it would be a happy idea to import the European feeing system into America. I believe it would result in getting even the bells of the Philadelphia hotels answered, and cheerful service rendered.

The greatest American hotels keep a number of clerks and a cashier, and pay them salaries which mount up to a considerable total in the course of a year. The great continental hotels keep a cashier on a trifling salary, and a portier *who pays the hotel a salary*. By the latter system both the hotel and the public save money and are better served than by our system. One of our consuls told me that the portier of a great Berlin hotel paid $5,000 a year for his position, and yet cleared $6,000 for himself. The position of portier in the chief hotels of Saratoga, Long Branch, New York, and similar centres of resort, would be one which the holder could afford to pay even more than $5,000 for, perhaps.

When we borrowed the feeing fashion from Europe a dozen years ago, the salary system ought to have been discontinued, of course. We might make this correction now, I should think. And we might add the portier, too. Since I first began to study the portier, I have had opportunities to observe him in the chief cities of Germany, Switzerland, and Italy; and the more I have seen of him the more I have wished that he might be adopted in America, and become there, as he is in Europe, the stranger's guardian angel.

Yes, what was true eight hundred years ago, is just as true to-day: "Few there be that can keep hotel." Perhaps it is because the landlords and their subordinates have in too many cases taken up their trade without first learning it. In Europe the trade of hotel keeper is taught. The apprentice begins at the bottom of the ladder and masters the several grades one after the other. Just as in our country printing-offices the apprentice first learns how to sweep out and bring water; then learns to "roll"; then to sort "pi"; then to set type; and finally rounds and completes his education with job-work and press-work: so the landlord-apprentice serves as call-boy; then as under-waiter; then as a parlor-waiter; then as head waiter, in which position he often has to make out all the bills; then as clerk or cashier; then as portier. His trade is learned now, and by and by he will assume the style and dignity of landlord, and be found conducting a hotel of his own.

Now in Europe, the same as in America, when a man has kept a hotel so thoroughly well during a number of years as to give it a great reputation, he has his reward. He can live prosperously on that reputation. He can let his hotel run down to the last degree of shabbiness and yet have it full of people all the time. For instance, there is the Hotel de Ville, in Milan. It swarms with mice and fleas, and if the rest of the world were destroyed it could furnish dirt enough to start another one with. The food would create an insurrection in a poor-house; and yet if you go outside to get your meals that hotel makes up its loss by overcharging you on all sorts of trifles, – and without making any denials or excuses about it, either. But the Hotel de Ville's old excellent reputation still keeps its dreary rooms crowded with travelers who would be elsewhere if they had only had some wise friend to warn them.

B

HEIDELBERG CASTLE

Heidelberg Castle must have been very beautiful before the French battered and bruised and scorched it two hundred years ago. The stone is brown, with a pinkish tint, and does not seem to stain easily. The dainty and elaborate ornamentation upon its two chief fronts is as delicately carved as if it had been intended for the interior of a drawing-room rather than for the outside of a house. Many fruit and flower-clusters, human heads and grim projecting lions' heads are still as perfect in every detail as if they were new. But the statues which are ranked between the windows have suffered. These are life-size statues of old-time emperors, electors, and similar grandees, clad in mail and bearing ponderous swords. Some have lost an arm, some a head, and one poor fellow is chopped off at the middle. There is a saying that if a stranger will pass over the draw-bridge and walk across the court to the castle front without saying any thing, he can make a wish and it will be fulfilled. But they say that the truth of this thing has never had a chance to be proved, for the reason that before any stranger can walk from the draw-bridge to the appointed place, the beauty of the palace front will extort an exclamation of delight from him.

A ruin must be rightly situated, to be effective. This one could not have been better placed. It stands upon a commanding elevation, it is buried in green woods, there is no level ground about it, but on the contrary there are wooded terraces upon terraces, and one looks down through shining leaves into profound chasms and abysses where twilight reigns and the sun cannot intrude. Nature knows how to garnish a ruin to get the best effect. One of these old towers is split down the middle, and one half has tumbled aside. It tumbled in such a way as to establish itself in a picturesque attitude. Then all it lacked was a fitting drapery, and Nature has furnished that; she has robed the rugged mass in flowers and verdure, and made it a charm to the eye. The standing half exposes its arched and cavernous rooms to you, like open, toothless mouths; there, too, the vines and flowers have done their work of grace. The rear portion of the tower has not been neglected, either, but is clothed with a clinging garment of polished ivy which hides the wounds and stains of time. Even the top is not left bare, but is crowned with a flourishing group of trees and shrubs. Misfortune has done for this old tower what it has done for the human character sometimes – improved it.

A gentleman remarked, one day, that it might have been fine to live in the castle in the day of its prime, but that we had one advantage which its vanished inhabitants lacked – the advantage of having a charming ruin to visit and muse over. But that was a hasty idea. Those people had the advantage of *us*. They had the fine castle to live in, and they could cross the Rhine valley and muse over the stately ruin of Trifels besides. The Trifels people, in their day, five hundred years ago, could go and muse over majestic ruins which have vanished, now, to the last stone. There have always been ruins, no doubt; and there have always been pensive people to sigh over them, and asses to scratch upon them their names and the important date of their visit. Within a hundred years after Adam left Eden, the guide probably gave the usual general flourish with his hand and said: "Place where the animals were named, ladies and gentlemen; place where the tree of the forbidden fruit stood; exact spot where Adam and Eve first met; and here, ladies and gentlemen, adorned and hallowed by the names and addresses of three generations of tourists, we have the crumbling remains of Cain's altar, – fine old ruin!" Then, no doubt, he taxed them a shekel apiece and let them go.

An illumination of Heidelberg Castle is one of the sights of Europe. The Castle's picturesque shape; its commanding situation, midway up the steep and wooded mountain side; its vast size, – these features combine to make an illumination a most effective spectacle. It is necessarily an expensive show, and consequently rather infrequent. Therefore whenever one of these exhibitions is to take place, the news goes about in the papers and Heidelberg is sure to be full of people on that night. I and my agent had one of these opportunities, and improved it.

About half-past seven on the appointed evening we crossed the lower bridge, with some American students, in a pouring rain, and started up the road which borders the Neunheim side of the river. This roadway was densely packed with carriages and foot passengers; the former of all ages, and the latter of all ages and both sexes. This black and solid mass was struggling painfully onward, through the slop, the darkness, and the deluge. We waded along for three-quarters of a mile, and finally took up a position in an unsheltered beer garden directly opposite the Castle. We could not *see* the Castle, – or any thing else, for that matter, – but we could dimly discern the outlines of the mountain over the way, through the pervading blackness, and knew whereabouts the Castle was located. We stood on one of the hundred benches in the garden, under our umbrellas; the other ninety-nine were occupied by standing men and women, and they also had umbrellas. All the region round about, and up and down the river-road, was a dense wilderness of humanity hidden under an unbroken pavement of carriage tops and umbrellas. Thus we stood during two drenching hours. No rain fell on my head, but the converging whalebone points of a dozen neighboring umbrellas poured little cooling streams of water down my neck, and sometimes into my ears, and thus kept me from getting hot and impatient. I had the rheumatism, too, and had heard that this was good for it. Afterward, however, I was led to believe that the water treatment is *not* good for rheumatism. There were even little girls in that dreadful place. A man held one in his arms, just in front of me, for as much as an hour, with umbrella-drippings soaking into her clothing all the time.

In the circumstances, two hours was a good while for us to have to wait, but when the illumination did at last come, we felt repaid. It came unexpectedly, of course, – things always do, that have been long looked and longed for. With a perfectly breath-taking suddenness several vast sheaves of vari-colored rockets were vomited skyward out of the black throats of the castle towers, accompanied by a thundering crash of sound, and instantly every detail of the prodigious ruin stood revealed against the mountain side and glowing with an almost intolerable splendor of fire and color. For some little time the whole building was a blinding crimson mass, the towers continued to spout thick columns of rockets aloft, and overhead the sky was radiant with arrowy bolts which clove their way to the zenith, paused, curved gracefully downward, then burst into brilliant fountain sprays of richly colored sparks. The red fires died slowly down, within the castle, and presently the shell grew nearly black outside; the angry glare that shone out through the broken arches and innumerable sashless windows, now, reproduced the aspect which the Castle must have borne in the old time when the French spoilers saw the monster bonfire which they had made there fading and smouldering toward extinction.

While we still gazed and enjoyed, the ruin was suddenly enveloped in rolling and tumbling volumes of vaporous green fire; then in dazzling purple ones; then a mixture of many colors followed, and drowned the great fabric in its blended splendors. Meantime the nearest bridge had been illuminated, and from several rafts anchored in the river, meteor showers of rockets, Roman candles, bombs, serpents, and Catherine wheels were being discharged in wasteful profusion into the sky, – a marvelous sight indeed to a person as little used to such spectacles as I was. For a while the whole region about us seemed as bright as day, and yet the rain was falling in torrents all the time. The evening's entertainment presently closed, and we joined the innumerable caravan of half-drowned spectators, and waded home again.

The Castle grounds are very ample and very beautiful; and as they joined the Hotel grounds, with no fences to climb, but only some nobly shaded stone stairways to descend, we spent a part of nearly every day in idling through their smooth walks and leafy groves. There was an attractive spot among the trees where were a great many wooden tables and benches; and there one could sit in the shade and pretend to sip at his foamy beaker of beer while he inspected the crowd. I say pretend, because I only pretended to sip, without really sipping. That is the polite way; but when you are ready to go, you empty the beaker at a draught. There was a brass band, and it furnished excellent music every afternoon. Sometimes so many people came that every seat was occupied, every table filled. And never a rough in the assemblage, – all nicely dressed fathers and mothers, young gentlemen and ladies and children; and plenty of university students and glittering officers; with here and there a gray professor, or a peaceful old lady with her knitting; and always a sprinkling of gawky foreigners. Every body had his glass of beer before him, or his cup of coffee, or his bottle of wine, or his hot cutlet and potatoes; young ladies chatted, or fanned themselves, or wrought at their crocheting or embroidering; the students fed sugar to their dogs, or discussed duels, or illustrated new fencing-tricks with their little canes; and every where was comfort and enjoyment, and every where peace and good-will to men. The trees were jubilant with birds, and the paths with rollicking children. One could have a seat in that place and plenty of music, any afternoon, for about eight cents, or a family ticket for the season for two dollars.

For a change, when you wanted one, you could stroll to the Castle, and burrow among its dungeons, or climb about its ruined towers, or visit its interior shows, – the great Heidelberg Tun, for instance. Every body has heard of the great Heidelberg Tun, and most people have seen it, no doubt. It is a wine cask as big as a cottage, and some traditions say it holds eighteen hundred thousand bottles, and other traditions say it holds eighteen hundred million barrels. I think it likely that one of these statements is a mistake, and the other one a lie. However, the mere matter of capacity is a thing of no sort of consequence, since the cask is empty, and indeed has always been empty, history says. An empty cask the size of a cathedral could excite but little emotion in me. I do not see any wisdom in building a monster cask to hoard up emptiness in, when you can get a better quality, outside, any day, free of expense. What could this cask have been built for? The more one studies over that, the more uncertain and unhappy he becomes. Some historians say that thirty couples, some say thirty thousand couples, can dance on the head of this cask at the same time. Even this does not seem to me to account for the building of it. It does not even throw light on it. A profound and scholarly Englishman, – a specialist, – who had made the great Heidelberg Tun his sole study for fifteen years, told me he had at last satisfied himself that the ancients built it to make German cream in. He said that the average German cow yielded from one to two and a half teaspoonfuls of milk, when she was not worked in the plow or the hay-wagon more than eighteen or nineteen hours a day. This milk was very sweet and good, and of a beautiful transparent bluish tint; but in order to get cream from it in the most economical way, a peculiar process was necessary. Now he believed that the habit of the ancients was to collect several milkings in a teacup, pour it into the Great Tun, fill up with water, and then skim off the cream from time to time as the needs of the German Empire demanded.

This began to look reasonable. It certainly began to account for the German cream which I had encountered and marveled over in so many hotels and restaurants. But a thought struck me, –

"Why did not each ancient dairyman take his own teacup of milk and his own cask of water, and mix them, without making a government matter of it?"

"Where could he get a cask large enough to contain the right proportion of water?"

Very true. It was plain that the Englishman had studied the matter from all sides. Still I thought I might catch him on one point; so I asked him why the modern empire did not make the nation's cream in the Heidelberg Tun, instead of leaving it to rot away unused. But he answered as one prepared, –

"A patient and diligent examination of the modern German cream has satisfied me that they do not use the Great Tun now, because they have got a *bigger* one hid away somewhere. Either that is the case or they empty the spring milkings into the mountain torrents and then skim the Rhine all summer."

There is a museum of antiquities in the castle, and among its most treasured relics are ancient manuscripts connected with German history. There are hundreds of these, and their dates stretch back through many centuries. One of them is a decree signed and sealed by the hand of a successor of Charlemagne, in the year 896. A signature made by a hand which vanished out of this life near a thousand years ago, is a more impressive thing than even a ruined castle. Luther's wedding ring was shown me; also a fork belonging to a time anterior to our era, and an early boot-jack. And there was a plaster cast of the head of a man who was assassinated about sixty years ago. The stab-wounds in the face were duplicated with unpleasant fidelity. One or two real hairs still remained sticking in the eyebrows of the cast. That trifle seemed to almost change the counterfeit into a corpse.

There are many aged portraits, – some valuable, some worthless; some of great interest, some of none at all. I bought a couple, – one a gorgeous duke of the olden time, and the other a comely blue-eyed damsel, a princess, may be. I bought them to start a portrait gallery of my ancestors with. I paid a dollar and a half for the duke and two and a half for the princess. One can lay in ancestors at even cheaper rates than these, in Europe, if he will mouse among old picture shops and look out for chances.

C

THE AWFUL GERMAN LANGUAGE

A little learning makes the whole world kin.
– PROVERBS XXXII, 7

I went often to look at the collection of curiosities in Heidelberg Castle, and one day I surprised the keeper of it with my German. I spoke entirely in that language. He was greatly interested; and after I had talked awhile he said my German was very rare, possibly a "unique;" and wanted to add it to his museum.

If he had known what it had cost me to acquire my art, he would also have known that it would break any collector to buy it. Harris and I had been hard at work on our German during several weeks at that time, and although we had made good progress, it had been accomplished under great difficulty and annoyance, for three of our teachers had died in the meantime. A person who has not studied German can form no idea of what a perplexing language it is.

Surely there is not another language that is so slip-shod and systemless, and so slippery and elusive to the grasp. One is washed about in it, hither and hither, in the most helpless way; and when at last he thinks he has captured a rule which offers firm ground to take a rest on amid the general rage and turmoil of the ten parts of speech, he turns over the page and reads, "Let the pupil make careful note of the following *exceptions*." He runs his eye down and finds that there are more exceptions to the rule than instances of it. So overboard he goes again, to hunt for another Ararat and find another quicksand. Such has been, and continues to be, my experience. Every time I think I have got one of these four confusing "cases" where I am master of it, a seemingly insignificant preposition intrudes itself into my sentence, clothed with an awful and unsuspected power, and crumbles the ground from under me. For instance, my book inquires after a certain bird – (it is always inquiring after things which are of no sort of consequence to anybody): "Where is the bird?" Now the answer to this question, – according to the book, – is that the bird is waiting in the blacksmith shop on account of the rain. Of course no bird would do that, but then you must stick to the book. Very well, I begin to cipher out the German for that answer. I begin at the wrong end, necessarily, for that is the German idea. I say to myself, "*Regen*, (rain,) is masculine – or maybe it is feminine – or possibly neuter – it is too much trouble to look, now. Therefore, it is either *der* (the) Regen, or *die* (the) Regen, or *das* (the) Regen, according to which gender it may turn out to be when I look. In the interest of science, I will cipher it out, on the hypothesis that it is masculine. Very well – then *the* rain is *der* Regen, if it is simply in the quiescent state of being *mentioned*, without enlargement or discussion – Nominative case; but if this rain is lying around, in a kind of a general way on the ground, it is then definitely located, it is *doing some thing* – that is, *resting*, (which is one of the German grammar's ideas of doing some thing,) and this throws the rain into the Dative case, and makes it *dem* Regen. However, this rain is not resting, but is doing some thing *actively*, – it is falling, – to interfere with the bird, likely, – and this indicates *movement*, which has the effect of sliding it into the Accusative case and changing *dem* Regen into *den* Regen." Having completed the grammatical horoscope of this matter, I answer up confidently and state in German that the bird is staying in the blacksmith shop "wegen (on account of) *den*

Regen." Then the teacher lets me softly down with the remark that whenever the word "wegen" drops into a sentence, it *always* throws that subject into the *Genitive* case, regardless of consequences – and that therefore this bird staid in the blacksmith shop "wegen *des* Regens."

N. B. I was informed, later, by a higher authority, that there was an "exception" which permits one to say "wegen *den* Regen" in certain peculiar and complex circumstances, but that this exception is not extended to anything *but* rain.

There are ten parts of speech, and they are all troublesome. An average sentence, in a German newspaper, is a sublime and impressive curiosity; it occupies a quarter of a column; it contains all the ten parts of speech – not in regular order, but mixed; it is built mainly of compound words constructed by the writer on the spot, and not to be found in any dictionary – six or seven words compacted into one, without joint or seam – that is, without hyphens; it treats of fourteen or fifteen different subjects, each enclosed in a parenthesis of its own, with here and there extra parentheses which re-enclose three or four of the minor parentheses, making pens within pens; finally, all the parentheses and re-parentheses are massed together between a couple of king-parentheses, one of which is placed in the first line of the majestic sentence and the other in the middle of the last line of it – *after which comes the* VERB, and you find out for the first time what the man has been talking about; and after the verb – merely by way of ornament, as far as I can make out, – the writer shovels in "*haben sind gewesen gehabt haben geworden sein*," or words to that effect, and the monument is finished. I suppose that this closing hurrah is in the nature of the flourish to a man's signature – not necessary, but pretty. German books are easy enough to read when you hold them before the looking-glass or stand on your head, – so as to reverse the construction, – but I think that to learn to read and understand a German newspaper is a thing which must always remain an impossibility to a foreigner.

Yet even the German books are not entirely free from attacks of the Parenthesis distemper – though they are usually so mild as to cover only a few lines, and therefore when you at last get down to the verb it carries some meaning to your mind because you are able to remember a good deal of what has gone before.

Now here is a sentence from a popular and excellent German novel, – with a slight parenthesis in it. I will make a perfectly literal translation, and throw in the parenthesis-marks and some hyphens for the assistance of the reader, – though in the original there are no parenthesis-marks or hyphens, and the reader is left to flounder through to the remote verb the best way he can:

"But when he, upon the street, the (in-satin-and-silk-covered-now-very-unconstrainedly-after-the-newest-fashion-dressed) government counsellor's wife *met*," etc., etc.*

That is from "The Old Mamselle's Secret," by Mrs. Marlitt. And that sentence is constructed upon the most approved German model. You observe how far that verb is from the reader's base of operations; well, in a German newspaper they put their verb away over on the next page; and I have heard that sometimes after stringing along on exciting preliminaries and parentheses for a column or two, they get in a hurry and have to go to press without getting to the verb at all. Of course, then, the reader is left in a very exhausted and ignorant state.

We have the Parenthesis disease in our literature, too; and one may see cases of it every day in our books and newspapers: but with us it is the mark and sign of an unpracticed writer or a cloudy intellect, whereas with the Germans it is doubtless the mark and sign of a practiced pen and of the presence of that sort of luminous intellectual fog which stands for clearness among these people. For surely it is *not* clearness, – it necessarily can't be clearness. Even a jury would have penetration enough to discover that. A writer's ideas must be a good deal confused, a good deal out of line and sequence, when he starts out to say that a man met a counsellor's wife in the street, and then right in the midst of this so simple undertaking halts these approaching people and makes them stand still until he jots down an inventory of the woman's dress. That is manifestly absurd. It reminds a person of those dentists who secure your instant and breathless interest in a tooth by taking a grip on it with the forceps, and then stand there and drawl through a tedious anecdote before they give the dreaded jerk. Parentheses in literature and dentistry are in bad taste.

The Germans have another kind of parenthesis, which they make by splitting a verb in two and putting half of it at the beginning of an exciting chapter and the *other half* at the end of it. Can any one conceive of anything more confusing than that? These things are called "separable verbs." The German grammar is blistered all over with separable verbs; and the wider the two portions of one of them are

* "Wenn er aber auf der Strasse der in Sammt und Seide gehüllten jetz sehr ungenirt nach der neusten mode gekleideten Regierungsrathin begegnet."

spread apart, the better the author of the crime is pleased with his performance. A favorite one is *reiste ab*, – which means, *departed*. Here is an example which I culled from a novel and reduced to English:

"The trunks being now ready, he DE- after kissing his mother and sisters, and once more pressing to his bosom his adored Gretchen, who, dressed in simple white muslin, with a single tube-rose in the ample folds of her rich brown hair, had tottered feebly down the stairs, still pale from the terror and excitement of the past evening, but longing to lay her poor aching head yet once again upon the breast of him whom she loved more dearly than life itself, PARTED."

However, it is not well to dwell too much on the separable verbs. One is sure to lose his temper early; and if he sticks to the subject, and will not be warned, it will at last either soften his brain or petrify it. Personal pronouns and adjectives are a fruitful nuisance in this language, and should have been left out. For instance, the same sound, *sie*, means *you*, and it means *she*, and it means *her*, and it means *it*, and it means *they*, and it means *them*. Think of the ragged poverty of a language which has to make one word do the work of six, – and a poor little weak thing of only three letters at that. But mainly, think of the exasperation of never knowing which of these meanings the speaker is trying to convey. This explains why, whenever a person says *sie* to me, I generally try to kill him, if a stranger.

Now observe the Adjective. Here was a case where simplicity would have been an advantage; therefore, for no other reason, the inventor of this language complicated it all he could. When we wish to speak of our "good friend or friends," in our enlightened tongue, we stick to the one form and have no trouble or hard feeling about it; but with the German tongue it is different. When a German gets his hands on an adjective, he declines it, and keeps on declining it until the common sense is all declined out of it. It is as bad as Latin. He says, for instance:

SINGULAR

Nominative – Mein gut*er* Freund, my good friend.
Genitive – Mein*es* gut*en* Freund*es*, of my good friend.
Dative – Mein*em* gut*en* Freund, to my good friend.
Accusative – Mein*en* gut*en* Freund, my good friend.

PLURAL

N. – Mein*e* gut*en* Freund*e*, my good friends.
G. – Mein*er* gut*en* Freund*e*, of my good friends.

D. – Mein*en* gut*en* Freund*en*, to my good friends.
A. – Mein*e* gut*en* Freund*e*, my good friends.

Now let the candidate for the asylum try to memorize those variations, and see how soon he will be elected. One might better go without friends in Germany than take all this trouble about them. I have shown what a bother it is to decline a good (male) friend; well, this is only a third of the work, for there is a variety of new distortions of the adjective to be learned when the object is feminine, and still another when the object is neuter. Now there are more adjectives in this language than there are black cats in Switzerland, and they must all be as elaborately declined as the examples above suggested. Difficult? – troublesome? – these words cannot describe it. I heard a Californian student in Heidelberg, say, in one of his calmest moods, that he would rather decline two drinks than one German adjective.

The inventor of the language seems to have taken pleasure in complicating it in every way he could think of. For instance, if one is casually referring to a house, *Haus*, or a horse, *Pferd*, or a dog, *Hund*, he spells these words as I have indicated; but if he is referring to them in the Dative case, he sticks on a foolish and unnecessary *e* and spells them Hause, Pferde, Hunde. So, as an added *e* often signifies the plural, as the *s* does with us, the new student is likely to go on for a month making twins out of a Dative dog before he discovers his mistake; and on the other hand, many a new student who could ill afford loss, has bought and paid for two dogs and only got one of them, because he ignorantly bought that dog in the Dative singular when he really supposed he was talking plural, – which left the law on the seller's side, of course, by the strict rules of grammar, and therefore a suit for recovery could not lie.

In German, all the Nouns begin with a capital letter. Now that is a good idea; and a good idea, in this language, is necessarily conspicuous from its lonesomeness. I consider this capitalizing of nouns a good idea, because by reason of it you are almost always able to tell a noun the minute you see it. You fall into error occasionally, because you mistake the name of a person for the name of a thing, and waste a good deal of time trying to dig a meaning out of it. German names almost always do mean some thing, and this helps to deceive the student. I translated a passage one day, which said that "the infuriated tigress broke loose and utterly ate up the unfortunate fir-forest," (*Tannenwald.*) When I was girding up my loins to doubt this, I found out that Tannenwald, in this instance, was a man's name.

Every noun has a gender, and there is no sense or system in the distribution; so the gender of each must be learned separately and by heart. There is no other way. To do this, one has to have a memory like a memorandum-book. In German, a young lady has no sex, while a turnip has. Think what overwrought reverence that shows for the turnip, and what callous disrespect for the girl. See how it looks in print – I translate this from a conversation in one of the best of the German Sunday School books:

GRETCHEN. Wilhelm, where is the turnip?
WILHELM. She has gone to the kitchen.
GRETCHEN. Where is the accomplished and beautiful English maiden?
WILHELM. It has gone to the opera.

To continue with the German genders: a tree is male, its buds are female, its leaves are neuter; horses are sexless, dogs are male, cats are female, – Tom-cats included, of course; a person's mouth, neck, bosom, elbows, fingers, nails, feet, and body, are of the male sex, and his head is male or neuter according to the word selected to signify it, and *not* according to the sex of the individual who wears it, – for in Germany all the women wear either male heads or sexless ones; a person's nose, lips, shoulders, breast, hands, hips, and toes are of the female sex; and his hair, ears, eyes, chin, legs, knees, heart, and conscience, haven't any sex at all. The inventor of the language probably got what he knew about a conscience from hearsay.

Now, by the above dissection, the reader will see that in Germany a man may *think* he is a man, but when he comes to look into the matter closely, he is bound to have his doubts; he finds that in sober truth he is a most ridiculous mixture; and if he ends by trying to comfort himself with the thought that he can at least depend on a third of this mess as being manly and masculine, the humiliating second thought will quickly remind him that in this respect he is no better off than any woman or cow in the land.

In the German it is true that by some oversight of the inventor of the language, a Woman is a female; but a Wife, (*Weib*,) is not, – which is unfortunate. A Wife, here, has no sex; she is neuter; so, according to the grammar, a fish is *he*, his scales are *she*, but a fishwife is neither. To describe a wife as sexless, may be called under-description; that is bad enough, but over-description is surely worse. A German speaks of an Englishman as the *Engländer*; to change the sex, he adds *inn*, and that stands for Englishwoman, – *Engländerinn*. That seems descriptive enough, but still it is not exact enough for a German; so he precedes the word with that article which indicates that the creature to follow is feminine, and writes it down thus: "*die* Englander*inn*," – which means "the *she-Englishwoman*." I consider that that person is over-described.

Well, after the student has learned the sex of a great number of nouns, he is still in a difficulty, because he finds it impossible to persuade his tongue to refer to things as "*he*" and "*she*," and "*him*" and "*her*," which it has been always accustomed to refer to as "*it*." When he even frames a German sentence in his mind, with the hims and hers in the right places, and then works up his courage to the utterance-point, it is no use, – the moment he begins to speak his tongue flies the track and all those labored males and females come out as "*its*." And even when he is reading German to himself, he always calls those things "*it*;" whereas he ought to read in this way:

TALE OF THE FISHWIFE AND ITS SAD FATE*

It is a bleak Day. Hear the Rain, how he pours, and the Hail, how he rattles; and see the Snow, how he drifts along, and oh the Mud, how deep he is! Ah the poor Fishwife, it is stuck fast in the Mire; it has dropped its Basket of Fishes; and its Hands have been cut by the Scales as it seized some of the falling Creatures; and one Scale has even got into its Eye, and it cannot get her out. It opens its Mouth to cry for Help; but if any Sound comes out of him, alas he is drowned by the raging of the Storm. And now a Tom-cat has got one of the Fishes and she will surely escape with him. No, she bites off a Fin, she holds her in her Mouth, – will she swallow her? No, the Fishwife's brave Mother-Dog deserts his Puppies and rescues the Fin, – which he eats, himself, as his Reward. O, horror, the Lightning has struck the Fishbasket; he sets him on Fire; see the Flame, how she licks the doomed Utensil with her red and angry

*I capitalize the nouns, in the German (and ancient English) fashion.

Tongue; now she attacks the helpless Fishwife's Foot, – she burns him up, all but the big Toe, and even *she* is partly consumed; and still she spreads, still she waves her fiery Tongues; she attacks the Fishwife's Leg and destroys *it*; she attacks its Hand and destroys *her*; she attacks its poor worn Garment and destroys *her* also; she attacks its Body and consumes *him*; she wreathes herself about its Heart and *it* is consumed; next about its Breast, and in a Moment *she* is a Cinder; now she reaches its Neck, – *he* goes; now its Chin, – *it* goes; now its Nose, – *she* goes. In another Moment, except Help come, the Fishwife will be no more. Time presses, – is there none to succor and save? Yes! Joy, joy, with flying Feet the she-Englishwoman comes! But alas, the generous she-Female is too late: where now is the fated Fishwife? It has ceased from its Sufferings, it has gone to a better Land; all that is left of it for its loved Ones to lament over, is this poor smouldering Ash-heap. Ah, woful, woful Ash-heap! Let us take him up tenderly, reverently, upon the lowly Shovel, and bear him to his long Rest, with the Prayer that when he rises again it will be in a Realm where he will have one good square responsible Sex, and have it all to himself, instead of having a mangy lot of assorted Sexes scattered all over him in Spots.

There, now, the reader can see for himself that this pronoun-business is a very awkward thing for the unaccustomed tongue.

I suppose that in all languages the similarities of look and sound between words which have no similarity in meaning are a fruitful source of perplexity to the foreigner. It is so in our tongue, and it is notably the case in the German. Now there is that troublesome word *vermählt:* to me it has so close a resemblance, – either real or fancied, – to three or four other words, that I never know whether it means despised, painted, suspected, or married; until I look in the dictionary, and then I find it means the latter. There are lots of such words, and they are a great torment. To increase the difficulty there are words which *seem* to resemble each other, and yet do not; but they make just as much trouble as if they did. For instance, there is the word *vermiethen*, (to let, to lease, to hire); and the word *verheirathen*, (another way of saying to *marry*.) I heard of an Englishman who knocked at a man's door in Heidelberg and proposed, in the best German he could command, to "verheirathen" that house. Then there are some words which mean one thing when you emphasize the first syllable, but mean something very different if you throw the emphasis on the last syllable. For instance, there is a word which means a runaway, or the act of glancing through a book, according to the placing of the emphasis; and another word which signifies to *associate* with a man, or to *avoid* him, according to where you put the emphasis, – and you can generally depend on putting it in the wrong place and getting into trouble.

There are some exceedingly useful words in this language. *Schlag*, for example; and *Zug*. There are three-quarters of a column of Schlags in the dictionary; and a column and a half of Zugs. The word Schlag means Blow, Stroke, Dash, Hit, Shock, Clap, Slap, Time, Bar, Coin, Stamp, Kind, Sort, Manner, Way, Apoplexy, Wood-Cutting, Enclosure, Field, Forest-Clearing. This is its simple and *exact* meaning, – that is to say, its restricted, its fettered meaning; but there are ways by which you can set it free, so that it can soar away, as on the wings of the morning, and never be at rest. You can hang any word you please to its tail, and make it mean any thing you want to. You can begin with *Schlag-ader*, which means artery, and you can hang on the whole dictionary, word by word, clear through the alphabet to *Schlag-wasser*, which means bilge-water, – and including *Schlagmutter*, which means mother-in-law.

Just the same with *Zug*. Strictly speaking, Zug means Pull, Tug, Draught, Procession, March, Progress, Flight, Direction, Expedition, Train, Caravan, Passage, Stroke, Touch, Line, Flourish, Trait of Character, Feature, Lineament, Chess-move, Organ-stop, Team, Whiff, Bias, Drawer, Propensity, Inhalation, Disposition: but that thing which it does *not* mean, – when all its legitimate pendants have been hung on, has not been discovered yet.

One cannot over-estimate the usefulness of Schlag and Zug. Armed just with these two, and the word *Also*, what cannot the foreigner on German soil accomplish? The German word *Also* is the equivalent of the English phrase "You know," and does not mean any thing at all, – in *talk*, though it sometimes does in print. Every time a German opens his mouth an *Also* falls out; and every time he shuts it he bites one in two that was trying to *get* out.

Now, the foreigner, equipped with these three noble words, is master of the situation. Let him talk right along, fearlessly; let him pour his indifferent German forth, and when he lacks for a word, let him heave a *Schlag* into the vacuum; all the chances are, that it fits it like a plug; but if it doesn't, let him promptly heave a *Zug* after it; the two together can hardly fail to bung the hole; but if, by a miracle, they *should* fail, let him simply say *Also!* and this will give him a moment's chance to think of the needful word. In Germany, when you load your conversational gun it is always best to throw in a *Schlag* or two and a *Zug* or two; because it doesn't make any difference how much the rest of the charge may scatter, you are bound to bag something with *them*. Then you blandly say *Also*, and load up again. Nothing gives such an air of grace and elegance and unconstraint to a German or an English conversation as to scatter it full of "Also's" or "You-knows."

In my notebook I find this entry:

> *July* 1. – In the hospital, yesterday, a word of thirteen syllables was successfully removed from a patient, – a North-German from near Hamburg; but as most unfortunately the surgeons had opened him in the wrong place, under the impression that he contained a panorama, he died. The sad event has cast a gloom over the whole community.

That paragraph furnishes a text for a few remarks about one of the most curious and notable features of my subject, – the length of German words. Some German words are so long that they have a perspective. Observe these examples:

Freundschaftsbezeigungen.
Dilletantenaufdringlichkeiten.
Stadtverordnetenversammlungen.

These things are not words, they are alphabetical processions. And they are not rare; one can open a German newspaper any time and see them marching majestically across the page, – and if he has any imagination he can see the banners and hear the music, too. They impart a martial thrill to the meekest subject. I take a great interest in these curiosities. Whenever I come across a good one, I stuff it and put it in my museum. In this way I have made quite a valuable collection. When I get duplicates, I exchange with other collectors, and thus increase the variety of my stock. Here are some specimens which I lately bought at an auction sale of the effects of a bankrupt bric-a-brac hunter:

GENERALSTAATSVERORDNETENVERSAMMLUNGEN.
ALTERTHUMSWISSENSCHAFTEN.
KINDERBEWAHRUNGSANSTALTEN.
UNABHAENGIGKEITSERKLAERUNGEN.

WIEDERHERSTELLUNGSBESTREBUNGEN.
WAFFENSTILLSTANDSUNTERHANDLUNGEN.

Of course when one of these grand mountain ranges goes stretching across the printed page, it adorns and ennobles that literary landscape, – but at the same time it is a great distress to the new student, for it blocks up his way; he cannot crawl under it, or climb over it or tunnel through it. So he resorts to the dictionary for help; but there is no help there. The dictionary must draw the line somewhere, – so it leaves this sort of words out. And it is right, because these long things are hardly legitimate words, but are rather combinations of words, and the inventor of them ought to have been killed. They are compound words, with the hyphens left out. The various words used in building them are in the dictionary, but in a very scattered condition; so you can hunt the materials out, one by one, and get at the meaning at last, but it is a tedious and harassing business. I have tried this process upon some of the above examples. "Freundschaftsbezeigungen" seems to be "Friendship demonstrations," which is only a foolish and clumsy way of saying "demonstrations of friendship." "Unabhaengigkeitserklaerungen" seems to be "Independencedeclarations," which is no improvement upon "Declarations of Independence," as far as I can see. "Generalstaatsverordnetenversammlungen" seems to be "Generalstatesrepresentativesmeetings," as nearly as I can get at it, – a mere rhythmical, gushy euphuism for "meetings of the legislature," I judge. We used to have a good deal of this sort of crime in our literature, but it has gone out, now. We used to speak of a thing as a "never-to-be-forgotten" circumstance, instead of cramping it into the simple and sufficient word "memorable" and then going calmly about our business as if nothing had happened. In those days we were not content to embalm the thing and bury it decently, we wanted to build a monument over it.

But in our newspapers the compounding-disease lingers a little to the present day, but with the hyphens left out, in the German fashion. This is the shape it takes: instead of saying "Mr. Simmons, clerk of the county and district courts, was in town yesterday," the new form puts it thus: "Clerk of the County and District Court Simmons was in town yesterday." This saves neither time nor ink, and has an awkward sound besides. One often sees a remark like this in our papers: "*Mrs.* Assistant District Attorney Johnson returned to her city residence yesterday for the season." That is a case of really unjustifiable compounding; because it not only saves no time or trouble, but confers a title on Mrs. Johnson which she has no right to. But these little instances are trifles indeed, contrasted with the ponderous and dismal German system of piling jumbled compounds together. I wish to submit the following local item, from a Mannheim journal, by way of illustration:

"In the daybeforeyesterdayshortlyaftereleveno'clock Night, the inthistownstandingtavern called 'The Wagoner' was downburnt. When the fire to the onthedownburninghouseresting Stork's Nest reached, flew the parent Storks away. But when the bytheraging, firesurrounded Nest *itself* caught Fire, straightway plunged the quickreturning Mother-Stork into the Flames and died, her Wings over her young ones outspread."

Even the cumbersome German construction is not able to take the pathos out of that picture, – indeed it somehow seems to strengthen it. This item is dated away back yonder months ago. I could have used it sooner, but I was waiting to hear from the Father-Stork. I am still waiting.

"*Also!*" If I have not shown that the German is a difficult language, I have at least intended to do it. I have heard of an American student who was asked how he was getting along with his German, and who answered promptly: "I am not getting along at all. I have worked at it hard for three level months, and all I have got to show for it is one solitary German phrase, – '*Zwei glas,*'" (two glasses of beer.) He paused a moment, reflectively, then added with feeling, "But I've got that *solid!*"

And if I have not also shown that German is a harassing and infuriating study, my execution has been at fault, and not my intent. I heard lately of a worn and sorely tried American student who used to fly to a certain German word for relief when he could bear up under his aggravations no longer, – the only word in the whole language whose sound was sweet and precious to his ear and healing to his lacerated spirit. This was the word *Damit.* It was only the *sound* that helped him, not the meaning;* and so, at last, when he learned that the emphasis was not on the first syllable, his only stay and support was gone, and he faded away and died.

I think that a description of any loud, stirring, tumultuous episode must be tamer in German than in English. Our descriptive words of this character have such a deep, strong, resonant sound, while their German equivalents do seem so thin and mild and

*It merely means, in its general sense, "herewith."

energyless. Boom, burst, crash, roar, storm, bellow, blow, thunder, explosion; howl, cry, shout, yell, groan; battle, hell. These are magnificent words; they have a force and magnitude of sound befitting the things which they describe. But their German equivalents would be ever so nice to sing the children to sleep with, or else my awe-inspiring ears were made for display and not for superior usefulness in analyzing sounds. Would any man want to die in a battle which was called by so tame a term as a *Schlacht?* Or would not a consumptive feel too much bundled up, who was about to go out, in a shirt collar and a seal ring, into a storm which the bird-song word *Gewitter* was employed to describe? And observe the strongest of the several German equivalents for explosion, – *Ausbruch.* Our word Toothbrush is more powerful than that. It seems to me that the Germans could do worse than import it into their language to describe particularly tremendous explosions with. The German word for hell, – Hölle, – sounds more like *helly* than anything else; therefore, how necessarily chipper, frivolous and unimpressive it is. If a man were told in German to go there, could he really rise to the dignity of feeling insulted?

Having now pointed out, in detail, the several vices of this language, I now come to the brief and pleasant task of pointing out its virtues. The capitalizing of the nouns, I have already mentioned. But far before this virtue stands another, – that of spelling a word according to the sound of it. After one short lesson in the alphabet, the student can tell how any German word is pronounced, without having to ask; whereas in our language if a student should inquire of us "What does B, O, W, spell?" we should be obliged to reply, "Nobody can tell what it spells, when you set it off by itself, – you can only tell by referring to the context and finding out what it signifies, – whether it is a thing to shoot arrows with, or a nod of one's head, or the forward end of a boat."

There are some German words which are singularly and powerfully effective. For instance, those which describe lowly, peaceful and affectionate home life; those which deal with love, in any and all forms, from mere kindly feeling and honest good-will toward the passing stranger, clear up to courtship; those which deal with outdoor Nature, in its softest and loveliest aspects, – with meadows, and forests, and birds and flowers, the fragrance and sunshine of summer, and the moonlight of peaceful winter nights; in a word, those which deal with any and all forms of rest, repose, and peace; those also which deal with the creatures and marvels of fairy-land; and lastly and chiefly, in those words which express pathos, is the language surpassingly rich and effective. There are German songs which can make a stranger to the language cry. That shows that the *sound* of the words is correct, – it interprets the meanings with truth and with exactness; and so the ear is informed, and through the ear, the heart.

The Germans do not seem to be afraid to repeat a word when it is the right one. They repeat it several times, if they choose. That is wise. But in English when we have used a word a couple of times in a paragraph, we imagine we are growing tautological, and so we are weak enough to exchange it for some other word which only approximates exactness, to escape what we wrongly fancy is a greater blemish. Repetition may be bad, but surely inexactness is worse.

There are people in the world who will take a great deal of trouble to point out the faults in a religion or a language, and then go blandly about their business without suggesting any remedy. I am not that kind of a person. I have shown that the German language needs reforming. Very well, I am ready to reform it. At least I am ready to make the proper suggestions. Such a course as this might be immodest in another; but I have devoted upwards of nine full weeks, first and last, to a careful and critical study of this tongue, and thus have acquired a confidence in my ability to reform it which no mere superficial culture could have conferred upon me.

In the first place, I would leave out the Dative Case. It confuses the plurals; and besides, nobody ever knows when he is in the Dative Case, except he discover it by accident, – and then he does not know when or where it was that he got into it, or how long he has been in it, or how he is ever going to get out of it again. The Dative Case is but an ornamental folly, – it is better to discard it.

In the next place, I would move the Verb further up to the front. You may load up with ever so good a Verb, but I notice that you never really bring down a subject with it at the present German range, – you only cripple it. So I insist that this important part of speech should be brought forward to a position where it may be easily seen with the naked eye.

Thirdly, I would import some strong words from the English tongue, – to swear with, and also to use in describing all sorts of vigorous things in a vigorous way.*

* "*Verdammt*," and its variations and enlargements, are words which have plenty of meaning, but the *sounds* are so mild and ineffectual that German ladies can use them without sin. German ladies who could not be induced to commit a sin by any

Fourthly, I would reorganize the sexes, and distribute them according to the will of the Creator. This as a tribute of respect, if nothing else.

Fifthly, I would do away with those great long compounded words; or require the speaker to deliver them in sections, with intermissions for refreshments. To wholly do away with them would be best, for ideas are more easily received and digested when they come one at a time than when they come in bulk. Intellectual food is like any other; it is pleasanter and more beneficial to take it with a spoon than with a shovel.

Sixthly, I would require a speaker to stop when he is done, and not hang a string of those useless "haben sind gewesen gehabt haben geworden seins" to the end of his oration. This sort of gewgaws undignify a speech, instead of adding a grace. They are therefore an offense, and should be discarded.

Seventhly, I would discard the Parenthesis. Also the re-Parenthesis, the re-re-parenthesis, and the re-re-re-re-re-re-parentheses, and likewise the final wide-reaching all-enclosing King-parenthesis. I would require every individual, be he high or low, to unfold a plain straight-forward tale, or else coil it and sit on it and hold his peace. Infractions of this law should be punishable with death.

And eighthly and lastly, I would retain *Zug* and *Schlag*, with their pendants, and discard the rest of the vocabulary. This would simplify the language.

I have now named what I regard as the most necessary and important changes. These are perhaps all I could be expected to name for nothing; but there are other suggestions which I can and will make in case my proposed application shall result in my being formally employed by the government in the work of reforming the language.

My philological studies have satisfied me that a gifted person ought to learn English (barring spelling and pronouncing), in 30 hours, French in 30 days, and German in 30 years. It seems manifest, then, that the latter tongue ought to be trimmed down and repaired. If it is to remain as it is, it ought to be gently and reverently set aside among the dead languages, for only the dead have time to learn it.

---

persuasion or compulsion, promptly rip out one of these harmless little words when they tear their dresses or don't like the soup. It sounds about as wicked as our "My gracious." German ladies are constantly saying, "Ach! Gott!" "Mein Gott!" "Gott in Himmel!" "Herr Gott!" "Der Herr Jesus!" etc. They think our ladies have the same custom, perhaps, for I once heard a gentle and lovely old German lady say to a sweet young American girl, "The two languages arc so alike – how pleasant that is; we say 'Ach! Gott!' You say '*Goddam.*'"

A FOURTH OF JULY ORATION IN THE GERMAN TONGUE, DELIVERED AT A BANQUET OF THE ANGLO-AMERICAN CLUB OF STUDENTS BY THE AUTHOR OF THIS BOOK

Gentlemen: Since I arrived, a month ago, in this old wonderland, this vast garden of Germany, my English tongue has so often proved a useless piece of baggage to me, and so troublesome to carry around, in a country where they haven't the checking system for luggage, that I finally set to work, last week, and learned the German language. Also! Es freüt mich dass dies so ist, denn es muss, in ein hauptsächlich degree, höflich sein, dass man aüf ein occasion like this, sein Rede in die Sprache des Landes worin he boards, aüssprechen soll. Dafür habe ich, aüs reinische Verlegenheit, – no Vergangenheit, – no, I mean Höflichkeit, – aüs reinische Höflichkeit habe ich resolved to tackle this business in the German language, üm Gottes willen! Also! Sie müssen so freündlich sein, ünd verzeih mich die interlarding von ein oder zwei Englischer Worte, hie ünd da, denn ich finde dass die deütche is not a very copious language, and so when you've really got any thing to say, you've got to draw on a language that can stand the strain.

Wenn aber man kann nicht meinem Rede verstehen, so werde ich ihm später dasselbe übersetz, wenn er solche Dienst verlangen wollen haben werden sollen sein hätte. (I don't know what wollen haben werden sollen sein hätte means, but I notice they always put it at the end of a German sentence – merely for general literary gorgeousness, I suppose.)

This is a great and justly honored day, – a day which is worthy of the veneration in which it is held by the true patriots of all climes and nationalities, – a day which offers a fruitful theme for thought and speech; ünd meinem Freünde, – no, mein*en* Freüd*en*, – mein*es* Freünd*es*, – well, take your choice, they're all the same price; I don't know which one is right, – also! ich habe gehabt haben worden gewesen sein, as Goethe says, in his Paradise Lost, – ich, – ich, – that is to say, – ich, – but let us change cars.

Also! Die Anblick so viele Grossbrittanischer ünd Amerikanischer hier zusammengetroffen in Bruderliche concord, ist zwar a welcome and inspiriting spectacle. And what has moved you to it? Can the terse German tongue rise to the expression of this impulse? Is it Freündschaftsbezeigüngenstadtverordnetenversammlungenfamilieneigenhümlichkeiten Nein, o nein! This is a crisp and noble word, but it fails to pierce the marrow of the impulse which has gathered this friendly meeting and produced diese Anblick, – eine Anblick welche ist güt zu sehen, – güt für die Aügen in a foreign land and a far country, – eine Anblick solche als in die gewönliche Heidelberger phrase nennt man ein "schönes Aussicht!" Ja, freilich natürlich wahrscheinlich ebensowohl! Also! Die Aussicht auf dem Königstuhl mehr grösserer ist, aber geistlische sprechend nicht so schön, lob' Gott! Because sie sind hier zusammengetroffen, in Bruderlichem concord, ein grossen Tag zu feiern, whose high benefits were not for one land and one locality only, but have conferred a measure of good upon all lands that know liberty to-day, and love it. Hündert Jahre vorüber, waren die Engländer ünd die Amerikaner Feinde; aber heüte sind sie herzlichen Freünde, Gott sei Dank! May this good fellowship endure; may these banners here blended in amity, so remain; may they never any more wave over opposing hosts, or be stained with blood which was kindred, is kindred, and always will be kindred, until a line drawn upon a map shall be able to say, "*This* bars the ancestral blood from flowing in the veins of the descendant!"

From

LIFE ON THE MISSISSIPPI

1883

THE "BATON ROUGE."

CHAPTER I

THE RIVER AND ITS HISTORY

THE MISSISSIPPI IS well worth reading about. It is not a commonplace river, but on the contrary is in all ways remarkable. Considering the Missouri its main branch, it is the longest river in the world – four thousand three hundred miles. It seems safe to say that it is also the crookedest river in the world, since in one part of its journey it uses up one thousand three hundred miles to cover the same ground that the crow would fly over in six hundred and seventy-five. It discharges three times as much water as the St. Lawrence, twenty-five times as much as the Rhine, and three hundred and thirty-eight times as much as the Thames. No other river has so vast a drainage-basin: it draws its water supply from twenty-eight States and Territories; from Delaware, on the Atlantic seaboard, and from all the country between that and Idaho on the Pacific slope – a spread of forty-five degrees of longitude. The Mississippi receives and carries to the Gulf water from fifty-four subordinate rivers that are navigable by steamboats, and from some hundreds that are navigable by flats and keels. The area of its drainage-basin is as great as the combined areas of England, Wales, Scotland, Ireland, France, Spain, Portugal, Germany, Austria, Italy, and Turkey; and almost all this wide region is fertile; the Mississippi valley, proper, is exceptionally so.

It is a remarkable river in this: that instead of widening toward its mouth, it grows narrower; grows narrower and deeper. From the junction of the Ohio to a point half way down to the sea, the width averages a mile in high water: thence to the sea the width steadily diminishes, until, at the "Passes," above the mouth, it is but little over half a mile. At the junction of the Ohio the Mississippi's depth is eighty-seven feet; the depth increases gradually, reaching one hundred and twenty-nine just above the mouth.

The difference in rise and fall is also remarkable – not in the upper, but in the lower river. The rise is tolerably uniform down to Natchez (three hundred and sixty miles above the mouth) – about fifty feet. But at Bayou La Fourche the river rises only twenty-four feet; at New Orleans only fifteen, and just above the mouth only two and one half.

An article in the New Orleans "Times-Democrat," based upon reports of able engineers, states that the river annually empties four hundred and six million tons of mud into the Gulf of Mexico – which brings to mind Captain Marryat's rude name for the Mississippi – "the Great Sewer." This mud, solidified, would make a mass a mile square and two hundred and forty-one feet high.

The mud deposit gradually extends the land – but only gradually; it has extended it not quite a third of a mile in the two hundred years which have elapsed since the river took its place in history. The belief of the scientific people is, that the mouth used to be at Baton Rouge, where the hills cease, and that the two hundred miles of land between there and the Gulf was built by the river. This gives us the age of that piece of country, without any trouble at all – one hundred and twenty thousand years. Yet it is much the youthfulest batch of country that lies around there anywhere.

The Mississippi is remarkable in still another way – its disposition to make prodigious jumps by cutting through narrow necks of land, and thus straightening and shortening itself. More than once it has shortened itself thirty miles at a single jump! These cut-offs have had curious effects: they have thrown several river towns out into the rural districts, and built up sand-bars and forests in front of them. The town of Delta used to be three miles below Vicksburg: a recent cut-off has radically changed the position, and Delta is now *two miles above* Vicksburg.

Both of these river towns have been retired to the country by that cut-off. A cut-off plays havoc with boundary lines and jurisdictions: for instance, a man is living in the State of Mississippi to-day, a cut-off occurs to-night, and to-morrow the man finds himself and his land over on the other side of the river, within the boundaries and subject to the laws of the State of Louisiana! Such a thing, happening in the upper river in the old times, could have transferred a slave from Missouri to Illinois and made a free man of him.

The Mississippi does not alter its locality by cut-offs alone: it is always changing its habitat *bodily* – is always moving bodily *sidewise*. At Hard Times, La., the river is two miles west of the region it used to occupy. As a result, the original *site* of that settlement is not now in Louisiana at all, but on the other side of the river, in the State of Mississippi. *Nearly the whole of that one thousand three hundred miles of old Mississippi River which La Salle floated down in his canoes, two hundred years ago, is good solid dry ground now.* The river lies to the right of it, in places, and to the left of it in other places.

Although the Mississippi's mud builds land but slowly, down at the mouth, where the Gulf's billows interfere with its work, it builds fast enough in better protected regions higher up: for instance, Prophet's Island contained one thousand five hundred acres of land thirty years ago; since then the river has added seven hundred acres to it.

But enough of these examples of the mighty stream's eccentricities for the present – I will give a few more of them further along in the book.

Let us drop the Mississippi's physical history, and say a word about its historical history – so to speak. We can glance briefly at its slumberous first epoch in a couple of short chapters; at its second and wider-awake epoch in a couple more; at its flushest and widest-awake epoch in a good many succeeding chapters; and then talk about its comparatively tranquil present epoch in what shall be left of the book.

The world and the books are so accustomed to use, and over-use, the word "new" in connection with our country, that we early get and permanently retain the impression that there is nothing old about it. We do of course know that there are several comparatively old dates in American history, but the mere figures convey to our minds no just idea, no distinct realization, of the stretch of time which they represent. To say that De Soto, the first white man who ever saw the Mississippi River, saw it in 1542, is a remark which states a fact without interpreting it: it is something like giving the dimensions of a sunset by astronomical measurements, and cataloguing the colors by their scientific names; – as a result, you get the bald fact of the sunset, but you don't see the sunset. It would have been better to paint a picture of it.

The date 1542, standing by itself, means little or nothing to us; but when one groups a few neighboring historical dates and facts around it, he adds perspective and color, and then realizes that this is one of the American dates which is quite respectable for age.

For instance, when the Mississippi was first seen by a white man, less than a quarter of a century had elapsed since Francis I.'s defeat at Pavia; the death of Raphael; the death of Bayard, *sans peur et sans reproche;* the driving out of the Knights-Hospitallers from Rhodes by the Turks; and the placarding of the Ninety-Five Propositions, – the act which began the Reformation. When De Soto took his glimpse of the river, Ignatius Loyola was an obscure name; the order of the Jesuits was not yet a year old; Michael Angelo's paint was not yet dry on the Last Judgment in the Sistine Chapel; Mary Queen of Scots was not yet born, but would be before the year closed.

Catherine de Medici was a child; Elizabeth of England was not yet in her teens; Calvin, Benvenuto Cellini, and the Emperor Charles V. were at the top of their fame, and each was manufacturing history after his own peculiar fashion; Margaret of Navarre was writing the "Heptameron" and some religious books, – the first survives, the others are forgotten, wit and indelicacy being sometimes better literature-preservers than holiness; lax court morals and the absurd chivalry business were in full feather, and the joust and the tournament were the frequent pastime of titled fine gentlemen who could fight better than they could spell, while religion was the passion of their ladies, and the classifying their offspring into children of full rank and children by brevet their pastime. In fact, all around, religion was in a peculiarly blooming condition: the Council of Trent was being called; the Spanish Inquisition was roasting, and racking, and burning, with a free hand; elsewhere on the continent the nations were being persuaded to holy living by the sword and fire; in England, Henry VIII. had suppressed the monasteries, burnt Fisher and another bishop or two, and was getting his English reformation and his harem effectively started. When De Soto stood on the banks of the Mississippi, it was still two years before Luther's death; eleven years before the burning of Servetus; thirty years before the St. Bartholomew slaughter; Rabelais was not yet published; "Don Quixote" was not yet written; Shakespeare was not yet born; a hundred long years must still elapse before Englishmen would hear the name of Oliver Cromwell.

Unquestionably the discovery of the Mississippi is a datable fact which considerably mellows and modifies the shiny newness of our country, and gives her a most respectable outside-aspect of rustiness and antiquity.

De Soto merely glimpsed the river, then died and was buried in it by his priests and soldiers. One would expect the priests and the soldiers to multiply the river's dimensions by ten – the Spanish custom of the day – and thus move other adventurers to go at once and explore it. On the contrary, their narratives when they reached home, did not excite that amount of curiosity. The Mississippi was left unvisited by whites during a term of years which seems incredible in our energetic days. One may "sense" the interval to his mind, after a fashion, by dividing it up in this way: After De Soto glimpsed the river, a fraction short of a quarter of a century elapsed, and then Shakespeare was born; lived a trifle more than half a century, then died; and when he had been in his grave considerably more than half a century, the *second* white man saw the Mississippi. In our day we don't allow a hundred and thirty years to elapse between glimpses of a marvel. If some body should discover a creek in the county next to the one that the North Pole is in, Europe and America would start fifteen costly expeditions thither: one to explore the creek, and the other fourteen to hunt for each other.

For more than a hundred and fifty years there had been white settlements on our Atlantic coasts. These people were in intimate communication with the Indians: in the south the Spaniards were robbing, slaughtering, enslaving and converting them; higher up, the English were trading beads and blankets to them for a consideration, and throwing in civilization and whiskey, "for lagniappe"; and in Canada the French were schooling them in a rudimentary way, missionarying among them, and drawing whole populations of them at a time to Quebec, and later to Montreal, to buy furs of them. Necessarily, then, these various clusters of whites must have heard of the great river of the far west; and indeed, they did hear of it vaguely, – so vaguely and indefinitely, that its course, proportions, and locality were hardly even guessable. The mere mysteriousness of the matter ought to have fired curiosity and compelled exploration; but this did not occur. Apparently nobody happened to want such a river, nobody needed it, nobody was curious about it; so, for a century and a half the Mississippi remained out of the market and undisturbed. When De Soto found it, he was not hunting for a river, and had no present occasion for one; consequently he did not value it or even take any particular notice of it.

But at last La Salle the Frenchman conceived the idea of seeking out that river and exploring it. It always happens that when a man seizes upon a neglected and important idea, people inflamed with the same notion crop up all around. It happened so in this instance.

Naturally the question suggests itself, Why did these people want the river now when nobody had wanted it in the five preceding generations? Apparently it was because at this late day they thought they had discovered a way to make it useful; for it had come to be believed that the Mississippi emptied into the Gulf of California, and therefore afforded a short cut from Canada to China. Previously the supposition had been that it emptied into the Atlantic, or Sea of Virginia.

CHAPTER IV

THE BOYS' AMBITION

WHEN I WAS a boy, there was but one permanent ambition among my comrades in our village* on the west bank of the Mississippi River. That was, to be a steamboatman. We had transient ambitions of other sorts, but they were only transient. When a circus came and went, it left us all burning to become clowns; the first negro minstrel show that came to our section left us all suffering to try that kind of life; now and then we had a hope that if we lived and were good, God would permit us to be pirates. These ambitions faded out, each in its turn; but the ambition to be a steamboatman always remained.

Once a day a cheap, gaudy packet arrived upward from St. Louis, and another downward from Keokuk. Before these events, the day was glorious with expectancy; after them, the day was a dead and empty thing. Not only the boys, but the whole village, felt this. After all these years I can picture that old time to myself now, just as it was then: the white town drowsing in the sunshine of a summer's morning; the streets empty, or pretty nearly so; one or two clerks sitting in front of the Water Street stores, with their splint-bottomed chairs tilted back against the wall, chins on breasts, hats slouched over their faces, asleep – with shingle-shavings enough around to show what broke them down; a sow and a litter of pigs loafing along the sidewalk, doing a good business in watermelon rinds and seeds; two or three lonely little freight piles scattered about the "levee"; a pile of "skids" on the slope of the stone-paved wharf, and the fragrant town drunkard asleep in the shadow of them; two or three wood flats at the head of the wharf, but nobody to listen to the peaceful lapping of the wavelets against them; the great Mississippi, the majestic, the magnificent Mississippi, rolling its mile-wide tide along, shining in the sun; the dense forest away on the other side; the "point" above the town, and the "point" below, bounding the river-glimpse and turning it into a sort of sea, and withal a very still and brilliant and lonely one. Presently a film of dark smoke appears above one of those remote "points"; instantly a negro drayman, famous for his quick eye and prodigious voice, lifts up the cry, "S-t-e-a-m-boat a-comin'!" and the scene changes!

*Hannibal, Missouri.

The town drunkard stirs, the clerks wake up, a furious clatter of drays follows, every house and store pours out a human contribution, and all in a twinkling the dead town is alive and moving. Drays, carts, men, boys, all go hurrying from many quarters to a common centre, the wharf. Assembled there, the people fasten their eyes upon the coming boat as upon a wonder they are seeing for the first time. And the boat *is* rather a handsome sight, too. She is long and sharp and trim and pretty; she has two tall, fancy-topped chimneys, with a gilded device of some kind swung between them; a fanciful pilot-house, all glass and "gingerbread," perched on top of the "texas" deck behind them; the paddle-boxes are gorgeous with a picture or with gilded rays above the boat's name; the boiler deck, the hurricane deck, and the texas deck are fenced and ornamented with clean white railings; there is a flag gallantly flying from the jack-staff; the furnace doors are open and the fires glaring bravely; the upper decks are black with passengers; the captain stands by the big bell, calm, imposing, the envy of all; great volumes of the blackest smoke are rolling and tumbling out of the chimneys – a husbanded grandeur created with a bit of pitch pine just before arriving at a town; the crew are grouped on the forecastle; the broad stage is run far out over the port bow, and an envied deck-hand stands picturesquely on the end of it with a coil of rope in his hand; the pent steam is screaming through the gauge-cocks; the captain lifts his hand, a bell rings, the wheels stop; then they turn back, churning the water to foam, and the steamer is at rest. Then such a scramble as there is to get aboard, and to get ashore, and to take in freight and to discharge freight, all at one and the same time; and such a yelling and cursing as the mates facilitate it all with! Ten minutes later the steamer is under way again, with no flag on the jack-staff and no black smoke issuing from the chimneys. After ten more minutes the town is dead again, and the town drunkard asleep by the skids once more.

My father was a justice of the peace, and I supposed he possessed the power of life and death over all men and could hang anybody that offended him. This was distinction enough for me as a general thing; but the desire to be a steamboatman kept intruding, nevertheless. I first wanted to be a cabin-boy, so that I could come out with a white apron on and shake a table-cloth over the side, where all my old comrades could see me; later I thought I would rather be the deck-hand who stood on the end of the stage-plank with the coil of rope in his hand, because he was particularly conspicuous. But these were only day-dreams, – they were too heavenly to be contemplated as real possibilities. By and by one of our boys went away. He was not heard of for a long time. At last he turned up as apprentice engineer or "striker" on a steamboat. This thing shook the bottom out of all my Sunday School teachings. That boy had been notoriously worldly, and I just the reverse; yet he was exalted to this eminence, and I left in obscurity and misery. There was nothing generous about this fellow in his greatness. He would always manage to have a rusty bolt to scrub while his boat tarried at our town, and he would sit on the inside guard and scrub it, where we could all see him and envy him and loathe him. And whenever his boat was laid up he would come home and swell around the town in his blackest and greasiest clothes, so that nobody could help remembering that he was a steamboatman; and he used all sorts of steamboat technicalities in his talk, as if he were so used to them that he forgot common people could not understand them. He would speak of the "labboard" side of a horse in an easy, natural way that would make one wish he was dead. And he was always talking about "St. Looy" like an old citizen; he would refer casually to occasions when he "was coming down Fourth Street," or when he was "passing by the Planter's House," or when there was a fire and he took a turn on the brakes of "the old Big Missouri"; and then he would go on and lie about how many towns the size of ours were burned down there that day. Two or three of the boys had long been persons of consideration among us because they had been to St. Louis once and had a vague general knowledge of its wonders, but the day of their glory was over now. They lapsed into a humble silence, and learned to disappear when the ruthless "cub"-engineer approached. This fellow had money, too, and hair oil. Also an ignorant silver watch and a showy brass watch chain. He wore a leather belt and used no suspenders. If ever a youth was cordially admired and hated by his comrades, this one was. No girl could withstand his charms. He "cut out" every boy in the village. When his boat blew up at last, it diffused a tranquil contentment among us such as we had not known for months. But when he came home the next week, alive, renowned, and appeared in church all battered up and bandaged, a shining hero, stared at and wondered over by every body, it seemed to us that the partiality of Providence for an undeserving reptile had reached a point where it was open to criticism.

This creature's career could produce but one result, and it speedily followed. Boy after boy managed to get on the river. The minister's son became an engineer. The doctor's and the post-master's sons became "mud clerks"; the wholesale liquor dealer's son became a bar-keeper on a boat; four sons of the chief merchant, and two sons of the county judge, became pilots. Pilot was the grandest position of all. The pilot, even in those days of trivial wages, had a princely salary – from a hundred and fifty to two hundred and fifty dollars a month, and no board to pay. Two months of his wages would pay a preacher's salary for a year. Now some of us were left disconsolate. We could not get on the river – at least our parents would not let us.

So by and by I ran away. I said I never would come home again till I was a pilot and could come in glory. But somehow I could not manage it. I went meekly aboard a few of the boats that lay packed together like sardines at the long St. Louis wharf, and very humbly inquired for the pilots, but got only a cold shoulder and short words from mates and clerks. I had to make the best of this sort of treatment for the time being, but I had comforting day-dreams of a future when I should be a great and honored pilot, with plenty of money, and could kill some of these mates and clerks and pay for them.

CHAPTER V

I WANT TO BE A CUB-PILOT

MONTHS AFTERWARD THE hope within me struggled to a reluctant death, and I found myself without an ambition. But I was ashamed to go home. I was in Cincinnati, and I set to work to map out a new career. I had been reading about the recent exploration of the river Amazon by an expedition sent out by our government. It was said that the expedition, owing to difficulties, had not thoroughly explored a part of the country lying about the head-waters, some four thousand miles from the mouth of the river. It was only about fifteen hundred miles from Cincinnati to New Orleans, where I could doubtless get a ship. I had thirty dollars left; I would go and complete the exploration of the Amazon. This was all the thought I gave to the subject. I never was great in matters of detail. I packed my valise, and took passage on an ancient tub called the "Paul Jones," for New Orleans. For the sum of sixteen dollars I had the scarred and tarnished splendors of "her" main saloon principally to myself, for she was not a creature to attract the eye of wiser travelers.

When we presently got under way and went poking down the broad Ohio, I became a new being, and the subject of my own admiration. I was a traveler! A word never had tasted so good in my mouth before. I had an exultant sense of being bound for mysterious lands and distant climes which I never have felt in so uplifting a degree since. I was in such a glorified condition that all ignoble feelings departed out of me, and I was able to look down and pity the untraveled with a compassion that had hardly a trace of contempt in it. Still, when we stopped at villages and wood-yards, I could not help lolling carelessly upon the railings of the boiler deck to enjoy the envy of the country boys on the bank. If they did not seem to discover me, I presently sneezed to attract their attention, or moved to a position where they could not help seeing me. And as soon as I knew they saw me I gaped and stretched, and gave other signs of being mightily bored with traveling.

I kept my hat off all the time, and stayed where the wind and the sun could strike me, because I wanted to get the bronzed and weather-beaten look of an old traveler. Before the second day was half gone, I experienced a joy which filled me with the purest gratitude; for I saw that the skin had begun to blister and peel off my face and neck. I wished that the boys and girls at home could see me now.

We reached Louisville in time – at least the neighborhood of it. We stuck hard and fast on the rocks in the middle of the river, and lay there four days. I was now beginning to feel a strong sense of being a part of the boat's family, a sort of infant son to the captain and younger brother to the officers. There is no estimating the pride I took in this grandeur, or the affection that began to swell and grow in me for those people. I could not know how the lordly steamboatman scorns that sort of presumption in a mere landsman. I particularly longed to acquire the least trifle of notice from the big stormy mate, and I was on the alert for an opportunity to do him a service to that end. It came at last. The riotous pow-wow of setting a spar was going on down on the forecastle, and I went down there and stood around in the way – or mostly skipping out of it – till the mate suddenly roared a general order for somebody to bring him a capstan bar. I sprang to his side and said: "Tell me where it is – I'll fetch it!"

If a rag-picker had offered to do a diplomatic service for the Emperor of Russia, the monarch could not have been more astounded than the mate was. He even stopped swearing. He stood and stared down at me. It took him ten seconds to scrape his disjointed remains together again. Then he said impressively: "Well, if this don't beat hell!" and turned to his work with the air of a man who had been confronted with a problem too abstruse for solution.

I crept away, and courted solitude for the rest of the day. I did not go to dinner; I stayed away from supper until every body else had finished. I did not feel so much like a member of the boat's family now as before. However, my spirits returned, in instalments, as we pursued our way down the river. I was sorry I hated the mate so, because it was not in (young) human nature not to admire him. He was huge and muscular, his face was bearded and whiskered all over; he had a red woman and a blue woman tattooed on his right arm, – one on each side of a blue anchor with a red rope to it; and in the matter of profanity he was sublime. When he was getting out cargo at a landing, I was always where I could see and hear. He felt all the majesty of his great position, and made the world feel it, too. When he gave even the simplest order, he discharged it like a blast of lightning, and sent a long, reverberating peal of profanity thundering after it. I could not help contrasting the way in which the average landsman would give an order, with the mate's way of doing it. If the landsman should wish the gang-plank moved a foot farther forward, he would probably say: "James, or William, one of you push that plank forward, please"; but put the mate in his place, and he would roar out: "Here, now, start that gang-plank for'ard! Lively, now! *What*'re you about! Snatch it! *snatch* it! There! there! Aft again! aft again! Don't you hear me? Dash it to dash! are you going to *sleep* over it! *'Vast* heaving. 'Vast heaving, I tell you! Going to heave it clear astern? WHERE're you going with that barrel! *for'ard* with it 'fore I make you swallow it, you dash-dash-dash-*dashed* split between a tired mud-turtle and a crippled hearse-horse!"

I wished I could talk like that.

When the soreness of my adventure with the mate had somewhat worn off, I began timidly to make up to the humblest official connected with the boat – the night watchman. He snubbed my advances at first, but I presently ventured to offer him a new chalk pipe, and that softened him. So he allowed me to sit with him by the big bell on the hurricane deck, and in time he melted into conversation. He could not well have helped it, I hung with such homage on his words and so plainly showed that I felt honored by his notice. He told me the names of dim capes and shadowy islands as we glided by them in the solemnity of the night, under the winking stars, and by and by got to talking about himself. He seemed over-sentimental for a man whose salary was six dollars a week – or rather he might have seemed so to an older person than I. But I drank in his words hungrily, and with a faith that might have moved mountains if it had been applied judiciously. What was it to me that he was soiled and seedy and fragrant with gin? What was it to me that his grammar was bad, his construction worse, and his profanity so void of art that it was an element of weakness rather than strength in his conversation? He was a wronged man, a man who had seen trouble, and that was enough for me. As he mellowed into his plaintive history his tears dripped upon the lantern in his lap, and I cried, too, from sympathy. He said he was the son of an English nobleman – either an earl or an alderman, he could not remember which, but believed was both; his father, the nobleman, loved him, but his mother hated him from the cradle; and so while he was still a little boy he was sent to "one of them old, ancient colleges" – he couldn't remember which; and by and by his father died and his mother seized the property and "shook" him, as he phrased it. After his mother shook him, members of the nobility with whom he was acquainted used their influence to get him the position of "loblolly-boy in a ship"; and from that point my watchman threw off all trammels of date and locality and branched out into a narrative that bristled all along with incredible adventures; a narrative that was so reeking with bloodshed and so crammed with hair-breadth escapes and the most engaging and unconscious personal villainies, that I sat speechless, enjoying, shuddering, wondering, worshiping.

It was a sore blight to find out afterwards that he was a low, vulgar, ignorant, sentimental, half-witted humbug, an untraveled native of the wilds of Illinois, who had absorbed wild-cat literature and appropriated its marvels, until in time he had woven odds and ends of the mess into this yarn, and then gone on telling it to fledglings like me, until he had come to believe it himself.

CHAPTER VI

A CUB-PILOT'S EXPERIENCE

WHAT WITH LYING on the rocks four days at Louisville, and some other delays, the poor old "Paul Jones" fooled away about two weeks in making the voyage from Cincinnati to New Orleans. This gave me a chance to get acquainted with one of the pilots, and he taught me how to steer the boat, and thus made the fascination of river life more potent than ever for me.

It also gave me a chance to get acquainted with a youth who had taken deck passage – more's the pity; for he easily borrowed six dollars of me on a promise to return to the boat and pay it back to me the day after we should arrive. But he probably died or forgot, for he never came. It was doubtless the former, since he had said his parents were wealthy, and he only traveled deck passage because it was cooler.*

I soon discovered two things. One was that a vessel would not be likely to sail for the mouth of the Amazon under ten or twelve years; and the other was that the nine or ten dollars still left in my pocket would not suffice for so imposing an exploration as I had planned, even if I could afford to wait for a ship. Therefore it followed that I must contrive a new career. The "Paul Jones" was now bound for St. Louis. I planned a siege against my pilot, and at the end of three hard days he surrendered. He agreed to teach me the Mississippi River from New Orleans to St. Louis for five hundred dollars, payable out of the first wages I should receive after graduating. I entered upon the small enterprise of "learning" twelve or thirteen hundred miles of the great Mississippi River with the easy confidence of my time of life. If I had really known what I was about to require of my faculties, I should not have had the courage to begin. I supposed that all a pilot had to do was to keep his boat in the river, and I did not consider that that could be much of a trick, since it was so wide.

The boat backed out from New Orleans at four in the afternoon, and it was "our watch" until eight. Mr. Bixby, my chief, "straightened her up," plowed her along past the sterns of the other boats that lay at the Levee, and then said, "Here, take her; shave those steamships as close as you'd peel an apple." I took the wheel, and my heart-beat fluttered up into the hundreds; for it seemed to me that we were about to scrape the side off every ship in the line, we were so close. I held my breath and began to claw the boat away from the danger; and I had my own opinion of the pilot who had known no better than to get us into such peril, but I was too wise to express it. In half a minute I had a wide margin of safety intervening between the "Paul Jones" and the ships; and within ten seconds more I was set aside in disgrace, and Mr. Bixby was going into danger

* "Deck" passage – *i.e.*, steerage passage.

again and flaying me alive with abuse of my cowardice. I was stung, but I was obliged to admire the easy confidence with which my chief loafed from side to side of his wheel, and trimmed the ships so closely that disaster seemed ceaselessly imminent. When he had cooled a little he told me that the easy water was close ashore and the current outside, and therefore we must hug the bank, up stream, to get the benefit of the former, and stay well out, down stream, to take advantage of the latter. In my own mind I resolved to be a down-stream pilot and leave the up-streaming to people dead to prudence.

Now and then Mr. Bixby called my attention to certain things. Said he, "This is Six-Mile Point." I assented. It was pleasant enough information, but I could not see the bearing of it. I was not conscious that it was a matter of any interest to me. Another time he said, "This is Nine-Mile Point." Later he said, "This is Twelve-Mile Point." They were all about level with the water's edge; they all looked about alike to me; they were monotonously unpicturesque. I hoped Mr. Bixby would change the subject. But no; he would crowd up around a point, hugging the shore with affection, and then say: "The slack water ends here, abreast this bunch of China-trees; now we cross over." So he crossed over. He gave me the wheel once or twice, but I had no luck. I either came near chipping off the edge of a sugar plantation, or I yawed too far from shore, and so dropped back into disgrace again and got abused.

The watch was ended at last, and we took supper and went to bed. At midnight the glare of a lantern shone in my eyes, and the night watchman said: –

"Come! turn out!"

And then he left. I could not understand this extraordinary procedure; so I presently gave up trying to, and dozed off to sleep. Pretty soon the watchman was back again, and this time he was gruff. I was annoyed. I said: –

"What do you want to come bothering around here in the middle of the night for? Now as like as not I'll not get to sleep again to-night."

The watchman said: –

"Well, if this an't good, I'm blest."

The "off-watch" was just turning in, and I heard some brutal laughter from them, and such remarks as "Hello, watchman! an't the new cub turned out yet? He's delicate, likely. Give him some sugar in a rag and send for the chamber-maid to sing rock-a-by-baby to him."

About this time Mr. Bixby appeared on the scene. Something like a minute later I was climbing the pilot-house steps with some of my clothes on and the rest in my arms. Mr. Bixby was close behind, commenting. Here was something fresh – this thing of getting up in the middle of the night to go to work. It was a detail in piloting that had never occurred to me at all. I knew that boats ran all night, but somehow I had never happened to reflect that somebody had to get up out of a warm bed to run them. I began to fear that piloting was not quite so romantic as I had imagined it was; there was some thing very real and work-like about this new phase of it.

It was a rather dingy night, although a fair number of stars were out. The big mate was at the wheel, and he had the old tub pointed at a star and was holding her straight up the middle of the river. The shores on either hand were not much more than half a mile apart, but they seemed wonderfully far away and ever so vague and indistinct. The mate said: –

"We've got to land at Jones's plantation, sir."

The vengeful spirit in me exulted. I said to myself, I wish you joy of your job, Mr. Bixby; you'll have a good time finding Mr. Jones's plantation such a night as this; and I hope you never *will* find it as long as you live.

Mr. Bixby said to the mate: –

"Upper end of the plantation, or the lower?"

"Upper."

"I can't do it. The stumps there are out of water at this stage. It's no great distance to the lower, and you'll have to get along with that."

"All right, sir. If Jones don't like it he'll have to lump it, I reckon."

And then the mate left. My exultation began to cool and my wonder to come up. Here was a man who not only proposed to find this plantation on such a night, but to find either end of it you preferred. I dreadfully wanted to ask a question, but I was carrying about as many short answers as my cargo-room would admit of, so I held my peace. All I desired to ask Mr. Bixby was the simple question whether he was ass enough to really imagine he was going to find that plantation on a night when all plantations were exactly alike and all the same color. But I held in. I used to have fine inspirations of prudence in those days.

Mr. Bixby made for the shore and soon was scraping it, just the same as if it had been daylight. And not only that, but singing –

"Father in heaven, the day is declining," etc.

It seemed to me that I had put my life in the keeping of a peculiarly reckless outcast. Presently he turned on me and said: –

"What's the name of the first point above New Orleans?"

I was gratified to be able to answer promptly, and I did. I said I didn't know.

"Don't *know*?"

This manner jolted me. I was down at the foot again, in a moment. But I had to say just what I had said before.

"Well, you're a smart one," said Mr. Bixby. "What's the name of the *next* point?"

Once more I didn't know.

"Well, this beats any thing. Tell me the name of *any* point or place I told you."

I studied a while and decided that I couldn't.

"Look here! What do you start out from, above Twelve-Mile Point, to cross over?"

"I – I – don't know."

"You – you – don't know?" mimicking my drawling manner of speech. "What *do* you know?"

"I – I – nothing, for certain."

"By the great Cæsar's ghost, I believe you! You're the stupidest dunderhead I ever saw or ever heard of, so help me Moses! The idea of *you* being a pilot – *you*! Why, you don't know enough to pilot a cow down a lane."

Oh, but his wrath was up! He was a nervous man, and he shuffled from one side of his wheel to the other as if the floor was hot. He would boil a while to himself, and then overflow and scald me again.

"Look here! What do you suppose I told you the names of those points for?"

I tremblingly considered a moment, and then the devil of temptation provoked me to say: –

"Well – to – to – be entertaining, I thought."

This was a red rag to the bull. He raged and stormed so (he was crossing the river at the time) that I judge it made him blind, because he ran over the steering-oar of a trading-scow. Of course the traders sent up a volley of red-hot profanity. Never was a man so grateful as Mr. Bixby was: because he was brim full, and here were subjects who would *talk back*. He threw open a window, thrust his head out, and such an irruption followed as I never had heard before. The fainter and farther away the scowmen's curses drifted, the higher Mr. Bixby lifted his voice and the weightier his adjectives grew. When he closed the window he was empty. You could have drawn a seine through his system and not caught curses enough to disturb your mother with. Presently he said to me in the gentlest way: –

"My boy, you must get a little memorandum-book, and every time I tell you a thing, put it down right away. There's only one way to be a pilot, and that is to get this entire river by heart. You have to know it just like A B C."

That was a dismal revelation to me; for my memory was never loaded with any thing but blank cartridges. However, I did not feel discouraged long. I judged that it was best to make some allowances, for doubtless Mr. Bixby was "stretching." Presently he pulled a rope and struck a few strokes on the big bell. The stars were all gone now, and the night was as black as ink. I could hear the wheels churn along the bank, but I was not entirely certain that I could see the shore. The voice of the invisible watchman called up from the hurricane deck: –

"What's this, sir?"

"Jones's plantation."

I said to myself, I wish I might venture to offer a small bet that it isn't. But I did not chirp. I only waited to see. Mr. Bixby handled the engine bells, and in due time the boat's nose came to the land, a torch glowed from the forecastle, a man skipped ashore, a darky's voice on the bank said, "Gimme de k'yarpet-bag, Mars' Jones," and the next moment we were standing up the river again, all serene. I reflected deeply a while, and then said, – but not aloud, – Well, the finding of that plantation was the luckiest accident that ever happened; but it couldn't happen again in a hundred years. And I fully believed it *was* an accident, too.

By the time we had gone seven or eight hundred miles up the river, I had learned to be a tolerably plucky up-stream steersman, in daylight, and before we reached St. Louis I had made a trifle of progress in night-work, but only a trifle. I had a notebook that fairly bristled with the names of towns, "points," bars, islands, bends, reaches, etc.; but the information was to be found only in the notebook – none of it was in my head. It made my heart ache to think I had only got half of the river set down; for as our watch was four hours off and four hours on, day and night, there was a long four-hour gap in my book for every time I had slept since the voyage began.

My chief was presently hired to go on a big New Orleans boat, and I packed my satchel and went with him. She was a grand affair. When I stood in her pilot-house I was so far above the water that I seemed perched on a mountain; and her decks stretched so far away, fore and aft, below me, that I wondered how I could ever have considered the little "Paul Jones" a large craft. There were other differences, too. The "Paul Jones's" pilot-house was a cheap, dingy, battered rattle-trap, cramped for room: but here was a sumptuous glass temple; room enough to have a dance in; showy red and gold window curtains; an imposing sofa; leather cushions and a back to the high bench where visiting pilots sit, to spin yarns and "look at the river"; bright, fanciful "cuspadores" instead of a broad wooden box filled with sawdust; nice new oilcloth on the floor; a hospitable big stove for winter; a wheel as high as my head, costly with inlaid work; a wire tiller-rope; bright brass knobs for the bells; and a tidy, white-aproned, black "texas-tender," to bring up tarts and ices and coffee during mid-watch, day and night. Now this was "something like"; and so I began to take heart once more to believe that piloting was a romantic sort of occupation after all. The moment we were under way I began to prowl about the great steamer and fill myself with joy. She was as clean and as dainty as a drawing-room; when I looked down her long, gilded saloon, it was like gazing through a splendid tunnel; she had an oil-picture, by some gifted sign-painter, on every state-room door; she glittered with no end of prism-fringed chandeliers; the clerk's office was elegant, the bar was marvellous, and the bar-keeper had been barbered and upholstered at incredible cost. The boiler deck (*i.e.*, the second story of the boat, so to speak), was as spacious as a church, it seemed to me; so with the forecastle; and there was no pitiful handful of deck-hands, firemen, and roustabouts down there, but a whole battalion of men. The fires were fiercely glaring from a long row of furnaces, and over them were eight huge boilers! This was unutterable pomp. The mighty engines – but enough of this. I had never felt so fine before. And when I found that the regiment of natty servants respectfully "sir'd" me, my satisfaction was complete.

CHAPTER VII

A DARING DEED

WHEN I RETURNED to the pilot-house St. Louis was gone and I was lost. Here was a piece of river which was all down in my book, but I could make neither head nor tail of it: you understand, it was turned around. I had seen it when coming up stream, but I had never faced about to see how it looked when it was behind me. My heart broke again, for it was plain that I had got to learn this troublesome river *both ways*.

The pilot-house was full of pilots, going down to "look at the river." What is called the "upper river" (the two hundred miles between St. Louis and Cairo, where the Ohio comes in) was low; and the Mississippi changes its channel so constantly that the pilots used to always find it necessary to run down to Cairo to take a fresh look, when their boats were to lie in port a week; that is, when the water was at a low stage. A deal of this "looking at the river" was done by poor fellows who seldom had a berth, and whose only hope of getting one lay in their being always freshly posted and therefore ready to drop into the shoes of some reputable pilot, for a single trip, on account of such pilot's sudden illness, or some other necessity. And a good many of them constantly ran up and down inspecting the river, not because they ever really hoped to get a berth, but because (they being guests of the boat) it was cheaper to "look at the river" than stay ashore and pay board. In time these fellows grew dainty in their tastes, and only infested boats that had an established reputation for setting good tables. All visiting pilots were useful, for they were always ready and willing, winter or summer, night or day, to go out in the yawl and help buoy the channel or assist the boat's pilots in any way they could. They were likewise welcome because all pilots are tireless talkers, when gathered together, and as they talk only about the river they are always understood and are always interesting. Your true pilot cares nothing about anything on earth but the river, and his pride in his occupation surpasses the pride of kings.

We had a fine company of these river-inspectors along, this trip. There were eight or ten; and there was abundance of room for them in our great pilot-house. Two or three of them wore polished silk hats, elaborate shirt-fronts, diamond breast-pins, kid gloves, and patent-leather boots. They were choice in their English, and bore themselves with a dignity proper to men of solid means and prodigious reputation as pilots. The others were more or less loosely clad, and wore upon their heads tall felt cones that were suggestive of the days of the Commonwealth.

I was a cipher in this august company, and felt subdued, not to say torpid. I was not even of sufficient consequence to assist at the wheel when it was necessary to put the tiller hard down in a hurry; the guest that stood nearest did that when occasion required – and this was pretty much all the time, because of the crookedness of the channel and the scant water. I stood in a corner; and the talk I listened to took the hope all out of me. One visitor said to another: –

"Jim, how did you run Plum Point, coming up?"

"It was in the night, there, and I ran it the way one of the boys on the 'Diana' told me; started out about fifty yards above the wood pile on the false point, and held on the cabin under Plum Point till I raised the reef – quarter less twain – then straightened up for the middle bar till I got well abreast the old one-limbed cotton-wood in the bend, then got my stern on the cotton-wood and head on the low place above the point, and came through a-booming – nine and a half."

"Pretty square crossing, an't it?"

"Yes, but the upper bar's working down fast."

Another pilot spoke up and said: –

"I had better water than that, and ran it lower down; started out from the false point – mark twain – raised the second reef abreast the big snag in the bend, and had quarter less twain."

One of the gorgeous ones remarked: –

"I don't want to find fault with your leadsmen, but that's a good deal of water for Plum Point, it seems to me."

There was an approving nod all around as this quiet snub dropped on the boaster and "settled" him. And so they went on talk-talk-talking. Meantime, the thing that was running in my mind was, "Now if my ears hear aright, I have not only to get the names of all the towns and islands and bends, and so on, by heart, but I must even get up a warm personal acquaintanceship with every old snag and one-limbed cotton-wood and obscure wood pile that ornaments the banks of this river for twelve hundred miles; and more than that, I must actually know where these things are in the dark, unless these guests are gifted with eyes that can pierce through two miles of solid blackness; I wish the piloting business was in Jericho and I had never thought of it."

At dusk Mr. Bixby tapped the big bell three times (the signal to land), and the captain emerged from his drawing-room in the forward end of the texas, and looked up inquiringly. Mr. Bixby said: –

"We will lay up here all night, captain."

"Very well, sir."

That was all. The boat came to shore and was tied up for the night. It seemed to me a fine thing that the pilot could do as he pleased, without asking so grand a captain's permission. I took my supper and went immediately to bed, discouraged by my day's observations and experiences. My late voyage's note-booking was but a confusion of meaningless names. It had tangled me all up in a knot every time I had looked at it in the day time. I now hoped for respite in sleep; but no, it reveled all through my head till sunrise again, a frantic and tireless nightmare.

Next morning I felt pretty rusty and low-spirited. We went booming along, taking a good many chances, for we were anxious to "get out of the river" (as getting out to Cairo was called) before night should overtake us. But Mr. Bixby's partner, the other pilot, presently grounded the boat, and we lost so much time getting her off that it was plain the darkness would overtake us a good long way above the mouth. This was a great misfortune, especially to certain of our visiting pilots, whose boats would have to wait for their return, no matter how long that might be. It sobered the pilot-house talk a good deal. Coming up stream, pilots did not mind low water or any kind of darkness; nothing stopped them but fog. But downstream work was different; a boat was too nearly helpless, with a stiff current pushing behind her; so it was not customary to run down stream at night in low water.

There seemed to be one small hope, however: if we could get through the intricate and dangerous Hat Island crossing before night, we could venture the rest, for we would have plainer sailing and better water. But it would be insanity to attempt Hat Island at night. So there was a deal of looking at watches all the rest of the day, and a constant ciphering upon the speed we were making; Hat Island was the eternal subject; sometimes hope was high and sometimes we were delayed in a bad crossing, and down it went again. For hours all hands lay under the burden of this suppressed excitement; it was even communicated to me, and I got to feeling so solicitous about Hat Island, and under such an awful pressure of responsibility, that I wished I might have five minutes on shore to draw a good, full, relieving breath, and start over again. We were standing no regular watches. Each of our pilots ran such portions of the river as he had run when coming up stream, because of his greater familiarity with it; but both remained in the pilot-house constantly.

An hour before sunset, Mr. Bixby took the wheel and Mr. W—— stepped aside. For the next thirty minutes every man held his watch in his hand and was restless, silent, and uneasy. At last some body said, with a doomful sigh, –

"Well yonder's Hat Island – and we can't make it."

All the watches closed with a snap, every body sighed and muttered some thing about its being "too bad, too bad – ah, if we could *only* have got here half an hour sooner!" and the place was thick with the atmosphere of disappointment. Some started to go out, but loitered, hearing no bell-tap to land. The sun dipped behind the horizon, the boat went on. Inquiring looks passed from one guest to another; and one who had his hand on the door-knob and had turned it, waited, then presently took away his hand and let the knob turn back again. We bore steadily down the bend. More looks were exchanged, and nods of surprised admiration – but no words. Insensibly the men drew together behind Mr. Bixby, as the sky darkened and one or two dim stars came out. The dead silence and sense of waiting became oppressive. Mr. Bixby pulled the cord, and two deep, mellow notes from the big bell floated off on the night. Then a pause, and one more note was struck. The watchman's voice followed, from the hurricane deck: –

"Labboard lead, there! Stabboard lead!"

The cries of the leadsmen began to rise out of the distance, and were gruffly repeated by the word-passers on the hurricane deck.

"M-a-r-k three! . . . M-a-r-k three! . . . Quarter-less-three! . . . Half twain! . . . Quarter twain! . . . M-a-r-k twain! . . . Quarter-less—"

Mr. Bixby pulled two bell-ropes, and was answered by faint jinglings far below in the engine room, and our speed slackened. The steam began to whistle through the gauge-cocks. The cries of the leadsmen went on – and it is a weird sound, always, in the night. Every pilot in the lot was watching now, with fixed eyes, and talking under his breath. Nobody was calm and easy but Mr. Bixby. He would put his wheel down and stand on a spoke, and as the steamer swung into her (to me) utterly invisible marks – for we seemed to be in the midst of a wide and gloomy sea – he would meet and fasten her there. Out of the murmur of half-audible talk, one caught a coherent sentence now and then – such as:

"There; she's over the first reef all right!"

After a pause, another subdued voice: –

"Her stern's coming down just *exactly* right, by *George*!"

"Now she's in the marks; over she goes!"

Some body else muttered: –

"Oh, it was done beautiful – *beautiful*!"

Now the engines were stopped altogether, and we drifted with the current. Not that I could see the boat drift, for I could not, the stars being all gone by this time. This drifting was the dismalest work; it held one's heart still. Presently I discovered a blacker gloom than that which surrounded us. It was the head of the island. We were closing right down upon it. We entered its deeper shadow, and so imminent seemed the peril that I was likely to suffocate; and I had the strongest impulse to do *some thing*, any thing, to save the vessel. But still Mr. Bixby stood by his wheel, silent, intent as a cat, and all the pilots stood shoulder to shoulder at his back.

"She'll not make it!" some body whispered.

The water grew shoaler and shoaler, by the leadsman's cries, till it was down to –

"Eight-and-a-half! . . . E-i-g-h-t feet! . . . E-i-g-h-t feet! . . . Seven-and—"

Mr. Bixby said warningly through his speaking tube to the engineer: –

"Stand by, now!"

"Aye-aye, sir!"

"Seven-and-a-half! Seven feet! *Six*-and—"

We touched bottom! Instantly Mr. Bixby set a lot of bells ringing, shouted through the tube, "*Now*, let her have it – every ounce you've got!" then to his partner, "Put her hard down! snatch her! snatch her!" The boat rasped and ground her way through the sand, hung upon the apex of disaster a single tremendous instant, and then over she went! And such a shout as went up at Mr. Bixby's back never loosened the roof of a pilot-house before!

There was no more trouble after that. Mr. Bixby was a hero that night; and it was some little time, too, before his exploit ceased to be talked about by river men.

Fully to realize the marvellous precision required in laying the great steamer in her marks in that murky waste of water, one should know that not only must she pick her intricate way through snags and blind reefs, and then shave the head of the island so closely as to brush the overhanging foliage with her stern, but at one place she must pass almost within arm's reach of a sunken and invisible wreck that would snatch the hull timbers from under her if she should strike it, and destroy a quarter of a million dollars' worth of steamboat and cargo in five minutes, and maybe a hundred and fifty human lives into the bargain.

The last remark I heard that night was a compliment to Mr. Bixby, uttered in soliloquy and with unction by one of our guests. He said: –

"By the Shadow of Death, but he's a lightning pilot!"

CHAPTER VIII

PERPLEXING LESSONS

AT THE END of what seemed a tedious while, I had managed to pack my head full of islands, towns, bars, "points," and bends; and a curiously inanimate mass of lumber it was, too. However, inasmuch as I could shut my eyes and reel off a good long string of these names without leaving out more than ten miles of river in every fifty, I began to feel that I could take a boat down to New Orleans if I could make her skip those little gaps. But of course my complacency could hardly get start enough to lift my nose a trifle into the air, before Mr. Bixby would think of some thing to fetch it down again. One day he turned on me suddenly with this settler: –

"What is the shape of Walnut Bend?"

He might as well have asked me my grandmother's opinion of protoplasm. I reflected respectfully, and then said I didn't know it had any particular shape. My gunpowdery chief went off with a bang, of course, and then went on loading and firing until he was out of adjectives.

I had learned long ago that he only carried just so many rounds of ammunition, and was sure to subside into a very placable and even remorseful old smooth-bore as soon as they were all gone. That word "old" is merely affectionate; he was not more than thirty-four. I waited. By and by he said, –

"My boy, you've got to know the *shape* of the river perfectly. It is all there is left to steer by on a very dark night. Everything else is blotted out and gone. But mind you, it hasn't the same shape in the night that it has in the day time."

"How on earth am I ever going to learn it, then?"

"How do you follow a hall at home in the dark? Because you know the shape of it. You can't see it."

"Do you mean to say that I've got to know all the million trifling variations of shape in the banks of this interminable river as well as I know the shape of the front hall at home?"

"On my honor, you've got to know them *better* than any man ever did know the shapes of the halls in his own house."

"I wish I was dead!"

"Now I don't want to discourage you, but—"

"Well, pile it on me; I might as well have it now as another time."

"You see, this has got to be learned; there isn't any getting around it. A clear starlight night throws such heavy shadows that if you didn't know the shape of a shore perfectly you would claw away from every bunch of timber, because you would take the black shadow of it for a solid cape; and you see you would be getting scared to death every fifteen minutes by the watch. You would be fifty yards from shore all the time when you ought to be within fifty feet of it. You can't see a snag in one of those shadows, but you know exactly where it is, and the shape of the river tells you when you are coming to it. Then there's your pitch-dark night; the river is a very different shape on a pitch-dark night from what it is on a starlight night. All shores seem to be straight lines, then, and mighty dim ones, too; and you'd *run* them for straight lines only you know better. You boldly drive your boat right into what seems to be a solid, straight wall (you knowing very well that in reality there is a curve there), and that wall falls back and makes way for you. Then there's your gray mist. You take a night when there's one of these grisly, drizzly, gray mists, and then there isn't *any* particular shape to a shore. A gray mist would tangle the head of the oldest man that ever lived. Well, then, different kinds of *moonlight* change the shape of the river in different ways. You see – "

"Oh, don't say any more, please! Have I got to learn the shape of the river according to all these five hundred thousand different ways? If I tried to carry all that cargo in my head it would make me stoop-shouldered."

"*No*! you only learn *the* shape of the river; and you learn it with such absolute certainty that you can always steer by the shape that's *in your head*, and never mind the one that's before your eyes."

"Very well, I'll try it; but after I have learned it can I depend on it? Will it keep the same form and not go fooling around?"

Before Mr. Bixby could answer, Mr. W—— came in to take the watch, and he said, –

"Bixby, you'll have to look out for President's Island and all that country clear away up above the Old Hen and Chickens. The banks are caving and the shape of the shores changing like everything. Why, you wouldn't know the point above 40. You can go up inside the old sycamore snag, now."*

So that question was answered. Here were leagues of shore changing shape. My spirits were down in the mud again. Two things seemed pretty apparent to me. One was, that in order to be a pilot a man had got to learn more than any one man ought to be allowed to know; and the other was, that he must learn it all over again in a different way every twenty-four hours.

That night we had the watch until twelve. Now it was an ancient river custom for the two pilots to chat a bit when the watch changed. While the relieving pilot put on his gloves and lit his cigar, his partner, the retiring pilot, would say something like this: –

"I judge the upper bar is making down a little at Hale's Point; had quarter twain with the lower lead and mark twain** with the other."

"Yes, I thought it was making down a little, last trip. Meet any boats?"

"Met one abreast the head of 21, but she was away over hugging the bar, and I couldn't make her out entirely. I took her for the 'Sunny South' – hadn't any skylights forward of the chimneys."

And so on. And as the relieving pilot took the wheel his partner*** would mention that we were in such-and-such a bend, and say we were abreast of such-and-such a man's wood-yard or plantation. This was courtesy; I supposed it was *necessity*. But Mr. W—— came on watch full twelve minutes late on this particular night, – a tremendous breach of etiquette; in fact, it is the unpardonable sin among pilots. So Mr. Bixby gave him no greeting whatever, but simply surrendered the wheel and marched out of the pilot-house without a word. I was appalled; it was a villainous night for blackness, we were in a particularly wide and blind part of the river, where there was no shape or substance to any thing, and it seemed

*It may not be necessary, but still it can do no harm to explain that "inside" means between the snag and the shore. – M. T.

**Two fathoms. Quarter twain is 2¼ fathoms, 13½ feet. Mark three is three fathoms.

***"Partner" is technical for "the other pilot."

incredible that Mr. Bixby should have left that poor fellow to kill the boat trying to find out where he was. But I resolved that I would stand by him any way. He should find that he was not wholly friendless. So I stood around, and waited to be asked where we were. But Mr. W—— plunged on serenely through the solid firmament of black cats that stood for an atmosphere, and never opened his mouth. Here is a proud devil, thought I; here is a limb of Satan that would rather send us all to destruction than put himself under obligations to me, because I am not yet one of the salt of the earth and privileged to snub captains and lord it over everything dead and alive in a steamboat. I presently climbed up on the bench; I did not think it was safe to go to sleep while this lunatic was on watch.

However, I must have gone to sleep in the course of time, because the next thing I was aware of was the fact that day was breaking, Mr. W—— gone, and Mr. Bixby at the wheel again. So it was four o'clock and all well – but me; I felt like a skinful of dry bones and all of them trying to ache at once.

Mr. Bixby asked me what I had stayed up there for. I confessed that it was to do Mr. W—— a benevolence, – tell him where he was. It took five minutes for the entire preposterousness of the thing to filter into Mr. Bixby's system, and then I judge it filled him nearly up to the chin; because he paid me a compliment – and not much of a one either. He said, –

"Well, taking you by-and-large, you do seem to be more different kinds of an ass than any creature I ever saw before. What did you suppose he wanted to know for?"

I said I thought it might be a convenience to him.

"Convenience! D–nation! Didn't I tell you that a man's got to know the river in the night the same as he'd know his own front hall?"

"Well, I can follow the front hall in the dark if I know it *is* the front hall; but suppose you set me down in the middle of it in the dark and not tell me which hall it is; how am *I* to know?"

"Well, you've *got* to, on the river!"

"All right. Then I'm glad I never said anything to Mr. W——."

"I should say so. Why, he'd have slammed you through the window and utterly ruined a hundred dollars' worth of window-sash and stuff."

I was glad this damage had been saved, for it would have made me unpopular with the owners. They always hated anybody who had the name of being careless, and injuring things.

I went to work now to learn the shape of the river; and of all the eluding and ungraspable objects that ever I tried to get mind or hands on, that was the chief. I would fasten my eyes upon a sharp, wooded point that projected far into the river some miles ahead of me, and go to laboriously photographing its shape upon my brain; and just as I was beginning to succeed to my satisfaction, we would draw up toward it and the exasperating thing would begin to melt away and fold back into the bank! If there had been a conspicuous dead tree standing upon the very point of the cape, I would find that tree inconspicuously merged into the general forest, and occupying the middle of a straight shore, when I got abreast of it! No prominent hill would stick to its shape long enough for me to make up my mind what its form really was, but it was as dissolving and changeful as if it had been a mountain of butter in the hottest corner of the tropics. Nothing ever had the same shape when I was coming down stream that it had borne when I went up. I mentioned these little difficulties to Mr. Bixby. He said, –

"That's the very main virtue of the thing. If the shapes didn't change every three seconds they wouldn't be of any use. Take this place where we are now, for instance. As long as that hill over yonder is only one hill, I can boom right along the way I'm going; but the moment it splits at the top and forms a V, I know I've got to scratch to starboard in a hurry, or I'll bang this boat's brains out against a rock; and then the moment one of the prongs of the V swings behind the other, I've got to waltz to larboard again, or I'll have a misunderstanding with a snag that would snatch the keelson out of this steamboat as neatly as if it were a sliver in your hand. If that hill didn't change its shape on bad nights there would be an awful steamboat graveyard around here inside of a year."

It was plain that I had got to learn the shape of the river in all the different ways that could be thought of, – upside down, wrong end first, inside out, fore-and-aft, and "thortships," – and then know what to do on gray nights when it hadn't any shape at all. So I set about it. In the course of time I began to get the best of this knotty lesson, and my self-complacency moved to the front once more. Mr. Bixby was all fixed, and ready to start it to the rear again. He opened on me after this fashion: –

"How much water did we have in the middle crossing at Hole-in-the-Wall, trip before last?"

I considered this an outrage. I said: –

"Every trip, down and up, the leadsmen are singing through that tangled place for three-quarters of an hour on a stretch. How do you reckon I can remember such a mess as that?"

"My boy, you've got to remember it. You've got to remember the exact spot and the exact marks the boat lay in when we had the shoalest water, in every one of the five hundred shoal places between St. Louis and New Orleans; and you mustn't get the shoal soundings and marks of one trip mixed up with the shoal soundings and marks of another, either, for they're not often twice alike. You must keep them separate."

When I came to myself again, I said, –

"When I get so that I can do that, I'll be able to raise the dead, and then I won't have to pilot a steamboat to make a living. I want to retire from this business. I want a slush-bucket and a brush; I'm only fit for a roustabout. I haven't got brains enough to be a pilot; and if I had I wouldn't have strength enough to carry them around, unless I went on crutches."

"Now drop that! When I say I'll learn* a man the river, I mean it. And you can depend on it, I'll learn him or kill him."

CHAPTER IX

CONTINUED PERPLEXITIES

THERE WAS NO use in arguing with a person like this. I promptly put such a strain on my memory that by and by even the shoal water and the countless crossing-marks began to stay with me. But the result was just the same. I never could more than get one knotty thing learned before another presented itself. Now I had often seen pilots gazing at the water and pretending to read it as if it were a book; but it was a book that told me nothing. A time came at last, however, when Mr. Bixby seemed to think me far enough advanced to hear a lesson on water-reading. So he began: –

"Do you see that long slanting line on the face of the water? Now, that's a reef. Moreover, it's a bluff reef. There is a solid sand-bar under it that is nearly as straight up and down as the side of a house. There is plenty of water close up to it, but mighty little on

* "Teach" is not in the river vocabulary.

top of it. If you were to hit it you would knock the boat's brains out. Do you see where the line fringes out at the upper end and begins to fade away?"

"Yes, sir."

"Well, that is a low place; that is the head of the reef. You can climb over there, and not hurt any thing. Cross over, now, and follow along close under the reef – easy water there – not much current."

I followed the reef along till I approached the fringed end. Then Mr. Bixby said, –

"Now get ready. Wait till I give the word. She won't want to mount the reef; a boat hates shoal water. Stand by – wait – *wait* – keep her well in hand. *Now* cramp her down! Snatch her! snatch her!"

He seized the other side of the wheel and helped to spin it around until it was hard down, and then we held it so. The boat resisted, and refused to answer for a while, and next she came surging to starboard, mounted the reef, and sent a long, angry ridge of water foaming away from her bows.

"Now watch her; watch her like a cat, or she'll get away from you. When she fights strong and the tiller slips a little, in a jerky, greasy sort of way, let up on her a trifle; it is the way she tells you at night that the water is too shoal; but keep edging her up, little by little, toward the point. You are well up on the bar, now; there is a bar under every point, because the water that comes down around it forms an eddy and allows the sediment to sink. Do you see those fine lines on the face of the water that branch out like the ribs of a fan? Well, those are little reefs; you want to just miss the ends of them, but run them pretty close. Now look out – look out! Don't you crowd that slick, greasy-looking place; there ain't nine feet there; she won't stand it. She begins to smell it; look sharp, I tell you! Oh blazes, there you go! Stop the starboard wheel! Quick! Ship up to back! Set her back!"

The engine bells jingled and the engines answered promptly, shooting white columns of steam far aloft out of the 'scape pipes, but it was too late. The boat had "smelt" the bar in good earnest; the foamy ridges that radiated from her bows suddenly disappeared, a great dead swell came rolling forward and swept ahead of her, she careened far over to larboard, and went tearing away toward the other shore as if she were about scared to death. We were a good mile from where we ought to have been, when we finally got the upper hand of her again.

During the afternoon watch the next day, Mr. Bixby asked me if I knew how to run the next few miles. I said: –

"Go inside the first snag above the point, outside the next one, start out from the lower end of Higgins's wood-yard, make a square crossing and—"

"That's all right. I'll be back before you close up on the next point."

But he wasn't. He was still below when I rounded it and entered upon a piece of river which I had some misgivings about. I did not know that he was hiding behind a chimney to see how I would perform. I went gayly along, getting prouder and prouder, for he had never left the boat in my sole charge such a length of time before. I even got to "setting" her and letting the wheel go, entirely, while I vaingloriously turned my back and inspected the stern marks and hummed a tune, a sort of easy indifference which I had prodigiously admired in Bixby and other great pilots. Once I inspected rather long, and when I faced to the front again my heart flew into my mouth so suddenly that if I hadn't clapped my teeth together I should have lost it. One of those frightful bluff reefs was stretching its deadly length right across our bows! My head was gone in a moment; I did not know which end I stood on; I gasped and could not get my breath; I spun the wheel down with such rapidity that it wove itself together like a spider's web; the boat answered and turned square away from the reef, but the reef followed her! I fled, and still it followed, still it kept – right across my bows! I never looked to see where I was going, I only fled. The awful crash was imminent – why didn't that villain come! If I committed the crime of ringing a bell, I might get thrown overboard. But better that than kill the boat. So in blind desperation I started such a rattling "shivaree" down below as never had astounded an engineer in this world before, I fancy. Amidst the frenzy of the bells the engines began to back and fill in a furious way, and my reason forsook its throne – we were about to crash into the woods on the other side of the river. Just then Mr. Bixby stepped calmly into view on the hurricane deck. My soul went out to him in gratitude. My distress vanished; I would have felt safe on the brink of Niagara, with Mr. Bixby on the hurricane deck. He blandly and sweetly took his tooth-pick out of his mouth between his fingers, as if it were a cigar, – we were just in the act of climbing an overhanging big tree, and the passengers were scudding astern like rats, – and lifted up these commands to me ever so gently: –

"Stop the starboard. Stop the larboard. Set her back on both."

The boat hesitated, halted, pressed her nose among the boughs a critical instant, then reluctantly began to back away.

"Stop the larboard. Come ahead on it. Stop the starboard. Come ahead on it. Point her for the bar."

I sailed away as serenely as a summer's morning. Mr. Bixby came in and said, with mock simplicity, –

"When you have a hail, my boy, you ought to tap the big bell three times before you land, so that the engineers can get ready."

I blushed under the sarcasm, and said I hadn't had any hail.

"Ah! Then it was for wood, I suppose. The officer of the watch will tell you when he wants to wood up."

I went on consuming, and said I wasn't after wood.

"Indeed? Why, what could you want over here in the bend, then? Did you ever know of a boat following a bend up stream at this stage of the river?"

"No, sir, – and *I* wasn't trying to follow it. I was getting away from a bluff reef."

"No, it wasn't a bluff reef; there isn't one within three miles of where you were."

"But I saw it. It was as bluff as that one yonder."

"Just about. Run over it!"

"Do you give it as an order?"

"Yes. Run over it."

"If I don't, I wish I may die."

"All right; I am taking the responsibility."

I was just as anxious to kill the boat, now, as I had been to save her before. I impressed my orders upon my memory, to be used at the inquest, and made a straight break for the reef. As it disappeared under our bows I held my breath; but we slid over it like oil.

"Now don't you see the difference? It wasn't any thing but a *wind* reef. The wind does that."

"So I see. But it is exactly like a bluff reef. How am I ever going to tell them apart?"

"I can't tell you. It is an instinct. By and by you will just naturally *know* one from the other, but you never will be able to explain why or how you know them apart."

It turned out to be true. The face of the water, in time, became a wonderful book – a book that was a dead language to the uneducated passenger, but which told its mind to me without reserve, delivering its most cherished secrets as clearly as if it uttered them with a voice. And it was not a book to be read once and thrown aside, for it had a new story to tell every day. Throughout the long twelve hundred miles there was never a page that was void of interest, never one that you could leave unread without loss, never one that you would want to skip, thinking you could find higher enjoyment in some other thing. There never was so wonderful a book written by man; never one whose interest was so absorbing, so unflagging, so sparklingly renewed with every re-perusal. The passenger who could not read it was charmed with a peculiar sort of faint dimple on its surface (on the rare occasions when he did not overlook it altogether); but to the pilot that was an *italicized* passage; indeed, it was more than that, it was a legend of the largest capitals, with a string of shouting exclamation points at the end of it; for it meant that a wreck or a rock was buried there that could tear the life out of the strongest vessel that ever floated. It is the faintest and simplest expression the water ever makes, and the most hideous to a pilot's eye. In truth, the passenger who could not read this book saw nothing but all manner of pretty pictures in it, painted by the sun and shaded by the clouds, whereas to the trained eye these were not pictures at all, but the grimmest and most dead-earnest of reading-matter.

Now when I had mastered the language of this water and had come to know every trifling feature that bordered the great river as familiarly as I knew the letters of the alphabet, I had made a valuable acquisition. But I had lost something, too. I had lost something which could never be restored to me while I lived. All the grace, the beauty, the poetry had gone out of the majestic river! I still keep in mind a certain wonderful sunset which I witnessed when steamboating was new to me. A broad expanse of the river was turned to blood; in the middle distance the red hue brightened into gold, through which a solitary log came floating, black and conspicuous; in one place a long, slanting mark lay sparkling upon the water; in another the surface was broken by boiling, tumbling rings, that were as many-tinted as an opal; where the ruddy flush was faintest, was a smooth spot that was covered with graceful circles and radiating lines, ever so delicately traced; the shore on our left was densely wooded, and the sombre shadow that fell from this forest was broken in one place by a long, ruffled trail that shone like silver; and high above the forest wall a clean-stemmed dead tree waved a single leafy bough that glowed like a flame in the unobstructed splendor that was flowing from the sun. There were graceful curves, reflected images, woody heights, soft distances; and over the whole scene, far and near, the dissolving lights drifted steadily, enriching it, every passing moment, with new marvels of coloring.

I stood like one bewitched. I drank it in, in a speechless rapture. The world was new to me, and I had never seen any thing like this at home. But as I have said, a day came when I began to cease from noting the glories and the charms which the moon and the sun and the twilight wrought upon the river's face; another day came when I ceased altogether to note them. Then, if that sunset scene had been repeated, I should have looked upon it without rapture, and should have commented upon it, inwardly, after this fashion: This sun means that we are going to have wind to-morrow; that floating log means that the river is rising, small thanks to it; that slanting mark on the water refers to a bluff reef which is going to kill some body's steamboat one of these nights, if it keeps on stretching out like that; those tumbling "boils" show a dissolving bar and a changing channel there; the lines and circles in the slick water over yonder are a warning that that troublesome place is shoaling up dangerously; that silver streak in the shadow of the forest is the "break" from a new snag, and he has located himself in the very best place he could have found to fish for steamboats; that tall dead tree, with a single living branch, is not going to last long, and then how is a body ever going to get through this blind place at night without the friendly old landmark?

No, the romance and the beauty were all gone from the river. All the value any feature of it had for me now was the amount of usefulness it could furnish toward compassing the safe piloting of a steamboat. Since those days, I have pitied doctors from my heart. What does the lovely flush in a beauty's cheek mean to a doctor but a "break" that ripples above some deadly disease? Are not all her visible charms sown thick with what are to him the signs and symbols of hidden decay? Does he ever see her beauty at all, or doesn't he simply view her professionally, and comment upon her unwholesome condition all to himself? And doesn't he sometimes wonder whether he has gained most or lost most by learning his trade?

CHAPTER X

COMPLETING MY EDUCATION

WHOSOEVER HAS DONE me the courtesy to read my chapters which have preceded this may possibly wonder that I deal so minutely with piloting as a science. It was the prime purpose of those chapters; and I am not quite done yet. I wish to show, in the most patient and painstaking way, what a wonderful science it is. Ship channels are buoyed and lighted, and therefore it is a comparatively easy undertaking to learn to run them; clear-water rivers, with gravel bottoms, change their channels very gradually, and therefore one needs to learn them but once; but piloting becomes another matter when you apply it to vast streams like the Mississippi and the Missouri, whose alluvial banks cave and change constantly, whose snags are always hunting up new quarters, whose sand-bars are never at rest, whose channels are forever dodging and shirking, and whose obstructions must be confronted in all nights and all weathers without the aid of a single light-house or a single buoy; for there is neither light nor buoy to be found anywhere in all this three or four thousand miles of villainous river.* I feel justified in enlarging upon this great science for the reason that I feel sure no one has ever yet written a paragraph about it who had piloted a steamboat himself, and so had a practical knowledge of the subject. If the theme were hackneyed, I should be obliged to deal gently with the reader; but since it is wholly new, I have felt at liberty to take up a considerable degree of room with it.

When I had learned the name and position of every visible feature of the river; when I had so mastered its shape that I could shut my eyes and trace it from St. Louis to New Orleans; when I had learned to read the face of the water as one would cull the news from the morning paper; and finally, when I had trained my dull memory to treasure up an endless array of soundings and crossing-marks, and keep fast hold of them, I judged that my education was complete: so I got to tilting my cap to the side of my head, and wearing a tooth-pick in my mouth at the wheel. Mr. Bixby had his eye on these airs. One day he said, –

"What is the height of that bank yonder, at Burgess's?"

"How can I tell, sir? It is three-quarters of a mile away."

"Very poor eye – very poor. Take the glass."

I took the glass, and presently said, –

"I can't tell. I suppose that that bank is about a foot and a half high."

"Foot and a half! That's a six-foot bank. How high was the bank along here last trip?"

*True at the time referred to: not true now (1882).

"I don't know; I never noticed."

"You didn't? Well, you must always do it hereafter."

"Why?"

"Because you'll have to know a good many things that it tells you. For one thing, it tells you the stage of the river – tells you whether there's more water or less in the river along here than there was last trip."

"The leads tell me that." I rather thought I had the advantage of him there.

"Yes, but suppose the leads lie? The bank would tell you so, and then you'd stir those leadsmen up a bit. There was a ten-foot bank here last trip, and there is only a six-foot bank now. What does that signify?"

"That the river is four feet higher than it was last trip."

"Very good. Is the river rising or falling?"

"Rising."

"No it ain't."

"I guess I am right, sir. Yonder is some drift-wood floating down the stream."

"A rise *starts* the drift-wood, but then it keeps on floating a while after the river is done rising. Now the bank will tell you about this. Wait till you come to a place where it shelves a little. Now here; do you see this narrow belt of fine sediment? That was deposited while the water was higher. You see the drift-wood begins to strand, too. The bank helps in other ways. Do you see that stump on the false point?"

"Ay, ay, sir."

"Well, the water is just up to the roots of it. You must make a note of that."

"Why?"

"Because that means that there's seven feet in the chute of 103."

"But 103 is a long way up the river yet."

"That's where the benefit of the bank comes in. There is water enough in 103 *now*, yet there may not be by the time we get there; but the bank will keep us posted all along. You don't run close chutes on a falling river, up stream, and there are precious few of them that you are allowed to run at all down stream. There's a law of the United States against it. The river may be rising by the time we get to 103, and in that case we'll run it. We are drawing – how much?"

"Six feet aft, – six and a half forward."

"Well, you do seem to know some thing."

"But what I particularly want to know is, if I have got to keep up an everlasting measuring of the banks of this river, twelve hundred miles, month in and month out?"

"Of course!"

My emotions were too deep for words for a while. Presently I said, –

"And how about these chutes? Are there many of them?"

"I should say so. I fancy we shan't run any of the river this trip as you've ever seen it run before – so to speak. If the river begins to rise again, we'll go up behind bars that you've always seen standing out of the river, high and dry like the roof of a house; we'll cut across low places that you've never noticed at all, right through the middle of bars that cover three hundred acres of river; we'll creep through cracks where you've always thought was solid land; we'll dart through the woods and leave twenty-five miles of river off to one side; we'll see the hind-side of every island between New Orleans and Cairo."

"Then I've got to go to work and learn just as much more river as I already know."

"Just about twice as much more, as near as you can come at it."

"Well, one lives to find out. I think I was a fool when I went into this business."

"Yes, that is true. And you are yet. But you'll not be when you've learned it."

"Ah, I never can learn it."

"I will see that you *do*."

By and by I ventured again: –

"Have I got to learn all this thing just as I know the rest of the river – shapes and all – and so I can run it at night?"

"Yes. And you've got to have good fair marks from one end of the river to the other, that will help the bank tell you when there is water enough in each of these countless places, – like that stump, you know. When the river first begins to rise, you can run half a dozen of the deepest of them; when it rises a foot more you can run another dozen; the next foot will add a couple of dozen, and so on: so you see you have to know your banks and marks to a dead moral certainty, and never get them mixed; for when you start through one of those cracks, there's no backing out again, as there is in the big river; you've got to go through, or stay there six months if you get caught on a falling river. There are about fifty of these cracks which you can't run at all except when the river is brim full and over the banks."

"This new lesson is a cheerful prospect."

"Cheerful enough. And mind what I've just told you; when you start into one of those places you've got to go through. They are too narrow to turn around in, too crooked to back out of, and the shoal water is always *up at the head;* never elsewhere. And the head of them is always likely to be filling up, little by little, so that the marks you reckon their depth by, this season, may not answer for next."

"Learn a new set, then, every year?"

"Exactly. Cramp her up to the bar! What are you standing up through the middle of the river for?"

The next few months showed me strange things. On the same day that we held the conversation above narrated, we met a great rise coming down the river. The whole vast face of the stream was black with drifting dead logs, broken boughs, and great trees that had caved in and been washed away. It required the nicest steering to pick one's way through this rushing raft, even in the day time, when crossing from point to point; and at night the difficulty was mightily increased; every now and then a huge log, lying deep in the water, would suddenly appear right under our bows, coming head-on; no use to try to avoid it then; we could only stop the engines, and one wheel would walk over that log from one end to the other, keeping up a thundering racket and careening the boat in a way that was very uncomfortable to passengers. Now and then we would hit one of these sunken logs a rattling bang, dead in the centre, with a full head of steam, and it would stun the boat as if she had hit a continent. Sometimes this log would lodge, and stay right across our nose, and back the Mississippi up before it; we would have to do a little crawfishing, then, to get away from the obstruction. We often hit *white* logs, in the dark, for we could not see them till we were right on them; but a black log is a pretty distinct object at night. A white snag is an ugly customer when the daylight is gone.

Of course, on the great rise, down came a swarm of prodigious timber-rafts from the head-waters of the Mississippi, coal barges from Pittsburgh, little trading-scows from every where, and broad-horns from "Posey County," Indiana, freighted with "fruit and furniture" – the usual term for describing it, though in plain English the freight thus aggrandized was hoop-poles and pumpkins. Pilots bore a mortal hatred to these craft; and it was returned with usury. The law required all such helpless traders to keep a light burning, but it was a law that was often broken. All of a sudden, on a murky night, a light would hop up, right under our bows, almost, and an agonized voice, with the backwoods "whang" to it, would wail out: –

"Whar'n the —— you goin' to! Cain't you see nothin', you dash-dashed aig-suckin', sheep-stealin', one-eyed son of a stuffed monkey!"

Then for an instant, as we whistled by, the red glare from our furnaces would reveal the scow and the form of the gesticulating orator as if under a lightning-flash, and in that instant our firemen and deck-hands would send and receive a tempest of missiles and profanity, one of our wheels would walk off with the crashing fragments of a steering-oar, and down the dead blackness would shut again. And that flatboatman would be sure to go into New Orleans and sue our boat, swearing stoutly that he had a light burning all the time, when in truth his gang had the lantern down below to sing and lie and drink and gamble by, and no watch on deck. Once, at night, in one of those forest-bordered crevices (behind an island) which steamboatmen intensely describe with the phrase "as dark as the inside of a cow," we should have eaten up a Posey County family, fruit, furniture, and all, but that they happened to be fiddling down below and we just caught the sound of the music in time to sheer off, doing no serious damage, unfortunately, but coming so near it that we had good hopes for a moment. These people brought up their lantern, then, of course; and as we backed and filled to get away, the precious family stood in the light of it – both sexes and various ages – and cursed us till everything turned blue. Once a coal-boatman sent a bullet through our pilot-house, when we borrowed a steering-oar of him in a very narrow place.

CHAPTER XI

THE RIVER RISES

DURING THIS BIG rise these small-fry craft were an intolerable nuisance. We were running chute after chute, – a new world to me, – and if there was a particularly cramped place in a chute, we would be pretty sure to meet a broad-horn there; and if he failed to be there, we would find him in a still worse locality, namely, the head of the chute, on the shoal water. And then there would be no end of profane cordialities exchanged.

Sometimes, in the big river, when we would be feeling our way cautiously along through a fog, the deep hush would suddenly be broken by yells and a clamor of tin pans, and all in an instant a log raft would appear vaguely through the webby veil, close upon us; and then we did not wait to swap knives, but snatched our engine bells out by the roots and piled on all the steam we had, to scramble out of the way! One doesn't hit a rock or a solid log raft with a steamboat when he can get excused.

You will hardly believe it, but many steamboat clerks always carried a large assortment of religious tracts with them in those old departed steamboating days. Indeed they did. Twenty times a day we would be cramping up around a bar, while a string of these small-fry rascals were drifting down into the head of the bend away above and beyond us a couple of miles. Now a skiff would dart away from one of them, and come fighting its laborious way across the desert of water. It would "ease all," in the shadow of our forecastle, and the panting oarsmen would shout, "Gimme a pa-a-per!" as the skiff drifted swiftly astern. The clerk would throw over a file of New Orleans journals. If these were picked up *without comment*, you might notice that now a dozen other skiffs had been drifting down upon us without saying any thing. You understand, they had been waiting to see how No. 1 was going to fare. No. 1 making no comment, all the rest would bend to their oars and come on, now; and as fast as they came the clerk would heave over neat bundles of religious tracts, tied to shingles. The amount of hard swearing which twelve packages of religious literature will command when impartially divided up among twelve raftsmen's crews, who have pulled a heavy skiff two miles on a hot day to get them, is simply incredible.

As I have said, the big rise brought a new world under my vision. By the time the river was over its banks we had forsaken our old paths and were hourly climbing over bars that had stood ten feet out of water before; we were shaving stumpy shores, like that at the foot of Madrid Bend, which I had always seen avoided before; we were clattering through chutes like that of 82, where the opening at the foot was an unbroken wall of timber till our nose was almost at the very spot. Some of these chutes were utter solitudes. The dense, untouched forest overhung both banks of the crooked little crack, and one could believe that human creatures had never intruded there before. The swinging grape-vines, the grassy nooks and vistas glimpsed as we swept by, the flowering creepers waving their red blossoms from the tops of dead trunks, and all the spendthrift richness of the forest foliage, were wasted and thrown away there. The chutes were lovely places to steer in; they were deep, except at the head; the current was gentle; under the "points" the water was absolutely dead, and the invisible banks so bluff that where the tender willow thickets projected you could bury your boat's broadside in them as you tore along, and then you seemed fairly to fly.

Behind other islands we found wretched little farms, and wretcheder little log-cabins; there were crazy rail fences sticking a foot or two above the water, with one or two jeans-clad, chills-racked, yellow-faced male miserables roosting on the top-rail, elbows on knees, jaws in hands, grinding tobacco and discharging the result at floating chips through crevices left by lost teeth; while the rest of the family and the few farm-animals were huddled together in an empty wood-flat riding at her moorings close at hand. In this flatboat the family would have to cook and eat and sleep for a lesser or greater number of days (or possibly weeks), until the river should fall two or three feet and let them get back to their log-cabin and their chills again – chills being a merciful provision of an all-wise Providence to enable them to take exercise without exertion. And this sort of watery camping out was a thing which these people were rather liable to be treated to a couple of times a year: by the December rise out of the Ohio, and the June rise out of the Mississippi. And yet these were kindly dispensations, for they at least enabled the poor things to rise from the dead now and then, and look upon life when a steamboat went by. They appreciated the blessing, too, for they spread their mouths and eyes wide open and made the most of these occasions. Now what *could* these banished creatures find to do to keep from dying of the blues during the low-water season!

Once, in one of these lovely island chutes, we found our course completely bridged by a great fallen tree. This will serve to show how narrow some of the chutes were. The passengers had an hour's recreation in a virgin wilderness, while the boat-hands chopped the bridge away; for there was no such thing as turning back, you comprehend.

From Cairo to Baton Rouge, when the river is over its banks, you have no particular trouble in the night, for the thousand-mile wall of dense forest that guards the two banks all the way is only gapped with a farm or wood-yard opening at intervals, and so you can't "get out of the river" much easier than you could get out of a fenced lane; but from Baton Rouge to New Orleans it is a different matter. The river is more than a mile wide, and very deep – as much as two hundred feet, in places. Both banks, for a good deal over a hundred miles, are shorn of their timber and bordered by continuous sugar plantations, with only here and there a scattering sapling or row of ornamental China-trees. The timber is shorn off clear to the rear of the plantations, from two to four miles. When the first frost threatens to come, the planters snatch off their crops in a hurry. When they have finished grinding the cane, they form the refuse of the stalks (which they call *bagasse*) into great piles and set fire to them, though in other sugar countries the bagasse is used for fuel in the furnaces of the sugar mills. Now the piles of damp bagasse burn slowly, and smoke like Satan's own kitchen.

An embankment ten or fifteen feet high guards both banks of the Mississippi all the way down that lower end of the river, and this embankment is set back from the edge of the shore from ten to perhaps a hundred feet, according to circumstances; say thirty or forty feet, as a general thing. Fill that whole region with an impenetrable gloom of smoke from a hundred miles of burning bagasse piles, when the river is over the banks, and turn a steamboat loose along there at midnight and see how she will feel. And see how you will feel, too! You find yourself away out in the midst of a vague dim sea that is shoreless, that fades out and loses itself in the murky distances; for you cannot discern the thin rib of embankment, and you are always imagining you see a straggling tree when you don't. The plantations themselves are transformed by the smoke, and look like a part of the sea. All through your watch you are tortured with the exquisite misery of uncertainty. You hope you are keeping in the river, but you do not know. All that you are sure about is that you are likely to be within six feet of the bank *and* destruction, when you think you are a good half-mile from shore. And you are sure, also, that if you chance suddenly to fetch up against the embankment and topple your chimneys overboard, you will have the small comfort of knowing that it is about what you were expecting to do. One of the great Vicksburg packets darted out into a sugar plantation one night, at such a time, and had to stay there a week. But there was no novelty about it; it had often been done before.

I thought I had finished this chapter, but I wish to add a curious thing, while it is in my mind. It is only relevant in that it is connected with piloting. There used to be an excellent pilot on the river, a Mr. X., who was a somnambulist. It was said that if his mind was troubled about a bad piece of river, he was pretty sure to get up and walk in his sleep and do strange things. He was once fellow-pilot for a trip or two with George Ealer, on a great New Orleans passenger packet. During a considerable part of the first trip George was uneasy, but got over it by and by, as X. seemed content to stay in his bed when asleep. Late one night the boat was approaching Helena, Arkansas; the water was low, and the crossing above the town in a very blind and tangled condition. X. had seen the crossing since Ealer had, and as the night was particularly drizzly, sullen, and dark, Ealer was considering whether he had not better have X. called to assist in running the place, when the door opened and X. walked in. Now on very dark nights, light is a deadly enemy to piloting; you are aware that if you stand in a lighted room, on such a night, you can not see things in the street to any purpose; but if you put out the lights and stand in the gloom you can make out objects in the street pretty well. So, on very dark nights, pilots do not smoke; they allow no fire in the pilot-house stove if there is a crack which can allow the least ray to escape; they order the furnaces to be curtained with huge tarpaulins and the skylights to be closely blinded. Then no light whatever issues from the boat. The undefinable shape that now entered the pilot-house had Mr. X.'s voice. This said, –

"Let me take her, George; I've seen this place since you have, and it is so crooked that I reckon I can run it myself easier than I could tell you how to do it."

"It is kind of you, and I swear *I* am willing. I haven't got another drop of perspiration left in me. I have been spinning around and around the wheel like a squirrel. It is so dark I can't tell which way she is swinging till she is coming around like a whirligig."

So Ealer took a seat on the bench, panting and breathless. The black phantom assumed the wheel without saying anything, steadied the waltzing steamer with a turn or two, and then stood at ease, coaxing her a little to this side and then to that, as gently and as sweetly as if the time had been noonday. When Ealer observed this marvel of steering, he wished he had not confessed! He stared, and wondered, and finally said, –

"Well, I thought I knew how to steer a steamboat, but that was another mistake of mine."

X. said nothing, but went serenely on with his work. He rang for the leads; he rang to slow down the steam; he worked the boat carefully and neatly into invisible marks, then stood at the centre of the wheel and peered blandly out into the blackness, fore and aft, to verify his position; as the leads shoaled more and more, he stopped the engines entirely, and the dead silence and suspense of "drifting" followed; when the shoalest water was struck, he cracked on the steam, carried her handsomely over, and then began to work her warily into the next system of shoal marks; the same patient, heedful use of leads and engines followed, the boat slipped through without touching bottom, and entered upon the third and last intricacy of the crossing; imperceptibly she moved through the gloom, crept by inches into her marks, drifted tediously till the shoalest water was cried, and then, under a tremendous head of steam, went swinging over the reef and away into deep water and safety!

Ealer let his long-pent breath pour out in a great, relieving sigh, and said: –

"That's the sweetest piece of piloting that was ever done on the Mississippi River! I wouldn't believed it could be done, if I hadn't seen it."

There was no reply, and he added: –

"Just hold her five minutes longer, partner, and let me run down and get a cup of coffee."

A minute later Ealer was biting into a pie, down in the "texas," and comforting himself with coffee. Just then the night watchman happened in, and was about to happen out again, when he noticed Ealer and exclaimed, –

"Who is at the wheel, sir?"

"X."

"Dart for the pilot-house, quicker than lightning!"

The next moment both men were flying up the pilot-house companion-way, three steps at a jump! Nobody there! The great steamer was whistling down the middle of the river at her own sweet will! The watchman shot out of the place again; Ealer seized the wheel, set an engine back with power, and held his breath while the boat reluctantly swung away from a "towhead" which she was about to knock into the middle of the Gulf of Mexico!

By and by the watchman came back and said, –

"Didn't that lunatic tell you he was asleep, when he first came up here?"

"No."

"Well, he was. I found him walking along on top of the railings, just as unconcerned as another man would walk a pavement; and I put him to bed; now just this minute there he was again, away astern, going through that sort of tight-rope deviltry the same as before."

"Well, I think I'll stay by, next time he has one of those fits. But I hope he'll have them often. You just ought to have seen him take this boat through Helena crossing. *I* never saw any thing so gaudy before. And if he can do such gold-leaf, kid-glove, diamond-breast-pin piloting when he is sound asleep, what *couldn't* he do if he was dead!"

CHAPTER XII

SOUNDING

WHEN THE RIVER is very low, and one's steamboat is "drawing all the water" there is in the channel, – or a few inches more, as was often the case in the old times, – one must be painfully circumspect in his piloting. We used to have to "sound" a number of particularly bad places almost every trip when the river was at a very low stage.

Sounding is done in this way. The boat ties up at the shore, just above the shoal crossing; the pilot not on watch takes his "cub" or steersman and a picked crew of men (sometimes an officer also), and goes out in the yawl – provided the boat has not that rare and sumptuous luxury, a regularly-devised "sounding-boat" – and proceeds to hunt for the best water, the pilot on duty watching his movements through a spy-glass, meantime, and in some instances assisting by signals of the boat's whistle, signifying "try higher up" or "try lower down"; for the surface of the water, like an oil-painting, is more expressive and intelligible when inspected from a little distance than very close at hand. The whistle signals are seldom necessary, however; never, perhaps, except when the wind confuses the significant ripples upon the water's surface. When the yawl has reached the shoal place, the speed is slackened, the pilot begins to sound the depth with a pole ten or twelve feet long, and the steersman at the tiller obeys the order to "hold her up to starboard"; or "let her fall off to larboard*"; or "steady – steady as you go."

When the measurements indicate that the yawl is approaching the shoalest part of the reef, the command is given to "ease all!" Then the men stop rowing and the yawl drifts with the current. The

*The term "larboard" is never used at sea, now, to signify the left hand; but was always used on the river in my time.

next order is, "Stand by with the buoy!" The moment the shallowest point is reached, the pilot delivers the order, "Let go the buoy!" and over she goes. If the pilot is not satisfied, he sounds the place again; if he finds better water higher up or lower down, he removes the buoy to that place. Being finally satisfied, he gives the order, and all the men stand their oars straight up in the air, in line; a blast from the boat's whistle indicates that the signal has been seen; then the men "give way" on their oars and lay the yawl alongside the buoy; the steamer comes creeping carefully down, is pointed straight at the buoy, husbands her power for the coming struggle, and presently, at the critical moment, turns on all her steam and goes grinding and wallowing over the buoy and the sand, and gains the deep water beyond. Or maybe she doesn't; maybe she "strikes and swings." Then she has to wile away several hours (or days) sparring herself off.

Sometimes a buoy is not laid at all, but the yawl goes ahead, hunting the best water, and the steamer follows along in its wake. Often there is a deal of fun and excitement about sounding, especially if it is a glorious summer day, or a blustering night. But in winter the cold and the peril take most of the fun out of it.

A buoy is nothing but a board four or five feet long, with one end turned up; it is a reversed schoolhouse bench, with one of the supports left and the other removed. It is anchored on the shoalest part of the reef by a rope with a heavy stone made fast to the end of it. But for the resistance of the turned-up end of the reversed bench, the current would pull the buoy under water. At night, a paper lantern with a candle in it is fastened on top of the buoy, and this can be seen a mile or more, a little glimmering spark in the waste of blackness.

Nothing delights a cub so much as an opportunity to go out sounding. There is such an air of adventure about it; often there is danger; it is so gaudy and man-of-war-like to sit up in the sternsheets and steer a swift yawl; there is some thing fine about the exultant spring of the boat when an experienced old sailor crew throw their souls into the oars; it is lovely to see the white foam stream away from the bows; there is music in the rush of the water; it is deliciously exhilarating, in summer, to go speeding over the breezy expanses of the river when the world of wavelets is dancing in the sun. It is such grandeur, too, to the cub, to get a chance to give an order; for often the pilot will simply say, "Let her go about!" and leave the rest to the cub, who instantly cries, in his sternest tone of command, "Ease starboard! Strong on the larboard! Starboard give way! With a will, men!" The cub enjoys sounding for the further reason that the eyes of the passengers are watching all the yawl's movements with absorbing interest if the time be daylight; and if it be night he knows that those same wondering eyes are fastened upon the yawl's lantern as it glides out into the gloom and dims away in the remote distance.

One trip a pretty girl of sixteen spent her time in our pilot-house with her uncle and aunt, every day and all day long. I fell in love with her. So did Mr. Thornburg's cub, Tom G——. Tom and I had been bosom friends until this time; but now a coolness began to arise. I told the girl a good many of my river adventures, and made myself out a good deal of a hero; Tom tried to make himself appear to be a hero, too, and succeeded to some extent, but then he always had a way of embroidering. However, virtue is its own reward, so I was a barely perceptible trifle ahead in the contest. About this time some thing happened which promised handsomely for me: the pilots decided to sound the crossing at the head of 21. This would occur about nine or ten o'clock at night, when the passengers would be still up; it would be Mr. Thornburg's watch, therefore my chief would have to do the sounding. We had a perfect love of a sounding-boat – long, trim, graceful, and as fleet as a greyhound; her thwarts were cushioned; she carried twelve oarsmen; one of the mates was always sent in her to transmit orders to her crew, for ours was a steamer where no end of "style" was put on.

We tied up at the shore above 21, and got ready. It was a foul night, and the river was so wide, there, that a landsman's uneducated eyes could discern no opposite shore through such a gloom. The passengers were alert and interested; everything was satisfactory. As I hurried through the engine room, picturesquely gotten up in storm toggery, I met Tom, and could not forbear delivering myself of a mean speech: –

"Ain't you glad *you* don't have to go out sounding?"

Tom was passing on, but he quickly turned, and said, –

"Now just for that, you can go and get the sounding-pole yourself. I was going after it, but I'd see you in Halifax, now, before I'd do it."

"Who wants you to get it? *I* don't. It's in the sounding-boat."

"It ain't, either. It's been new-painted; and it's been up on the ladies cabin guards two days, drying."

I flew back, and shortly arrived among the crowd of watching and wondering ladies just in time to hear the command:

"Give way, men!"

I looked over, and there was the gallant sounding-boat booming away, the unprincipled Tom presiding at the tiller, and my chief sitting by him with the sounding-pole which I had been sent on a fool's errand to fetch. Then that young girl said to me, –

"Oh, how awful to have to go out in that little boat on such a night! Do you think there is any danger?"

I would rather have been stabbed. I went off, full of venom, to help in the pilot-house. By and by the boat's lantern disappeared, and after an interval a wee spark glimmered upon the face of the water a mile away. Mr. Thornburg blew the whistle, in acknowledgment, backed the steamer out, and made for it. We flew along for a while, then slackened steam and went cautiously gliding toward the spark. Presently Mr. Thornburg exclaimed, –

"Hello, the buoy-lantern's out!"

He stopped the engines. A moment or two later he said, –

"Why, there it is again!"

So he came ahead on the engines once more, and rang for the leads. Gradually the water shoaled up, and then began to deepen again! Mr. Thornburg muttered: –

"Well, I don't understand this. I believe that buoy has drifted off the reef. Seems to be a little too far to the left. No matter, it is safest to run over it, any how."

So, in that solid world of darkness we went creeping down on the light. Just as our bows were in the act of plowing over it, Mr. Thornburg seized the bell-ropes, rang a startling peal, and exclaimed, –

"My soul, it's the sounding-boat!"

A sudden chorus of wild alarms burst out far below – a pause – and then a sound of grinding and crashing followed. Mr. Thornburg exclaimed, –

"There! the paddle-wheel has ground the sounding-boat to lucifer matches! Run! See who is killed!"

I was on the main deck in the twinkling of an eye. My chief and the third mate and nearly all the men were safe. They had discovered their danger when it was too late to pull out of the way; then, when the great guards overshadowed them a moment later, they were prepared and knew what to do; at my chief's order they sprang at the right instant, seized the guard, and were hauled aboard. The next moment the sounding-yawl swept aft to the wheel and was struck and splintered to atoms. Two of the men and the cub Tom, were missing – a fact which spread like wildfire over the boat. The passengers came flocking to the forward gangway, ladies and all, anxious-eyed, white-faced, and talked in awed voices of the dreadful thing. And often and again I heard them say, "Poor fellows! poor boy, poor boy!"

By this time the boat's yawl was manned and away, to search for the missing. Now a faint call was heard, off to the left. The yawl had disappeared in the other direction. Half the people rushed to one side to encourage the swimmer with their shouts; the other half rushed the other way to shriek to the yawl to turn about. By the callings, the swimmer was approaching, but some said the sound showed failing strength. The crowd massed themselves against the boiler-deck railings, leaning over and staring into the gloom; and every faint and fainter cry wrung from them such words as "Ah, poor fellow, poor fellow! is there *no* way to save him?"

But still the cries held out, and drew nearer, and presently the voice said pluckily, –

"I can make it! Stand by with a rope!"

What a rousing cheer they gave him! The chief mate took his stand in the glare of a torch-basket, a coil of rope in his hand, and his men grouped about him. The next moment the swimmer's face appeared in the circle of light, and in another one the owner of it was hauled aboard, limp and drenched, while cheer on cheer went up. It was that devil Tom.

The yawl crew searched every where, but found no sign of the two men. They probably failed to catch the guard, tumbled back, and were struck by the wheel and killed. Tom had never jumped for the guard at all, but had plunged head-first into the river and dived under the wheel. It was nothing; I could have done it easy enough, and I said so; but every body went on just the same, making a wonderful to-do over that ass, as if he had done something great. That girl couldn't seem to have enough of that pitiful "hero" the rest of the trip; but little I cared; I loathed her, any way.

The way we came to mistake the sounding-boat's lantern for the buoy-light was this. My chief said that after laying the buoy he fell away and watched it till it seemed to be secure; then he took up a position a hundred yards below it and a little to one side of the steamer's course, headed the sounding-boat up stream, and waited. Having to wait some time, he and the officer got to talking; he looked up when he judged that the steamer was about on the reef; saw that the buoy was gone, but supposed that the steamer had already run over it; he went on with his talk; he noticed that the steamer was getting very close down on him, but that was the correct thing; it was her business to shave him closely, for convenience in taking him aboard; he was expecting her to sheer off, until the last moment; then it flashed upon him that she was trying to run him down, mistaking his lantern for the buoy-light; so he sang out, "Stand by to spring for the guard, men!" and the next instant the jump was made.

CHAPTER XIII

A PILOT'S NEEDS

BUT I AM wandering from what I was intending to do, that is, make plainer than perhaps appears in the previous chapters, some of the peculiar requirements of the science of piloting. First of all, there is one faculty which a pilot must incessantly cultivate until he has brought it to absolute perfection. Nothing short of perfection will do. That faculty is memory. He cannot stop with merely thinking a thing is so and so; he must *know* it; for this is eminently one of the "exact" sciences. With what scorn a pilot was looked upon, in the old times, if he ever ventured to deal in that feeble phrase "I think," instead of the vigorous one "I know!" One cannot easily realize what a tremendous thing it is to know every trivial detail of twelve hundred miles of river and know it with absolute exactness. If you will take the longest street in New York, and travel up and down it, conning its features patiently until you know every house and window and door and lamp-post and big and little sign by heart, and know them so accurately that you can instantly name the one you are abreast of when you are set down at random in that street in the middle of an inky black night, you will then have a tolerable notion of the amount and the exactness of a pilot's knowledge who carries the Mississippi River in his head. And then if you will go on until you know every street crossing, the character, size, and position of the crossing-stones, and the varying depth of mud in each of those numberless places, you will have some idea of what the pilot must know in order to keep a Mississippi steamer out of trouble. Next, if you will take half of the signs in that long street, and *change their places* once a month, and still manage to know their new positions accurately on dark nights, and keep up with these repeated changes without making any mistakes, you will understand what is required of a pilot's peerless memory by the fickle Mississippi.

I think a pilot's memory is about the most wonderful thing in the world. To know the Old and New Testaments by heart, and be able to recite them glibly, forward or backward, or begin at random anywhere in the book and recite both ways and never trip or make a mistake, is no extravagant mass of knowledge, and no marvellous facility, compared to a pilot's massed knowledge of the Mississippi and his marvellous facility in the handling of it. I make this comparison deliberately, and believe I am not expanding the truth when I do it. Many will think my figure too strong, but pilots will not.

And how easily and comfortably the pilot's memory does its work; how placidly effortless is its way; how *unconsciously* it lays up its vast stores, hour by hour, day by day, and never loses or mislays a single valuable package of them all! Take an instance. Let a leadsman cry, "Half twain! half twain! half twain! half twain! half twain!" until it becomes as monotonous as the ticking of a clock; let conversation be going on all the time, and the pilot be doing his share of the talking, and no longer consciously listening to the leadsman; and in the midst of this endless string of half twains let a single "quarter twain!" be interjected, without emphasis, and then the half twain cry go on again, just as before: two or three weeks later that pilot can describe with precision the boat's position in the river when that quarter twain was uttered, and give you such a lot of head marks, stern marks, and side marks to guide you, that you ought to be able to take the boat there and put her in that same spot again yourself! The cry of "quarter twain" did not really take his mind from his talk, but his trained faculties instantly photographed the bearings, noted the change of depth, and laid up the important details for future reference without requiring any assistance from *him* in the matter. If you were walking and talking with a friend, and another friend at your side kept up a monotonous repetition of the vowel sound A, for a couple of blocks, and then in the midst interjected an R, thus, A, A, A, A, A, R, A, A, A, etc., and gave the R no emphasis, you would not be able to state, two or three weeks afterward, that the R had been put in, nor be able to tell what objects you were passing at the moment it was done. But you could if your memory had been patiently and laboriously trained to do that sort of thing mechanically.

Give a man a tolerably fair memory to start with, and piloting will develop it into a very colossus of capability. But *only in the matters it is daily drilled in.* A time would come when the man's faculties could not help noticing landmarks and soundings, and his memory could not help holding on to them with the grip of a vice; but if you asked that same man at noon what he had had for breakfast, it would be ten chances to one that he could not tell you. Astonishing things can be done with the human memory if you will devote it faithfully to one particular line of business.

At the time that wages soared so high on the Missouri River, my chief, Mr. Bixby, went up there and learned more than a thousand miles of that stream with an ease and rapidity that were astonishing. When he had seen each division *once* in the day time and *once* at night, his education was so nearly complete that he took out a "daylight" license; a few trips later he took out a full license, and went to piloting day and night, – and he ranked A 1, too.

Mr. Bixby placed me as steersman for a while under a pilot whose feats of memory were a constant marvel to me. However, his memory was born in him, I think, not built. For instance, some body would mention a name. Instantly Mr. Brown would break in: –

"Oh, I knew *him.* Sallow-faced, red-headed fellow, with a little scar on the side of his throat, like a splinter under the flesh. He was only in the Southern trade six months. That was thirteen years ago. I made a trip with him. There was five feet in the upper river then; the 'Henry Blake' grounded at the foot of Tower Island drawing four and a half; the 'George Elliott' unshipped her rudder on the wreck of the 'Sunflower'—"

"Why, the 'Sunflower' didn't sink until—"

"*I* know when she sunk; it was three years before that, on the 2d of December; Asa Hardy was captain of her, and his brother John was first clerk; and it was his first trip in her, too; Tom Jones told me these things a week afterward in New Orleans; he was first mate of the 'Sunflower.' Captain Hardy stuck a nail in his foot the 6th of July of the next year, and died of the lock-jaw on the 15th. His brother John died two years after, – 3d of March, – erysipelas. I never saw either of the Hardys, – they were Alleghany River men, – but people who knew them told me all these things. And they said Captain Hardy wore yarn socks winter and summer just the same, and his first wife's name was Jane Shook, – she was from New England, – and his second one died in a lunatic asylum. It was in the blood. She was from Lexington, Kentucky. Name was Horton before she was married."

And so on, by the hour, the man's tongue would go. He could *not* forget any thing. It was simply impossible. The most trivial details remained as distinct and luminous in his head, after they had lain there for years, as the most memorable events. His was not simply a pilot's memory; its grasp was universal. If he were talking about a trifling letter he had received seven years before, he was pretty sure to deliver you the entire screed from memory. And then without observing that he was departing from the true line of his talk, he was more than likely to hurl in a long-drawn parenthetical biography of the writer of that letter; and you were lucky indeed if he did not take up that writer's relatives, one by one, and give you their biographies, too.

Such a memory as that is a great misfortune. To it, all occurrences are of the same size. Its possessor cannot distinguish an interesting circumstance from an uninteresting one. As a talker, he is bound to clog his narrative with tiresome details and make himself an insufferable bore. Moreover, he cannot stick to his subject. He picks up every little grain of memory he discerns in his way, and so is led aside. Mr. Brown would start out with the honest intention of telling you a vastly funny anecdote about a dog. He would be "so full of laugh" that he could hardly begin; then his memory would start with the dog's breed and personal appearance; drift into a history of his owner; of his owner's family, with descriptions of weddings and burials that had occurred in it, together with recitals of congratulatory verses and obituary poetry provoked by the same; then this memory would recollect that one of these events occurred during the celebrated "hard winter" of such and such a year, and a minute description of that winter would follow, along with the names of people who were frozen to death, and statistics showing the high figures which pork and hay went up to. Pork and hay would suggest corn and fodder; corn and fodder would suggest cows and horses; cows and horses would suggest the circus and certain celebrated bare-back riders; the transition from the circus to the menagerie was easy and natural; from the elephant to equatorial Africa was but a step; then of course the heathen savages would suggest religion; and at the end of three or four hours' tedious jaw, the watch would change, and Brown would go out of the pilot-house muttering extracts from sermons he had heard years before about the efficacy of prayer as a means of grace. And the original first mention would be all you had learned about that dog, after all this waiting and hungering.

A pilot must have a memory; but there are two higher qualities which he must also have. He must have good and quick judgment and decision, and a cool, calm courage that no peril can shake. Give a man the merest trifle of pluck to start with, and by the time he has become a pilot he cannot be unmanned by any danger a steamboat can get into; but one cannot quite say the same for judgment. Judgment is a matter of brains, and a man must *start* with a good stock of that article or he will never succeed as a pilot.

The growth of courage in the pilot-house is steady all the time, but it does not reach a high and satisfactory condition until some time after the young pilot has been "standing his own watch," alone and under the staggering weight of all the responsibilities connected with the position. When an apprentice has become pretty thoroughly acquainted with the river, he goes clattering along so fearlessly with his steamboat, night or day, that he presently begins to imagine that it is *his* courage that animates him; but the first time the pilot steps out and leaves him to his own devices he finds out it was the other man's. He discovers that the article has been left out of his own cargo altogether. The whole river is bristling with exigencies in a moment; he is not prepared for them; he does not know how to meet them; all his knowledge forsakes him; and within fifteen minutes he is as white as a sheet and scared almost to death. Therefore pilots wisely train these cubs by various strategic tricks to look danger in the face a little more calmly. A favorite way of theirs is to play a friendly swindle upon the candidate.

Mr. Bixby served me in this fashion once, and for years afterward I used to blush even in my sleep when I thought of it. I had become a good steersman; so good, indeed, that I had all the work to do on our watch, night and day; Mr. Bixby seldom made a suggestion to me; all he ever did was to take the wheel on particularly bad nights or in particularly bad crossings, land the boat when she needed to be landed, play gentleman of leisure nine-tenths of the watch, and collect the wages. The lower river was about bank-full, and if anybody had questioned my ability to run any crossing between Cairo and New Orleans without help or instruction, I should have felt irreparably hurt. The idea of being afraid of any crossing in the lot, in the *day time*, was a thing too preposterous for contemplation. Well, one matchless summer's day I was bowling down the bend above island 66, brimful of self-conceit and carrying my nose as high as a giraffe's, when Mr. Bixby said, –

"I am going below a while. I suppose you know the next crossing?"

This was almost an affront. It was about the plainest and simplest crossing in the whole river. One couldn't come to any harm, whether he ran it right or not; and as for depth, there never had been any bottom there. I knew all this, perfectly well.

"Know how to *run* it? Why, I can run it with my eyes shut."

"How much water is there in it?"

"Well, that is an odd question. I couldn't get bottom there with a church steeple."

"You think so, do you?"

The very tone of the question shook my confidence. That was what Mr. Bixby was expecting. He left, without saying any thing more. I began to imagine all sorts of things. Mr. Bixby, unknown to me, of course, sent some body down to the forecastle with some mysterious instructions to the leadsmen, another messenger was sent to whisper among the officers, and then Mr. Bixby went into hiding behind a smoke-stack where he could observe results. Presently the captain stepped out on the hurricane deck; next the chief mate appeared; then a clerk. Every moment or two a straggler was added to my audience; and before I got to the head of the island I had fifteen or twenty people assembled down there under my nose. I began to wonder what the trouble was. As I started across, the captain glanced aloft at me and said, with a sham uneasiness in his voice, –

"Where is Mr. Bixby?"

"Gone below, sir."

But that did the business for me. My imagination began to construct dangers out of nothing, and they multiplied faster than I could keep the run of them. All at once I imagined I saw shoal water ahead! The wave of coward agony that surged through me then came near dislocating every joint in me. All my confidence in that crossing vanished. I seized the bell-rope; dropped it, ashamed; seized it again; dropped it once more; clutched it tremblingly once again, and pulled it so feebly that I could hardly hear the stroke myself. Captain and mate sang out instantly, and both together, –

"Starboard lead there! and quick about it!"

This was another shock. I began to climb the wheel like a squirrel; but I would hardly get the boat started to port before I would see new dangers on that side, and away I would spin to the other; only to find perils accumulating to starboard, and be crazy to get to port again. Then came the leadsman's sepulchral cry: –

"D-e-e-p four!"

Deep four in a bottomless crossing! The terror of it took my breath away.

"M-a-r-k three! . . . M-a-r-k three . . . Quarter less three! . . . Half twain!"

This was frightful! I seized the bell-ropes and stopped the engines.

"Quarter twain! Quarter twain! *Mark* twain!"

I was helpless. I did not know what in the world to do. I was quaking from head to foot, and I could have hung my hat on my eyes, they stuck out so far.

"Quarter *less* twain! Nine and a *half*!"

We were *drawing* nine! My hands were in a nerveless flutter. I could not ring a bell intelligibly with them. I flew to the speaking tube and shouted to the engineer, –

"Oh, Ben, if you love me, *back* her! Quick, Ben! Oh, back the immortal *soul* out of her!"

I heard the door close gently. I looked around, and there stood Mr. Bixby, smiling a bland, sweet smile. Then the audience on the hurricane deck sent up a thundergust of humiliating laughter. I saw it all, now, and I felt meaner than the meanest man in human history. I laid in the lead, set the boat in her marks, came ahead on the engines, and said: –

"It was a fine trick to play on an orphan, *wasn't* it? I suppose I'll never hear the last of how I was ass enough to heave the lead at the head of 66."

"Well, no, you won't, may be. In fact I hope you won't; for I want you to learn some thing by that experience. Didn't you *know* there was no bottom in that crossing?"

"Yes, sir, I did."

"Very well, then. You shouldn't have allowed me or anybody else to shake your confidence in that knowledge. Try to remember that. And another thing: when you get into a dangerous place, don't turn coward. That isn't going to help matters any."

It was a good enough lesson, but pretty hardly learned. Yet about the hardest part of it was that for months I so often had to hear a phrase which I had conceived a particular distaste for. It was, "Oh, Ben, if you love me, back her!"

CHAPTER XIV

RANK AND DIGNITY OF PILOTING

IN MY PRECEDING chapters I have tried, by going into the minutiæ of the science of piloting, to carry the reader step by step to a comprehension of what the science consists of; and at the same time

I have tried to show him that it is a very curious and wonderful science, too, and very worthy of his attention. If I have seemed to love my subject, it is no surprising thing, for I loved the profession far better than any I have followed since, and I took a measureless pride in it. The reason is plain: a pilot, in those days, was the only unfettered and entirely independent human being that lived in the earth. Kings are but the hampered servants of parliament and people; parliaments sit in chains forged by their constituency; the editor of a newspaper cannot be independent, but must work with one hand tied behind him by party and patrons, and be content to utter only half or two-thirds of his mind; no clergyman is a free man and may speak the whole truth, regardless of his parish's opinions; writers of all kinds are manacled servants of the public. We write frankly and fearlessly, but then we "modify" before we print. In truth, every man and woman and child has a master, and worries and frets in servitude; but in the day I write of, the Mississippi pilot had *none*. The captain could stand upon the hurricane deck, in the pomp of a very brief authority, and give him five or six orders while the vessel backed into the stream, and then that skipper's reign was over. The moment that the boat was under way in the river, she was under the sole and unquestioned control of the pilot. He could do with her exactly as he pleased, run her when and whither he chose, and tie her up to the bank whenever his judgment said that that course was best. His movements were entirely free; he consulted no one, he received commands from nobody, he promptly resented even the merest suggestions. Indeed, the law of the United States forbade him to listen to commands or suggestions, rightly considering that the pilot necessarily knew better how to handle the boat than anybody could tell him. So here was the novelty of a king without a keeper, an absolute monarch who was absolute in sober truth and not by a fiction of words. I have seen a boy of eighteen taking a great steamer serenely into what seemed almost certain destruction, and the aged captain standing mutely by, filled with apprehension but powerless to interfere. His interference, in that particular instance, might have been an excellent thing, but to permit it would have been to establish a most pernicious precedent. It will easily be guessed, considering the pilot's boundless authority, that he was a great personage in the old steamboating days. He was treated with marked courtesy by the captain and with marked deference by all the officers and servants; and this deferential spirit was quickly communicated to the passengers, too. I think pilots were about the only people I ever knew who failed to show, in some degree, embarrassment in the presence of traveling foreign princes. But then, people in one's own grade of life are not usually embarrassing objects.

By long habit, pilots came to put all their wishes in the form of commands. It "gravels" me, to this day, to put my will in the weak shape of a request, instead of launching it in the crisp language of an order.

In those old days, to load a steamboat at St. Louis, take her to New Orleans and back, and discharge cargo, consumed about twenty-five days, on an average. Seven or eight of these days the boat spent at the wharves of St. Louis and New Orleans, and every soul on board was hard at work, except the two pilots; *they* did nothing but play gentleman up town, and receive the same wages for it as if they had been on duty. The moment the boat touched the wharf at either city, they were ashore; and they were not likely to be seen again till the last bell was ringing and everything in readiness for another voyage.

When a captain got hold of a pilot of particularly high reputation, he took pains to keep him. When wages were four hundred dollars a month on the Upper Mississippi, I have known a captain to keep such a pilot in idleness, under full pay, three months at a time, while the river was frozen up. And one must remember that in those cheap times four hundred dollars was a salary of almost inconceivable splendor. Few men on shore got such pay as that, and when they did they were mightily looked up to. When pilots from either end of the river wandered into our small Missouri village, they were sought by the best and the fairest, and treated with exalted respect. Lying in port under wages was a thing which many pilots greatly enjoyed and appreciated; especially if they belonged in the Missouri River in the hey-day of that trade (Kansas times), and got nine hundred dollars a trip, which was equivalent to about eighteen hundred dollars a month. Here is a conversation of that day. A chap out of the Illinois River, with a little stern-wheel tub, accosts a couple of ornate and gilded Missouri River pilots: –

"Gentlemen, I've got a pretty good trip for the up-country, and shall want you about a month. How much will it be?"

"Eighteen hundred dollars apiece."

"Heavens and earth! You take my boat, let me have your wages, and I'll divide!"

I will remark, in passing, that Mississippi steamboatmen were important in landsmen's eyes (and in their own, too, in a degree) according to the dignity of the boat they were on. For instance, it was a proud thing to be of the crew of such stately craft as the "Aleck Scott" or the "Grand Turk." Negro firemen, deck-hands, and barbers belonging to those boats were distinguished personages in their grade of life, and they were well aware of that fact, too. A stalwart darky once gave offence at a negro ball in New Orleans by putting on a good many airs. Finally one of the managers bustled up to him and said, –

"Who *is* you, any way? Who *is* you? dat's what *I* wants to know!"

The offender was not disconcerted in the least, but swelled himself up and threw that into his voice which showed that he knew he was not putting on all those airs on a stinted capital.

"Who *is* I? Who *is* I? I let you know mighty quick who I is! I want you niggers to understan' dat I fires de middle do'* on de 'Aleck Scott!'"

That was sufficient.

The barber of the "Grand Turk" was a spruce young negro, who aired his importance with balmy complacency, and was greatly courted by the circle in which he moved. The young colored population of New Orleans were much given to flirting, at twilight, on the banquettes of the back streets. Some body saw and heard something like the following, one evening, in one of those localities. A middle-aged negro woman projected her head through a broken pane and shouted (very willing that the neighbors should hear and envy), "You Mary Ann, come in de house dis minute! Stannin' out dah foolin' 'long wid dat low trash, an' heah's de barber off'n de 'Gran' Turk' wants to conwerse wid you!"

My reference, a moment ago, to the fact that a pilot's peculiar official position placed him out of the reach of criticism or command, brings Stephen W—— naturally to my mind. He was a gifted pilot, a good fellow, a tireless talker, and had both wit and humor in him. He had a most irreverent independence, too, and was deliciously easy-going and comfortable in the presence of age, official dignity, and even the most august wealth. He always had work, he never saved a penny, he was a most persuasive borrower, he was in debt to every pilot on the river, and to the majority of the captains. He could throw a sort of splendor around a bit of harum-scarum, devil-may-care piloting, that made it almost fascinating – but not to every body. He made a trip with good old Captain Y—— once, and

*Door.

was "relieved" from duty when the boat got to New Orleans. Some body expressed surprise at the discharge. Captain Y—— shuddered at the mere mention of Stephen. Then his poor, thin old voice piped out something like this: –

"Why, bless me! I wouldn't have such a wild creature on my boat for the world – not for the whole world! He swears, he sings, he whistles, he yells – I never saw such an Injun to yell. All times of the night – it never made any difference to him. He would just yell that way, not for any thing in particular, but merely on account of a kind of devilish comfort he got out of it. I never could get into a sound sleep but he would fetch me out of bed, all in a cold sweat, with one of those dreadful war-whoops. A queer being, – very queer being; no respect for any thing or anybody. Sometimes he called me 'Johnny.' And he kept a fiddle, and a cat. He played execrably. This seemed to distress the cat, and so the cat would howl. Nobody could sleep where that man – and his family – was. And reckless? There never was any thing like it. Now you may believe it or not, but as sure as I am sitting here, he brought my boat a-tilting down through those awful snags at Chicot under a rattling head of steam, and the wind a-blowing like the very nation, at that! My officers will tell you so. They saw it. And, sir, while he was a-tearing right down through those snags, and I a-shaking in my shoes and praying, I wish I may never speak again if he didn't pucker up his mouth and go to *whistling*! Yes, sir; whistling 'Buffalo gals, can't you come out to-night, can't you come out to-night, can't you come out to-night'; and doing it as calmly as if we were attending a funeral and weren't related to the corpse. And when I remonstrated with him about it, he smiled down on me as if I was his child, and told me to run in the house and try to be good, and not be meddling with my superiors!"*

Once a pretty mean captain caught Stephen in New Orleans out of work and as usual out of money. He laid steady siege to Stephen, who was in a very "close place," and finally persuaded him to hire with him at one hundred and twenty-five dollars per month, just half wages, the captain agreeing not to divulge the secret and so bring down the contempt of all the guild upon the poor fellow. But the boat was not more than a day out of New Orleans before Stephen discovered that the captain was boasting of his exploit, and that all

*Considering a captain's ostentatious but hollow chieftainship, and a pilot's real authority, there was something impudently apt and happy about that way of phrasing it.

the officers had been told. Stephen winced, but said nothing. About the middle of the afternoon the captain stepped out on the hurricane deck, cast his eye around, and looked a good deal surprised. He glanced inquiringly aloft at Stephen, but Stephen was whistling placidly, and attending to business. The captain stood around a while in evident discomfort, and once or twice seemed about to make a suggestion; but the etiquette of the river taught him to avoid that sort of rashness, and so he managed to hold his peace. He chafed and puzzled a few minutes longer, then retired to his apartments. But soon he was out again, and apparently more perplexed than ever. Presently he ventured to remark, with deference, –

"Pretty good stage of the river now, ain't it, sir?"

"Well, I should say so! Bank-full *is* a pretty liberal stage."

"Seems to be a good deal of current here."

"Good deal don't describe it! It's worse than a mill-race."

"Isn't it easier in toward shore than it is out here in the middle?"

"Yes, I reckon it is; but a body can't be too careful with a steamboat. It's pretty safe out here; can't strike any bottom here, you can depend on that."

The captain departed, looking rueful enough. At this rate, he would probably die of old age before his boat got to St. Louis. Next day he appeared on deck and again found Stephen faithfully standing up the middle of the river, fighting the whole vast force of the Mississippi, and whistling the same placid tune. This thing was becoming serious. In by the shore was a slower boat clipping along in the easy water and gaining steadily; she began to make for an island chute; Stephen stuck to the middle of the river. Speech was *wrung* from the captain. He said, –

"Mr. W——, don't that chute cut off a good deal of distance?"

"I think it does, but I don't know."

"Don't know! Well, isn't there water enough in it now to go through?"

"I expect there is, but I am not certain."

"Upon my word this is odd! Why, those pilots on that boat yonder are going to try it. Do you mean to say that you don't know as much as they do?"

"*They!* Why, *they* are two-hundred-and-fifty-dollar pilots! But don't you be uneasy; I know as much as any man can afford to know for a hundred and twenty-five!"

The captain surrendered.

Five minutes later Stephen was bowling through the chute and showing the rival boat a two-hundred-and-fifty-dollar pair of heels.

CHAPTER XV

THE PILOTS' MONOPOLY

ONE DAY, ON board the "Aleck Scott," my chief, Mr. Bixby, was crawling carefully through a close place at Cat Island, both leads going, and every body holding his breath. The captain, a nervous, apprehensive man, kept still as long as he could, but finally broke down and shouted from the hurricane deck, –

"For gracious' sake, give her steam, Mr. Bixby! give her steam! She'll never raise the reef on this headway!"

For all the effect that was produced upon Mr. Bixby, one would have supposed that no remark had been made. But five minutes later, when the danger was past and the leads laid in, he burst instantly into a consuming fury, and gave the captain the most admirable cursing I ever listened to. No bloodshed ensued; but that was because the captain's cause was weak; for ordinarily he was not a man to take correction quietly.

Having now set forth in detail the nature of the science of piloting, and likewise described the rank which the pilot held among the fraternity of steamboatmen, this seems a fitting place to say a few words about an organization which the pilots once formed for the protection of their guild. It was curious and noteworthy in this, that it was perhaps the compactest, the completest, and the strongest commercial organization ever formed among men.

For a long time wages had been two hundred and fifty dollars a month; but curiously enough, as steamboats multiplied and business increased, the wages began to fall little by little. It was easy to discover the reason of this. Too many pilots were being "made." It was nice to have a "cub," a steersman, to do all the hard work for a couple of years, gratis, while his master sat on a high bench and smoked; all pilots and captains had sons or nephews who wanted to be pilots. By and by it came to pass that nearly every pilot on the river had a steersman. When a steersman had made an amount of progress that was satisfactory to any two pilots in the trade, they could get a pilot's license for him by signing an application directed to the United States Inspector. Nothing further was needed; usually no questions were asked, no proofs of capacity required.

Very well, this growing swarm of new pilots presently began to undermine the wages, in order to get berths. Too late – apparently – the knights of the tiller perceived their mistake. Plainly, some thing had to be done, and quickly; but what was to be the needful thing? A close organization. Nothing else would answer. To compass this seemed an impossibility; so it was talked, and talked, and then dropped. It was too likely to ruin whoever ventured to move in the matter. But at last about a dozen of the boldest – and some of them the best – pilots on the river launched themselves into the enterprise and took all the chances. They got a special charter from the legislature, with large powers, under the name of the Pilots' Benevolent Association; elected their officers, completed their organization, contributed capital, put "association" wages up to two hundred and fifty dollars at once – and then retired to their homes, for they were promptly discharged from employment. But there were two or three unnoticed trifles in their by-laws which had the seeds of propagation in them. For instance, all idle members of the association, in good standing, were entitled to a pension of twenty-five dollars per month. This began to bring in one straggler after another from the ranks of the new-fledged pilots, in the dull (summer) season. Better have twenty-five dollars than starve; the initiation fee was only twelve dollars, and no dues required from the unemployed.

Also, the widows of deceased members in good standing could draw twenty-five dollars per month, and a certain sum for each of their children. Also, the said deceased would be buried at the association's expense. These things resurrected all the superannuated and forgotten pilots in the Mississippi Valley. They came from farms, they came from interior villages, they came from every where. They came on crutches, on drays, in ambulances, – any way, so they got there. They paid in their twelve dollars, and straightway began to draw out twenty-five dollars a month and calculate their burial bills.

By and by, all the useless, helpless pilots, and a dozen first-class ones, were in the association, and nine-tenths of the best pilots out of it and laughing at it. It was the laughing-stock of the whole river. Every body joked about the by-law requiring members to pay ten per cent. Of their wages, every month, into the treasury for the support of the association, whereas all the members were outcast and tabooed, and no one would employ them. Every body was derisively grateful to the association for taking all the worthless pilots out of the way and leaving the whole field to the excellent and the deserving; and every body was not only jocularly grateful for that, but for a result which naturally followed, namely, the gradual advance of wages as the busy season approached. Wages had gone up from the low figure of one hundred dollars a month to one hundred and twenty-five, and in some cases to one hundred and fifty; and it was great fun to enlarge upon the fact that this charming thing had been accomplished by a body of men not one of whom received a particle of benefit from it. Some of the jokers used to call at the association rooms and have a good time chaffing the members and offering them the charity of taking them as steersmen for a trip, so that they could see what the forgotten river looked like. However, the association was content; or at least it gave no sign to the contrary. Now and then it captured a pilot who was "out of luck," and added him to its list; and these later additions were very valuable, for they were good pilots; the incompetent ones had all been absorbed before. As business freshened, wages climbed gradually up to two hundred and fifty dollars – the association figure – and became firmly fixed there; and still without benefiting a member of that body, for no member was hired. The hilarity at the association's expense burst all bounds, now. There was no end to the fun which that poor martyr had to put up with.

However, it is a long lane that has no turning. Winter approached, business doubled and trebled, and an avalanche of Missouri, Illinois, and Upper Mississippi River boats came pouring down to take a chance in the New Orleans trade. All of a sudden, pilots were in great demand, and were correspondingly scarce. The time for revenge was come. It was a bitter pill to have to accept association pilots at last, yet captains and owners agreed that there was no other way. But none of these outcasts offered! So there was a still bitterer pill to be swallowed: they must be sought out and asked for their services. Captain —— was the first man who found it necessary to take the dose, and he had been the loudest derider of the organization. He hunted up one of the best of the association pilots and said, –

"Well, you boys have rather got the best of us for a little while, so I'll give in with as good a grace as I can. I've come to hire you; get your trunk aboard right away. I want to leave at twelve o'clock."

"I don't know about that. Who is your other pilot?"

"I've got I. S——. Why?"

"I can't go with him. He don't belong to the association."

"What!"

"It's so."

"Do you mean to tell me that you won't turn a wheel with one of the very best and oldest pilots on the river because he don't belong to your association?"

"Yes, I do."

"Well, if this isn't putting on airs! I supposed I was doing you a benevolence; but I begin to think that I am the party that wants a favor done. Are you acting under a law of the concern?"

"Yes."

"Show it to me."

So they stepped into the association rooms, and the secretary soon satisfied the captain, who said, –

"Well, what am I to do? I have hired Mr. S—— for the entire season."

"I will provide for you," said the secretary. "I will detail a pilot to go with you, and he shall be on board at twelve o'clock."

"But if I discharge S——, he will come on me for the whole season's wages."

"Of course that is a matter between you and Mr. S——, captain. We cannot meddle in your private affairs."

The captain stormed, but to no purpose. In the end he had to discharge S——, pay him about a thousand dollars, and take an association pilot in his place. The laugh was beginning to turn the other way, now. Every day, thenceforward, a new victim fell; every day some outraged captain discharged a non-association pet, with tears and profanity, and installed a hated association man in his berth. In a very little while, idle non-associationists began to be pretty plenty, brisk as business was, and much as their services were desired. The laugh was shifting to the other side of their mouths most palpably. These victims, together with the captains and owners, presently ceased to laugh altogether, and began to rage about the revenge they would take when the passing business "spurt" was over.

Soon all the laughers that were left were the owners and crews of boats that had two non-association pilots. But their triumph was not very long-lived. For this reason: It was a rigid rule of the association that its members should never, under any circumstances whatever, give information about the channel to any "outsider." By this time about half the boats had none but association pilots, and the other half had none but outsiders. At the first glance one would suppose that when it came to forbidding information about the river these two parties could play equally at that game; but this was not so. At every good-sized town from one end of the river to the other, there was a "wharf-boat" to land at, instead of a wharf or a pier. Freight was stored in it for transportation; waiting passengers slept in its cabins. Upon each of these wharf-boats the association's officers placed a strong box, fastened with a peculiar lock which was used in no other service but one – the United States mail service. It was the letter-bag lock, a sacred governmental thing. By dint of much beseeching the government had been persuaded to allow the association to use this lock. Every association man carried a key which would open these boxes. That key, or rather a peculiar way of holding it in the hand when its owner was asked for river information by a stranger, – for the success of the St. Louis and New Orleans association had now bred tolerably thriving branches in a dozen neighboring steamboat trades, – was the association man's sign and diploma of membership; and if the stranger did not respond by producing a similar key and holding it in a certain manner duly prescribed, his question was politely ignored. From the association's secretary each member received a package of more or less gorgeous blanks, printed like a bill-head, on handsome paper, properly ruled in columns; a bill-head worded something like this: –

STEAMER GREAT REPUBLIC.

JOHN SMITH, MASTER.

Pilots, John Jones and Thomas Brown.

CROSSINGS.	SOUNDINGS.	MARKS.	REMARKS.

These blanks were filled up, day by day, as the voyage progressed, and deposited in the several wharf-boat boxes. For instance, as soon as the first crossing, out from St. Louis, was completed, the items would be entered upon the blank, under the appropriate headings, thus: –

"St. Louis. Nine and a half (feet). Stern on court-house, head on dead cotton-wood above wood-yard, until you raise the first reef, then pull up square." Then under head of Remarks: "Go just outside the wrecks; this is important. New snag just where you straighten down; go above it."

The pilot who deposited that blank in the Cairo box (after adding to it the details of every crossing all the way down from St. Louis) took out and read half a dozen fresh reports (from upward-bound steamers) concerning the river between Cairo and Memphis, posted himself thoroughly, returned them to the box, and went back aboard his boat again so armed against accident that he could not possibly get his boat into trouble without bringing the most ingenious carelessness to his aid.

Imagine the benefits of so admira[illegible] in a piece of river twelve or thirteen hundred miles long, [illegible]annel was shifting every day! The pilot who had formerly be[illegible]d to put up with seeing a shoal place once or possibly twice a [illegible]had a hundred sharp eyes to watch it for him, now, and bushel[illegible]lligent brains to tell him how to run it. His information ab[illegible]was seldom twenty-four hours old. If the reports in the last box c[illegible]d to leave any misgivings on his mind concerning a treacherou[illegible]sing, he had his remedy; he blew his steam-whistle in a peculiar w[illegible]s soon as he saw a boat approaching; the signal was answered in a [illegible]uliar way if that boat's pilots were association men; and then the [illegible]vo steamers ranged alongside and all uncertainties were swept away by fresh information furnished to the inquirer by word of mouth and in minute detail.

The first thing a pilot did when he reached New Orleans or St. Louis was to take his final and elaborate report to the association parlors and hang it up there, – *after* which he was free to visit his family. In these parlors a crowd was always gathered together, discussing changes in the channel, and the moment there was a fresh arrival, every body stopped talking till this witness had told the newest news and settled the latest uncertainty. Other craftsmen can "sink the shop," sometimes, and interest themselves in other matters. Not so with a pilot; he must devote himself wholly to his profession and talk of nothing else; for it would be small gain to be perfect one day and imperfect the next. He has no time or words to waste if he would keep "posted."

But the outsiders had a hard time of it. No particular place to meet and exchange information, no wharf-boat reports, none but chance and unsatisfactory ways of getting news. The consequence was that a man sometimes had to run five hundred miles of river on information that was a week or ten days old. At a fair stage of the river that might have answered; but when the dead low water came it was destructive.

Now came another perfectly logical result. The outsiders began to ground steamboats, sink them, and get into all sorts of trouble, whereas accidents seemed to keep entirely away from the association men. Wherefore even the owners and captains of boats furnished exclusively with outsiders, and previously considered to be wholly independent of the association and free to comfort themselves with brag and laughter, began to feel pretty uncomfortable. Still, they made a show of keeping up the brag, until one black day

e lot was formally ordered to immediately
when every ca s and take association pilots in their stead.
discharge his had the dashing presumption to do that? Alas,
And who w wer behind the throne that was greater than the
it came fro as the underwriters!
throne its me to "swap knives." Every outsider had to take his
It was at once. Of course it was supposed that there was col-
trunk a ween the association and the underwriters, but this was
lusion The latter had come to comprehend the excellence of the
not "re rt" system of the association and the safety it secured, and so
th y had made their decision among themselves and upon plain
business principles.

There was weeping and wailing and gnashing of teeth in the camp of the outsiders now. But no matter, there was but one course for them to pursue, and they pursued it. They came forward in couples and groups, and proffered their twelve dollars and asked for membership. They were surprised to learn that several new by-laws had been long ago added. For instance, the initiation fee had been raised to fifty dollars; that sum must be tendered, and also ten per cent. of the wages which the applicant had received each and every month since the founding of the association. In many cases this amounted to three or four hundred dollars. Still, the association would not entertain the application until the money was present. Even then a single adverse vote killed the application. Every member had to vote yes or no in person and before witnesses; so it took weeks to decide a candidacy, because many pilots were so long absent on voyages. However, the repentant sinners scraped their savings together, and one by one, by our tedious voting process, they were added to the fold. A time came, at last, when only about ten remained outside. They said they would starve before they would apply. They remained idle a long while, because of course nobody could venture to employ them.

By and by the association published the fact that upon a certain date the wages would be raised to five hundred dollars per month. All the branch associations had grown strong, now, and the Red River one had advanced wages to seven hundred dollars a month. Reluctantly the ten outsiders yielded, in view of these things, and made application. There was *another* new by-law, by this time, which required them to pay dues not only on all the wages they had received since the association was born, but also on what they would have received if they had continued at work up to the time of their application, instead of going off to pout in idleness. It turned out to be a difficult matter to elect them, but it was accomplished at last. The most virulent sinner of this batch had stayed out and allowed "dues" to accumulate against him so long that he had to send in six hundred and twenty-five dollars with his application.

The association had a good bank account now, and was very strong. There was no longer an outsider. A by-law was added forbidding the reception of any more cubs or apprentices for five years; after which time a limited number would be taken, not by individuals, but by the association, upon these terms: the applicant must not be less than eighteen years old, and of respectable family and good character; he must pass an examination as to education, pay a thousand dollars in advance for the privilege of becoming an apprentice, and must remain under the commands of the association until a great part of the membership (more than half, I think) should be willing to sign his application for a pilot's license.

All previously-articled apprentices were now taken away from their masters and adopted by the association. The president and secretary detailed them for service on one boat or another, as they chose, and changed them from boat to boat according to certain rules. If a pilot could show that he was in infirm health and needed assistance, one of the cubs would be ordered to go with him.

The widow and orphan list grew, but so did the association's financial resources. The association attended its own funerals in state, and paid for them. When occasion demanded, it sent members down the river upon searches for the bodies of brethren lost by steamboat accidents; a search of this kind sometimes cost a thousand dollars.

The association procured a charter and went into the insurance business, also. It not only insured the lives of its members, but took risks on steamboats.

The organization seemed indestructible. It was the tightest monopoly in the world. By the United States law, no man could become a pilot unless two duly licensed pilots signed his application; and now there was nobody outside of the association competent to sign. Consequently the making of pilots was at an end. Every year some would die and others become incapacitated by age and infirmity; there would be no new ones to take their places. In time, the association could put wages up to any figure it chose; and as long as it should be wise enough not to carry the thing too far and provoke the national government into amending the licensing system, steamboat owners would have to submit, since there would be no help for it.

The owners and captains were the only obstruction that lay between the association and absolute power; and at last this one was removed. Incredible as it may seem, the owners and captains deliberately did it themselves. When the pilots' association announced, months beforehand, that on the first day of September, 1861, wages would be advanced to five hundred dollars per month, the owners and captains instantly put freights up a few cents, and explained to the farmers along the river the necessity of it, by calling their attention to the burdensome rate of wages about to be established. It was a rather slender argument, but the farmers did not seem to detect it. It looked reasonable to them that to add five cents freight on a bushel of corn was justifiable under the circumstances, overlooking the fact that this advance on a cargo of forty thousand sacks was a good deal more than necessary to cover the new wages.

So, straightway the captains and owners got up an association of their own, and proposed to put captains' wages up to five hundred dollars, too, and move for another advance in freights. It was a novel idea, but of course an effect which had been produced once could be produced again. The new association decreed (for this was before all the outsiders had been taken into the pilots' association) that if any captain employed a non-association pilot, he should be forced to discharge him, and also pay a fine of five hundred dollars. Several of these heavy fines were paid before the captains' organization grew strong enough to exercise full authority over its membership; but that all ceased, presently. The captains tried to get the pilots to decree that no member of their corporation should serve under a non-association captain; but this proposition was declined. The pilots saw that they would be backed up by the captains and the underwriters any how, and so they wisely refrained from entering into entangling alliances.

As I have remarked, the pilots' association was now the compactest monopoly in the world, perhaps, and seemed simply indestructible. And yet the days of its glory were numbered. First, the new railroad stretching up through Mississippi, Tennessee, and Kentucky, to Northern railway centres, began to divert the passenger travel from the steamers; next the war came and almost entirely annihilated the steamboating industry during several years, leaving most of the pilots idle, and the cost of living advancing all the time;

then the treasurer of the St. Louis association put his hand into the till and walked off with every dollar of the ample fund; and finally, the railroads intruding every where, there was little for steamers to do, when the war was over, but carry freights; so straightway some genius from the Atlantic coast introduced the plan of towing a dozen steamer cargoes down to New Orleans at the tail of a vulgar little tug-boat; and behold, in the twinkling of an eye, as it were, the association and the noble science of piloting were things of the dead and pathetic past!

CHAPTER XVI

RACING DAYS

IT WAS ALWAYS the custom for the boats to leave New Orleans between four and five o'clock in the afternoon. From three o'clock onward they would be burning rosin and pitch pine (the sign of preparation), and so one had the picturesque spectacle of a rank, some two or three miles long, of tall, ascending columns of coal-black smoke; a colonnade which supported a sable roof of the same smoke blended together and spreading abroad over the city. Every outward-bound boat had its flag flying at the jack-staff, and sometimes a duplicate on the verge staff astern. Two or three miles of mates were commanding and swearing with more than usual emphasis; countless processions of freight barrels and boxes were spinning athwart the levee and flying aboard the stage-planks; belated passengers were dodging and skipping among these frantic things, hoping to reach the forecastle companion-way alive, but having their doubts about it; women with reticules and bandboxes were trying to keep up with husbands freighted with carpet sacks and crying babies, and making a failure of it by losing their heads in the whirl and roar and general distraction; drays and baggage-vans were clattering hither and thither in a wild hurry, every now and then getting blocked and jammed together, and then during ten seconds one could not see them for the profanity, except vaguely and dimly; every windlass connected with every fore-hatch, from one end of that long array of steamboats to the other, was keeping up a deafening whiz and whir, lowering freight into the hold, and the half-naked crews of perspiring negroes that worked them were roaring such songs as "De Las' Sack! De Las' Sack!" – inspired to unimaginable exaltation by the chaos of turmoil and racket that was driving every body else mad. By this time the hurricane and boiler decks of the steamers would be packed and black with passengers. The "last bells" would begin to clang, all down the line, and then the pow-wow seemed to double; in a moment or two the final warning came, – a simultaneous din of Chinese gongs, with the cry, "All dat ain't goin', please to git asho'!" – and behold, the pow-wow quadrupled! People came swarming ashore, overturning excited stragglers that were trying to swarm aboard. One more moment later a long array of stage-planks was being hauled in, each with its customary latest passenger clinging to the end of it with teeth, nails, and everything else, and the customary latest procrastinator making a wild spring shoreward over his head.

Now a number of the boats slide backward into the stream, leaving wide gaps in the serried rank of steamers. Citizens crowd the decks of boats that are not to go, in order to see the sight. Steamer after steamer straightens herself up, gathers all her strength, and presently comes swinging by, under a tremendous head of steam, with flag flying, black smoke rolling, and her entire crew of firemen and deck-hands (usually swarthy negroes) massed together on the forecastle, the best "voice" in the lot towering from the midst (being mounted on the capstan), waving his hat or a flag, and all roaring a mighty chorus, while the parting cannons boom and the multitudinous spectators swing their hats and huzza! Steamer after steamer falls into line, and the stately procession goes winging its flight up the river.

In the old times, whenever two fast boats started out on a race, with a big crowd of people looking on, it was inspiring to hear the crews sing, especially if the time were night-fall, and the forecastle lit up with the red glare of the torch-baskets. Racing was royal fun. The public always had an idea that racing was dangerous; whereas the opposite was the case – that is, after the laws were passed which restricted each boat to just so many pounds of steam to the square inch. No engineer was ever sleepy or careless when his heart was in a race. He was constantly on the alert, trying gauge-cocks and watching things. The dangerous place was on slow, plodding boats, where the engineers drowsed around and allowed chips to get into the "doctor" and shut off the water supply from the boilers.

In the "flush times" of steamboating, a race between two notoriously fleet steamers was an event of vast importance. The date was set for it several weeks in advance, and from that time forward, the whole Mississippi Valley was in a state of consuming excitement. Politics and the weather were dropped, and people talked only of the coming race. As the time approached, the two steamers "stripped" and got ready. Every incumbrance that added weight, or exposed a resisting surface to wind or water, was removed, if the boat could possibly do without it. The "spars," and sometimes even their supporting derricks, were sent ashore, and no means left to set the boat afloat in case she got aground. When the "Eclipse" and the "A. L. Shotwell" ran their great race many years ago, it was said that pains were taken to scrape the gilding off the fanciful device which hung between the "Eclipse's" chimneys, and that for that one trip the captain left off his kid gloves and had his head shaved. But I always doubted these things.

If the boat was known to make her best speed when drawing five and a half feet forward and five feet aft, she was carefully loaded to that exact figure – she wouldn't enter a dose of homœopathic pills on her manifest after that. Hardly any passengers were taken, because they not only add weight but they never will "trim boat." They always run to the side when there is any thing to see, whereas a conscientious and experienced steamboatman would stick to the centre of the boat and part his hair in the middle with a spirit level.

No way-freights and no way-passengers were allowed, for the racers would stop only at the largest towns, and then it would be only "touch and go." Coal-flats and wood-flats were contracted for before-hand, and these were kept ready to hitch on to the flying steamers at a moment's warning. Double crews were carried, so that all work could be quickly done.

The chosen date being come, and all things in readiness, the two great steamers back into the stream, and lie there jockeying a moment, and apparently watching each other's slightest movement, like sentient creatures; flags drooping, the pent steam shrieking through safety-valves, the black smoke rolling and tumbling from the chimneys and darkening all the air. People, people every where; the shores, the house-tops, the steamboats, the ships, are packed with them, and you know that the borders of the broad Mississippi are going to be fringed with humanity thence northward twelve hundred miles, to welcome these racers.

Presently tall columns of steam burst from the 'scape-pipes of both steamers, two guns boom a good-bye, two red-shirted heroes mounted on capstans wave their small flags above the massed crews on the forecastles, two plaintive solos linger on the air a few waiting seconds, two mighty choruses burst forth – and here they come! Brass bands bray Hail Columbia, huzza after huzza thunders from the shores, and the stately creatures go whistling by like the wind.

Those boats will never halt a moment between New Orleans and St. Louis, except for a second or two at large towns, or to hitch thirty-cord wood-boats alongside. You should be on board when they take a couple of those wood-boats in tow and turn a swarm of men into each; by the time you have wiped your glasses and put them on, you will be wondering what has become of that wood.

Two nicely matched steamers will stay in sight of each other day after day. They might even stay side by side, but for the fact that pilots are not all alike, and the smartest pilots will win the race. If one of the boats has a "lightning" pilot, whose "partner" is a trifle his inferior, you can tell which one is on watch by noting whether that boat has gained ground or lost some during each four-hour stretch. The shrewdest pilot can delay a boat if he has not a fine genius for steering. Steering is a very high art. One must not keep a rudder dragging across a boat's stern if he wants to get up the river fast.

There is a great difference in boats, of course. For a long time I was on a boat that was so slow we used to forget what year it was we left port in. But of course this was at rare intervals. Ferry-boats used to lose valuable trips because their passengers grew old and died, waiting for us to get by. This was at still rarer intervals. I had the documents for these occurrences, but through carelessness they have been mislaid. This boat, the "John J. Roe," was so slow that when she finally sunk in Madrid Bend, it was five years before the owners heard of it. That was always a confusing fact to me, but it is according to the record, any way. She was dismally slow; still, we often had pretty exciting times racing with islands, and rafts, and such things. One trip, however, we did rather well. We went to St. Louis in sixteen days. But even at this rattling gait I think we changed watches three times in Fort Adams reach, which is five miles long. A "reach" is a piece of straight river, and of course the current drives through such a place in a pretty lively way.

That trip we went to Grand Gulf, from New Orleans, in four days (three hundred and forty miles); the "Eclipse" and "Shotwell" did it in one. We were nine days out, in the chute of 63 (seven hundred miles); the "Eclipse" and "Shotwell" went there in two days.

Something over a generation ago, a boat called the "J. M. White" went from New Orleans to Cairo in three days, six hours, and forty-four minutes. In 1853 the "Eclipse" made the same trip in three days, three hours, and twenty minutes.* In 1870 the "R. E. Lee" did it in three days and *one* hour. This last is called the fastest trip on record. I will try to show that it was not. For this reason: the distance between New Orleans and Cairo, when the "J. M. White" ran it, was about eleven hundred and six miles; consequently her average speed was a trifle over fourteen miles per hour. In the "Eclipse's" day the distance between the two ports had become reduced to one thousand and eighty miles; consequently her average speed was a shade under fourteen and three-eighths miles per hour. In the "R. E. Lee's" time the distance had diminished to about one thousand and thirty miles; consequently her average was about fourteen and one-eighth miles per hour. Therefore the "Eclipse's" was conspicuously the fastest time that has ever been made.

THE RECORD OF SOME FAMOUS TRIPS.

[*From Commodore Rollingpin's Almanac.*]

FAST TIME ON THE WESTERN WATERS.

FROM NEW ORLEANS TO NATCHEZ – 268 MILES.

		D.	H.	M.
1814.	Orleans made the run in	6	6	40
1814.	Comet " "	5	10	
1815.	Enterprise " "	4	11	20
1817.	Washington " "	4		
1817.	Shelby " "	3	20	
1819.	Paragon " "	3	8	
1828.	Tecumseh " "	3	1	20
1834.	Tuscarora " "	1	21	
1838.	Natchez " "	1	17	
1840.	Ed. Shippen " "	1	8	
1842.	Belle of the West "	1	18	

		H.	M.
1844.	Sultana...made the run in	19	45
1851.	Magnolia " "	19	50
1853.	A. L. Shotwell " "	19	49
1853.	Southern Belle " "	20	3
1853.	Princess (No. 4) " "	20	26
1853.	Eclipse " "	19	47
1855.	Princess (New) " "	18	53
1855.	Natchez (New) " "	17	30
1856.	Princess (New) " "	17	30
1870.	Natchez " "	17	17
1870.	R. E. Lee " "	17	11

FROM NEW ORLEANS TO CAIRO – 1,024 MILES.

		D.	H.	M.
1844.	J. M. White made the run in	3	6	44
1852.	Reindeer " "	3	12	45
1853.	Eclipse " "	3	4	4
1853.	A. L. Shotwell " "	3	3	40

		D.	H.	M.
1869.	Dexter...made the run in	3	6	20
1870.	Natchez " "	3	4	34
1870.	R. E. Lee " "	3	1	

*Time disputed. Some authorities add 1 hour and 16 minutes to this.

TIME TABLE.—*Continued*

FROM NEW ORLEANS TO LOUISVILLE – 1,440 MILES.

Year	Boat	D.	H.	M.
1815.	Enterprise made the run in	25	2	40
1817.	Washington " "	25		
1817.	Shelby " "	20	4	20
1819.	Paragon " "	18	10	
1828.	Tecumseh " "	8	4	
1834.	Tuscarora " "	7	16	
1837.	Gen. Brown " "	6	22	
1837.	Randolph " "	6	22	
1837.	Empress " "	6	17	
1837.	Sultana " "	6	15	
1840.	Ed. Shippen made the run in	5	14	
1842.	Belle of the West " "	6	14	
1843.	Duke of Orleans " "	5	23	
1844.	Sultana " "	5	12	
1849.	Bostona " "	5	8	
1851.	Belle Key " "	4	28	
1852.	Reindeer " "	4	20	45
1852.	Eclipse " "	4	19	
1853.	A. L. Shotwell " "	4	10	20
1853.	Eclipse " "	4	9	30

FROM NEW ORLEANS TO DONALDSVILLE – 78 MILES.

Year	Boat	H.	M.
1852.	A. L. Shotwell made the run in	5	42
1852.	Eclipse " "	5	42
1854.	Sultana " "	5	12
1856.	Princess " "	4	51
1860.	Atlantic...made the run in	5	11
1860.	Gen. Quitman " "	5	6
1865.	Ruth " "	4	43
1870.	R. E. Lee " "	4	59

FROM NEW ORLEANS TO ST. LOUIS – 1,218 MILES.

Year	Boat	D.	H.	M.
1844.	J. M. White made the run in	3	23	9
1849.	Missouri " "	4	19	
1869.	Dexter " "	4	9	
1870.	Natchez...made the run in	3	21	58
1870.	R. E. Lee " "	3	18	14

FROM LOUISVILLE TO CINCINNATI – 141 MILES.

Year	Boat	D.	H.	M.
1819.	Gen. Pike made the run in	1	16	
1819.	Paragon " "	1	14	20
1822.	Wheeling Packet " "	1	10	
1837.	Moselle " "		12	
1843.	Duke of Orleans " "		12	
1843.	Congress...made the run in		12	20
1846.	Ben Franklin (No. 6) "		11	45
1852.	Alleghaney " "		10	38
1852.	Pittsburgh " "		10	23
1853.	Telegraph No. 3 " "		9	52

FROM LOUISVILLE TO ST. LOUIS – 750 MILES.

Year	Boat	D.	H.	M.
1843.	Congress...made the run in	2	1	
1854.	Pike " "	1	23	
1854.	Northerner made the run in	1	22	30
1855.	Southerner " "	1	19	

FROM CINCINNATI TO PITTSBURG – 490 MILES.

Year	Boat	D.	H.
1850.	Telegraph No. 2 made the run in	1	17
1851.	Buckeye State " "	1	16
1852.	Pittsburgh...made the run in	1	15

FROM ST. LOUIS TO ALTON – 30 MILES.

Year	Boat	H.	M.
1853.	Altona...made the run in	1	35
1876.	Golden Eagle " "	1	37
1876.	War Eagle...made the run in	1	37

MISCELLANEOUS RUNS.

In June, 1859, the St. Louis and Keokuk Packet, City of Louisiana, made the run from St. Louis to Keokuk (214 miles) in 16 hours and 20 minutes, the best time on record.

In 1868 the steamer Hawkeye State, of the Northern Line Packet Company, made the run from St. Louis to St. Paul (800 miles) in 2 days and 20 hours. Never was beaten.

In 1853 the steamer Polar Star made the run from St. Louis to St. Joseph, on the Missouri River, in 64 hours. In July, 1856, the steamer Jas. H. Lucas, Andy Wineland, Master, made the same run in 60 hours and 57 minutes. The distance between the ports is 600 miles, and when the difficulties of navigating the turbulent Missouri are taken into consideration, the performance of the Lucas deserves especial mention.

The time made by the R. E. Lee from New Orleans to St. Louis in 1870, in her famous race with the Natchez, is the best on record, and, inasmuch as the race created a national interest, we give below her time table from port to port.

Left New Orleans, Thursday, June 30th, 1870, at 4 o'clock and 55 minutes, P.M.; reached

	D.	H.	M.
Carrollton			27½
Harry Hills		1	00½
Red Church		1	39
Bonnet Carre		2	38
College Point		3	50½
Donaldsonville		4	59
Plaquemine		7	05½
Baton Rouge		8	25
Bayou Sara		10	26
Red River		12	56
Stamps		13	56
Bryaro		15	51½
Hinderson's		16	29
Natchez		17	11
Cole's Creek		19	21
Waterproof		18	53
Rodney		20	45
St. Joseph		21	02
Grand Gulf		22	06
Hard Times		22	18
Half Mile Below Warrenton	1		
Vicksburg	1		38
Milliken's Bend	1	2	37
Bailey's	1	3	48
Lake Providence	1	5	47
Greenville	1	10	55
Napoleon	1	16	22
White River	1	16	56
Australia	1	19	
Helena	1	23	25
Half Mile Below St. Francis	2		
Memphis	2	6	9
Foot of Island 37	2	9	
Foot of Island 26	2	13	30
Tow-head, Island 14	2	17	23
New Madrid	2	19	50
Dry Bar No. 10	2	20	37
Foot of Island 8	2	21	25
Upper Tow-head – Lucas Bend	3		
Cairo	3	1	
St. Louis	3	18	14

The Leo landed at St. Louis at 11.25 A.M., on July 4th, 1870 – six hours and thirty-six minutes ahead of the Natchez. The officers of the Natchez claimed seven hours and one minute stoppage on account of fog and repairing machinery. The R. E. Lee was commanded by Captain John W. Cannon, and the Natchez was in charge of that veteran Southern boatman, Captain Thomas P. Leathers.

CHAPTER XVII

CUT-OFFS AND STEPHEN

THESE DRY DETAILS are of importance in one particular. They give me an opportunity of introducing one of the Mississippi's oddest peculiarities, – that of shortening its length from time to time. If you will throw a long, pliant apple-paring over your shoulder, it will pretty fairly shape itself into an average section of the Mississippi River; that is, the nine or ten hundred miles stretching from Cairo, Illinois, southward to New Orleans, the same being wonderfully crooked, with a brief straight bit here and there at wide intervals. The two-hundred-mile stretch from Cairo northward to St. Louis is by no means so crooked, that being a rocky country which the river cannot cut much.

The water cuts the alluvial banks of the "lower" river into deep horseshoe curves; so deep, indeed, that in some places if you were to get ashore at one extremity of the horseshoe and walk across the neck, half or three-quarters of a mile, you could sit down and rest a couple of hours while your steamer was coming around the long elbow, at a speed of ten miles an hour, to take you aboard again. When the river is rising fast, some scoundrel whose plantation is back in the country, and therefore of inferior value, has only to watch his chance, cut a little gutter across the narrow neck of land some dark night, and turn the water into it, and in a wonderfully short time a miracle has happened: to wit, the whole Mississippi has taken possession of that little ditch, and placed the countryman's plantation on its bank (quadrupling its value), and that other party's formerly valuable plantation finds itself away out yonder on a big island; the old watercourse around it will soon shoal up, boats can not approach within ten miles of it, and down goes its value to a fourth of its former worth. Watches are kept on those narrow necks, at needful times, and if a man happens to be caught cutting a ditch across them, the chances are all against his ever having another opportunity to cut a ditch.

Pray observe some of the effects of this ditching business. Once there was a neck opposite Port Hudson, Louisiana, which was only half a mile across, in its narrowest place. You could walk across there in fifteen minutes; but if you made the journey around the cape on a raft, you traveled thirty-five miles to accomplish the same thing. In 1722 the river darted through that neck, deserted its old bed, and thus shortened itself thirty-five miles. In the same way it shortened itself twenty-five miles at Black Hawk Point in 1699. Below Red River Landing, Raccourci cut-off was made (forty or fifty years ago, I think). This shortened the river twenty-eight miles. In our day, if you travel by river from the southernmost of these three cut-offs to the northernmost, you go only seventy miles. To do the same thing a hundred and seventy-six years ago, one had to go a hundred and fifty-eight miles! – a shortening of eighty-eight miles in that trifling distance. At some forgotten time in the past, cut-offs were made above Vidalia, Louisiana; at island 92; at island 84; and at Hale's Point. These shortened the river, in the aggregate, seventy-seven miles.

Since my own day on the Mississippi, cut-offs have been made at Hurricane Island; at island 100; at Napoleon, Arkansas; at Walnut Bend; and at Council Bend. These shortened the river, in the aggregate, sixty-seven miles. In my own time a cut-off was made at American Bend, which shortened the river ten miles or more.

Therefore, the Mississippi between Cairo and New Orleans was twelve hundred and fifteen miles long one hundred and seventy-six years ago. It was eleven hundred and eighty after the cut-off of 1722. It was one thousand and forty after the American Bend cut-off. It has lost sixty-seven miles since. Consequently its length is only nine hundred and seventy-three miles at present.

Now, if I wanted to be one of those ponderous scientific people, and "let on" to prove what had occurred in the remote past by what had occurred in a given time in the recent past, or what will occur in the far future by what has occurred in late years, what an opportunity is here! Geology never had such a chance, nor such exact data to argue from! Nor "development of species," either! Glacial epochs are great things, but they are vague – vague. Please observe: –

In the space of one hundred and seventy-six years the Lower Mississippi has shortened itself two hundred and forty-two miles. That is an average of a trifle over one mile and a third per year. Therefore, any calm person, who is not blind or idiotic, can see that in the Old Oölitic Silurian Period, just a million years ago next November, the Lower Mississippi River was upwards of one million three hundred thousand miles long, and stuck out over the Gulf of Mexico like a fishing-rod. And by the same token any person can see that seven hundred and forty-two years from now the Lower Mississippi will be only a mile and three-quarters long, and Cairo and New Orleans will have joined their streets together, and be plodding comfortably along under a single mayor and a mutual board of aldermen. There is something fascinating about science. One gets such wholesale returns of conjecture out of such a trifling investment of fact.

When the water begins to flow through one of those ditches I have been speaking of, it is time for the people thereabouts to move. The water cleaves the banks away like a knife. By the time the ditch has become twelve or fifteen feet wide, the calamity is as good as accomplished, for no power on earth can stop it now. When the width has reached a hundred yards, the banks begin to peel off in slices half an acre wide. The current flowing around the bend traveled formerly only five miles an hour; now it is tremendously increased by the shortening of the distance. I was on board the first boat that tried to go through the cut-off at American Bend, but we did not get through. It was toward midnight, and a wild night it was – thunder, lightning, and torrents of rain. It was estimated that the current in the cut-off was making about fifteen or twenty miles an hour; twelve or thirteen was the best our boat could do, even in tolerably slack water, therefore perhaps we were foolish to try the cut-off. However, Mr. Brown was ambitious, and he kept on trying.

The eddy running up the bank, under the "point," was about as swift as the current out in the middle; so we would go flying up the shore like a lightning express train, get on a big head of steam, and "stand by for a surge" when we struck the current that was whirling by the point. But all our preparations were useless. The instant the current hit us it spun us around like a top, the water deluged the forecastle, and the boat careened so far over that one could hardly keep his feet. The next instant we were away down the river, clawing with might and main to keep out of the woods. We tried the experiment four times. I stood on the forecastle companion-way to see. It was astonishing to observe how suddenly the boat would spin around and turn tail the moment she emerged from the eddy and the current struck her nose. The sounding concussion and the quivering would have been about the same if she had come full speed against a sandbank. Under the lightning-flashes one could see the plantation cabins and the goodly acres tumble into the river; and the crash they made was not a bad effort at thunder. Once, when we spun around, we only missed a house about twenty feet, that had a light burning in the window; and in the same instant that house went overboard. Nobody could stay on our forecastle; the water swept across it in a torrent every time we plunged athwart the current. At the end of our fourth effort we brought up in the woods two miles below the cut-off; all the country there was overflowed, of course. A day or two later the cut-off was three-quarters of a mile wide, and boats passed up through it without much difficulty, and so saved ten miles.

The old Raccourci cut-off reduced the river's length twenty-eight miles. There used to be a tradition connected with it. It was said that a boat came along there in the night and went around the enormous elbow the usual way, the pilots not knowing that the cut-off had been made. It was a grisly, hideous night, and all shapes were vague and distorted. The old bend had already begun to fill up, and the boat got to running away from mysterious reefs, and occasionally hitting one. The perplexed pilots fell to swearing, and finally uttered the entirely unnecessary wish that they might never get out of that place. As always happens in such cases, that particular prayer was answered, and the others neglected. So to this day that phantom steamer is still butting around in that deserted river, trying to find her way out. More than one grave watchman has sworn to me that on drizzly, dismal nights, he has glanced fearfully down that forgotten river as he passed the head of the island, and seen the faint glow of the spectre steamer's lights drifting through the distant gloom, and heard the muffled cough of her 'scape-pipes and the plaintive cry of her leadsmen.

In the absence of further statistics, I beg to close this chapter with one more reminiscence of "Stephen."

Most of the captains and pilots held Stephen's note for borrowed sums, ranging from two hundred and fifty dollars upward. Stephen never paid one of these notes, but he was very prompt and very zealous about renewing them every twelve-month.

Of course there came a time, at last, when Stephen could no longer borrow of his ancient creditors; so he was obliged to lie in wait for new men who did not know him. Such a victim was good-hearted, simple-natured young Yates (I use a fictitious name, but the real name began, as this one does, with a Y). Young Yates graduated as a pilot, got a berth, and when the month was ended and he stepped up to the clerk's office and received his two hundred and fifty dollars in crisp new bills, Stephen was there! His silvery tongue began to wag, and in a very little while Yates's two hundred and fifty dollars had changed hands. The fact was soon known at pilot headquarters, and the amusement and satisfaction of the old creditors were large and generous. But innocent Yates never suspected that

Stephen's promise to pay promptly at the end of the week was a worthless one. Yates called for his money at the stipulated time; Stephen sweetened him up and put him off a week. He called then, according to agreement, and came away sugar-coated again, but suffering under another postponement. So the thing went on. Yates haunted Stephen week after week, to no purpose, and at last gave it up. And then straightway Stephen began to haunt Yates! Wherever Yates appeared, there was the inevitable Stephen. And not only there, but beaming with affection and gushing with apologies for not being able to pay. By and by, whenever poor Yates saw him coming, he would turn and fly, and drag his company with him, if he had company; but it was of no use; his debtor would run him down and corner him. Panting and red-faced, Stephen would come, with outstretched hands and eager eyes, invade the conversation, shake both of Yates's arms loose in their sockets, and begin: –

"My, what a race I've had! I saw you didn't see me, and so I clapped on all steam for fear I'd miss you entirely. And here you are! there, just stand so, and let me look at you! Just the same old noble countenance." [To Yates's friend:] "Just look at him! *Look* at him! Ain't it just *good* to look at him! *Ain't* it now? Ain't he just a picture! *Some* call him a picture; *I* call him a panorama! That's what he is – an entire panorama. And now I'm reminded! How I do wish I could have seen you an hour earlier! For twenty-four hours I've been saving up that two hundred and fifty dollars for you; been looking for you every where. I waited at the Planter's from six yesterday evening till two o'clock this morning, without rest or food; my wife says, 'Where have you been all night?' I said, 'This debt lies heavy on my mind.' She says, 'In all my days I never saw a man take a debt to heart the way you do.' I said, 'It's my nature; how can *I* change it?' She says, 'Well, do go to bed and get some rest.' I said, 'Not till that poor, noble young man has got his money.' So I set up all night, and this morning out I shot, and the first man I struck told me you had shipped on the 'Grand Turk' and gone to New Orleans. Well, sir, I had to lean up against a building and cry. So help me goodness, I couldn't help it. The man that owned the place come out cleaning up with a rag, and said he didn't like to have people cry against his building, and then it seemed to me that the whole world had turned against me, and it wasn't any use to live anymore; and coming along an hour ago, suffering no man knows what agony, I met Jim Wilson and paid him the two hundred and fifty dollars on account;

and to think that here you are, now, and I haven't got a cent! But as sure as I am standing here on this ground on this particular brick, – there, I've scratched a mark on the brick to remember it by, – I'll borrow that money and pay it over to you at twelve o'clock sharp, to-morrow! Now, stand so; let me look at you just once more."

And so on. Yates's life became a burden to him. He could not escape his debtor and his debtor's awful sufferings on account of not being able to pay. He dreaded to show himself in the street, lest he should find Stephen lying in wait for him at the corner.

Bogart's billiard saloon was a great resort for pilots in those days. They met there about as much to exchange river news as to play. One morning Yates was there; Stephen was there, too, but kept out of sight. But by and by, when about all the pilots had arrived who were in town, Stephen suddenly appeared in the midst, and rushed for Yates as for a long-lost brother.

"*Oh*, I am so glad to see you! Oh my soul, the sight of you is such a comfort to my eyes! Gentlemen, I owe all of you money; among you I owe probably forty thousand dollars. I want to pay it; I intend to pay it – every last cent of it. You all know, without my telling you, what sorrow it has cost me to remain so long under such deep obligations to such patient and generous friends; but the sharpest pang I suffer – by far the sharpest – is from the debt I owe to this noble young man here; and I have come to this place this morning especially to make the announcement that I have at last found a method whereby I can pay off all my debts! And most especially I wanted *him* to be here when I announced it. Yes, my faithful friend, – my benefactor, I've found the method! I've found the method to pay off *all* my debts, and you'll get your money!" Hope dawned in Yates's eye; then Stephen, beaming benignantly, and placing his hand upon Yates's head, added, "I am going to pay them off in alphabetical order!"

Then he turned and disappeared. The full significance of Stephen's "method" did not dawn upon the perplexed and musing crowd for some two minutes; and then Yates murmured with a sigh: –

"Well, the Y's stand a gaudy chance. He won't get any further than the C's in *this* world, and I reckon that after a good deal of eternity has wasted away in the next one, I'll still be referred to up there as 'that poor, ragged pilot that came here from St. Louis in the early days!' "

CHAPTER XVIII

I TAKE A FEW EXTRA LESSONS

DURING THE TWO or two and a half years of my apprenticeship, I served under many pilots, and had experience of many kinds of steamboatmen and many varieties of steamboats; for it was not always convenient for Mr. Bixby to have me with him, and in such cases he sent me with some body else. I am to this day profiting somewhat by that experience; for in that brief, sharp schooling, I got personally and familiarly acquainted with about all the different types of human nature that are to be found in fiction, biography, or history. The fact is daily borne in upon me, that the average shore-employment requires as much as forty years to equip a man with this sort of an education. When I say I am still profiting by this thing, I do not mean that it has constituted me a judge of men – no, it has not done that; for judges of men are born, not made. My profit is various in kind and degree; but the feature of it which I value most is the zest which that early experience has given to my later reading. When I find a well-drawn character in fiction or biography, I generally take a warm personal interest in him, for the reason that I have known him before – met him on the river.

The figure that comes before me oftenest, out of the shadows of that vanished time, is that of Brown, of the steamer "Pennsylvania" – the man referred to in a former chapter, whose memory was so good and tiresome. He was a middle-aged, long, slim, bony, smooth-shaven, horse-faced, ignorant, stingy, malicious, snarling, fault-hunting, mote-magnifying tyrant. I early got the habit of coming on watch with dread at my heart. No matter how good a time I might have been having with the off-watch below, and no matter how high my spirits might be when I started aloft, my soul became lead in my body the moment I approached the pilot-house.

I still remember the first time I ever entered the presence of that man. The boat had backed out from St. Louis and was "straightening down"; I ascended to the pilot-house in high feather, and very proud to be semi-officially a member of the executive family of so fast and famous a boat. Brown was at the wheel. I paused in the middle of the room, all fixed to make my bow, but Brown did not look around. I thought he took a furtive glance at me out of the corner of his eye, but as not even this notice was repeated, I judged I had been mistaken. By this time he was picking his way among some dangerous "breaks" abreast the wood-yards; therefore it would not be proper to interrupt him; so I stepped softly to the high bench and took a seat.

There was silence for ten minutes; then my new boss turned and inspected me deliberately and painstakingly from head to heel for about – as it seemed to me – a quarter of an hour. After which he removed his countenance and I saw it no more for some seconds; then it came around once more, and this question greeted me: –

"Are you Horace Bigsby's cub?"

"Yes, sir."

After this there was a pause and another inspection. Then: –

"What's your name?"

I told him. He repeated it after me. It was probably the only thing he ever forgot; for although I was with him many months he never addressed himself to me in any other way than "Here!" and then his command followed.

"Where was you born?"

"In Florida, Missouri."

A pause. Then: –

"Dern sight better staid there!"

By means of a dozen or so of pretty direct questions, he pumped my family history out of me.

The leads were going now, in the first crossing. This interrupted the inquest. When the leads had been laid in, he resumed: –

"How long you been on the river?"

I told him. After a pause: –

"Where'd you get them shoes?"

I gave him the information.

"Hold up your foot!"

I did so. He stepped back, examined the shoe minutely and contemptuously, scratching his head thoughtfully, tilting his high sugar-loaf hat well forward to facilitate the operation, then ejaculated, "Well, I'll be dod derned!" and returned to his wheel.

What occasion there was to be dod derned about it is a thing which is still as much of a mystery to me now as it was then. It must have been all of fifteen minutes – fifteen minutes of dull, homesick silence – before that long horse-face swung round upon me again – and then, what a change! It was as red as fire, and every muscle in it was working. Now came this shriek: –

"Here! – You going to set there all day?"

I lit in the middle of the floor, shot there by the electric suddenness of the surprise. As soon as I could get my voice I said, apologetically: –

"I have had no orders, sir."

"You've had no *orders*! My, what a fine bird we are! We must have *orders*! Our father was a *gentleman* – owned slaves – and *we've* been to *school*. Yes, *we* are a gentleman, *too*, and got to have *orders*! ORDERS, is it? ORDERS is what you want! Dod dern my skin, *I'll* learn you to swell yourself up and blow around *here* about your dod-derned *orders*! G'way from the wheel!" (I had approached it without knowing it.)

I moved back a step or two, and stood as in a dream, all my senses stupefied by this frantic assault.

"What you standing there for? Take that ice-pitcher down to the texas-tender – come, move along, and don't you be all day about it!"

The moment I got back to the pilot-house, Brown said: –

"Here! What was you doing down there all this time?"

"I couldn't find the texas-tender; I had to go all the way to the pantry."

"Derned likely story! Fill up the stove."

I proceeded to do so. He watched me like a cat. Presently he shouted: –

"Put down that shovel! Derndest numskull I ever saw – ain't even got sense enough to load up a stove."

All through the watch this sort of thing went on. Yes, and the subsequent watches were much like it, during a stretch of months. As I have said, I soon got the habit of coming on duty with dread. The moment I was in the presence, even in the darkest night, I could feel those yellow eyes upon me, and knew their owner was watching for a pretext to spit out some venom on me. Preliminarily he would say: –

"Here! Take the wheel."

Two minutes later: –

"*Where* in the nation you going to? Pull her down! pull her down!"

After another moment: –

"Say! You going to hold her all day? Let her go – meet her! meet her!"

Then he would jump from the bench, snatch the wheel from me, and meet her himself, pouring out wrath upon me all the time.

George Ritchie was the other pilot's cub. He was having good times now; for his boss, George Ealer, was as kind-hearted as Brown wasn't. Ritchie had steered for Brown the season before; consequently he knew exactly how to entertain himself and plague me, all by the one operation. Whenever I took the wheel for a moment on Ealer's watch, Ritchie would sit back on the bench and play Brown, with continual ejaculations of "Snatch her! snatch her! Derndest mud-cat I ever saw!" "Here! Where you going *now?* Going to run over that snag?" "Pull her *down*! Don't you hear me? Pull her *down*!" "There she goes! *Just* as I expected! I *told* you not to cramp that reef. G'way from the wheel!"

So I always had a rough time of it, no matter whose watch it was; and sometimes it seemed to me that Ritchie's good-natured badgering was pretty nearly as aggravating as Brown's dead-earnest nagging.

I often wanted to kill Brown, but this would not answer. A cub had to take everything his boss gave, in the way of vigorous comment and criticism; and we all believed that there was a United States law making it a penitentiary offense to strike or threaten a pilot who was on duty. However, I could *imagine* myself killing Brown; there was no law against that; and that was the thing I used always to do the moment I was abed. Instead of going over my river in my mind as was my duty, I threw business aside for pleasure, and killed Brown. I killed Brown every night for months; not in old, stale, commonplace ways, but in new and picturesque ones, – ways that were sometimes surprising for freshness of design and ghastliness of situation and environment.

Brown was *always* watching for a pretext to find fault; and if he could find no plausible pretext, he would invent one. He would scold you for shaving a shore, and for not shaving it; for hugging a bar, and for not hugging it; for "pulling down" when not invited, and for *not* pulling down when not invited; for firing up without orders, and for waiting *for* orders. In a word, it was his invariable rule to find fault with *everything* you did; and another invariable rule of his was to throw all his remarks (to you) into the form of an insult.

One day we were approaching New Madrid, bound down and heavily laden. Brown was at one side of the wheel, steering; I was at the other, standing by to "pull down" or "shove up." He cast a furtive glance at me every now and then. I had long ago learned what that meant; viz., he was trying to invent a trap for me. I wondered what shape it was going to take. By and by he stepped back from the wheel and said in his usual snarly way: –

"Here! – See if you've got gumption enough to round her to."

This was simply *bound* to be a success; nothing could prevent it; for he had never allowed me to round the boat to before; consequently, no matter how I might do the thing, he could find free fault with it. He stood back there with his greedy eye on me, and the result was what might have been foreseen: I lost my head in a quarter of a minute, and didn't know what I was about; I started too early to bring the boat around, but detected a green gleam of joy in Brown's eye, and corrected my mistake; I started around once more while too high up, but corrected myself again in time; I made other false moves, and still managed to save myself; but at last I grew so confused and anxious that I tumbled into the very worst blunder of all – I got too far *down* before beginning to fetch the boat around. Brown's chance was come.

His face turned red with passion; he made one bound, hurled me across the house with a sweep of his arm, spun the wheel down, and began to pour out a stream of vituperation upon me which lasted till he was out of breath. In the course of this speech he called me all the different kinds of hard names he could think of, and once or twice I thought he was even going to swear – but he had never done that, and he didn't this time. "Dod dern" was the nearest he ventured to the luxury of swearing, for he had been brought up with a wholesome respect for future fire and brimstone.

That was an uncomfortable hour; for there was a big audience on the hurricane deck. When I went to bed that night, I killed Brown in seventeen different ways – all of them new.

CHAPTER XIX

BROWN AND I EXCHANGE COMPLIMENTS

TWO TRIPS LATER, I got into serious trouble. Brown was steering; I was "pulling down." My younger brother appeared on the hurricane deck, and shouted to Brown to stop at some landing or other a mile or so below. Brown gave no intimation that he had heard any thing. But that was his way: he never condescended to take notice of an under clerk. The wind was blowing; Brown was deaf (although he always pretended he wasn't), and I very much doubted if he had heard the order. If I had had two heads, I would have spoken; but as I had only one, it seemed judicious to take care of it; so I kept still.

Presently, sure enough, we went sailing by that plantation. Captain Klinefelter appeared on the deck, and said: –

"Let her come around, sir, let her come around. Didn't Henry tell you to land here?"

"*No*, sir!"

"I sent him up to do it."

"He *did* come up; and that's all the good it done, the dod-derned fool. He never said any thing."

"Didn't *you* hear him?" asked the captain of me.

Of course I didn't want to be mixed up in this business, but there was no way to avoid it; so I said: –

"Yes, sir."

I knew what Brown's next remark would be, before he uttered it; it was: –

"Shut your mouth! you never heard any thing of the kind."

I closed my mouth according to instructions. An hour later, Henry entered the pilot-house, unaware of what had been going on. He was a thoroughly inoffensive boy, and I was sorry to see him come, for I knew Brown would have no pity on him. Brown began, straightway: –

"Here! why didn't you tell me we'd got to land at that plantation?"

"I did tell you, Mr. Brown."

"It's a lie!"

I said: –

"You lie, yourself. He did tell you."

Brown glared at me in unaffected surprise; and for as much as a moment he was entirely speechless; then he shouted to me: –

"I'll attend to your case in a half a minute!" then to Henry, "And you leave the pilot-house; out with you!"

It was pilot law, and must be obeyed. The boy started out, and even had his foot on the upper step outside the door, when Brown, with a sudden access of fury, picked up a ten-pound lump of coal and sprang after him; but I was between, with a heavy stool, and I hit Brown a good honest blow which stretched him out.

I had committed the crime of crimes, – I had lifted my hand against a pilot on duty! I supposed I was booked for the penitentiary sure, and couldn't be booked any surer if I went on and squared my long account with this person while I had the chance; consequently I stuck to him and pounded him with my fists a considerable time, – I do not know how long, the pleasure of it probably made it seem longer than it really was; – but in the end he struggled free and jumped up and sprang to the wheel: a very natural solicitude, for, all this time, here was this steamboat tearing down the river at the rate of fifteen miles an hour and nobody at the helm! However, Eagle Bend was two miles wide at this bank-full stage, and correspondingly long and deep; and the boat was steering herself straight down the middle and taking no chances. Still, that was only luck – a body *might* have found her charging into the woods.

Perceiving, at a glance, that the "Pennsylvania" was in no danger, Brown gathered up the big spy-glass, war-club fashion, and ordered me out of the pilot-house with more than Comanche bluster. But I was not afraid of him now; so, instead of going, I tarried, and criticized his grammar; I reformed his ferocious speeches for him, and put them into good English, calling his attention to the advantage of pure English over the bastard dialect of the Pennsylvanian collieries whence he was extracted. He could have done his part to admiration in a cross-fire of mere vituperation, of course; but he was not equipped for this species of controversy; so he presently laid aside his glass and took the wheel, muttering and shaking his head; and I retired to the bench. The racket had brought every body to the hurricane deck, and I trembled when I saw the old captain looking up from the midst of the crowd. I said to myself, "Now I *am* done for!" – For although, as a rule, he was so fatherly and indulgent toward the boat's family, and so patient of minor shortcomings, he could be stern enough when the fault was worth it.

I tried to imagine what he *would* do to a cub-pilot who had been guilty of such a crime as mine, committed on a boat guard-deep with costly freight and alive with passengers. Our watch was nearly ended. I thought I would go and hide somewhere till I got a chance to slide ashore. So I slipped out of the pilot-house, and down the steps, and around to the texas door, – and was in the act of gliding within, when the captain confronted me! I dropped my head, and he stood over me in silence a moment or two, then said impressively, –

"Follow me."

I dropped into his wake; he led the way to his parlor in the forward end of the texas. We were alone, now. He closed the after door; then moved slowly to the forward one and closed that. He sat down; I stood before him. He looked at me some little time, then said, –

"So you have been fighting Mr. Brown?"

I answered meekly: –

"Yes, sir."

"Do you know that that is a very serious matter?"

"Yes, sir."

"Are you aware that this boat was plowing down the river fully five minutes with no one at the wheel?"

"Yes, sir."

"Did you strike him first?"

"Yes, sir."

"What with?"

"A stool, sir."

"Hard?"

"Middling, sir."

"Did it knock him down?"

"He – he fell, sir."

"Did you follow it up? Did you do any thing further?"

"Yes, sir."

"What did you do?"

"Pounded him, sir."

"Pounded him?"

"Yes, sir."

"Did you pound him much? – that is, severely?"

"One might call it that, sir, may be."

"I'm deucéd glad of it! Hark ye, never mention that I said that. You have been guilty of a great crime; and don't you ever be guilty of it again, on this boat. *But* – lay for him ashore! Give him a good sound thrashing, do you hear? I'll pay the expenses. Now go – and mind you, not a word of this to anybody. Clear out with you! – you've been guilty of a great crime, you whelp!"

I slid out, happy with the sense of a close shave and a mighty deliverance; and I heard him laughing to himself and slapping his fat thighs after I had closed his door.

When Brown came off watch he went straight to the captain, who was talking with some passengers on the boiler deck, and demanded that I be put ashore in New Orleans – and added: –

"I'll never turn a wheel on this boat again while that cub stays."

The captain said: –

"But he needn't come round when you are on watch, Mr. Brown."

"I won't even stay on the same boat with him. *One* of us has got to go ashore."

"Very well," said the captain, "let it be yourself;" and resumed his talk with the passengers.

During the brief remainder of the trip, I knew how an emancipated slave feels; for I was an emancipated slave myself. While we lay at landings, I listened to George Ealer's flute; or to his readings from his two bibles, that is to say, Goldsmith and Shakespeare; or I played chess with him – and would have beaten him sometimes, only he always took back his last move and ran the game out differently.

CHAPTER XX

A CATASTROPHE

WE LAY THREE days in New Orleans, but the captain did not succeed in finding another pilot; so he proposed that I should stand a daylight watch, and leave the night watches to George Ealer. But I was afraid; I had never stood a watch of any sort by myself, and I believed I should be sure to get into trouble in the head of some chute, or ground the boat in a near cut through some bar or other. Brown remained in his place; but he would not travel with me. So the captain gave me an order on the captain of the "A. T. Lacey," for a passage to St. Louis, and said he would find a new pilot there and my steersman's berth could then be resumed. The "Lacey" was to leave a couple of days after the "Pennsylvania."

The night before the "Pennsylvania" left, Henry and I sat chatting on a freight pile on the levee till midnight. The subject of the chat, mainly, was one which I think we had not exploited before – steamboat disasters. One was then on its way to us, little as we suspected it; the water which was to make the steam which should cause it, was washing past some point fifteen hundred miles up the river while we talked; – but it would arrive at the right time and the right place. We doubted if persons not clothed with authority were of much use in cases of disaster and attendant panic; still, they might be of *some* use; so we decided that if a disaster ever fell within our experience we would at least stick to the boat, and give such minor service as chance might throw in the way. Henry remembered this, afterward, when the disaster came, and acted accordingly.

The "Lacey" started up the river two days behind the "Pennsylvania." We touched at Greenville, Mississippi, a couple of days out, and somebody shouted: –

"The 'Pennsylvania' is blown up at Ship Island, and a hundred and fifty lives lost!"

At Napoleon, Arkansas, the same evening, we got an extra, issued by a Memphis paper, which gave some particulars. It mentioned my brother, and said he was not hurt.

Further up the river we got a later extra. My brother was again mentioned; but this time as being hurt beyond help. We did not get full details of the catastrophe until we reached Memphis. This is the sorrowful story: –

It was six o'clock on a hot summer morning. The "Pennsylvania" was creeping along, north of Ship Island, about sixty miles below Memphis on a half-head of steam, towing a wood-flat which was fast being emptied. George Ealer was in the pilot-house – alone, I think; the second engineer and a striker had the watch in the engine room; the second mate had the watch on deck; George Black, Mr. Wood, and my brother, clerks, were asleep, as were also Brown and the head engineer, the carpenter, the chief mate, and one striker; Capt. Klinefelter was in the barber's chair, and the barber was preparing to shave him. There were a good many cabin passengers aboard, and three or four hundred deck passengers – so it was said at the time – and not very many of them were astir. The wood being nearly all out of the flat now, Ealer rang to "come ahead" full steam, and the next moment four of the eight boilers exploded with a thunderous crash, and the whole forward third of the boat was hoisted toward the sky! The main part of the mass, with the chimneys, dropped upon the boat again, a mountain of riddled and chaotic rubbish – and then, after a little, fire broke out.

Many people were flung to considerable distances, and fell in the river; among these were Mr. Wood and my brother, and the carpenter. The carpenter was still stretched upon his mattress when he struck the water seventy-five feet from the boat. Brown, the pilot, and George Black, chief clerk, were never seen or heard of after the explosion. The barber's chair, with Captain Klinefelter in it and unhurt, was left with its back overhanging vacancy – everything forward of it, floor and all, had disappeared; and the stupefied barber, who was also unhurt, stood with one toe projecting over space, still stirring his lather unconsciously, and saying not a word.

When George Ealer saw the chimneys plunging aloft in front of him, he knew what the matter was; so he muffled his face in the lapels of his coat, and pressed both hands there tightly to keep this protection in its place so that no steam could get to his nose or mouth. He had ample time to attend to these details while he was going up and returning. He presently landed on top of the unexploded boilers, forty feet below the former pilot-house, accompanied by his wheel and a rain of other stuff, and enveloped in a cloud of scalding steam. All of the many who breathed that steam, died; none escaped. But Ealer breathed none of it. He made his way to the free air as quickly as he could; and when the steam cleared away he returned and climbed up on the boilers again, and patiently hunted out each and every one of his chessmen and the several joints of his flute.

By this time the fire was beginning to threaten. Shrieks and groans filled the air. A great many persons had been scalded, a great many crippled; the explosion had driven an iron crowbar through one man's body – I think they said he was a priest. He did not die at once, and his sufferings were very dreadful. A young French naval cadet, of fifteen, son of a French admiral, was fearfully scalded, but bore his tortures manfully. Both mates were badly scalded, but they stood to their posts, nevertheless. They drew the wood-boat aft, and they and the captain fought back the frantic herd of frightened immigrants till the wounded could be brought there and placed in safety first.

When Mr. Wood and Henry fell in the water, they struck out for shore, which was only a few hundred yards away; but Henry presently said he believed he was not hurt (what an unaccountable error!), and therefore would swim back to the boat and help save the wounded. So they parted, and Henry returned.

By this time the fire was making fierce headway, and several persons who were imprisoned under the ruins were begging piteously for help. All efforts to conquer the fire proved fruitless; so the buckets were presently thrown aside and the officers fell-to with axes and tried to cut the prisoners out. A striker was one of the captives; he said he was not injured, but could not free himself; and when he saw that the fire was likely to drive away the workers, he begged that some one would shoot him, and thus save him from the more dreadful death. The fire did drive the axmen away, and they had to listen, helpless, to this poor fellow's supplications till the flames ended his miseries.

The fire drove all into the wood-flat that could be accommodated there; it was cut adrift, then, and it and the burning steamer floated down the river toward Ship Island. They moored the flat at the head of the island, and there, unsheltered from the blazing sun, the half-naked occupants had to remain, without food or stimulants, or help for their hurts, during the rest of the day. A steamer came along, finally, and carried the unfortunates to Memphis, and there the most lavish assistance was at once forthcoming. By this time Henry was insensible. The physicians examined his injuries and saw that they were fatal, and naturally turned their main attention to patients who could be saved.

Forty of the wounded were placed upon pallets on the floor of a great public hall, and among these was Henry. There the ladies of Memphis came every day, with flowers, fruits, and dainties and delicacies of all kinds, and there they remained and nursed the wounded. All the physicians stood watches there, and all the medical students; and the rest of the town furnished money, or whatever else was wanted. And Memphis knew how to do all these things well; for many a disaster like the "Pennsylvania's" had happened near her doors, and she was experienced, above all other cities on the river, in the gracious office of the Good Samaritan.

The sight I saw when I entered that large hall was new and strange to me. Two long rows of prostrate forms – more than forty, in all – and every face and head a shapeless wad of loose raw cotton. It was a gruesome spectacle. I watched there six days and nights, and a very melancholy experience it was. There was one daily incident which was peculiarly depressing: this was the removal of the doomed to a chamber apart. It was done in order that the *morale* of the other patients might not be injuriously affected by seeing one of their number in the death-agony. The fated one was always carried out with as little stir as possible, and the stretcher was always hidden from sight by a wall of assistants; but no matter: every body knew what that cluster of bent forms, with its muffled step and its slow movement meant; and all eyes watched it wistfully, and a shudder went abreast of it like a wave.

I saw many poor fellows removed to the "death-room," and saw them no more afterward. But I saw our chief mate carried thither more than once. His hurts were frightful, especially his scalds. He was clothed in linseed oil and raw cotton to his waist, and resembled nothing human. He was often out of his mind; and then his pains would make him rave and shout and sometimes shriek. Then, after a period of dumb exhaustion, his disordered imagination would suddenly transform the great apartment into a forecastle, and the hurrying throng of nurses into the crew; and he would come to a sitting posture and shout, "Hump yourselves, *hump* yourselves, you petrifactions, snail-bellies, pall-bearers! going to be all *day* getting that hatful of freight out?" and supplement this explosion with a firmament-obliterating irruption of profanity which nothing could stay or stop till his crater was empty. And now and then while these frenzies possessed him, he would tear off handfuls of the cotton and expose his cooked flesh to view. It was horrible. It was bad for the others, of course – this noise and these exhibitions; so the doctors tried to give him morphine to quiet him. But, in his mind or out of it, he would not take it. He said his wife had been killed by that treacherous drug, and he would die before he would take it. He suspected that the doctors were concealing it in his ordinary medicines and in his water – so he ceased from putting either to his lips. Once, when he had been without water during two sweltering days, he took the dipper in his hand, and the sight of the limpid fluid, and the misery of his thirst, tempted him almost beyond his strength; but he mastered himself and threw it away, and after that he allowed no more to be brought near him. Three times I saw him carried to the death-room, insensible and supposed to be dying; but each time he revived, cursed his attendants, and demanded to be taken back. He lived to be mate of a steamboat again.

But he was the only one who went to the death-room and returned alive. Dr. Peyton, a principal physician, and rich in all the attributes that go to constitute high and flawless character, did all that educated judgment and trained skill could do for Henry; but, as the newspapers had said in the beginning, his hurts were past help. On the evening of the sixth day his wandering mind busied itself with matters far away, and his nerveless fingers "picked at his coverlet." His hour had struck; we bore him to the death-room, poor boy.

CHAPTER XXI

A SECTION IN MY BIOGRAPHY

IN DUE COURSE I got my license. I was a pilot now, full fledged. I dropped into casual employments; no misfortunes resulting, intermittent work gave place to steady and protracted engagements. Time drifted smoothly and prosperously on, and I supposed – and hoped – that I was going to follow the river the rest of my days, and die at the wheel when my mission was ended. But by and by the war came, commerce was suspended, my occupation was gone.

I had to seek another livelihood. So I became a silver miner in Nevada; next, a newspaper reporter; next, a gold miner, in California;

next, a reporter in San Francisco; next, a special correspondent in the Sandwich Islands; next, a roving correspondent in Europe and the East; next, an instructional torch-bearer on the lecture platform; and, finally, I became a scribbler of books, and an immovable fixture among the other rocks of New England.

In so few words have I disposed of the twenty-one slow-drifting years that have come and gone since I last looked from the windows of a pilot-house.

Let us resume, now.

CHAPTER LIII

MY BOYHOOD'S HOME

WE TOOK PASSAGE in one of the fast boats of the St. Louis and St. Paul Packet Company, and started up the river.

When I, as a boy, first saw the mouth of the Missouri River, it was twenty-two or twenty-three miles above St. Louis, according to the estimate of pilots; the wear and tear of the banks has moved it down eight miles since then; and the pilots say that within five years the river will cut through and move the mouth down five miles more, which will bring it within ten miles of St. Louis.

About night-fall we passed the large and flourishing town of Alton, Illinois; and before daylight next morning the town of Louisiana, Missouri, a sleepy village in my day, but a brisk railway centre now; however, all the towns out there are railway centres now. I could not clearly recognize the place. This seemed odd to me, for when I retired from the rebel army in '61 I retired upon Louisiana in good order; at least in good enough order for a person who had not yet learned how to retreat according to the rules of war, and had to trust to native genius. It seemed to me that for a first attempt at a retreat it was not badly done. I had done no advancing in all that campaign that was at all equal to it.

There was a railway bridge across the river here well sprinkled with glowing lights, and a very beautiful sight it was.

At seven in the morning we reached Hannibal, Missouri, where my boyhood was spent. I had had a glimpse of it fifteen years ago, and another glimpse six years earlier, but both were so brief that they hardly counted. The only notion of the town that remained in my mind was the memory of it as I had known it when I first quitted it twenty-nine years ago. That picture of it was still as clear and vivid to me as a photograph. I stepped ashore with the feeling of one who returns out of a dead-and-gone generation. I had a sort of realizing sense of what the Bastille prisoners must have felt when they used to come out and look upon Paris after years of captivity, and note how curiously the familiar and the strange were mixed together before them. I saw the new houses – saw them plainly enough – but they did not affect the older picture in my mind, for through their solid bricks and mortar I saw the vanished houses, which had formerly stood there, with perfect distinctness.

It was Sunday morning, and every body was abed yet. So I passed through the vacant streets, still seeing the town as it was, and not as it is, and recognizing and metaphorically shaking hands with a hundred familiar objects which no longer exist; and finally climbed Holiday's Hill to get a comprehensive view. The whole town lay spread out below me then, and I could mark and fix every locality, every detail. Naturally, I was a good deal moved. I said, "Many of the people I once knew in this tranquil refuge of my childhood are now in heaven; some, I trust, are in the other place."

The things about me and before me made me feel like a boy again – convinced me that I was a boy again, and that I had simply been dreaming an unusually long dream; but my reflections spoiled all that; for they forced me to say, "I see fifty old houses down yonder, into each of which I could enter and find either a man or a woman who was a baby or unborn when I noticed those houses last, or a grandmother who was a plump young bride at that time."

From this vantage ground the extensive view up and down the river, and wide over the wooded expanses of Illinois, is very beautiful, – one of the most beautiful on the Mississippi, I think; which is a hazardous remark to make, for the eight hundred miles of river between St. Louis and St. Paul afford an unbroken succession of lovely pictures. It may be that my affection for the one in question biases my judgment in its favor; I can not say as to that. No matter, it was satisfyingly beautiful to me, and it had this advantage over all the other friends whom I was about to greet again: it had suffered no change; it was as young and fresh and comely and gracious as ever it had been; whereas, the faces of the others would be old, and scarred with the campaigns of life, and marked with their griefs and defeats, and would give me no upliftings of spirit.

An old gentleman, out on an early morning walk, came along, and we discussed the weather, and then drifted into other matters.

I could not remember his face. He said he had been living here twenty-eight years. So he had come after my time, and I had never seen him before. I asked him various questions; first about a mate of mine in Sunday School – what became of him?

"He graduated with honor in an Eastern college, wandered off into the world somewhere, succeeded at nothing, passed out of knowledge and memory years ago, and is supposed to have gone to the dogs."

"He was bright, and promised well when he was a boy."

"Yes, but the thing that happened is what became of it all."

I asked after another lad, altogether the brightest in our village school when I was a boy.

"He, too, was graduated with honors, from an Eastern college; but life whipped him in every battle, straight along, and he died in one of the Territories, years ago, a defeated man."

I asked after another of the bright boys.

"He is a success, always has been, always will be, I think."

I inquired after a young fellow who came to the town to study for one of the professions when I was a boy.

"He went at some thing else before he got through – went from medicine to law, or from law to medicine – then to some other new thing; went away for a year, came back with a young wife; fell to drinking, then to gambling behind the door; finally took his wife and two young children to her father's, and went off to Mexico; went from bad to worse, and finally died there, without a cent to buy a shroud, and without a friend to attend the funeral."

"Pity, for he was the best-natured, and most cheery and hopeful young fellow that ever was."

I named another boy.

"Oh, he is all right. Lives here yet; has a wife and children, and is prospering."

Same verdict concerning other boys.

I named three school-girls.

"The first two live here, are married and have children; the other is long ago dead – never married."

I named, with emotion, one of my early sweethearts.

"She is all right. Been married three times; buried two husbands, divorced from the third, and I hear she is getting ready to marry an old fellow out in Colorado somewhere. She's got children scattered around here and there, most everywheres."

The answer to several other inquiries was brief and simple, –

"Killed in the war."

I named another boy.

"Well, now, his case *is* curious! There wasn't a human being in this town but knew that that boy was a perfect chuckle-head; perfect dummy; just a stupid ass, as you may say. Every body knew it, and every body said it. Well, if that very boy isn't the first lawyer in the State of Missouri to-day, I'm a Democrat!"

"Is that so?"

"It's actually so. I'm telling you the truth."

"How do you account for it?"

"Account for it? There ain't any accounting for it, except that if you send a damned fool to St. Louis, and you don't tell them he's a damned fool *they'll* never find it out. There's one thing sure – if I had a damned fool I should know what to do with him: ship him to St. Louis – it's the noblest market in the world for that kind of property. Well, when you come to look at it all around, and chew at it and think it over, *don't* it just bang any thing you ever heard of?"

"Well, yes, it does seem to. But don't you think may be it was the Hannibal people who were mistaken about the boy, and not the St. Louis people?"

"Oh, nonsense! The people here have known him from the very cradle – they knew him a hundred times better than the St. Louis idiots *could* have known him. No, if you have got any damned fools that you want to realize on, take my advice – send them to St. Louis."

I mentioned a great number of people whom I had formerly known. Some were dead, some were gone away, some had prospered, some had come to naught; but as regarded a dozen or so of the lot, the answer was comforting:

"Prosperous – live here yet – town littered with their children."

I asked about Miss ——.

"Died in the insane asylum three or four years ago – never was out of it from the time she went in; and was always suffering, too; never got a shred of her mind back."

If he spoke the truth, here was a heavy tragedy, indeed. Thirty-six years in a madhouse, that some young fools might have some fun! I was a small boy, at the time; and I saw those giddy young ladies come tip-toeing into the room where Miss —— sat reading at midnight by a lamp. The girl at the head of the file wore a shroud and a doughface; she crept behind the victim, touched her on the shoulder, and she looked up and screamed, and then fell into convulsions. She did not recover from the fright, but went mad. In these days it seems incredible that people believed in ghosts so short a time ago. But they did.

After asking after such other folk as I could call to mind, I finally inquired about *myself:*

"Oh, he succeeded well enough – another case of damned fool. If they'd sent him to St. Louis, he'd have succeeded sooner."

It was with much satisfaction that I recognized the wisdom of having told this candid gentleman, in the beginning, that my name was Smith.

CHAPTER LIV

PAST AND PRESENT

BEING LEFT TO myself, up there, I went on picking out old houses in the distant town, and calling back their former inmates out of the moldy past. Among them I presently recognized the house of the father of Lem Hackett (fictitious name). It carried me back more than a generation in a moment, and landed me in the midst of a time when the happenings of life were not the natural and logical results of great general laws, but of special orders, and were freighted with very precise and distinct purposes – partly punitive in intent, partly admonitory; and usually local in application.

When I was a small boy, Lem Hackett was drowned – on a Sunday. He fell out of an empty flat-boat, where he was playing. Being loaded with sin, he went to the bottom like an anvil. He was the only boy in the village who slept that night. We others all lay awake, repenting. We had not needed the information, delivered from the pulpit that evening, that Lem's was a case of special judgment – we knew that, already. There was a ferocious thunderstorm, that night, and it raged continuously until near dawn. The winds blew, the windows rattled, the rain swept along the roof in pelting sheets, and at the briefest of intervals the inky blackness of the night vanished, the houses over the way glared out white and blinding for a quivering instant, then the solid darkness shut down again and a splitting peal of thunder followed which seemed to rend everything in the neighborhood to shreds and splinters. I sat up in bed quaking and shuddering, waiting for the destruction of the world, and expecting it. To me there was nothing strange or incongruous in heaven's making such an uproar about Lem Hackett. Apparently it was the right and proper thing to do. Not a doubt entered my mind that all the angels were grouped together, discussing this boy's case and observing the awful bombardment of our beggarly little village with satisfaction and approval. There was one thing which disturbed me in the most serious way; that was the thought that this centring of the celestial interest on our village could not fail to attract the attention of the observers to people among us who might otherwise have escaped notice for years. I felt that I was not only one of those people, but the very one most likely to be discovered. That discovery could have but one result: I should be in the fire with Lem before the chill of the river had been fairly warmed out of him. I knew that this would be only just and fair. I was increasing the chances against myself all the time, by feeling a secret bitterness against Lem for having attracted this fatal attention to me, but I could not help it – this sinful thought persisted in infesting my breast in spite of me. Every time the lightning glared I caught my breath, and judged I was gone. In my terror and misery, I meanly began to suggest other boys, and mention acts of theirs which were wickeder than mine, and peculiarly needed punishment – and I tried to pretend to myself that I was simply doing this in a casual way, and without intent to divert the heavenly attention to them for the purpose of getting rid of it myself. With deep sagacity I put these mentions into the form of sorrowing recollections and left-handed sham-supplications that the sins of those boys might be allowed to pass unnoticed – "Possibly they may repent." "It is true that Jim Smith broke a window and lied about it – but may be he did not mean any harm. And although Tom Holmes says more bad words than any other boy in the village, he probably intends to repent – though he has never said he would. And whilst it is a fact that John Jones did fish a little on Sunday, once, he didn't really catch any thing but only just one small useless mud-cat; and maybe that wouldn't have been so awful if he had thrown it back – as he says he did, but he didn't. Pity but they would repent of these dreadful things – and may be they will yet."

But while I was shamefully trying to draw attention to these poor chaps – who were doubtless directing the celestial attention to me at the same moment, though I never once suspected that – I had heedlessly left my candle burning. It was not a time to neglect even trifling precautions. There was no occasion to add any thing to the facilities for attracting notice to me – so I put the light out.

It was a long night to me, and perhaps the most distressful one I ever spent. I endured agonies of remorse for sins which I knew I had committed, and for others which I was not certain about, yet was sure that they had been set down against me in a book by an angel who was wiser than I and did not trust such important matters to memory. It struck me, by and by, that I had been making a most foolish and calamitous mistake, in one respect: doubtless I had not only made my own destruction sure by directing attention to those other boys, but had already accomplished theirs! – Doubtless the lightning had stretched them all dead in their beds by this time! The anguish and the fright which this thought gave me made my previous sufferings seem trifling by comparison.

Things had become truly serious. I resolved to turn over a new leaf instantly; I also resolved to connect myself with the church the next day, if I survived to see its sun appear. I resolved to cease from sin in all its forms, and to lead a high and blameless life forever after. I would be punctual at church and Sunday School; visit the sick; carry baskets of victuals to the poor (simply to fulfil the regulation conditions, although I knew we had none among us so poor but they would smash the basket over my head for my pains); I would instruct other boys in right ways, and take the resulting trouncings meekly; I would subsist entirely on tracts; I would invade the rum shop and warn the drunkard – and finally, if I escaped the fate of those who early become too good to live, I would go for a missionary.

The storm subsided toward daybreak, and I dozed gradually to sleep with a sense of obligation to Lem Hackett for going to eternal suffering in that abrupt way, and thus preventing a far more dreadful disaster – my own loss.

But when I rose refreshed, by and by, and found that those other boys were still alive, I had a dim sense that perhaps the whole thing was a false alarm; that the entire turmoil had been on Lem's account and nobody's else. The world looked so bright and safe that there did not seem to be any real occasion to turn over a new leaf. I was a little subdued, during that day, and perhaps the next; after that, my purpose of reforming slowly dropped out of my mind, and I had a peaceful, comfortable time again, until the next storm.

That storm came about three weeks later; and it was the most unaccountable one, to me, that I had ever experienced; for on the afternoon of that day, "Dutchy" was drowned. Dutchy belonged to our Sunday School. He was a German lad who did not know enough to come in out of the rain; but he was exasperatingly good, and had a prodigious memory. One Sunday he made himself the envy of all the youth and the talk of all the admiring village, by reciting three thousand verses of Scripture without missing a word; then he went off the very next day and got drowned.

Circumstances gave to his death a peculiar impressiveness. We were all bathing in a muddy creek which had a deep hole in it, and in this hole the coopers had sunk a pile of green hickory hoop-poles to soak, some twelve feet under water. We were diving and "seeing who could stay under longest." We managed to remain down by holding on to the hoop-poles. Dutchy made such a poor success of it that he was hailed with laughter and derision every time his head appeared above water. At last he seemed hurt with the taunts, and begged us to stand still on the bank and be fair with him and give him an honest count – "be friendly and kind just this once, and not miscount for the sake of having the fun of laughing at him." Treacherous winks were exchanged, and all said "All right, Dutchy – go ahead, we'll play fair."

Dutchy plunged in, but the boys, instead of beginning to count, followed the lead of one of their number and scampered to a range of blackberry bushes close by and hid behind it. They imagined Dutchy's humiliation, when he should rise after a superhuman effort and find the place silent and vacant, nobody there to applaud. They were "so full of laugh" with the idea, that they were continually exploding into muffled cackles. Time swept on, and presently one who was peeping through the briers, said, with surprise: –

"Why, he hasn't come up, yet!"

The laughing stopped.

"Boys, it's a splendid dive," said one.

"Never mind that," said another, "the joke on him is all the better for it."

There was a remark or two more, and then a pause. Talking ceased, and all began to peer through the vines. Before long, the boys' faces began to look uneasy, then anxious, then terrified. Still there was no movement of the placid water. Hearts began to beat fast, and faces to turn pale. We all glided out, silently, and stood on the bank, our horrified eyes wandering back and forth from each other's countenances to the water.

"Some body must go down and see!"

Yes, that was plain; but nobody wanted that grisly task.

"Draw straws!"

So we did – with hands which shook so, that we hardly knew what we were about. The lot fell to me, and I went down. The water was so muddy I could not see any thing, but I felt around among the hoop-poles, and presently grasped a limp wrist which gave me no response – and if it had I should not have known it, I let it go with such a frightened suddenness.

The boy had been caught among the hoop-poles and entangled there, helplessly. I fled to the surface and told the awful news. Some of us knew that if the boy were dragged out at once he might possibly be resuscitated, but we never thought of that. We did not think of any thing; we did not know what to do, so we did nothing – except that the smaller lads cried, piteously, and we all struggled frantically into our clothes, putting on anybody's that came handy, and getting them wrong-side-out and upside down, as a rule. Then we skurried away and gave the alarm, but none of us went back to see the end of the tragedy. We had a more important thing to attend to: we all flew home, and lost not a moment in getting ready to lead a better life.

The night presently closed down. Then came on that tremendous and utterly unaccountable storm. I was perfectly dazed; I could not understand it. It seemed to me that there must be some mistake. The elements were turned loose, and they rattled and banged and blazed away in the most blind and frantic manner. All heart and hope went out of me, and the dismal thought kept floating through my brain, "If a boy who knows three thousand verses by heart is not satisfactory, what chance is there for anybody else?"

Of course I never questioned for a moment that the storm was on Dutchy's account, or that he or any other inconsequential animal was worthy of such a majestic demonstration from on high; the lesson of it was the only thing that troubled me; for it convinced me that if Dutchy, with all his perfections, was not a delight, it would be vain for me to turn over a new leaf, for I must infallibly fall hopelessly short of that boy, no matter how hard I might try. Nevertheless I did turn it over – a highly educated fear compelled me to do that – but succeeding days of cheerfulness and sunshine came bothering around, and within a month I had so drifted backward that again I was as lost and comfortable as ever.

Breakfast time approached while I mused these musings and called these ancient happenings back to mind; so I got me back into the present and went down the hill.

On my way through town to the hotel, I saw the house which was my home when I was a boy. At present rates, the people who now occupy it are of no more value than I am; but in my time they would have been worth not less than five hundred dollars apiece. They are colored folk.

After breakfast, I went out alone again, intending to hunt up some of the Sunday Schools and see how this generation of pupils might compare with their progenitors who had sat with me in those places and had probably taken me as a model – though I do not remember as to that now. By the public square there had been in my day a shabby little brick church called the "Old Ship of Zion," which I had attended as a Sunday School scholar; and I found the locality easily enough, but not the old church; it was gone, and a trig and rather hilarious new edifice was in its place. The pupils were better dressed and better looking than were those of my time; consequently they did not resemble their ancestors; and consequently there was nothing familiar to me in their faces. Still, I contemplated them with a deep interest and a yearning wistfulness, and if I had been a girl I would have cried; for they were the offspring, and represented, and occupied the places, of boys and girls some of whom I had loved to love, and some of whom I had loved to hate, but all of whom were dear to me for the one reason or the other, so many years gone by – and, Lord, where be they now!

I was mightily stirred, and would have been grateful to be allowed to remain unmolested and look my fill; but a bald-summited superintendent who had been a tow-headed Sunday School mate of mine on that spot in the early ages, recognized me, and I talked a flutter of wild nonsense to those children to hide the thoughts which were in me, and which could not have been spoken without a betrayal of feeling that would have been recognized as out of character with me.

Making speeches without preparation is no gift of mine; and I was resolved to shirk any new opportunity, but in the next and larger Sunday School I found myself in the rear of the assemblage; so I was very willing to go on the platform a moment for the sake of getting a good look at the scholars. On the spur of the moment I could not recall any of the old idiotic talks which visitors used to insult me with when I was a pupil there; and I was sorry for this, since it would have given me time and excuse to dawdle there and take a long and satisfying look at what I feel at liberty to say was an array of fresh young comeliness not matchable in another Sunday School of the same size. As I talked merely to get a chance to inspect; and as I strung out the random rubbish solely to prolong the inspection, I judged it but decent to confess these low motives, and I did so.

If the Model Boy was in either of these Sunday Schools, I did not see him. The Model Boy of my time – we never had but the one – was perfect: perfect in manners, perfect in dress, perfect in conduct, perfect in filial piety, perfect in exterior godliness; but at bottom he was a prig; and as for the contents of his skull, they could have changed place with the contents of a pie and nobody would have been the worse off for it but the pie. This fellow's reproachlessness was a standing reproach to every lad in the village. He was the admiration of all the mothers, and the detestation of all their sons. I was told what became of him, but as it was a disappointment to me, I will not enter into details. He succeeded in life.

CHAPTER LV

A VENDETTA AND OTHER THINGS

DURING MY THREE days' stay in the town, I woke up every morning with the impression that I was a boy – for in my dreams the faces were all young again, and looked as they had looked in the old times – but I went to bed a hundred years old, every night – for meantime I had been seeing those faces as they are now.

Of course I suffered some surprises, along at first, before I had become adjusted to the changed state of things. I met young ladies who did not seem to have changed at all; but they turned out to be the daughters of the young ladies I had in mind – sometimes their grand-daughters. When you are told that a stranger of fifty is a grandmother, there is nothing surprising about it; but if, on the contrary, she is a person whom you knew as a little girl, it seems impossible. You say to yourself, "How can a little girl be a grandmother?" It takes some little time to accept and realize the fact that while you have been growing old, your friends have not been standing still, in that matter.

I noticed that the greatest changes observable were with the women, not the men. I saw men whom thirty years had changed but slightly; but their wives had grown old. These were good women; it is very wearing to be good.

There was a saddler whom I wished to see; but he was gone. Dead, these many years, they said. Once or twice a day, the saddler used to go tearing down the street, putting on his coat as he went;

and then every body knew a steamboat was coming. Every body knew, also, that John Stavely was not expecting anybody by the boat – or any freight, either; and Stavely must have known that every body knew this, still it made no difference to him; he liked to seem to himself to be expecting a hundred thousand tons of saddles by this boat, and so he went on all his life, enjoying being faithfully on hand to receive and receipt for those saddles, in case by any miracle they should come. A malicious Quincy paper used always to refer to this town, in derision as "Stavely's Landing." Stavely was one of my earliest admirations; I envied him his rush of imaginary business, and the display he was able to make of it, before strangers, as he went flying down the street struggling with his fluttering coat.

But there was a carpenter who was my chiefest hero. He was a mighty liar, but I did not know that; I believed everything he said. He was a romantic, sentimental, melodramatic fraud, and his bearing impressed me with awe. I vividly remember the first time he took me into his confidence. He was planing a board, and every now and then he would pause and heave a deep sigh; and occasionally mutter broken sentences – confused and not intelligible – but out of their midst an ejaculation sometimes escaped which made me shiver and did me good: one was, "O God, it is his blood!" I sat on the tool-chest and humbly and shudderingly admired him; for I judged he was full of crime. At last he said in a low voice: –

"My little friend, can you keep a secret?"

I eagerly said I could.

"A dark and dreadful one?"

I satisfied him on that point.

"Then I will tell you some passages in my history; for oh, I *must* relieve my burdened soul, or I shall die!"

He cautioned me once more to be "as silent as the grave"; then he told me he was a "red-handed murderer." He put down his plane, held his hands out before him, contemplated them sadly, and said: –

"Look – with these hands I have taken the lives of thirty human beings!"

The effect which this had upon me was an inspiration to him, and he turned himself loose upon his subject with interest and energy. He left generalizing, and went into details, – began with his first murder; described it, told what measures he had taken to avert suspicion; then passed to his second homicide, his third, his fourth, and so on. He had always done his murders with a bowie knife, and he made all my hairs rise by suddenly snatching it out and showing it to me.

At the end of this first *séance* I went home with six of his fearful secrets among my freightage, and found them a great help to my dreams, which had been sluggish for a while back. I sought him again and again, on my Saturday holidays; in fact I spent the summer with him – all of it which was valuable to me. His fascinations never diminished, for he threw some thing fresh and stirring, in the way of horror, into each successive murder. He always gave names, dates, places – everything. This by and by enabled me to note two things: that he had killed his victims in every quarter of the globe, and that these victims were always named Lynch. The destruction of the Lynches went serenely on, Saturday after Saturday, until the original thirty had multiplied to sixty, – and more to be heard from yet; then my curiosity got the better of my timidity, and I asked how it happened that these justly punished persons all bore the same name.

My hero said he had never divulged that dark secret to any living being; but felt that he could trust me, and therefore he would lay bare before me the story of his sad and blighted life. He had loved one "too fair for earth," and she had reciprocated "with all the sweet affection of her pure and noble nature." But he had a rival, a "base hireling" named Archibald Lynch, who said the girl should be his, or he would "dye his hands in her heart's best blood." The carpenter, "innocent and happy in love's young dream," gave no weight to the threat, but led his "golden-haired darling to the altar," and there, the two were made one; there also, just as the minister's hands were stretched in blessing over their heads, the fell deed was done – with a knife – and the bride fell a corpse at her husband's feet. And what did the husband do? He plucked forth that knife, and kneeling by the body of his lost one, swore to "consecrate his life to the extermination of all the human scum that bear the hated name of Lynch."

That was it. He had been hunting down the Lynches and slaughtering them, from that day to this – twenty years. He had always used that same consecrated knife; with it he had murdered his long array of Lynches, and with it he had left upon the forehead of each victim a peculiar mark – a cross, deeply incised. Said he: –

"The cross of the Mysterious Avenger is known in Europe, in America, in China, in Siam, in the Tropics, in the Polar Seas, in the deserts of Asia, in all the earth. Wherever in the uttermost parts of the globe, a Lynch has penetrated, there has the Mysterious Cross been seen, and those who have seen it have shuddered and said, 'it is his mark, he has been here.' You have heard of the Mysterious Avenger – look upon him, for before you stands no less a person! But beware – breathe not a word to any soul. Be silent, and wait. Some morning this town will flock aghast to view a gory corpse; on its brow will be seen the awful sign, and men will tremble and whisper, 'he has been here, – it is the Mysterious Avenger's mark!' You will come here, but I shall have vanished; you will see me no more."

This ass has been reading the "Jibbenainosay," no doubt, and had had his poor romantic head turned by it; but as I had not yet seen the book then, I took his inventions for truth, and did not suspect that he was a plagiarist.

However, we had a Lynch living in the town; and the more I reflected upon his impending doom, the more I could not sleep. It seemed my plain duty to save him, and a still plainer and more important duty to get some sleep for myself, so at last I ventured to go to Mr. Lynch and tell him what was about to happen to him – under strict secrecy. I advised him to "fly," and certainly expected him to do it. But he laughed at me; and he did not stop there; he led me down to the carpenter's shop, gave the carpenter a jeering and scornful lecture upon his silly pretensions, slapped his face, made him get down on his knees and beg – then went off and left me to contemplate the cheap and pitiful ruin of what, in my eyes, had so lately been a majestic and incomparable hero. The carpenter blustered, flourished his knife, and doomed this Lynch in his usual volcanic style, the size of his fateful words undiminished; but it was all wasted upon me; he was a hero to me no longer but only a poor, foolish, exposed humbug. I was ashamed of him, and ashamed of myself; I took no further interest in him, and never went to his shop anymore. He was a heavy loss to me, for he was the greatest hero I had ever known. The fellow must have had some talent; for some of his imaginary murders were so vividly and dramatically described that I remember all their details yet.

The people of Hannibal are not more changed than is the town. It is no longer a village; it is a city, with a mayor, and a council, and water-works, and probably a debt. It has fifteen thousand people, is a thriving and energetic place, and is paved like the rest of the west and south – where a well-paved street and a good sidewalk are things so seldom seen, that one doubts them when he does see them. The customary half dozen railways centre in Hannibal now, and there is a new depot which cost a hundred thousand dollars. In my time the town had no specialty, and no commercial grandeur; the daily packet usually landed a passenger and bought a catfish, and took away another passenger and a hatful of freight; but now a huge commerce in lumber has grown up and a large miscellaneous commerce is one of the results. A deal of money changes hands there now.

Bear Creek – so called, perhaps, because it was always so particularly bare of bears – is hidden out of sight now, under islands and continents of piled lumber, and nobody but an expert can find it. I used to get drowned in it every summer regularly, and be drained out, and inflated and set going again by some chance enemy; but not enough of it is unoccupied now to drown a person in. It was a famous breeder of chills and fever in its day. I remember one summer when every body in town had this disease at once. Many chimneys were shaken down, and all the houses were so racked that the town had to be rebuilt. The chasm or gorge between Lover's Leap and the hill west of it is supposed by scientists to have been caused by glacial action. This is a mistake.

There is an interesting cave a mile or two below Hannibal, among the bluffs. I would have liked to revisit it, but had not time. In my time the person who then owned it turned it into a mausoleum for his daughter, aged fourteen. The body of this poor child was put into a copper cylinder filled with alcohol, and this was suspended in one of the dismal avenues of the cave. The top of the cylinder was removable; and it was said to be a common thing for the baser order of tourists to drag the dead face into view and examine it and comment upon it.

CHAPTER LVI

A QUESTION OF LAW

THE SLAUGHTER-HOUSE IS gone from the mouth of Bear Creek and so is the small jail (or "calaboose") which once stood in its neighborhood. A citizen asked, "Do you remember when Jimmy Finn, the town drunkard, was burned to death in the calaboose?"

Observe, now, how history becomes defiled, through lapse of time and the help of the bad memories of men. Jimmy Finn was not burned in the calaboose, but died a natural death in a tan vat, of a combination of delirium tremens and spontaneous combustion. When I say natural death, I mean it was a natural death for Jimmy Finn to die. The calaboose victim was not a citizen; he was a poor stranger, a harmless whiskey-sodden tramp. I know more about his case than anybody else; I knew too much of it, in that bygone day, to relish speaking of it. That tramp was wandering about the streets one chilly evening, with a pipe in his mouth, and begging for a match; he got neither matches nor courtesy; on the contrary, a troop of bad little boys followed him around and amused themselves with nagging and annoying him. I assisted; but at last, some appeal which the wayfarer made for forbearance, accompanying it with a pathetic reference to his forlorn and friendless condition, touched such sense of shame and remnant of right feeling as were left in me, and I went away and got him some matches, and then hied me home and to bed, heavily weighted as to conscience, and unbuoyant in spirit. An hour or two afterward, the man was arrested and locked up in the calaboose by the marshal – large name for a constable, but that was his title. At two in the morning, the church bells rang for fire, and every body turned out, of course – I with the rest. The tramp had used his matches disastrously: he had set his straw bed on fire, and the oaken sheathing of the room had caught. When I reached the ground, two hundred men, women, and children stood massed together, transfixed with horror, and starting at the grated windows of the jail. Behind the iron bars, and tugging frantically at them, and screaming for help, stood the tramp; he seemed like a black object set against a sun, so white and intense was the light at his back. That marshal could not be found, and he had the only key. A battering-ram was quickly improvised, and the thunder of its blows upon the door had so encouraging a sound that the spectators broke into wild cheering, and believed the merciful battle won. But it was not so. The timbers were too strong; they did not yield. It was said that the man's death-grip still held fast to the bars after he was dead; and that in this position the fires wrapped him about and consumed him. As to this, I do not know. What was seen after I recognized the face that was pleading through the bars was seen by others, not by me.

I saw that face, so situated, every night for a long time afterward; and I believed myself as guilty of the man's death as if I had given him the matches purposely that he might burn himself up with them. I had not a doubt that I should be hanged if my connection with this tragedy were found out. The happenings and the impressions of that time are burnt into my memory, and the study of them entertains me as much now as they themselves distressed me then. If anybody spoke of that grisly matter, I was all ears in a moment, and alert to hear what might be said, for I was always dreading and expecting to find out that I was suspected; and so fine and so delicate was the perception of my guilty conscience, that it often detected suspicion in the most purposeless remarks, and in looks, gestures, glances of the eye which had no significance, but which sent me shivering away in a panic of fright, just the same. And how sick it made me when some body dropped, howsoever carelessly and barren of intent, the remark that "murder will out!" For a boy of ten years, I was carrying a pretty weighty cargo.

All this time I was blessedly forgetting one thing – the fact that I was an inveterate talker in my sleep. But one night I awoke and found my bed-mate – my younger brother – sitting up in bed and contemplating me by the light of the moon. I said: –

"What is the matter?"

"You talk so much I can't sleep."

I came to a sitting posture in an instant, with my kidneys in my throat and my hair on end.

"What did I say? Quick – out with it – what did I say?"

"Nothing much."

"It's a lie – you know everything."

"Everything about what?"

"You know well enough. About *that.*"

"About *what*? – I don't know what you are talking about. I think you are sick or crazy or some thing. But any way, you're awake, and I'll get to sleep while I've got a chance."

He fell asleep and I lay there in a cold sweat, turning this new terror over in the whirling chaos which did duty as my mind. The burden of my thought was, How much did I divulge? How much does he know? – what a distress is this uncertainty! But by and by I evolved an idea – I would wake my brother and probe him with a supposititious case. I shook him up, and said –

"Suppose a man should come to you drunk—"

"This is foolish – I never get drunk."

"I don't mean you, idiot – I mean the man. Suppose a *man* should come to you drunk, and borrow a knife, or a tomahawk, or a pistol, and you forgot to tell him it was loaded, and—"

"How could you load a tomahawk?"

"I don't mean the tomahawk, and I didn't *say* the tomahawk; I said the pistol. Now don't you keep breaking in that way, because this is serious. There's been a man killed."

"What! In this town?"

"Yes, in this town."

"Well, go on – I won't say a single word."

"Well, then, suppose you forgot to tell him to be careful with it, because it was loaded, and he went off and shot himself with that pistol, – fooling with it, you know, and probably doing it by accident, being drunk. Well, would it be murder?"

"No – suicide."

"No, no. I don't mean *his* act, I mean yours: would you be a murderer for letting him have that pistol?"

After deep thought came this answer, –

"Well, I should think I was guilty of something – may be murder – yes, probably murder, but I don't quite know."

This made me very uncomfortable. However, it was not a decisive verdict. I should have to set out the real case – there seemed to be no other way. But I would do it cautiously, and keep a watch out for suspicious effects. I said: –

"I was supposing a case, but I am coming to the real one now. Do you know how the man came to be burned up in the calaboose?"

"No."

"Haven't you the least idea?"

"Not the least."

"Wish you may die in your tracks if you have?"

"Yes, wish I may die in my tracks."

"Well, the way of it was this. The man wanted some matches to light his pipe. A boy got him some. The man set fire to the calaboose with those very matches, and burnt himself up."

"Is that so?"

"Yes, it is. Now, is that boy a murderer, do you think?"

"Let me see. The man was drunk?"

"Yes, he was drunk."

"Very drunk?"

"Yes."

"And the boy knew it?"

"Yes, he knew it."

There was a long pause. Then came this heavy verdict: –

"If the man was drunk, and the boy knew it, the boy murdered that man. This is certain."

Faint, sickening sensations crept along all the fibres of my body, and I seemed to know how a person feels who hears his death sentence pronounced from the bench. I waited to hear what my brother would say next. I believed I knew what it would be, and I was right. He said, –

"I know the boy."

I had nothing to say; so I said nothing. I simply shuddered. Then he added, –

"Yes, before you got half through telling about the thing, I knew perfectly well who the boy was; it was Ben Coontz!"

I came out of my collapse as one who rises from the dead. I said, with admiration: –

"Why, how in the world did you ever guess it?"

"You told it in your sleep."

I said to myself, "How splendid that is! This is a habit which must be cultivated."

My brother rattled innocently on: –

"When you were talking in your sleep, you kept mumbling some thing about 'matches,' which I couldn't make any thing out of; but just now, when you began to tell me about the man and the calaboose and the matches, I remembered that in your sleep you mentioned Ben Coontz two or three times; so I put this and that together, you see, and right away I knew it was Ben that burnt that man up."

I praised his sagacity effusively. Presently he asked, –

"Are you going to give him up to the law?"

"No," I said; "I believe that this will be a lesson to him. I shall keep an eye on him, of course, for that is but right; but if he stops where he is and reforms, it shall never be said that I betrayed him."

"How good you are!"

"Well, I try to be. It is all a person can do in a world like this."

And now, my burden being shifted to other shoulders, my terrors soon faded away.

The day before we left Hannibal, a curious thing fell under my notice, – the surprising spread which longitudinal time undergoes there. I learned it from one of the most unostentatious of men, – the colored coachman of a friend of mine, who lives three miles from town. He was to call for me at the Park Hotel at 7:30 P.M., and drive me out. But he missed it considerably, – did not arrive till ten. He excused himself by saying: –

"De time is mos' an hour en a half slower in de country en what it is in de town; you'll be in plenty time, boss. Sometimes we shoves out early for church, Sunday, en fetches up dah right plum in de middle er de sermon. Diffunce in de time. A body can't make no calculations 'bout it."

I had lost two hours and a half; but I had learned a fact worth four.

NON-FICTION IN EVERYMAN'S LIBRARY

JOHN JAMES AUDUBON
The Audubon Reader

AUGUSTINE
The Confessions

SIMONE DE BEAUVOIR
The Second Sex

HECTOR BERLIOZ
The Memoirs of Hector Berlioz

THE BIBLE
(King James Version)
The Old Testament
The New Testament

JAMES BOSWELL
The Life of Samuel Johnson
The Journal of a Tour to the Hebrides

JEAN ANTHELME BRILLAT-SAVARIN
The Physiology of Taste

EDMUND BURKE
Reflections on the Revolution in France and Other Writings

GIACOMO CASANOVA
History of My Life

BENVENUTO CELLINI
The Autobiography of Benvenuto Cellini

G. K. CHESTERTON
The Everyman Chesterton

CARL VON CLAUSEWITZ
On War

CONFUCIUS
The Analects

THOMAS CRANMER
The Book of Common Prayer
(UK only)

CHARLES DARWIN
The Origin of Species
The Voyage of the Beagle
(in 1 vol.)

JOAN DIDION
We Tell Ourselves Stories in Order to Live (US only)

W.E.B. DU BOIS
The Souls of Black Folk (US only)

JOHN EVELYN
The Diary of John Evelyn
(UK only)

ANNE FRANK
The Diary of a Young Girl
(US only)

BENJAMIN FRANKLIN
The Autobiography and Other Writings

EDWARD GIBBON
The Decline and Fall of the Roman Empire
Vols 1 to 3: The Western Empire
Vols 4 to 6: The Eastern Empire

KAHLIL GIBRAN
The Collected Works

HERODOTUS
The Histories

MICHAEL HERR
Dispatches (US only)

HINDU SCRIPTURES
(tr. R. C. Zaehner)

SAMUEL JOHNSON
A Journey to the Western Islands of Scotland

SØREN KIERKEGAARD
Fear and Trembling and The Book on Adler

MAXINE HONG KINGSTON
The Woman Warrior and China Men
(US only)

THE KORAN
(tr. Marmaduke Pickthall)

NICCOLÒ MACHIAVELLI
The Prince

MARCUS AURELIUS
Meditations

W. SOMERSET MAUGHAM
The Skeptical Romancer
(US only)

JOHN STUART MILL
On Liberty and Utilitarianism

MARY WORTLEY MONTAGU
Letters

This book is set in BASKERVILLE. John Baskerville of Birmingham formed his ideas of letter-design during his early career as a writing-master and engraver of inscriptions. He retired in middle age, set up a press of his own and produced his first book in 1757.